introduction to

WEB TECHNOLOGY

introduction to WEB TECHNOLOGY

[For BTech(CSE/IT) and all Computer Science Students]

Tanweer Alam
*M.Sc, MCA, M.Tech (IT), M.Phil (CS), Ph.D (CSE)**

MCA Department, Meerut Institute of Engineering and Technology
Meerut, Uttar Pradesh (INDIA)

KHANNA BOOK PUBLISHING CO. (P) LTD.

Publisher of Engineering and Computer Books

4C/4344, Ansari Road, Darya Ganj, New Delhi-110002
Phone : 011-23244447-48 **Mobile:** +91-9910909320
E-mail : contact@khannabooks.com
Website : www.khannabooks.com

Dear Readers,

To prevent the piracy, this book is secured with HIGH SECURITY HOLOGRAM on the front title cover. In case you don't find the hologram on the front cover title, please write us to at contact@khannabooks.com or whatsapp us at +91-99109 09320 and avail special gift voucher for yourself.

Specimen of Hologram on front Cover title:

Moreover, there is a SPECIAL DISCOUNT COUPON for you with EVERY HOLOGRAM.

How to avail this SPECIAL DISCOUNT:

Step 1: Scratch the hologram
Step 2: Under the scratch area, your "coupon code" is available
Step 3: Logon to www.khannabooks.com
Step 4: Use your "coupon code" in the shopping cart and get your copy at a special discount
Step 5: Enjoy your reading!

Thanks,
Khanna Publishing House

ISBN: 978-93-80016-86-3

Introduction To Web Technology
by Tanweer Alam

First Edition: 2010
Reprint: 2025, 2026

To view complete list of books, please scan the QR Code:

Published by:
Khanna Book Publishing Co. (P) Ltd.
CIN: U22110DL1998PTC095547

Visit us at: www.khannabooks.com
Write us at: contact@khannabooks.com

Printed in Bharat.

Dedication to

My Family,
My Parents: **Dr. Tahir Hasan and Mrs. Zurera**
My Wife: **Anjum and**
My cute Son: **Aatif Alam**

PREFACE

The Internet provides new opportunities for any individual or organization in the world. It represents a low cost opportunity for businesses to promote their products and services world wide. The Internet is a global data communications system. It is a hardware and software Infrastructure that provides connectivity between computers. The web is one of the services communicated via the Internet. Web Applications are using web technologies such as web browsers and web servers.

Web Technologies definitely has a future in teaching and research, as well as web development. The objective of this book is to promote that future by spreading the use of the web technologies as widely as possible.

This book will be of great help to web developers. They can upgrade their skills through this book and achieve great height in the world of web programming.

The book is self contained. The chapters in this book are arranged in a sequence order. The programs presented in this book are just to understand the application. The objective of this book is the serve as a textbook for the subject "Introduction to Web Technology" in various course viz. BTech(CS/IT)/MCA/MTech etc.

I am sure that the text's user friendly approach will encourage the students to read the book and will make them understand the concept in an easy way.

I always welcome suggestions from researchers, academicians, students and others to improve the quality of this book.

Tanweer Alam

ACKNOWLEDGEMENTS

All praise be to ALLAH for his limitless help and guidance. Peace and Blessings of ALLAH be upon his messenger Mohammad.

I heartily take this opportunity to acknowledge my great debt to my parents for their valuable help, cooperation, support and advice. My thanks go out to everyone who helped me to produce this book, particularly to my wife **Anjum** for her valuable contributions to the development of this book.

I express my sincere and heart felt thanks to **Dr Shamimul Qamar**, Professor and Head of Dept of IT, SRM University, NCR Campus, **Dr Parveen Kumar**, Professor and Director of Dept of MCA, Meerut Institute of Engineering and Technology, Meerut and my departmental friends for their whole hearted support.

I want to thanks the Department of MCA, Meerut Institute of Engineering and Technology, Meerut for giving me permission to do the necessary work and to use departmental resource and data.

Thanks is also due to Mr. Mayank Prashar (System Administrator), MIET, Meerut for provide me lab facility to do the necessary work and hearted support for development of this book.

Thanks to **Mr. Puneet Khanna**, **Mr Mukul Seth** and Khanna Publication, who managed the publishing agreement and the production process so smoothly.

My child, **Aatif Alam**, who left me in peace long enough to get things finished!

Now all that remains is to wish you, Dear Reader, lots of fun with **"Introduction to web Technology"**!

Tanweer Alam

CONTENTS

CHAPTER 1

WEB DEVELOPMENT

The term Internet and World Wide Web (WWW) are often used in everyday speech without much distinction. However the Internet and the World Wide Web are not one and the same. The Internet is a global data communications system. It is a hardware and software Infrastructure that provides connectivity between computers. The web is one of the services communicated via the Internet. It is a collection of interconnected documents and other resources linked by hyperlinks and URLs.

1.0 INTRODUCTION

The World Wide Web or Web or WWW is a system of Internet servers that supports hypertext. WWW is used to access several Internet protocols on a single interface. This creates a convenient and user-friendly environment. This includes e-mail, FTP, Telnet and Usenet News. The WWW consists of files, called pages or home pages, containing links to documents and resources throughout the Internet. HTML is an evolving language, with new tags being added as each upgrade of the language is developed and released. Programming languages such as Java, Visual Basic, JavaScript, Cold Fusion and XML extend the capabilities of the Web. Much information on the Web is served dynamically from content stored in databases.

1.1 HISTORY OF WEB

The Internet was created on Jan 2, 1969 when United States computer scientists began researching computer networking. This research was founded by the Advanced Research Projects Agency (ARPA), which gave the Internet its first name, THE ARPANET. THE ARPANET was used to test the use of packet-switched Networks, which are computer networks that transfer information in the form of little packets that are move independent of each other through various networks until they reach their final destination. ARPANET users started sharing the resources of the computers by telenetworking using a protocol called Telnet. This protocol shares remote computers resources through a telephone.

In 1975, Vinton Cerf of standard University developed a transport layer of protocol. This protocol is called Transmission Control Protocol (TCP). He also developed network layer protocol called Internet Protocol (IP). TCP/IP means the use of TCP (or UDP) at the transport layer and the use of IP at the network layer.

In 1980 The National Science Foundation (NSF) founded the TCP/IP Network to establish a Network, NSFNET. Initially NSFNET used digital exchanges and a speed of 56 kbps over the Telephone Lines. In 1983, the SRPANET was reserved for civilian use, while MILNET was created for military use.

In 1988, Traffic increased so quickly that there was an immediate necessity for upgrading the network again. So there was an introduction of T3 lines which are 45 mbps lines.

In 1991, The NSF established a new network that is known a NREN (National Research and Education Network)

Table 1.0: History of Internet

Year	History of the Internet
Jan 2, 1969	The Internet was created. This research was founded by the Advanced Research Projects Agency (ARPA), which gave the Internet its first name, THE ARPANET.
1975	Vinton Cerf developed a transport layer of protocol.
1980	The National Science Foundation (NSF) founded the TCP/IP Network to establish a Network, NSFNET. Initially NSFNET used digital exchanges and a speed of 56 kpbs over the Telephone Lines.
1983	The SRPANET was reserved for civilian use, while MILNET was created for military use.
1988	Traffic increased so quickly that there was an immediate necessity for upgrading the network again. So there was an introduction of T3 lines which are 45mbps lines.
1991	The NSF established a new network that is known a NREN (National Research and Education Network).
1992	WWW was introduced by NSFNET, upgraded to T3 lines.

In 1992, WWW was introduced by NSFNET, upgraded to T3 lines. Tim Berners-lee introduced WWW to the Internet, which has the ability to link data together if that data was located in files on the server. He did this by bringing together three main elements.

1. HTTP (WWW Protocol)
2. HTML (The language for the web)
3. URL (for addressing web sites anywhere in the world)

1.2 PROTOCOLS GOVERNING WEB

A protocol is a standard that controls or enables the connection, communication and data transfer between two computing devices. Protocol is the most fundamental concepts of network communication. A protocol is a formal set of rules that must be followed in order to communicate. We may not realize it that the use of protocols every day. In other words, protocol is the set of rules by which data is formatted in the form for exchanging between computing devices. For example computer A wants to sends to data to computer B and computer B wants to receive data then the computer A needs to format the data such that B will be able to understand it. So there must exits a set of rules by which the data is formatted. Furthermore computer B needs to be error control and retransmission rules if it is to be capable of repackaging the data into the correct format. These rules are known as protocol.

The following are the common protocols that are used to govern the web.

(i) HTTP (Hypertext Transfer Protocol)
(ii) IP (Internet Protocol)
(iii) TCP (Transmission Control Protocol)
(iv) UDP (User Datagram Protocol)
(v) Telnet (Telnet Remote Protocol)
(vi) FTP (File Transfer Protocol)
(vii) DHCP (Dynamic Host Configuration Protocol)
(viii) SMTP (Simple Mail Transfer Protocol)
(ix) IMAP (Internet Message Access Protocol)
(x) POP3 (Post Office Protocol 3)
(xi) SSH (Secure Shell Remote Protocol)
(xii) ARP (Address Resolution Protocol)
(xiii) DNS (Domain Name Service)
(xiv) DSN (Data Source Name)
(xv) ICMP (Internet Control Message Protocol)
(xvi) SSL (Secure Sockets Layer)

The Internet Protocol is a protocol used for communicating data across a packet-switched inter network. IP is a network layer protocol in the Internet protocol suite and is encapsulated in a data link layer protocol (e.g., Ethernet). The Transmission Control Protocol is one of the core protocols of the Internet protocol suite. TCP provides reliable, in-order delivery of a stream of bytes, making it suitable for applications like file transfer and e-mail. It is so important in the Internet protocol suite that sometimes the entire suite is referred to as TCP/IP. File Transfer Protocol is a network protocol used to transfer data from one computer to another through a network, such as the Internet. FTP is a file transfer protocol for exchanging and manipulating files over any TCP-based computer network. A FTP client may connect to a FTP server to manipulate files on that server. FTP is a popular choice for exchanging files independent of the operating systems involved. TELNET (TELecommunication NETwork) is a network protocol used on the Internet or local area network (LAN) connections.

1.3 CONNECTING TO INTERNET

Before you can connect to the internet and access the www, you need to have certain equipment. In brief, you must have a computer, a modem and access to a telephone line or a Local area network (LAN) that is in turn connected to the internet and connection software that will allow you to establish an account with a service provider and access the internet. The following steps are used to connect to the Internet:

1. Start → Control Panel → Network Connections.

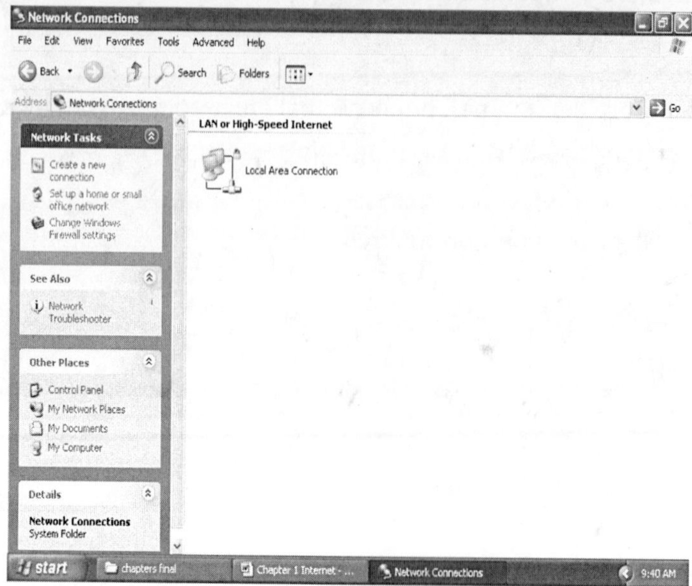

2. Ensure Enable this connection is turned on.
   Right click on Local area connection and click on Enable.

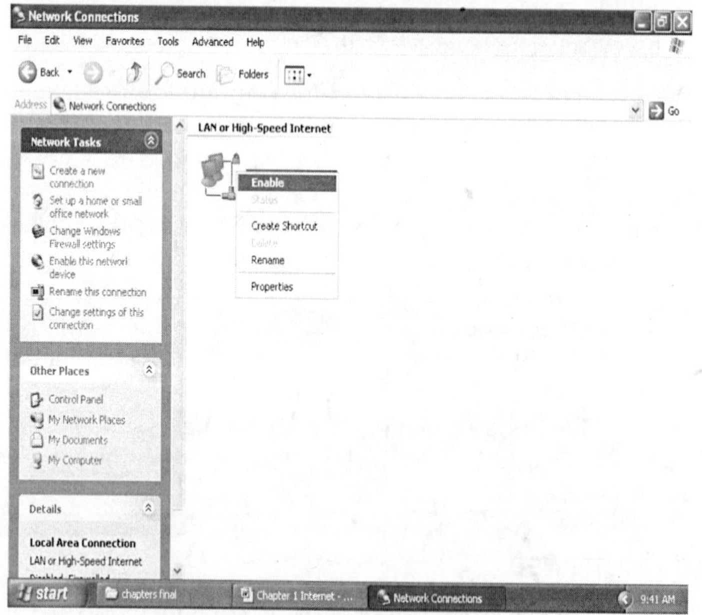

3. Select the connection you wish to use, and then click Properties.

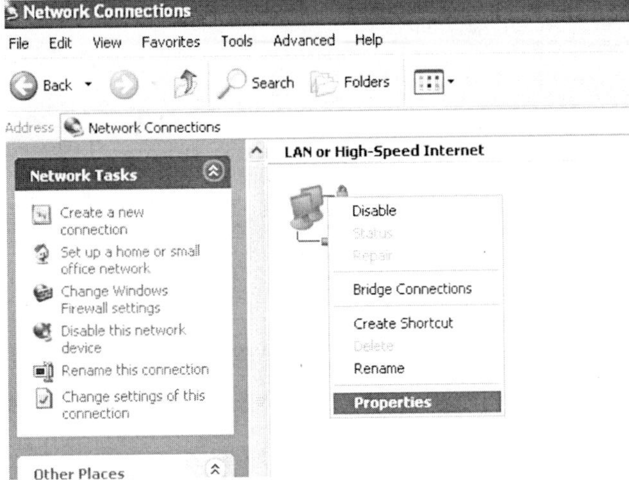

4. If ISP or network administrator has given you an IP address, set Configuration to Static IP address, then enter the address in the IP address field and click **OK**. Otherwise, set Configuration to DHCP and click **OK**.

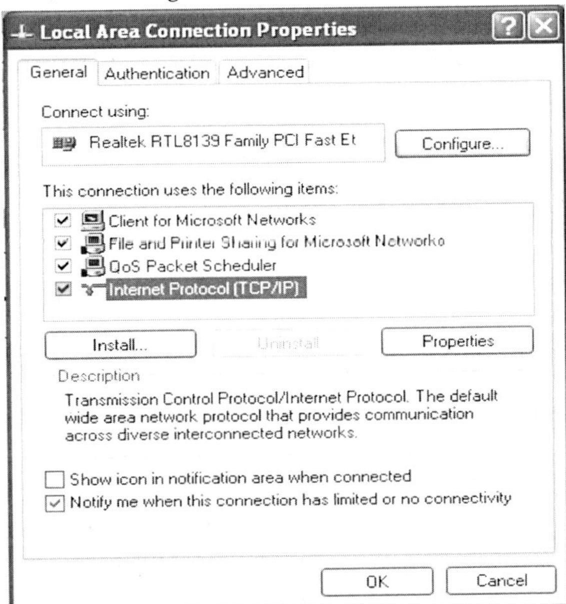

Double click on Internet Protocol (TCP/IP).

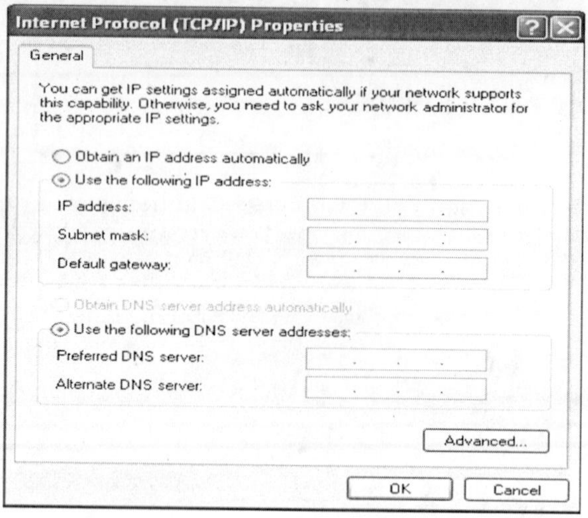

Internet Protocol (TCP/IP) Properties

General

You can get IP settings assigned automatically if your network supports this capability. Otherwise, you need to ask your network administrator for the appropriate IP settings.

Obtain an IP address automatically

Use the following IP address:

IP address:

Subnet mask:

Default gateway:

Obtain DNS server address automatically

Use the following DNS server addresses:

Preferred DNS server:

Alternate DNS server:

Advanced...

OK Cancel

For Example:

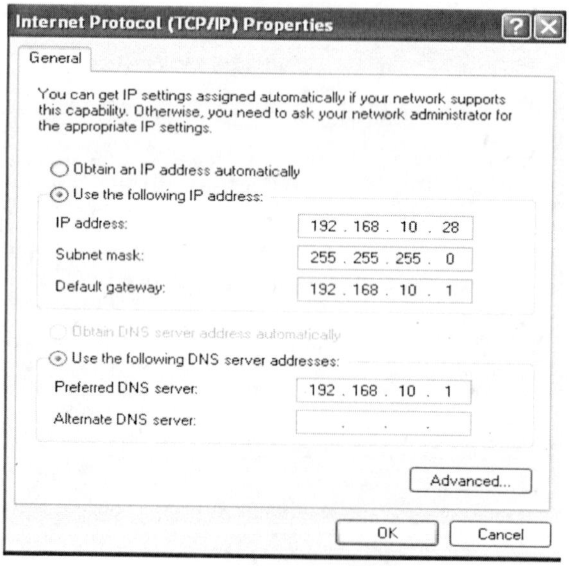

Internet Protocol (TCP/IP) Properties

General

You can get IP settings assigned automatically if your network supports this capability. Otherwise, you need to ask your network administrator for the appropriate IP settings.

Obtain an IP address automatically

Use the following IP address:

IP address: 192 . 168 . 10 . 28

Subnet mask: 255 . 255 . 255 . 0

Default gateway: 192 . 168 . 10 . 1

Obtain DNS server address automatically

Use the following DNS server addresses:

Preferred DNS server: 192 . 168 . 10 . 1

Alternate DNS server:

Advanced...

OK Cancel

To activate or deactivate network connections, select your connection and then click Activate/Deactivate.

Note: A modem is not needed when accessing the internet through a LAN.

The Right Hardware

To operate most of the current web browsers and online services, you should have a workstation (computer) with at least 8MB RAM and 10MB of free disk space. If you are accessing the internet outside of a LAN environment, you will need a modem that will connect you with other computers and interpret the data being sent back and forth. You must also have access to a live telephone line.

The Right Software

To make your connection complete you will need connection software that allows your computer to dial into an internet access provider, establish an account and work with the data in a straight forward manner. Many access providers will give you software that will allow you to access their system using all-in-one custom interface. Some internet access providers may allow you to establish a serial line interface protocol (SLIP) or Point to Point protocol (PPP) connection. SLIP/PPP connection allows you to one independent software packages such as web browsers, either one at a time or simultaneously.

Connection Option

Until recently, the two primary methods of accessing the Internet are network connections and dial up connection. The network connections are allowing users of LAN to go online through their workplace system and dial up connection through a modem and telephone line. The following are some of the newer connections options that you might want to investigate.

Cable Internet

These systems allow your computer to connect to the Internet through the same cable that carrier your TV signal.

Satellite Connections

Direct PC allows you to download Internet files via a satellite connection.

Integrated services Digital Network (ISDN)

An ISDN line is a type of digital phone line that can transmit data many times faster than a modern and phone line.

Wireless Connections

Cellular phones, personal digital assistants (PDAs) now Allow Internet access from notifications of Email to limited web Connections.

Web TV

Web TV Provides web and E-mail access through ordinary television Sets. The connection is made through a custom high speed modem.

1.4 Creating Websites for individual and Corporate World

In India the development of Web started in the year 1995 the day was 15th of August, when the first time VSNL (Videsh Sanchar Nigam Limited, now BSNL), India's first internet service provider started its services for accessing the Internet. Since that day Web Development Companies in India provided Web site Development for Individuals and Corporate World. The following are the some examples of such Web site development:

(i) Application Service Providers Web Site Development

Application Service Providers (ASPs) are third-party entities that manage and distribute software-based services and solutions to customers across a wide area network from a central data center. ASPs give customers to implement complex systems themselves. In some cases, ASPs even provide customers with a comprehensive alternative to desining and managing internal information technology operations. ASP customers are also able to control more precisely the total cost of technology ownership through scheduled payment schemes.

(ii) B2B and B2C Portal Development

B2B portals provide a full range of web services, including applications and e-commerce support for a customized, integrated e-business hub. B2C portals allow companies to deploy customer, consumer or community Internet sites to provide a centralized full service starting point that can eventually be customized.

(iii) Database Driven Web Site Development

A database-driven Web site combines databases with the Web ability to distribute information, database-powered Web sites are a key driver of today's e-commerce revolution. Companies today are faced with an opportunity to transform their Web sites from collections of static, text-based information into dynamic business tools. Database driven pages offer some advanced capabilities, such as publishing data from corporate databases into Web pages and customizing a visitor's view of a site around their individual needs and preferences.

Web Site Development

The Internet represents a low cost opportunity for businesses to promote their products and services globally. It provides new opportunities for any individual or company in the world. They offer web development services for all types of businesses. They have experience in different web design technology areas including basic HTML, DHTML, Java Script, VBScript, CSS, ASP and other technologies. Functional capabilities include forums, group email, database access & management, Flash and ecommerce.

Technical Requirements for Web Site Development

HTML, DHTML, SQL, CSS, Java Script, VBScript, ASP, JSP

HTML Basics

HTML is a scripting language that is used to design the web pages. It is most powerful and basic required tool for web site development. Normally it started with an opening tag and ended with a closing tag:

```
<html> </html>
<p></p>, <h2></h2>, ..........
```

Some tags do not have a closing tags: <br>, <hr>, etc.

Attributes

Extra parameters are in the opening tags to change some behaviors of the tag.

For example:

<tag attr1="value1" attr2="value2" .....>
<tag attr1='value1' attr2='value2' .....>
<tag attr1=value1 attr2=value2 .....>

Color

Color may be specified as the value of an attribute or represented by pre-defined name or RGB code. The following list represents the color name as well as color code.

Color Name	Color Code
Aqua	#00ffff
Black	#000000
Blue	#0000ff
Fuchsia	#ff00ff
Gray	#808080
Green	#008080
Lime	#00ff00
Maroon	#800000
Navy	#000080
Olive	#808000
Purple	#800080
Red	#ff0000
Silver	#c0c0c0
Teal	#008080
White	#ffffff
Yellow	#ffff00

Special characters

Some characters are used for HTML constructs and cannot be used directly. And, some characters are hard to type, eg. ©. Human cannot remember numbers. So, mnemonic is normally used instead.

© = ©

Some important special characters are as follows:

Special Character	Code
Non-breakable space	

"	"
&	&
<	<
>	>

Cascading Style Sheet (CSS)

Cascading Style Sheets allow us to specify the style of our page elements separately from the structure of our document. This separation of structure from content allows greater manageability and makes changing the style of our document easier. We can do following through CSS:

- Colors and Backgrounds
- Fonts
- Letter Spacing
- Text Decoration
- Clipping
- Margins
- Text Indent
- Position and Z-index
- Line Height

JavaScript

JavaScript is an Object oriented programming language. It is used to write programs that are executed by a Web browser within the context of a Web Page. To embed JavaScript in HTML, use the <script> tag.

Example:

```
<script language="JavaScript">
//statements
</script>
```

The script tag may be placed in either the head or the body of an HTML document. JavaScript supports several primitive types of values and complex types.

Primitive types:

Number: Consists of integer and floating-point numbers and the special NaN (not a number) value.

Boolean: Consists of the logical values true and false.

String: Consists of string values that are enclosed in single or double quotes.

Complex types:

- Array

- Object

In JavaScript, we do not declare the type of a variable as you do in other languages, such as Java and C++.

Boolean Values

JavaScript, like Java and unlike C, supports a pure Boolean type that consists of the two values true and false.

String Values

JavaScript provides built-in support for strings of characters. A string is a sequence of zero or more characters that are enclosed by double or single quotes. If a string begins with a double quote, then it must end with a double quote. JavaScript defines special formatting characters for use in strings.

Character	Meaning
\'	Single quote
\"	Double quote
\\	backslash
\n	new line
\r	carriage return
\f	formfeed
\t	horizontal tab
\b	backspace

JavaScript comments

- "//" for single line comments (everything are ignored from "//" to the end of line)
- "/*", "*/" block for multi-line comments (everything are ignore in between "/*" and "*/")

Unlike Java, semi-colon is not necessary for the end of statement. It is used only if multiple statements are put in the same line. "{" and "}" are used to group statements as one single statement.

Events Handling

Events are actions that usually occur as a result of something the user does. JavaScript applications in browsers are event-driven. For example, clicking a button or moving the mouse over a link are events. For our script to react to an event, we define event handlers, such as onChange and onClick.

The general syntax is:

<input type=button name=submit onclick="JavaScript: window.alert(this.name)">

1.5 CYBER LAWS

Introduction to Cyber laws in India

The Cyber laws Act-2000 aims to provide the legal infrastructure for e-commerce in India and would have a major impact for e-business and the new economy in India. In May 2000 both the houses of the India parliament passed the information technology bill. The bill received the assent of the president in August-2000 and Come to be unknown as the information technology Act-2000 cyber laws are contained in the IT act-2000. In IT Act-2000 also aims to provide the legal framework under which legal sanctity is accorded to all electronic records and other activities carried out by electronic means.

The following are the main objectives of the act:

(i) To facilitate electronic filling of documents with departments.

(ii) To facilitate electronic storage of data.

(iii) To grant legal recognition for transactions carried out by means of electronic data interchange and other means of electronic communication common known as e-commerce in place of paper based method communication.

(iv) To give a legal recognition to digital signature for authentication of any information or matter that requires authentication under any law.

(v) To facilitate and give legal sanction to electronic fund transfer between banks and financial institution.

The act-2000 consists of 94-section spread over thirteen chapters and four schedules to the Act. The various chapters are clearly mentioned in detail. The schedule to the Act contain related amendments made in other acts as outlined in the objectives of the act, namely, the Indian evidence Act,1972, the bankers book evidence Act,1981 and the Reserve Bank of India,1934.

The various chapters are ....

Chapter-1: Scope of the Act and definitions.

Chapter-2: Authentication of Electronic Records using Digital Signature.

Chapter-3: Electronic Governance.

Chapter-4: ATTRIBUTION, RECEIPT and DISPATCH of electronic Records.

Chapter-5: Secure Electronic records and secure Digital signature.

Chapter-6: Regulation of certifying authorities.

Chapter-7: Digital signature certification.

Chapter-8: Duties of subscribers.

Chapter-9: Panaties and Adjudication.

Chapter-10: Cyber Regulations Appellate Tribunal.

Chapter-11: OFFENCES.

Chapter-12: Network Service Providers not be liable in certain cases.

Chapter-13: miscellaneous (power of central and state Govt. to make rules, cyber Regulations Advisory committee etc.)

1.6 WEB APPLICATIONS

Web Applications are using web technologies such as web browsers and web servers. The original purpose of the World Wide Web was merely presenting information. Web applications are use the Internet's infrastructure to deliver their functionality. Recent reports indicate that web applications represent more than thirty present of software applications across all industry sectors. A website comprises from one or more web pages. A document on the World Wide Web, consisting of an HTML file and any related files for scripts and graphics and often hyperlinked to other documents on the Web.

The server receives the HTTP request and dispatches the request and its associated data (headers + query) to the desired resource residing on the server. In the simplest case, the server responds with a static HTML page, which the browser interprets and presents to the user. In more complex web applications, the server must perform other functions such as the following:

(i) Build the HTML response page dynamically to be passed back to the browser

(ii) Execute business logic

(iii) Exchange data with legacy systems

(iv) Retrieve data according to query parameters

(v) Reestablish a session from a former request

(vi) Authenticate and authorize users

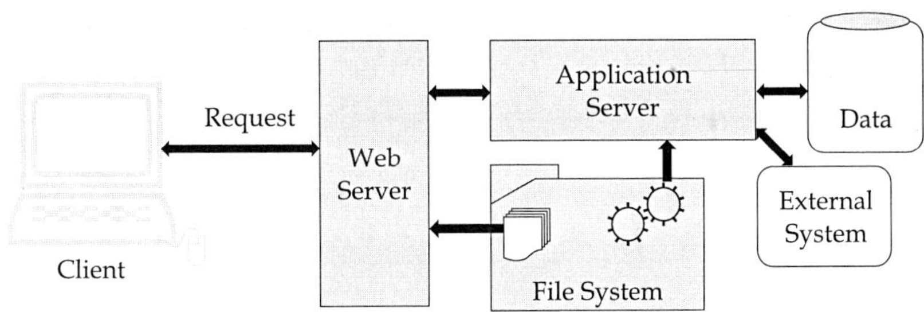

Figure: Web Application Architecture

The following are two reasons that preferred Web applications over traditional applications:

1. Web applications are more accessible. The HTTP protocol used in web applications is a standard protocol that can travel across corporate firewalls.
2. Web applications have a lower maintenance and deployment costs.

Since Web applications are running in web browser, they do not depend on installing client software on each user's computer. Web applications can be maintained by modifying code that resides on a server. This reduces the time and the cost of upgrade and deployment of web applications compared to traditional client/server applications. Web applications are not limited to one type of application. They can range from simple static web pages to sophisticated applications.

Types of Web Applications

(i) Brochure Web Applications

This is the first generation of Web Applications. They are composed of static web pages. When developing focus on content development and the layout of graphics and text. For example personal web pages that contains their resume and personal information or web pages about a company's product.

(ii) Service oriented applications

Service oriented applications contain the programming logic needed to implement the service. These sites are used to offer a service to web users. The layout of the data is often a secondary concern. During maintenance the developers need a good understanding of the control logic. For example web mail services or online word-processing systems.

(iii) Data intensive applications

These are sites that provide an interface to browse and query large amount of data. The main emphasis in these applications is on the data, with minimal amount of programming logic involved. During maintenance the developers need a good understanding of the data flow. For example online library catalogues.

(iv) Information system applications

Information System applications combine the Service Oriented Applications and the Data Intensive Applications. Developers are concerned with the data flow and control flow. For example online banking System.

Web Application Architecture

A Web Application Architecture proposed by Kruchten, can build upon the four views:

(i) Logical view

(ii) Development view

(iii) Physical view

(iv) Process view

Each view captures specific decisions and all views must be examined together to gain a good understanding of the whole applications.

(i) The Logical View

The Logical view provides a high level abstraction of the system based on the domain of the problem. The application is represented by different components and the interaction between them. The Presentation Logic tier shows the interaction between the components responsible for the generation of the User Interface. Web Applications can be organized as 2-tiers or as 3 tiers. The database system used for the implementation can easily be changed without affecting the Business Logic. The Database tier contains all the data components that are used to provide persistent storage for the application data.

(ii) The Development View

The Development view presents that actual software module organization in the development environment. It focuses on the mapping of the Logical view conceptual components to the actual implementation artifacts. The Development View for Web Applications must highlight the following points:

(a) The link structure of the application pages

(b) User's session management techniques

(c) Application page generation technology

Examples of this technology are PHP and Java Server Pages (JSP).

(iii) The Physical View

It presents the mappings of the components in the Development view to the components in the environment. In this view use the following components:

(a) Web browsers

(b) Web servers

(c) Application servers

(d) Distributes objects (i.e. Enterprise Java Beans)

(e) Databases

(iv) The Process View

It presents the concurrency and distribution of process in the application.

1.7 WRITING WEB PROJECTS

If we are writing web projects or if we have ever been tempted to write web projects, we can use Java technologies and tools. A web programmer must understand concepts related to distributed applications and services, the HTTP protocol, Common Gateway Interface (CGI) programming, HTML/JavaScript programming, user authentication and authorization, session management, data exchange from disparate sources and so on.

1.7.1 Stages of Web Project developing process

The Four stages are used for the Web Project Developing as follows:

(i) **Strategy Phase** – In this phase, a strategic planner executive or project manager or client is determining the objective for the site based on a dedicated research effort.

(ii) **Design Phase** – In this phase the technical and creative teams are doing a parallel design of the site. technical team is designing the back-end applications that will be used on the site and the creative team is designing the user interface and interactions.

(iii) **Production Phase-** In this phase, we are building the site. If the client requests a change at this point a change order is issued. Any major changes in functionality and features have to monitor closely.

(iv) **Testing Phase-** In this phase, we are testing the site and getting ready to publish it on the Web server.

1.7.2 Web Project Characteristics

The following are the web project characteristics.

(i) **Project managers are not always client managers** – if you are project manager then you are not responsible for the client's expectations.

(ii) **Development schedules are dramatically short** - people on both sides (client & developer) underestimate the time and resources need to complete the project.

1.7.3 Technical Specifications

The users of the technical specification are other engineers who may bring in to work on the project, as well as the client's technical team. The technical specification is a document that clearly details how a technical component will be built.

1.8 WEB TEAM

The Internet provides new opportunities for businesses to promote their products and services globally. Further it allows companies to penetrate new markets and to establish a presence. The team of IT professionals develops fully functional, highly interactive web sites for entrepreneurs and companies which automatically become an asset to any business. They offer web development services for all types of businesses. They have experience in different web design technology areas including basic HTML, DHTML, SQL, CSS, Java Script, VBScript, ASP, and other leading edge technologies. Functional capabilities include forums, group email, database access & management, Flash and ecommerce. Determined to reach your target market, meet company goals and sales strategies, you need to develop a dynamic web site to enhance the particular business needs.

Skills of web team / Roles of Team

The following is a list of skills that require in project managers:

(i) Superior written and verbal communication skills.

(ii) Understanding of scheduling, budgeting and resource allocation.

(iii) Software project management experience.

(iv) Ability to lead effective meetings.

(v) Detail oriented.

(vi) Good sense of humor.

(vii) Development or production experience in Web multimedia software.

(viii) Pragmatic.

(ix) Ability to stay calm during disasters.

There are three compositions of Team Members based on certain types of Web projects.

1. Core
2. Extended
3. Special

Core team members

- Project Manager / Producer
- Web Production Specialist
- Creative Lead
- Designers
- Technical Lead
- Production Artist
- Quality Assurance Lead

Extend team members

- Account Manager
- Programmer
- Network Engineer
- Information Architect
- Copywriter
- Tester

Special team members

- Web Cast Specialist
- Strategic Planner
- Security Expert
- Media Buyer
- Video Engineer
- Audio Engineer
- 3-D Modeler
- Feasibility and Software Testing

In software testing, the technical team tests all software that is to be used on the site, such as e-commerce server software, so that they can get up to speed with the features and the application programming interfaces.

1.9 PLANNING AND PROCESS DEVELOPMENT

To become an effective plan and process development, web designer will be much time spent on the following points:

- Define the problem
- Thinking
- Analyzing what needs to be done
- Talking with your client and their customers
- Planning on paper
- Devise a solution

Planning has three types.

(i) Early Planning

The following are the functions of early planning.

(i) Plan,"what the web site is to do".

(ii) We will require background information to understand the company/ product/organization and so put our work and the whole design process in context.

(iii) Gather information about the organization.

(iv) Gather information about the type of customer.

(v) Gather information about the product's market conditions.

(vi) Gather information about its pricing.

(vii) Gather information about advertising plans.

(viii) Gather information about the competitive situation.

(ix) Gather information about positioning or market stance of the company/ organization.

From this context, establish with the client what the web site needs to do.

(ii) Technical Planning

When we are going through this process always keep in mind the overall web goal statement. The overall model used for the site structure is probably going to be a combination of hierarchy and hypertext.

Hierarchy

This is also known as a top-down approach, as it literally works from a high, general level, and works itself down into increasing levels.

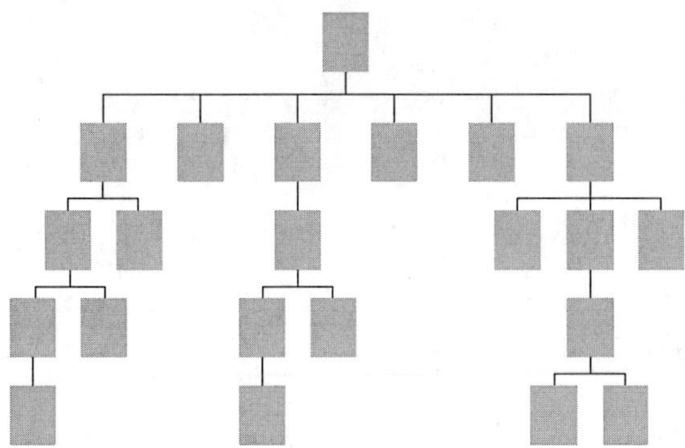

Each rectangle represents a web page. One choice logically progresses to the next. Overall it is a good model and structure to use.

Hypertext

The hypertext structure is a fundamental to the web. It will also be vital to the design of the web site. It allows free movement around the site in the sense of breaking down a linear hierarchy.

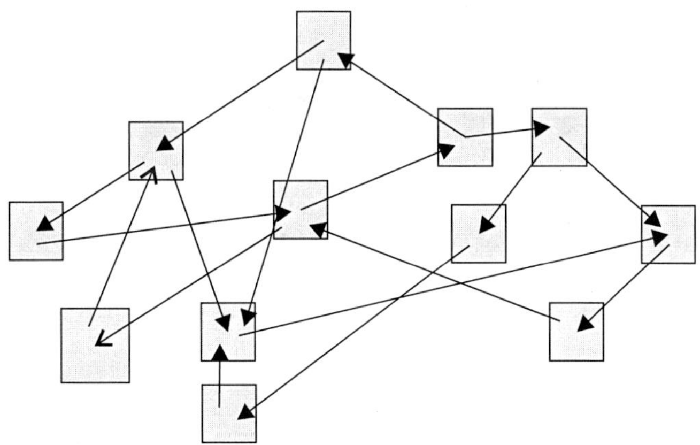

Hierarchy and Hypertext

By combining both models, we can achieve the best of both worlds. The pages gain a logical structure but gain freedom to allow the user to move across levels. This can usefully reduce the number of stages a user has to go through to get to where they want.

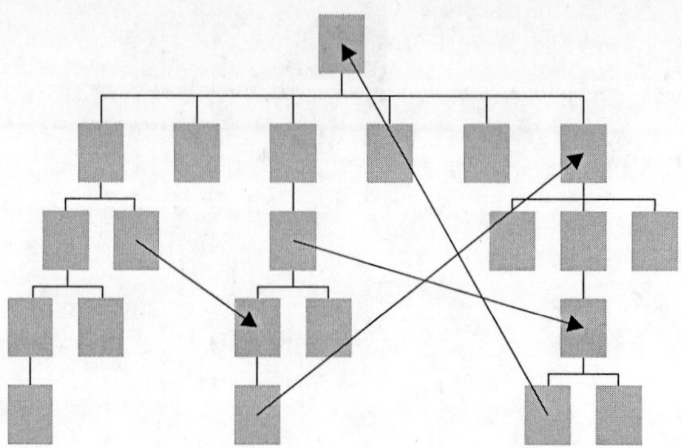

Linear Arrangement

A variation on the above two models is a linear, sequential arrangement of pages. It is appropriate for any information that must be viewed in sequence. It could form part of a larger site's design that means it could be built into a hierarchy/hypertext system.

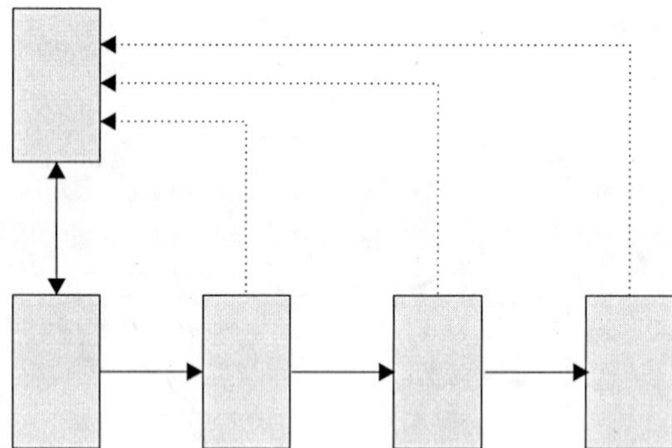

(iii) Production Planning

Directory Structure

When we want to rearrange our web site, we may cause broken links in our site. We first launch our site; it may comprise a small, manageable number of files. So don't dump all our files into the same directory on the server. But it will grow. So from the start, arrange our server hierarchy logically and neatly, with specific directories for images and content. Then further divide content directories by topic.

Hosting

ISP allows us to use URL like mydomain.com rather than myisp.com/mydirectory. The following facility provided by the ISP.

- Works properly in different server
- Use relative URLs
- Database access
- Search Engine

- Don't need to resolve domain name
- CGI access
- Transfer limit

Site Integrity

- There are commercial programs to search broken links.
- There is a free resource available to check for broken links.
- Broken links give very bad impression to visitors.

Site Performance

ISP provides log files that are used to know how many hits our pages have received, where the requests came from and so on.

Log files

Upon receiving the request from a browser, your Web server will try to service the request. We can analyze this data to get a picture of how our audience is using our site. If we want to perform really sophisticated analysis, we may need a commercial analysis tool.

SUMMARY

The Internet represents a low cost opportunity for businesses to promote their products and services globally. It provides new opportunities for any individual or company in the world. A protocol is a standard that controls or enables the connection, communication and data transfer between two computing devices. Protocol is the most fundamental concepts of network communication. The Internet Protocol is a protocol used for communicating data across a packet-switched inter network. TCP provides reliable, in-order delivery of a stream of bytes, making it suitable for applications like file transfer and e-mail. It is so important in the Internet protocol suite that sometimes the entire suite is referred to as TCP/IP. File Transfer Protocol is a network protocol used to transfer data from one computer to another through a network, such as the Internet. The team of IT professionals develops fully functional, highly interactive web sites for entrepreneurs and companies which automatically become an asset to any business. Web Applications are using web technologies such as web browsers and web servers. The original purpose of the World Wide Web was merely presenting information. Web applications are use the Internet's infrastructure to deliver their functionality. Recent reports indicate that web applications represent more than thirty present of software applications across all industry sectors.

EXERCISE

1. Explain the development of web.
2. Explain the protocols governing web.
3. Write the short notes on Cyber laws.

4. How to write web projects?
5. Explain web teams.
6. What is Planning and Process Development?
7. Explain web development strategies.

*****

CHAPTER 2

HTML

HTML stands for Hyper Text Mark-up Language. It allows images and objects to be embedded and can be used to create interactive forms. It is written in the form of HTML elements consisting of "tags" surrounded by angle brackets within the web page content.

2.1 INTRODUCTION

HTML is a technique to design web pages. HTML is not a programming language, it is a markup language. A markup language is a set of markup tags. It uses markup tags to describe web pages.

HTML Tags

HTML markup tags are usually called HTML tags. HTML tags are keywords surrounded by angle brackets like <html>.HTML tags normally come in pairs like <b> and </b>. The first tag in a pair is the start tag and the second tag is the end tag. Start and end tags are also called opening tags and closing tags.

HTML Documents = Web Pages

HTML documents describe web pages. It contains HTML tags and plain text. HTML documents are also called web pages. The purpose of a web browser (like Internet Explorer or Firefox) is to read HTML documents and display them as web pages. The browser does not display the HTML tags, but uses the tags to interpret the content of the page.

```
<html>
<body>
<h1>My First Heading</h1>
<p>My first paragraph</p>
</body>
</html>
```

Save the above program with extension .html like f1.html.

Now double click on f1.html.

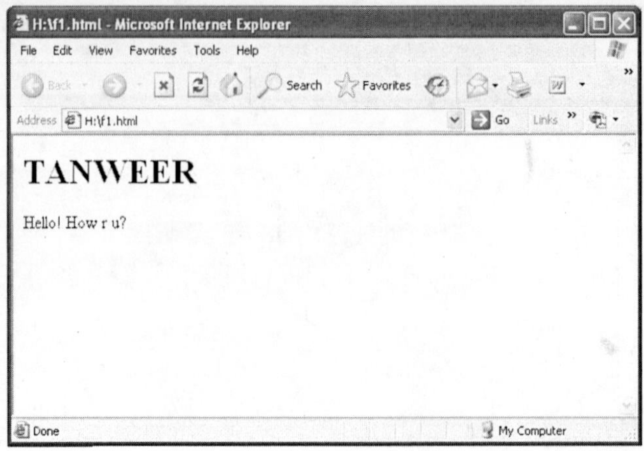

2.2 HTML Basics

All HTML documents must contain the following elements.

- HTML
- HEAD
- BODY

```
<HTML>
<HEAD>
<TITLE>MY FIRST WEB PAGE</TITLE>
</HEAD>
<BODY>
WELCOME HTML!
</BODY>
</HTML>
```

The text between <html> and </html> describes the web page.

The text between <title> and </title> describes the title of web page.

The text between <body> and </body> is the visible page content.

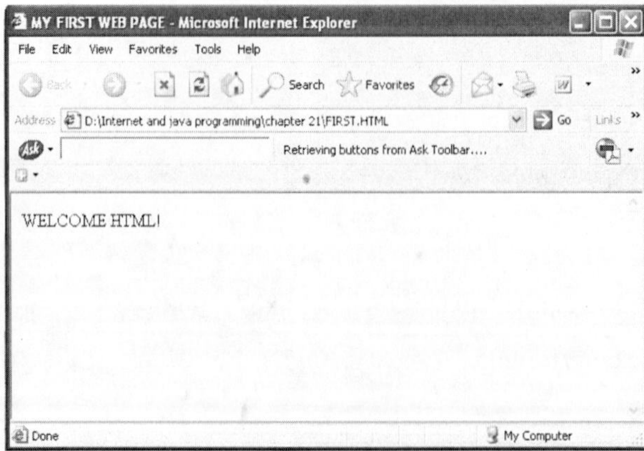

BODY element has the following attributes.

- BGCOLOR
- LEFTMARGIN
- TOPMARGIN

```
<HTML>
<HEAD>
<TITLE>MY FIRST WEB PAGE</TITLE>
</HEAD>
<BODY BGCOLOR="#C0C0C0" LEFTMARGIN ="50" TOPMARGIN= "100">
HTML BODY ATTRIBUTES ARE SET AS FOLLOWS.
BACKGROUND COLOR: SILVER <BR>
LEFTMARGIN = 50 <BR>
TOPMARGIN= 100 <BR>
</BODY>
</HTML>
```

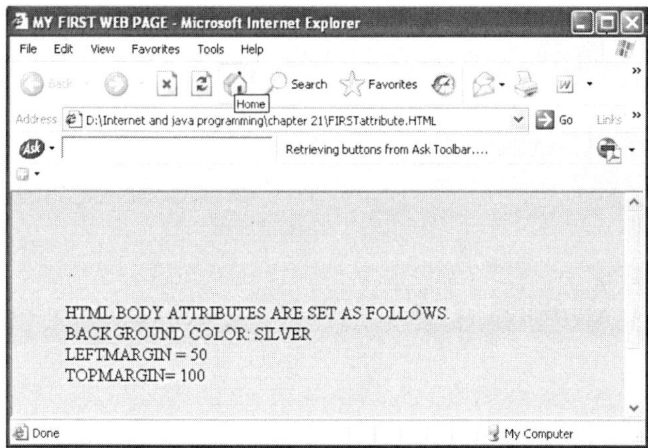

2.2 FORMATTING AN HTML DOCUMENTS

The following table defines the formatting tags long with description.

Tag	Description
<b>	Defines bold text
<big>	Defines big text
<em>	Defines emphasized text
<i>	Defines italic text
<small>	Defines small text
<strong>	Defines strong text
<sub>	Defines subscripted text
<sup>	Defines superscripted text
<ins>	Defines inserted text
<del>	Defines deleted text

Character Formatting

Bold

The Syntax is as follows.

<B>.... </B>

```
<HTML>
<HEAD>
<TITLE>MY FIRST WEB PAGE</TITLE>
</HEAD>
<BODY BGCOLOR="#C0C0C0" LEFTMARGIN ="50" TOPMARGIN= "100">
<B>
You are visiting our website first time.<br>
Have a nice day.<br>
</B>
</BODY>
</HTML>
```

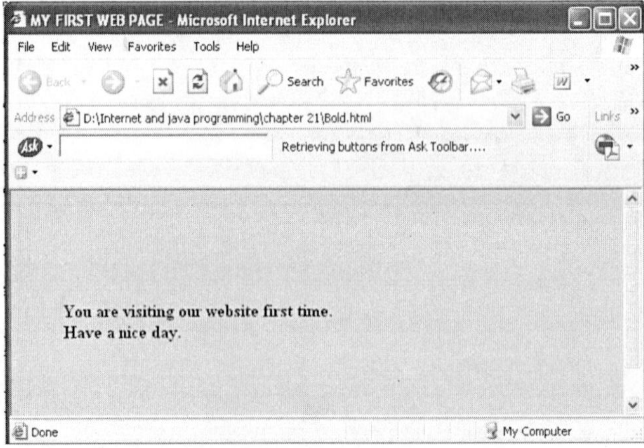

Italic

The Syntax is as follows.

<I> </I>

```
<HTML>
<HEAD>
<TITLE>MY FIRST WEB PAGE</TITLE>
</HEAD>
<BODY BGCOLOR="#C0C0C0" LEFTMARGIN ="50" TOPMARGIN= "100">
<I>
You are visiting our website first time.<br> Have a nice day.<br>
</I>
</BODY>
</HTML>
```

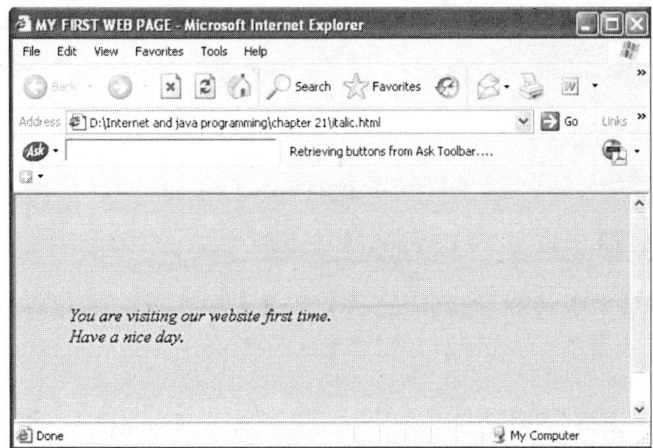

Underline

The Syntax is as follows.

<U> …. </U>

```
<HTML>
<HEAD>
<TITLE>MY FIRST WEB PAGE</TITLE>
</HEAD>
<BODY BGCOLOR="#C0C0C0" LEFTMARGIN ="50" TOPMARGIN= "100">
<U>
You are visiting our website first time.<br>
Have a nice day.<br>
</U>
</BODY>
</HTML>
```

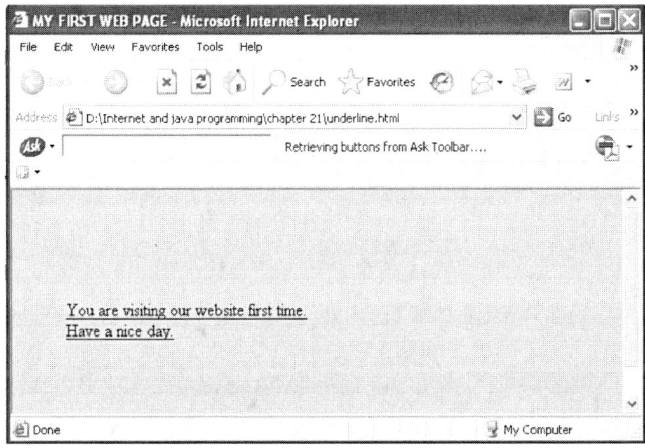

BIG

The Syntax is as follows.

<BIG> </BIG>

```
<HTML>
<HEAD>
<TITLE>MY FIRST WEB PAGE</TITLE>
</HEAD>
<BODY BGCOLOR="#C0C0C0" LEFTMARGIN ="50" TOPMARGIN= "100">
You are visiting our website first time.<br>
<BIG>
Have a nice day.<br>
</BIG>
</BODY>
</HTML>
```

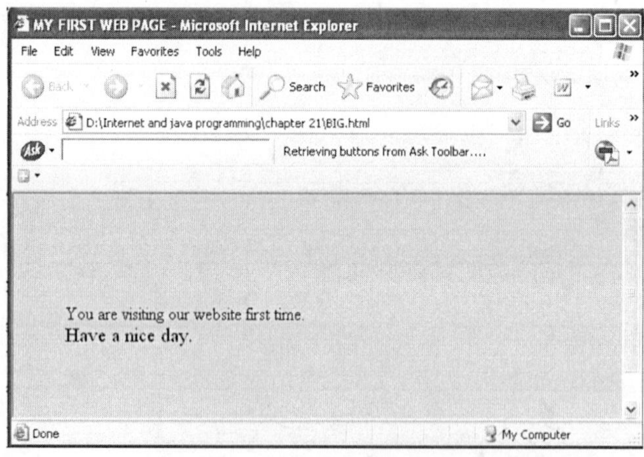

SMALL

The Syntax is as follows.

<SMALL>

….

</SMALL>

```
<HTML>
<HEAD>
<TITLE>MY FIRST WEB PAGE</TITLE>
</HEAD>
<BODY BGCOLOR="#C0C0C0" LEFTMARGIN ="50" TOPMARGIN= "100">
<B>You are visiting our website first time.<br></B>
<SMALL>
Have a nice day.<br>
```

```
</SMALL>
</BODY>
</HTML>
```

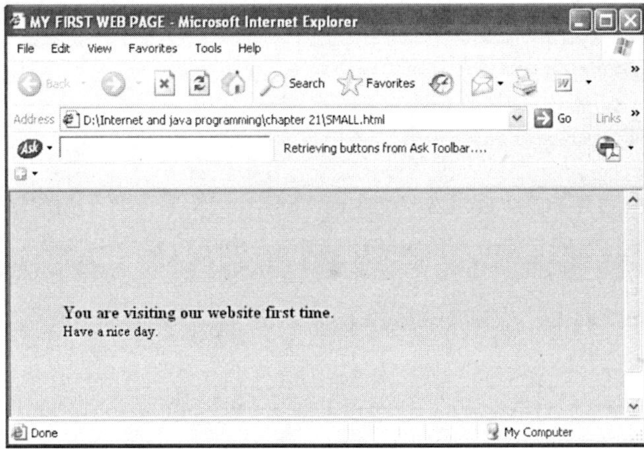

Subscript

The Syntax is as follows.

_{....}

```
<HTML>
<HEAD>
<TITLE>MY FIRST WEB PAGE</TITLE>
</HEAD>
<BODY BGCOLOR="#C0C0C0" LEFTMARGIN ="50" TOPMARGIN= "100">
<B>You are visiting our website first time.<br></B>
<SMALL>
Have a <SUB> nice </SUB>day.<br>
</SMALL>
</BODY>
</HTML>
```

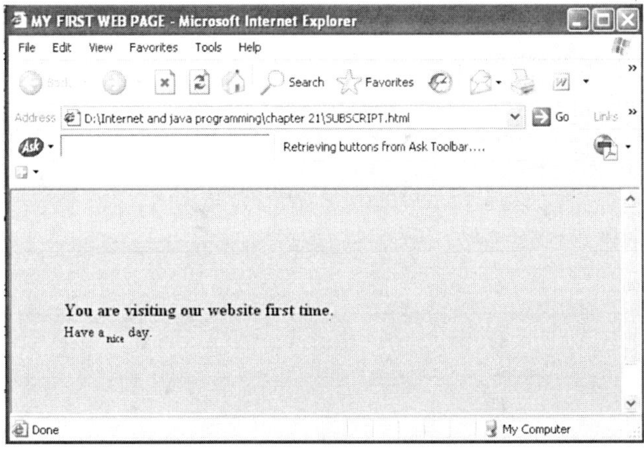

Superscript

The Syntax is as follows.

^{……}

```
<HTML>
<HEAD>
<TITLE>MY FIRST WEB PAGE</TITLE>
</HEAD>
<BODY BGCOLOR="#C0C0C0" LEFTMARGIN ="50" TOPMARGIN= "100">
<B>You are visiting our website first time.<br></B>
<SMALL>
Have a <SUP> nice </SUP>day.<br>
</SMALL>
</BODY>
</HTML>
```

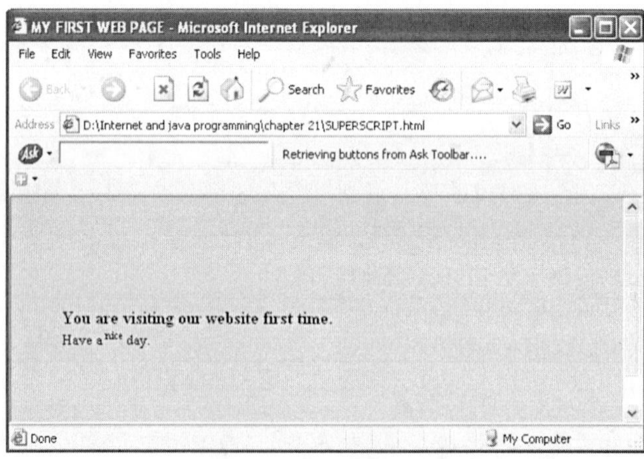

Block Formatting

Line Break

The Syntax is as follows.


```
<HTML>
<HEAD>
<TITLE>Line Break</TITLE>
</HEAD>
<BODY>
You are visiting our website first time.<br>Have a nice day.<br>
</BODY>
</HTML>
```

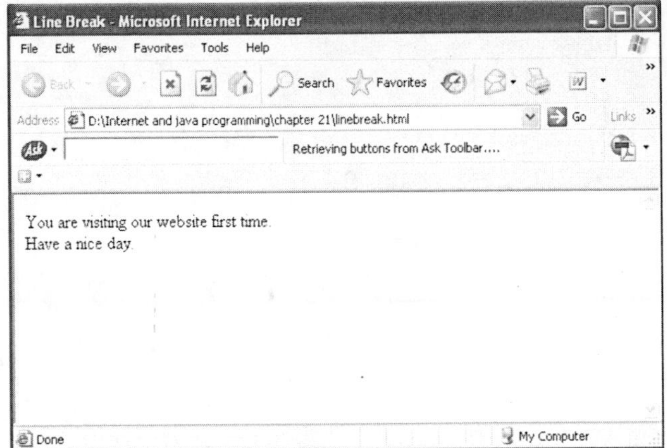

Paragraph

HTML paragraphs are defined with the <p> tag.

The syntax is as follows.

<p> ….. </p>

<P ALIGN=value> … </P>

Value can be

- LEFT
- RIGHT
- CENTER

For example:

```
<p>This is First paragraph</p>
<p>This is another paragraph</p>
```

```
<HTML>
<HEAD>
<TITLE>Paragraph</TITLE>
</HEAD>
<BODY>
<P ALIGN=CENTER>
You are visiting our website first time.<br>Have a nice day.<br>
</P>
</BODY>
</HTML>
```

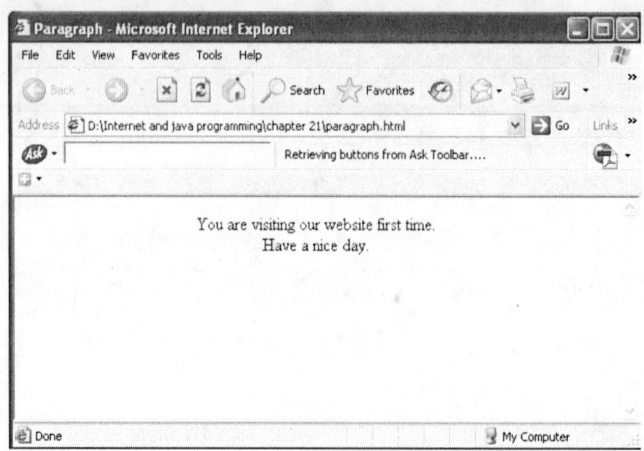

Address

The syntax is as follows.

<ADDRESS>....</ADDRESS>

```
<HTML>
<HEAD>
<TITLE>Address</TITLE>
</HEAD>
<BODY>
<ADDRESS>
Tanweer Alam<br>MCA Department<br>MIET, Meerut
</ADDRESS>
</BODY>
</HTML>
```

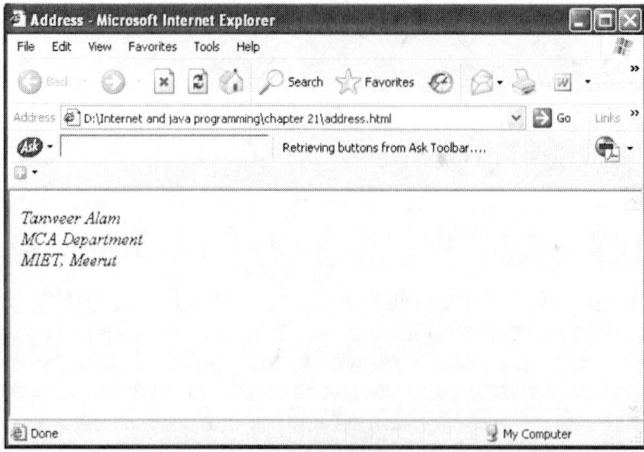

Heading

HTML headings are defined with the <h1> to <h6> tags.

The syntax is as follows.

```
<h1> This is a heading1</h1>
<h2> This is a heading2</h2>
<h3> This is a heading3</h3>
<h4> This is a heading4</h4>
<h5> This is a heading5</h5>
<h6> This is a heading6</h6>
```

```
<HTML>
<HEAD>
<TITLE>Address</TITLE>
</HEAD>
<BODY>
<H1>Tanweer Alam</H1>
<H2>Tanweer Alam</H2>
<H3>Tanweer Alam</H3>
<H4>Tanweer Alam</H4>
<H5>Tanweer Alam</H5>
<H6>Tanweer Alam</H6>
</BODY>
</HTML>
```

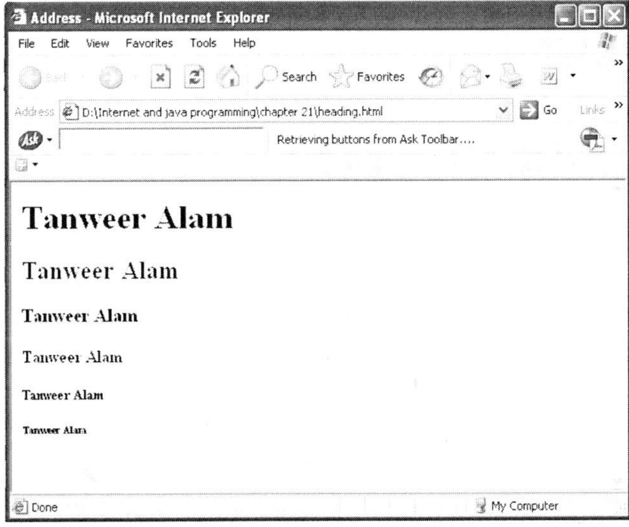

Blockquote

The syntax is as follows.

```
<BLOCKQUOTE>.... </BLOCKQUOTE>
```

```
<HTML>
<HEAD>
<TITLE>BLOCKQUOTE</TITLE>
</HEAD>
<BODY>
<BLOCKQUOTE>
"God helps those who help themselves."
</BLOCKQUOTE>
</BODY>
</HTML>
```

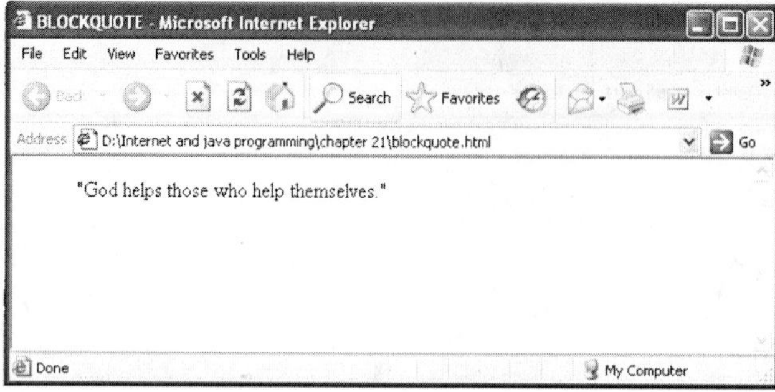

Horizontal rule

The syntax is as follows.

<HR>

```
<HTML>
<HEAD>
<TITLE>Horizontal Rule</TITLE>
</HEAD>
<BODY>
<HR>
This is Tanweer Alam.<BR>
<HR>This is ANJUM.<BR>
<HR>This is AAtif.<BR>
</BODY>
</HTML>
```

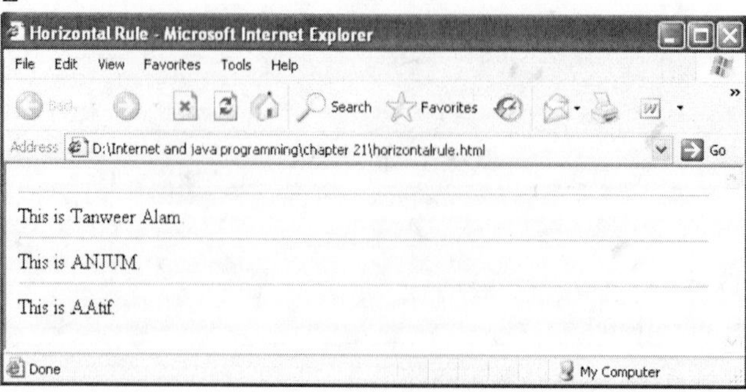

MARQUEE

The syntax is as follows.

```
<MARQUEE> Write Text here. </MARQUEE>
```

```
<HTML>
<HEAD>
<TITLE>MARQUEE</TITLE>
</HEAD>
<BODY>
<MARQUEE>
Write Scrolling Text here.
</MARQUEE>
</BODY>
</HTML>
```

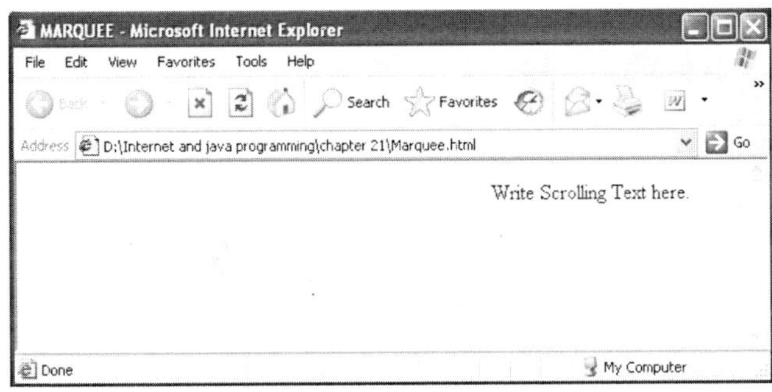

ATTRIBUTES:

(a) BGCOLOR

```
<HTML>
<HEAD>
<TITLE>MARQUEE</TITLE>
</HEAD>
<BODY>
<MARQUEE BGCOLOR="#00FF00">
Write Scrolling Text here.
</MARQUEE>
</BODY>
</HTML>
```

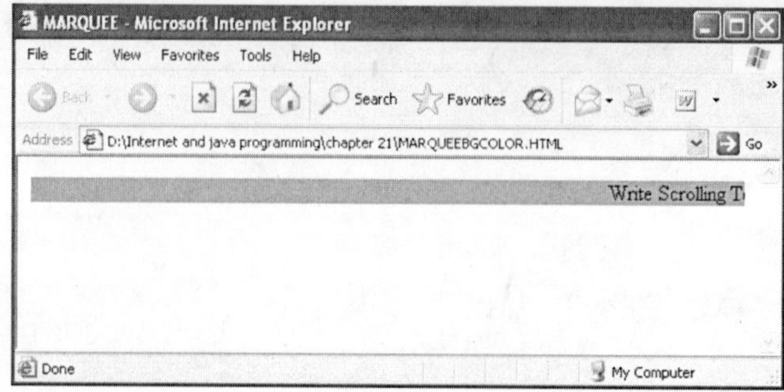

(b) **BEHAVIOR**

ATTRIBUTE:

(a) **SCROLL**

```
<HTML>
<HEAD>
<TITLE>MARQUEE</TITLE>
</HEAD>
<BODY>
<MARQUEE BEHAVIOR=SCROLL>
Write Scrolling Text here.
</MARQUEE>
</BODY>
</HTML>
```

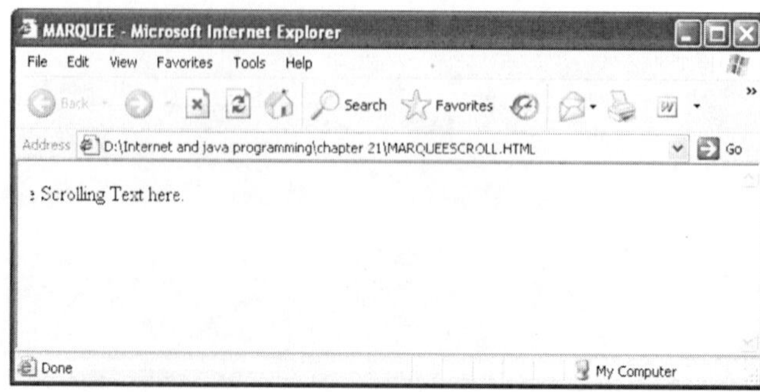

(b) **SLIDE**

```
<HTML>
<HEAD>
<TITLE>MARQUEE</TITLE>
</HEAD>
<BODY>
<MARQUEE BEHAVIOR=SLIDE>
Write Scrolling Text here.
</MARQUEE>
</BODY>
</HTML>
```

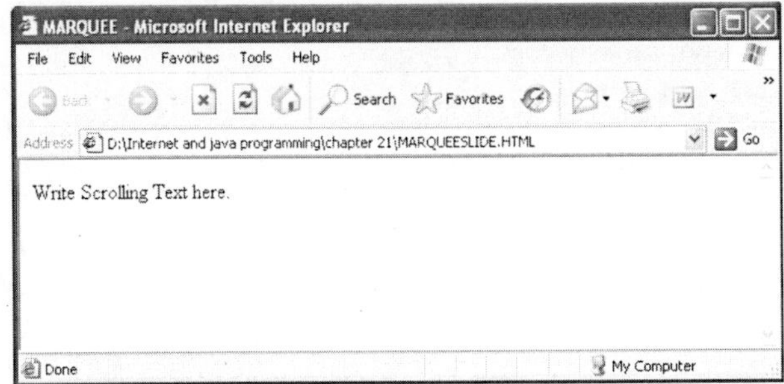

(c) ALTERNATE

```
<HTML>
<HEAD>
<TITLE>MARQUEE</TITLE>
</HEAD>
<BODY>
<MARQUEE BEHAVIOR=ALTERNATE>
Write Scrolling Text here.
</MARQUEE>
</BODY>
</HTML>
```

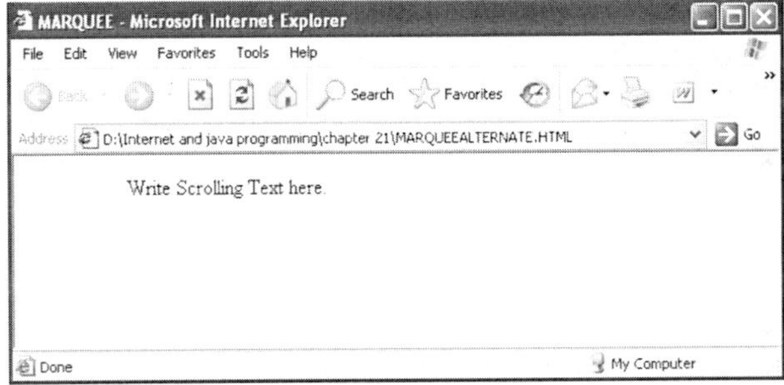

(d) DIRECTION

ATTRIBUTE:

(a) LEFT

```
<HTML>
<HEAD>
<TITLE>MARQUEE</TITLE>
</HEAD>
<BODY>
<MARQUEE DIRECTION=LEFT>
Write Scrolling Text here.
</MARQUEE>
</BODY>
</HTML>
```

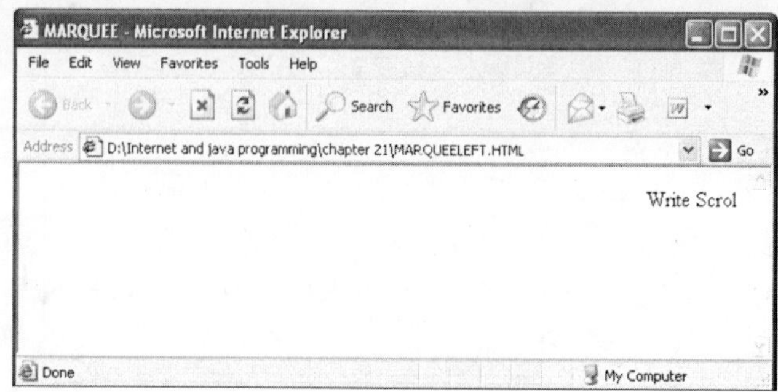

(b) RIGHT

```
<HTML>
<HEAD>
<TITLE>MARQUEE</TITLE>
</HEAD>
<BODY>
<MARQUEE DIRECTION=RIGHT>
Write Scrolling Text here.
</MARQUEE>
</BODY>
</HTML>
```

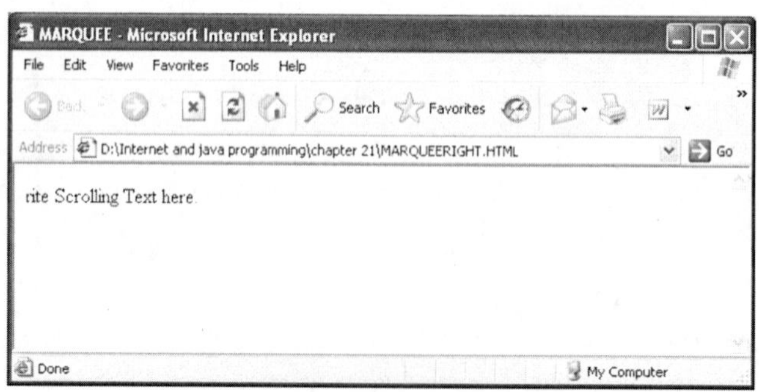

(c) HEIGHT

```
<HTML>
<HEAD>
<TITLE>MARQUEE</TITLE>
</HEAD>
<BODY>
<MARQUEE HEIGHT=10>
Write Scrolling Text here.
</MARQUEE>
</BODY>
</HTML>
```

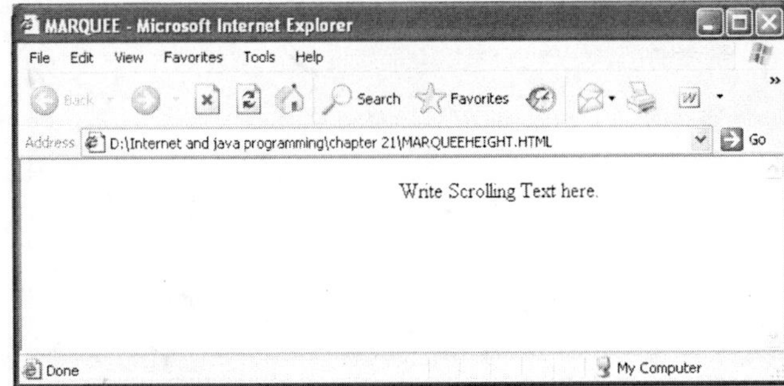

(d) HSPACE

```
<HTML>
<HEAD>
<TITLE>MARQUEE</TITLE>
</HEAD>
<BODY>
<MARQUEE HSPACE=100>
Write Scrolling Text here.
</MARQUEE>
</BODY>
</HTML>
```

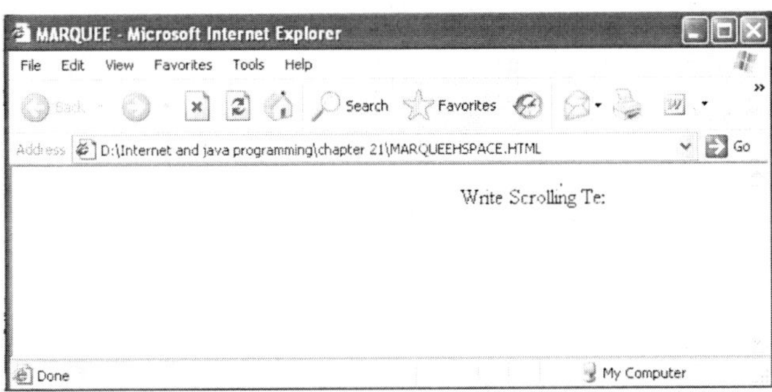

(e) VSPACE

```
<HTML>
<HEAD>
<TITLE>MARQUEE</TITLE>
</HEAD>
<BODY>
<MARQUEE VSPACE=100>
Write Scrolling Text here.
</MARQUEE>
</BODY>
</HTML>
```

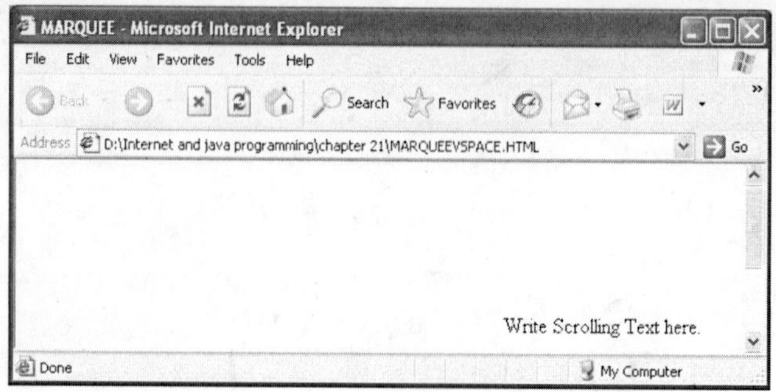

(f) LOOP

```
<HTML>
<HEAD>
<TITLE>MARQUEE</TITLE>
</HEAD>
<BODY>
<MARQUEE LOOP=2>
Write Scrolling Text here.
</MARQUEE>
</BODY>
</HTML>
```

OUTPUT AFTER TWO LOOPS.

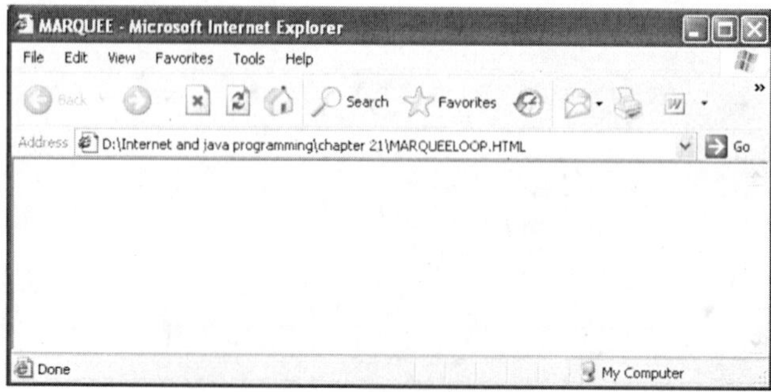

(g) SCROLLAMOUNT

```
<HTML>
<HEAD>
<TITLE>MARQUEE</TITLE>
</HEAD>
<BODY>
<MARQUEE SCROLLAMOUNT=100>
Write Scrolling Text here.
</MARQUEE>
</BODY>
</HTML>
```

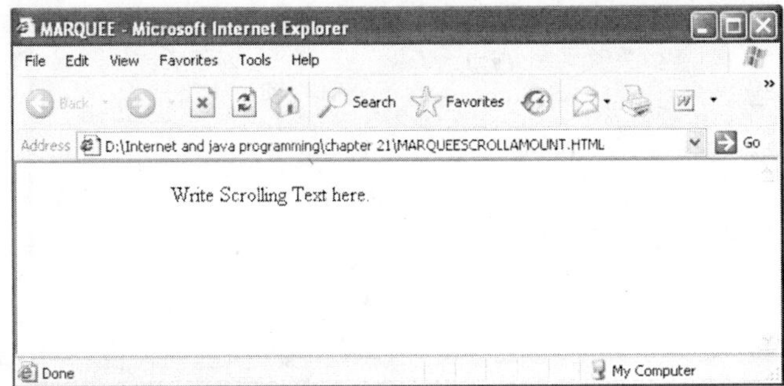

(h) SCROLLDELAY

```
<HTML>
<HEAD>
<TITLE>MARQUEE</TITLE>
</HEAD>
<BODY>
<MARQUEE SCROLLDELAY=100>
Write Scrolling Text here.
</MARQUEE>
</BODY>
</HTML>
```

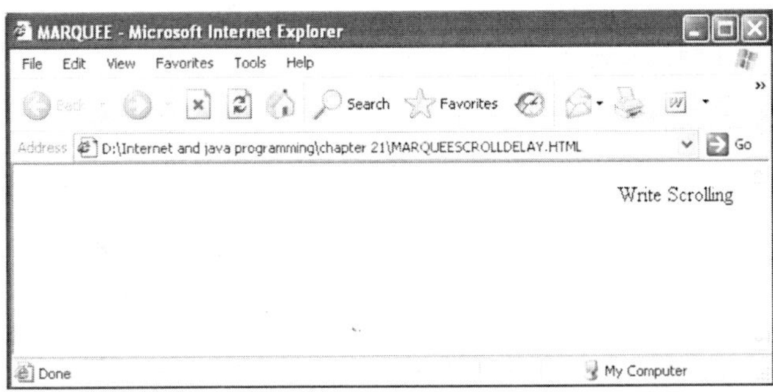

(i) Pre-formatted text

```
<HTML>
<HEAD>
<TITLE>PRE FORMATTED TEXT</TITLE>
</HEAD>
<BODY>
TANWEER ALAM, ANJUM, AATIF ALAM
<PRE>
Pre-Formatted Text here.
TANWEER ALAM, ANJUM, AATIF ALAM
</PRE>
</BODY>
</HTML>
```

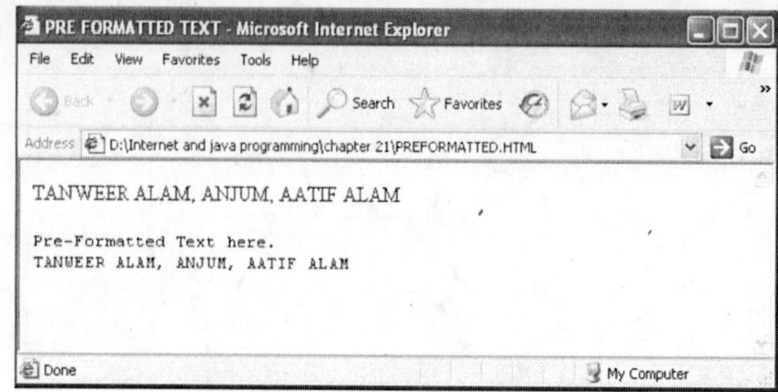

(j) Define

```
<HTML>
<HEAD>
<TITLE>DEFINE</TITLE>
</HEAD>
<BODY>
<DFN>
JAVA IS SIMPLE,OBJECT ORIENTED, DISTRIBUTED.
</DFN>
</BODY>
</HTML>
```

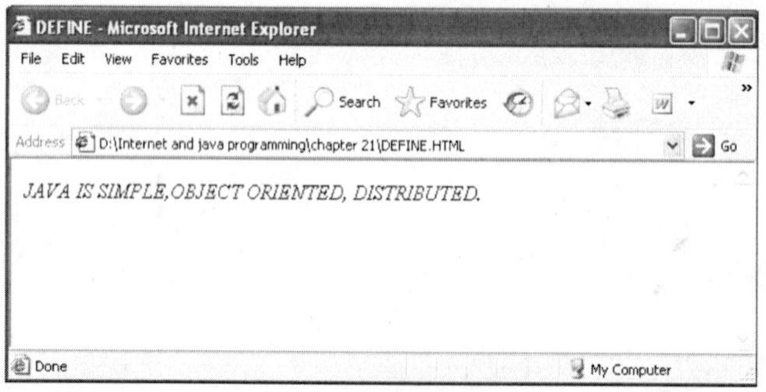

(k) No break

```
<HTML>
<HEAD>
<TITLE>DEFINE</TITLE>
</HEAD>
<BODY>
<NOBR>
JAVA IS SIMPLE,
OBJECT ORIENTED,
DISTRIBUTED.
</NOBR>
</BODY>
</HTML>
```

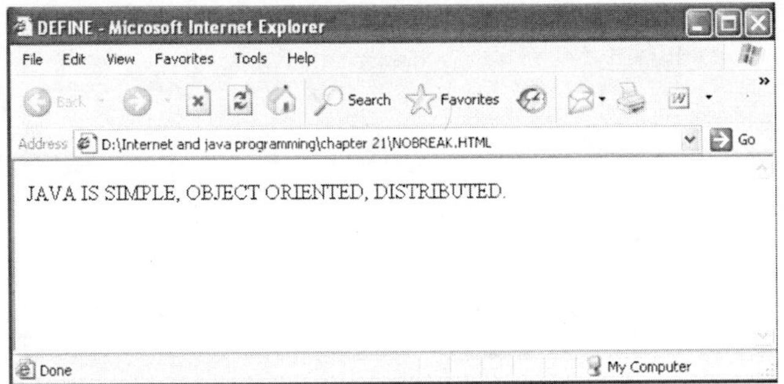

2.3 HYPER LINKS

The syntax is as follows.

```
<A HREF="program.html">Click Here</A>
```

```
<HTML>
<HEAD>
<TITLE>Tanweer Alam's Books</TITLE>
</HEAD>
<BODY>
<H1>List of My Books is as follows.</H1><br><br>
<B>
1. .Net Framework and C# Progrmming<br>
2. Computer Graphics<br>
3. Computer based Optimization Techniques<br>
4. Computer Graphics and Animation<br>
5. Object Oriented Systems with Java2.0<br>
</B>
</BODY>
</HTML>
```

Save the above file as books.html

Now write the following code and save as hyperlink.html

```
<HTML>
<HEAD>
<TITLE>My Books</TITLE>
</HEAD>
<BODY>
For My books information please
<B>
<A HREF="books.html">Click Here</A>
</B>
</BODY>
</HTML>
```

Output

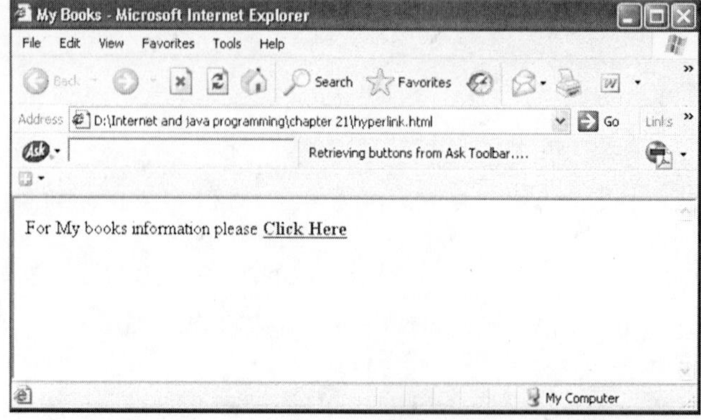

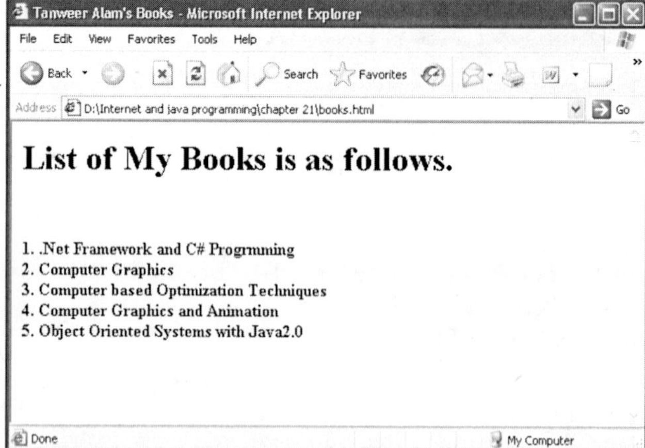

2.4 FONTS AND COLORS

(i) SIZE

```
<HTML>
<HEAD>
<TITLE>FONT SIZE</TITLE>
</HEAD>
<BODY>
<FONT SIZE=18>
TANWEER ALAM<BR>ANJUM<BR>AATIF ALAM<BR>
</FONT>
</BODY>
</HTML>
```

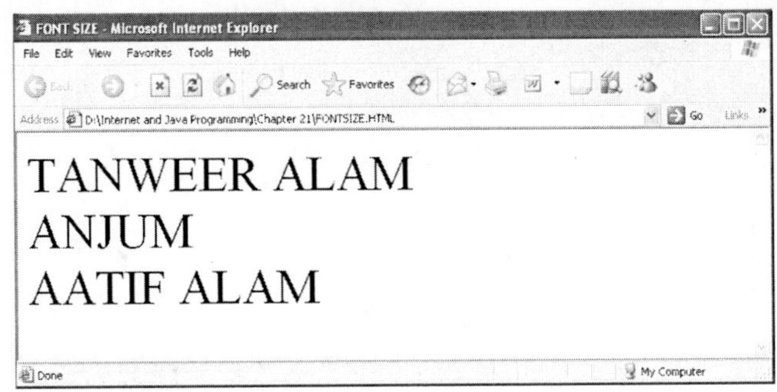

(ii) COLOR

```
<HTML>
<HEAD>
<TITLE>FONT COLOR</TITLE>
</HEAD>
<BODY>
<FONT COLOR=RED>
TANWEER ALAM<BR>ANJUM<BR>AATIF ALAM<BR>
</FONT>
</BODY>
</HTML>
```

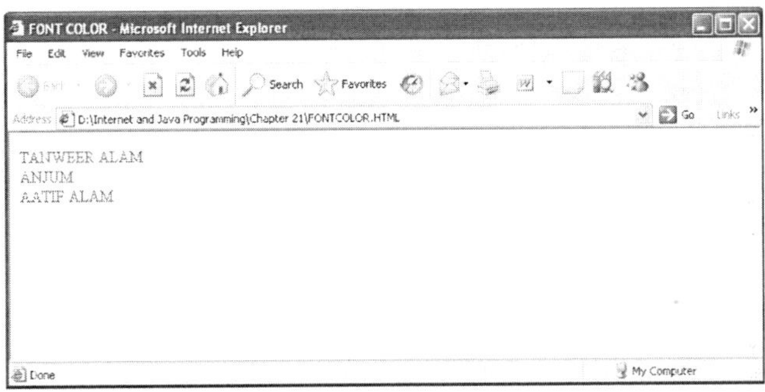

(iii) FACE

```
<HTML>
<HEAD>
<TITLE>FONT FACE</TITLE>
</HEAD>
<BODY>
<FONT FACE="Tw Cen MT">
TANWEER ALAM<BR>ANJUM<BR>AATIF ALAM<BR>
</FONT>
</BODY>
</HTML>
```

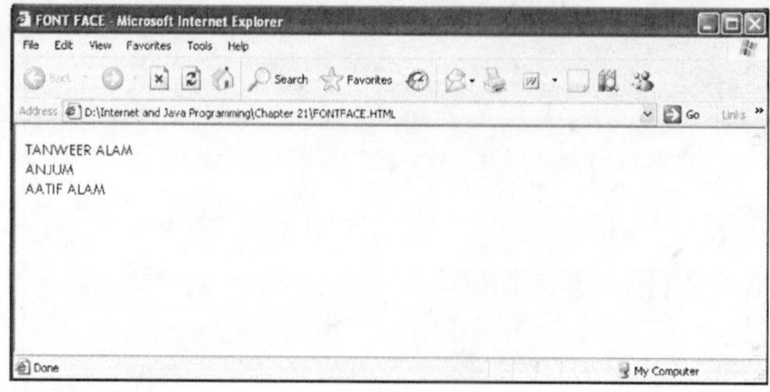

2.5 LISTS

(i) Unordered lists

The syntax is as follows.

```
<UL>
<LI>item1
<LI>item2
<LI>item3
</UL>
```

```
<HTML>
<HEAD>
<TITLE>UNORDERED LISTS</TITLE>
</HEAD>
<BODY>
Unordered Lists
<UL>
<LI>TANWEER ALAM
<LI>ANJUM
<LI>AATIF ALAM
</UL>
</BODY>
</HTML>
```

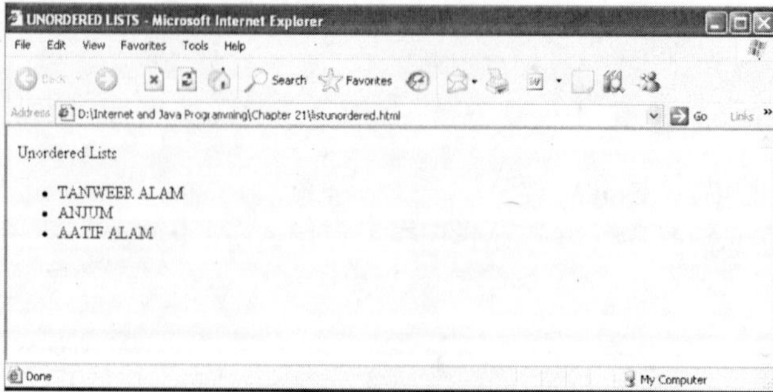

(ii) Ordered lists

The syntax is as follows.

```
<OL>
<LI>item1
<LI>item2
</OL>
```

```
<HTML>
<HEAD>
<TITLE>Ordered Lists</TITLE>
</HEAD>
<BODY>
Ordered Lists
<OL>
<LI>TANWEER ALAM
<LI>ANJUM
<LI>AATIF ALAM
</OL>
</BODY>
</HTML>
```

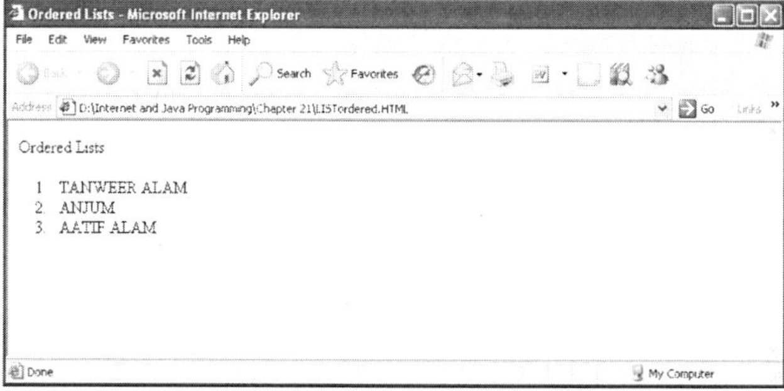

(iii) Definition lists

The syntax is as follows.

```
<DL>
<DT>item1
<DT>item2
</DL>
```

```
<HTML>
<HEAD>
<TITLE>Definition Lists</TITLE>
</HEAD>
```

```
<BODY>
Definition Lists display all data term tags followed by the data definition tags.
<DL>
<DT>TANWEER ALAM
<DT>ANJUM
<DD>AATIF ALAM
</DL>
</BODY>
</HTML>
```

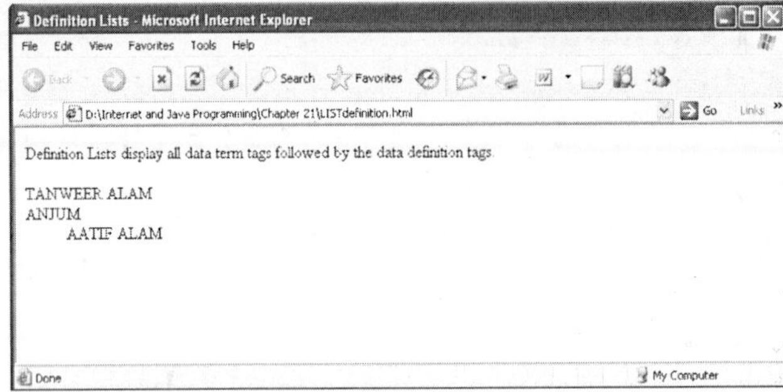

2.6 TABLES

Tables are the collection of rows and columns. Tables are defined with the tag <table>. A table is divided into rows (<tr>), and each row is divided into data cells (<td>). We can enter the contents into datacell using <td>. A data cell can contain text, paragraphs, tables, images, lists, forms, horizontal rules, etc. If we do not specify a border attribute then the table will be displayed without any borders. Sometimes this can be useful, but most of the time, you want the borders to show. To display a table with borders, we will have to use the border attribute:

```
<html>
<Body>
<table border="1">
<tr>
<td>row 1, cell 1</td>
<td>row 1, cell 2</td>
</tr>
<tr>
<td>row 2, cell 1</td>
<td>row 2, cell 2</td>
</tr>
</table>
<Body>
<html>
```

It looks in a browser:

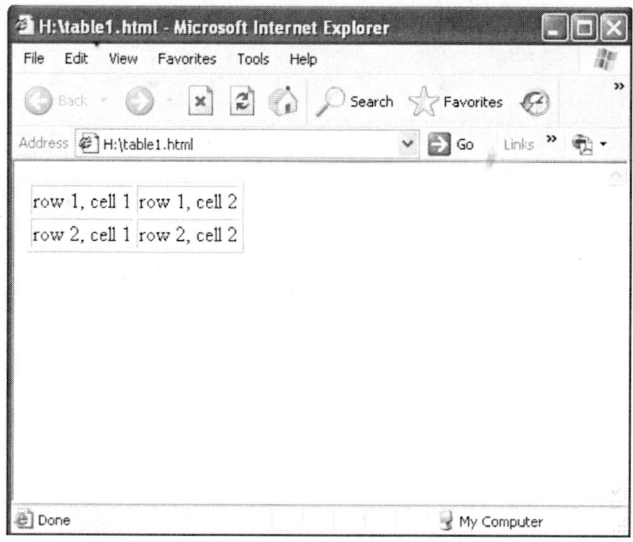

Headings in a Table

Headings in a table are defined with the <th> tag.

```
<html>
<body>
<table border="1">
<tr>
<th>Name</th>
<th>Roll No</th>
</tr>
<tr>
<td>Tanweer</td>
<td>53</td>
</tr>
<tr>
<td>AAtif</td>
<td>74</td>
</tr>
</table>
<body>
<html>
```

It looks in a browser:

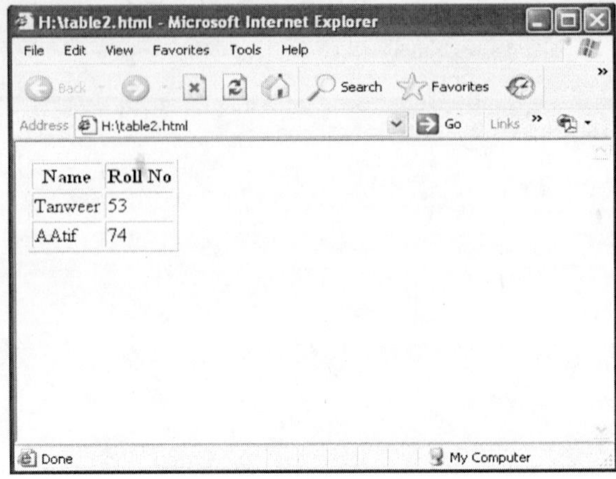

Empty Cells in a Table

Table cells with no content are not displayed very well in most browsers.

```
<html>
<body>
<table border="1">
<tr>
<td>Tanweer</td>
<td>Alam</td>
</tr>
<tr>
<td>Anjum</td>
<td></td>
</tr>
</table>
</body>
</html>
```

How it looks in a browser:

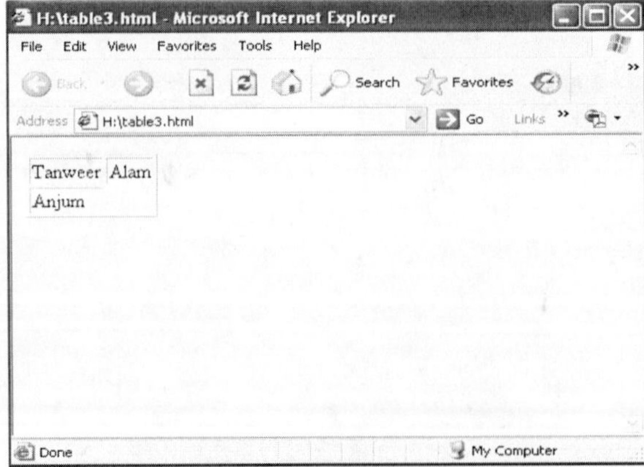

2.7 FRAMES

(i) Cols

```
<HTML>
<HEAD>
<TITLE>Frame</TITLE>
</HEAD>
<FRAMESET COLS="50%,50%">
<FRAME NAME=FIRST SRC=FONTCOLOR.HTML>
<FRAME NAME=SECOND SRC=FONTSIZE.HTML>
</FRAMESET>
<BODY>
</BODY>
</HTML>
```

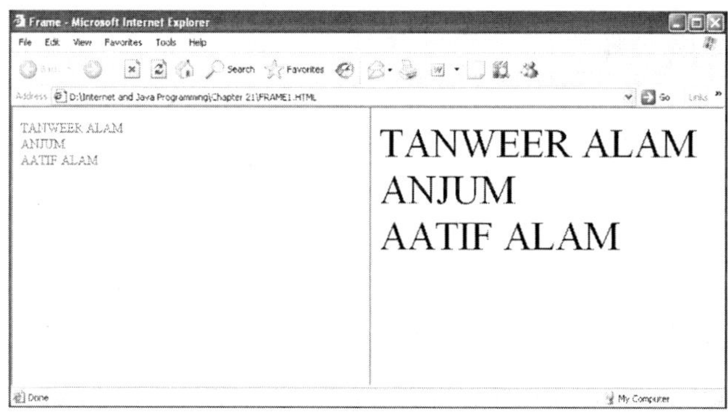

(ii) Rows

```
<HTML>
<HEAD>
<TITLE>Frame</TITLE>
</HEAD>
<FRAMESET ROWS="50%,50%">
<FRAME NAME=FIRST SRC=FONTCOLOR.HTML>
<FRAME NAME=SECOND SRC=FONTSIZE.HTML>
</FRAMESET>
<BODY>
</BODY>
</HTML>
```

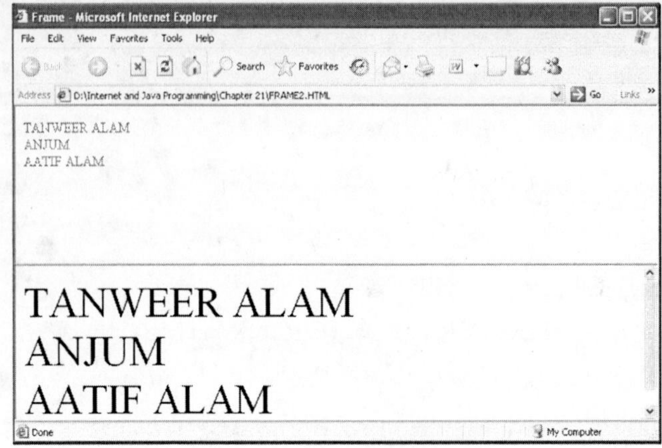

(iii) Inline Frame

```
<HTML>
<HEAD>
<TITLE>IN LINE Frame</TITLE>
</HEAD>
<BODY>
THIS IS INLINE FRAME<BR>
<IFRAME SRC=FONTCOLOR.HTML>
</IFRAME>
</BODY>
</HTML>
```

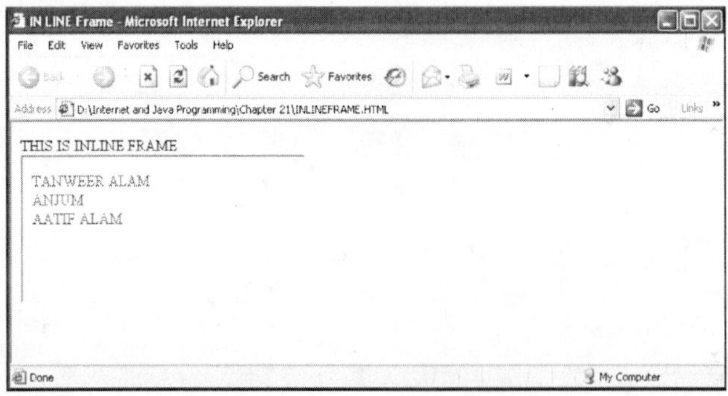

2.8 FORMS

A form is an area that can contain form elements.

Form elements are elements that allow the user to enter information (like text fields, textarea fields, drop-down menus, radio buttons, checkboxes, etc.) in a form.

A form is defined with the <form> tag.

```
<form>
.
input elements
.
</form>
```

Input

The most used form tag is the <input> tag. The type of input is specified with the type attribute. The most commonly used input types are explained below.

Text Fields

Text fields are used when you want the user to type letters, numbers, etc. in a form.

```
<html>
<body>
<form>
First name:
<input type="text" name="Name" />
<br />
Last name:
<input type="text" name="Roll No" />
</form>
</body>
</html>
```

How it looks in a browser:

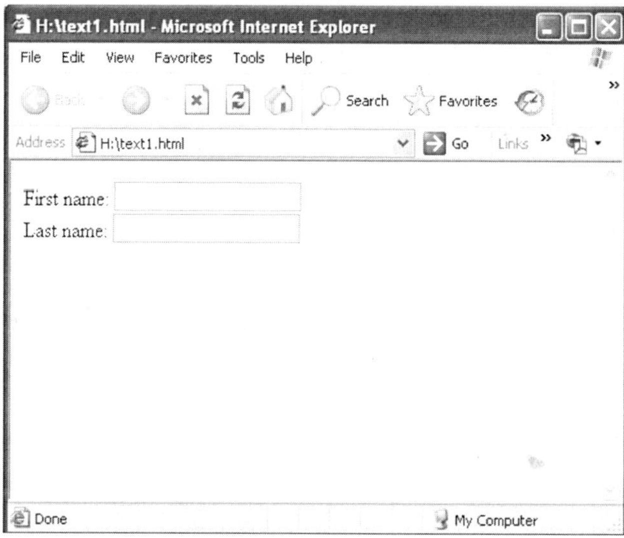

Note that the form itself is not visible. Also note that in most browsers, the width of the text field is 20 characters by default.

Radio Buttons

Radio Buttons are used when you want the user to select one of a limited number of choices.

```
<html>
<body>
<form>
<input type="radio" name="sex" value="male" /> Male
<br />
<input type="radio" name="sex" value="female" /> Female
</form>
</body>
</html>
```

How it looks in a browser:
Note that only one option can be chosen.

Checkboxes

Checkboxes are used when you want the user to select one or more options of a limited number of choices.

```
<html>
<body>
<form>
I have a Computer:
<input type="checkbox" name="a" value="computer" />
<br />
I have a Bike:
<input type="checkbox" name="a" value="Bike" />
<br />
I have a room:
<input type="checkbox" name="a" value="room" />
</form>
</body>
</html>
```

How it looks in a browser:

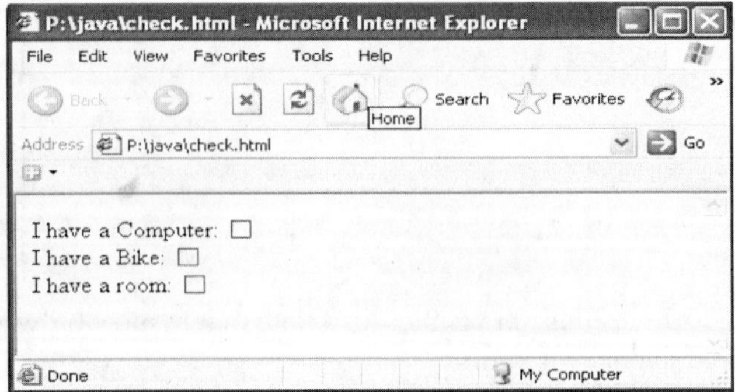

Submit Button

When the user clicks on the "Submit" button, the content of the form is sent to the server. The form's action attribute defines the name of the file to send the content to. The file defined in the action attribute usually does something with the received input.

```
<html>
<body>
<form name="input" action="table2.html" method="get">
Username:
<input type="text" name="user" />
<input type="submit" value="Submit" />
</form>
</body>
</html>
```

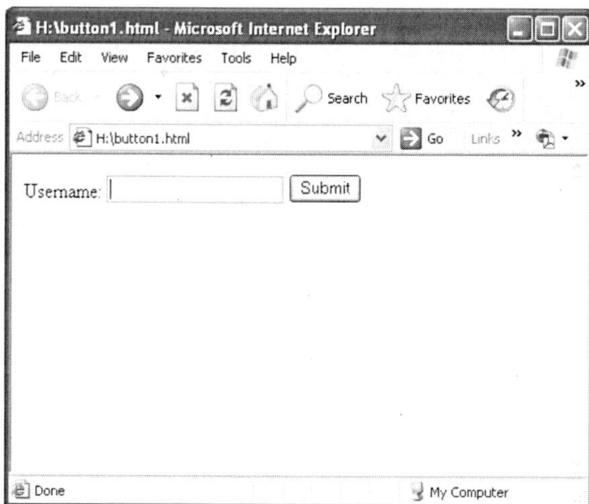

Now click on submit button. The output is as follows.

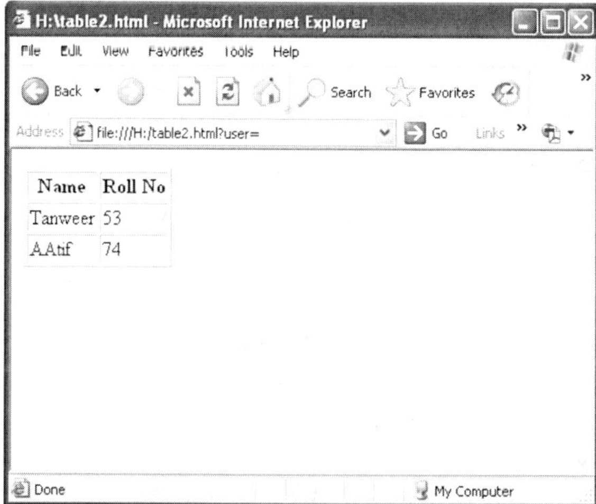

2.9 IMAGES

The Image Tag and the Src Attribute

In HTML, images are defined with the <img> tag. The <img> tag is empty, which means that it contains attributes only and it has no closing tag. To display an image on a page, we need to use the src attribute. Src stands for "source". The value of the src attribute is the URL of the image you want to display on your page.

The syntax of defining an image:

```
<img src="url" />
```

The Alt Attribute

The alt attribute is used to define an "alternate text" for an image.

```
<img src="tanweer.gif" alt="Tanweer Alam" />
```

The browser will display the alternate text instead of the image.

The following are the components of image.

- Width
- Height
- Hspace
- Vspace
- Align
- Alt

```
<HTML>
<HEAD>
<TITLE>IMAGES</TITLE>
</HEAD>
<BODY>
<IMG SRC="aa.gif" WIDTH=400 HEIGHT=300>
</BODY>
</HTML>
```

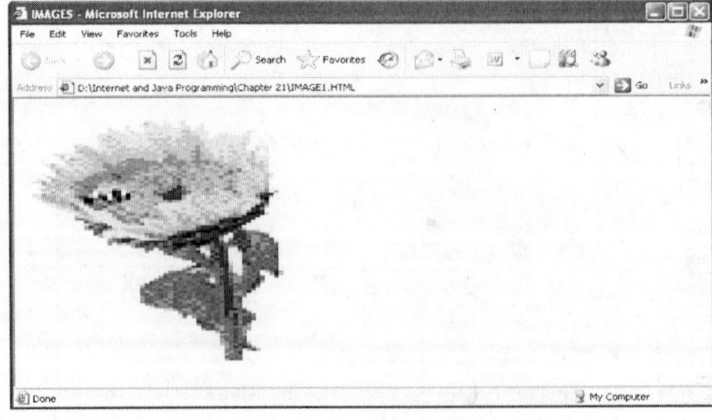

2.10 STYLE SHEETS

How to Use Styles

When a browser reads a style sheet, it will format the document according to it. There are three ways of inserting a style sheet:

External Style Sheet

An external style sheet is ideal when the style is applied to many pages. With an external style sheet, you can change the look of an entire Web site by changing one file

```
<head>
<link rel="stylesheet" type="text/css" href="mystyle.css">
</head>
```

Internal Style Sheet

An internal style sheet should be used when a single document has a unique style. We define internal styles in the head section with the <style> tag.

```
<head>
<style type="text/css">
body {background-color: red}
p {margin-left: 20px}
</style>
</head>
```

Inline Styles

An inline style should be used when a unique style is to be applied to a single occurrence of an element. To use inline styles you use the style attribute in the relevant tag. The style attribute can contain any CSS property.

```
<p style="color: red; margin-left: 20px">
This is a paragraph
</p>
```

Style Tags

Tag	Description
<style>	Defines a style definition
<center>	Deprecated. Use styles instead
<div>	Defines a section in a document
<span>	Defines a section in a document
<font>	Deprecated. Use styles instead
<link>	Defines a resource reference
<basefont>	Deprecated. Use styles instead

```
<HTML>
<HEAD>
<TITLE>Style Sheets</TITLE>
```

```
<STYLE TYPE="text/css">
H1 {font-style:bold;background:yellow;color:red}
</STYLE>
</HEAD>
<BODY>
<H1>TANWEER ALAM</H1>
<P>THE STYLE DEFINITION ARE DEFINE IN STYLE TAGS.</P>
</BODY>
</HTML>
```

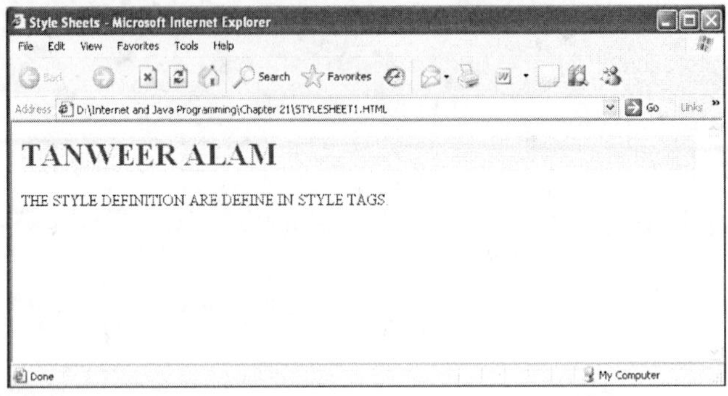

2.11 SOME HTML PROGRAMS

2.11.1 Design a HTML page to display your CV.

```
<html>
   <head>

   </head>

   <body>
      <center> <h1><b> <u>CURRICULUM VITAE</u> </h1>
      <br> <br>
      <hr /><br>
      <table border=1 cellpadding="6" cellspacing="1" bordercolor="black">
      <tr>
      <td>
      <table cellpadding="6" cellspacing="1" bordercolor="black">
         <tr>
            <td align="left" width="900">
               <h2> AAtif Alam</h2>

               <h3><u><i>E-mail:</i></u> <font face="Arial" size="3"
                     >tanweer03@gmail.com</font></h3>
```

```
        <h3><u><i>Cell No.:</i></u><font face="Arial" size="3"
            >9999999999</font></h3

        <h3><u><i><b>Address for Correspondence:</b></i></u></h3>
        <h3> <font face="Arial" size="3" >ABC
        <br>XYZ
        </font></h3>
      </td>
    </tr>

  </table>
  <table>
    <tr>
      <td width="900" align="left">
        <h3><u><i>Objective:</i></u></h3>
          <p><font face="Arial" size="3" >To learn, gather & attain
              knowledge & experience as much as possible in the field of
              software developement & to utilize
          my knowledge to proof myself an asset to theassociated
             organization.</font></p>
      </td>
    </tr>
    <tr>
    </tr>
    <tr>
      <td width="900" align="left"><h3><u><i>Presently Doing:</i></u></
              h3>
        • <font face="Arial" size="3">
            Pursuing <b>MCA</b>, from <b>Meerut Institute of Engineering
                  & Technology</b>
            (U.P.T.U. University), Meerut with aggregate <b>80%</b>
          </font>
      </td>
    </tr>
    <tr>
    </tr>
    <tr>
    </tr>
    <tr>
      <td>
        <h3><u><i>Academic Qualifications:</i></u></h3>
      </td>
    </tr>
```

```
        </table>
        <table border="1" cellpadding="6" cellspacing="1" bordercolor="black">
          <tr align="center">
            <td width="900" colspan="5"><h4>ACADEMIC QUALIFICATIONS</
h4></td>
          </tr>
          <tr align="center">
            <td width="8%"><b>S. No.</b></td>
            <td width="30%"><b>Degree</b></td>
            <td><b>Board/University</b></td>
            <td width="16%"><b>Year of Passing</b></td>
            <td width="15%"><b>Percentage %</b></td>
          </tr>
          <font face="Arial" size="3">
          <tr align="center">
            <td>1.</td>
            <td><font face="Arial" size="3">Graduation BSc (Maths)</td>
            <td><font face="Arial" size="3">C.C.S. University</td>
            <td><font face="Arial" size="3">2008</td>
            <td><font face="Arial" size="3">70</td>
          </tr>
          <tr align="center">
            <td>2.</td>
            <td><font face="Arial" size="3">Intermidiate</td>
            <td><font face="Arial" size="3">C.B.S.E.</td>
            <td><font face="Arial" size="3">1995</td>
            <td><font face="Arial" size="3">75</td>
          </tr>
          <tr align="center">
            <td>3.</td>
            <td><font face="Arial" size="3">Highschool</td>
            <td><font face="Arial" size="3">C.B.S.E.</td>
            <td><font face="Arial" size="3">1993</td>
            <td><font face="Arial" size="3">83</td>
          </tr>
          </font>
        </table>
        <br>
        <table>
          <tr>
          </tr>
          <tr>
            <td width="900" align="left">
              <h4><u><i>TECHNICAL SKILLS:</i></u></h4>
            </td>
          </tr>
```

```
</table>

<table >
    <tr align="center">
      <td width="350"><font face="Arial" size="3"><b>Operating
            platforms</b></td>
      <td width="50">:</td>
      <td width="400"><font face="Arial" size="3">Windows 9X, Linux</
            td>
    </tr>
    <tr align="center">
      <td width="350"><font face="Arial" size="3"><b>Development
            Tools & Lang. </b></td>
      <td width="50">:</td>
      <td width="400"><font face="Arial" size="3"> JAVA, JDBC, C, C++,
            C#.Net</td>
    </tr>
    <tr align="center">
      <td width="350"><font face="Arial" size="3"><b>Internet
            Technologies</b></td>
      <td width="50">:</td>
      <td width="400"><font face="Arial" size="3">HTML, DHTML, Java
            Script</td>
    </tr>
    <tr align="center">
      <td width="350"><font face="Arial" size="3"><b>Database
            Management</b></td>
      <td width="50">:</td>
      <td width="400"><font face="Arial" size="3">Oracle (9.0), MS-
            Access, SQL Server</td>
    </tr>
</table>
<br>
<table>
  <tr>
  </tr>
  <tr>
    <tr><td width="900" align="left">
      <h3><u><i>Extra Curricular Activities:</i></u></h3>
    </td></tr>
          <tr><td>
    • <font face="Arial" size="3"> I have got many prizes in Debate
            Competitions at school and interschool level.
    </td></tr>
```

```
          <tr><td>
             • <font face="Arial" size="3"> I have attended the workshop of .net
          </td></tr>

       </tr>
    </table>
    <br>
    <table>
       <tr>
       </tr>
       <tr>
          <td width="900" align="left">
             <h3><u><i>Personal Detail:</i></u></h3>
          </td>
       </tr>
    </table>
    <table >
          <tr align="center">
             <td width="350"><font face="Arial" size="3"><b> DOB </b></td>
             <td width="50">:</td>
             <td width="400"><font face="Arial" size="3">dd mm yyyy</td>
          </tr>
          <tr align="center">
             <td width="350"><font      face="Arial"      size="3"><b>Language
                         Proficiency</b></td>
             <td width="50">:</td>
             <td width="400"><font face="Arial" size="3">Hindi and English</
                         td>
          </tr>
          <tr align="center">
             <td width="350"><font  face="Arial"  size="3"><b>Hobbies</b></
                         td>
             <td width="50">:</td>
             <td width="400"><font face="Arial" size="3">Dancing, Cooking </
                         td>
          </tr>
    </td>
    </tr>
    </table>
    </center>
  </body>
</html>
```

Output:

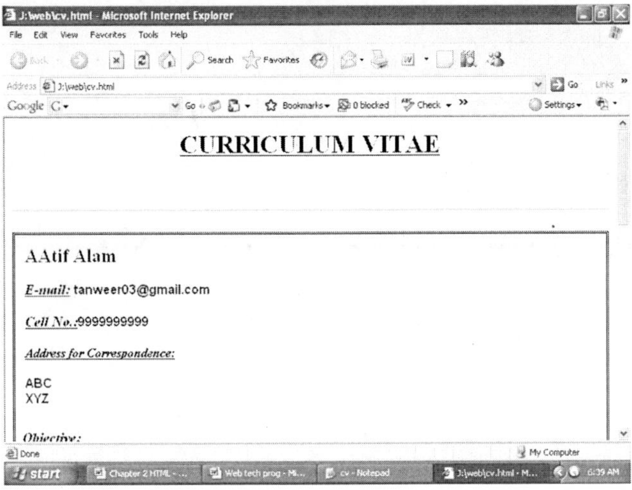

2.11.2 Create a web page giving the following train details :-

(a) Train Name

(b) Starting Place

(c) Arrival and Departure time

Place a border for the table and use cell padding to present the cell data with clarity. Align the table the center of the screen .Use a caption saying "Time Table".Let the output as be shown in the diagram.

Name of the train	Starting Place	Destination	Time	
			Arrival	Time
Madras Mail	Bombay	Madras	9:00	10:00
Intercity Exp.	Delhi	Bareilly	11:00	16:30

```
<HTML>
  <Head>
    <Title>The Time Table of Trains</Title>
  </Head>
  <Body>
    <Table border="1" align="center" cellpadding="25" >
      <caption><h1>Time Table</h1></caption>
      <tr>
        <td rowspan="2" width="150" align="center"
 valign="middle"><b><center>Name of the train</center></b></td>
        <td rowspan="2" width="150" align="center"
valign="middle"><b>Starting Place</b></td>
        <td rowspan="2" width="150" align="center"
```

```
valign="middle"><b>Destination</b></td>
        <td colspan="2" width="150" align="center"
valign="middle"><b>Time</b></td>
       </tr>
       <tr>
<td width="150" align="center"
valign="middle"><b>Arrival</b></td>
         <td width="150" align="center"
valign="middle"><b>Departure</b></td>
       </tr>
       <tr>
         <td align="center" valign="middle">Madras Mail</td>
         <td align="center" valign="middle">Bombay</td>
         <td align="center" valign="middle">Madras</td>
         <td align="center" valign="middle">9:00</td>
         <td align="center" valign="middle">10:00</td>
       </tr>
       <tr>
         <td align="center" valign="middle">Intercity Express</td>
         <td align="center" valign="middle">Delhi</td>
         <td align="center" valign="middle">Bareilly</td>
         <td align="center" valign="middle">11:00</td>
         <td align="center" valign="middle">16:30</td>
       </tr>
     </Table>
   </Body>
</HTML>
```

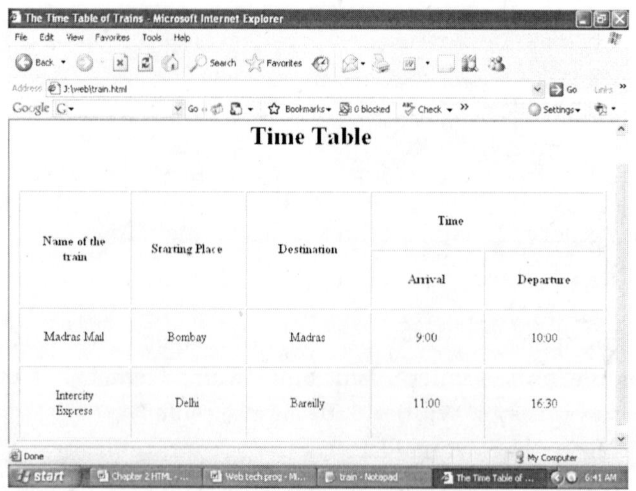

2.11.3 **Create a specimen of corporate webpage. Divide the browser screen into two frames. The frame of the left will be a menu consisting of hyperlinks, clicking on any one of these links will lead to new page, which must open in the target frame, which is on the right hand side.**

Coding:

P3.html

```
<HTML>
      <Head>
         <Title>The Time Table of Trains</Title>
      </Head>
      <frameset cols="20%,*">
         <frame name="first" src="first.html">
         <frame name="second" src="second.html">
      </frameset>
</HTML>
```

first.html

```
<html>
      <head>
      </head>
   <body>
      <center>
         <a href="home.html" target="second">Home</a><br><br><br><br>
         <a href="Product.html" target="second">Product</a><br><br><br><br>
         <a href="Services.html" target="second">Services</
                 a><br><br><br><br>
         <a href="Contact_us.html" target="second">Contact</
                 a><br><br><br><br>
   </body>
</html>
```

second.html

```
   <html>
<head>
</head>
<body><center>
         <marquee><h1>Hello ,This is Nokia Showroom web site.</h1></
                       marquee>
</body>
</html>
```

home.html

```
<html>
   <head>
   </head>
   <body bgcolor="00ff00">
      <center>
         <h1> Home Page </h1><br><br><br><br><br>
         <img src="C:\Mouse.jpg" width="500" height="400">
   </body>
</html>
```

product.html

```
<html>
   <head>
      <title>The Products
      </title>
   </head>
   <body bgcolor=yellow>
   <center><h1>Nokia product list</h1><br><br><br><br><br>
      <table>
      <tr> <td>


      <ol>
         <li>Nokia 5130</li>
         <li>Nokia 2310</li>
         <li>Nokia 6270</li>
         <li>Nokia 6020</li>
         <li>Nokia N-95</li>
         <li>Nokia N-91</li>
         <li>Nokia N-93</li>
      </ol>
      </td> </tr>
      </table>
   </body>
</html>
```

services.html

```
<html>
   <head>
      <title>Services
      </title>
   </head>
   <body bgcolor="#ff00ff">
      <h1>The folowing service is provided</h1><br>
```

```
    <ol>
        <li>S/W Loading/Insatllation
        <li>Mobile Repairing
        <li>Formatting
        <li>Accessories

    </ol>
  </body>
</html>
```

Contact_us.html

```
<html>
  <head>
    <title>The Contact
    </title>
  </head>
  <body bgcolor="ffff00"><center>
    <br><br><br><br><br><br>
    <div>
    <b>Tanweer Alam</b><br>
    Meerut Institute of Engineering & Technology,Meerut<br>
    <font color="#0000ff">
    email: tanweer03@gmail.com<br>
         </font><br>
    Mobile No.->9319390001
    </div>
  </body>

</html>
```

Output

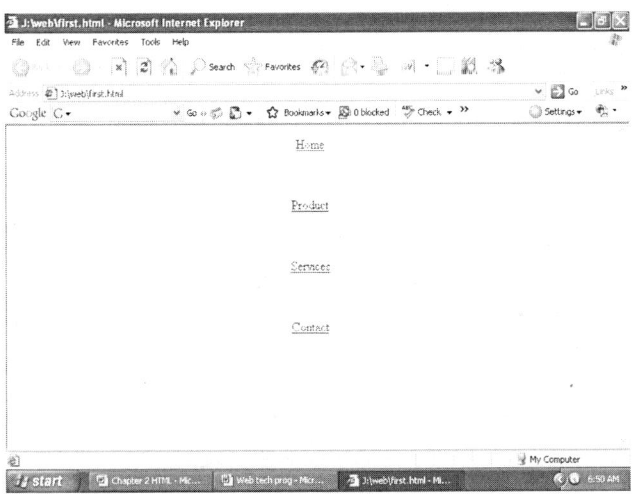

Click on home.

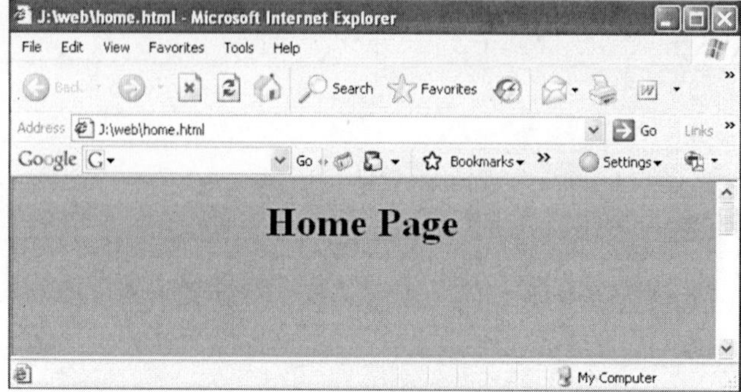

Click on product.

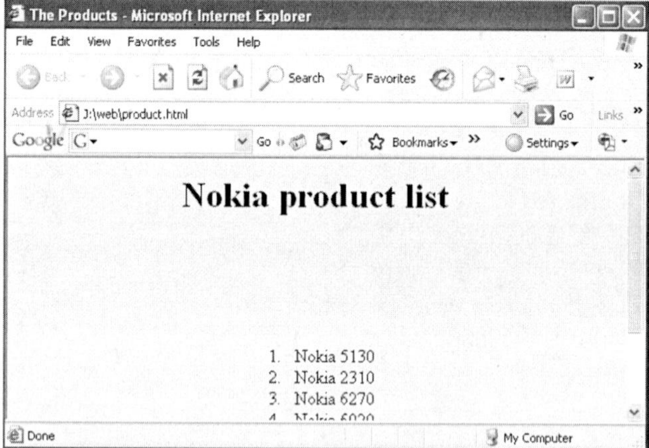

Click on services.

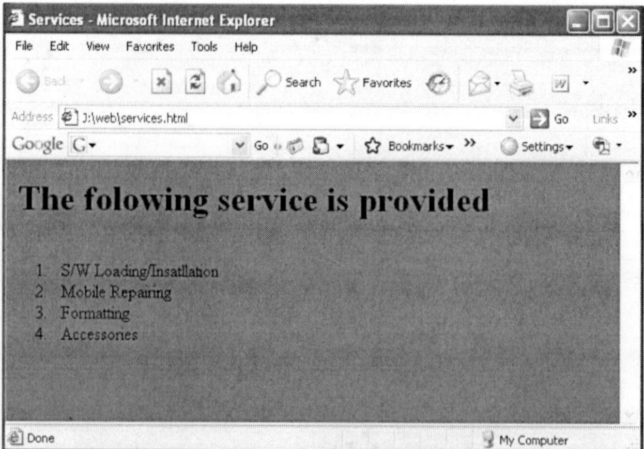

Click on contact us.

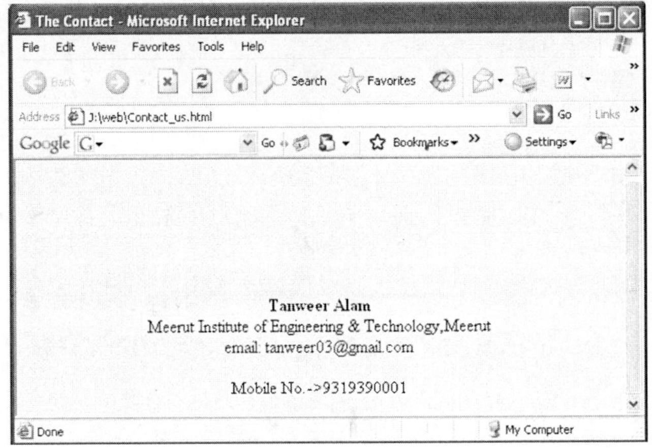

2.11.4 Design a HTML form to reserve a railway ticket.

```
<!--HTML code for Railway Reservation Form -->
<HTML>
  <Head>
    <Title>Railway Reservation Form</Title>
  </Head>
  <body>
    <center>
    <form name="frm1">
      <h1>Railway Reservation System</h1>
      <table>
        <tr>
          <td>From :</td>
          <td><input type="text" name="txt1" ></td>
        </tr>\
        <tr>
          <td>To :</td>
          <td><input type="text" name="txt2" ></td>
        </tr>
        <tr>
          <td>Name :</td>
          <td><input type="text" name="txt3" ></td>
        </tr>
        <tr>
          <td>Age :</td>
          <td><input type="text" name="txt4" ></td>
        </tr>
```

```
            <tr>
              <td>Address :</td>
              <td><Textarea></Textarea></td>
            </tr>
            <tr>
              <td>Account Type :</td>
              <td><input type="Radio" name="cc">Credit card</td>
            </tr>
            <tr>
              <td></td>
              <td><input type="Radio" name="dc">Debit Card</td>
            </tr>
            <tr>
              <td></td>
              <td><input type="Radio" name="other">Other</td>
            </tr>
            <tr>
              <td></td>
            <td><input type="button" name="btn1"
value="Submit"
OnClick="f1();" ></td>
<td><input type="button" name="btn2" value="Cancel"
></td>
            </tr>
        </table>
    </body>
</HTML>
```

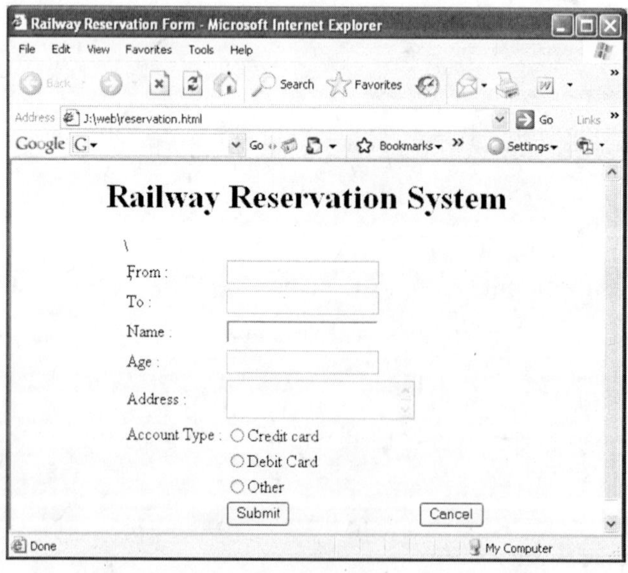

SUMMARY

HTML is not a programming language, it is a markup language. A markup language is a set of markup tags. It uses markup tags to describe web pages. HTML documents are also called web pages. The purpose of a web browser (like Internet Explorer or Firefox) is to read HTML documents and display them as web pages.

EXERCISE

1. Explain HTML.
2. Define Style tags in HTML.
3. What are the formatting an HTML Documents?
4. Define Style Sheets.

*****

CHAPTER 3

XML

XML stand for Extensible Markup Language. It is a set of rules for encoding documents electronically. XML is designed to transport and store data. XML is important to know, and very easy to learn. It is defined in the XML 1.0 Specification produced by the W3C. The design goals of XML emphasize simplicity, usability and generality over the Internet. XML is a cross-platform, software and hardware independent tool for transmitting information.

3.0 INTRODUCTION

XML is a markup language much more like HTML. The tags of XML are not predefined. We must define our own tags. It is common for XML to be used in interchanging data over the Internet. XML was designed to carry data, not to display data while HTML is designed to display data.

For example

In HTML, we write the following code.

```
<b>Tanweer Alam<b>
<i>931939<i>
<i> 30 </i>
```

In XML we represent it as.

```
<Personnel>
 <Student>
 <Name>Tanweer Alam</Name>
 < MobileNo>931939</MobileNo>
 <Age>30</Age>
 </Student>
</Personnel>
```

3.1 DIFFERENCES BETWEEN XML AND HTML

The following table represents the differences between XML and HTML.

XML	HTML
XML was designed to transport and store data.	HTML was designed to display data.
XML focus on what data is.	HTML focus on how data looks.
XML is about carrying information.	HTML is about displaying information.

3.2 USE OF XML

MetaContent

It is used to describe the contents of a document.

Messaging

It is used to exchanges data between applications or organizations.

Database

Database is a collection of Data. The data extracted from the database can be preserved with original information and it can be used more than one application or organization in different ways. We can express it as one application might just display the data and the other application might perform some complex calculation on this data.

3.3 ADVANTAGES OF XML

The following are the advantages of XML.

(i) Language Independent

XML documents are language independent. For example a Java program can generate a XML which can be parsed by a program written in Perl or C++.

(ii) OS Independent

XML files are Operating System independent

(iii) Readability

XML document is plain text and human readable, to edit or view XML documents any simple text editor will use.

(iv) Hierarchical

XML document has a hierarchical (tree) structure which is powerful to express complex data and simple to understand.

3.4 WORKING WITH AN XML DOCUMENTS

The following rules are used to work with an XML document.

(i) XML documents must have a root element

(ii) XML elements must be properly nested

(iii) XML attribute values must be quoted

(iv) XML elements must have a closing tag

(v) XML tags are case sensitive

For example

```
<?xml version="1.0" encoding="ISO-8859-1"?>
<Student>
<Name>AAtif Alam</Name>
<RollNo>001</RollNo>
</ Student>
```

Save the above file with extension .xml.

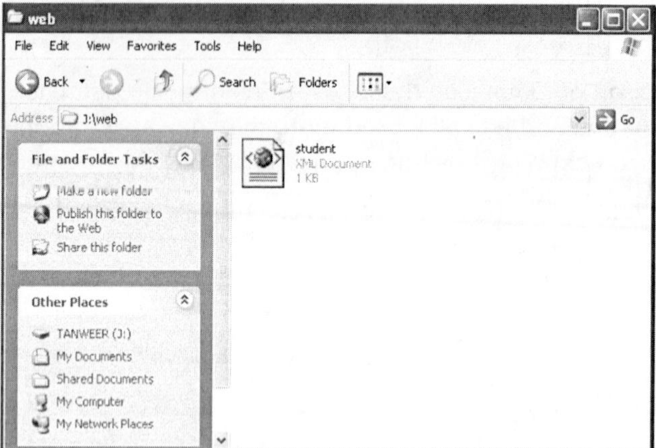

Double click on xml file.

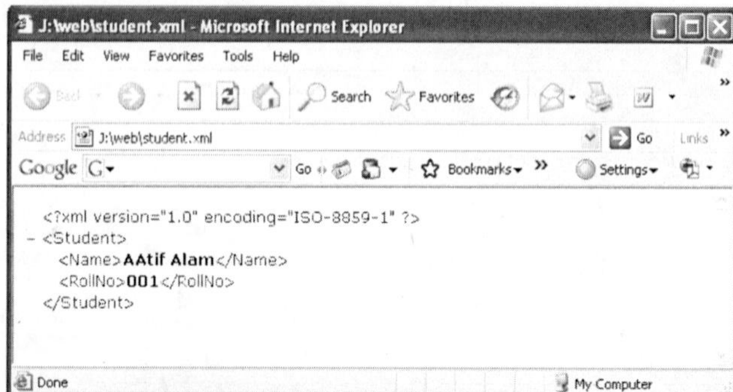

3.5 HOW TO ACCESS XML FILE USING HTML

Step 1: Create the XML file as follows

```
<?xml version="1.0" encoding="ISO-8859-1"?>
<Student>
<Name>AAtif Alam</Name>
<RollNo>001</RollNo>
</ Student>
```

Save the above file as student.xml

Step 2: Now create a HTML file using Java Script as follows

```
<html>
<head>
<script language="JavaScript" for="window" event="onload">
var xmlDoc = new ActiveXObject("Microsoft.XMLDOM")
xmlDoc.async="false"
xmlDoc.load("student.xml")
nodes = xmlDoc.documentElement.childNodes
Name.innerText = nodes.item(0).text
RollNo.innerText = nodes.item(1).text
</script>
<title>HTML using XML data</title>
</head>
<body bgcolor="yellow">
<h1>Display XML Data</h1>
<b>Name is: </b><span id="Name"></span>
<br>
<b>Roll No is: </b><span id="RollNo"></span>
<hr>
</body>
</html>
```

Save the above program as xmltohtml.html.

Now double click on html file, the result is as follows.

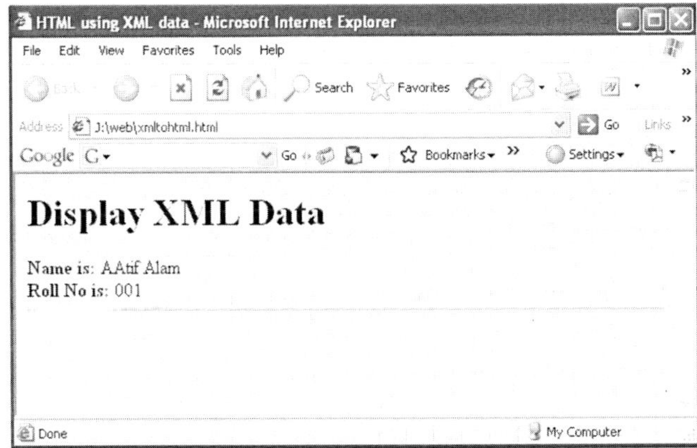

3.6 SYNTAX RULES

The syntax rules of XML are very simple and logical. The rules are easy to learn, and easy to use.

(i) All XML Elements Must Have a Closing Tag

Unlike HTML, In XML, it is illegal to omit the closing tag. All elements must have a closing tag.

For Example

```
<p>paragraph 1</p>
<p>paragraph 2</p>
```

(ii) XML Tags are Case Sensitive

Unlike HTML, XML tags are case sensitive. In XML, the tag <Student> is different from the tag <student>.

Opening and closing tags must be written with the same case.

(iii) XML Elements Must be Properly Nested

Unlike HTML, In XML, all elements must be properly nested within each other.

For Example

In HTML, we might see improperly nested elements:

```
<b><i>bold and italic</b></i>
```

In XML, all elements must be properly nested like below.

```
<b><i>bold and italic</i></b>
```

(iv) XML Documents Must Have a Root Element

XML documents must contain one element that is the parent of all other elements. This element is called the root element.

```
<root>
 <child>
 <subchild>.....</subchild>
 </child>
</root>
```

(v) XML Attribute Values Must be Quoted

In XML the attribute value must always be quoted.

```
<Personnel date="5/5/2010">
 <to>AAtif</to>
 <from>Tanweer</from>
</Personnel>
```

(vi) Comments in XML

Comments in XML are similar to that of HTML.

```
<!-- comment -->
```

(vii) White-space is Preserved in XML

Unlike HTML, In XML, the white-space in a document is not truncated.

For example

HTML truncates multiple white-space characters to one single white-space:

HTML/XML Document:	Hello AAtif
Output of HTML:	Hello AAtif
Output of XML:	Hello AAtif

3.7 DOCUMENT TYPE DEFINITION (DTD)

The purpose of a DTD is to define the legal building blocks of an XML document. It describes syntax that explains which elements may appear in the XML document and what are the element contents and attributes. The purpose of a DTD is to define the structure of an XML document. It defines the structure with a list of legal elements:

```
<!DOCTYPE student
[
<!ELEMENT student (Name,RollNo)>
<!ELEMENT Name (#Tanweer)>
<!ELEMENT RollNo (#53)>
]>
```

Types of DTD

Internal DTD: DTD can be embedded into XML document.

External DTD: DTD can be in a separate file.

Internal DTD

Internal DTD are embedded in the XML document itself. It is used when constraints are applied to a single document. The syntax is as follows.

```
<! DOCTYPE root[assignments]>
```

For example

```
<?xml version='1.0' encoding='utf-8'?>
<!DOCTYPE student
[
<!ELEMENT student (Name,RollNo)>
<!ELEMENT Name (#PCDATA)>
<!ELEMENT RollNo (#PCDATA)>
]>

<student>
<Info>
```

```
<Name>Tanweer</Name>
<RollNo>53</RollNo>
</Info>
</student>
```

Above when viewed in IE 6.0 or above

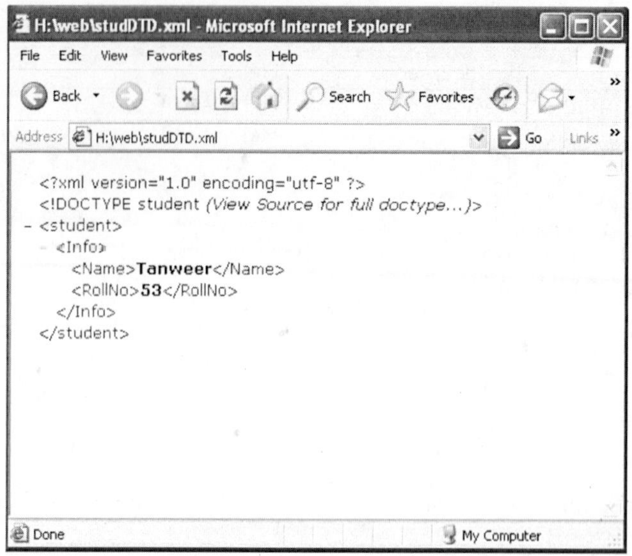

External DTD

In External DTD, DTD is present in separate file and a reference is placed to its location in the document. External DTD's are easy to apply to multiple documents. External DTD's are of two Types.

1. **Public:** These are publicly available set of rules for writing XML Document.
2. **NonPublic:** These are created by private organizations.

3.8 WORKING WITH XML SCHEMA

An XML Schema describes the structure of an XML document. An XML Schema serves the same purpose as a DTD. W3C supports an XML-based alternative to DTD, called XML Schema. An XML Schema conforms to the W3C XML Schema Recommendation. The XML Schema Recommendation defines an XML markup vocabulary for specifying the structure of an XML document.

For example

```
<?xml version='1.0' encoding='utf-8'?>
<xs:schema xmlns:xs="http://www.w3.org/2001/XMLSchema">
<xs:element name="Student">
<xs:complexType>
 <xs:sequence>
```

```
<xs:element name="Name" type="xs:string"/>
<xs:element name="RollNo" type="xs:string"/>
</xs:sequence>
</xs:complexType>
</xs:element>
</xs:schema>
```

Save the above schema with schema.xml

Now double click on this file.

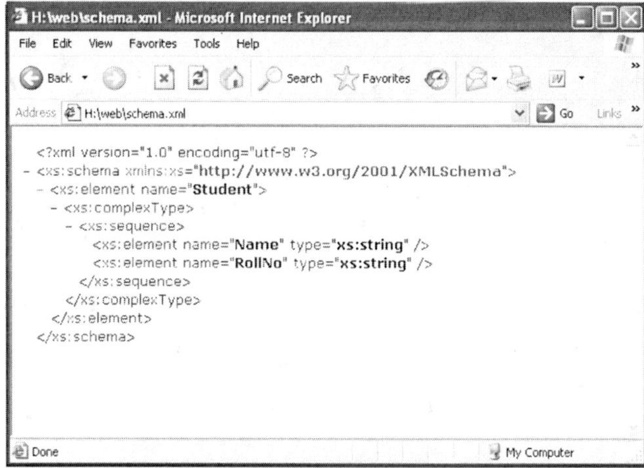

An XML Schema:

(i) Explain the data types for elements and attributes.

(ii) Explain the elements that can appear in a document.

(iii) Explain attributes that can appear in a document.

(iv) Defines which elements are child elements.

(v) Defines the order of child elements.

(vi) Defines the number of child elements.

3.9 PRESENTING XML

Presenting XML is a Java web based application framework for presenting HTML, DHTML, WML and PDF etc. in a device independent manner. It supports several types of content including XML files, dynamic content, SQL result sets and flat files. It may be used as a framework for a servlet-based web application. There are presenting XML examples for converting flat files to XML (and vice versa), for converting SQL results to XML.

3.9.1 Convert XML to MSAccess Database

Step 1:Create database in XML as follows

```
<?xml version="1.0" encoding="ISO-8859-1"?>
```

```
<Student>
<Record>
<Name>Tanweer Alam</Name>
<RollNo>051</RollNo>
</Record>
<Record>
<Name>AAtif Alam</Name>
<RollNo>052</RollNo>
</Record>
</Student>
```

Save the above file as Database.xml

Step 2:Open MS Access database as follows

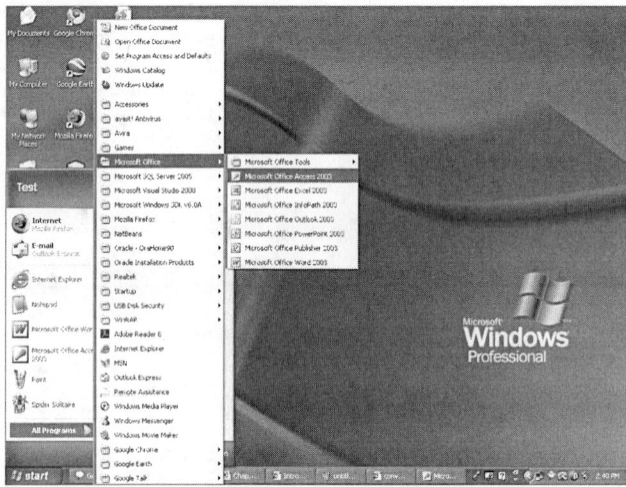

Click on start>all programs> Microsoft Office Access 2003.

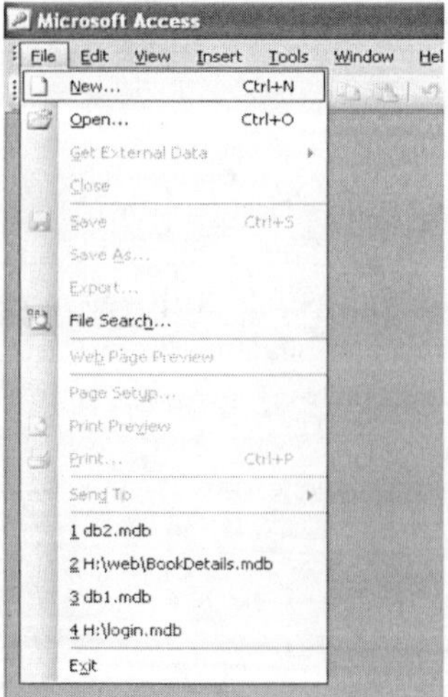

Click on file> New.

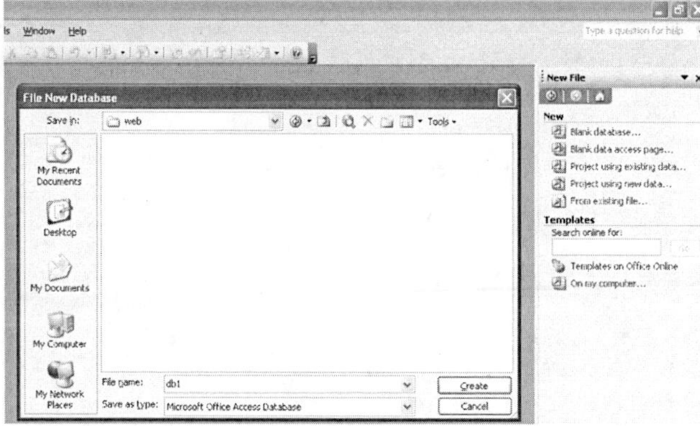

Select Blank database and click create.

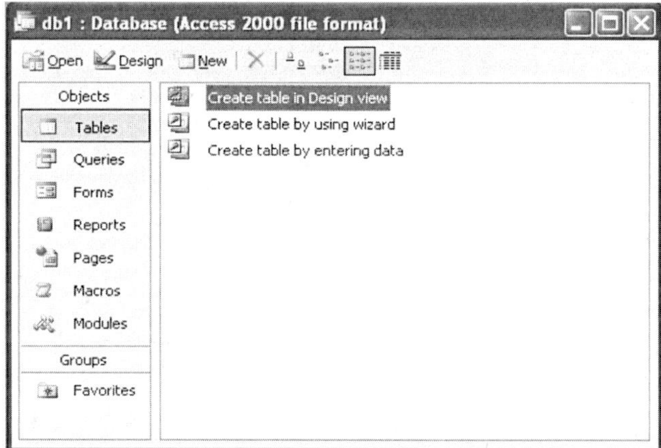

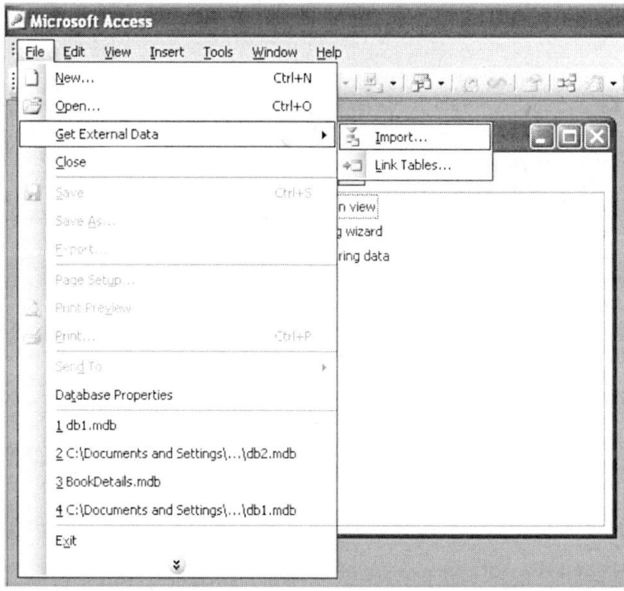

Click on file>Get External Data>Import….

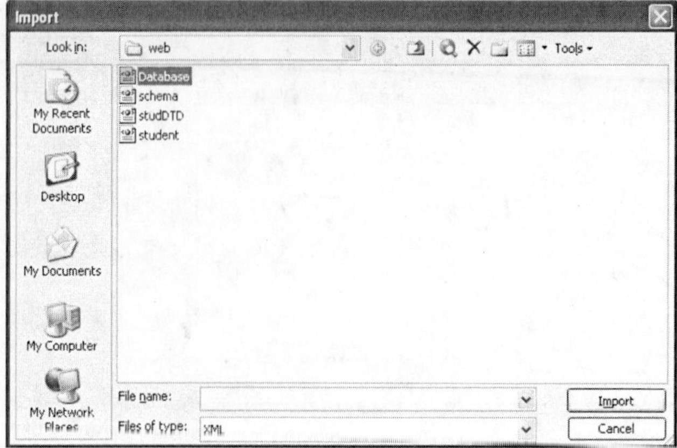

Select Files of Type: XML, select XML file and click import.

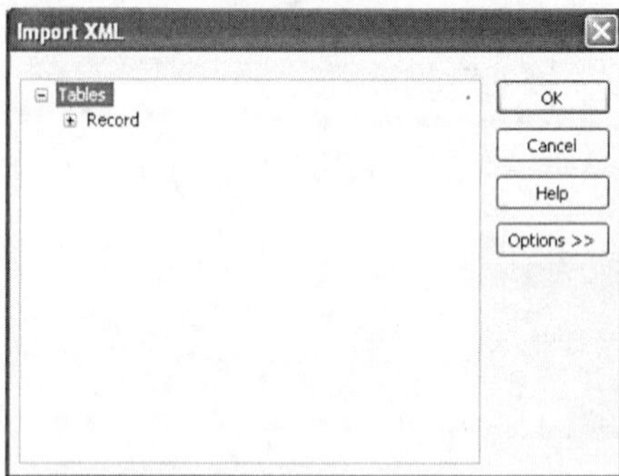

Click OK.

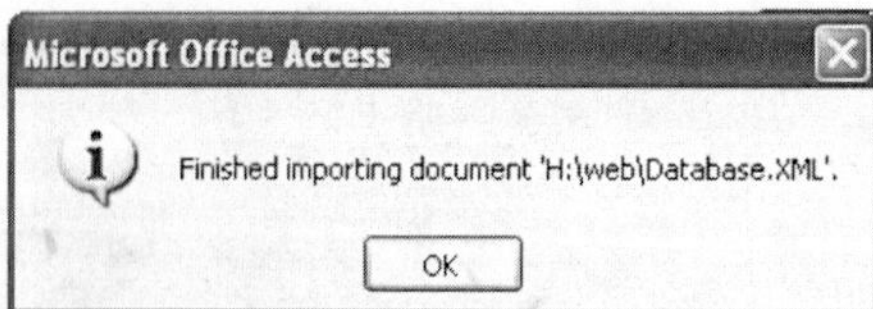

Click OK.

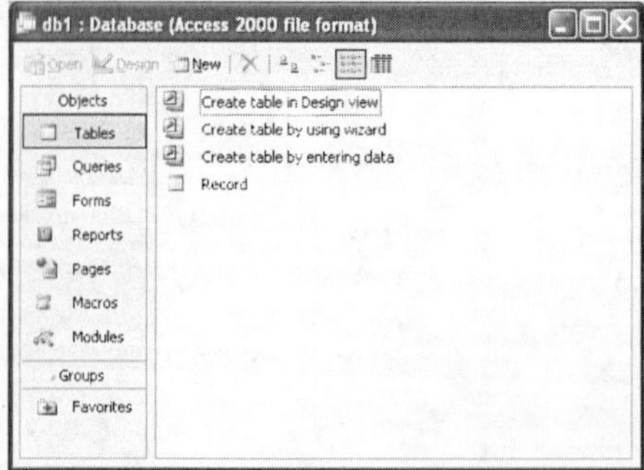

Double click on Record table.

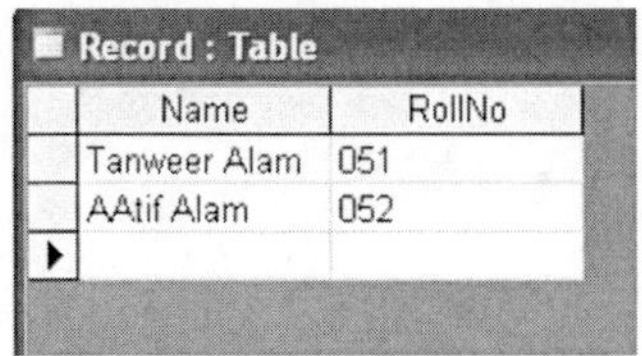

Record : Table

Name	RollNo
Tanweer Alam	051
AAtif Alam	052

3.9.2 Convert MS Access database to XML

Step 1:Create Database in MS Access

Create database in MS Access as follows

login : Table

id	password	firstname	lastname	department	mobileno	subspeci	address
administrator	12345678	amit	garg	mca	76789908097	data structure	meerut
faculty1	111	tanweer	alam	mca	57879890896	java	meerut
faculty2	222	aakansha	rastogi	mca	64786544336	oos	meerut
faculty3	333	kanika	kapoor	mca	42355467677	cbot	meerut
faculty4	444	tapesh	tyagi	mca	45346656256	daa	meerut
faculty5	555	vinay	goyal	mca	63463666344	dm	modinagar

Now double click on database and right click on table and click Export.

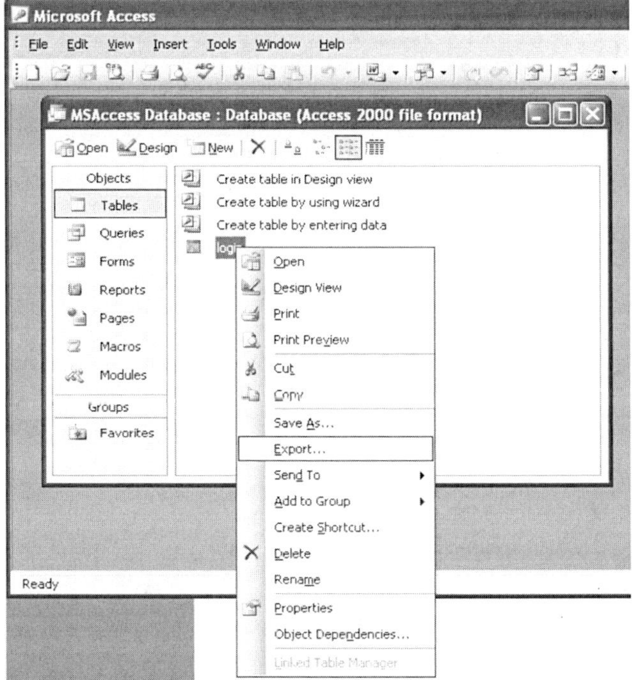

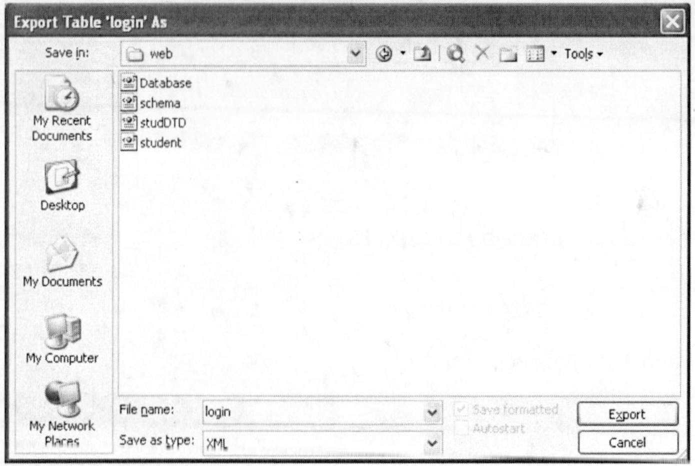

Click Export.

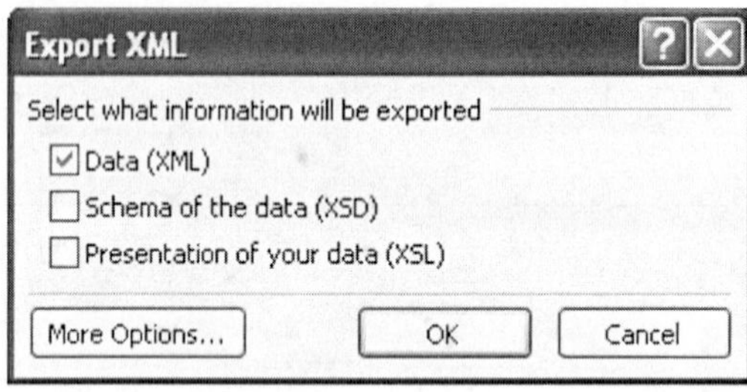

Click OK.

Now XML file has been generated.

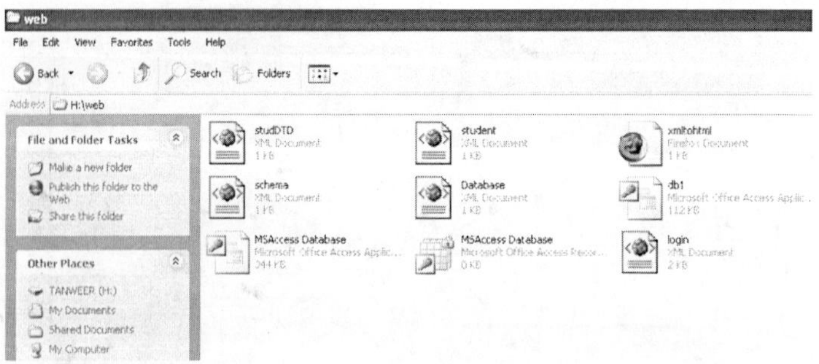

Double click on login.xml file.

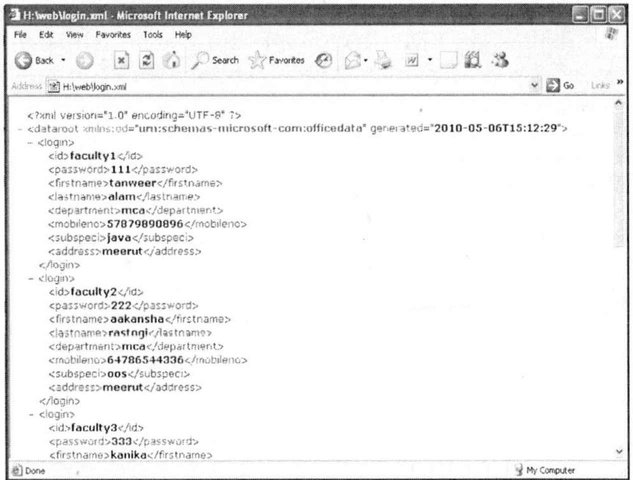

3.10 USING XML PROCESSORS: DOM AND SAX

An XML Parser is a parser that is designed to read XML and create a way for programs to use XML. Every program must implement or call on an XML parser. The main types of parsers are known as: SAX, DOM and pull. For each type, there are some excellent implementations freely available for a variety of languages like C#, Java, C++, PHP, Ruby, Perl, Python and so on.

SAX (Simple API For XML) parser: Event Based API

SAX is used to obtain the content of an XML document as a sequence of events. The SAX parser implements the SAX API and it is event driven interface. As it parses it invokes the callback methods. For example, we'll be notified when the parsing starts and ends, when a start / end tag is found.

When to use SAX parser

(i) No structural modification

(ii) Huge XML files

DOM (Document Object Model) parser: Tree Structure based API

The Dom parser implements the dom api and it creates a DOM tree in memory for a XML document.

When to use DOM parser

(i) We can manipulate the document

(ii) We can traverse the document back and forth

(iii) Small XML files

Well Formed

The XML specification defines an XML document as a text which is well-formed, i.e., it satisfies a list of syntax rules provided in the specification. A well formed XML must satisfy the following constraints.

(i) All tags must have a corresponding ending tag

For example:

Well Formed

```
<Personnel>
 <record>
 <Name>Tanweer Alam</Name>
 <RollNo> 53 </RollNo>
 <Age>30</Age>
 </record>
</Personnel>
```

Not Well formed

```
<Personnel>
 <record>
 <Name>Tanweer Alam</Name>
 <RollNo> 53 </RollNo>
 <Age>30
 </record>
</Personnel>
```

(Missing ending tag for Age)

(ii) No overlapping tags

For example:

Well Formed

```
<Personnel>
 <record>
 <Name>Tanweer Alam</Name>
 <RollNo> 53 </RollNo>
 <Age>30</Age>
 </record>
</Personnel>
```

Not Well formed

```
<Personnel>
 <record>
 <Name>Tanweer Alam</Name>
 <RollNo> 53 </RollNo>
 <Age>30</Age>
 </Personnel>
</record>
```

Note: </record> and </Personnel> tags are not in the right order.

Pull parsing

A pull parser creates an iterator that sequentially visits the various elements, attributes, and data in an XML document. Pull parsing treats the document as a series of items which are read in sequence using the iterator design pattern. The recursive-descent approach tends to lend itself to keeping data as typed local variables in the code doing the parsing, while SAX, for instance, typically requires a parser to manually maintain intermediate data within a stack of elements which are parent elements of the element being parsed. Examples of pull parsers include StAX in the Java programming language, SimpleXML in PHP and System.Xml.XmlReader in the .NET Framework. . Pull-parsing code can be more straightforward to understand and maintain than SAX parsing code.

3.11 XML STYLE SHEETS (XSL)

We can add display information With Cascading Style Sheets (CSS) to an XML document. Style Sheets can be associated with an XML document by using a processing instruction whose target is xml-style sheet. XSL is as a language that can transform XML into HTML, a language that can filter and sort XML data and a language that can format XML data, based on the data value, like displaying negative numbers in red.

XSL consists of two parts:

(i) Method to transform XML documents

(ii) Method to format XML documents

XML Style Sheets can be used to define how an XML file should be displayed by transforming the XML file into a format that is recognizable to a browser. One such format is HTML. Normally XSL does this by transforming each XML element into an HTML element. XSL can also add completely new elements into the output file, or remove elements. It can rearrange and sort the elements, test and make decisions about which elements to display.

3.12 SOME APPLICATIONS OF XML

The following are the few applications of XML.

(i) **Cell Phones**: Some Cell Phone is the application of XML. XML data is sent to some cell phones, which is then formatted by the specification of the cell phone software designer to display text, images and even play sounds.

(ii) **File Converters:** Many applications or software have been written to convert existing documents into the XML standard. An example is a MS Access Database to XML converter.

(iii) **EDI Transactions:** XML allows data to be exchanged. XML has made electronic data interchange transactions accessible to a broader set of users.

(iv) **VoiceXML**: Converts XML documents into an audio format so that a user can listen to an XML document.

SUMMARY

XML is a markup language much more like HTML. The tags of XML are not predefined. XML is a simple, very flexible text format derived from SGML (ISO 8879). XML is a cross-platform, software and hardware independent tool for transmitting information. Originally designed to meet the challenges of large-scale electronic publishing, XML is also playing an increasingly important role in the exchange of a wide variety of data on the Web and elsewhere. We must define our own tags. It is common for XML to be used in interchanging data over the Internet.

EXERCISE

1. Explain XML.
2. What is XML Style Sheets?
3. Define Document Type Definition (DTD).
4. How to Access XML File using HTML?

*****

CHAPTER 4

JAVA SCRIPT

JavaScript is the most popular scripting language on the internet. JavaScript was designed to add interactivity to HTML pages and works in all major browsers, such as Internet Explorer, Safari, Chrome, Opera and Firefox. Java and JavaScript are different in both concept and design. Java is a powerful programming language in the same category as C and C++ while Java script is a scripting language. Everyone can use JavaScript without purchasing a license of Java script software.

4.0 INTRODUCTION

A scripting language is a lightweight programming language. JavaScript is a scripting language that is usually embedded directly into HTML pages. JavaScript is an interpreted language means that scripts execute without preliminary compilation. The following are the advantages of JavaScript.

(i) **It gives HTML designers a programming tool –** web page designers are normally not programmers, but JavaScript is a scripting language with a very simple syntax. Almost anyone can put small code into their HTML pages.

(ii) **It can read and write HTML elements -** A JavaScript can read and change the content of an HTML element.

(iii) **JavaScript can put dynamic text into an HTML page -** A JavaScript statement as follows:

```
document.write("<h1>" + name + "</h1>")
```

We can write a variable text into an HTML page.

(iv) **JavaScript can react to events -** A JavaScript can be set to execute when something happens, like when a user clicks on an HTML element.

(v) **JavaScript can be used to validate data -** A JavaScript can be used to validate form data before it is submitted to a server. This saves the server from extra processing.

(vi) **JavaScript can be used to create cookies** - A JavaScript can be used to store and retrieve information on the visitor's computer.

4.1 FEATURES OF JAVA SCRIPTS

The following are the features of Java script.

4.1.1 Java Script is Imperative and structured

JavaScript supports all the syntax of structured programming like if statements, while loops, switch statements, etc. Like C, JavaScript makes a distinction between expressions and statements.

4.1.2 Dynamic

As in most scripting languages, types are associated with values, not variables. JavaScript is almost entirely object-based. JavaScript objects are associative arrays, augmented with prototypes. JavaScript includes an evaluation function that can execute statements provided as strings at run-time.

4.1.3 Functional

Java Script is functional. Functions are first-class, they are objects themselves. As such, they have properties and can be passed around and interacted with like any other object. Inner functions (functions defined within other functions) are created each time the outer function is invoked and variables of the outer functions for that invocation continue to exist as long as the inner functions still exist, even after that invocation is finished this is the mechanism behind closures within JavaScript.

4.1.4 Prototype-based

JavaScript uses prototypes instead of classes for inheritance. It is possible to simulate many class-based features with prototypes in JavaScript.

4.1.5 Miscellaneous

(i) **Run-time environment:** JavaScript typically relies on a run-time environment (e.g. in a web browser) to provide objects and methods by which scripts can interact with the outside world. In fact, it relies on the environment to provide the ability to include/import scripts.

(ii) An indefinite number of parameters can be passed to a function. The function can access them through formal parameters and also through the local arguments object.

(iii) **Array and object literals:** Like many scripting languages, arrays and objects can each be created with shortcut syntax.

(iv) **Regular expressions:** JavaScript also supports regular expressions in a manner similar to Perl, which provide a powerful syntax for text manipulation that is more sophisticated than the built-in string functions.

4.2 JAVASCRIPT STATEMENTS

JavaScript is a sequence of statements that is executed by the browser. A JavaScript statement is a command to a browser. The purpose of the command is to tell the browser what to do. Each statement is executed by the browser in the sequence they are written. For example to write “Hello AAtif” to the web page, the command is as follows:

```
document.write("Hello AAtif");
```

It is normal to add a semicolon at the end of each executable statement. The semicolon is optional and the browser is supposed to interpret the end of the line as the end of the statement.

```
<script type="text/javascript">
document.write("<h1>This is a heading 1</h1>");
document.write("<h2>This is a heading 2</h2>");
document.write("<p>This is a paragraph 1.</p>");
document.write("<p>This is a paragraph 2.</p>");
</script>
```

JavaScript statements can be grouped together in blocks. Blocks start with a left curly bracket {, and ends with a right curly bracket }.

```
<script type="text/javascript">
{
document.write("<h1>This is a heading 1</h1>");
document.write("<h2>This is a heading 2</h2>");
document.write("<p>This is a paragraph 1.</p>");
document.write("<p>This is a paragraph 2.</p>");
}
</script>
```

Now add the above script to the HTML page as follows.

```
<HTML>
<BODY>
<script type="text/javascript">
{
document.write("<h1>This is a heading 1</h1>");
document.write("<h2>This is a heading 2</h2>");
document.write("<p>This is a paragraph 1.</p>");
document.write("<p>This is a paragraph 2.</p>");
}
</script>
</BODY>
</HTML>
```

The output is as follows.

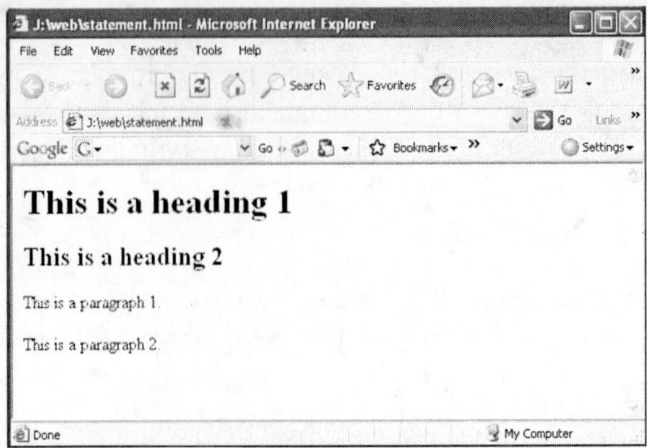

4.3 WHERE TO PUT THE JAVASCRIPT

JavaScripts in a web page will be executed immediately while the web page loads into the web browser. This is not always what we want. Sometimes we wanna execute a script when a page loads or at a later event, such as when a user clicks a button.

Scripts in <head>

Scripts are executed when they are called. Put your functions in the head section as follows.

```
<html>
<head>
<script type="text/javascript">
function msg()
{
alert("Hi, it is fire when load");
}
</script>
</head>
<body onload="msg()">
</body>
</html>
```

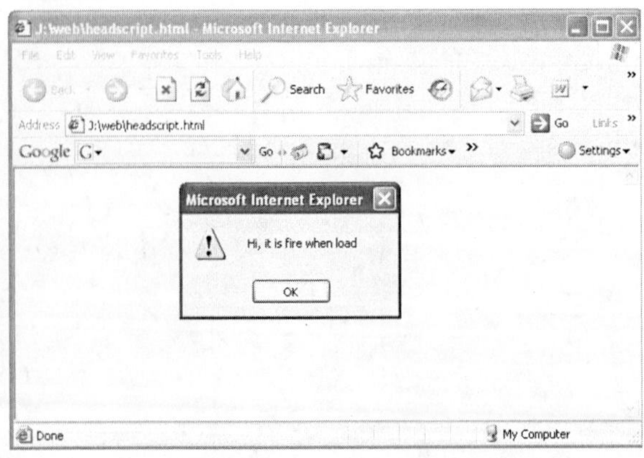

Scripts in <body>

If we don't want our script to be placed inside a function, or if our script should write page content, it should be placed in the body section as follows.

```
<html>
<head>
</head>
<body>
<script type="text/javascript">
document.write("Java Script in body");
</script>
</body>
</html>
```

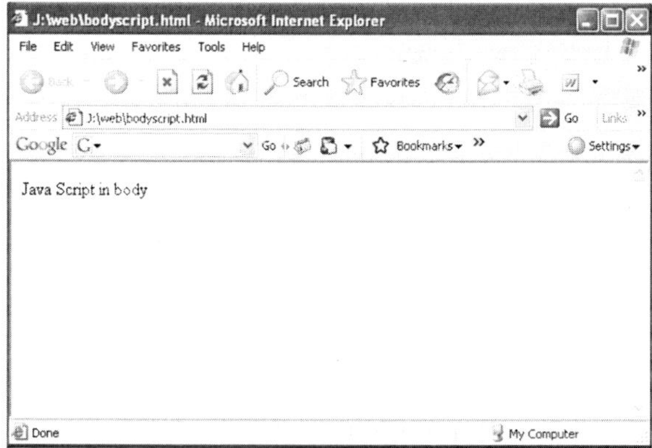

Scripts in <head> and <body>

You can place an unlimited number of scripts in your document, so you can have scripts in both the body and the head section.

```
<html>
<head>
<script type="text/javascript">
function msg()
{
alert("Java Script in Head");
}
</script>
</head>
<body onload="msg()">
<script type="text/javascript">
document.write("Java Script in Body");
</script>
</body>
</html>
```

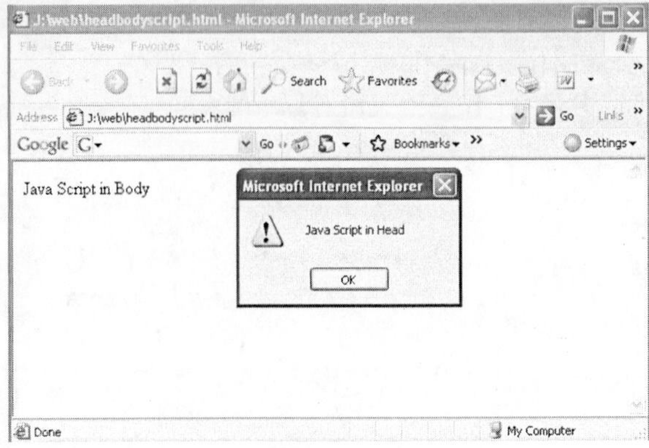

External JavaScript

If we want to run the same JavaScript on several pages, without having to write the same script on every page, we can write a JavaScript in an external file. Save the external JavaScript file with a .js file extension. Write the following code and save it as msg.js

```
function msg1()
{
alert("Hi, This is external java script file");
}
```

Remember: The external script cannot contain the <script></script> tags.

To use the external script, point to the .js file in the "src" attribute of the <script> tag:

Now write the following program and save it as external.html.

```
<html>
<head>
<script type="text/javascript" src="msg.js"></script>
</head>
<body onload="msg1()">
</body>
</html>
```

Now out put is as follows.

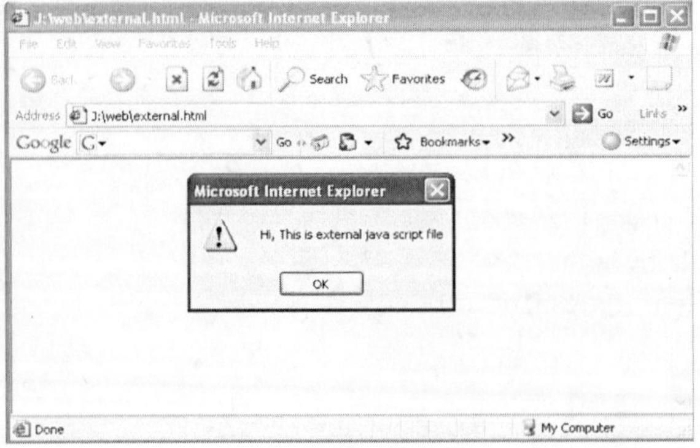

4.3 USE IN WEB PAGES

JavaScript code can run locally in a web browser rather than on a remote server. it can respond to user actions quickly, making an application feel more responsive. Applications such as Gmail take advantage of this: much of the user-interface logic is written in JavaScript, and JavaScript dispatches requests for information to the web server. A JavaScript engine is an interpreter that interprets JavaScript source code and executes the script accordingly. The first JavaScript engine was created by Brendan Eich at Netscape Communications Corporation, for the Netscape Navigator web browser. The engine named SpiderMonkey is implemented in C. A JavaScript webserver would expose host objects representing an HTTP request and response objects, which a JavaScript program could then manipulate to dynamically generate web pages.

For example

```
<html>
 <head><title>simple page</title></head>
 <body>
 <script type="text/javascript">
 document.write('Hello Java Script!');
 </script>
 <noscript>
Our browser either does not support JavaScript, or We have JavaScript turned off.
 </noscript>
 </body>
</html>
```

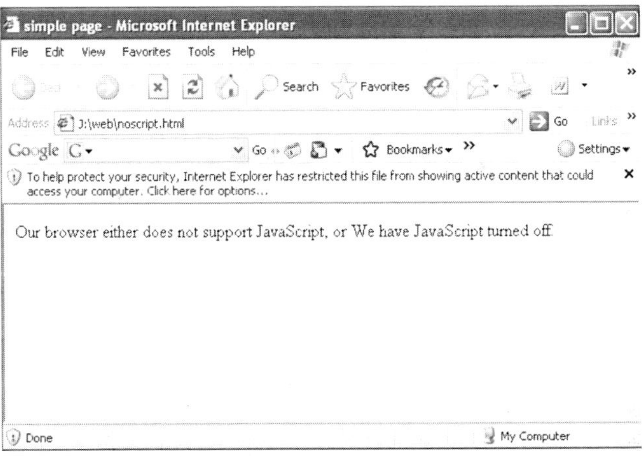

Right click as follows

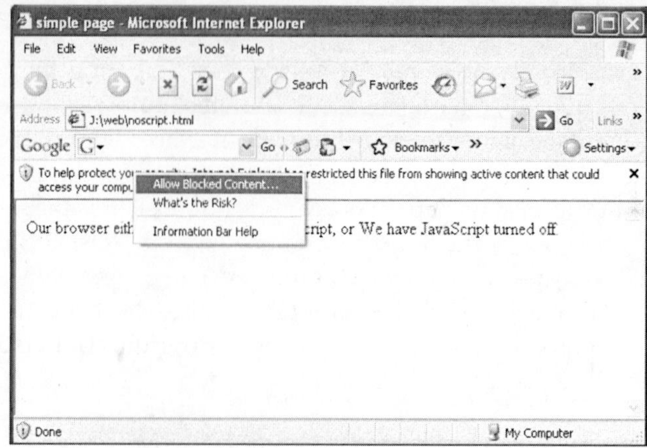

Now select Allow Blocked Contents….

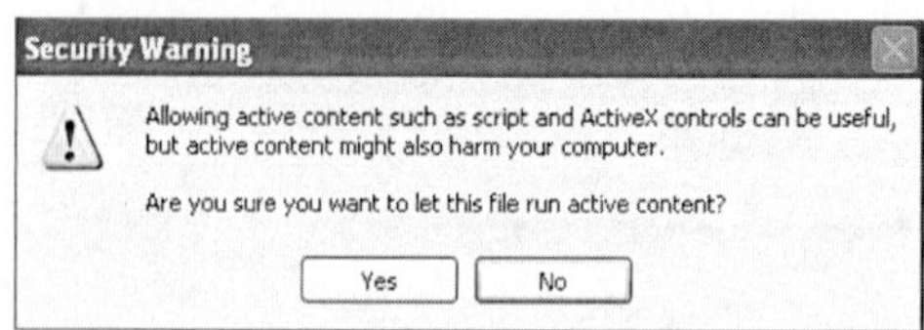

Click yes.

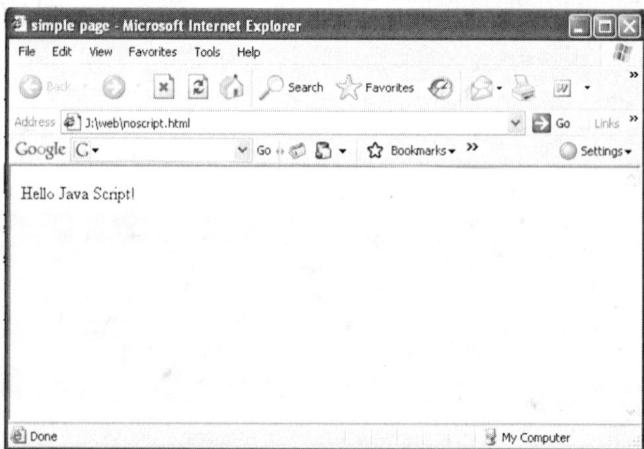

Browser Detection

The Navigator object contains all information about the visitor's browser:

```
<html>
<body>
<script type="text/javascript">
document.write("Browser Name is: " + navigator.appName);
document.write("<br>Browser Code is: " + navigator.appCodeName);
document.write("<br>Browser Version No is: " + navigator.appVersion);
```

```
document.write("<br>Platform is: " + navigator.platform);
document.write("<br>User agent Header: " + navigator.userAgent);
document.write("<br>Cookies Enabled is: " + navigator.cookieEnabled);
</script>
</body>
</html>
```

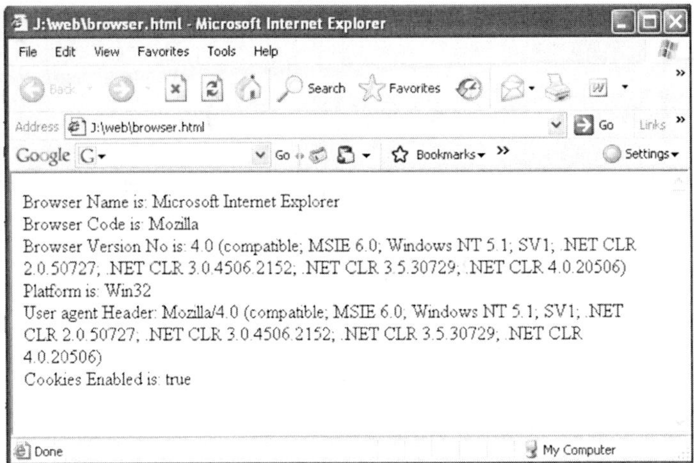

4.4 JAVASCRIPT OBJECTS

JavaScript is an Object Oriented Programming scripting language. An Object Oriented Programming language allows us to define own objects and make variable types. Properties are the values associated with an object. In the following example we are using the length property of the String object to return the number of characters in a string.

```
<html>
 <head><title>To Find Length of a Text</title></head>
 <body>
 <script type="text/javascript">
 var s="Hello Tanweer!";
 document.write(s);
 document.write(" The Length of text is::");
 document.write(s.length);
 </script>
 </body>
</html>
```

Output is as follows.

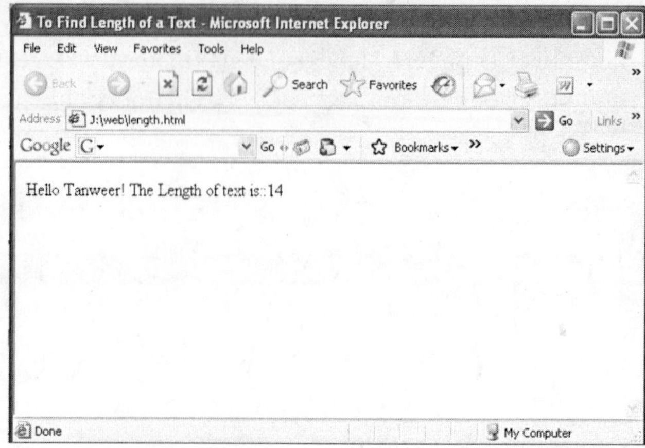

Methods are the actions that can be performed on objects. In the following example we are using the toUpperCase() and toLowerCase() method of the String object to display a text in uppercase and lowercase letters:

```
<html>
<head><title>To Find Length of a Text</title></head>
<body>
<script type="text/javascript">
var s="Hello Tanweer!";
document.write(s+"<br>");
document.write("Upper Case::");
document.write(s.toUpperCase());
document.write("<br>Lower Case::");
document.write(s.toLowerCase());
</script>
</body>
</html>
```

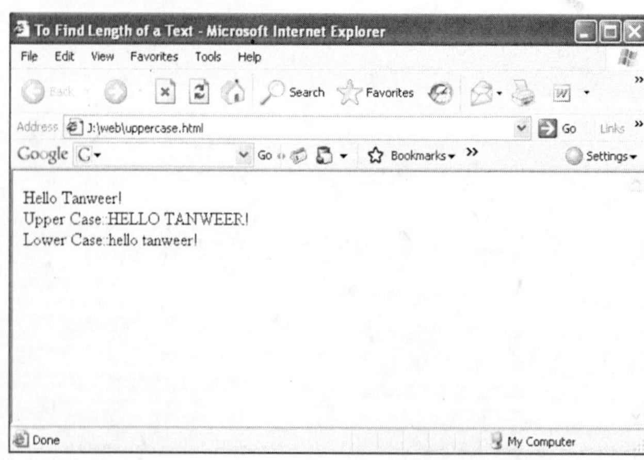

JavaScript Date Object

Return date and time using Date object of java script that are created with the Date() constructor. There are four ways of instantiating a date:

```
new Date() // current date and time
new Date(milliseconds) //milliseconds since 1970/01/01
new Date(String)
new Date(year, month, day, hours, minutes, seconds, milliseconds)
```

Some examples of instantiating a date:

```
today = new Date()
d1 = new Date("August 11, 1993 10:14:00")
d2 = new Date(80,6,22)
d3 = new Date(88,6,21,12,15,0)
```

Example 1:

```
<html>
 <head><title>Current Date and Time</title></head>
 <body>
 <script type="text/javascript">
 var d=new Date();
 document.write(d);
 </script>
 </body>
</html>
```

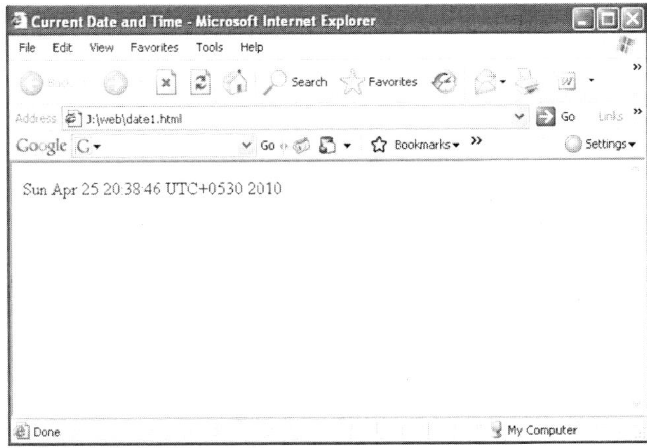

Example 2:

```
<html>
 <head><title>To Get the Date</title></head>
 <body>
```

```
<script type="text/javascript">
var today=new Date();
document.write(today.getDate());
</script>
</body>
</html>
```

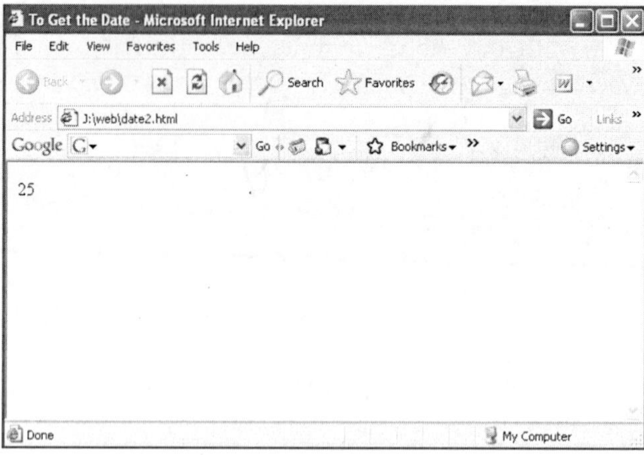

Math Objects

The Math object allows us to perform mathematical tasks. We can use several mathematical constants and methods. Methods of Math can be called by using Math as an object without creating it. The syntax is as follows.

Syntax:

```
var val_sqrt=Math.sqrt(value);
var val_pi=Math.PI;
```

JavaScript provides eight mathematical constants that is accessed from the Math object.

```
Math.PI //value of PI
Math.LOG10E //base-10 log of E
Math.E //Value of e
Math.SQRT2 //square root of 2
Math.SQRT1_2 //square root of 1/2
Math.LN2 //natural log of 2
Math.LN10 //natural log of 10
Math.LOG2E //base-2 log of E
//Program
<html>
<body>
<script type="text/javascript">
document.write("<B>Value of PI:"+Math.PI+"</B><br>");
```

```
document.write("<B>Value of base-10 log of E:"+Math.LOG10E+"</B><br>");
document.write("<B> Value of E:"+Math.E +"</B><br>");
document.write("<B>SQRT of 2:"+Math.SQRT2+"</B><br>");
document.write("<B>SQRT of 1/2 is: "+Math.SQRT1_2 +"</B><br>");
document.write("<B>Value of natural log of 2:"+Math.LN2 +"</B><br>");
document.write("<B>Value of natural log of 10"+Math.LN10+"</B><br>");
document.write("<B>Value of base-2 log of E:"+Math.LOG2E+"</B><br>");
</script>
</body>
</html>
```

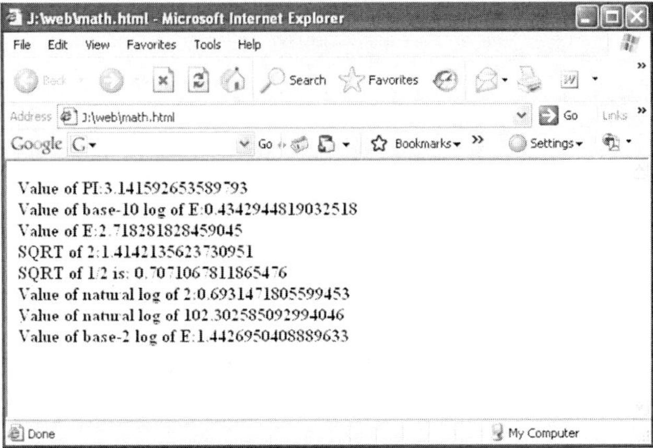

Mathematical Methods

There are also several mathematical methods available.

(i) **round():** it is used to round a number to the nearest integer.

```
document.write(Math.round(6.9));
```

The output is as follows:

7

(ii) **random():** it is used to return a random number between 0 and 1:

```
document.write(Math.random());
```

The output is as follows:

0.3074066661885156

(iii) **floor():** floor() and random() methods of the Math object to return a random number between 0 and 10.

```
document.write(Math.floor(Math.random()*11));
```

The output is as follows:

10

4.5 ARRAY IN JAVA SCRIPT

An array is a special variable, which can hold more than one value, at a time. An array can hold all our variable values under a single name. And we can access the values by referring to the array name. We can declare the array as follows.

```
var Arrayname=new Array();
We can insert the values in array as follows.
Arrayname[0]="Tanweer";
Arrayname[1]="AAtif";
Or
var Arrayname=new Array("Tanweer","AAtif");
or
var Arrayname=["Tanweer","AAtif"];
```

We can access the array as follows.

```
document.write(Arrayname[0]);
```

```
//Program
<html>
 <head><title>Array</title></head>
 <body>
 <script type="text/javascript">
 var arr=new Array();
 arr[0]="Tanweer";
 arr[1]="AAtif";
 document.write(arr[0]+"<br>");
 document.write(arr[1]);
 </script>
 </body>
</html>
```

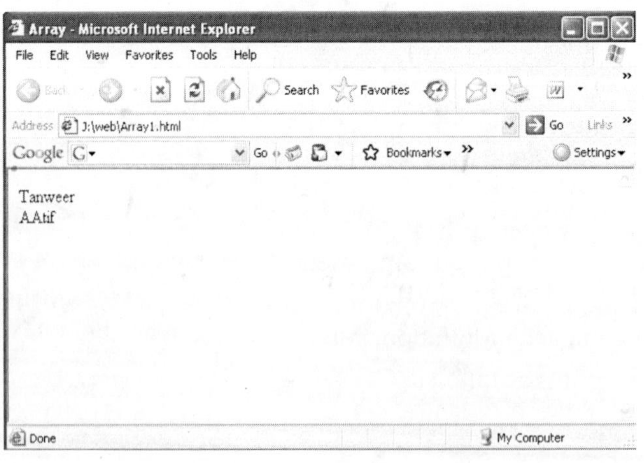

4.6 CONTROL STRUCTURE IN JAVA SCRIPT

The Control Structure has the following types.

4.6.1 Conditional Statement

Conditional statement is performed different actions based on different conditions. JavaScript has the following conditional statements:

if statement - if a specified condition is true then this statement is used to execute some code.

Syntax

```
if (condition)
{
 //Statements to be executed if condition is true
}
//Program
<html>
 <head><title>Array</title></head>
 <body>
 <script type="text/javascript">
 var a=10;
 if (a==10)
 {
 document.write("<b><H1>Good Morning</H1></b>");
 }
 </script>
 </body>
</html>
```

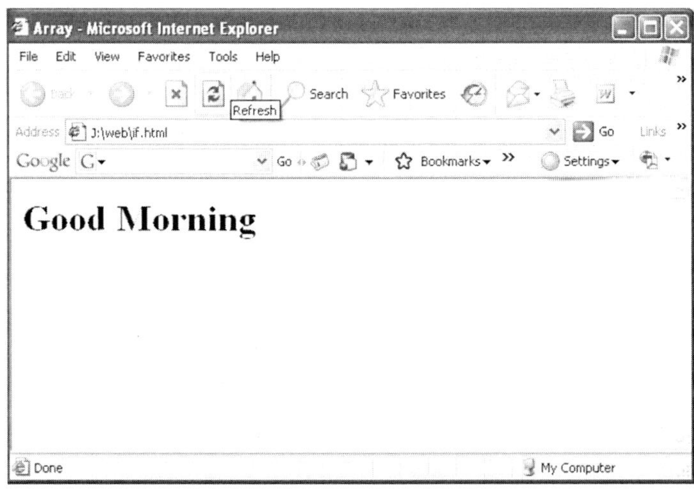

if...else statement - if a specified condition is true then this statement is used to execute some code and another code if the condition is false.

Syntax

```
if (condition)
{
//Statement to be executed if condition is true
}
else
{
//statement to be executed if condition is not true
}
```

//Program

```
<html>
 <head><title>Array</title></head>
 <body>
 <script type="text/javascript">
 var a=10;
 if (a<10)
 {
 document.write("<b><H1>Good Morning</H1></b>");
 }
else
{
 document.write("<b><H1>Good Evening</H1></b>");
}
 </script>
 </body>
</html>
```

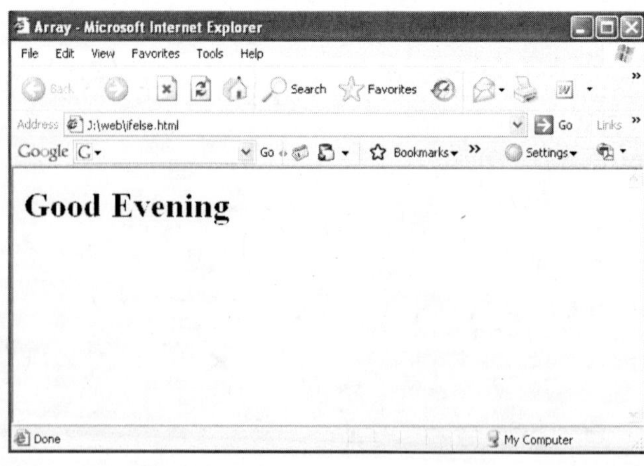

Nested if (if...else if....else) statement - this statement is used to select one of many blocks of code to be executed.

Syntax:

```
if (condition1)
{
   //statements to be executed if condition1 is true
}
else if (condition2)
{
   //statements to be executed if condition2 is true
}
else
{
   //statements to be executed if condition1 and condition2 are not true
}
//Program
<html>
 <head><title>Array</title></head>
 <body>
 <script type="text/javascript">
var d = new Date()
var t = d.getHours()
if (t<10)
 {
 document.write("<b><H1>Good morning</H1></b>");
 }
else if (t>10 && t<16)
 {
 document.write("<b><H2>Have a nice day</H2></b>");
 }
else
 {
 document.write("<b>Hello AAtif!</b>");
 }
</script>
 </body>
</html>
```

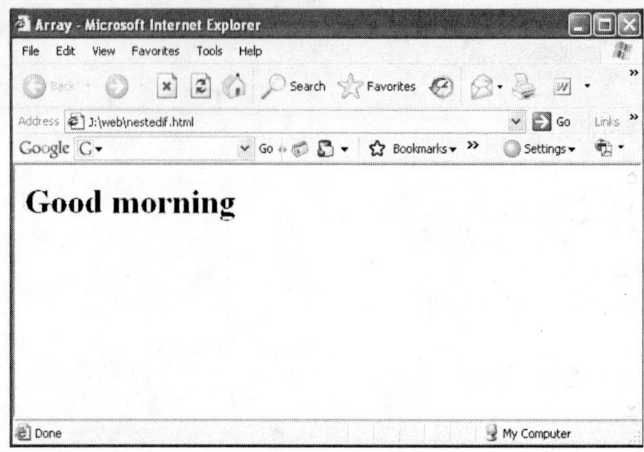

switch statement - this statement is used to select one of many blocks of code to be executed.

Syntax

```
switch(ch)
{
case 1:
 // execute block code 1
 break;
case 2:
 //execute block code 2
 break;
default:
 //code to be executed if ch is different from case 1 and 2
}
```

//Program

```
<html>
 <head><title>Array</title></head>
 <body>
 <script type="text/javascript">
var d=new Date();
day=d.getDay();
switch (day)
{

case 0:
 document.write("Sunday");
 break;

case 1:
 document.write("Monday");
 break;
```

```
case 2:
 document.write("Tuesday");
 break;
case 3:
 document.write("Wedensday");
 break;
case 4:
 document.write("Thursday");
 break;
case 5:
 document.write("Friday");
 break;
case 6:
 document.write("Satday");
 break;
default:
 document.write("Wrong Choice");
}
</script>
 </body>
</html>
```

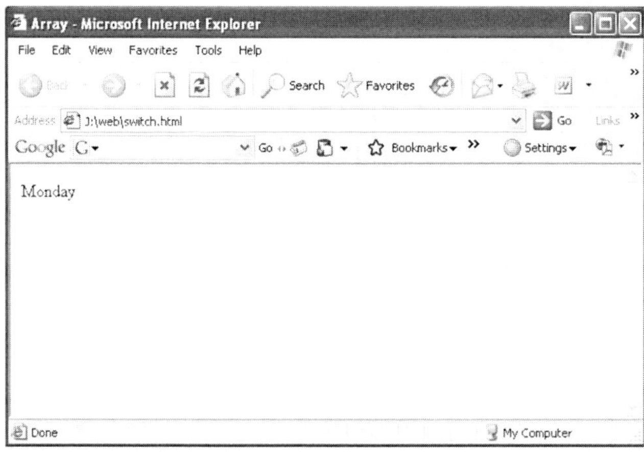

4.6.2 Control Flow (Loops)

Loops execute a block of code a specified number of times or while a specified condition is true. There are three types of Loops.

For loop

For loop is used when we know in advance how many times the script should run.

Syntax

```
for (initialization; Condition; increment/decrement)
{
//code to be executed
}
```

Example:

Print the table of 5.

```
<html>
<body>
<script type="text/javascript">
var i=1;
for (i=1;i<=10;i++)
{
document.write(i*5+"<br>");
}
</script>
</body>
</html>
```

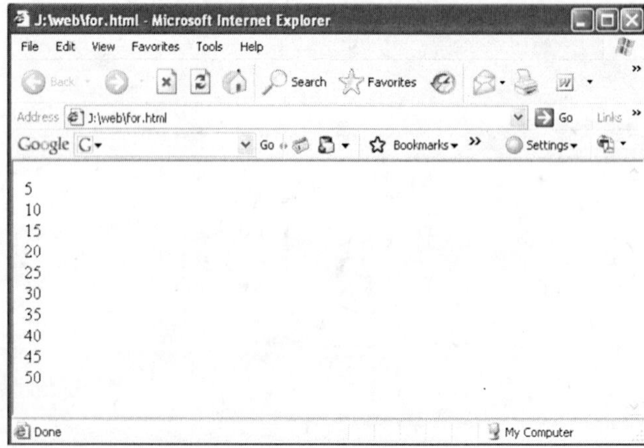

Example 2:

Use the for...in statement to loop through an array.

```
<html>
<body>
<script type="text/javascript">
var i;
var name = new Array();
name[0] = "Tanweer";
name[1] = "Anjum";
name[2] = "AAtif";
```

```
for (i in name)
{
document.write(“<B>”+name[i] + “</B><br>”);
}
</script>
</body>
</html>
```

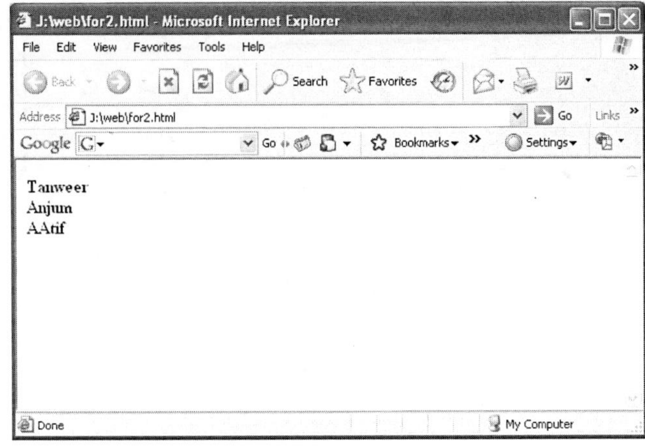

While loop

The while loop is used to loop through a block of code while a specified condition is true.

Syntax

```
while (Condition)
      {
//Statements
}
```

Example:

Print numbers 0 to 10.

```
<html>
<body>
<script type=″text/javascript″>
 var i=0;
 while (i<=10)
 {
 document.write(“<B>Number:″ + i+″</B><br>”);
 i++;
 }
</script>
</body>
</html>
```

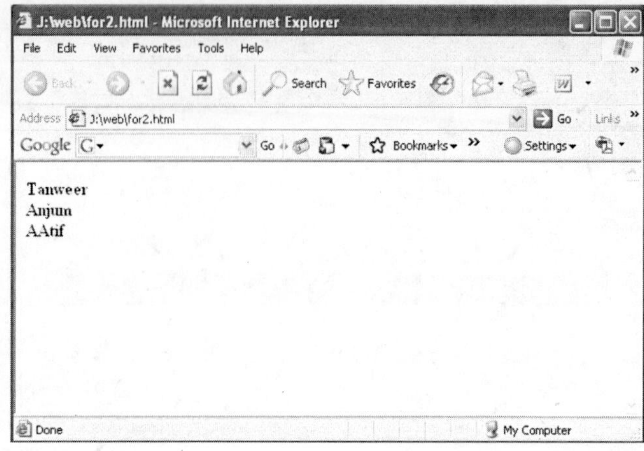

The do...while Loop

The do...while loop is similar to while loop but this loop will execute the block of code once if condition wrong and if specified condition is true then it will repeat the loop until the condition is true.

Syntax

```
do
{
//Statements
}
while (Condition);
```

//Program

```
<html>
<body>
<script type="text/javascript">
 var i=0;
 do
 {
 document.write("<B>Number:" + i+"</B><br>");
 i++;
 }while (i<=3)
</script>
</body>
</html>
```

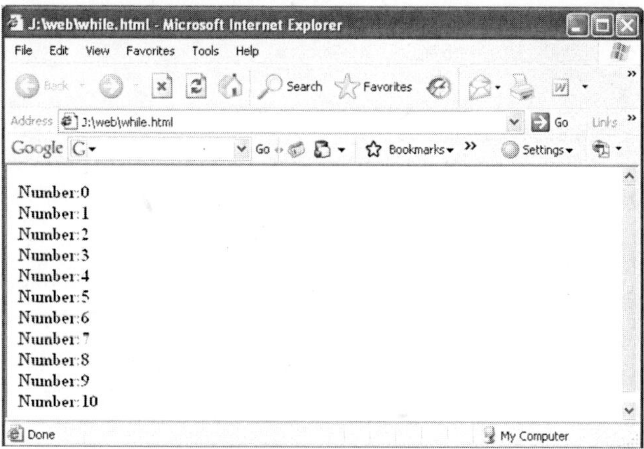

4.7 ERROR HANDING IN JAVA SCRIPTS

The try...catch statement is used to test a block of code for errors. The try block contains the code to be run, and the catch block contains the code to be executed if an error occurs.

Syntax

```
try
 {
 // code
 }
catch(e)
 {
 //Handle errors
 }
```

//Program

```
<html>
<head>
<script type="text/javascript">
var s="";
function msg()
{
try
 {
 adddlert("Welcome Visitor!"); //Error in syntax
 }
catch(e)
 {
 s="Error on this page.\n\n";
 s=s+"Error description: " + e.description + "\n\n";
```

```
s=s+"Click OK Button to continue.\n\n";
 alert(s);
 }
}
</script>
</head>
<body>
<input type="button" value="Click Here for msg" onclick="msg()" />
</body>
</html>
```

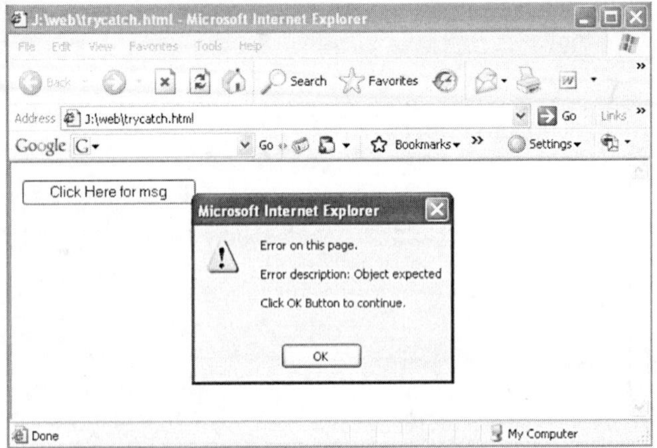

If the program is as follows.

```
<html>
<head>
<script type="text/javascript">
var s="";
function msg()
{
try
 {
alert("Welcome Visitor!"); //there is no error
 }
catch(e)
 {
 s="Error on this page.\n\n";
 s=s+"Error description: " + e.description + "\n\n";
s=s+"Click OK Button to continue.\n\n";
 alert(s);
 }
}
```

```
</script>
</head>
<body>
<input type="button" value="Click Here for msg" onclick="msg()" />
</body>
</html>
```

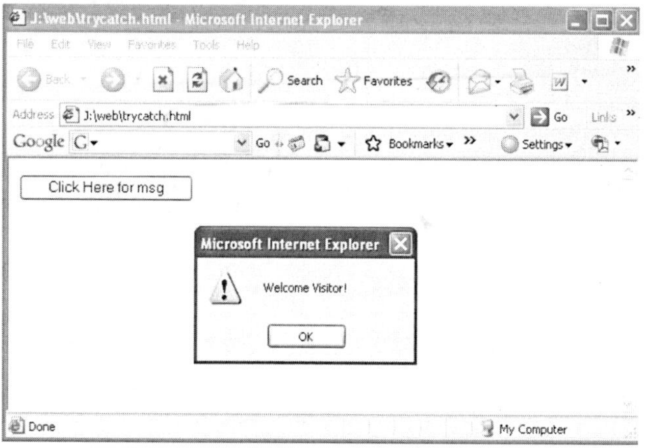

The Throw Statement

The throw statement allows us to create an exception. If we use this statement together with the try...catch statement, we can control program flow and generate accurate error messages. The throw is written in lowercase letters. Using uppercase letters will generate a JavaScript error. The syntax is as follows.

Syntax

throw(e)

Where e is the exception. The exception can be a string, integer, Boolean or an object.

```
//Program
<html>
<body>
<script type="text/javascript">
var input=prompt("Enter a positive number","");
try
{
if(isNaN(input))
{
throw "Error 1";
}
else if(input<0)
{
```

```
throw "Error 2";
}
}
catch(e)
{
if(e=="Error 1")
{
alert("Error! The Input value is not a number");
}
if(e=="Error 2")
{
alert("Error! The value is Negative");
}

}
</script>
</body>
</html>
```

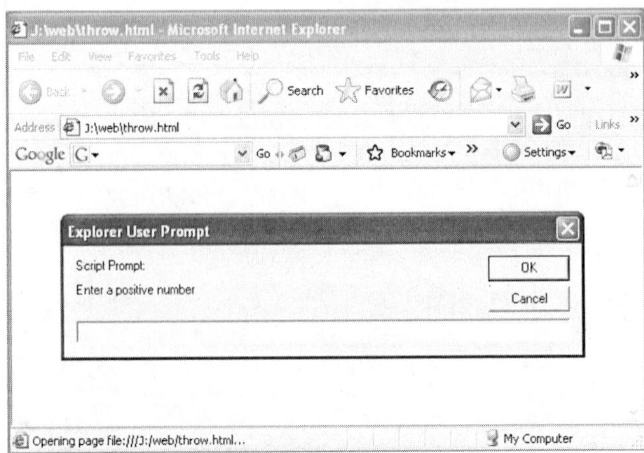

Enter a String and click OK.

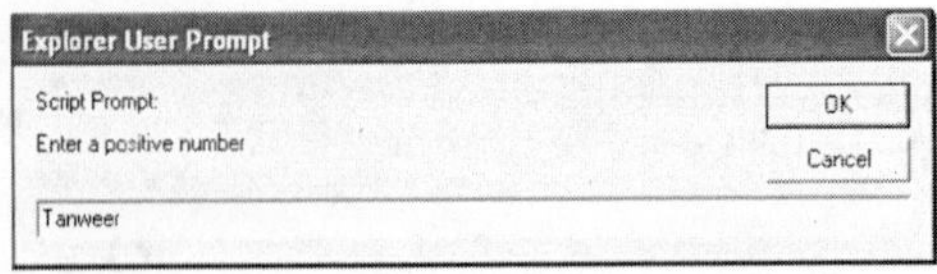

The output is as follows.

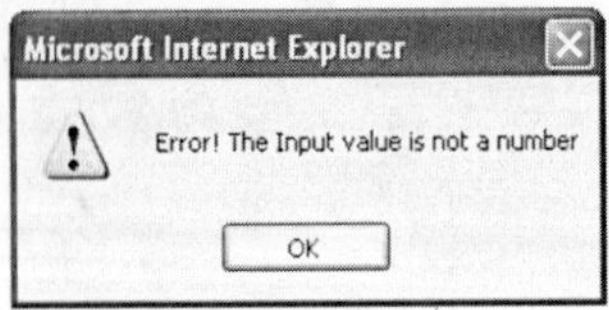

Now enter a negative no.

Click Ok.

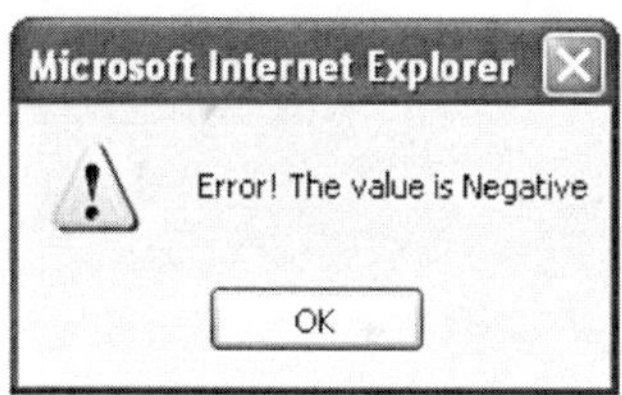

4.8 DYNAMIC HTML WITH JAVA SCRIPT

We can create dynamic web pages using JavaScript. In JavaScript, Events are actions. Every element on a web page has certain events which can trigger by JavaScript. We define the events in the HTML tags. For example, we can use the onClick event of a button element to indicate that a function will run when a user clicks on the button. The onLoad events are triggered when the user load the web page. The function of Events will not be executed before the event occurs.

The following are the examples of events:

(i) A mouse click on button

(ii) A web page loading or Unloading

(iii) An image loading

(iv) Submitting an HTML form etc.

The following events are triggered when the user want to perform the specific events.

(i) onLoad

The onLoad events are triggered when the user enters the page. The onLoad event is often used to load the proper version of the web page based on the information.

Syntax

```
<body onLoad="function()" >
```

//Program

```
<html>
<head>
<script type="text/javascript">
function load()
```

```
{
 alert("This is the loading message");
}
</script>
</head>
<body onLoad="load()" >
<input type="button" value="Hii" />
</body>
</html>
```

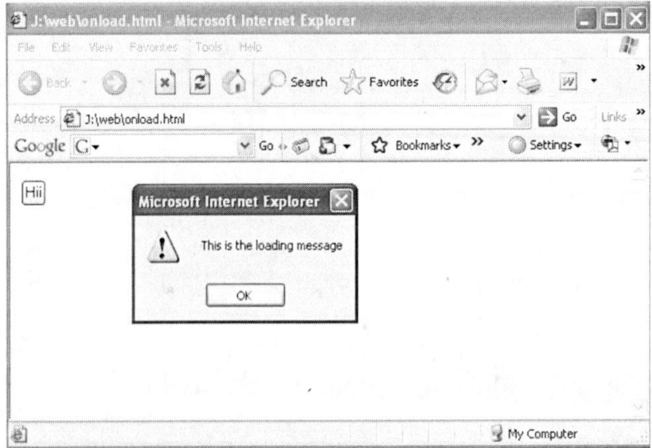

(ii) onUnload

The onUnload events are triggered when the user leaves the page.

Syntax

```
<body onUnload="unload()" >
```

//Program

```
<html>
<head>
<script type="text/javascript">
function unload()
{
 alert("This is the message of unloading");
}
</script>
</head>
<body onUnload="unload()" >
<input type="button" value="unload" />
</body>
</html>
```

When refresh the web form the output is as follows.

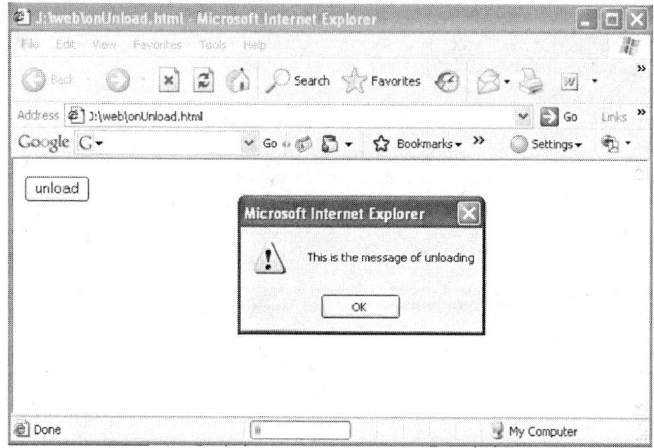

(iii) onSubmit

The onSubmit event is used to validate ALL form fields before submitting it.

Syntax

```
<form method="post" action="xxx.html" onsubmit="checkForm()">
```

(iv) onFocus

The onFocus, onBlur and onChange events are often used in combination with validation of form fields.

Below is an example of how to use the onChange event. The checkEmail() function will be called whenever the user changes the content of the field:

```
<input type="text" size="30" id="email" onchange="checkEmail()">
```

Syntax

//Program

```
<html>
<head>
<script type="text/javascript">
function submit1()
{
 alert("Enter on focus");
}
</script>
</head>
<body>
<input type="text" size="30" onFocus="submit1()">
<input type="button" value="Hi" />
</body>
</html>
```

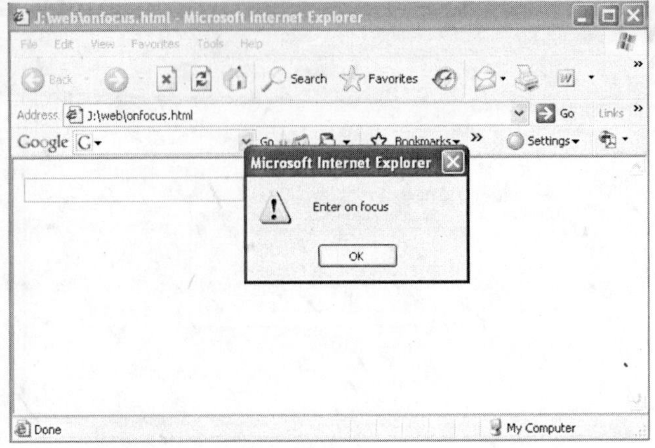

(v) onChange

Syntax

//Program

```
<html>
<head>
<script type="text/javascript">
function submit1()
{
 alert("Dont Enter");
}
</script>
</head>
<body>
<input type="text" size="30" onchange="submit1()">
<input type="button" value="Hi" />
</body>
</html>
```

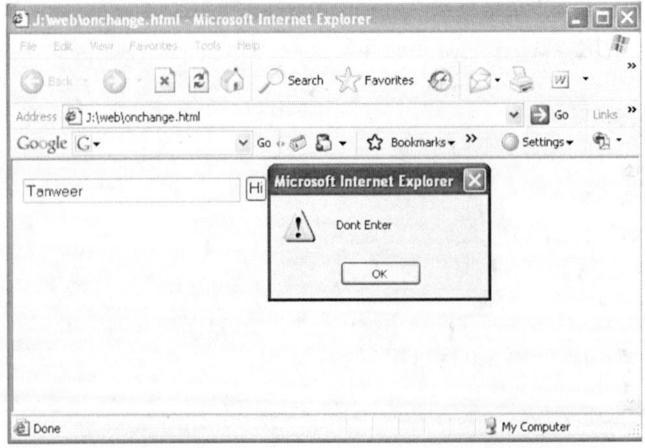

(vi) onBlur

Syntax

//Program

```
<html>
<head>
<script type="text/javascript">
function submit1()
{
 alert("Enter on blur");
}
</script>
</head>
<body>
<input type="text" size="30" onBlur="submit1()">
<input type="button" value="Hi" />
</body>
</html>
```

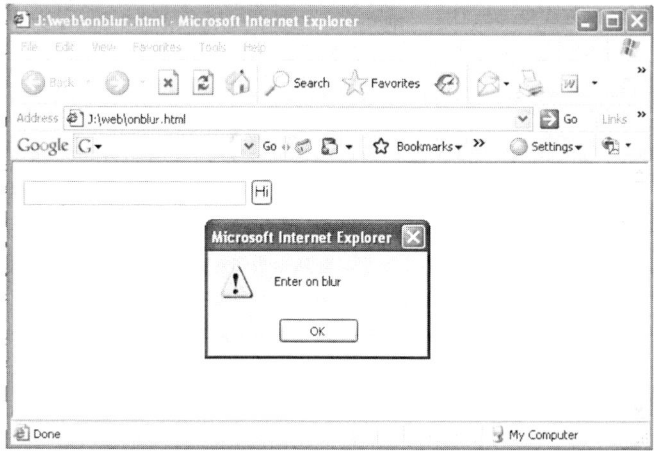

(vii) onMouseOver

Syntax

//Program

```
<html>
<head>
<script type="text/javascript">
function submit1()
{
 alert("Enter on mouse over");
}
```

```
</script>
</head>
<body>
<input type="text" size="30" onMouseOver="submit1()">
<input type="button" value="Hi" />
</body>
</html>
```

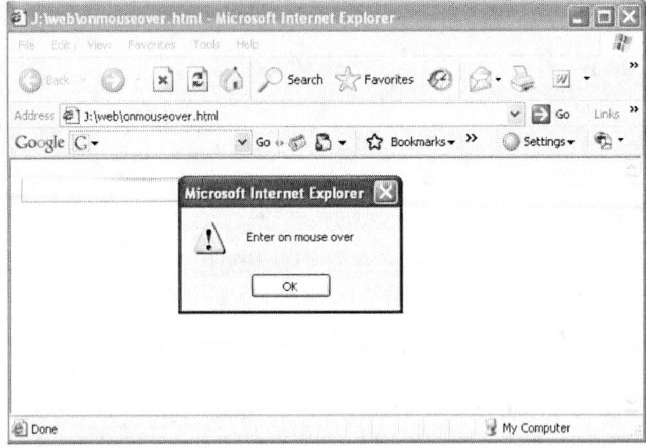

onMouseOver and onMouseOut are often used to create "animated" buttons.

Below is an example of an onMouseOver event. An alert box appears when an onMouseOver event is detected:

(viii) onMouseOut

Syntax

//Program

```
<html>
<head>
<script type="text/javascript">
function submit1()
{
 alert("msg on mouse out");
}
</script>
</head>
<body>
<input type="text" size="30" onMouseOut="submit1()">
<input type="button" value="Hi" />
</body>
html>
```

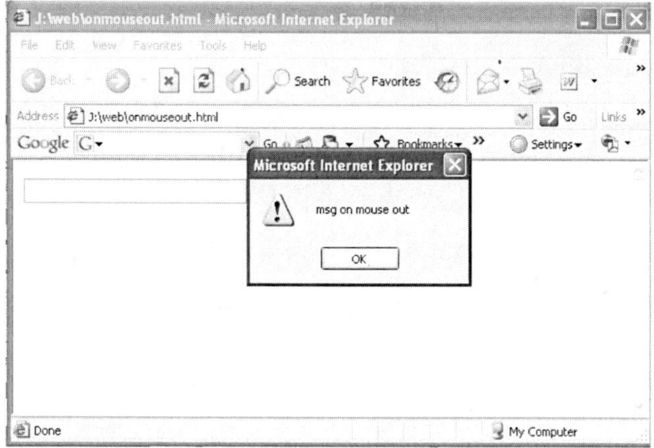

(ix) onClick

Syntax

```
//Program
<html>
<head>
<script type="text/javascript">
function submit1()
{
 alert("Hi,How r u?");
}
</script>
</head>
<body>
<input type="button" value="Hi" onClick="submit1()"/>
</body>
</html>
```

Output

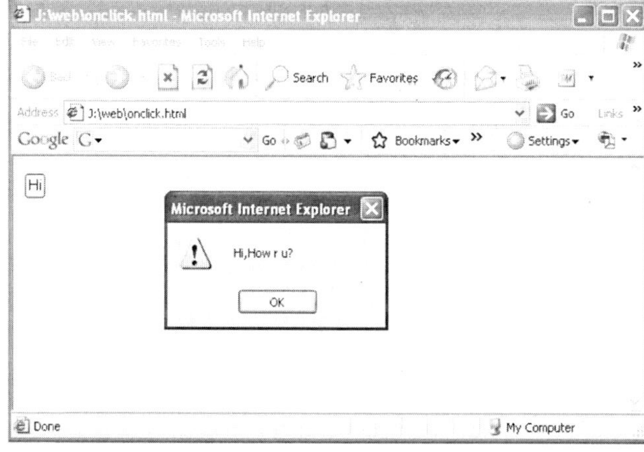

4.9 CONNECTIVITY WITH DATABASE

The following steps are used.

Step 1: Create a Connection

```
var cn = new ActiveXObject("ADODB.Connection");
var strConn = "Provider=Microsoft.Jet.OLEDB.4.0;Data Source = C:\\mydatabase.
mdb";
```

Step 2: Create a resultset and Command

```
var rs = new ActiveXObject("ADODB.Recordset");
var SQL = "select * from stud";
```

Step 3: Open the Connection

```
cn.Open(strConn);
rs.Open(SQL,cn);
```

Step 4: Display the Records.

```
while(!rs.EOF)
{
document.write(rs(0) + " " +rs(1)+"<br>");
rs.MoveNext();
}
```

Step 5: Close the resultset and Connection.

```
rs.Close();
cn.Close();
```

Select:

We can display all records of database using select command.

Database:

stud : Table

Name	RollNo
Tanweer	53
Aatif	01
Sameer	02

Coding

```
<html>
<head>
<title>Entitled Document</title>
<script language="JavaScript">
function getSubmit()
```

```
{ var i=0;
var cn = new ActiveXObject("ADODB.Connection");
var strConn = "Provider=Microsoft.Jet.OLEDB.4.0;Data Source = C:\\mydatabase.
mdb";
var rs = new ActiveXObject("ADODB.Recordset");
var SQL = "select * from stud";
cn.Open(strConn);
rs.Open(SQL,cn);
alert("Display Record");
while(!rs.EOF)
{
document.write(rs(0) + " " +rs(1)+"<br>");
rs.MoveNext();
}
rs.Close();
cn.Close();
}
</script>
</head>
<body onLoad="getSubmit()"></body>
</html>
```

Output

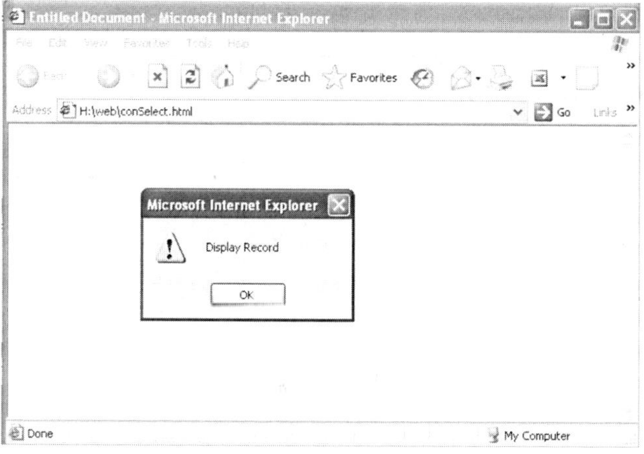

Click OK.

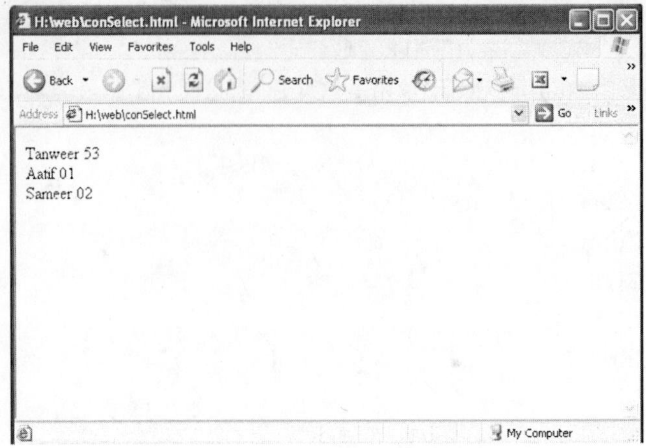

Update:

We can update any record of database using update command.

The database is as follows.

stud : Table

Name	RollNo
Tanweer	53
Aatif	01
Sameer	02

Coding:

```
<html>
<head>
<title>Entitled Document</title>
<script language="JavaScript">
function getSubmit()
{
var cn = new ActiveXObject("ADODB.Connection");
var strConn = "Provider=Microsoft.Jet.OLEDB.4.0;Data Source = C:\\mydatabase.
mdb";
var rs = new ActiveXObject("ADODB.Recordset");
var SQL = "UPDATE stud SET Name='Anjum' WHERE Name='Tanweer'";
cn.Open(strConn);
rs.Open(SQL, cn);
alert("Database Updated");
rs.Close();
```

```
cn.Close();
}
</script>
</head>
<body onLoad="getSubmit()"></body>
</html>
```

Output:

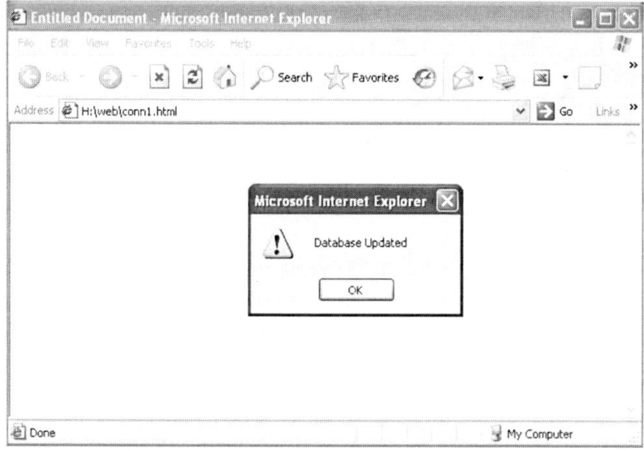

Now updated database is

stud : Table

Name	RollNo
Anjum	53
Aatif	01
Sameer	02

Insert:

We can insert any record into database using insert command.

Coding:

```
<html>
<head>
<title>Entitled Document</title>
<script language="JavaScript">
function getSubmit()
{
var cn = new ActiveXObject("ADODB.Connection");
```

```
var strConn = "Provider=Microsoft.Jet.OLEDB.4.0;Data Source = C:\\mydatabase.
mdb";
var rs = new ActiveXObject("ADODB.Recordset");
var SQL = "insert into stud values('Alam','43')";
cn.Open(strConn);
rs.Open(SQL, cn);
alert("Record Inserted");
rs.Close();
cn.Close();
}
</script>
</head>
<body onLoad="getSubmit()"></body>
</html>
```

Output:

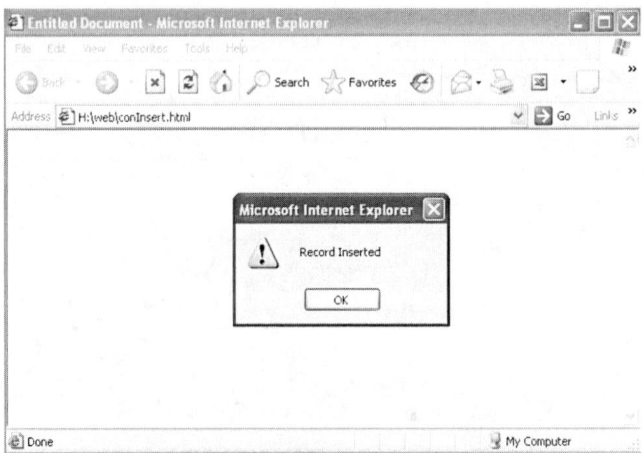

Now database is as follows.

stud : Table

Name	RollNo
Anjum	53
Aatif	01
Sameer	02
Alam	43

Delete:

Coding:

```
<html>
```

```
<head>
<title>Entitled Document</title>
<script language="JavaScript">
function getSubmit()
{
var cn = new ActiveXObject("ADODB.Connection");
var strConn = "Provider=Microsoft.Jet.OLEDB.4.0;Data Source = C:\\mydatabase.mdb";
var rs = new ActiveXObject("ADODB.Recordset");
var SQL = "delete from stud where RollNo='43'";
cn.Open(strConn);
rs.Open(SQL, cn);
alert("Record Deleted");
rs.Close();
cn.Close();
}
</script>
</head>
<body onLoad="getSubmit()"></body>
</html>
```

Output:

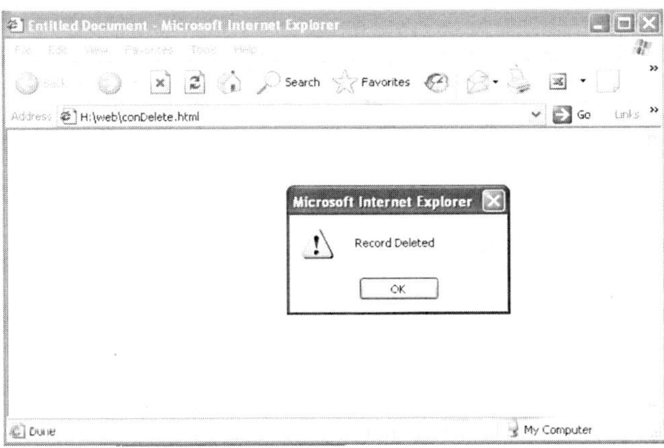

Now database is as follows.

stud : Table

Name	RollNo
Anjum	53
Aatif	01
Sameer	02

4.6 SOME JAVA SCRIPT PROGRAMS

Program: 1

Write a java script program that finds the greatest common divisor of two numbers.

```
<html>
<head>
<title>The Greatest Common Divisor
</title>
<script language="JavaScript">
var a=prompt("Enter the First value","");
var b=prompt("Enter the Second value","");
if(a==b)
{
          document.write("<b>"+a+" is gcd</b>");
}
else
{
          if(a%b==0)
          {
            document.write("<b>"+b +" is gcd</b>");
          }
          else
          {
            if(b%a==0)
            {
              document.write("<b>"+a+" is gcd</b>");
            }
            else
            {
              document.write("<b>1 is gcd</b>");
            }
          }
}
</script>
</head>
<body>

</body>
</html>
```

Output

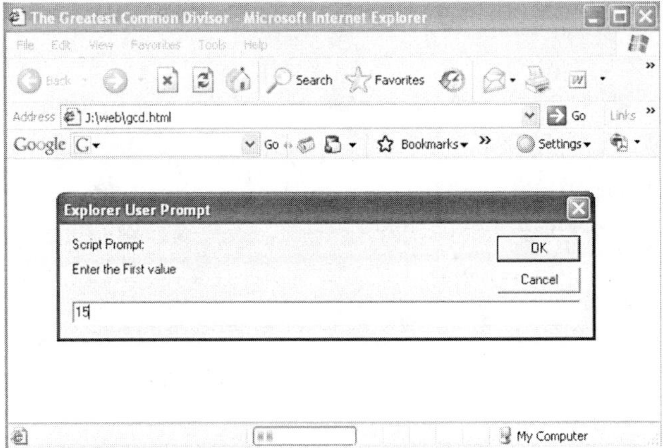

Click OK.

Again click OK.

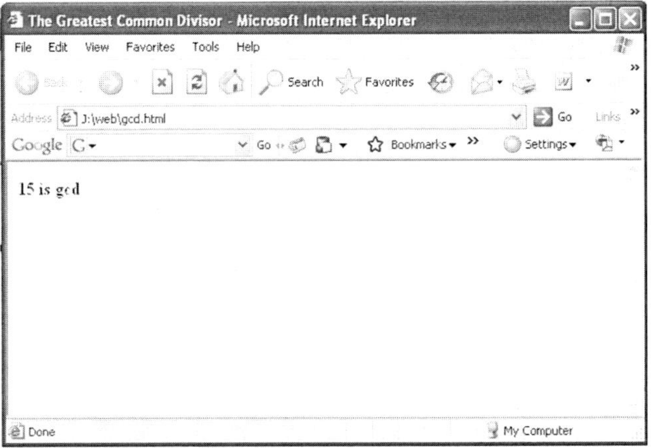

Program: 2

Design a HTML form to reserve a railway ticket.

```
<!--HTML code for Railway Reservation Form -->
<HTML>
  <Head>
    <Title>Railway Reservation Form</Title>
  </Head>
```

```
<body>
   <center>
   <form name="frm1">
      <h1>Railway Reservation System</h1>
      <table>
         <tr>
            <td>From :</td>
            <td><input type="text" name="txt1" ></td>
         </tr>
         <tr>
            <td>To :</td>
            <td><input type="text" name="txt2" ></td>
         </tr>
         <tr>
            <td>Name :</td>
            <td><input type="text" name="txt3" ></td>
         </tr>
         <tr>
            <td>Age :</td>
            <td><input type="text" name="txt4" ></td>
         </tr>
         <tr>
            <td>Address :</td>
            <td><Textarea></Textarea></td>
         </tr>
         <tr>
            <td>Account Type :</td>
            <td><input type="Radio" name="cc">Credit card</td>
         </tr>
         <tr>
            <td></td>
            <td><input type="Radio" name="dc">Debit Card</td>
         </tr>
         <tr>
            <td></td>
            <td><input type="Radio" name="other">Other</td>
         </tr>
         <tr>
            <td></td>
         <td><input type="button" name="btn1"
value="Submit"
OnClick="f1();" ></td>
<td><input type="button" name="btn2" value="Cancel"
```

```
></td>
        </tr>
    </table>
  </body>
</HTML>
```

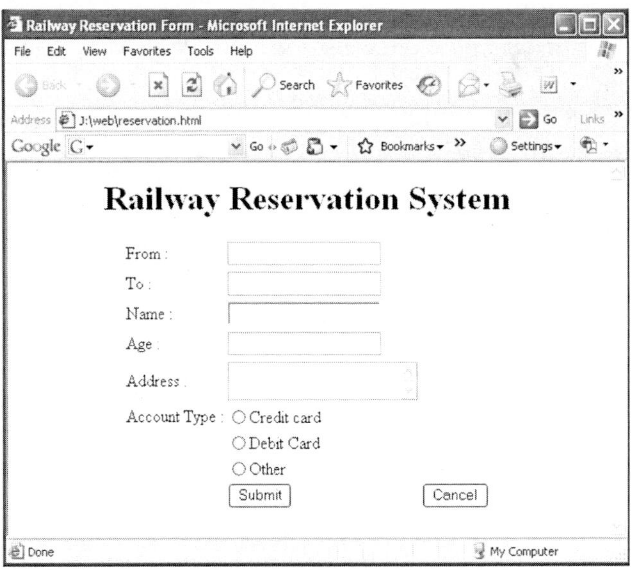

Program: 3

In the above form to reserve a railway ticket add the following validations using Java Script.

(i) From city and to city are two different cities.

(ii) Age of the passenger should not be greater than 150.

(iii) Name of the passenger should be a string of maximum length20.

```
<HTML>
  <Head>
    <Title>The Time Table of Trains</Title>
    <script language="JavaScript">
      function f1()
      {
      // Validation->From city and to city are two different cities.
        var len=parseInt(frm1.txt4.value);
        if(len>150)
        {
          alert("Enter the age less than 150");
        }
      // Validation->Age of the passenger should not be greater than 150.
```

```
            var str1=frm1.txt1.value;
            var str2=frm1.txt2.value;
            if(str1==str2)
            {
         alert("Please select diffrent cities for FROM and DESTINATION");
            }
//Validation->Name of the passenger should be a string of maximum length20
            var str3=frm1.txt3.value;
            var len1=str3.length;
            if(len1>20)
            {
               alert("Enter max. 20 characters in NAME field");
            }
         }
      </script>
   </Head>
   <body>
   <center>
      <form name="frm1">
      <h1>Railway Reservation System</h1>
         <table>
            <tr>
               <td>From :</td>
               <td><input type="text" name="txt1" ></td>
            </tr>
<img src="india2.jpg">
            <tr>
               <td>To :</td>
               <td><input type="text" name="txt2" ></td>
            </tr>

            <tr>
               <td>Name :</td>
               <td><input type="text" name="txt3" ></td>
            </tr>

            <tr>
               <td>Age :</td>
               <td><input type="text" name="txt4" ></td>
            </tr>

            <tr>
               <td>Address :</td>
```

```
                <td><Textarea></Textarea></td>
            </tr>
            <tr>
               <td>Account Type :</td>
               <td><input type="Radio" name="cc">Credit card</td>
            </tr>

            <tr>
               <td></td>
               <td><input type="Radio" name="dc">Debit Card</td>
            </tr>
            <tr>
               <td></td>
               <td><input type="Radio" name="other">Other</td>
            </tr>
            <tr>
               <td></td>
               <td><input type="button" name="btn1"
value="Submit" OnClick="f1();" ></td>
<td><input type="button" name="btn2"
value="Cancel" ></td>
            </tr>
        </table>
    </body>
</HTML>
```

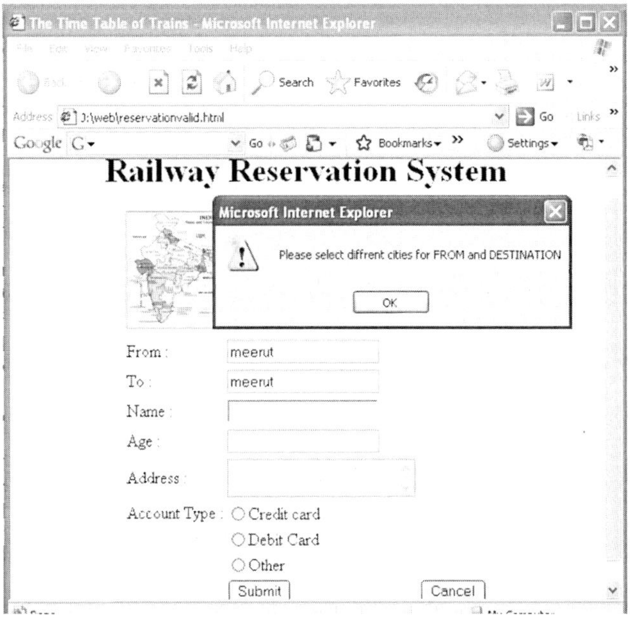

Program: 4

Write a java script code block to find largest of three integers.

```
<!-- JavaScript Code to find largest of three numbers -->
<html>
  <head>
    <title>Largest of Three Numbers</title>
  </head>
  <script language="JavaScript">
    var a,b,c;
    a=parseInt(prompt("Enter integer value for a",""));
    b=parseInt(prompt("Enter integer value for b",""));
    c=parseInt(prompt("Enter integer value for c",""));
    if( a > b && a > c )
      document.write("Value a = "+a+" is largest");
    else if( b > a && b > c )
      document.write("Value b = "+b+" is largest");
    else
      document.write("Value c = "+c+" is largest");
  </script>
</html>
```

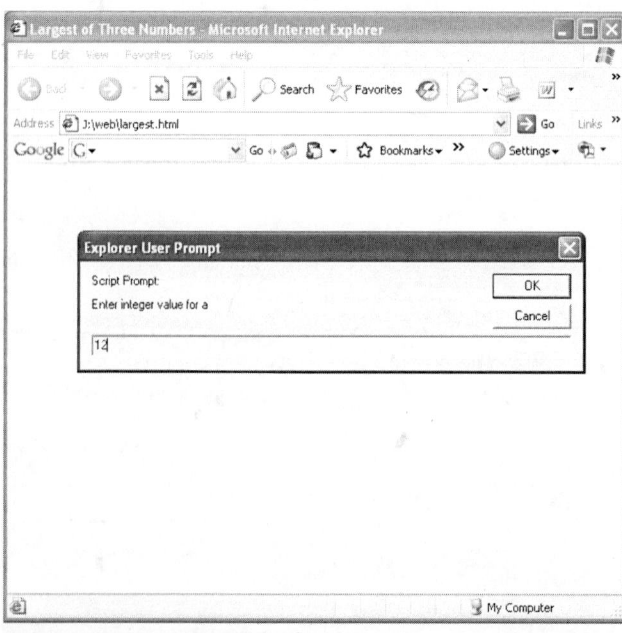

Program: 5

Write a java script code block to check whether the given string is palindrome or not.

```
<!-- JavaScript Code to check that given string is palindrome or not -->
<html>
  <head>
    <title>Palindrome Checker</title>
  </head>
  <script language="JavaScript">
    var i,len,j,flag=0;
    var str = new Array(20);
    str=prompt("Enter any string to check","");
    len=str.length;
    j=len-1
    for(i=0;i<len/2;i++)
    {
      if(str.charAt(i)==str.charAt(j))
      {
        j--;
        flag=1;
      }
      else
      {
        flag=0;
        break;
      }
```

```
      }
      if(flag==1)
         document.write("Given string is a palindrome");
      else
         document.write("Given string is not a palindrome");
   </script>
</html>
```

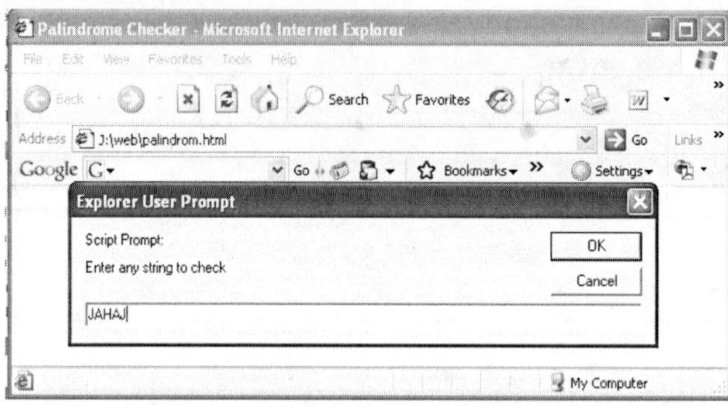

Program: 6

Write a java script code block to check whether the given number is prime or not.

```
<!-- JavaScript Code to check that given number is prime or not -->

<html>
   <head>
      <title>Prime Number Checker</title>
   </head>
   <script language="JavaScript">
      var i,flag=0,number;
      number=prompt("Enter any number to check","");
      for(i=2;i<number;i++)
      {
         if(number%i==0)
         {
```

```
            flag=1;
            break;
         }
      }
      if(flag==1)
         document.write("Given Number is not a prime number");
      else
         document.write("Given Number is a prime number");
   </script>
</html>
```

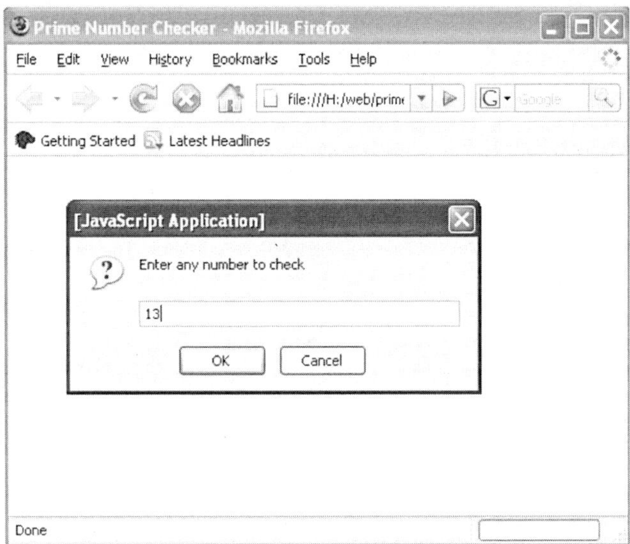

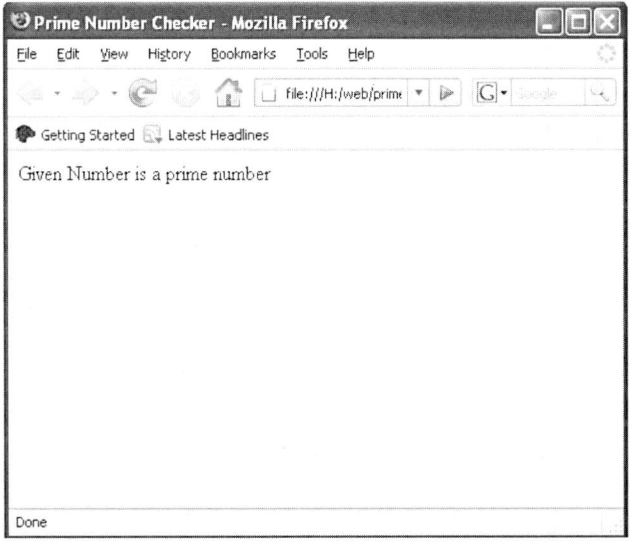

Program: 7

Write a java script code block to print a pyramid.

```
<!-- JavaScript Code to print the pyramid -->

<html>
   <head>
      <title>Pyramid Builder</title>
   </head>
   <script language="JavaScript">
      var i,j,k,n=9;
      for(i=0;i<n;i++)
      {
         for(j=0;j<n-i;j++)
            document.write(" ");
         for(k=0;k<i;k++)
            document.write(" *");
         document.write("<br>");
      }
   </script>
</html>
```

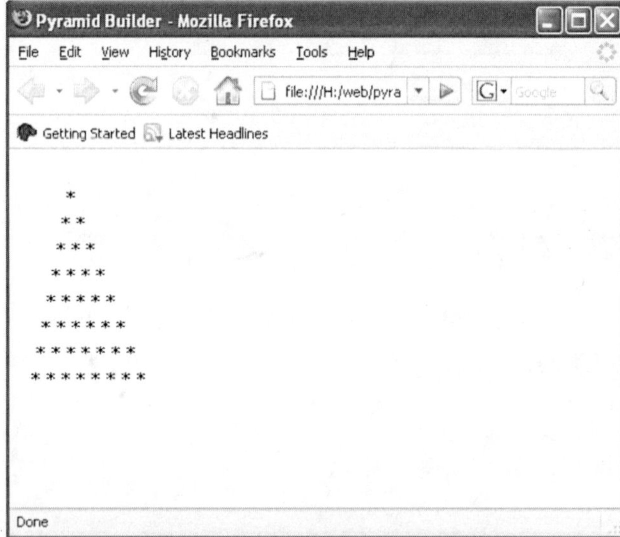

Program: 8

Write a java script code block to find Fibonacci series of iterative method using user-defined function.

```
<!-- JavaScript Code to find fibonacci series using user- defined functions -->

<html>
```

```
  <head>
    <title>Fibonacci Series</title>
  </head>
  <script language="JavaScript">
    function printseries(val)
    {
      var a=1,b=1,c;
      document.write("<H1>Fibonacci Series</H1>");
      document.write("<HR>");
      document.write(a+"<br>");
      document.write(b+"<br>");
      for(i=0;i<val-2;i++)
      {
        c=a+b;
        document.write(c+"<br>");
        a=b;
        b=c;
      }
    }
  </script>
  <body>
    <table border="0">
      <tr>
        <td><p>Enter total numbers in series to print</p></td>
        <td><input type="text" name="txt1"></td>
      </tr>
      <tr>
        <td><input type="button" name="bt1" value="Print Series"
onClick="printseries(txt1.value)"></td>
      </tr>
    </table>
</html>
```

Program: 9

Write a java script code block to find factorial of n by recursion using user-defined function.

```
<!-- JavaScript Code to find factorial of a number by using recursion -->
<html>
  <head>
    <title>Factorial</title>
  </head>
  <script language="JavaScript">
    var f=1;
```

```
        function printfact(val)
        {
            if(val>1)
                return val*(printfact(val-1));
            else
                return 1;
        }
        val=parseInt(prompt("Enter any number to calculate factorial",""));
        f=printfact(val);
        document.write("Factorial is : "+f);
    </script>
</html>
```

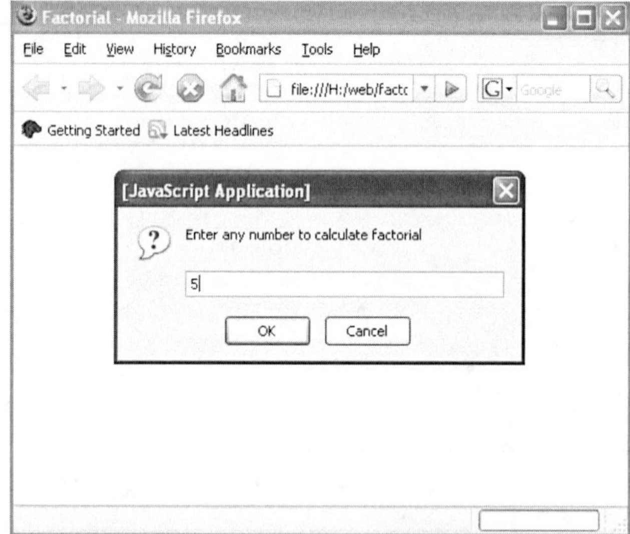

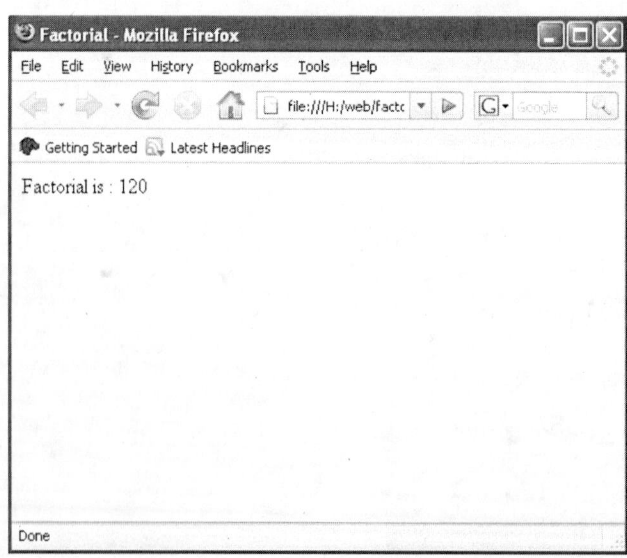

Program: 10

Write a java script code block to find sum and average of n integers using array.

```
<!-- JavaScript Code to find sum and average of n integers using array -->

<html>
   <head>
      <title>Sum and Average</title>
   </head>
   <script language="JavaScript">
      var arr = new Array(10);
      var avg=0,sum=0,i;
      for(i=0;i<10;i++)
      {
         arr[i]=parseInt(prompt("Enter array element",""));
         sum=sum+arr[i];
      }
      avg=sum/10;
      document.write("Sum is : "+sum+" Average is : "+avg);
   </script>
</html>
```

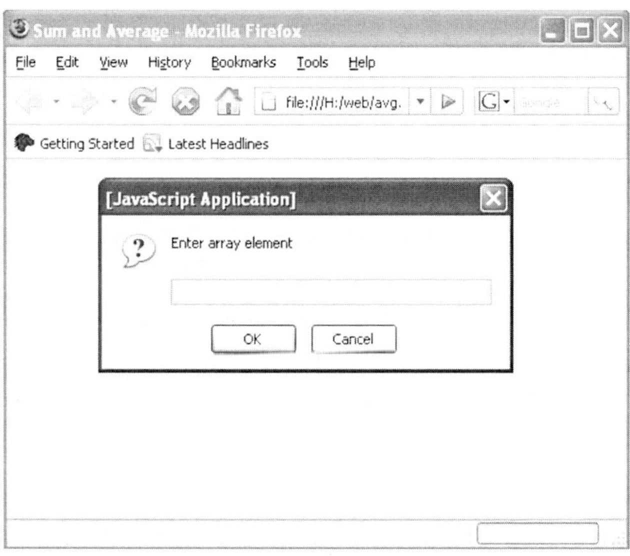

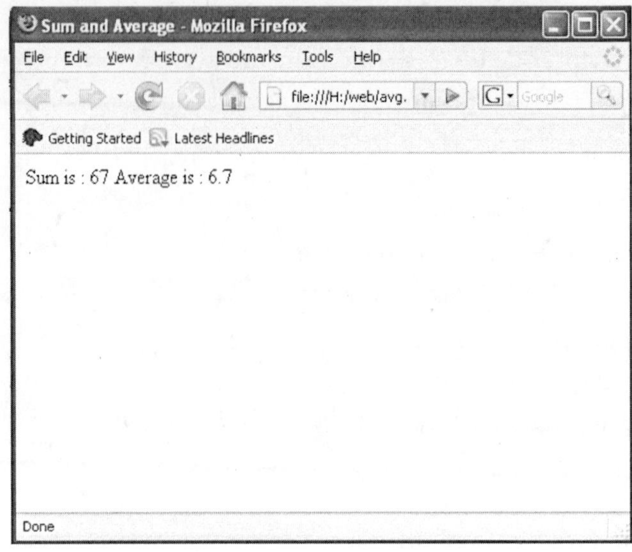

SUMMARY

Java is a powerful programming language in the same category as C and C++ while Java script is a scripting language. Everyone can use JavaScript without purchasing a license of Java script software. JavaScript is a scripting language that is usually embedded directly into HTML pages. JavaScript is an interpreted language means that scripts execute without preliminary compilation. JavaScript is an Object Oriented Programming scripting language. An Object Oriented Programming language allows us to define own objects and make variable types. Properties are the values associated with an object.

EXERCISE

1. What is Math object in Java Script?
2. Define JavaScript.
3. Explain events in Java Script.
4. What are prompt in Java script?

*****

CHAPTER 5

JAVA: GETTING START

Java is a high-level, third generation programming language, like C, COBOL, PASCAL, BASIC, FORTRAN, Perl, Smalltalk and many others. Java is related to C++, which is a direct descendent of C. Unlike C++ Java is not a superset of C. A Java compiler won't compile C code, and most large C programs need to be changed substantially before they can become Java programs. You can use Java to write computer applications that process words, play games, crunch numbers, store data or do any of the thousands of other things computer software can do. The original motivation of Java was the need for a platform independent language. This platform independence is exactly what is needed for Internet programming. The secret of the platform independent characteristic of Java lies in byte code and JVM (Java Virtual machine).When we compile a java program it is converted to byte code and then Java Virtual Machine executes the byte code.

5.1 INTRODUCTION

Java was developed by a group of programmers at Sun Microsystems in 1991. Earlier it was named Oak. In some sense Java is what C++ might have been if it was not required to be backward compatible with C. Java was originally called Oak but that turned out to be a copyrighted name so after some brainstorming they chose the name Java. It doesn't really mean Just another Vague Acronym. Java has gone through two major upgrades from the original version 1.0.2 to version 1.1 and now to version 1.2 (also called Java 2). There are major changes in the language between the versions.

5.2 Java's Past, Present and Future

The Java language was developed at Sun Microsystems in 1991 as part of a research project to develop software for consumer electronics devices like television sets, toasters, VCRs and the other sorts of machines you can buy at any department store. At first glance, it may appear that Java was developed specifically for the World Wide Web. However, Java was developed independently of the web, and went through several stages of metamorphosis before reaching its current status of de facto programming language for the World Wide Web. Java's goals at that time were to be small, fast, efficient, and easily portable to a wide range of hardware devices. Those same goals made Java an ideal language for distributing executable programs via the World Wide Web and also a general-purpose programming language for developing programs that are easily usable and portable across different platforms.

The Java language was used in several projects within Sun (under the name Oak), but did not get very much commercial attention until it was paired with Hot Java. Bill Joy, currently a vice president at Sun Microsystems, is widely believed to have been the person to conceive of the idea of a programming language that later became Java. In January of 1991, Bill Joy, Mike Sheradin, James Gosling, Patrick Naughton and several other individuals met in Aspen, Colorado for the first time to discuss the ideas for the Stealth Project. The goal of the Stealth Project was to do research in the area of application of computers in the consumer electronics market.

The vision of the project was to develop "smart" consumer electronic devices that could all be centrally controlled and programmed from a handheld-remote-control-like device. Gosling, who had joined Sun in 1984, had previously developed the commercially unsuccessful NEWS windowing system. He began with C++, but soon after was convinced that C++ was inadequate for this particular project. His extensions and modifications to C++, were the first steps towards the development of an independent language that would fit the project objectives.

(i) Sun is developing a number of new features for the Java environment, including a number of new class libraries for database integration, multimedia, electronic commerce, and other uses. Sun also has a Java-based Web server, a Java-based hardware chip (with which you can write Java-specific systems), and a Java-based operating system. You'll learn about all these things later in this book. The 1.1 release of the JDK will include many of these features; others will be released as separate packages.

(ii) Sun is also developing a framework called Java Beans, which will allow the development of component objects in Java, similarly to Microsoft's ActiveX (OLE) technology. These different components can then are easily combined and interact with each other using standard component assembly tools. You'll learn more about Java Beans later in this book.

(iii) Java capabilities will be incorporated into a wide variety of operating systems, including Solaris, Windows 95, and Mac OS. This means that Java applications (as opposed to applets) can run nearly anywhere without needing additional software to be installed.

(iv) Many companies are working on performance enhancements for Java programs, including the aforementioned Java chip and what are called just-in-time compilers.

The Present: Java 2

Java 2 was released in December 1998, providing many improvements and additions. The most notable addition is Swing, which is a new user interface toolkit with capabilities far exceeding AWT's. (Swing, AWT, and some other packages are now called the JFC, or Java Foundation Classes.) Here's a brief overview of the most important features of the core Java 2 API:

(i) JDBC (Java Database Connectivity)

A general facility for interacting with databases. (Introduced with Java 1.1.)

(ii) RMI (Remote Method Invocation)

Java's distributed objects system. RMI lets you call methods on objects hosted by a server running somewhere else on the network. (Introduced with Java 1.1.)

(iii) Java Security

A facility for controlling access to system resources, combined with a uniform interface to cryptography. Java Security is the basis for signed classes, which were discussed earlier.

(iv) JFC (Java Foundation Classes)

A catch-all for a number of new features, including the Swing user interface components; "pluggable look-and-feel," which means the ability of the user interface to adapt itself to the "look-and-feel" of the platform you're using; drag and drop; and accessibility, which means the ability to integrate with special software and hardware for people with disabilities.

(v) Java 2D

Part of JFC; enables high-quality graphics, font manipulation, and printing.

Internationalization The ability to write programs that adapt themselves to the language the user wants to use; the program automatically displays text in the appropriate language. (Introduced with Java 1.1.)

The following features aren't part of the core Java 2 definition; you may have to download them separately. Most of them are what Sun calls "standard extensions":

(vi) JNDI (Java Naming and Directory Interface)

A very general service for looking up resources. JNDI unifies access to directory services like LDAP, Novell's NDS, and others.

(vii) JavaMail

A uniform API for writing email software.

(viii) Java 3D

A facility for developing applications with 3D graphics.

(ix) Java Media

Another catch-all that includes Java 2D, Java 3D, the Java Media Framework (a framework for coordinating the display of many different kinds of media), Java Speech (for speech recognition and synthesis), Java Sound (high-quality audio), Java TV (for interactive television and similar applications), and others.

(x) *Java Servlets*

A facility that lets you write custom Internet servers. It is most frequently used to write web server applications, but it's much more general.

(xi) *Java Cryptography*

Actual implementations of cryptographic algorithms. (This package was separated from Java Security for legal reasons.)

(xii) *JavaHelp*

A facility for writing help systems and incorporating them in Java programs.

(xiii) *Enterprise JavaBeans*

A component architecture for building distributed server-side applications.

(xiv) *Jini*

An extremely interesting catch-all that is designed to enable massively distributed computing, including computing on common household appliances. In a few years, your stereo may be able to execute Java programs.

(xv) *Java Card*

A version of Java for very small (i.e., credit card-sized) devices, which have severe limitations on speed and memory.

5.3 FEATURES OF JAVA

Sun described Java as: *Java is* a simple, object-oriented, distributed, interpreted, robust, secure, architecture neutral, portable, high-performance, multithreaded, and dynamic language. The features of Java are as follows.

- Simple
- Object Oriented
- Robust
- Distributed
- Interpreted
- Secure
- Portable
- Platform Independent
- Architecture Neutral
- Multithreaded

(i) Simple

Java is simple, it is easy to read and write. Java was designed to make it much easier to write bug free code. It is easy to learn and can be used effectively. If you are familiar with C++, learning Java will be particularly easy for you because you have most of the foundation already. Although Java looks similar to C and C++, most of the more complex parts of those languages have been excluded from Java, making the language simpler without sacrificing much of its power. There are no pointers in Java, nor is there pointer arithmetic. Strings and arrays are real objects in Java. Memory management is automatic. To an experienced programmer, these omissions may be difficult to get used to, but to beginners or programmers who have worked in other languages, they make the Java language far easier to learn.

(ii) Object Oriented

The object-oriented programming technique is merely a way of organizing programs, and it can be accomplished using any language. Working with a real object-oriented language and programming environment, however, enables you to take full advantage of object-oriented methodology and its capabilities for creating flexible, modular programs and reusing code.

In object-oriented programs data is represented by objects. Objects have two sections, fields (instance variables) and methods. Fields tell you what an object is. Methods tell you what an object does. These fields and methods are closely tied to the object's real world characteristics and behavior. When a program is run messages are passed back and forth between objects. When an object receives a message it responds accordingly as defined by its methods.

Object oriented programming is alleged to have a number of advantages including:

- Simpler, easier to read programs
- More efficient reuse of code
- Faster time to market
- More robust, error-free code

(iii) Robust

Garbage collection and Exception handling make Java a robust language. In garbage collection the user doesn't have to bother about the memory allocation as, when the object is no longer in use it is automatically deleted to release memory space.

(iv) Distributed

The widely used protocols like HTTP and FTP are developed in java. Internet programmers can call functions on these protocols and can get access the files from any remote machine on the internet rather than writing codes on their local system.

(v) Interpreted

The Java code is compiled into the byte code (.class file). The byte code is then interpreted to the machine language by the JVM environment. The Java compiler generates byte-codes for the Java Virtual Machine (JVM), rather than native machine code.

(vi) Secure

The Java language has built-in capabilities to ensure that violations of security do not occur. There is a concept of applets in Java, which can be downloaded without virus or malicious contents because the Java programs are confined to Java execution environment (JVM) and are not allowed to access other parts of the CPU.

(vii) Portable

By porting an interpreter for the Java Virtual Machine to any computer hardware or operating system, one is assured that all code compiled for it will run on that system. This forms the basis for Java's portability. The Java programs called Applets run in the JVM environment that is in every browser therefore the programs can run anywhere.

(viii) Platform Independent

Platform independence means that a program can run on any computer system. Java programs can run on any system for which a Java virtual machine has been installed. Platform independence in Java doesn't stop at the source level, however. Java compiled binary files are also platform independent and can run on multiple platforms (if they have a Java virtual machine available) without the need to recompile the source. Java bytecodes are a special set of machine instructions that are not specific to any one processor or computer system. A platform-specific bytecode interpreter executes the Java bytecodes. The bytecode interpreter is also called the Java virtual machine or the Java runtime interpreter.

(ix) Architecture Neutral

The compiler generates an architecture-neutral object file format to enable a Java application to execute anywhere on the network and then the compiled code is executed on many processors, given the presence of the Java runtime system. The Java compiler compiles source code to a stage which is intermediate between source and native machine code. This intermediate stage is known as the bytecode, which is neutral. The bytecode conforms to the specification of a hypothetical machine called the Java Virtual Machine and can be efficiently converted into native code for a particular processor.

In other words, we can say, "Write once, run anywhere".

JVM = interpreter + run-time system, ported to various platforms.

(x) Multithreaded

Multithreading means a single program having different threads executing independently at the same time. Multiple threads execute instructions according to the program code in a process or a program. A single threaded application has one thread of execution running at all times and such programs can do only one task at a time. A multi-threaded application can have several threads of execution running independently and simultaneously. These threads may communicate and cooperate and will appear to be a single program to the user.

5.4 DIFFERENCES BETWEEN JAVA AND C++

Java and C++ use different techniques for splitting up code in multiple source files. Java uses a package system that dictates the file name and path for all program definitions. In addition to running a compiled Java program, computers running Java applications must also run the Java Virtual Machine JVM, while compiled C++ programs can be run without external applications.

Java	C++
Java does not support typedefs, defines, or a preprocessor.	C++ support typedefs, defines, or a preprocessor.
Java does not support enums	C++ support enums
Java supports classes, but does not support structures or unions	C++ supports classes, structures or unions.
Java does not support multiple inheritance.	C++ supports multiple inheritance.
Runs in a protected virtual machine.	Exposes low-level system facilities.
Java has No Pointers	C++ has Pointers
Java Does Not Support Templates	C++ Support Templates
Java compiler produce Java bytecode	C++ compiler produce native machine code

C++ Features Not Found in Java

1. **Java does not support Multiple Inheritance**

   C++ supports multiple inheritance of method implementations from more than one super class at a time. While it seems like a very useful feature, adding it to the language turns out to introduce many complexities. The Java language designers chose to avoid the added complexity by using interfaces instead.

   Thus, a class in Java can only inherit method implementations from a single super class, but it can inherit method declarations from any number of interfaces. In practice, this is not any particular hardship.

2. **Java has no Global Variables**

   The fields and methods of a class are known as the members of a class. In Java, every field and method is declared within a class (not out side the class or globally) and forms part of that class.

3. **No Preprocessor**

   Java does not include any kind of preprocessor like the C++ preprocessor. It may seem hard to imagine programming without #define, #ifdef and #include but in fact Java really does not require these constructs.

4. **Java has no Pointers**

Pointers are a source of bugs. Eliminating them simplifies the language and eliminates many potential bugs.The referencing and dereferencing of objects is handled for you automatically by Java. Java does not allow you to manipulate memory addresses or pointers of any type:

- It does not allow you to do pointer arithmetic.
- It does not allow you to array references or cast object into integers or vice versa.
- It does not allow you to compute the size in bytes of any object or primitive type.

5. **Java does not support Templates**

C++ supports templates that allow you to implement a Stack and then instantiate it as Stack <int> or Stack <double> to produce two separate types: a stack of integers and a stack of floating point values. Java has no such facility. However, the fact that every class in Java is a subclass of Object means that every object can be cast to an instance of Object. Thus, in Java, it is often sufficient to define a data structure that operates on Object values.

6. **Java Does Not Allow Operator Overloading**

C++ allows you to define operators that perform arbitrary operations on instances of your class. In effect, it allows extending the syntax of the language. In practice however, it tends to make code hard to understand. The Java language designers decided to omit such operator overloading from the language. Note, though, that the use of the + operator for string concatenation in Java is at least reminiscent of operator overloading.

5.5 THE JAVA VIRTUAL MACHINE

JVM is a platform-independent execution environment that converts Java bytecode into machine language and executes it. A Java virtual machine (JVM) is an implementation of the Java Virtual Machine Specification, interprets compiled Java binary code (called bytecode) for a computer's processor so that it can perform a Java program's instructions. Java was designed to allow application programs to be built that could be run on any platform without having to be rewritten or recompiled by the programmer for each separate platform. Most programming languages compile source code directly into machine code that is designed to run on a specific microprocessor architecture or operating system, such as Windows or UNIX.

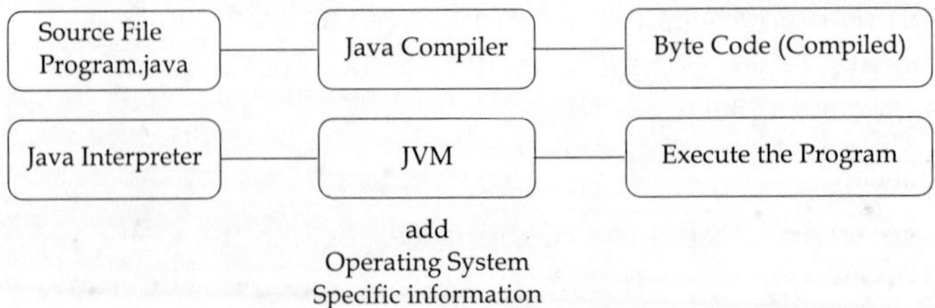

Figure 5.1: Java Virtual Machine

A program written in Java cannot be run directly on any computer. First, it has to be translated into machine language. This translation is done by a program called a compiler. A compiler takes a Java program and translates it into an executable machine-language program. Once the translation is completed, the machine-language program can be run many times, but of course it can only be run on same type of computers (since same type of computer has its own individual machine language). If the program is to run on another type of computer it has to be re-translated, using a different compiler, into the appropriate machine language. There is an alternative to compiling a Java program. Instead of using a compiler, which translates the program all at once, the interpreter, this translates it instruction-by-instruction, as necessary. An interpreter is a program that acts much like a CPU, with a kind of fetch-and-execute cycle. In order to execute a program, the interpreter runs in a loop in which it repeatedly reads one instruction from the program, decides what is necessary to carry out that instruction, and then performs the appropriate machine-language commands to do so. The designers of Java use a combination of compilation and interpretation. Programs written in Java are compiled into machine language, but it is a machine language for a computer that doesn't really exist, known as the Java virtual machine. The machine language for the Java virtual machine is called Java bytecode. However, one of the main selling points of Java is that it can actually be used on any computer. All that the computer needs is an interpreter for Java bytecode. Such an interpreter simulates the Java virtual machine in the same way that Virtual PC simulates a PC computer.

5.6 JAVA PROGRAM STRUCTURE

```
public class ClassName
{
//class body
public static void main (String[] args)
{
//method body
}
}
```

```
public class Hello
{
public static void main(String[] args)
{
 System.out.println("Hello");
 }
}
```

Save this program in the folder say C:\javaprogram. The name of the class is the same as the name of the file. When you're creating a stand-alone program such as this one, one of the classes in the file must have the same name as the file. (The compiler complains if you don't do this.)

Compiling and running

Compile the First program as follows.

In order to compile the program open the command prompt and go to your directory and write this command.

I:\program>**javac Hello.java**

I am assuming that Hello.java is in a directory called program. The java compiler creates a file called Hello.class in the directory program (check that it is there!). This class contains the program but in bytecode form ready to run. Run the program as follows.

I:\program>**java Hello**

The output of this program is **Hello**

NOTE :

1. java is case sensitive, **first** is different from **First**.
2. By convention the name of the file should match the name of the class.

Figure 5.2: Output Hello.java

5.7 CREATING A JAVA APPLICATION

Java applications are different from Java applets. Java applications, however, are more general programs written in the Java language. Java applications don't require a browser to run; in fact, Java can be used to create all the kinds of applications that you would normally use a more conventional programming language to create.

5.7.1 Program Code

```
/*This is the first java program hence named first.java*/
class first
{
public static void main(String[] args)
{
System.out.println("This is a java program");
}
}
```

4.7.2 How to set PATH

(i) Firstly install JDK 1.6

(ii) Copy the following path:

C:\Program Files\Java\jdk1.6.0\bin;

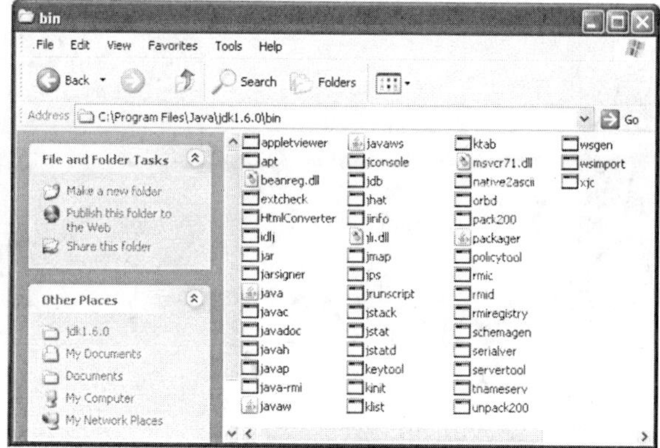

Figure 5.3: Path C:\Program Files\Java\jdk1.6.0\bin

(iii) Now right click on My Computer

Figure 5.4: Right Click on My Computer

Select Properties

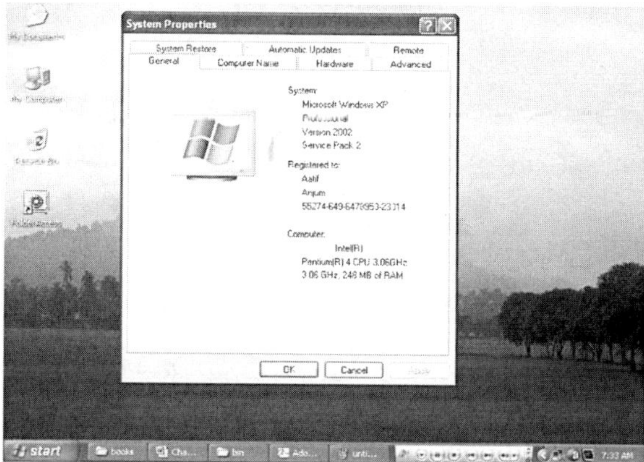

Figure 5.5: Select Properties

Now Select Advanced

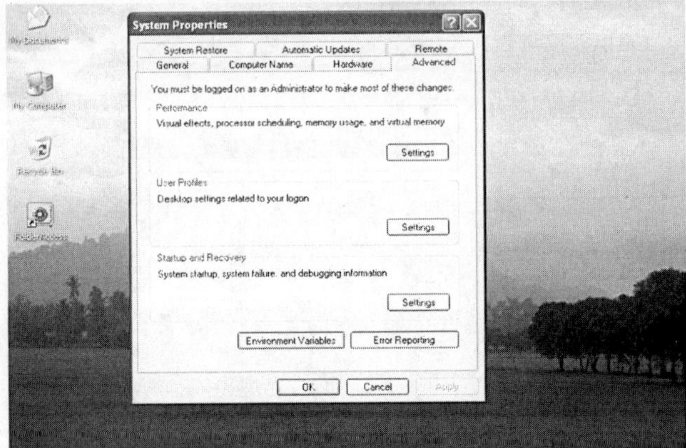

Figure 5.6: Select Advanced

Now Select Environmental Variable

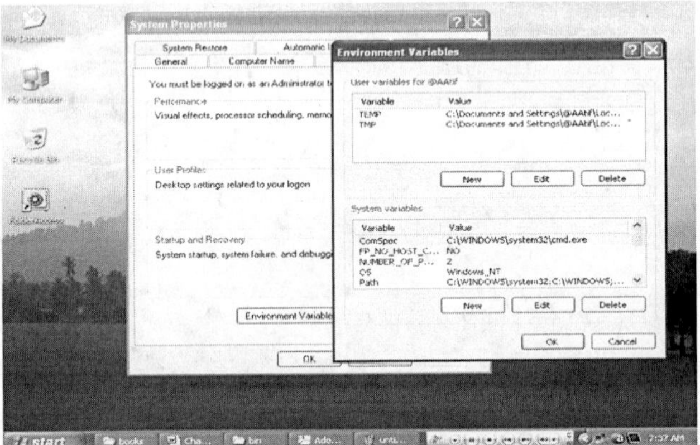

Figure 5.7: Select Environmental Variable

Now Click on New.

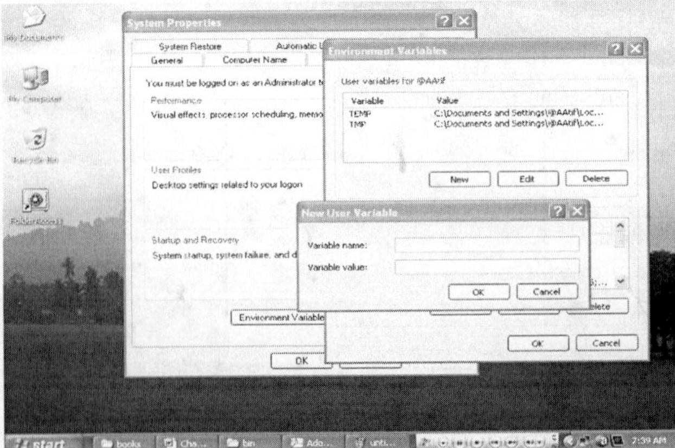

Figure 5.8: Enter variable name and value

Now enter the following values.

Varible Name: path

Variable Value: C:\Program Files\Java\jdk1.6.0\bin;

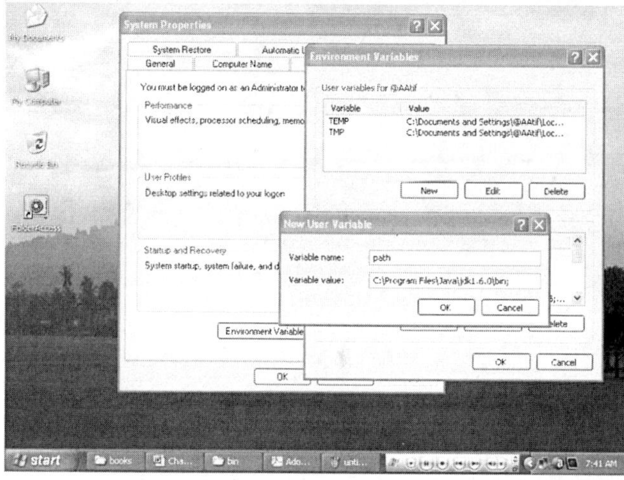

Figure 5.9: Enter variable name and value

Now click OK.

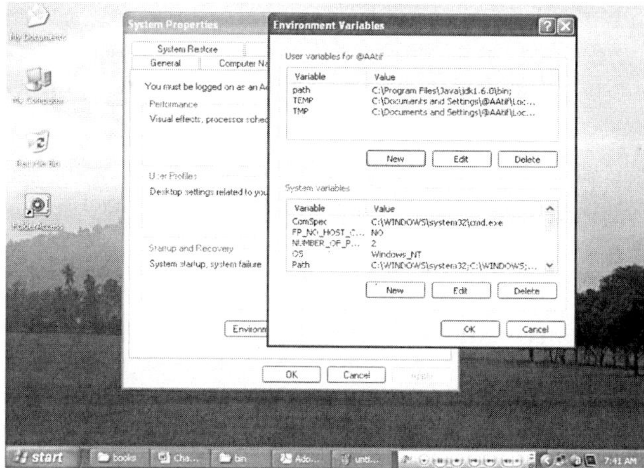

Figure 5.10: Path setting

Now again click OK then again click OK.

Now path has been set.

Now Test path, it is set or not.

Write javac on command prompt and press ENTER, if information about java compiler is displayed, then path has been set otherwise display an internal or external error.

Figure 5.11: check java compiler

5.7.3 Understanding Java Programs

You have already seen the making and executing of a Java program. Understanding a program is the most important task. Have a closer look at *"first.java"*.

By default java import a package java.lang and in this package we have a System class, and System class has a static object out of PrintStream class. Since it's static you don't need to create anything. The out object is always there and provides a println( ) function, which is used to print the string on the console and end with a new line." Thus, in any Java program you write you can say System.out.println("things") whenever you want to print something to the console.

Line 1:

/* Multiline Comment*/

The comments on program are enclosed within it. The compiler ignores these lines and hence no error is generated. Writing comments is not binding on the user.

Line 2:

class first

This is the second line of our java program. Here we have created a class named *"first"*. Creating a class is binding on the programmer as Java is strictly object oriented. Everything is encapsulated within a class.

Line 3:

{

Opening braces

Braces play a vital role in programming. A group of statements are enclosed in braces called blocks. Brace, here depicts that the class has begin.

Line 4:

public static void main(String args[])

In this line we have created a method or function using a list of java *"keywords"*. A **keyword** is a special word that is recognized by the compiler and has a special use.

Keywords

(i). **public:** An access specifier, The public keyword means that the method is available to the outside world.

(ii). **static**: We have created a static method named *"main"*. The static keyword means that no need to create an object of this class to access the main function. In the context of methods "static" keyword means that this method is independent of any object. As main is executed before any other method, we need to make it static so that we can call other methods by creating their instances here.

(iii). **void:** You will learn in the upcoming chapters that a method can even return a value. The *"void"* keyword here means that the method does not return any value. If these things seem too complicated to you, have patience!! Soon each and every detail will be clear.

(iv). **main (String args[])**: We have now specified the main method. The main keyword is the name of the main function from where the execution will start and args are the command line arguments. The brackets enclose within themselves 'the parameters'. Here we have an array of instances of String class. (Arrays are a group of one kind of data and String is a predefined class in Java that stores series of characters in itself).

Line 5:

{

Opening Brace

By this brace we come to know that our method has begun. It defines the starting point of method.

Line 6:

System.out.println("This is a java program");

This is an output statement. Well, there is good reason for this line working like magic and sincerely you don't need to mug it up. In Java we take input and output in forms of *"Streams"*. Imagine it as a flow of data. System.out.println(); directs all the contents within the brackets as *"Output Streams"* to the console. Here System is a predefined class, out an object and println() a method. Once you have studied in detail about classes and objects, you will understand this scary business much better.

// Printing a statement

This is another way of writing comments. The difference being that this is a single line comment.

It has a scope till the end of line. For commenting on the next line, we have to again insert //.

Remember – Writing comments are not binding on the programmer but it is a good practice to insert comments in your code. It makes the code clean, readable and understandable.

Line 7:

}

Closing Braces

These braces tell us that the method has ended. Now all other statements will not be considered as a part of that method.

Line 8:

}

These braces illustrate the ending of class.

5.7.4 Output

Figure 5.12: Output of First.java

5.8 HOW TO CREATE BATCH FILE OF YOUR JAVA PROGRAM

Batch files are not programs. They are lists of command line instructions that are batched together in one file. The following steps are used to create a Batch file.

1. Open Notepad(NOT word or wordpad)
2. Type the following text:

   @echo off

   title Compile

   javac <Program Name>.java

   title Run

   java <Program Name>

   pause
3. Save this as **batchfile.bat**
4. Double-click the batchfile icon

Note: make sure there is no .txt extension after the .bat

For Example

Write the following code and save with batch.java.

```
class batch
{
public static void main(String[] args)
{
System.out.println("Program for Creating a Batch File");
}
}
```

Now write the following code and save with extension .bat as follows.

```
@echo off
title Compile
javac batch.java
title Run
java batch
pause
```

Save as batch.bat

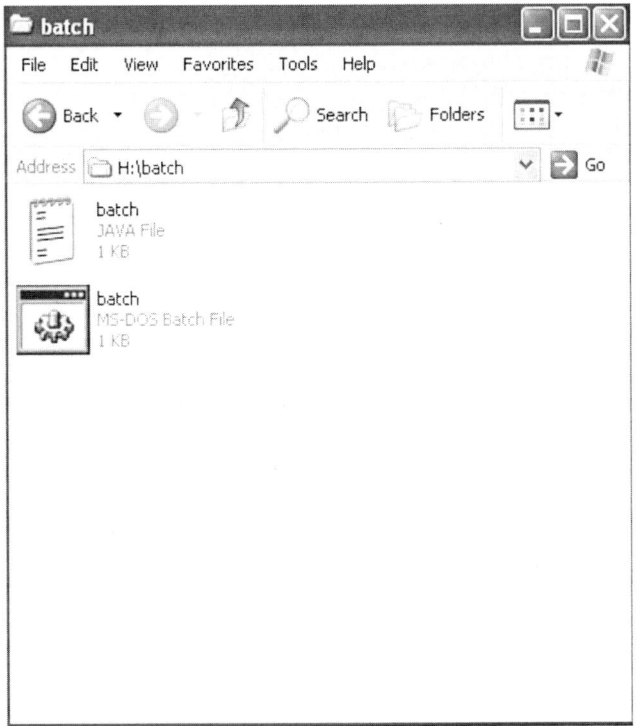

Now double click on batch file icon.

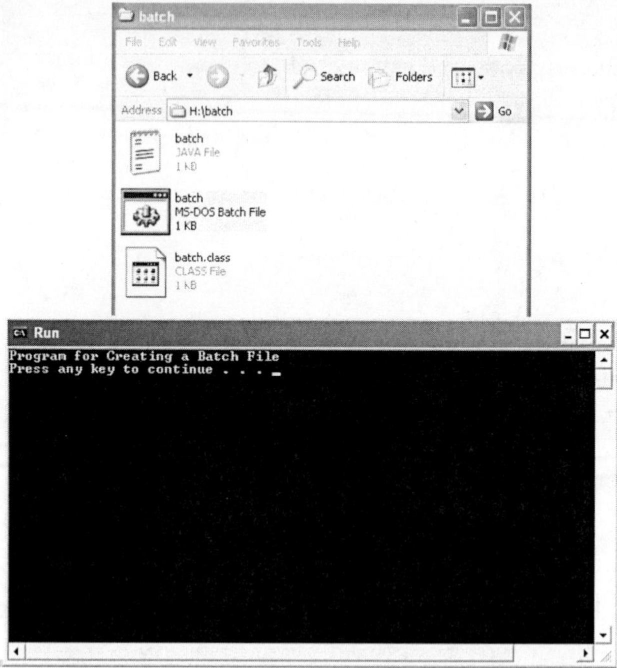

5.9 JAVA TOKEN:

A java program is a collection of tokens, comments and white spaces. In a Java program, all characters are grouped into symbols called tokens. Larger language features are built from the first five categories of tokens (the sixth kind of token is recognized, but is then discarded by the Java compiler from further processing).

- Identifier
- Keyword
- Literal
- Separator
- Operator
- Comments
    - Line
    - Block

5.10 IDENTIFIERS

The Java identifiers are the names given for classes, objects, methods, variables, labels, exceptions, packages and interfaces in a program. Here are the rules for creating a properly formed identifier:

- Java Identifiers are names for classes, methods, or variables.
- Java Identifiers begin with a *letter*, underscore (_), or dollar sign ($).

- Java Identifiers are case sensitive
- Java Identifiers have no maximum length.
- Java Identifiers must not begin with digit.
- Identifiers must be meaningful, short enough to be quickly and easily typed and long enough to be descriptive and easily read.

5.11 Keywords

Keywords are identifiers that Java reserves for its own use. These identifiers have built-in meanings that cannot change. Thus, programmers cannot use these identifiers for anything other than their built-in meanings. Technically, Java classifies identifiers and keywords as separate categories of tokens.

Table 5.1: Keywords

abstract	assert	protected	continue	switch
package	default	strictfp	private	public
case	import	break	throws	throw
goto	double	do	this	static
byte	for	instanceof	interface	new
implements	extends	int	short	try
catch	final	long	return	char
boolean	finally	if	else	volatile
class	float	native	super	while
const	synchronized	void	transient	

The keywords const and goto are reserved, even though they are not currently used. This may allow a Java compiler to produce better error messages if these C++ keywords incorrectly appear in programs.

5.12 Literals

All values that we write in a program are literals: each belongs to one of Java's four primitive types (**int**, **double**, **boolean**, **char**) or belongs to the special reference type **String**. Literal in java are a sequence of characters (digits, letters, and other characters) that represent constant values to be stored in variables. Java language specifies five major types of literals. They are:

Integer Literal
Double Literal (Floating-Point Literal)
Boolean Literal
Character Literal
String Literal
Null Literal

For Example

Table 5.2: Literal

Literal	Type
1	int
3.14	double (1. is a double too)
true	boolean
'3'	char ('P' and '+' are char too)
"Tanweer"	String
null	any reference type

5.13 OPERATORS

An operator is a symbol that takes one or more arguments and operates on them to produce a result. Java includes 37 operators that are listed in the table below.

Table 5.3: Operators

<table>
<tr><td>=</td><td>==</td><td>!=</td><td>!</td><td>&</td><td>&&</td><td>||</td><td>++</td></tr>
<tr><td>--</td><td>></td><td><</td><td><=</td><td>>=</td><td>?</td><td>:</td><td>^</td></tr>
<tr><td>~</td><td>+</td><td>-</td><td>*</td><td>/</td><td>%</td><td>|</td><td>&=</td></tr>
<tr><td><<</td><td>>></td><td>>>></td><td>+=</td><td>-=</td><td>*=</td><td>/=</td><td>%=</td></tr>
<tr><td>^=</td><td>|=</td><td><<=</td><td>>>=</td><td>>>>=</td><td></td><td></td><td></td></tr>
</table>

The keywords **instanceof** and **new** are also considered operators in Java.

5.14 SEPARATORS

This category of token is a **Separator** (also known as a punctuator). There are exactly nine, single character separators in Java Separators are symbols used to indicate where groups of code are divided and arranged. They basically define the shape and function of our code. The following ASCII characters are the separators:

Separator:	*one of*
;	Semicolon
,	Comma
.	Period
( )	Parentheses
{ }	Braces
[ ]	Brackets

For example the Java code **Math.max(count,limit);** contains nine tokens

1. an identifier (**Math**), followed by
2. a separator (a period), followed by
3. another identifier (**max**), followed by
4. a separator (the left parenthesis delimiter), followed by

5. an identfier (**count**), followed by
6. a separator (a comma), followed by
7. another identifier(**limit**), followed by
8. a separator (the right parenthesis delimiter), followed by
9. a separator (a semicolon)

5.15 COMMENTS

There are two kinds of *comments*

1. **A traditional comment:** /* *text* */
   All the text from the ASCII characters.
   /* to the ASCII characters */ is ignored (as in C and C++).

2. **A end-of-line comment:** // *text*
   All the text from the ASCII characters.
   // to the end of the line is ignored (as in C++).

5.16 WHITE SPACE

White space is defined as the ASCII space, horizontal tab, and form feed characters, as well as line terminators

WhiteSpace:
the ASCII SP character, also known as "space"
the ASCII HT character, also known as "horizontal tab"
the ASCII FF character, also known as "form feed"
LineTerminator

5.17 CONSTANTS

- A constant is an identifier that is similar to a variable except that it holds one value for its entire existence
- The compiler will issue an error if you try to change a constant
- In Java, we use the final modifier to declare a constant final int count = 100;

5.18 BACKSLASH CHARACTER CONSTANTS

Constants	Meanings
'\n'	new line
'\b'	back space
'\f'	form feed
'\r'	carriage return
'\t'	horizontal tab
\v	**vertical tab**
'\''	single quote
'\"'	double quote
'\\'	backslash

SUMMARY

Java is a programming language, similar to C or C++, in which you can develop a wide range of programs. Java's strengths lie in its portability-both at the source and at the binary level, in its object-oriented design and in its simplicity. Each of these features helps make applets possible, but they also make Java an excellent language for writing more general-purpose programs that do not require a Java-enabled browser to run. These general-purpose Java programs are called applications.

Java still has a great deal of power and flexibility. Java's initial design goals was to be small and simple, and therefore easier to write, easier to compile, easier to debug, and, best of all, easy to learn. Keeping the language small also makes it more robust because there are fewer chances for programmers to make mistakes that are difficult to fix.

There were five primary goals in the creation of the Java language.

1. It should be "simple, object oriented and familiar".
2. It should be "robust and secure".
3. It should be "architecture neutral and portable".
4. It should execute with "high performance".
5. It should be "interpreted, threaded, and dynamic".

In brief

- In Java all object variables, arguments and return types are references.
- Java does not support complex numbers and since it does not support operator overloading we can't build complex numbers ourselves as is done in C++.
- Java does not support operator overloading.
- Java does not allow default arguments.
- Java does not support templates. In Java all classes inherit from a single class called Object so that it is not difficult to write generalized classes building on the Object class as the base type.
- Java has a streamlined approach to memory allocation.
- Java does not support multiple inheritance. Java does support the interface, which is similar to abstract classes in C++, and does give a form of multiple inheritance.

EXERCISE

1. Discuss the evolution of Java.
2. How is the platform independent feature of Java implemented?
3. Explain Inheritance, Encapsulation and Polymorphism.
4. Write a short note on jdk and its tools.
5. What is an IDE?
6. Can we use Ms Word for writing java programs?
7. Write a program that prints the following two lines------
   "Java is a powerful language"
   "Executing a Java program"
8. What are Java "keywords"? Explain some of them.
9. Why are comments important in our program?

CHAPTER 6

JAVA LANGUAGE BASICS

Variables are locations in memory in which values can be stored. Each one has a name, a type, and a value. Variables can be declared anywhere in the method definition and can be initialized during their declaration. They are commonly declared before usage at the beginning of the definition. Before you can use a variable, you have to declare it. After it is declared, you can then assign values to it. Java provides a rich operator environment. Most of its operators can be divided into the following four groups: arithmetic, bitwise, relational, and logical. Java also defines some additional operators that handle certain special situations.

6.1 VARIABLES

A variable stores a value of a particular type. Each variable has a name, a type, and a value. In Java, variables can only store values of primitive data types and references to objects. A variable is an identifier that denotes a storage location used to store a data value.

6.1.1 Variable Names

A variable name can be chosen by the programmer in a meaningful way. Variable name may consist of alphabets, digits and the underscore (_) and dollar character ($), subject to the following conditions:

(i) They must not begin with a digit. After the first character, your variable names can include any letter or number.

(ii) Variable name can be of any length.

(iii) Uppercase and lowercase are different in Java because Java is case-sensitive. This means that the variable Abc is not equal to abc or ABC.

(iv) White space is not allowed.

(v) It should not be a keyword.

Every variable must have a data type. A variable's data type determines the values that the variable can contain, size it takes in memory and the operations that can be performed on it.

6.1.2 Variable Types

Each variable declaration must have a type, which defines what values that variable can hold. The variable type can be one of three things:

(i) One of the eight basic primitive data types
(ii) The name of a class
(iii) An array

The eight primitive data types handle common types for integers, floating-point numbers, characters or boolean values (true or false). They are called primitive because they're built into the system and are not actual objects, which make them more efficient to use. Note: These data types are machine-independent, which means that you can rely on their sizes and characteristics to be consistent across your Java programs.

6.1.3 Lifetime of Variables

Lifetime of a variable is the time, a variable is accessible during execution, is determined by the context in which it is declared. We distinguish between lifetimes of variables in three contexts:

(i) Instance variables
Members of a class and created for each object of the class. In other words, every object of the class will have its own copies of these variables, which are local to the object. The values of these variables at any given time constitute the state of the object. Instance variables exist as long as the object they belong to exists.

(ii) Static variables
Also members of a class, but not created for any object of the class and, therefore, belong only to the class. They are created when the class is loaded at runtime, and exist as long as the class exists.

(iii) Local variables (also called method automatic variables)
Declared in methods and in blocks and created for each execution of the method or block. After the execution of the method or block completes, local (non-final) variables are no longer accessible.

6.1.4 Scope of Variables

A variable's scope determines when the system creates and destroys memory for the variable. The concept of scope is tightly linked to blocks and is very important when working with variables in Java. Scope refers to blocks affect the lifetime of variables. Every variable declared in a program has an associated scope, meaning that the variable is used only in that particular part of the program.

Scope is distinct from visibility, which applies only to member variables and determines whether the variable can be used from outside of the class within which it is declared. Visibility is set with an access modifier. Class variables are global to a class and belong to the entire set of objects that class creates. Only one memory location is created for each class variable. Local variables can also be declared inside program blocks that are defined between an opening brace {and a closing brace}.These variables are visible to the program only from the beginning of its program block to the end of the program block. When the program control leaves a block, all the variables in the block will cease to exist.

In Java, source code is broken into parts separated by opening and closing curly braces: {and}. Everything between curly braces is considered a block and exists more or less independently of everything outside of the braces. Scope is determined by blocks. To better understand blocks, take a look of the following example of the proper indentation of blocks in Java:

```
for (int i = 0; i < 4; i++)
{
 if (i < 3)
 {
 System.out.println(i);
 }
}
```

6.2 DATA TYPE IN JAVA

Data types define the storage methods available for representing information. Data types are linked tightly to the storage of variables in memory because the data type of a variable determines how the compiler interprets the contents of the memory. To create a variable in memory, you must declare it by providing the type of the variable.

Data types in Java are divided into two categories:

1. Primitive
2. Non-Primitive (Reference type)

The primitive types are boolean, byte, char, short, int, long, float and double. All non-primitive types are reference types, so classes, which specify the types of objects, are reference types. Programs use variables of reference types to store the locations of objects in the computer's memory.

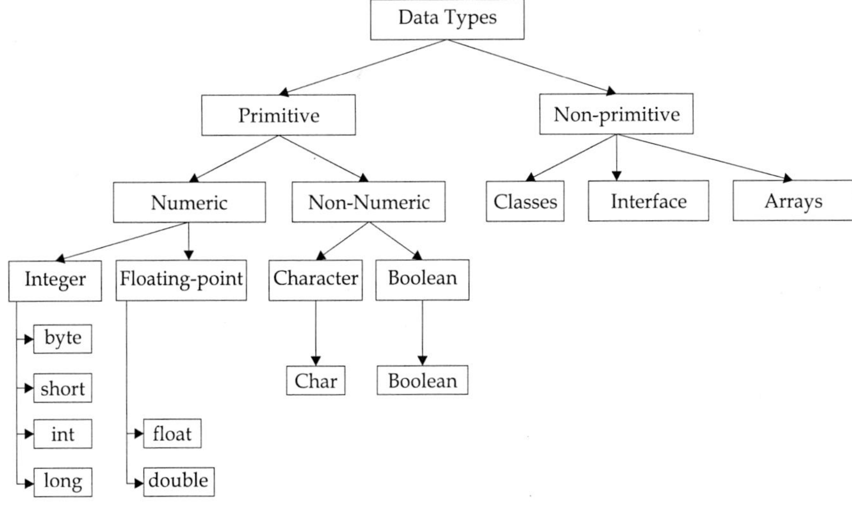

Figure 6.1: Data Types

Primitive Data Types

The following table lists, by keyword, all of the primitive data types supported by Java, their sizes, range and a brief description of each.

Table 6.1: Primitive Data Types

Keyword	Description	Size	Negative Minimal	Positive Minimal
Byte	Byte-length integer	One byte	-128(-2^7)	127(2^7-1)
Short	Short integer	Two bytes	-32768(-2^{15})	32767(2^{15}-1)
Int	Integer	Four bytes	-2147483648(-2^{31})	2147483647(2^{31}-1)
Long	Long integer	Eight bytes	-9223372036854775808 (-2^{63})	9223372036854775807 (2^{63}-1)
Float	Single-precision floating point	Four bytes	1.40239846e-45	3.40282347e38
Double	Double-precision floating point	Eight bytes	4.94065645841246544e-324	1.79769313486231570e308
Char	A single character	Two bytes (Unicode character)	'\u0000'	'\uffff'
Boolean	A Boolean value (true or false)	true or false	False	true

Examples of Literal Values and Their Data Types

Table 6.2: Literal Values and Their Data Types

Literal	Data Type
212	Int
123L	Long
21.75	Double
21.75D	Double
23.543F	Float
23.543e3	Float
' a '	Char
True	Boolean
False	Boolean

6.2.1 Byte

byte is the smallest integer type. This is a signed 8-bit (1-byte) type that has a range from –128 to 127. Byte variables are declared by use of the **byte** keyword.

For example, the following declares two **byte** variables called **x** and **y**:

byte x, y;

6.2.2 Short

short is a signed 2-bytes type. The range of short is starting from –32,768 to 32,767.

Here are some examples of **short** variable declarations:

```
short x;
short y;
```

6.2.3 Int

int is the most commonly used integer type. It is a signed 4-byte(32-bit) type that has a range starting from –2,147,483,648 to 2,147,483,647. int is useful to control loops and to index arrays.

Here are some examples of **int** variable declarations:

```
int x;
int y;
```

6.2.4 Long

long is a signed 8-byte(64-bit) type and is useful for those cases where an **int** type is not large enough to hold the desired value. The range of a **long** is quite large. This makes it useful when big, whole numbers are needed.

Here are some examples of **long** variable declarations:

```
long days;
long seconds;
long distance;
```

6.2.5 Float

float specifies a *single-precision* value that uses 32 bits of storage. Single precision takes half as much space as double precision so that is faster on some processors. Variables of type **float** are useful for fractional component.

Here are some examples of **float** variable declarations:

```
float hightemp, lowtemp;
```

6.2.6 Double

double uses 8-byte(64 bits) to store a value. Double precision is faster than single precision on some processors to optimize for high-speed mathematical calculations. All transcendental math functions, such as **sqrt( ), sin( )** and **cos( )**, return **double** values. When we need to maintain accuracy over many iterative calculations, **double** is the best choice.

```
// Compute the area of a circle.

class Area
{
public static void main(String args[])
{
```

```
double pi, rd, area1;
rd = 6.8;
pi = 3.1416;
area1 = pi * rd * rd;
System.out.println("Area of circle is " + area1);
}
}
```

```
Command Prompt
H:\java>javac Area.java

H:\java>java Area
Area of circle is 145.267584

H:\java>\
```

Figure 6.2: Output of Area

6.2.7 Char

In Java **char** is a 16-bit type. The range of a **char** is 0 to 65,536. There are no negative **char**s.

```
class Char1
{
public static void main(String args[])
{
char char1;
char1 = 'A';
System.out.println("ch1 contains " + char1);
char1++;
System.out.println("ch1 is now " + char1);
}
}
```

The output generated by this program is shown here:

Figure 6.3: Output of Char1

In the above program, char1 is first given the value A. Next, char1 is incremented. This results in char1 containing B, the next character in the ASCII (and Unicode) sequence.

6.2.8 Boolean

boolean is a simple type that is used for logical values. It can be **true** or **false**. This is the type returned by all relational operators, such as **i < j.**

```
// Demonstrate boolean values.
class Boolean1
{
public static void main(String args[])
{
System.out.println("12 > 4 is " + (12 > 4));
}
}
```

The output generated by this program is shown here:

Figure 6.4: Output of Boolean1

6.2.9 Strings

String is an array of char. The Java API considers a String to be an object. Therefore, you benefit from built-in methods and property to help you handle strings.

6.3 OPERATORS

Operators are special symbols that perform specific operations on one, two, or three *operands*, and then return a result.

6.3.1 Arithmetic Operators

The Java programming language provides operators to perform addition, subtraction, multiplication, and division. The only one symbol that might look new to you is "%", which divides one operand by another operand and returns the remainder as its result.

Table 6.3: Arithmetic Operators

Operator	Name	Use	Description
+	Addition	Operand1 + Operand 2	Adds Operand 1 and Operand 2
-	Subtraction	Operand 1 - Operand 2	Subtracts Operand 2 from Operand 1
*	multiplication	Operand 1 * Operand 2	Multiplies Operand 1 by Operand 2
/	Division	Operand 1 / Operand 2	Divides Operand 1 by Operand 2
%	modulus (mod)	Operand 1 % Operand 2	Computes the remainder of dividing Operand 1 by Operand 2

The arithmetic operators return a number.

return value = <operand1> <operator> <operand2>;

Example:
total = num1 + num2;

(i) Addition(+)
- adds two numbers
- concatenates two string objects

(ii) subtraction (-)
- subtract one number from another

(iii) multiplication (*)
- multiply two numbers

(iv) division (/)
- divide two numbers

(v) modulus (%)
- the remainder of an integer division
- 5 % 3 = 2 Because 5/3 = 1 and leaves 2.
- myRemainder = 5 % 3;

```
// Use of Arithmetic Operators

class Arithmetic1 {
 public static void main (String[] args){
 int result = 3 + 2; // result is now 5
 System.out.println(result);
 result = result - 1; // result is now 4
 System.out.println(result);
 result = result * 2; // result is now 8
 System.out.println(result);
 result = result / 2; // result is now 4
 System.out.println(result);
 result = result + 8; // result is now 12
```

```
result = result % 7; // result is now 5
System.out.println(result);
}
}
```

The output is:

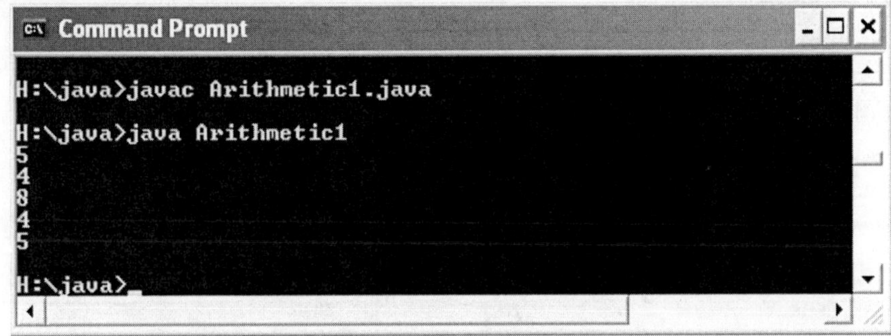

Figure 6.5: Output of Arithmetic1

6.3.2 Assignment Operator

One of the most common operators that you will encounter is the simple assignment operator "=". You use the assignment operator '=' to assign one value to another. The following list represents the Compound Assignment Operators.

Table 6.4: Assignment Operators

Operator	Use	Equivalent to
+=	Operand1 += Operand 2	Operand 1 = Operand 1 + Operand 2
-=	Operand 1 -= Operand 2	Operand 1 = Operand 1 - Operand 2
*=	Operand 1 *= Operand 2	Operand 1 = Operand 1 * Operand 2
/=	Operand 1 /= Operand 2	Operand 1 = Operand 1 / Operand 2
%=	Operand 1 %= Operand 2	Operand 1 = Operand 1 % Operand 2
&=	Operand 1 &= Operand 2	Operand 1 = Operand 1 & Operand 2
|=	Operand 1 |= Operand 2	Operand 1 = Operand 1 | Operand 2
^=	Operand 1 ^= Operand 2	Operand 1 = Operand 1 ^ Operand 2
<<=	Operand 1 <<= Operand 2	Operand 1 = Operand 1 << Operand 2
>>=	Operand 1 >>= Operand 2	Operand 1 = Operand 1 >> Operand 2
>>>=	Operand 1 >>>= Operand 2	Operand 1 = Operand 1 >>> Operand 2

6.3.3 Conditional Operator

The conditional operator is ?:, which is a shorthand for an if-then-else statement. ?: operator is also known as the ternary operator because it uses three operands.

Table 6.5: Conditional Operators

Operator	Use	Description
?:	Exp1 ? exp2 : exp3	If Exp1 is true, returns exp2. Otherwise, returns exp3.

```
// Conditional operator implementation

class Conditional
{
public static void main(String[] args)
{
 int value1 = 10;
 int value2 = 20;
 int result;
 boolean Condition = true;
 result = Condition ? value1 : value2;
 System.out.println(result);
 }
}
```

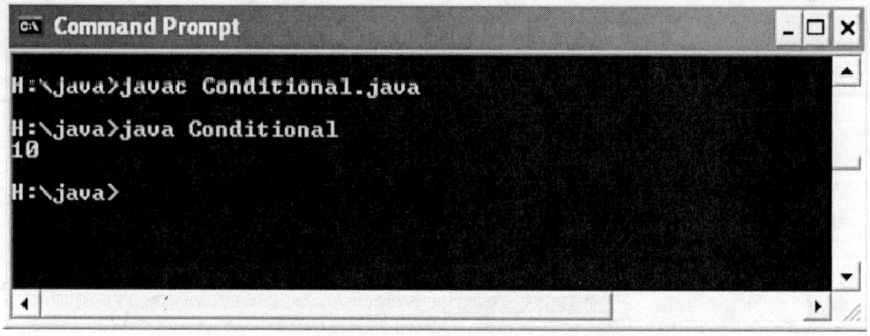

```
Command Prompt
H:\java>javac Conditional.java

H:\java>java Conditional
10

H:\java>
```

Figure 6.6: Output of Conditional

6.3.4 Relational Operators

Relational operators determine if one operand is greater than, less than, equal to, or not equal to another operand. Keep in mind, you must be use "==", not "=", when testing if two primitive values are equal. Logical operators *check* a condition by comparing values and return a boolean value (true or false).

Table 6.6: Relational Operators

==	equal to
!=	not equal to
>	greater than
>=	greater than or equal to
<	less than
<=	less than or equal to

```
// Comparison of two values

class Comparison
{
```

```
public static void main(String[] args)
{
 int value1 = 10;
 int value2 = 20;
 if(value1 == value2) System.out.println("value1 == value2");
 if(value1 != value2) System.out.println("value1 != value2");
 if(value1 > value2) System.out.println("value1 > value2");
 if(value1 < value2) System.out.println("value1 < value2");
 if(value1 <= value2) System.out.println("value1 <= value2");
 }
}
```

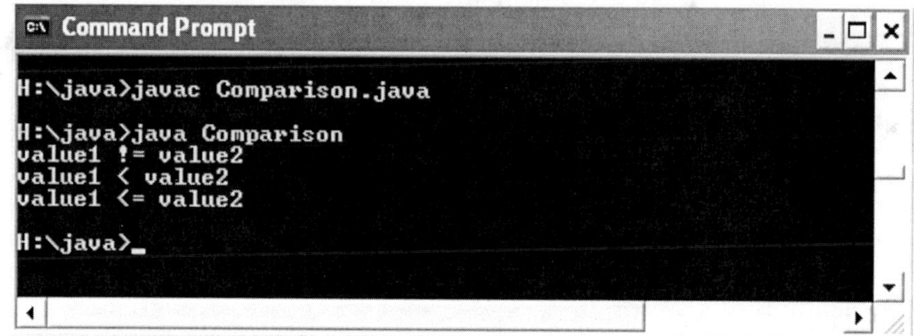

Figure 6.7: Output of Comparison

6.3.6 Boolean Logical Operators

Table 6.7: Boolean Logical Operators

<table>
<tr><th>Operator</th><th>Meaning</th></tr>
<tr><td>&</td><td>ampersand is the logical and operator</td></tr>
<tr><td>&&</td><td>double ampersand is the logical and operator that can "short circuit" when appropriate</td></tr>
<tr><td>|</td><td>the logical or operator is the "pipe" key</td></tr>
<tr><td>||</td><td>double "pipe" is the logical or operator that can "short circuit" when appropriate</td></tr>
</table>

Truth table

Table 6.8: Truth table of Boolean Logical Operators

<table>
<tr><th>Operand1</th><th>Operand2</th><th>==</th><th>!=</th><th>&&</th><th>||</th></tr>
<tr><td>true</td><td>true</td><td>True</td><td>false</td><td>true</td><td>true</td></tr>
<tr><td>true</td><td>false</td><td>False</td><td>true</td><td>false</td><td>true</td></tr>
<tr><td>False</td><td>true</td><td>False</td><td>true</td><td>false</td><td>true</td></tr>
<tr><td>False</td><td>false</td><td>True</td><td>false</td><td>false</td><td>false</td></tr>
</table>

6.3.7 Incrementing and Decrementing

The increment/decrement operators require only one operand; they perform various operations such as incrementing/decrementing a value by one. The increment/decrement operators can be applied before (prefix) or after (postfix) the operand.

Table 6.9: Increment/Decrement Operators

Operator	Meaning
++	Increment operator; increments a value by 1
--	Decrement operator; decrements a value by 1

Examples:

i++ Increments i by 1; evaluates to the value of i before it was incremented
++i Increments i by 1; evaluates to the value of i after it was incremented
i-- Decrements i by 1; evaluates to the value of i before it was decremented
--i Decrements i by 1; evaluates to the value of i after it was decremented

```
//implements increment decrement operators

class incr
{
public static void main(String[] args)
{
 int result = +10;
 System.out.println(result);
 result--;
 System.out.println(result);
 result++;
 System.out.println(result);
 --result;
 System.out.println(result);
 ++result;
 System.out.println(result);
 result = -result;
 System.out.println(result);
 boolean success = false;
 System.out.println(success);
 System.out.println(!success);
 }
}
```

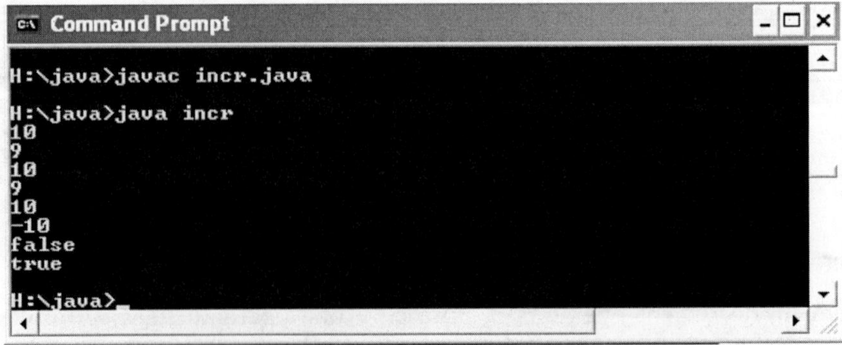

Figure 6.8: Output of incr

6.3.8 Bitwise Operators

Java provides operators that perform bitwise and bit shift operations. Bitwise operators are used for testing the bits, or shifting them to right or left. Bitwise operators may not be applied to float or double.

The bitwise & operator performs a bitwise AND operation.
The bitwise | operator performs a bitwise inclusive OR operation.
The bitwise ^ operator performs a bitwise exclusive OR operation.

Table 6.10: Bitwise Operators

Operator	Meaning
&	bitwise AND
!	bitwise OR
^	bitwise exclusive OR
~	one's complement
<<	shift left
>>	shift right
>>>	shift right with zero fill

```
//Program
class operator1
{
   public static void main(String[] ar)
   {
      int i=17;
      int j=5;
      int k1=i & j;
      int k2=i | j;
      int k3=i ^ j;
      boolean k=i>j;
      boolean k4=!k;
      System.out.println(k1);
      System.out.println(k2);
      System.out.println(k3);
      System.out.println(k4);
   }
}
```

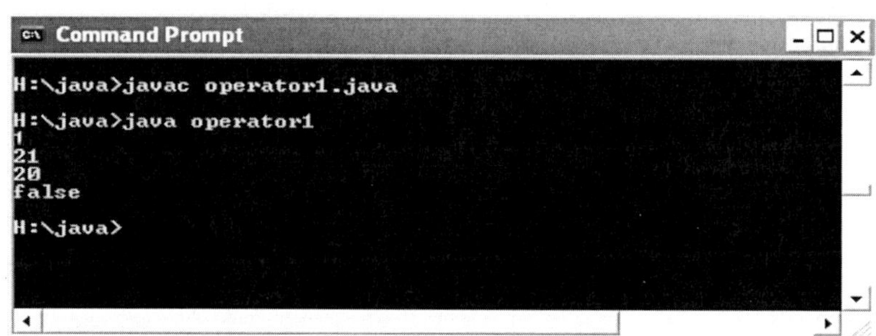

Figure 6.9: Output of operator1

6.3.9 Operator Precedence

The higher precedence Operators are evaluated before operators with relatively lower precedence. Operators, which on the same line have equal precedence. When operators of equal precedence appear in the same line, a rule must govern which is evaluated first. All binary operators except assignment operators are evaluated from left to right; assignment operators are evaluated right to left. The operators in the following table are listed according to precedence order.

Table 6.11 : Operators Precedence

<table>
<tr><td>Operators Precedence</td><td>Operator type</td></tr>
<tr><td>++expr --expr +expr -expr ~ !</td><td>Unary</td></tr>
<tr><td>* / %+ -</td><td>Arithmetic</td></tr>
<tr><td><< >> >>></td><td>Shift</td></tr>
<tr><td>> < >= <= instanceof</td><td>Relational</td></tr>
<tr><td>== !=</td><td>Equally</td></tr>
<tr><td>& | ^&& | |</td><td>Logical (and bitwise)</td></tr>
<tr><td>x > y ? a : b</td><td>Conditional (ternary)</td></tr>
<tr><td>= += -= *= /= %= &= ^= |= <<= >>= >>>=</td><td>Assignment</td></tr>
</table>

SUMMARY

Java supports four primitive data types: integer, floating point, Boolean and character. The integer has four types: byte, short, int and long. These types correspond to 1-byte, 2-byte, 4-byte, and 8-byte integer values respectively. The floating point has two types:float and double. These types correspond to 4-byte and 8-byte respectively. The boolean type consists of the literal values true and false.The character type uses the standard Unicode character set and is a 2-byte unsigned integer. Variables of the char type store single characters. The java.lang.String class is used to store strings of characters.

EXERCISE

1. What is Data Type in java? Define all with Examples.
2. Write a program in java to implement matrix multiplication.
3. Explain kinds of variables in Java?
4. What is thse Life cycle of a variable in Java?
5. Define Bitwise Operators in Java.
6. Write the minimum to maximum ranges of Integer Data Types.

*****

CHAPTER 7

OBJECT ORIENTATION

Java is an object-oriented language. Object-oriented programming requires a language that supports classes and objects. Both Java and C++ can be used for object-oriented programming. This chapter explains the means of "object-oriented" for Java. It covers the following object oriented concepts:

- Classes and objects in Java
- Creating object of class
- To create a subclass with extending base class
- Interface types and their implementation by classes
- Abstract classes
- Overriding class methods
- Garbage collection

A class is a way to encapsulate both data and the methods that operate on that data. We also learned about inheritance, which enables a class (subclass) to inherit the capabilities of a base class (superclass). Polymorphism enables us to create virtual methods that can be implemented differently in derived classes. A method is the object-oriented term for a procedure or a function. In Java all classes must be derived from some class. The top most class, the class from which all other classes are derived, is the Object class defined in java.lang.

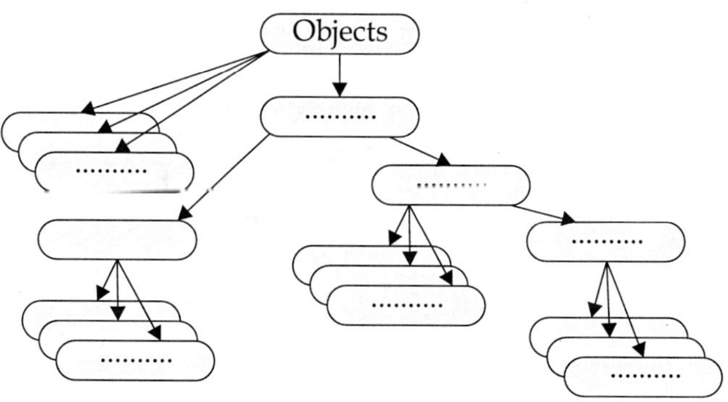

Figure 7.1: Object

7.1 CLASSES

A class is a collection of data and methods that operate on that data. The data and methods usually serve to define the contents and capabilities of some kind of object. A class is a blueprint that we can use to create many objects. An object that belongs to a class is said to be an instance of that class. A sample of a class is given below:

```
class college
{
 int faculty_id;
 void facultyData()
{
faculty_id=20;
System.out.println(faculty_id);
}
}
```

7.1.1 The Class Declaration

Defining classes is very easy. To define a class, use the class keyword and the name of the class that you are defining:

```
class <class name>
{
//variables declaration
//methods declaration
}
```

A class can contain any of the following variable types.

Local variables: These variables are defined inside the methods, constructors or blocks. The variable will be declared and initialized within the method body and the variable will be destroyed when the method has completed.

Instance variables: These variables are within a class but outside any method. These variables are instantiated when the class is loaded. Instance variables can be accessed from inside any method, constructor or blocks of that particular class.

Class variables: Class variables are variables declared with in a class, outside any method, with the static keyword.

A class can have any number of methods to access the value of various kinds of methods. See the following example.

//program to display the volume of a box.

```
class Box
{
int w=5;
int h=10;
```

```
int d=15;
int volume;
void display()
{
volume = w * h * d;
System.out.println("Volume is " + volume);
}
}
class BoxImp1
{
public static void main(String args[])
{
Box b = new Box();
b.display();
}
}
```

```
H:\java>javac BoxImp.java

H:\java>java BoxImp
Volume is 750

H:\java>_
```

```
class A
{
   public static void main(String[] ar)
   {
      B1 b1=new B1();
      b1.f1();
   }
}
class B1
{
   void f1()
   {
      System.out.println("F1");
   }
   static void f2()
   {
      System.out.println("F2");
   }
}
```

```
Command Prompt

H:\java>javac A.java

H:\java>java A
F1

H:\java>
```

//Or the following program, the result is same as above program

```
class Box
{
int w;
int h;
int d;
}
class BoxImp
{
public static void main(String args[])
{
Box b = new Box();
int volume;
b.w = 5;
b.h = 10;
b.d = 15;
volume = b.w * b.h * b.d;
System.out.println("Volume is " + volume);
}
}
```

7.1.2 Declaring a Class's Superclass

In Java language every subclass has a superclass. If we have not specified a superclass for our class then assumed to be the Object class. A subclass inherits variables and methods from its superclass. The syntax is as follows.

```
class <class name> extends <Super Class Name>
{
  //statements
}
```

7.1.3 Interfaces Implemented by a Class

An interface declares a set of methods and constants without body of the methods. When a class is to implement an interface then it is necessary to provide implementations for all of the methods that are declared in the interface.

```
class A extends B implements C
{
//statements
}
```

7.1.4 Class Declaration Summary

```
[Access modifiers] class <Class Name> [extends <SuperClassName>] [implements
        <InterfaceNames>]
{
//statements
}
```

Access modifiers is optional it may be public, abstract or final. Bydefault it is private.

The <Class Name> is the user defined name of class.
<SuperClassName> is the name of superclass
<InterfaceNames> is the name of interface that is implemented.

7.2 OBJECTS

An object is an instance of the class. Instances and objects are the same thing. An instance is the specific concrete representation of a class. Object is the more general term, but both instances and objects are the concrete representation of a class. When we write a Java program then we design and construct a set of classes. When our program runs the instances of these classes are created or discarded as needed.

7.2.1 Declaring Objects

For declaring the objects of a class is a two-step process.

(9) First, we must declare a variable of the class type. This variable is simply a variable that can refer to an object.

For example:

```
BoxImp b; // declare reference to object
```

After the above line executes, b contains the value null, which indicates that it does not yet point to an actual object.

(ii) Second, we must acquire an actual, physical copy of the object and assign it to that variable using the new operator. The new operator dynamically allocates memory for an object and returns a reference to it.

For example:

```
BoxImp b=new BoxImp(); // allocate a Box object
```

The line allocates an actual object and assigns a reference to it to b.

7.3 CONTROLLING ACCESS TO MEMBERS OF A CLASS

Access Specifier	class	subclass	package	Outside world
public	√	√	√	√
private	√	X	X	X
protected	√	√	√	X
package	√	X	√	X

7.3.1 Public

Any class, in any package, has access to a class's public members.

```
package p1;
public class A
{
public int numA;
public void display()
{
System.out.println("This is the public Method of Class A");
}
}
```

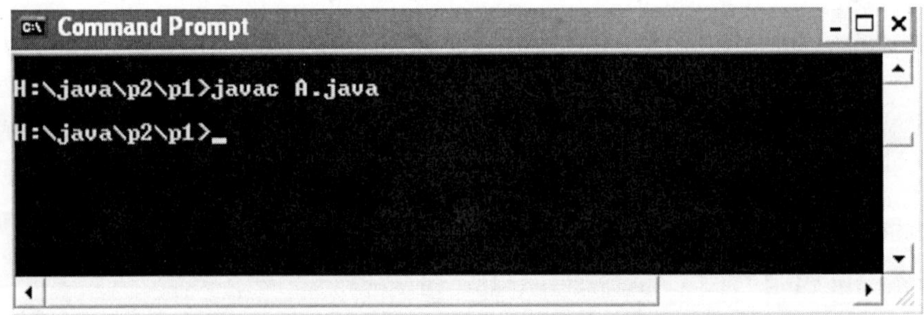


```
import p1.*;
package p2;
public class B
{
 void show()
 {
 A Obj = new A();
```

```
Obj.numA = 10; // legal
Obj.display(); // legal
}
}
```

Command Prompt

```
H:\java\p2\p1>cd..

H:\java\p2>javac B.java

H:\java\p2>_
```

```
import p2.*;
import p2.p1.*;
class program
{
public static void main(String args[])
{
B ObjB = new B();
ObjB.show(); // Illegal because show(0 is not public

}
}
```

Command Prompt

```
H:\java>javac program.java
program.java:8: cannot find symbol
symbol  : method show()
location: class B
        ObjB.show();    // Illegal because show() is not publ
            ^
1 error

H:\java>_
```

```
import p1.*;
class program1
{
public static void main(String args[])
{
A ObjA = new A();
ObjA.display(); // legal

}
}
```

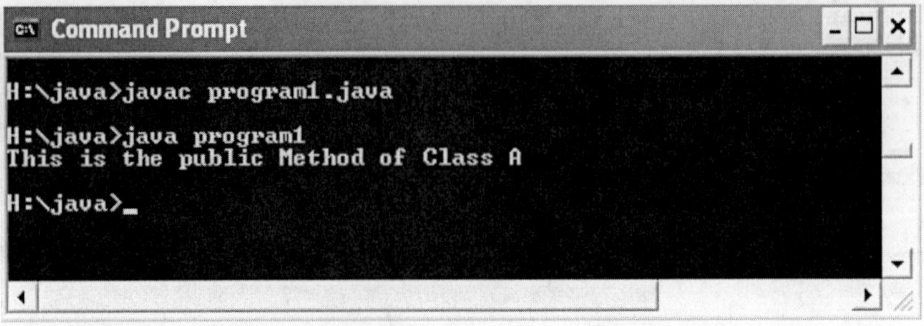

```
Command Prompt
H:\java>javac program1.java

H:\java>java program1
This is the public Method of Class A

H:\java>_
```

7.3.2 Private

Private is the most restrictive access level. A private member is accessible only to the class in which it is defined. For example

```
class A
{
 private int x;
 private void Method1()
{
 System.out.println("this is the private Method");
 }
}
class prog1
{
 public static void main(String args[])
 {
 A objA = new A();
 objA.x = 15; // illegal
 objA.Method1(); // illegal
 }
}
```

```
Command Prompt
H:\java>javac prog1.java
prog1.java:14: x has private access in A
        objA.x = 15;     // illegal
            ^
prog1.java:15: Method1() has private access in A
        objA.Method1();       // illegal
            ^
2 errors

H:\java>
```

7.3.3 Protected

Protected is allowed the class itself, subclasses, and all classes in the same package to access the members.

```
class A
{
 protected int x;
 protected void Method1()
 {
 System.out.println("this is the protected Method");
 }
}
class prog2 extends A
{
 public static void main(String args[])
 {
 A objA = new A();
 objA.x = 15; // illegal
 objA.Method1(); // illegal
 }
}
```

```
Command Prompt
O:\java>javac prog2.java

O:\java>java prog2
this is the protected Method

O:\java>
```

7.4 CREATING METHODS

Method is a block of code written to perform a specific task which may or may not return a value. The general form of a method is as follows:

```
<Type> <method name> (parameter-list)
{
// body of method
}
```

For example:

```
int sum(int x, int y)
{
return x+y;
}
```

Method definitions have four basic parts:

(i) The type of method returns

(ii) The name of method

(iii) A list of parameters

(iv) The body of the method

For example:

```
class Box
{
double w;
double h;
double d;
void volume()
{
System.out.println("Volume is"+(w * h * d));
}
}
class BoxImp2
{
public static void main(String args[])
{
Box b1 = new Box();
Box b2 = new Box();
b1.w = 8;
b1.h = 12;
b1.d = 6;
b1.volume();
b2.w = 12;
b2.h = 18;
b2.d = 9;
b2.volume();
}
}
```

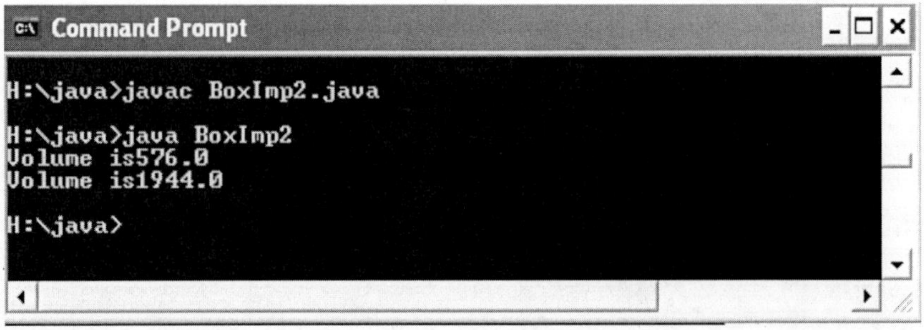

```
Command Prompt
H:\java>javac BoxImp2.java

H:\java>java BoxImp2
Volume is576.0
Volume is1944.0

H:\java>
```

7.5 CONSTRUCTORS

A constructor is a method that can be accessed anywhere in a program with the same name as the class name and it enables an object to initialize itself when it's created. A constructor initializes an object immediately upon creation. Constructor is the class type itself. It allows us to initialize variables and perform any other operations when an object is created from the class. Constructors have no return type, not even void. This is because the implicit return type of a class. Once defined, the constructor is automatically called immediately after the object is created. There are two types of constructor.

(i) Default constructor

If we don't define a constructor for a class then a default parameter less constructor is automatically created by the compiler. Default constructor is created only if there are no constructors. A default constructor with no arguments will be called automatically by the Java Virtual Machine (JVM).

(ii) Parameterized constructor

Constructors are used to assign initial values to instance variables of the class. If the method defines parameters inside the method in parenthesis, it is called parameterized constructor.

Example:

```
class Box
{
int w;
int h;
int d;
Box(int a, int b, int c)
{
w = a;
h = b;
d = c;
}
int volume()
{
return w * h * d;
}
}
class BoxImp3
{
public static void main(String args[])
{
Box b1 = new Box(5, 10, 12);
```

```
Box b2 = new Box(6, 12, 7);
int vol;
vol = b1.volume();
System.out.println("Volume is " + vol);
vol = b2.volume();
System.out.println("Volume is " + vol);
}
}
```

The output is shown below:

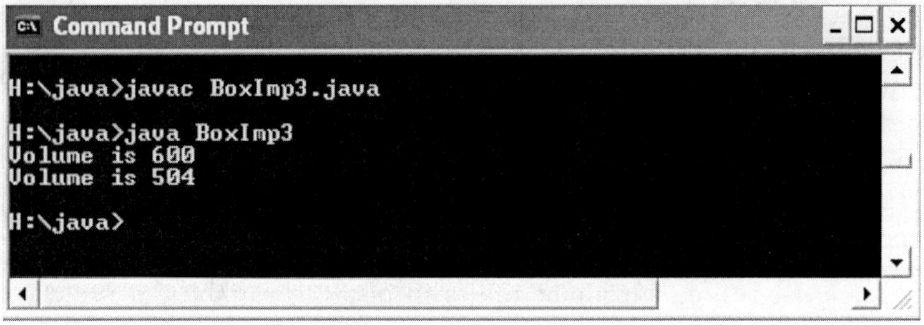

```
Command Prompt
H:\java>javac BoxImp3.java

H:\java>java BoxImp3
Volume is 600
Volume is 504

H:\java>
```

// another Example

```
class constructor1
{
int x,y;
constructor1(int a, int b)
{
x = a;
y = b;
}
constructor1()
{
x = 10;
y = 20;
}
int area()
{
int a1 = x*y;
return(a1);
}
}
public class con1
{
public static void main(String[] args)
{
```

```
constructor1 c1 = new constructor1();
System.out.println("Area of rectangle is= " + c1.area());
constructor1 c2 = new constructor1(12,15);
System.out.println("Area of rectangle is= " + c2.area());
}
}
```

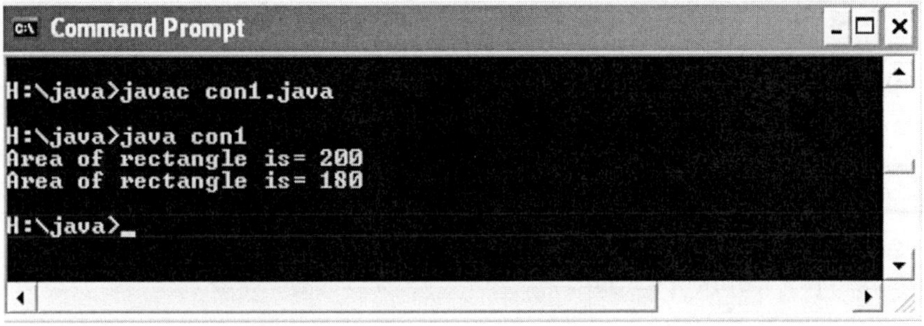

```
Command Prompt
H:\java>javac con1.java

H:\java>java con1
Area of rectangle is= 200
Area of rectangle is= 180

H:\java>_
```

Constructor Overloading

The JVM differentiates constructors on the basis of arguments passed in the constructor. So constructor provides the overloading they should have different arguments. Whenever we assign the name of the method same as class name. This method should not have any return type. This is called as constructor overloading.

For Example:

```
class Test
{
 int x,y;
 int i,k;

 Test(int x, int y)
 {
 this.x = x;
 this.y = y;
 }

 Test(int x, int y, int i, int k)
 {
 this(x,y);// Must be in first line
 this.i = i;
 this.k = k;
 }
public int display1()
{
return x*y;
```

```
}
public int display2()
{
return i*k;
}
}
class con3
{
public static void main(String args[])
{
Test t1=new Test(10,20);
System.out.println(t1.display1());
Test t2=new Test(5,10,15,20);
System.out.println(t2.display2());

}
}
```

// another example

```
class Rectangle
{
int l, b;
float p, q;
public Rectangle(int x, int y)
{
l = x;
b = y;
}
public int one()
{
return(l * b);
}
public Rectangle(int x)
{
```

```
l = x;
b = x;
}
public int two()
{
return(l * b);
}
public Rectangle(float x)
{
p = x;
q = x;
}
public float three()
{
return(p * q);
}
public Rectangle(float x, float y)
{
p = x;
q = y;
}
public float four()
{
return(p * q);
}
}
public class con2
{
public static void main(String args[])
{
Rectangle r1 = new Rectangle(12,13);
int a1= r1.one();
System.out.println(" The area of a rectangle in first constructor is : " + a1);
Rectangle r2 = new Rectangle(10);
int a2= r2.two();
System.out.println(" The area of a rectangle in first constructor is : " + a2);
Rectangle r3 = new Rectangle(20.0f);
float a3= r3.three();
System.out.println(" The area of a rectangle in first constructor is : " + a3);
Rectangle r4 = new Rectangle(13.0f,12.0f);
float a4= r4.four();
System.out.println(" The area of a rectangle in first constructor is : " + a4);
}
}
```

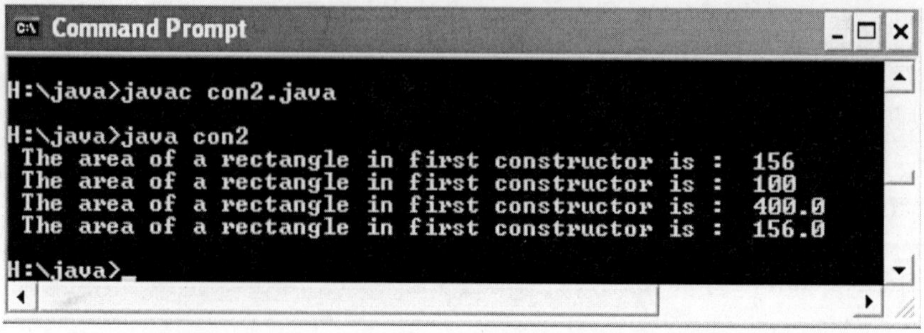

```
Command Prompt

H:\java>javac con2.java

H:\java>java con2
 The area of a rectangle in first constructor is :  156
 The area of a rectangle in first constructor is :  100
 The area of a rectangle in first constructor is :  400.0
 The area of a rectangle in first constructor is :  156.0

H:\java>_
```

7.6 DIFFERENCES BETWEEN METHODS AND CONSTRUCTORS

(i) No return type given in a constructor signature.

(ii) No return statement in the body of the constructor.

(iii) The first line of a constructor must either be a call on another constructor in the same class (using this keyword), or a call on the superclass constructor (using super keyword). If the first line is neither of these then the compiler automatically inserts a call to the parameterless super class constructor.

SUMMARY

A class is a collection of data and methods that operate on that data. The data and methods usually serve to define the contents and capabilities of some kind of object. A class is a blueprint that we can use to create many objects. A class is a way to encapsulate both data and the methods that operate on that data. Polymorphism enables us to create virtual methods that can be implemented differently in derived classes. A method is the object-oriented term for a procedure or a function. In Java all classes must be derived from some class. The top most class, the class from which all other classes are derived, is the Object class defined in java.lang. An object is an instance of the class. Instances and objects are the same thing. An instance is the specific concrete representation of a class.

EXERCISE

1. What is the difference between superclass & subclass?
2. What are constructors?
3. Explain class and Object.
4. What is Constructor Overloading?
5. What are the differences between methods and constructors?

*****

CHAPTER 8

APPLET PROGRAMMING

This chapter introduces the classes of the java.applet package and explains how applets are integrated within Web documents. When you use a Java technology-enabled browser to view a page that contains an applet, the applet's code is transferred to your system and executed by the browser's Java Virtual Machine (JVM). An applet is a Java program that can operate only within a compatible Web browser, such as Netscape Navigator or Microsoft Internet Explorer. Java applets can run in a Web browser using a Java Virtual Machine (JVM), using a java interpreter or in Sun's AppletViewer included in the java development kit, a stand-alone tool for testing applets. In order to run an applet it must be included in a web page, using HTML tags. When a user browses a web page containing an applet, the browser downloads the applet from the web server and runs it on the user's system.

8.1 INTRODUCTION

Java applets were introduced in the first version of the Java language in 1995. The applet programs are also written in Java. The first browser that could show applets was introduced in 1994, as "WebRunner" - later known as "The HotJava Browser". Java applications are stand-alone Java programs that can be run by using just the Java interpreter, for example, from a command line. Applets are not executed by the console-based Java run-time interpreter. Rather, they are executed by either a Web browser or an applet viewer. Java applets, however, are run from inside a World Wide Web browser. A reference to an applet is embedded in a Web page using a special HTML tag. All applets are subclasses of Applet. Thus, all applets must import java.applet. Applets do not have main() method. All applets must be declared public.

8.2 TYPES OF AN APPLET

An applet is a special kind of Java program which is used for internet programming. Basically applet has two types:

(i) Local Applet

(ii) Remote Applet

8.2.1 LOCAL APPLETS

A Local applet is the one which is stored on our local computer system. When browser try to access the applet, it is not necessary for our computer to be connected to The Internet.

When our Web page finds a local applet, it doesn't need to retrieve information from the Internet; in fact, your web browser doesn't even need to be connected to the Internet at that time.

Figure 8.1: Local Applet

As you can see in the following example, a local applet is specified by a path name and a file name.

Syntax to specifying a Local Applet

```
<APPLET CODEBASE="localApplet "
 CODE="localApplet.class"
 WIDTH=300
 HEIGHT=400>
</APPLET>
```

Where codebase specifies a path name on your system for the local applet and code specifies the name of the byte-code file (.class) that contains the applet's code. The path specified in codebase is relative to the folder containing the HTML document to references the applet.

8.2.2 Remote Applets

A Remote applet is the one which is not stored on our computer system but located on another computer system. We are required to be connected to the Internet. This computer system may be located in the internet. No matter, where the remote applet is located, it's downloaded onto our computer via the Internet. Our browser must be connected to the Internet at the time it needs to display the remote applet. To display the remote applet in your Web browser, you must know the URL of Applet (location of applet on Web) and the parameters and attributes are needed to supply in order to display the applet correctly. If you are not the author of applet then you will need to find the document that describes the applet's parameters and attributes. This document is usually written by the author of applet. The following example shows how to compose an HTML <applet> tag for accessing the remote applet.

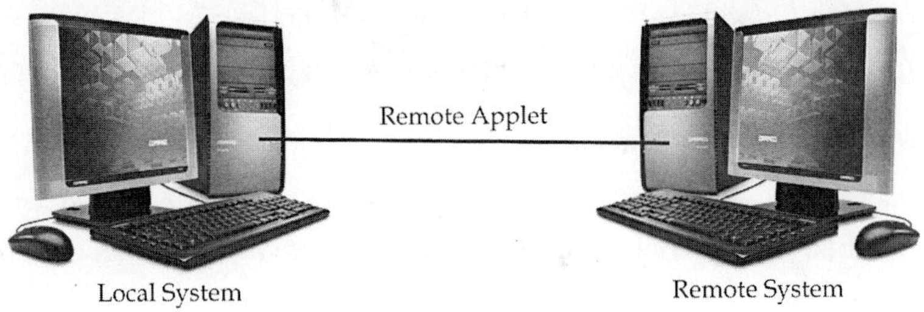

Figure 8.2: Remote Applet

Syntax to specifying a Remote Applet.

```
<APPLET CODEBASE=" http://www.myapplet.com/remoteapplets/"
 CODE="remoteApplet.class"
 WIDTH=300
 HEIGHT=400>
</APPLET>
```

The only difference between local applet and remote applet is the value of the codebase attribute. In the local applet, codebase specifies a local folder and in the remote applet, it specifies the URL, where the applet is located.

8.3 ADVANTAGES OF JAVA APPLET

(i) Applets run in a sandbox, so that user does not need to trust the code, so it can work without security approval.

(ii) Applets are platform independent and can run on Windows, Macintosh OS and Linux platform.

(iii) Applets are supported by most web browsers.

(iv) Applets running within a Web browser can easily cause HTML documents to be displayed

(v) Applets can invoke public methods of other applets on the same page.

(vi) Applets can make network connections to the host they came from

(vii) Applets can work on all the versions of Java Plug-Ins.

(viii) Applets are cached in most web browsers, so will be quick to load when returning to a web page

8.4 DISADVANTAGES OF JAVA APPLET

(i) Java plug-in is required to run any applet.

(ii) Applets can't make network connections except to the host that it came from.

(iii) Designing and build good user interfaces are difficult in applets compared to HTML.

(iv) Applet can't start any program on the host that's executing it.

(v) If applet is not already cached in the machine, it will be downloaded from internet and will take time

(vi) An applet can't load libraries or define native methods.

(vii) Applet can't read or write files on the host that's executing it.

8.5 HOW TO RUN APPLET PROGRAM

To run the applet program, we need to load the HTML file into an application that is used to run Java applet program. This application might be a java compatible web browser or appletviewer which is provided in the JDK.

Building Applet Code: An Example

```
//HelloApplet.java
import java.awt.* ;
import java.applet.*;
public class HelloApplet extends Applet
{
public void paint(Graphics g)
{
g.drawString ("My First Applet",50, 50);
}
}
```

Command Prompt

```
H:\java>javac HelloApplet.java

H:\java>
```

Embedding Applet in Web Page

```
// HelloApplet.html

<HTML>
<HEAD>
<TITLE>
Hello Applet
</TITLE>
</HEAD>
<BODY>
<H1>Hi, This is My First Applet Program on the Web! </H1>
<APPLET CODE= "HelloApplet.class" width= 400 height=400>
</APPLET>
</BODY>
</HTML>
```

Accessing Web page (runs Applet)

Start internet explorer.

Click file -> open -> Browse… -> select the file -> open

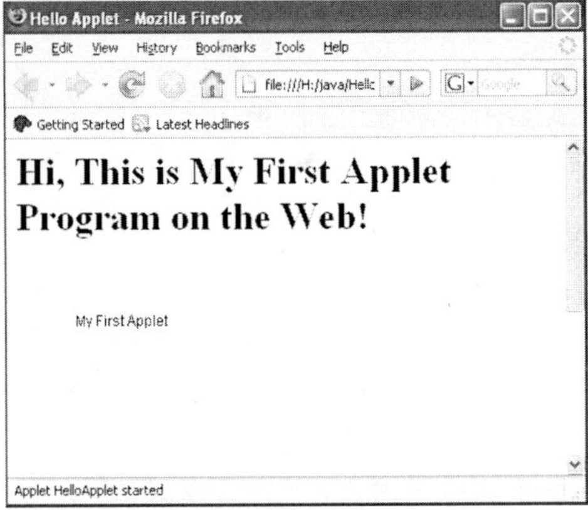

Embedding Applet in AppletViewer

Write the following command to the command prompt

>appletviewer HelloApplet.html

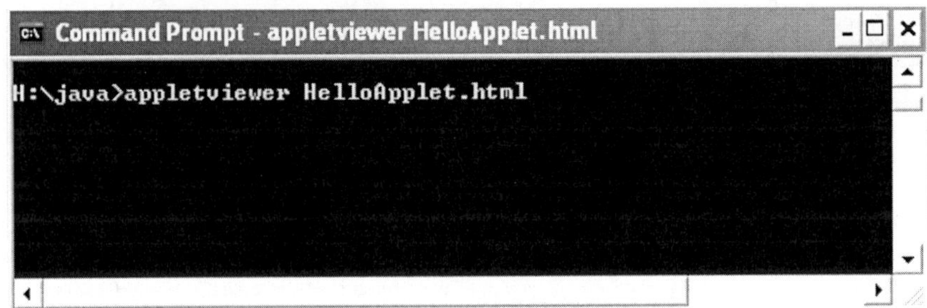

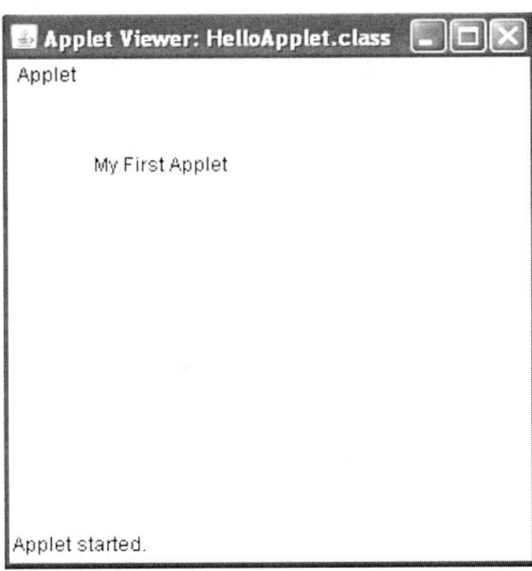

Or write the following code with the main program using comment line as follows.

```
/* <APPLET CODE= "HelloApplet.class" width= 400 height=400>
</APPLET>*/
import java.awt.* ;
import java.applet.*;
public class HelloApplet1 extends Applet
{
public void paint(Graphics g)
{
g.drawString ("My First Applet",50, 50);
}
}
```

Save the above program with HelloApplet1.java

Now compile and execute the program as follows.

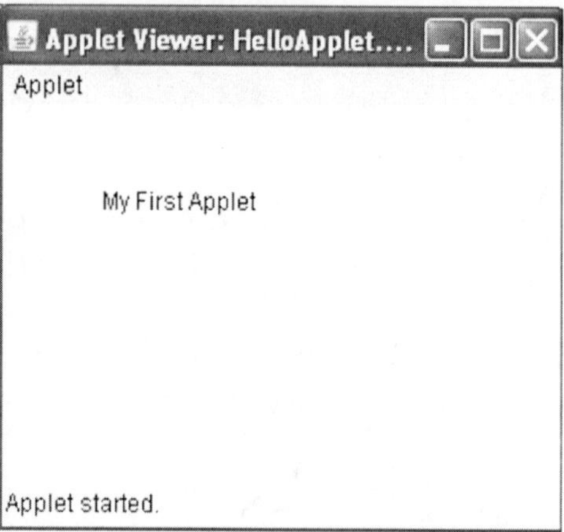

8.6 LIFECYCLE OF AN APPLET

Applets are automatically constructed by the runtime environment associated with a Web browser or the applet viewer. Applets have four lifecycle methods: init(), start(), paint(), stop(), and destroy().

8.6.1 init()

Initialization occurs when the applet is loaded. The init() is called before the applet begins execution, it is the first method called by an applet once it has been loaded by the AppletViewer or web browser., it can be overridden to perform any necessary initialization processing, such as loading images, establishing the connection to the data base, set layout or set Fonts.

Syntax:

```
public void init()
{
...
}
```

8.6.2 start()

After initialization an applet is started by the start() method. start( ) is called automatically to begin the actual execution of the applet. The start() method serves as the execution entry point for an applet when it is initially executed and restarted as the result of a user returning to the Web page that contains the applet.

Syntax:

```
public void start()
{
...
}
```

8.6.3 paint()

The applet overrides paint() method. The paint method is where the real work of this applet really occurs. The Graphics object passed into the paint() method holds the graphics state that is, the current features of the drawing surface.

```
public void paint(Graphics g)
{
...
}
```

8.6.4 stop()

The stop() method provides the capability to stop the execution of an applet. It is called by the web browser on that time when the user leaves one applet to go another applet. start() can occur if the applet is in a stopped state. An applet is stopped when the user goes to a different web page and comes back to the applet page.

Syntax:

```
public void stop()
```

```
{
...
}
```

8.6.5 destroy()

Like init() method, the destroy() method is called only one time in the life cycle of Applet. destroy( ) is called when an applet has completely finished the execution process, or when the browser needs to Shut down. This method is used at the end of an applet's life cycle to perform the process of termination of applet from web browser.

Syntax:

```
public void destroy()
{
...
}
```

Example:
LifeCycleApplet

```
import java.awt.*;
import java.applet.*;
import java.applet.*;
public class LifeCycleApplet extends Applet
{
   Font f = new Font("times new roman", Font.BOLD, 20);
   int i;
   String S1, S2;

public void paint(Graphics g)
{
   g.setFont(f);
   g.setColor(Color.RED);
   g.drawString(S1, 100, 50);
   g.drawString(S2, 100, 100);
}

public void init()
{
   i = 0;
   S1 = "";
   S2 = "This is the initialization state.";
   repaint();
   showStatus("The applet is initializing!");
}
```

```
public void start()
{
  i = 1;
  S1 = S2;
  S2 = "This is the starting state.";
  repaint();
  showStatus("The applet is starting!");
}

public void stop()
{
  i = 2;
  S1 = S2;
  S2 = "This is the stopping state.";
  repaint();
  showStatus("The applet is stopping!");
}

public void destroy()
{
  i = 3;
  S1 = S2;
  S2 = "This is the destroyed stat.";
  repaint();
  showStatus("The applet is being destroyed!");
  }
}
/* <APPLET CODE= "LifeCycleApplet.class" width= 400 height=400>
</APPLET>*/
```

Compile and run the program

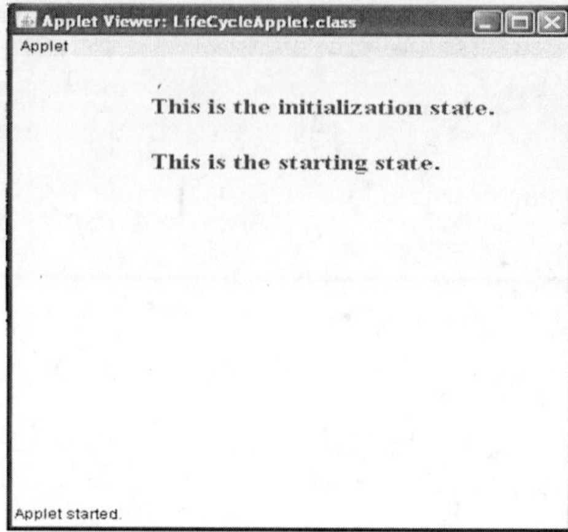

Select Applet and click on Stop.

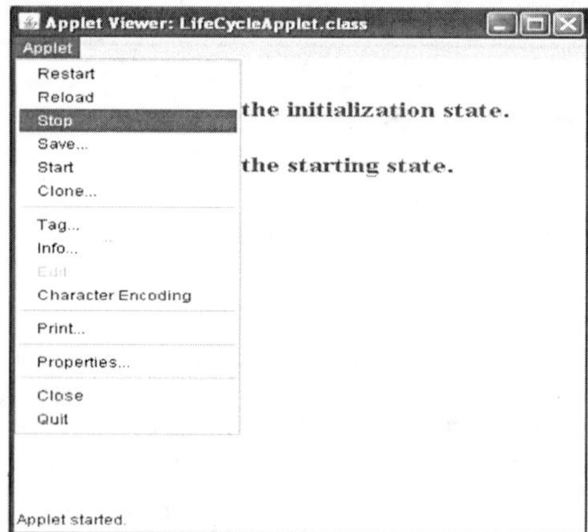

Now again click on start.

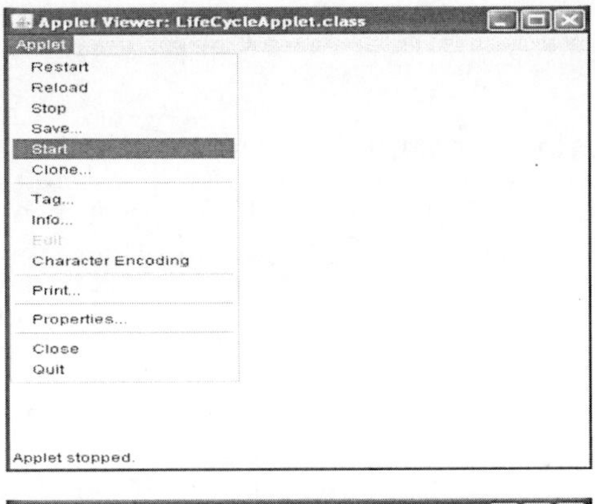

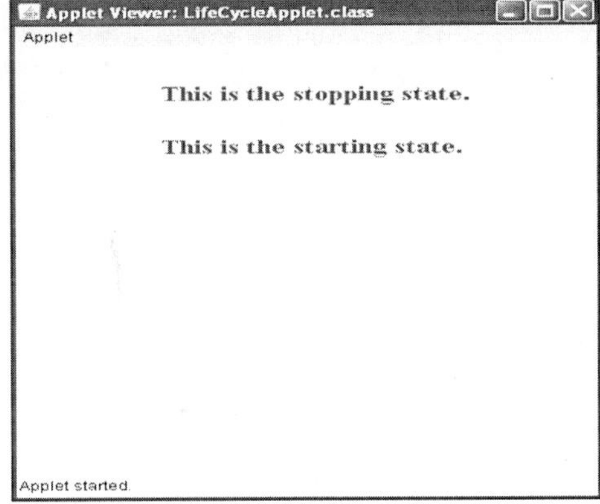

8.7 STATES TRANSITION DIAGRAM OF AN APPLET

If we have to create a basic Java application then our class must have one method, main(). When our application starts up then main() method is executed and from main() we can set up the behavior that our program needs. Applets are similar to Java application. Applets have many states that correspond to various major events in the life cycle of an applet, for example, initialization, painting, stopped or dead states. Each state has a corresponding method, so when an event occurs, the browser or AppletViewer calls those specific methods.

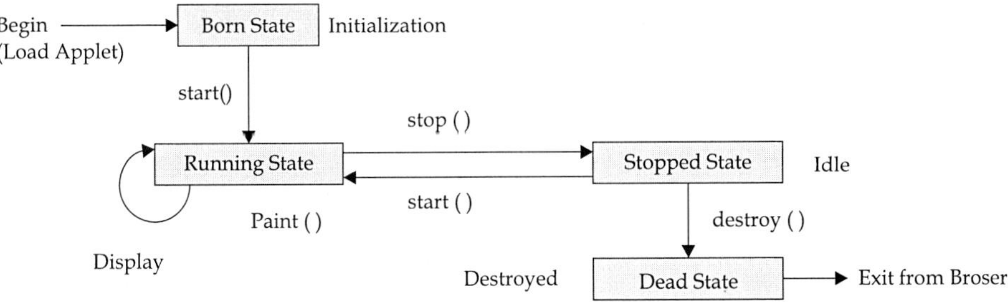

Figure 8.3: Life cycle of Applet

Here are five of the more important states in execution of an applet: initialization, starting, painting, stopping and destroying.

8.7.1 Born State-invokes init() - only once

When we want to provide behavior for loading the applet then override init() method. When the applet is loaded or reloaded, initialization occurs. In this state Initialization might include creating the objects and setting up an initial state, loading images or fonts or setting the parameters.

8.7.2 Running State invokes start() - more than once

We have to provide startup behavior for our applet then override the start() method. After initialization, it is started. Starting can occur if the applet was previously stopped. Note that starting can occur several times during an applet's life cycle, whereas initialization happens only once.

8.7.3 Display State invokes paint() - more than once

Display state override the paint() method for your applet to have an actual appearance on the screen. An applet actually draws something on the screen using paint(), be it text, a line, a colored background, or an image. Paint() can occur many hundreds of times during an applet's life cycle. Note that paint() takes an argument, an object of the class Graphics. This object is created and passed to paint method by the browser. The java.awt package has the class Graphics. So import this package in your Applet program.

8.7.4 Stopped State invokes stop() - more than once

Stopping state occurs when we leaves the page that contains a currently running applet, or we can stop the applet by calling stop() method. By overriding stop(), we can suspend execution of applet and then restart them if the applet is viewed again.

8.7.5 Dead State invokes destroy() - only once

Dead state occurs when the web browser exits. To provide clean up behavior for your applet, override the destroy() method. Destroying enables the applet to clean up before it is freed.

8.8 APPLET'S METHODS

Applet provides all of the necessary support and functionality for window-based programming. Applet provides more methods for applet execution, such as starting and stopping, load and display images, load and play audio clips. Applet extends the Applet class which exists in applet package. These classes provide support for Java's window-based, graphical user interface.

Table 8.1: Applet's Methods

Method	Result
Graphics( )	To constructs a new Graphics object.
create( )	To creates a new Graphics object.
dispose( )	To disposes of the current graphics context.
getColor( )	Gets the current color value.
setColor( )	Sets the current color value.
getFont( )	Gets the current font name.
setFont( )	Sets the font for all text operations.
drawRoundRect( )	Draws a rounded corner rectangle using the current color.
draw3DRect( )	Draws a 3-D rectangle.
drawOval( )	Draws an oval using the current color.
drawPolygon( )	Draws a polygon using an array of x points and y points.
drawString( )	Draws a string using the current font and color.
drawLine( )	Draws a line between two points(x1,y1) and (x2,y2).
drawRect( )	To draws a rectangle using the current color.
clipRect( )	Clips to a rectangle.
clearRect( )	Clears the specified rectangle using the current background color.
fillPolygon( )	To fills a polygon with the current color.
fillRect( )	To fills a rectangle using the current color.
fillRoundRect( )	To draws a filled rounded rectangle.
fill3DRect( )	Paints a 3-D rectangle filled with the current color.
fillOval( )	Fills an oval using the current color.

8.9 THE <APPLET> TAG

Use the <APPLET> tag, to include an applet on a Web page. <APPLET> is a special extension to HTML for including applets in Web pages. In order to view the applet, an HTML code has to be written. It has three attributes.

(i) **CODE** – Specifies the name of the applet class including the .class extension. For example code="applet1.class". In this case, the class file must be in the same directory as this HTML file.

(ii) **WIDTH** – Specifies the width of the applet window on the Web Page or the width of appletviewer window.

(iii) **HEIGHT** – Specifies the height of the applet window on the Web Page or the width of appletviewer window.

Other attribute that could be added to the <applet> tag are as follows.

(i) **ALIGN** – This could be set to LEFT,RIGHT,MIDDLE,TOP,BOTTOM

(ii) **HSPACE** – Controls the horizontal space to the left and right of the applet.

(iii) **VSPACE** – Controls the vertical space above and below the applet.

(iv) **CODEBASE** – Indicates an alternate web site for the web browser to specify the location of the applet.

ALT – Specifies the text to be display if the web browser understands the <applet> tag, but can't run Java applets.

8.10 SOME EXAMPLES OF APPLET

// Draw a string "Hello Applet" to web browser/AppletViewer

```
import java.awt.*;
import java.applet.*;
public class applet1 extends Applet
{
public void paint(Graphics g)
 {
 g.drawString("Hello Applet", 100, 100);
 }
}
/*<applet code="applet1.class" width=400 height=400></applet>*/
```

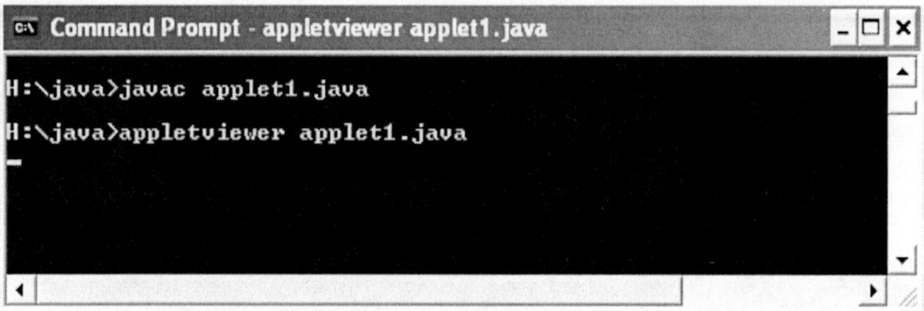

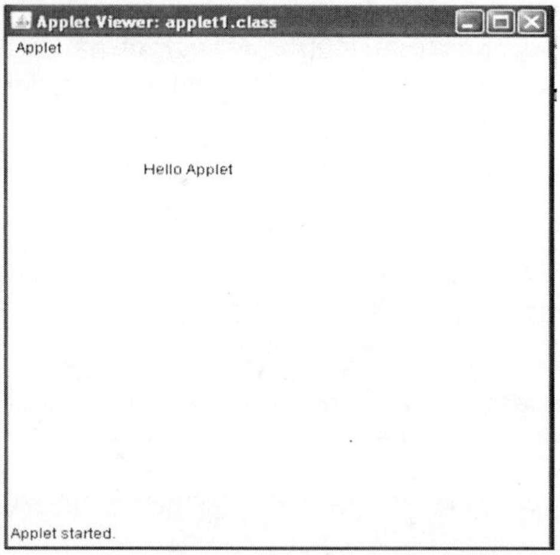

```
Command Prompt - appletviewer applet1.java

H:\java>javac applet1.java

H:\java>appletviewer applet1.java
```

```
Applet Viewer: applet1.class
Applet

Hello Applet

Applet started.
```

// Set the Color and Font of a string

```
import java.awt.*;
import java.applet.*;
public class applet1 extends Applet
{
```

```
Font f;
Public void init()
{
f = new Font("TimesRoman", Font.BOLD, 36);
}
public void paint(Graphics g)
 {
 g.setFont(f);
 g.setColor(Color.red);
 g.drawString("Hello Applet", 100, 100);
 }
}
/*<applet code="applet1.class" width=400 height=400></applet>*/
```

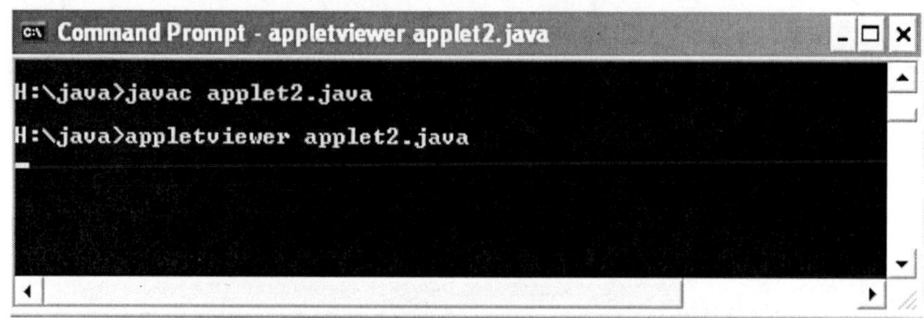

// Sum of Two Numbers

```
import java.awt.*;
import java.applet.*;
public class sum1 extends Applet
{
```

```
TextField t1,t2;
public void init()
{
t1 = new TextField(10);
t2 = new TextField(10);
t1.setText("0");
t2.setText("0");
add(t1);
add(t2);
}
public void paint(Graphics g) {
int a = 0;
int b = 0;
int sum;
String s1,s2,s3;
g.drawString("Enter Two Numbers", 20, 60);
try
{
s1 = t1.getText();
a = Integer.parseInt(s1);
s2 = t2.getText();
b = Integer.parseInt(s2);
}
catch(Exception e1)
{}

sum = a + b;
String str = "THE SUM OF TWO NO IS: "+String.valueOf(sum);
g.drawString (str,100, 125);
}
public boolean action(Event e, Object o)
{
repaint();
return true;
}
}
/* <APPLET CODE= "sum1.class" width= 400 height=400>
</APPLET>*/
```

Now compile and rum the program as follows.

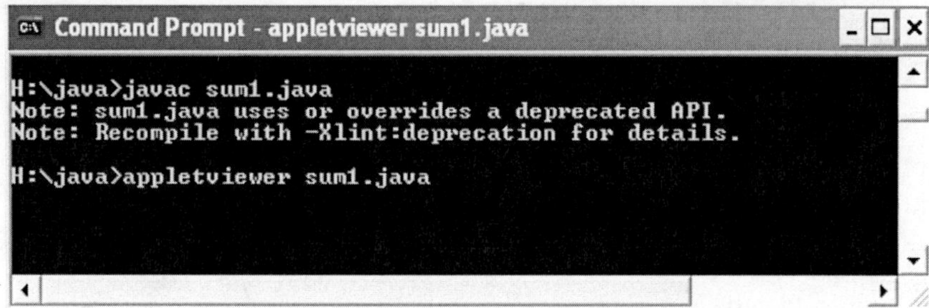

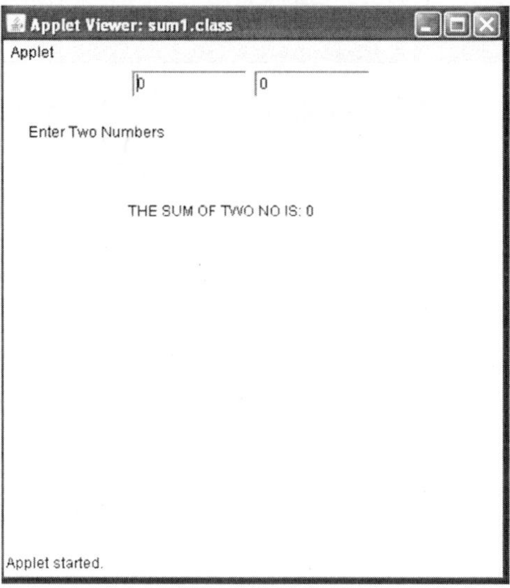

Enter the values and press enter key. The result is display as follows.

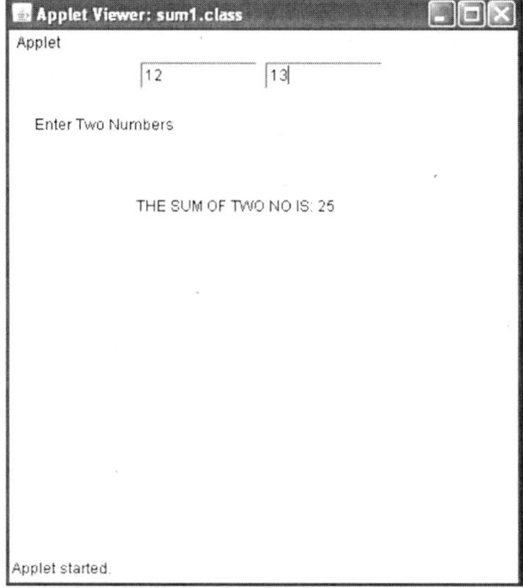

// Create a Back Buffer in Applet

```
import java.applet.*;
import java.awt.*;
import java.awt.event.*;
public class AppBackBuffer extends Applet
  implements MouseMotionListener {
  int width, height;
  Image i;
  Graphics g1;
  public void init() {
  width = getSize().width;
  height = getSize().height;
    i = createImage( width, height );
    g1 = i.getGraphics();
    g1.setColor( Color.black );
    g1.fillRect( 0, 0, width, height );
    g1.setColor( Color.white );
    addMouseMotionListener( this );
  }
  public void mouseMoved( MouseEvent e ) { }
  public void mouseDragged( MouseEvent e ) {
    int x = e.getX();
    int y = e.getY();
    g1.fillOval(x-5,y-5,10,10);
    repaint();
    e.consume();
  }
  public void update( Graphics g ) {
    g.drawImage( i, 0, 0, this );
  }
  public void paint( Graphics g ) {
    update( g );
  }
}/*<applet code="AppBackBuffer.class" width=400 height=400></applet>*/
```

Compile and Run the Program

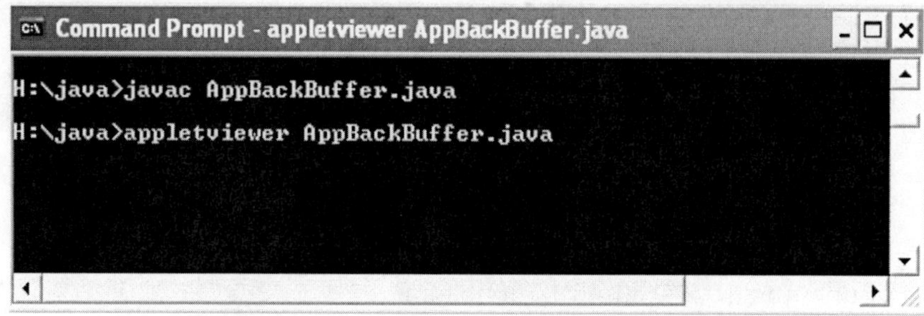

You can write anything using mouse dragging.

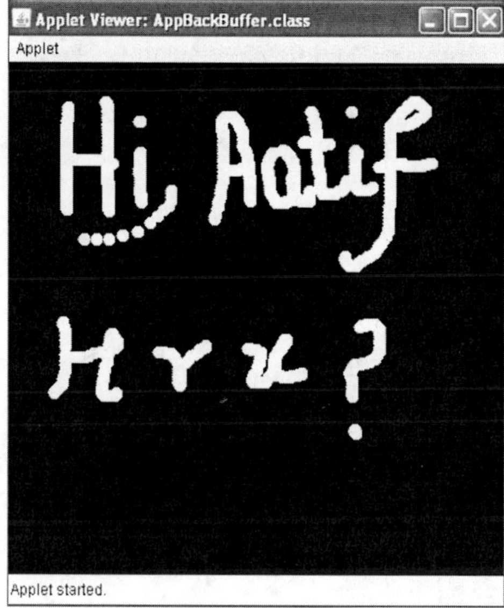

//Draw a circle of a string using Color Spectrum

```
import java.applet.*;
import java.awt.*;
import java.lang.Math;
public class AppCircleSpectrum extends Applet
{
   width, height;
   int n = 25;
   Color[] c;
   public void init() {
   width = getSize().width;
   height = getSize().height;
   setBackground( Color.BLACK );
   c = new Color[n];
   for ( int i = 0; i < n; ++i )
{
```

```
        c[i] = new Color( Color.HSBtoRGB(i/(float)n,1,1) );
    }
public void paint( Graphics g )
    {
        int r = width / 3;
        for ( int i = 0; i < n; ++i )
    {
        double angle = 2*Math.PI*i/(double)n;
        int x = (int)(r*Math.cos(angle));
        int y = (int)(r*Math.sin(angle));
        g.setColor(c[i]);
        g.drawString( “Tanweer”, width/2+x, height/2+y );
        }
    }
}
/*<applet code=”AppCircleSpectrum.class” width=400 height=400></applet>*/
```

Compile and run the Program

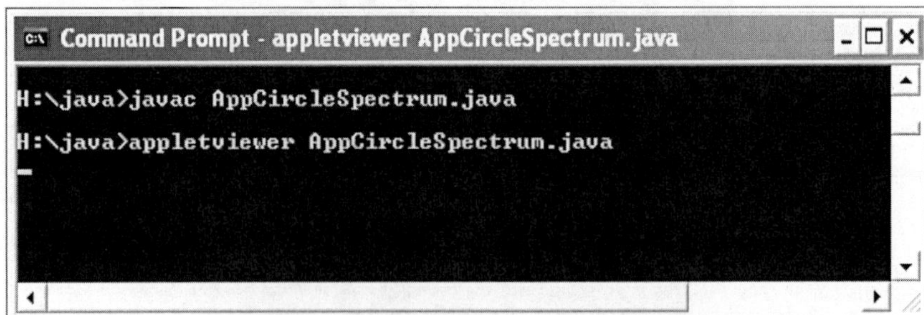

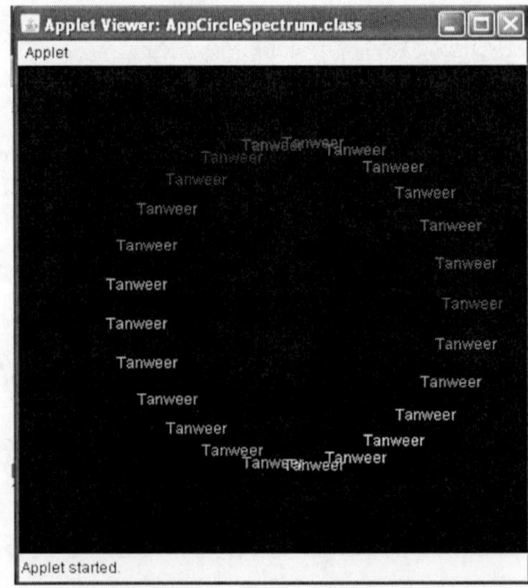

// Draw a Digital and Analog Watch on applet

```
import java.applet.*;
import java.awt.*;
import java.util.*;
import java.text.*;
public class AppWatch extends Applet implements Runnable {
   int width, height;
   hread t = null;
   boolean threadSuspended;
   int hours=0, minutes=0, seconds=0;
   String timeString = "";
   public void init() {
      width = getSize().width;
      height = getSize().height;
      setBackground( Color.green );
   }
public void start() {
   if ( t == null ) {
      t = new Thread( this );
      t.setPriority( Thread.MIN_PRIORITY );
      threadSuspended = false;
      t.start();
   }
   else {
         ( threadSuspended ) {
         threadSuspended = false;
         synchronized( this ) {
         notify();
         }
      }
   }
}

public void stop() {
   threadSuspended = true;
}

public void run() {
   try {
      while (true) {
         Calendar cal = Calendar.getInstance();
         hours = cal.get( Calendar.HOUR_OF_DAY );
         if ( hours > 12 ) hours -= 12;
         minutes = cal.get( Calendar.MINUTE );
```

```
        seconds = cal.get( Calendar.SECOND );
        SimpleDateFormat formatter
        = new SimpleDateFormat( "hh:mm:ss", Locale.getDefault() );
        Date date = cal.getTime();
        timeString = formatter.format( date );
// Now the thread checks to see if it should suspend itself
if ( threadSuspended ) {
   synchronized( this ) {
      while ( threadSuspended ) {
         wait();
         }
      }
   }
   repaint();
   t.sleep( 1000 ); // interval given in milliseconds
   }
}
(InterruptedException e) { }
}
void drawHand( double angle, int radius, Graphics g ) {
   angle -= 0.5 * Math.PI;
   int x = (int)( radius*Math.cos(angle) );
   int y = (int)( radius*Math.sin(angle) );
   g.drawLine( width/2, height/2, width/2 + x, height/2 + y );
}
void drawWedge( double angle, int radius, Graphics g ) {
   angle -= 0.5 * Math.PI;
   int x = (int)( radius*Math.cos(angle) );
   int y = (int)( radius*Math.sin(angle) );
   angle += 2*Math.PI/3;
   int x2 = (int)( 5*Math.cos(angle) );
   int y2 = (int)( 5*Math.sin(angle) );
   angle += 2*Math.PI/3;
   int x3 = (int)( 5*Math.cos(angle) );
   int y3 = (int)( 5*Math.sin(angle) );
   g.drawLine( width/2+x2, height/2+y2, width/2 + x, height/2 + y );
   g.drawLine( width/2+x3, height/2+y3, width/2 + x, height/2 + y );
   g.drawLine( width/2+x2, height/2+y2, width/2 + x3, height/2 + y3 );
}
public void paint( Graphics g ) {
   g.setColor( Color.gray );
   drawWedge( 2*Math.PI * hours / 12, width/5, g );
```

```
    drawWedge( 2*Math.PI * minutes / 60, width/3, g );
    drawHand( 2*Math.PI * seconds / 60, width/2, g );
    g.setColor( Color.white );
    g.drawString( timeString, 10, height-10 );
    }
}
/*<applet code="AppWatch.class" width=400 height=400></applet>*/
```

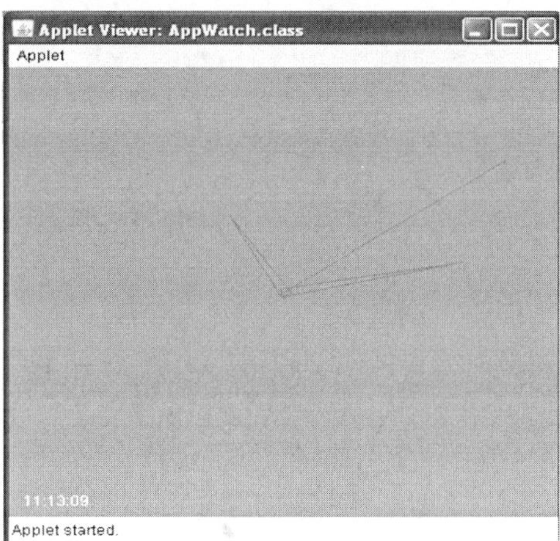

//Passing parameters to an applet

//The parameters are passed to applets by using the attribute PARAM in the applet tag.

```
import java.awt.*;
import java.applet.Applet;
public class AppParam extends Applet
{
Font f;
String s;
public void init()
{
f= new Font("Arial",Font.BOLD,24);
s= getParameter("s");
```

```
if(s==null)
s="Null";
}
public void paint(Graphics g)
{
g.setFont(f);
g.setColor(Color.BLUE);
g.drawString(s,100,50);
}
}
/*<applet code="AppParam.class" width=400 height=400>
<param name=s value="TANWEER ALAM">
</applet>*/
```

Compile and Run the Program.

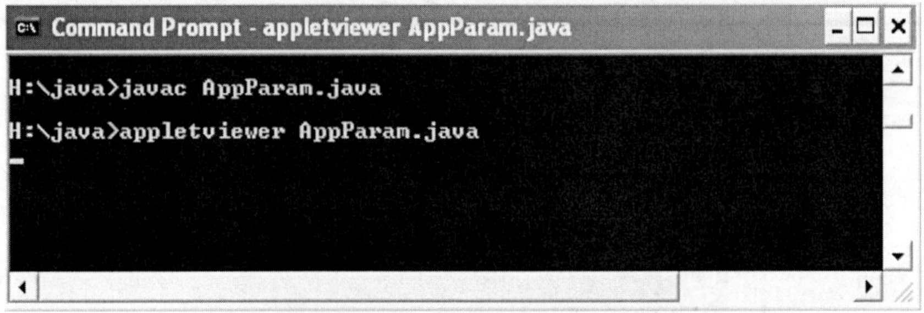

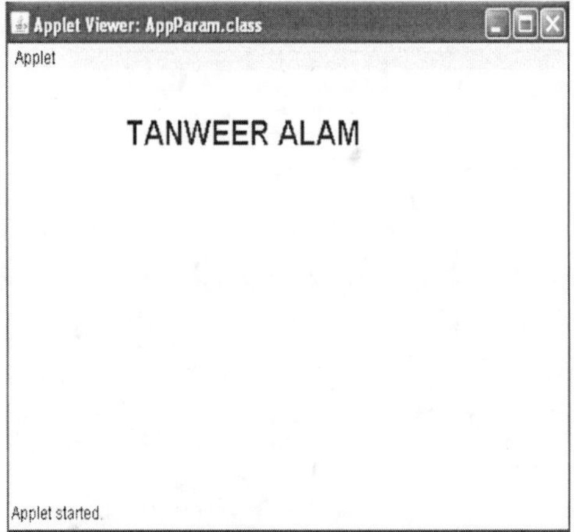

//Program to find the current date and Time

```
import java.awt.*;
import java.awt.event.*;
import java.applet.*;
import java.util.*;
```

```
public class dateApp extends Applet
{
   Button b1=new Button("Start");
   String s1="";
   public void init()
   {
      this.setLayout(null);
      this.setSize(300,300);
      b1.setBounds(50,200,100,30);
      b1.addActionListener(new ActionListener(){public void
               actionPerformed(ActionEvent e){b1_Click();}});
      this.add(b1);
   }
   public void paint(Graphics g)
   {setBackground(Color.YELLOW);
      Font f=new Font("Arial",Font.BOLD,20);
      g.setFont(f);
      g.drawString(s1,10,100);
   }
   class MT extends Thread
   {
      public void run()
      {
      try{
            while(true)
            {
               Date d=new Date();
               s1=d.toString();
               repaint();
               Thread.sleep(1000);
            }
         }catch(Exception ee){}
      }
   }
   class MT1 extends Thread
      {
         public void run()
         {
         try{
               while(true)
               {
                  Math.random();
                  repaint();
```

```
                Thread.sleep(1000);
            }
        }catch(Exception ee){}
    }
}
    void b1_Click()
    {
        MT t=new MT();
        MT1 t1=new MT1();
        t.start();
        t1.start();
    }
}/*<applet code="dateApp.class" width=400 height=400></applet>*/
```

```
Command Prompt - appletviewer dateApp.java

H:\java>javac AppParam.java
H:\java>appletviewer AppParam.java
H:\java>javac dateApp.java
H:\java>appletviewer dateApp.java
```

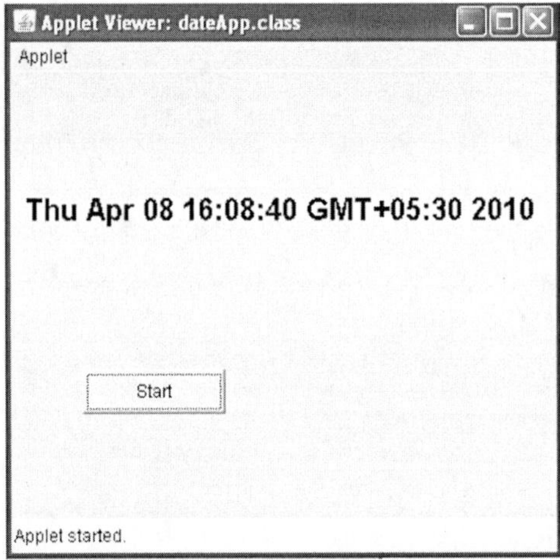

//To Change the color of text in above program every second.

```
import java.awt.*;
import java.awt.event.*;
import java.applet.*;
import java.util.*;
public class datecolorApp extends Applet
{
```

```
Button b1=new Button("Start");
String s1="";
Color c=Color.BLACK;
public void init()
{
   this.setLayout(null);
   this.setSize(300,300);
   b1.setBounds(50,10,100,30);
   b1.addActionListener(new ActionListener(){public void
          actionPerformed(ActionEvent e){b1_Click();}});
   this.add(b1);
}
public void paint(Graphics g)
{
   Font f=new Font("Arial",Font.BOLD,20);
   g.setFont(f);
   g.setColor(c);
   g.drawString(s1,10,100);
}
class MT extends Thread
{
   public void run()
   {
   try{
          while(true)
          {
             Date d=new Date();
             s1=d.toString();
             repaint();
             Thread.sleep(1000);
          }
      }catch(Exception ee){}
   }
}
class MT1 extends Thread
   {
      public void run()
      {
      try{
             while(true)
             {
                int r=(int)(Math.random()*255);
                int g=(int)(Math.random()*255);
```

```
                    int b=(int)(Math.random()*255);
                    c=new Color(r,g,b);
                    repaint();
                    Thread.sleep(200);
                }
            }catch(Exception ee){}
        }
    }
        void b1_Click()
        {
            MT t=new MT();
            MT1 t1=new MT1();
            t.start();
            t1.start();
        }
}/*<applet code="datecolorApp.class" width=400 height=400></applet>*/
```

```
Command Prompt - appletviewer datecolorApp.java

H:\java>javac datecolorApp.java

H:\java>appletviewer datecolorApp.java
```

/*Program to load an image to the applet when mouse is entered and exit when mouse is out from applet.*/

```
import java.awt.*;
import java.applet.*;
import java.awt.event.*;
```

```
import java.net.*;
public class imageApp extends Applet
{
   String s="";
   public void init()
   {
      this.setLayout(null);
      s="r7b.jpg";
      this.addMouseListener(new MouseAdapter(){public void
               mouseEntered(MouseEvent e){mouse_in();}});
      this.addMouseListener(new MouseAdapter(){public void
               mouseExited(MouseEvent e){mouse_out();}});
   }
   void mouse_in()
   {
      s="r7.jpg";
      repaint();
   }
   void mouse_out()
   {
      s="r7b.jpg";
      repaint();
   }
   public void paint(Graphics g)
   {
      try{
      URL u1=getCodeBase();
      String s1=u1.toString();
      s1=s1+s;
      URL u2=new URL(s1);
      Image img=getImage(u2);
      g.drawImage(img,10,60,300,300,this);
      }catch(Exception e){}
   }
}
/*<applet code="imageApp.class" width=400 height=400></applet>*/
```

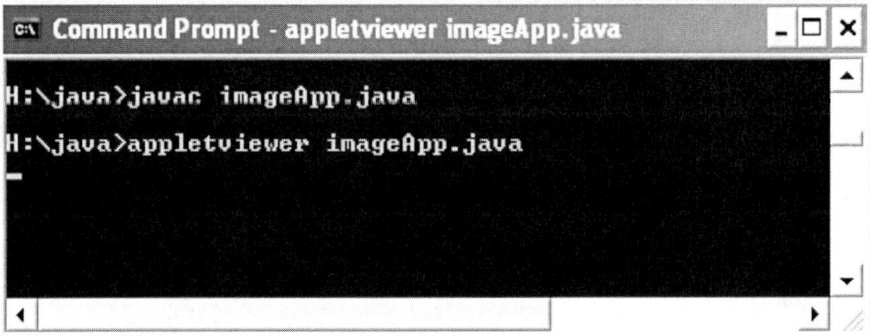

```
Command Prompt - appletviewer imageApp.java

H:\java>javac imageApp.java

H:\java>appletviewer imageApp.java
_
```

Output: when mouse is enterd.

When mouse is exited.

// Change Image when press a push Button

```
import java.awt.*;
import java.awt.event.*;
import java.applet.*;
import java.net.*;
public class changeImageApp extends Applet
{
   int i=1;
   public void init()
   {
```

```
        Button b1=new Button("Next>>");
        this.add(b1);
        b1.addActionListener(new ActionListener(){public void
                actionPerformed(ActionEvent e){b1_Click();}});
    }
    void b1_Click()
    {
        i=i+1;
        if(i==8) i=1;
        repaint();

    }
    public void paint(Graphics g)
    {
        try{
        URL u1=getCodeBase();
        String s1=u1.toString();
        URL u2=new URL(s1+"r" + i + ".jpg");
        Image img=getImage(u2);
        g.drawImage(img,10,10,this);
        showStatus("Displaying image " + i);
    }catch(Exception ee){}
  }
}/*<applet code="changeImageApp.class" width=400 height=400></applet>*/
```

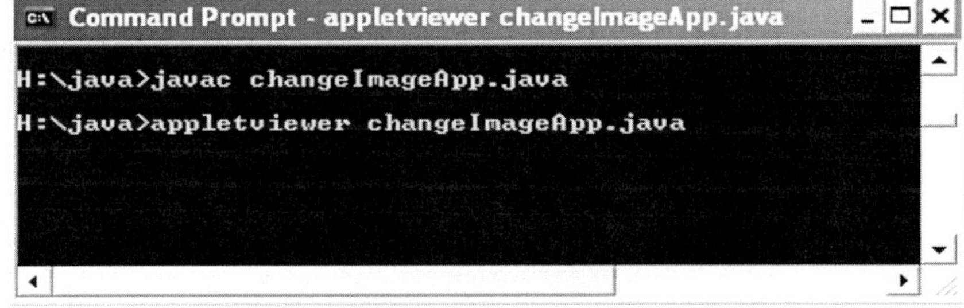

SUMMARY

An applet is a special kind of Java program which is used for internet programming. So an applet is included in an HTML page, like an image is included. In other words an applet is a java program that can be embedded in a web page. The applets reside in a server, can be downloaded from the server to the client machine and executed on client machine using a Java enabled web browser.

EXERCISE

1. Define Applet.
2. What is a local applet?
3. What is a remote applet?
4. Explain the client/server relationship as it applies to Java applets.
5. How will the client/server focus of the Internet change as applications start to flow two ways, both from and to a remote computer?
6. Explain why Java applets are secure and guaranteed not to crash the system on which they're executing.

*****

CHAPTER 9

ABSTRACT WINDOW TOOLKIT

Java provides a class library which is known as Abstract Window Toolkit (AWT). AWT is a set of classes, enabling the user to create a user friendly, graphical user Interface (GUI). AWT classes are used to create, implement and organize windows, implement GUI components like Buttons, labels, choice etc., handle events, draw graphics, image and text and access the native Windows implementation. AWT is platform-independent. A common set of tools is provided by the AWT for graphical user interface (GUI) design.

9.1 INTRODUCTION

AWT can be used by Java applications and applets. But Applets do not use frames and menus. The features implemented by the AWT are

- Graphics operations: Define colors, fonts, images, etc.
- Components: Standard GUI components like buttons, choice, windows, menus, etc.
- Layout Managers: Layouts responsible for actual positioning of components. Like FlowLayout, BorderLayout, GridLayout and Null layout etc.
- Use Graphics class for custom drawing
- Printing
- Menu Shortcuts
- Popup menus
- Event Handling

Abstract Window Toolkit supplies a number of classes, each class providing an interface component which can be combined with other components to build a complete Graphical User Interface.

9.2 A Component Hierarchy of AWT

AWT provides only the necessary components and functionality which are common to all major windowing systems. The GUI hierarchy of subclasses is directly from Object. The current version of the AWT has the following structure:

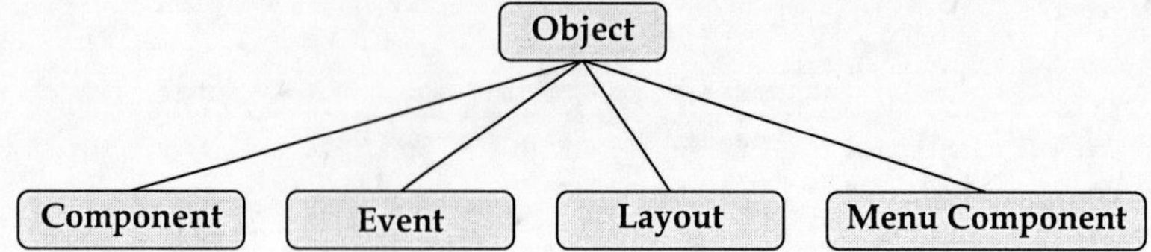

Figure 9.1: Class Hierarchy of AWT

- Containers used to contain Components, which are basic user interface controls.
- The "look-and-feel" of the application is dependant on the underlying GUIs.
- Layouts managers vs. fixed positioning of the components.
- Not very device-independent and the lack of ability to draw to the printer.
- Lacks a resource format.
- Class hierarchy is fairly shallow.

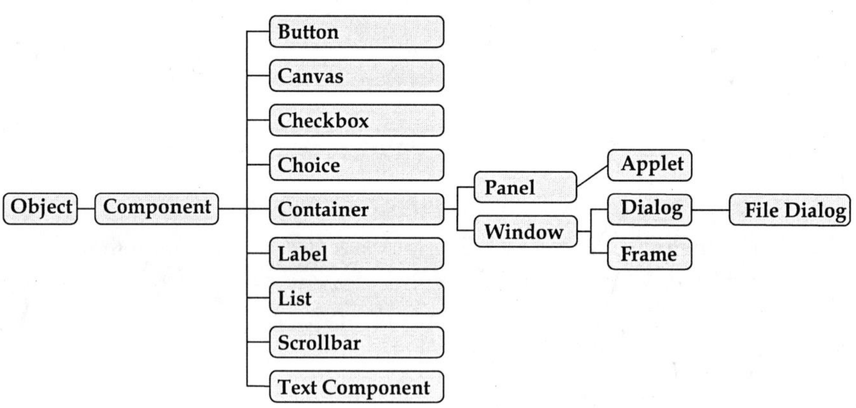

Figure 9.2: Component Hierarchy of AWT

AWT Menu Component

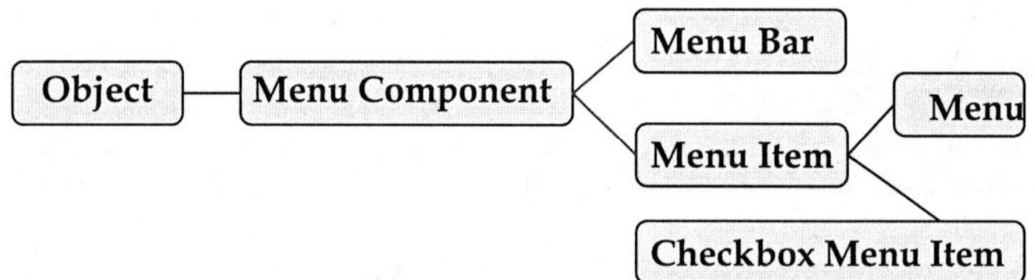

Figure 9.3: Menu Component Hierarchy of AWT

9.3 ADD /REMOVE A COMPONENT TO A CONTAINER

The Component class is the root class for almost components in the AWT. For any object of Component except a Window to display itself on screen, we must add it to a Container object. The Container class defines three methods for adding components:

(i) **add (Component c)**-this method is used to add the component to container.

(ii) **add (Component c, int position)**- this method specifying the integer position at which the component should be added.

(iii) **add (String position, Component c)**- in this method, string position specifies the component's position to the layout manager.

Remove method is used to remove the component from Container class.

void remove(Component c)

The Graphical user interface consists of the following three.

(i) **Component** – Anything that can be put on the component interface. This includes buttons, choice, Labels, TextFields etc.

(ii) **Containers** – This is a component that can contain other components.

(iii) **Layout managers** – Layout Managers define how the components will be arranged in a container.

Import java.awt.*; is used to imports all the containers, components and layout managers necessary for designing the user interface.

9.4 STEPS FOR STAND-ALONE APPLICATIONS USING THE AWT

Design the Interface: The following steps to create the interface.

(i) Create Frame

(ii) Initialize the fonts, colors, layouts and other resources

(iii) Create menus and menu bars

(iv) Create controls, dialogs, windows, etc.

Implementation: The following steps are used to implement the interface.

(i) Add event handlers.

(ii) Add functionality (i.e. networking, threading, etc).

(iii) Add exception-handling.

9.5 BUILDING GRAPHICAL USER INTERFACES

The following steps are used to design the GUI.

(i) Firstly import the awt package as import java.awt.*;

(ii) Use containers (Frame, Panel etc.)

(iii) Add basic components (like Button, TextField, List etc.)

(iv) set the positioning of the components

(v) use Layout Managers

(vi) Attach events for the user interaction with GUI.

9.6 AWT COMPONENTS

java.awt package has a big collection of controls. The ranging of controls from text labels and buttons to selection lists, windows and dialogs. The common methods of AWT components are as follow:

Methods	Description
setFont(Font)	Change the font of text within a component.
getBounds()	Get the current bounding Rectangle of component.
setVisible(boolean)	The component appears on the screen if setVisible() is set to true and if its set to false then the component will not appear on the screen.
getLocation()	Get position of the component, as a Point. The x and y parts of the location can be easily accessed by using getX() and getY().
getLocationOnScreen()	Get the position of the upper-left corner of the screen of the component, as a Point.
setBackground(Color)/ setForeground(Color)	change the background/foreground colors of the component
setEnabled(boolean)	The component will appear if set to true else if set to false then the component will not appear hence no user interaction will be there.
getSize()	Get the current size of component. use getWidth() and getHeight() methods to directly access the width and height of component.

9.6.1 Label

This is the simplest component of AWT. An instance of the Java Label class is used to provide the area upon which the text of a label is displayed. The display text is non editable. Label never performs any type of action.

Constructors Used

Constructor	Description
Label ()	Creates an empty Label
Label (string str)	creates a label with the string str
Label (string str, int Alignment)	Creates a label displaying string str with the alignment which can be one of the right, left or center, as specified

Methods Used

Methods	Description
setText(String str)	Sets the text displayed by label
getText()	obtains the text displayed by label
setAlignment(int Alignment)	Sets the alignment of the label
getAlignment()	obtains the alignment of the label

```
// implement label
import java.awt.*;
import java.applet.Applet;
public class label extends Applet
{
public void init()
{
Label l = new Label("Tanweer Alam",Label.CENTER);
add(l);
}
}
/*<applet code=label width=200 height=200></applet>*/
```

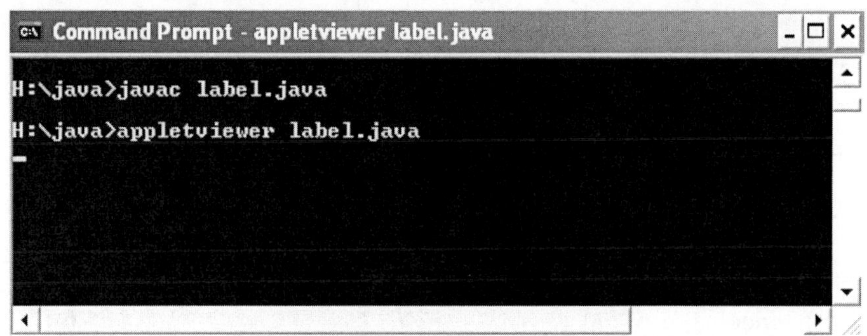

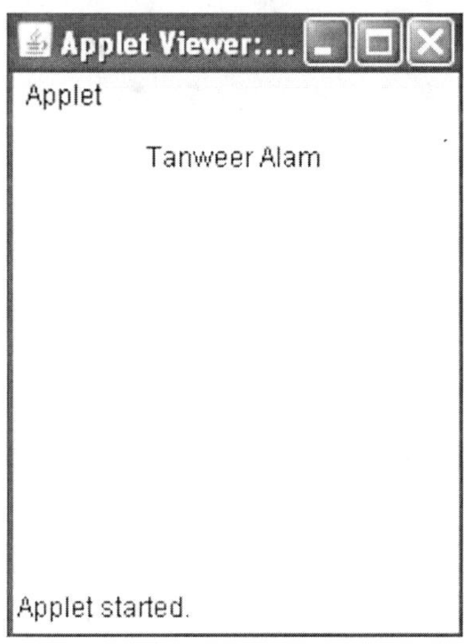

9.6.2 Button

Button class is a class that produces a labeled button component. Push buttons can be created from the Button class.

Constructors Used

Constructor	Description
Button ()	Constructs a Button with no label.
Button (string str)	Constructs a Button with the specified label str

Methods Used

Methods	Description
setLabel(String str)	Sets the Button with label str.
getLabel()	Obtains the label of the Button.
addActionListener(ActionListener)	Adds the specified action listener to receive action events from this button.
removeActionListener(ActionListener)	Removes the specified action listener so it no longer receives action events from this button.

Arguments

Arguments	Description
BackgroundColor	The color to be used for the background of the butt on.
Text	The text to appear next to the button.
TextFont	The font to be used for the text of the button.
TextColo r	The color to be used for the text of the button.
Handler	The object which handles action events from this combo box.
State	The enable state of the button (true or false.)
ActionText	The ActionCommand text for the event associated with the button.

```
// Implements Button
import java.awt.*;
import java.applet.Applet;
public class button extends Applet
{
public void init()
{
Button b = new Button("Hello");
add(b);
}
}
/*<applet code=button width=200 height=200></applet>*/
```

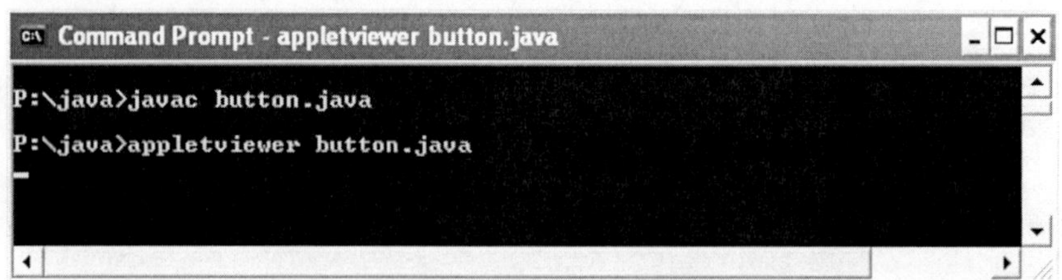

9.6.3 Checkbox

They are labeled or unlabeled boxes that can be either checked off or empty. They are used for selecting some option. Use one of the following to create them.

Constructors Used

Constructor	Description
Checkbox ()	Constructs a checkbox without any label
Checkbox(string str)	creates a checkbox with the Label str
Checkbox(String str, Boolean state)	Constructs a Checkbox with the label str and specified state.

Methods Used

Methods	Description
setLabel(String str)	Sets the Label to be displayed by the checkbox.
getLabel()	Obtains the label to be displayed by the checkbox.
setState(Boolean State)	Sets the State of checkbox.
getState()	Obtains the State of checkbox.
addItemListener(ItemListener il)	Adds the specified item listener to receive item events from this checkbox.
removeItemListener(ItemListener il)	Removes the specified item listener so it no longer receives item events from this checkbox.

```
import java.awt.*;

import java.applet.Applet;
public class checkbox extends Applet
{
public void init()
```

```
{
Checkbox c1 = new Checkbox ("Yes");
Checkbox c2 = new Checkbox ("No");
add(c1);
add(c2);
}
}
/*<applet code=checkbox width=500 height=500></applet>*/
```

Now compile and run the program as follows.

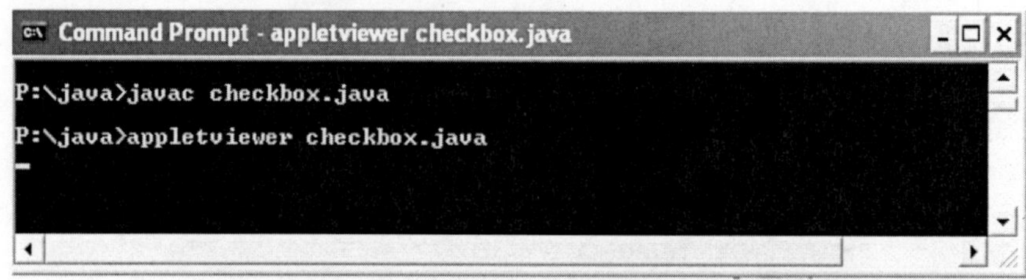

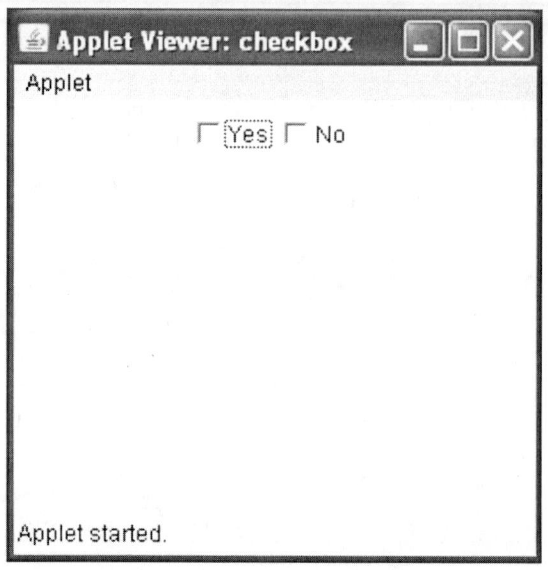

9.6.4 CheckboxGroup

CheckboxGroup is a class, used to create a multiple-exclusion scope for a set of checkbox buttons. Suppose we want to create a group of Checkbox buttons with the same CheckboxGroup object means radio buttons that only one of those Checkbox buttons will be allowed to be true state at a time. This class has only one constructor. The following statement creates a checkbox group.

```
CheckboxGroup cbg = new CheckboxGroup();
```

Now we have to create two checkboxes, belonging to CheckboxGroup, use the following statement.

```
Checkbox c1 = new Checkbox ("Yes", cbg, true);
Checkbox c2 = new Checkbox ("No", cbg, false);
```

Constructors Used

Constructor	Description
CheckboxGroup()	Creates a new CheckboxGroup
Checkbox(String, boolean, CheckboxGroup)	Constructs a Checkbox with the specified label, set to the specified state, and in the specified check box group.

Methods Used

Methods	Description
getSelectedCheckbox()	Gets the current choice. Returns type Checkbox
setSelectedCheckbox(Checkbox)	Sets the current choice to the specified Checkbox.
toString()	Returns the Str

```
import java.awt.*;

import java.applet.Applet;
public class checkboxgroup extends Applet
{
public void init()
{
CheckboxGroup cbg = new CheckboxGroup();
Checkbox c1 = new Checkbox ("Yes", cbg, true);
Checkbox c2 = new Checkbox ("No", cbg, false);
add(c1);
add(c2);
}
}
/*<applet code=checkboxgroup width=500 height=500></applet>*/
```

Now compile and run the program.

```
Command Prompt - appletviewer checkboxgroup.java

P:\java>javac checkboxgroup.java

P:\java>appletviewer checkboxgroup.java
```

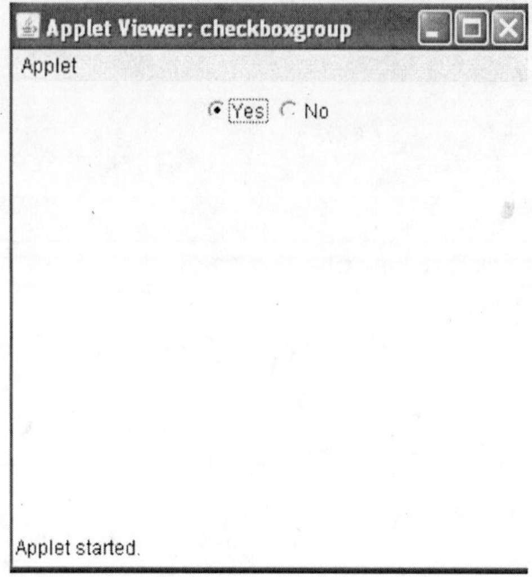

9.6.5 TextField

TextField is an editable component. This component is useful for obtaining short pieces of information from users. These components are limited to single line input. User enters data into a TextField or changes the focus of the TextField.

Constructor Used

Constructor	Description
TextField ()	Creates an empty text field.
TextField (string)	Creates a text field with the specified string.
TextField (string, int)	Creates a text field with specified string and specified width.

Methods Used

Methods	Description
setText(String str)	Sets the text displayed by TextField
getText()	obtains the text displayed by TextField
isEditable ()	This method returns a Boolean value indicating whether the filed is editable or not.
setEditable (Boolean)	This method decides whether the field should be editable or not depending upon the Boolean value

```
// implement TextField
import java.awt.*;
import java.applet.Applet;
public class textfield extends Applet
{
public void init()
{
```

```
TextField t = new TextField("Hello");
add(t);
}
}
/*<applet code=textfield width=200 height=200></applet>*/
```

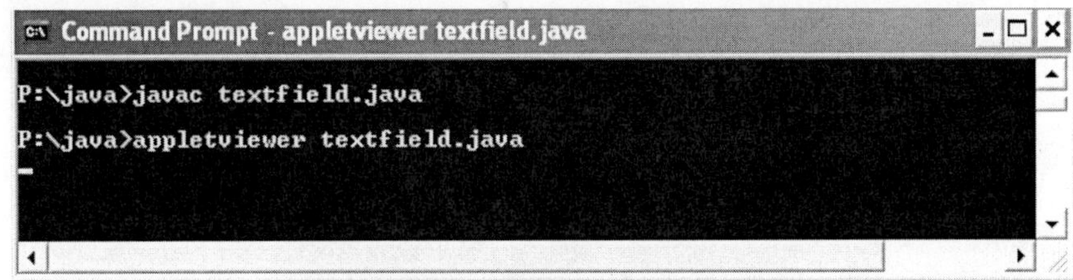

9.6.6 TextArea

TextArea component is useful for getting a large data from the user. TextArea is similar as TextField but there is multiple line input. A TextArea is a multi-line area that displays text. It can be set to allow editing text or read-only modes.

Constructor Used

Constructor	Description
TextArea ()	Creates an empty TextArea.
TextArea (int rows, int chars)	Creates a TextArea of rows specified and width to accommodate the characters specified.
TextArea (string str)	Creates a TextArea with string str.
TextArea (string str, int rows, int chars)	Creates a TextArea with string str, rows specified and width to accommodate the characters specified.
TextArea(String str, int rows, int chars, int alignment)	Constructs a new TextArea with the specified text and number of rows, columns and scrollbar.

The symbolic constants that can be used to specify information about the scrollbar in the fourth version of the constructor are:

(i) **SCROLLBARS_BOTH** Create and display both vertical and horizontal scrollbars.

(ii) **SCROLLBARS_HORIZONTAL_ONLY** Create and display horizontal scrollbar only.

(iii) **SCROLLBARS_NONE** Do not create or display any scrollbars for the text area.

(iv) **SCROLLBARS_VERTICAL_ONLY** Create and display vertical scrollbar only.

Methods Used

Methods	Description
insert(string str, int position)	This method inserts the indicated string at the position indicated by the second argument.
replace(string str, int startpos, int endpos)	This method replaces the text between the given integer positions with the indicated string.
append(String)	Appends the given text to the end.
replaceRange(String, int, int)	Replaces text from the indicated start to end position with the new text specified.

```
//applet to show TextArea
import java.awt.*;
import java.applet.Applet;
public class textarea extends Applet
{
public void init()
{
TextArea t = new TextArea(20,40);
   add(t);
}
}
/*<applet code=textarea width=100 height=100></applet>*/
```

Now compile and run the program as follows.

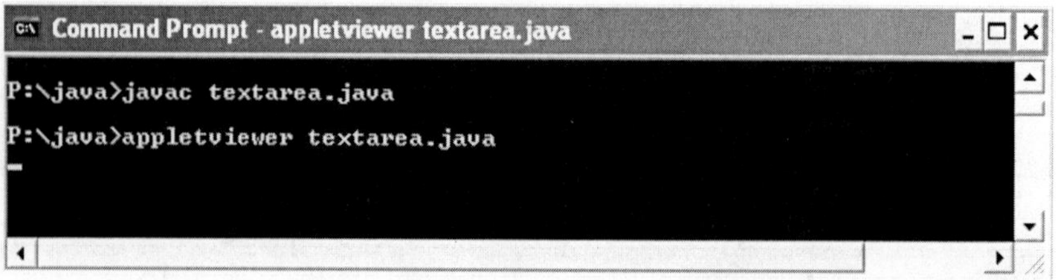

```
Command Prompt - appletviewer textarea.java
P:\java>javac textarea.java
P:\java>appletviewer textarea.java
```

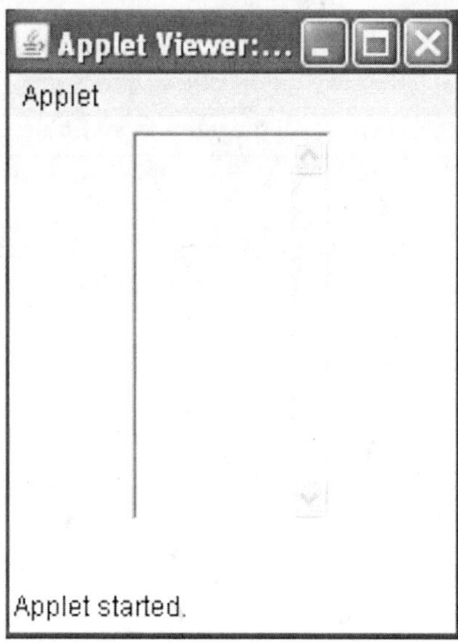

9.6.7 Choice

A Choice component is a combination of a TextField and dropdown list. The Choice class provides an option that allows the user to select a single item from a drop down list of choices. The following steps are used to create a Choice, insert items and add component:

(i) Create an instance of the class Choice.

(ii) Add items to the Choice by using the method addItem(string item) in the choice class.

(iii) Add the Choice component using the add(component) method.

Constructors Used

Constructor	**Description**
Choice()	Create a new Choice instance

Methods Used

Methods	Description
add(String item)	Add the item to the Choice.
insert(String item, int position)	Add the item at the specified position to the Choice.
clear()	Remove all items from Choice.
getSelectedItem ()	Returns the index position of the currently selected item.
getSelectedIndex ()	Returns the index position of the currently selected item.
select (pos)	Selects the item at the indicated index position.
select (text)	Selects the first in the list with the given text
getItem (index)	Returns text of the Choice item at the index position specified in the argument.
getItemCount ()	Returns the number of items in the Choice.

remove(int position)	Remove the item at index position from Choice.
remove(String item)	Remove the specified item from Choice.
removeAll()	Remove all the items from Choice.
addItemListener(ItemListener il)	Adds the specified ItemListener to receive item events from Choice.
removeItemListener (ItemListener il)	Removes the specified ItemListener so it no longer receives item events from this Choice.

```
// implement Choice

import java.awt.*;
import java.applet.Applet;
public class choice extends Applet
{
public void init()
{
Choice c = new Choice();
c.add("Tanweer Alam");
c.add("Anjum");
c.add("AAtif Alam");
add(c);
}
}

/*<applet code=choice width=200 height=200></applet>*/
```

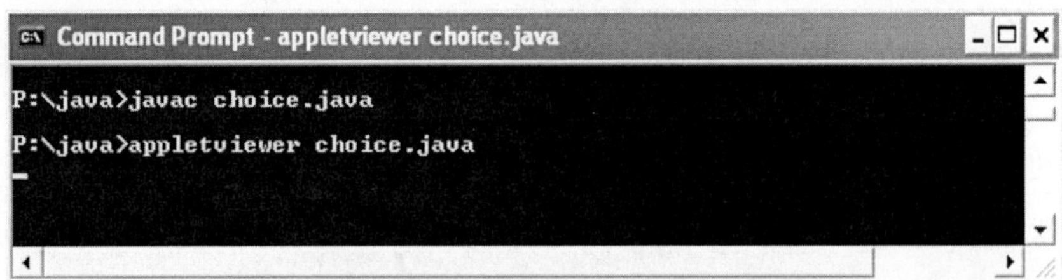

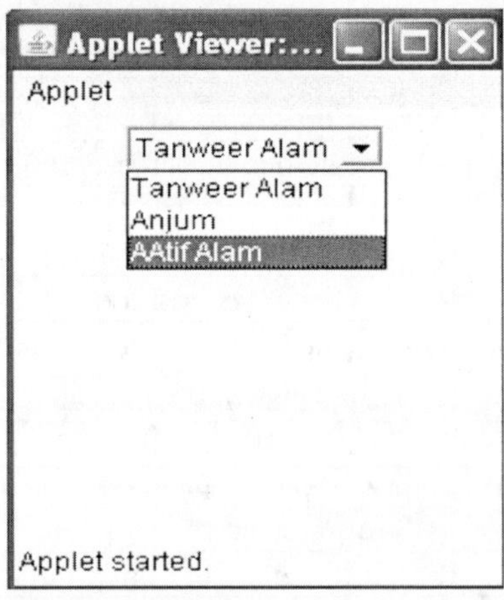

9.6.8 List

A List is similar to Choice. But in List we can choose more than one item at a time. A List component is a possibly scrolling list box. The List class provides an option that allows the user to select a single item or multiple items from the List. Scrolling lists do not pop up (as Choice). Multiple items are displayed at the same time.

The following steps are used to create a List, insert items and add component:

(i) Create an instance of the class List.

(ii) Add items to the List by using the method addItem(string item) in the List class.

(iii) Add the List component using the add(component) method.

Constructors Used

Constructor	Description
List()	Create a new List with the default number of items visible.
List(int n)	Create a new List with the specified number of items visible.
List (int n, Boolean state)	Created a new list with specified number of items visible. The Boolean state is allowed multiple selections, if it set to be true.

Methods Used

Methods	Description
add(String item)	Add the item to the List.
add(String item, int position)	Add the item at the specified position to the List.
clear()	Remove all items from List.
getSelectedItem ()	Returns the index position of the currently selected item.
getSelectedIndex ()	Returns the index position of the currently selected item.
select (pos)	Selects the item at the indicated index position.
select (text)	Selects the first in the list with the given text
getItem (index)	Returns text of the list item at the index position specified in the argument.
getItemCount ()	Returns the number of items in the list.
remove(int position)	Remove the item at index position from List.
remove(String item)	Remove the specified item from List.
removeAll()	Remove all the items from List.
addItemListener(ItemListener il)	Adds the specified ItemListener to receive item events from List.
removeItemListener(ItemListener il)	Removes the specified ItemListener so it no longer receives item events from this List.
replaceItem(String item, int position)	Replace the item with the specified item at the given position.
getSelectedIndexes ()	Returns the array index of the currently selected items.
getRow()	Obtain the number of currently visible items.
setMultipleMode(Boolean true)	Sets true or resets false multiple selection.
isMultipleMode()	Return true, if List is in Multiple mode.
makeVisible(int rows)	Make the specified rows visible in the scrolling List.

```
// shows the use of scrolling list.

import java.awt.*;
import java.applet.*;
public class list extends Applet
{
public void init()
{
List l = new List (3, true);
l.addItem("Tanweer");
l.addItem("Anjum");
l.addItem("AAtif");
add(l);
}
}

/*<applet code=list width=200 height=200></applet>*/
```

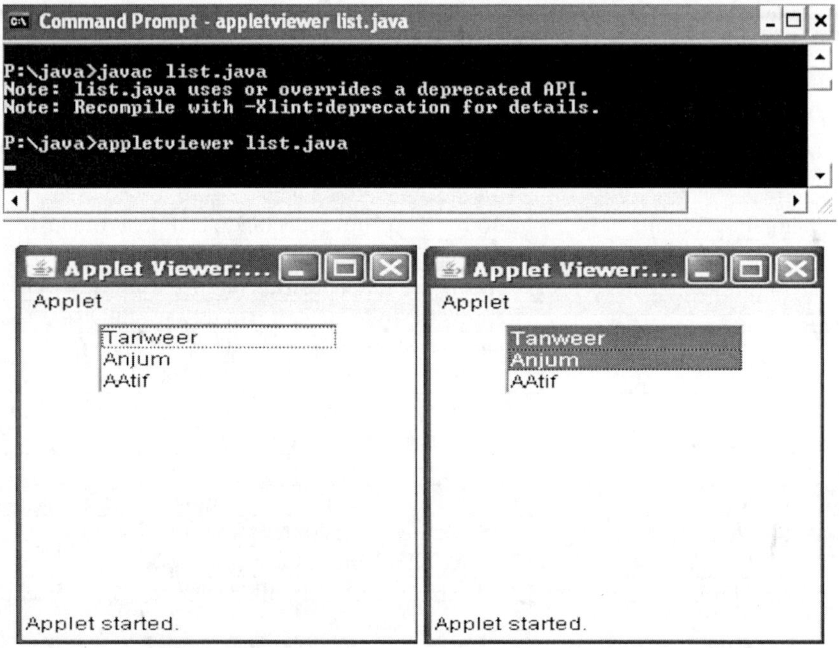
Command Prompt - appletviewer list.java
P:\java>javac list.java
Note: list.java uses or overrides a deprecated API.
Note: Recompile with -Xlint:deprecation for details.
P:\java>appletviewer list.java
Applet Viewer:...
Applet
Tanweer
Anjum
AAtif
Applet started.
Applet Viewer:...
Applet
Tanweer
Anjum
AAtif
Applet started.

9.6.9 Scrollbar

Scrollbar is a component that provides an area containing a slider which can be dragged from one end to another to indicate the value between its limit and arrow icons at each end for adjustment the slider. The characteristics of scrollbar are specified by integer values which are being set at the time of scrollbar construction. Both the types of Scrollbars are available i.e. horizontal and vertical.

Constructors Used

Constructor	Description
Scrollbar()	Create a new Scrollbar.
Scrollbar(int orientation)	Create a new scrollbar with specified orientation, by default orientation is horizontal.
Scrollbar(int orientation, int initialvalue, int size, int minimum, int maximum)	Create a new scrollbar with specified orientation, initial value, size, minimum and maximum value by default orientation is horizontal.

Methods Used

Methods	Description
setValue(int value)	Set the value of the scrollbar between minimum and maximum.
getValue()	Get the value of scrollbar
setOrientation(int orientation)	Set the orientation of the scrollbar.
getOrientation()	Get the orientation of scrollbar
setMinimum(int value)	Set the minimum value of the scrollbar.
getMinimum()	Get the minimum value of scrollbar
setMaximum(int value)	Set the maximum value of the scrollbar.
getMaximum()	Get the maximum value of scrollbar
setValue(int initialvalue, int size, int minimum, int maximum)	Set the value of the scrollbar.
setUnitIncrement(int value)	Set the unit value of the scrollbar.
getUnitIncrement()	Get the unit value of the scrollbar.
setVisibleAmount(int value)	Set the visible value of the scrollbar.
getVisibleAmount()	Get the visible value of the scrollbar.

```
// Scrollbar implementation

import java.awt.*;
import java.applet.Applet;

public class scrollbar extends Applet
{
	public void init()
{
	Scrollbar sb = new Scrollbar(Scrollbar.HORIZONTAL,10,10,50,100);
	add(sb);
    }
}
/*<applet code=scrollbar width=200 height=200></applet>*/
```

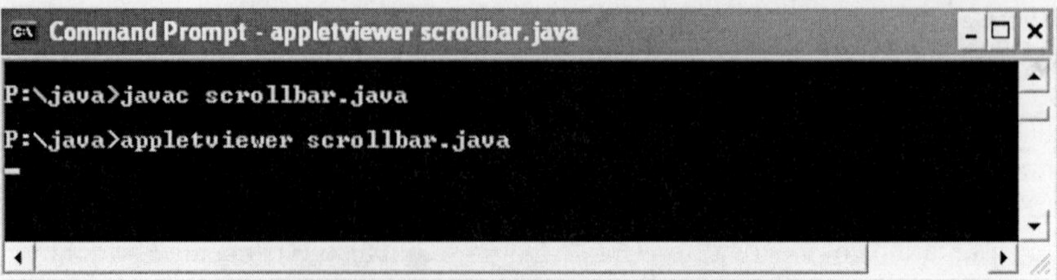

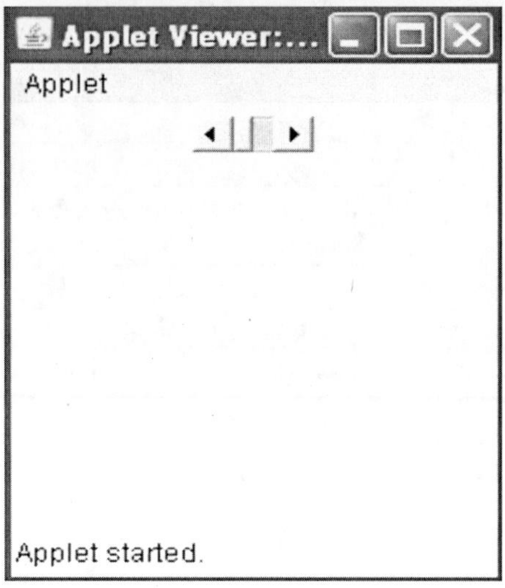

9.6.10 Canvas

The Canvas class is used for drawing because it implements a GUI object. It is most often used to display images and background for user drawing. Canvas provides the Graphics object for the drawing because Drawing is not implemented on the canvas itself. The AWT Canvas class is a generic Component class. The Canvas class is usually subclassed to implement a custom graphics object. Canvas can override the paint() method, which specifies how its Graphics object is to be updated.

Constructors used

Constructor	Description
Canvas()	Create a new canvas object.

Methods Used

Methods	Description
paint()	Can override the paint() method
repaint() :	Request an update of the applet display.
update()	Clears the applet display with the background color and then invokes the paint() method, be overridden.

```
// draw waveform using canvas

import java.applet.*;
import java.awt.*;
class canvas1 extends Canvas
{
public void paint(Graphics g)
{
g.setColor(Color.RED);
Dimension d = getSize();
g.drawRect(0, 0, d.width - 1, d.height - 1);
g.drawLine(0, d.height / 2, d.width - 1, d.height / 2 - 1);
g.drawLine(d.width / 2, 0, d.width / 2 - 1, d.height - 1);
g.setColor(Color.BLUE);
double dx = 4 * Math.PI / d.width;
double x = -2 * Math.PI;
int h = d.height;
for (int i = 0; i < d.width - 1; i++) {
int y1 = (int)((h - h * Math.sin(x)) / 2);
int y2 = (int)((h - h * Math.sin(x + dx)) / 2);
g.drawLine(i, y1, i + 1, y2);
x += dx;
}
}
}
public class canvas extends Applet
{
public void init()
{
canvas1 c = new canvas1();
c.setSize(400, 170);
add(c);
}
}
/*<applet code=canvas width=500 height=200></applet>*/
```

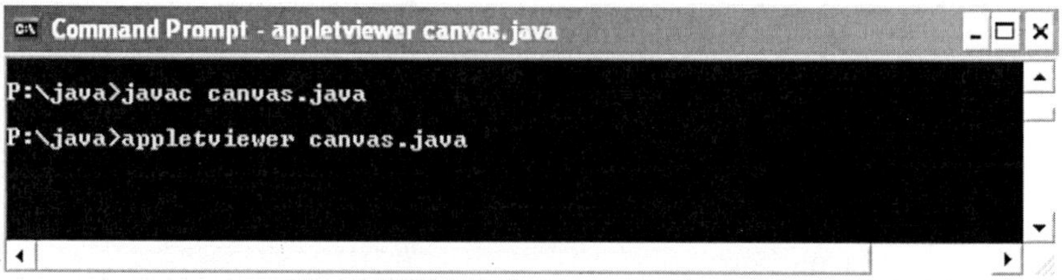

Command Prompt - appletviewer canvas.java

```
P:\java>javac canvas.java

P:\java>appletviewer canvas.java
```

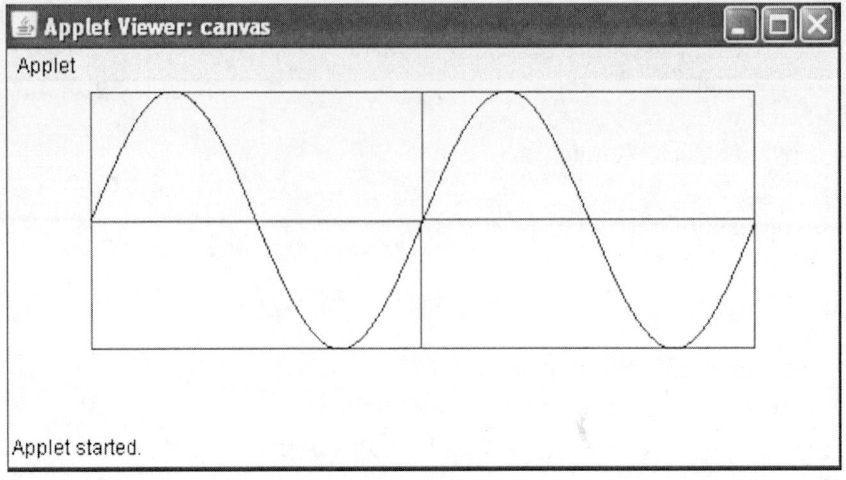

9.6.11 Frame

A Frame is a Window for Applet and stand alone applications with the entire window manager's like window title, borders, window minimize/maximize/close functionality added. It can include a menu bar. The default layout manager of Frame window is Border Layout. A Frame is providing the basic building block for screen-oriented applications. Frame allows you to change the mouse cursor, set an icon image, and have menus and menu bars. All graphical applications display their information inside a frame window.

Constructors used

Constructor	Description
Frame()	Create a frame without any title.
Frame(String title)	Create a frame with specified title.

Methods Used

Methods	Description
setTitle(String str)	Set the title of the frame.
getTitle()	Obtain the title of frame
MenuBar getMenuBar()	Obtain the MenuBar, which is set to Frame
setMenuBar(MenuBar mb)	Set the MenuBar to the Frame

To construct a frame window, the following steps are used:

(i) Create an object of the Frame class as follows.

```
Frame f = new Frame();
```

(ii) Set the size of the frame as follows:

```
f.setSize(500,500);
```

(iii) Set the title of the frame:

```
f.setTitle("My First Frame ");
```

(iv) Set the "default close operation":
f.setDefaultCloseOperation(Frame.EXIT_ON_CLOSE);

(v) Make the frame visible
f.setVisible(true);

(vi) Import the package java.awt:
import java.awt.*;

To see the component, add it to your frame.

(i) Construct a frame.

(ii) Construct an object of your component class.
Button b=new Button();

(iii) Add the component to the frame.
f.add(b);

(iv) Make the frame visible.
f.setVisible(true);

// Frame example

```
import java.awt.*;
public class frame1
{
    public static void main(String[] args)
{
    Frame f = new Frame("Welcome to Frame");
    Label l = new Label("This is my first Frame program",Label.CENTER);
    f.add(l);
    f.setSize(400,400);
    f.setVisible(true);
  }
}
```

```
Command Prompt - java frame1
P:\java>javac frame1.java
P:\java>java frame1
```

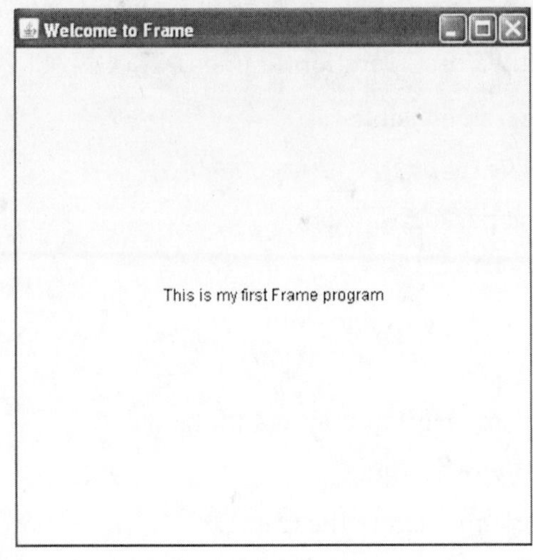


```
// create a new frame after click a button of applet

import java.applet.*;
import java.awt.*;
import java.awt.event.*;

class Frame2 extends Frame
{
Frame2(String title)
{
super(title);
addWindowListener(new WindowAdapter() {
public void windowClosing(WindowEvent we) {
dispose();}});
}
}

public class FrameApplet extends Applet implements ActionListener
{
public void init()
{
Button b = new Button("Create new Frame");
b.addActionListener(this);
add(b);
}
public void actionPerformed(ActionEvent ae)
{
Frame2 f = new Frame2("welcome Frame");
f.setSize(250, 250);
f.show();
```

```
}
}
/*<applet code=FrameApplet width=300 height=300></applet>*/
```

```
Command Prompt - appletviewer FrameApplet.java

P:\java>javac FrameApplet.java
Note: FrameApplet.java uses or overrides a deprecated API.
Note: Recompile with -Xlint:deprecation for details.

P:\java>appletviewer FrameApplet.java
```

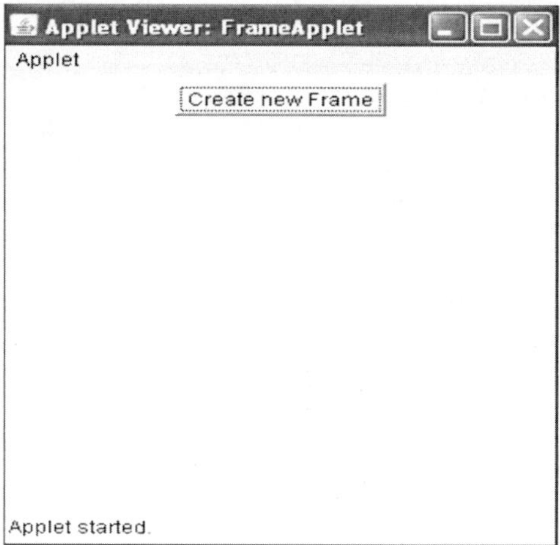

Press button.

9.6.12 Containers

Container is an abstract class. Container class is a Component class that can contain other Component objects. A Container is providing a rectangular area within which other components can be organized by the Layout Manager. Container is a subclass of Component. A Container can go inside another Container, which can go inside another Container, and so on. Container classes are the basic framework from which you build the GUI components of applets or applications.

Constructors used

Constructor	Description
Frame()	Create a new frame.
Panel()	Create a new Panel.
Dialog()	Create a new Dialog.

Methods Used

Methods	Description
getComponents();	Obtain an array of components.
add();	Add component to the container.
getComponentCount();	Return the total number of components
getComponent(int index);	Obtain the component with specified index.

The Container hierarchy can be divided into two categories:

(i) Panel classes

(ii) Window classes

(i) Panel classes

A Panel is the basic building block of an applet. Actually Applet class is not part of the java.awt package. Applet is contained in the java.applet package. Panel is not an abstract class but a subclass of Container and superclass of the Applet class and can be instantiated. Panel provides a multipurpose container with no special features. The default layout for a Panel is FlowLayout. Panels provide a convenient method of forming composite controls.

Constructors used

Constructor	Description
Panel()	Create a new Panel.

Methods Used

Methods	Description
add(Component c)	Add the component to the panel.
setLocation()	Sets the location of the panel.
setSize()	Sets the size of the panel.
setPreferredSize()	Sets the preferred size of the panel
setBounds()	Sets the bounds of the panel.

(ii) Window classes

Window class is derived from the Container class. It provides a top-level window on the screen, without borders and menu bar. Although it is not an abstract class but a subclass of Container and root class for two very useful classes: Frame and Dialog. We can create Window objects. These Window objects can have their own titles and menus and can be resizable. The default layout manager for a Window is BorderLayout.

Methods	Description
getToolkit()	Get the toolkit of window.
getWarningString()	Get the warning message.
pack()	Widow is packed using this method.
toBack()	Shift the window to the back.
toFront()	Shift the window to front.

```
import java.awt.*;
import java.awt.event.*;
    public class AppWin extends Frame
{
    public AppWin ()
    {
    super("ApplicationWindow");
    setSize(200, 200);
    addWindowListener(new WindowAdapter()
    {
      public void windowClosing(WindowEvent we)
      {
      setVisible(false);
      dispose();
      System.exit(0);
    }
  });
}
public static void main(String[] args)
{
    AppWin aw = new AppWin();
    aw.setVisible(true);
  }
}
```

```
Command Prompt - java AppWin

P:\java>javac AppWin.java

P:\java>java AppWin
_
```

```
//get the toolkit of window
import java.awt.*;
import java.awt.event.*;
public class AppWin extends Frame
{
      public AppWin ()
      {
      super("Application Window");
      setSize(200, 200);
      addWindowListener(new WindowAdapter()
      {
      public void windowClosing(WindowEvent we)
      {
      setVisible(false);
      dispose();
      System.exit(0);
   }
   });
 }
public static void main(String[] args)
{
      AppWin aw = new AppWin();
      aw.setVisible(true);
System.out.println(aw.getToolkit());
   }
}
```

```
Command Prompt - java AppWin

D:\>javac AppWin.java

D:\>java AppWin
sun.awt.windows.WToolkit@1270b73
_
```

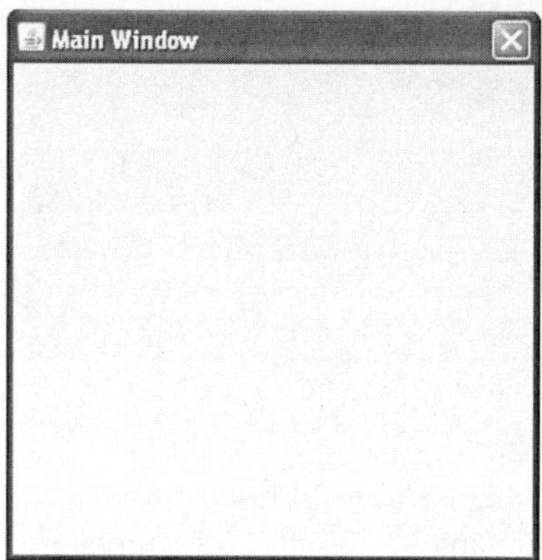

9.6.13 Dialog

A Dialog is an extension of the Window class. A Dialog is a Window that accepts input from the user. The state of a Dialog is by default false, it is constructed in an invisible state, it is shown using setVisible() with the argument true. When Dialog is no longer required then it can be hidden by using setVisible() method with the argument false. The default layout manager of Dialog is BorderLayout. It implements the Open/Save dialog provided by the native windowing system.

Constructors used

Constructor	**Description**
Dialog(Frame f)	Create a new dialog.
Dialog(Frame f, String title)	Create a new dialog with specified title.
Dialog(Frame f, Boolean model)	Create a new dialog with modality.
Dialog(Frame f, String title, Boolean model)	Create a new dialog with specified title and modelity.

Methods Used

Methods	**Description**
setTitle(String title)	Set the title of the Dialog.
getTitle()	Get the title of the Dialog.
setModel(Boolean modality)	Set the Model of the Dialog.
isModel()	Get the Model of the Dialog.
setVisible(Boolean visibility)	Set the visibility of the Dialog.
isVisible()	Return true, if Dialog is visible.
setResizable(Boolean state)	Determine the Dialog can be resized by the user.
isResizable()	Return true, if Dialog is resized.
toFront	Move the window above to any other window.
toBack	Move the window behind the other window.

```
import java.awt.*;
import java.awt.event.*;
class F1 extends Frame
{
   Button b1,b2;
   F1()
   {
      setLayout(null);
      this.setTitle("Main Window");
      this.setSize(700,700);
      this.addWindowListener(new WindowAdapter(){public void
            windowClosing(WindowEvent e){System.exit(0);}});
      b1=new Button("Open");
      b1.setBounds(50,50,100,30);
      this.add(b1);
      b1.addActionListener(new ActionListener(){public void
          actionPerformed(ActionEvent e){b1_Click();}});
   }
   void b1_Click()
   {
      F2 f=new F2(this);
      f.setVisible(true);
      b1.setLabel("Click");
   }
}
class F2 extends Dialog
{
   Button b1,b2;
   F2(Frame parent)
   {
      super(parent,true);
      setLayout(null);
      this.setTitle("Main Window");
      this.setSize(300,300);
      this.addWindowListener(new WindowAdapter(){public void
            windowClosing(WindowEvent e){setVisible(false);}});
   }
}
class dialog
{
   public static void main(String[] ar)
   {
      (new F1()).setVisible(true);
   }
}
```

9.6.14 FileDialog

A FileDialog is used to interact with the filesystem and provides a prebuilt Dialog boxes. We will primarily use FileDialog with applications since there is no guarantee that an applet can interact with the local filesystem.

There are two design approaches to using the Dialogs within an application.

(i) Create all the windows in an invisible state when the application initializes itself. The particular windows are then shown in response to the user's actions and are subsequently hidden when these windows are no longer required.

(ii) Not to create any windows upon initialization but when it is required then create each time and destroy them when they are no longer required.

The FileDialog can be created in two modes: open a file or save a file. The looking style of both the dialog boxes is similar but performs slightly differently. The difference is only the name of button (open or save). The Save button of the dialog box notifies the user that a file exists if a filename is given for a preexisting file.

Constructors used

Constructor	Description
FileDialog(Frame f)	Create a new filedialog.
FileDialog(Frame f, String title)	Create a new filedialog with specified title.
FileDialog(Frame f, String title, int type)	Create a new filedialog with specified title and type.

The int type has two types.

FileDialog.LOAD- select a file for reading.

FileDialog.SAVE- select a file for writing.

Methods Used

Methods	Description
setTitle(String title)	Set the title of the FileDialog.
getTitle()	Get the title of the FileDialog.
getFile()	Return the file name
getDirectory()	Return the Directory name

The following code is represented for both the open and save cases:

```
// File Open Dialog...
FileDialog openFileDialog;
openFileDialog = new FileDialog(this,"Open File", FileDialog.LOAD);
// File Save Dialog...
FileDialog saveFileDialog;
saveFileDialog = new FileDialog(this,"Save File", FileDialog.SAVE);
import java.awt.*;
import java.awt.event.*;
class F1 extends Frame
{
   Button b1,b2;
   F1()
   {
      setLayout(null);
      this.setTitle("Main Window");
      this.setSize(700,700);
      this.addWindowListener(new WindowAdapter(){public void
               windowClosing(WindowEvent e){System.exit(0);}});
      b1=new Button("Open");
      b1.setBounds(50,50,100,30);
      this.add(b1);
      b1.addActionListener(new ActionListener(){public void
```

```
                actionPerformed(ActionEvent e){b1_Click();}});
    }
    void b1_Click()
    {
        FileDialog fd=new FileDialog(this,"Save as...",FileDialog.LOAD);
        fd.setVisible(true);
    }
}
class filedialog
{
    public static void main(String[] ar)
    {
        (new F1()).setVisible(true);
    }
}
```

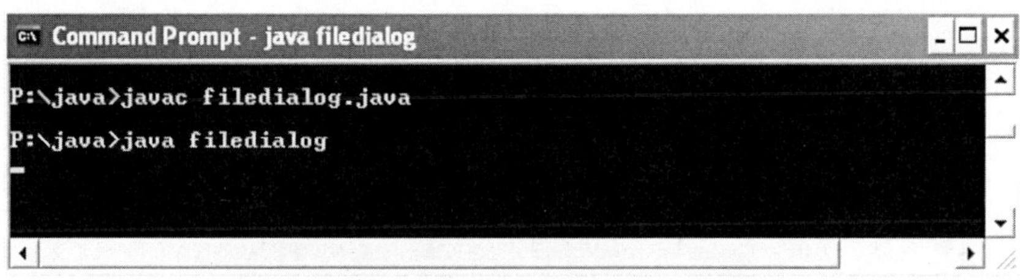

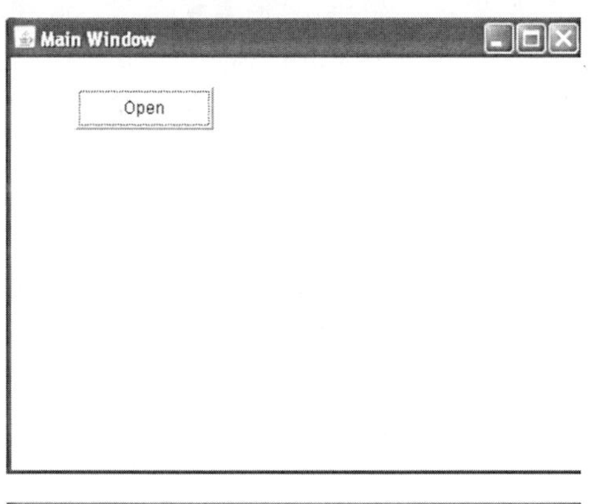

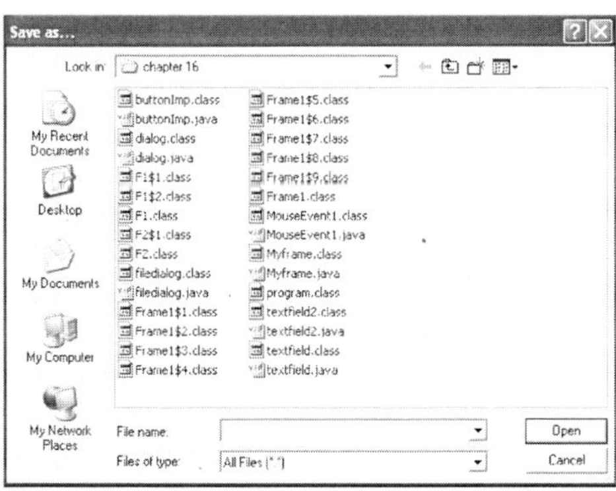

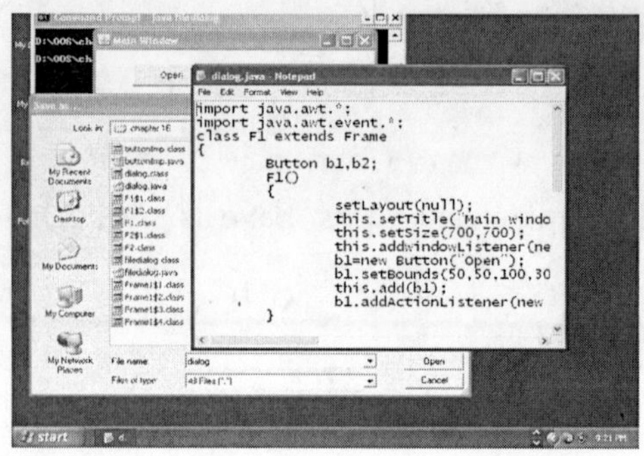

```
import java.awt.*;
import java.awt.event.*;
import java.io.*;
class F1 extends Frame
{
   Button b1,b2;
   TextArea ta=new TextArea();
   F1()
   {
      setLayout(null);
      this.setTitle("Main Window");
      this.setSize(700,700);
      this.addWindowListener(new WindowAdapter(){public void
            windowClosing(WindowEvent e){System.exit(0);}});
      b1=new Button("Open");
      b1.setBounds(10,30,100,30);
      this.add(b1);
      b1.addActionListener(new ActionListener(){public void
            actionPerformed(ActionEvent e){b1_Click();}});
      ta.setBounds(10,90,600,600);
      Font f=new Font("Arial",Font.PLAIN,18);
      ta.setFont(f);
      this.add(ta);
   }
   void b1_Click()
   {
      FileDialog fd=new FileDialog(this,"Open as...",FileDialog.LOAD);
      fd.setVisible(true);
      String s1=fd.getDirectory()+fd.getFile();
      try{
         FileReader fr=new FileReader(s1);
         String data="";
         int x=fr.read();
```

```
            while(x>=0)
            {
                data=data+(char)x;
                x=fr.read();
            }
            ta.setText(data);
        }catch(Exception e){}

    }
}
class filedialog2
{
    public static void main(String[] ar)
    {
        (new F1()).setVisible(true);
    }
}
```

Command Prompt - java filedialog2

```
P:\java>javac filedialog2.java

P:\java>java filedialog2
_
```

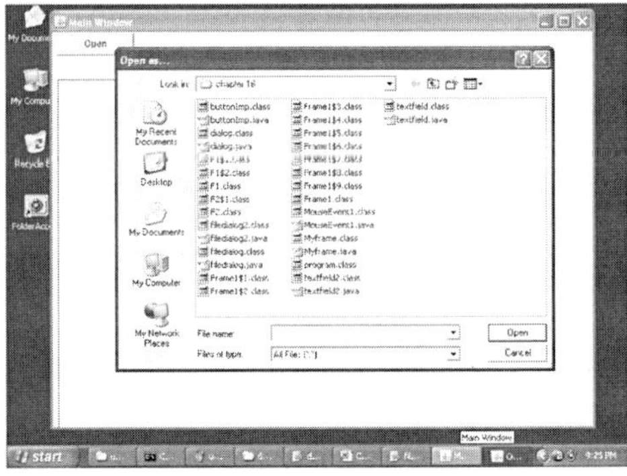

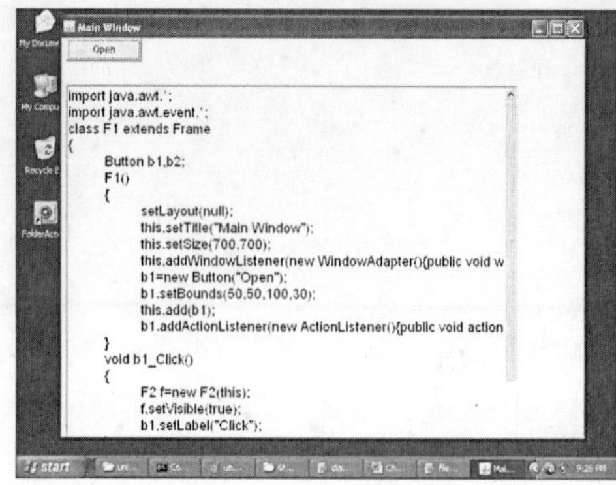

9.6.15 Menus

Most modern user interfaces are using menus. Java supports menus. Java provides several classes that allow menu bars to be constructed and attached to a Frame window. Java menus look like the menus in the windowing environment under which the program runs. Menus can only appear within a Frame. A Java Menu has three parts: MenuBar, Menu and MenuItem. MenuItems are added to Menu, Menu objects are added to MenuBar and MenuBar Object is added to Frame. MenuItem can be selected by the user with a click of a mouse.

Constructors used

Constructor	Description
Menu()	Create a new Menu
Menu(String name)	Name is the name of the Menu selection.
Menu(String name, Boolean stae)	If state is true, the Menu can be removed.
MenuItem()	Create a new MenuItem.
MenuItem(String name)	Name is the name of the MenuItem selection.
CheckboxMenuItem()	Create a new Checkbox MenuItem.
CheckboxMenuItem(String name)	Create a new Checkbox MenuItem with name specified.
CheckboxMenuItem(String name, Boolean state)	Create a new Checkbox MenuItem with name specified and if state is true then checkbox entry is initially checked.

Methods Used

Methods	Description
setEnabled(Boolean state)	If true the MenuItem is enabled.
isEnabled(Boolean state)	Return true, if MenuItem is enabled.
setLabel(String name)	Set the name of MenuItem.
getLabel()	Get the name of MenuItem
add()	Add the MenuItem to the menu or menu to the MenuBar.
setState(Boolean state)	Set the state of CheckboxMenuItem.
getState()	Get the state of CheckboxMenuItem.

Following steps are used to add MenuBar to Frame:

(i) Create a MenuBar object as follows.
MenuBar mb = new MenuBar();

(ii) Create a Menu Object as follows.
Menu menu = new Menu("File");

(iii) Add the MenuItem object to the Menu from top to bottom as follows.
menu.add(new MenuItem("Open"));
menu.add(new CheckboxMenuItem("Save"));

(iv) Add the Menu to the MenuBar.
menubar.add(menu);

(v) Set MenuBar to the Frame by using the method setMenuBar().
frame.setMenuBar(mb);

For Example:

```
import java.awt.*;
public class menu
{
      public static void main(String[] args)
      {
      Frame f = new Frame("Menu");
      f.setSize(300, 300);
      MenuBar mb=new MenuBar();
      Menu menu=new Menu("File");
      MenuItem m1=new MenuItem("New");
      MenuItem m2=new MenuItem("Open");
      menu.add(m1);
      menu.add(m2);
      mb.add(menu);
      f.setMenuBar(mb);
      f.setVisible(true);
   }
}
```

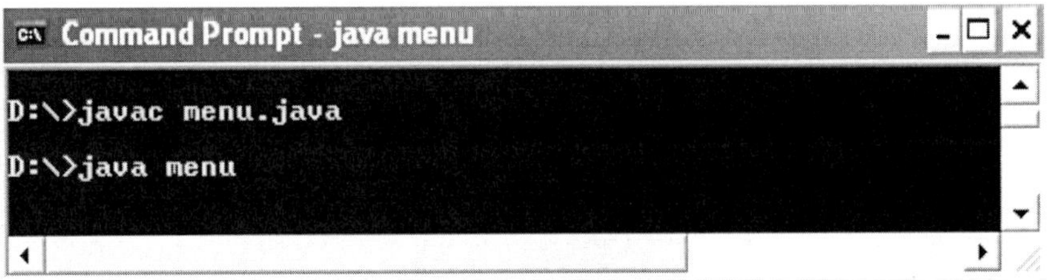

Command Prompt - java menu

```
D:\>javac menu.java

D:\>java menu
```

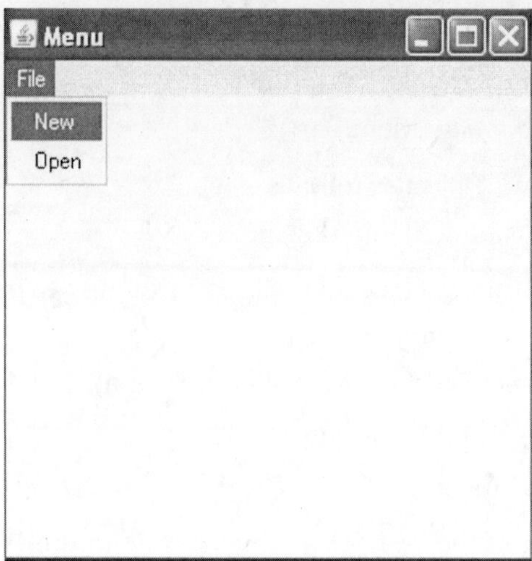

The program code given below creates an application window with a menu bar.

```
import java.awt.*;
import java.awt.event.*;

public class MenuApp extends Frame
{
   public MenuApp()
{
   super("Menu Application");
   setSize(300, 300);
filem fm = new filem(this);
   HelpMenu helpMenu = new HelpMenu(this);
   MenuBar mb = new MenuBar();
   mb.add(fm);
   mb.add(helpMenu);
   setMenuBar(mb);
   addWindowListener(new WindowAdapter()
{
   public void windowClosing(WindowEvent e)
{
      exit();
      }
   });
 }

public void exit()
{
   setVisible(false);
   dispose();
```

```
   System.exit(0);
}
public static void main(String args[])
{
   MenuApp w = new MenuApp();
   w.setVisible(true);
   }
}
class filem extends Menu implements ActionListener
{
   MenuApp mw;
   public filem(MenuApp m)
{
   super("File");
   mw = m;
   MenuItem mi;
   add(mi = new MenuItem("Open"));
   mi.addActionListener(this);
   add(mi = new MenuItem("Close"));
   mi.addActionListener(this);
   add(mi = new MenuItem("Exit"));
   mi.addActionListener(this);
}
public void actionPerformed(ActionEvent e)
{
   String item = e.getActionCommand();
   if (item.equals("Exit"))
   mw.exit();
   else
   System.out.println("Selected FileMenu " + item);
   }
}
class HelpMenu extends Menu implements ActionListener
{
   MenuApp mw;
   public HelpMenu(MenuApp m)
{
   super("Help");
   mw = m;
   MenuItem mi;
   add(mi = new MenuItem("Basics"));
```

```
    mi.addActionListener(this);
    add(mi = new MenuItem(“Advanced”));
    mi.addActionListener(this);
    addSeparator();
    add(mi = new CheckboxMenuItem(“Manual”));
    mi.addActionListener(this);
    Menu subMenu = new Menu(“Miscellaneous”);
    subMenu.add(mi = new MenuItem(“Help”));
    mi.addActionListener(this);
    subMenu.add(mi = new MenuItem(“Other Option”));
    mi.addActionListener(this);
    add(subMenu);
    }
public void actionPerformed(ActionEvent e)
{
    String item = e.getActionCommand();
    if (item.equals(“Basics”))
    System.out.println(“Basics Menu”);
    else if (item.equals(“Help”))
    System.out.println(“Help Menu”);
    }
}
```

```
Command Prompt - java MenuApp
P:\java>javac MenuApp.java
P:\java>java MenuApp
```

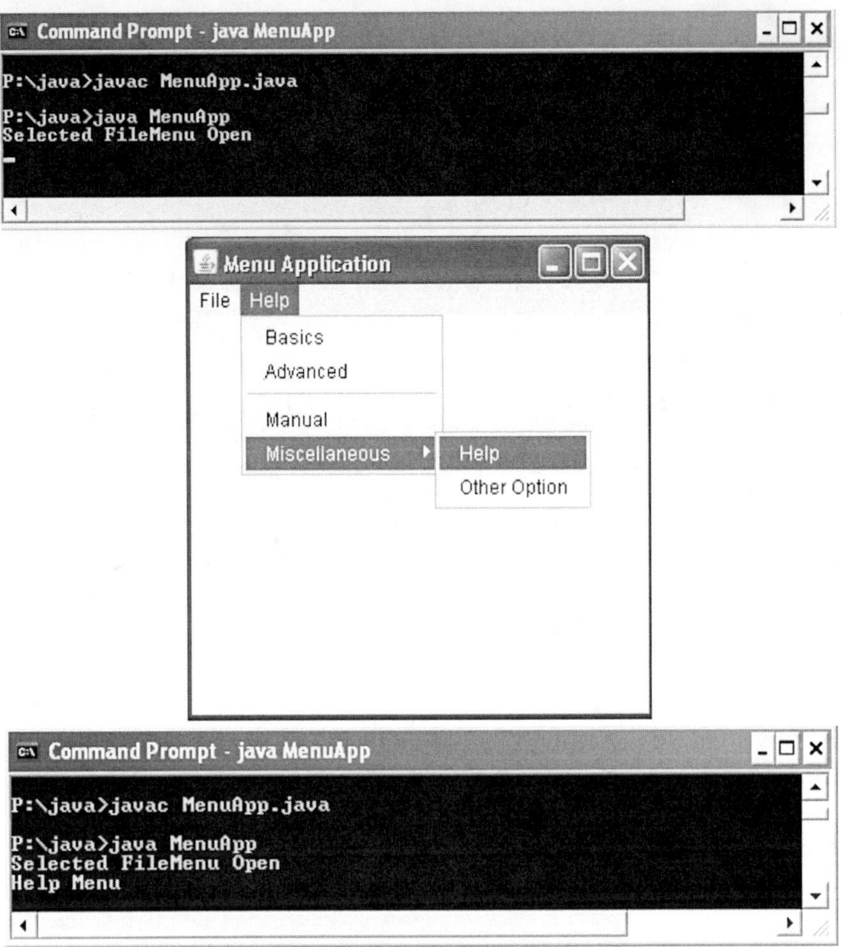

Menu Shortcuts

We can create a shortcut to any of the MenuItem with the help of MenuItem class. The MenuItem class provides a feature of menu shortcuts and speed keys. The menu shortcuts such as Ctrl-S which is used to give a save command to save the file rather than going to the File menu. The use of Ctrl for the shortcut key is defined by the method getMenuShortcutKeyMask(). For example creates menu items with speed keys i.e. Ctrl-P for Print and Shift-Ctrl-P for Print Preview:

```
filemenu.add (new MenuItem ("Print", new MenuShortcut('p')));
filemenu.add (new MenuItem ("Print Preview", new MenuShortcut('p', true)));
```

Constructors used

Constructor	Description
MenuItem(String name, MenuShortcut key)	Create a MenuItem with name and Shortcut Ctrl-Key.
MenuItem(String name, MenuShortcut (key, true))	Create a MenuItem with name and Shortcut Shift-Ctrl-Key.

Methods Used

Methods	Description
setShortcut(MenuShortcut shortcut)	Sets the shortcut for popup menu.
getShortcut()	Gets the shortcut.
deleteShortcut()	Delete the shortcut.

```
//program
import java.awt.*;
import java.awt.event.*;
public class MenuShort extends Frame
{
   public MenuShort()
{
   super("Menu Short cut Application");
   setSize(300, 300);
   MenuBar mb = new MenuBar();
   Menu top =new Menu("File");
   Menu sub =new Menu("Print");
   sub.add(new MenuItem("print",new MenuShortcut('P')));
   sub.add(new MenuItem("print preview",new MenuShortcut('P',true)));
   top.add(sub);
   mb.add(top);
   setMenuBar(mb);

}
public static void main(String[] args)
{
MenuShort ms=new MenuShort();
   ms.setVisible(true);
   }
}
```

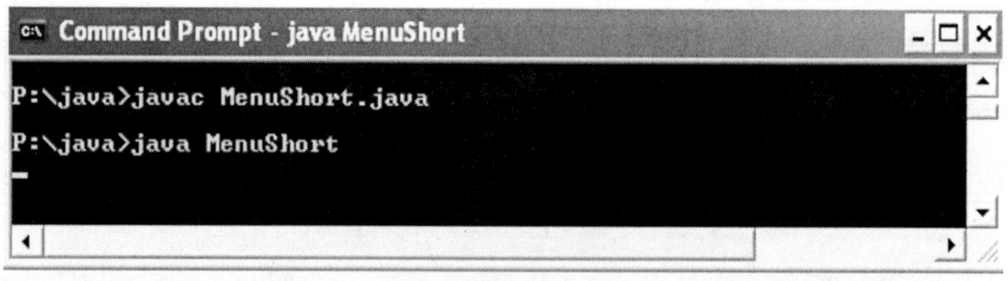

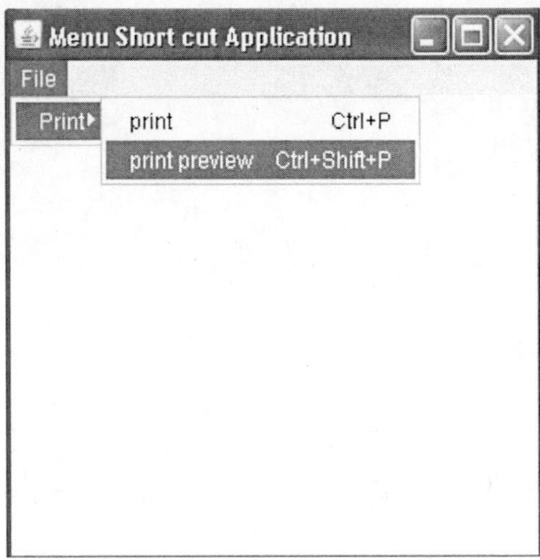

PopupMenu

The Pop-up Menu can not appear at the top of a Frame. But it can be popped over any component while generating the appropriate mouse event. Menu class can not add to an Applet but can add to the Frame. Pop-up menus can be used for component-level, context-sensitive menus. Pop-up menus can be associated with each Component can be its own popup menu. A PopupMenu class is similar to a Menu class as it contains MenuItem objects. The isPopupTrigger() method is used to trigger the MouseEvent that pops up the menu.

Constructors used

Constructor	Description
PopupMenu()	Creates an untitled popup menu.
PopupMenu(String title)	Creates a popup menu with the specified title.

Methods Used

Methods	Description
isPopupTrigger()	To trigger the MouseEvent.
addSeparator()	Adds a nonselectable horizontal line to the menu.
setShortcut(MenuShortcut shortcut)	Sets the shortcut for popup menu.
getShortcut()	Gets the shortcut.
deleteShortcut()	Delete the shortcut.
show(Component c, int x, int y)	Displays the popup menu at the specified location relative to the top-left corner of the component.

```
import java.awt.*;
import java.awt.event.*;
public class PopupMenuApp extends Frame
{
```

```
    Button b;
    TextField t;
    PopupAppMenu m;
    public PopupMenuApp()
{
    setSize(200, 200);
    b = new Button("Popup Menu Application");
    add(b, BorderLayout.NORTH);
    t = new TextField();
    t.setEditable(false);
    add(t, BorderLayout.SOUTH);
    m = new PopupAppMenu(this);
    add(m);
    b.addActionListener(new ActionListener(){
        public void actionPerformed(ActionEvent e){
        m.show(b, 25, 25);
        }
});
addMouseListener(new MouseAdapter()
{
    public void mousePressed(MouseEvent e)
{
    if (e.isPopupTrigger())
    m.show(e.getComponent(), e.getX(), e.getY());
    }
    public void mouseReleased(MouseEvent e)
{
    if (e.isPopupTrigger())
    m.show(e.getComponent(), e.getX(), e.getY());
    }
});
}
    public static void main(String[] args){
    PopupMenuApp app = new PopupMenuApp();
    app.setVisible(true);
    }
}
class PopupAppMenu extends PopupMenu implements ActionListener
{
    PopupMenuApp pm;
    public PopupAppMenu(PopupMenuApp pm)
{
```

```
super("File");
this.pm = pm;
MenuItem mi;
add(mi = new MenuItem("Cut"));
mi.addActionListener(this);
add(mi = new MenuItem("Copy"));
mi.addActionListener(this);
add(mi = new MenuItem("Paste"));
mi.addActionListener(this);
}
public void actionPerformed(ActionEvent e)
{
String s = e.getActionCommand();
pm.t.setText("Option Selected: " + s);
}
}
```

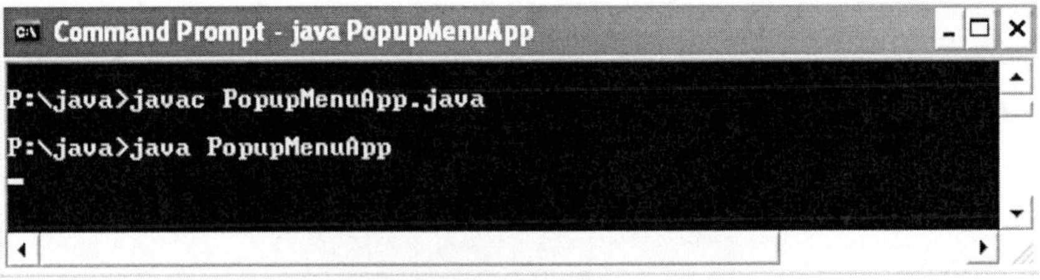
Command Prompt - java PopupMenuApp
P:\java>javac PopupMenuApp.java
P:\java>java PopupMenuApp

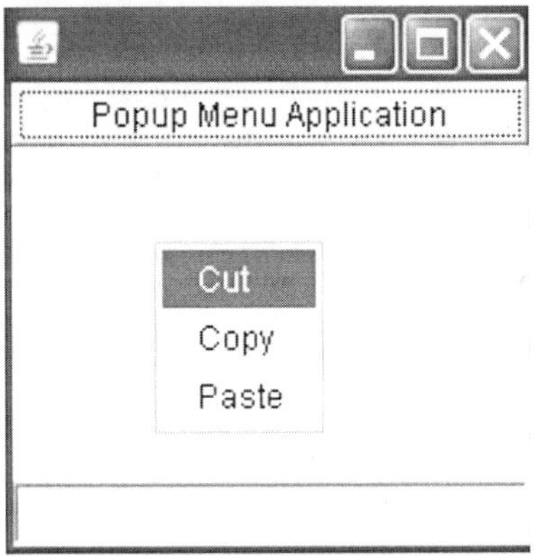
Popup Menu Application
Cut
Copy
Paste

9.7 LAYOUT MANAGERS

A layout manager is used to control the size and position of components inside a Container object. It is an object that allows you to format components on the screen in a platform-independent way. By default, Every Container has a layout manager, an object that implements the Layout Manager interface. If a Container's default layout manager doesn't suit your requirements, you can easily change it with another one. For example, a window is a container that contains components like buttons, choice and labels. The layout manager in effect for the window determines how the components are sized and positioned inside the window.

Methods Used

Methods	Description
setLayout (objectOfLayoutManager);	Sets the layout manager.
getMinimumSize()	Gets the minimum size of layout.
getMaximumSize()	Gets the maximum size of layout.
preferredSize()	Gets the preferred size of layout.
pack()	Sets the window's size so it is as small as possible.
setLocation()	Sets the location.

Types of Layout Manager

The java.awt package provides the following predefined layout managers that implement the java.awt.LayoutManager interface. It is easy to use the container. The setLayout method is used to change the layout manager and you can define your own layout manager by implementing the java.awt.LayoutManager interface.

(i) java.awt.FlowLayout

(ii) java.awt.GridLayout

(iii) java.awt.BorderLayout

(iv) java.awt.CardLayout

(v) java.awt.GridBagLayout

9.7.1 FlowLayout

FlowLayout is the default layout manager for all Applets and Panels. It places all panel components in rows according to the width of the panel and the number of components and size of the components. It simply lays out the components from left to right, if first row is complete then starting new rows if necessary. You start at row one, column one, move across the row until it's full and then continue on to the next row. If we resize an applet then the flow of component will change based upon the new width and height.

Constructors used

Constructor	Description
public FlowLayout()	Create a new flowlayout with centerd alignment and leaving a horizontal and vertical gap of 5 pixels.
public FlowLayout(int alignment)	Create a new flowlayout with specified alignment and leaving a horizontal and vertical gap of 5 pixels.
Public FlowLayout(int alignment, int hGap, int vGap)	Create a new flowlayout with specified alignment and leaving a horizontal and vertical gap as specified.

The alignment argument must have the value FlowLayout.LEFT, FlowLayout. RIGHT or FlowLayout.CENTER, FlowLayout.LEADING, FlowLayout.TRAILING. The hGap and vGap arguments specify the number of pixels to put between components. If you don't enter a gap value, by default FlowLayout takes 5 pixels for the gap value.

Methods Used

Methods	Description
getAlignment ()	The getAlignment() method retrieves the current alignment of the FlowLayout
setAlignment (int alignment)	Changes the FlowLayout alignment to alignment.
getHgap ()	retrieves the current horizontal gap setting
setHgap (int hgap)	Changes the current horizontal gap setting to hgap.
getVgap ()	Retrieves the current vertical gap setting.
setVgap (int hgap)	Changes the current vertical gap setting to vgap.

```
//Program
import java.awt.*;
import java.awt.event.*;
import java.applet.*;
public class flowLayoutManager extends Applet
{
    Button button1;
    Button button2;
    Button button3;
    Button button4;
    Button button5;
        public void init()
        {
            FlowLayout f=new FlowLayout();
            this.setLayout(f);
            button1 = new Button("Button 1");
            button2 = new Button("Button 2");
            button3 = new Button("Button 3");
            button4 = new Button("Button 4");
            button5 = new Button("Button 5");
            this.add(button1);
            this.add(button2);
            this.add(button3);
            this.add(button4);
            this.add(button5);
            }
    }
/*<applet code=flowLayoutManager.class width=300 height=300></applet>*/
```

```
Command Prompt - appletviewer flowLayoutManager.java

P:\java>javac flowLayoutManager.java

P:\java>appletviewer flowLayoutManager.java
```

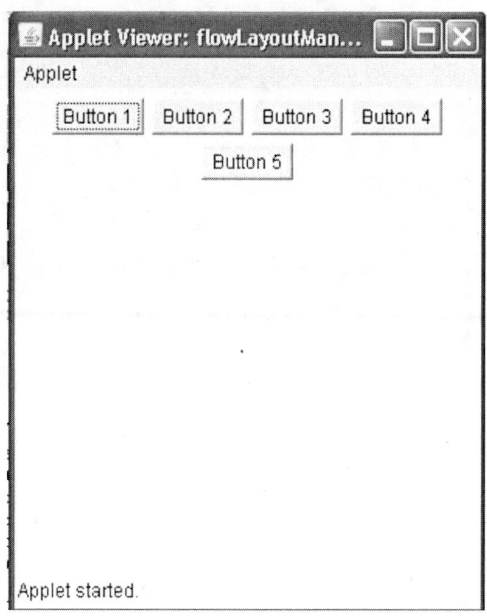

9.7.2 GridLayout

The Grid layout arranges components into a grid of rows and columns. Each row and each column in a grid layout will be the same size based on the largest component in the grid. The overall area available to the layout is divided into cells that are equally between the number of rows and the number of columns. Most components will be expanded to the size of the cells. GridLayout can resize or reposition objects after adding or removing components. Whenever the area is resized, the components within it are resized automatically.

Constructors used

Constructor	Description
GridLayout(int rows, int columns)	Creates a new grid layout with specified rows and columns.
GridLayout(int rows, int columns, int hgap, int vgap)	Creates a new grid layout with specified rows and columns and horizontal and vertical gap.

Methods Used

Methods	Description
getColumns ()	Retrieves the current column setting, which may differ from the number of columns displayed.
setColumns (int columns)	Changes the current column setting to columns.
getRows ()	Retrieves the current row setting; this may differ from the number of rows displayed.
setRows (int rows)	changes the current row setting to rows.
getHgap ()	retrieves the current horizontal gap setting
setHgap (int hgap)	Changes the current horizontal gap setting to hgap.
getVgap ()	Retrieves the current vertical gap setting.
setVgap (int hgap)	Changes the current vertical gap setting to vgap.

```
//Program
import java.awt.*;
import java.awt.event.*;
import java.applet.*;
public class gridLayoutManager extends Applet
{
   Button button1;
   Button button2;
   Button button3;
   Button button4;
   Button button5;
      public void init()
      {
      GridLayout f=new GridLayout(3,2);
      this.setLayout(f);
      button1 = new Button("Button 1");
      button2 = new Button("Button 2");
      button3 = new Button("Button 3");
      button4 = new Button("Button 4");
      button5 = new Button("Button 5");
      this.add(button1);
      this.add(button2);
      this.add(button3);
      this.add(button4);
      this.add(button5);
      }
}
```

/*<applet code=gridLayoutManager.class width=300 height=300></applet>*/

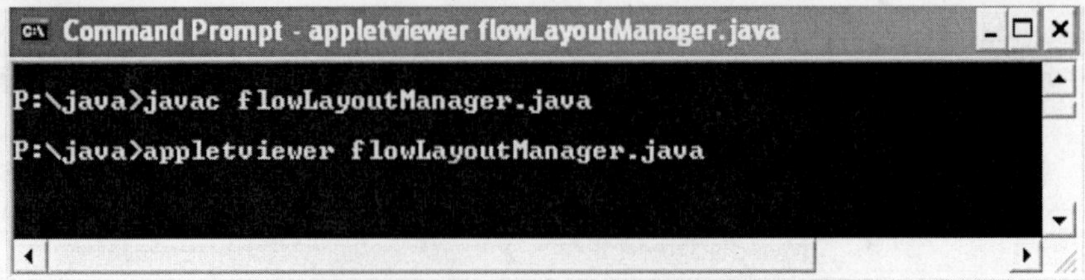

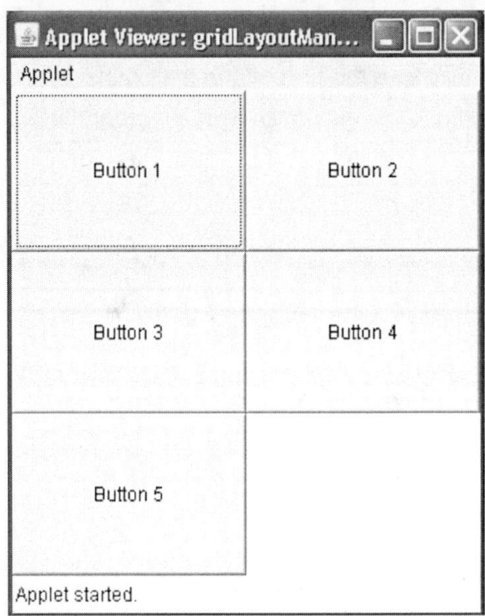

9.7.3 BorderLayout

BorderLayout is the default layout manager for all Windows like Frames and Dialogs. BorderLayout provides five areas to hold components. The names of these areas are North, South, East, West, and Center. The North and South areas are useful for toolbars and status bars. We can put only a single component in each area. When we add a component to the layout, we must specify which area to place it in. The order in which components are added to the screen is not important, although you can have only one component in each area. The following method is used to add the component.

add(Component c, int alignment)

Where alignment may be one of these constants:

- BorderLayout.NORTH
- BorderLayout.SOUTH
- BorderLayout.EAST
- BorderLayout.WEST
- BorderLayout.CENTER

Constructors used

Constructor	Description
BorderLayout()	Creates a new border layout.
BorderLayout (int hgap, int vgap)	Create a BorderLayout with a horizontal gap of hgap and vertical gap of vgap.

Methods Used

Methods	Description
getHgap ()	retrieves the current horizontal gap setting
setHgap (int hgap)	Changes the current horizontal gap setting to hgap.
getVgap ()	Retrieves the current vertical gap setting.
setVgap (int hgap)	Changes the current vertical gap setting to vgap.

```
//Program
import java.awt.*;
import java.awt.event.*;
import java.applet.*;
public class BorderLayoutManager extends Applet
{
   Button button1;
   Button button2;
   Button button3;
   Button button4;
   Button button5;
      public void init()
      {
      BorderLayout f=new BorderLayout();
      this.setLayout(f);
      button1 = new Button("Button 1");
      button2 = new Button("Button 2");
      button3 = new Button("Button 3");
      button4 = new Button("Button 4");
      button5 = new Button("Button 5");
      this.add(button1,BorderLayout.NORTH);
      this.add(button2,BorderLayout.SOUTH);
      this.add(button3,BorderLayout.EAST);
      this.add(button4,BorderLayout.WEST);
      this.add(button5,BorderLayout.CENTER);
      }
}
/*<applet code=BorderLayoutManager.class width=300 height=300></applet>*/
```

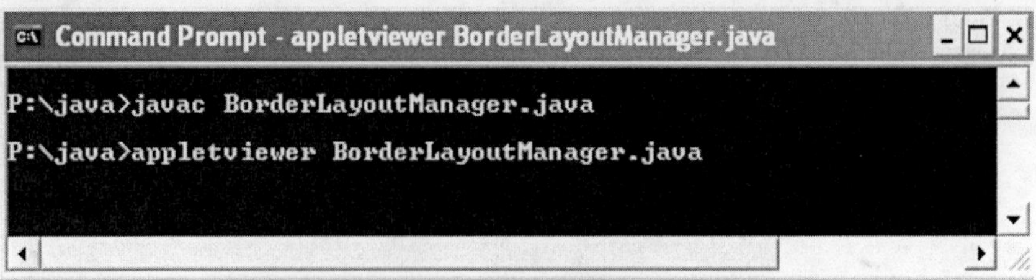

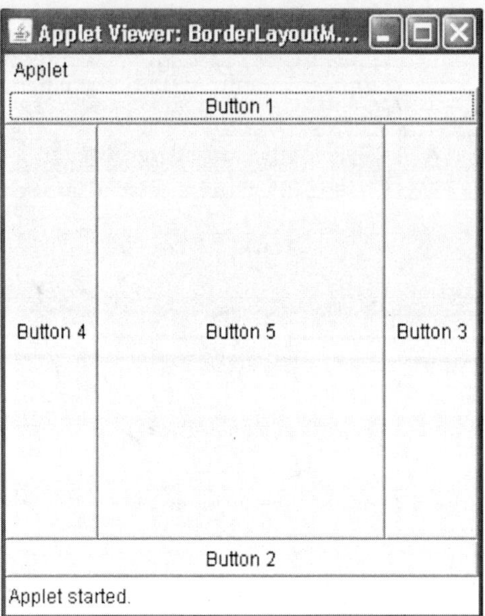

9.7.4 CardLayout

A CardLayout usually manages two or more components, displaying one of them at a time and hiding the others. The card layout uses a panel to display one out of many possible components. The CardLayout manages a group of Panels. Each panel contains several components of its own. A program can use this layout to show a different component to different users. For example, the interface shown to an administrator might have additional functionality from the interface shown to a regular user. With card layout, our program can show the appropriate interface depending on the type of user.

The Card layout manages the components in a sequence and display the first or last component in that sequence explicitly. We can ask for the next or previous component in that sequence. In this way, we can cycle through the components very easily. We can control component display to give a name to each component. If we take this approach, the Card layout allows us to select the component to be displayed using that name. We can add a component with a name as follows.

```
add(String name, Component c);
```

Constructors used

Constructor	Description
CardLayout()	Create a new card layout manager.
CardLayout (int hgap, int vgap)	Create a CardLayout with a horizontal gap of hgap and vertical gap of vgap.

Methods Used

Methods	Description
first(Container)	Display the first card.
last(Container)	Display the last card.
next(Container)	Display the next card.
previous(Container)	Display the previous card.
show(Container, String)	Display the card.
getHgap ()	retrieves the current horizontal gap setting
setHgap (int hgap)	Changes the current horizontal gap setting to hgap.
getVgap ()	Retrieves the current vertical gap setting.
setVgap (int hgap)	Changes the current vertical gap setting to vgap.

```
//Program
import java.awt.*;
import java.awt.event.*;
import java.applet.*;
public class cardLayoutManager extends Applet implements ActionListener
{
    Button button1;
    Button button2;
    Button button3;
    CardLayout crd;
    Panel p,p1,p2;
    public void init()
      {
      crd=new CardLayout();

      button1 = new Button("next");
      button2 = new Button("card1");
      button3 = new Button("card2");
setBackground(Color.yellow);
      p=new Panel();
      p1=new Panel();
      p2=new Panel();
      p.setLayout(crd);
p.setBackground(Color.red);
      add(button1);
```

```
        p1.add(button2);
        p2.add(button3);
        p.add(p1,"Hi");
        p.add(p2,"Hello");
    add(p);
        button1.addActionListener(this);
    }
    public void actionPerformed(ActionEvent e)
    {
        if(e.getSource()==button1)
        {
        crd.next(p);
        crd.show(p,"Hello");
        }
    }
    }
    /*
    <applet code="cardLayoutManager" width=300 height=300>
    </applet>
    */
```

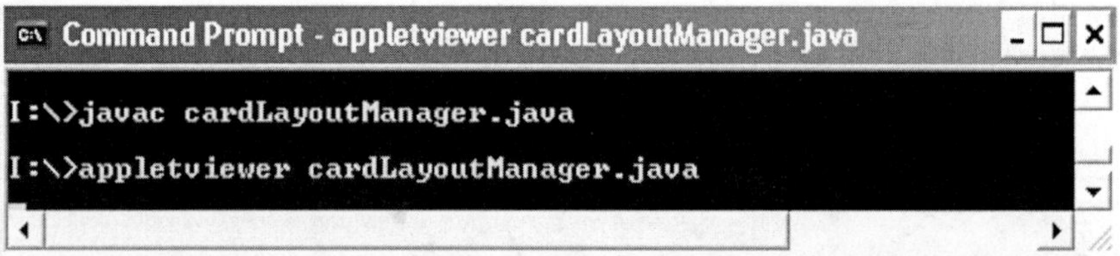

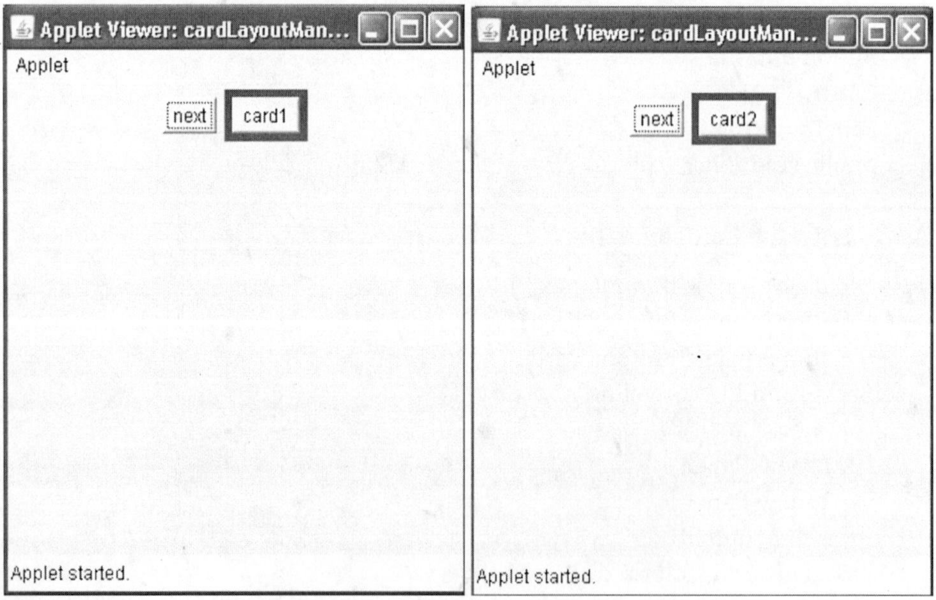

```
Command Prompt - appletviewer cardLayoutManager.java
I:\>javac cardLayoutManager.java
I:\>appletviewer cardLayoutManager.java
```

Applet Viewer: cardLayoutMan... — Applet — next | card1 — Applet started.

Applet Viewer: cardLayoutMan... — Applet — next | card2 — Applet started.

9.7.5 GridBagLayout

The Grid bag layout (like grid layout) arranges components into a grid of rows and columns. AWT provides the most flexible and complex layout manager called GridBagLayout. The GridBagLayout manager divides its container into an array of flexible cells unlike the cells of a Grid layout manager. Unlike the grid layout, the rows and columns are not constrained to be equal size. Essentially, GridBagLayout places components in cells in a grid and then uses the preferred sizes of components to determine how big the cells should be. With the GridBagLayout, we can organize components in multiple rows and columns. Different cell rows can have different heights and different cell columns can have different widths.

GridBagConstraints object is represents a set of constraints that defined a display area which provides a way in which it fills. These constraints are as follows.

(i) gridx/gridy
(ii) gridwidth/gridheight
(iii) fill
(iv) anchor
(v) ipadx/ipady
(vi) insets

Constructors used

Constructor	Description
GridBagLayout()	Creates a new grid bag layout.

Methods Used

Methods	Description
getLayoutOrigin ()	Returns the origin for the GridBagLayout.
getLayoutDimensions ()	Returns the array of layout dimensions.
getLayoutWeights ()	Returns the array of layout weights.

(i) gridx and gridy – To Choose a cell

A grid is created according to the cells that you add to it. With the help of gridx and gridy, we can choose where we want to place a given component.

gridbagconstraint.gridx = 2;
gridbagconstraint.gridy = 2;

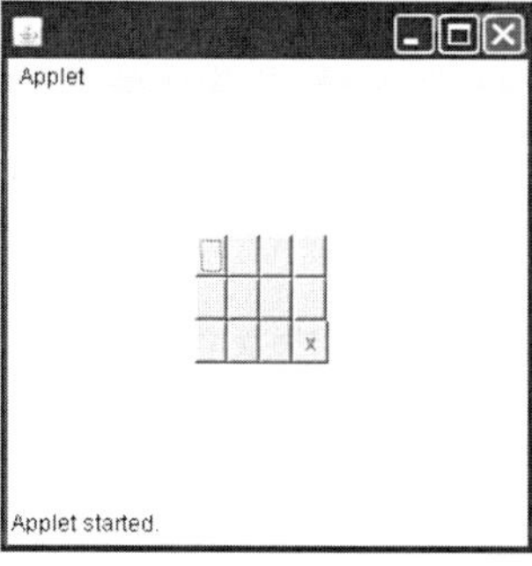

(ii) gridwidth and gridheight - To Control the size of a component

A component may use one or more cells, not just one. So we want to control the size of a component. This way, you can create very interesting layouts, not just chessboard-alike ones.

```
Gridbagconstraint.gridx = 2;
Gridbagconstraint.gridy = 2;
Gridbagconstraint.gridwidth = 2;
Gridbagconstraint.gridheight = 3;
```

z	z	z	

(iii) fill- To Control the stretch in cell

Using fill, we can determine whether a component to fill the available space, either horizontally, vertically or both.

Constants:

(i) GridBagConstraints.HORIZONTAL

(ii) GridBagConstraints.VERTICAL

(iii) GridBagConstraints.BOTH

(iv) GridBagConstraints.NONE

Example:

```
gridbagconstraint.fill = GridBagConstraints.HORIZONTAL;
```

HORIZONTAL	NONE

(iv) anchor - To Control the component position

anchor is used to control the position of cell. We find the corners of the cell where we want to place the component in. anchor is an int value that can use any of these constants.

(i) GridBagConstraints.CENTER

(ii) GridBagConstraints.NORTH

(iii) GridBagConstraints.NORTHEAST

(iv) GridBagConstraints.EAST

(v) GridBagConstraints.SOUTHEAST

(vi) GridBagConstraints.SOUTH

(vii) GridBagConstraints.SOUTHWEST

(viii) GridBagConstraints.WEST

(ix) GridBagConstraints.NORTHWEST

Example:

gridbagconstraint.anchor = GridBagConstraints.SOUTHEAST;

NW	*N*	*NE*
W	*C*	*E*
SW	*S*	*SE*

(v) weightx and weighty- To Allow rows and columns to stretch

This value applies only to rows and columns, not to individual cells. We can define the column (weightx) or the row (weighty) to stay still using a value of 0.

```
gridbagconstraint.weightx = 0;
```

If all columns have the value 0 and one has the value 1.0, that one will stretch to the maximum available space. Otherwise, we may consider the values to be percentages, for example:

```
gridbagconstraint.weightx = 25;
gridbagconstraint.gridx++;
gridbagconstraint.weightx =60;
```


(vi) insets

The setting of insets specifies the minimum space between the component and the edges of the component's display area. By default, the insets space is left blank, but it could be used to render a border and/or title. The inset setting takes a java.awt.insets object as its value.

```
//Example of Grid bag layout

import java.awt.*;
import java.awt.event.*;
import java.applet.*;
public class gridbagLayoutManager extends Applet
{
   public void init()
   {

   Frame f = new Frame("My Frame");
      f.setSize(300,150);
      GridBagConstraints gbc = new GridBagConstraints();
      GridBagLayout gbl = new GridBagLayout();
```

```
        f.setLayout(gbl);
        gbc.gridx = 0;
        gbc.gridy = 0;
        gbc.weightx = 150;
        gbc.fill = GridBagConstraints.HORIZONTAL;
        f.add(new Button("Tanweer"), gbc);
        gbc.fill = GridBagConstraints.BOTH;
        gbc.gridheight = 2;
        gbc.weightx = 20;
        gbc.gridx++;
        f.add(new Scrollbar(Scrollbar.VERTICAL), gbc);
        gbc.fill = GridBagConstraints.NONE;
        gbc.gridy = 1;
        gbc.gridx = 0;
        gbc.anchor = GridBagConstraints.WEST;
        f.add(new Button("AAtif"), gbc);
        f.setVisible(true);
    }
}
/*<applet code=gridbagLayoutManager.class width=300 height=300></
applet>*/
```

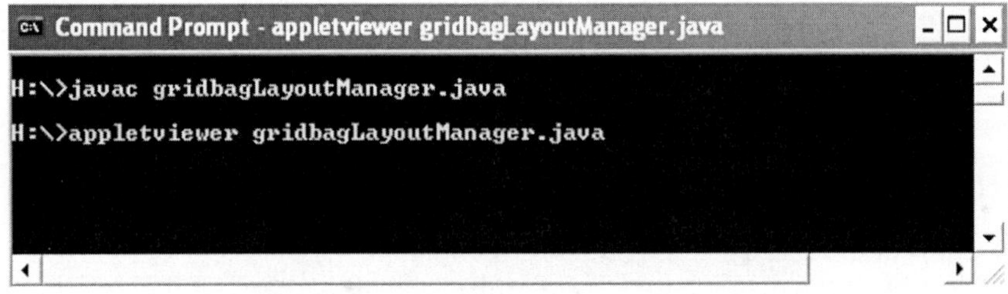

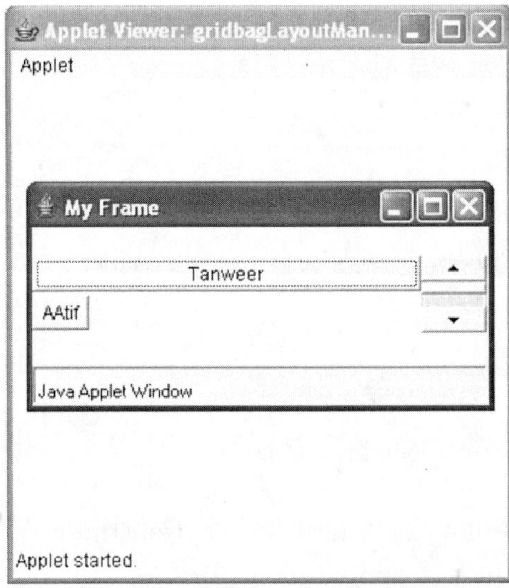

SUMMARY

The java.awt package provides a great deal of functionality and flexibility. The package goes well beyond the basics presented in this chapter. Do not be intimidated by the vast libraries available to you in Java. With the help of this book, you should get an excellent grasp of the java.awt, java.awt.image, java.awt.datatransfer, java.awt.event, and java.applet packages, along with some pieces of the proprietary sun.awt and sun.audio packages.Do not feel the need to read this book cover to cover. Pick the section that interests you most, where you feel you do not fully understand something, or where you have an immediate question to be answered and dive right in.

EXERCISE

1. What are layout managers? Define with example.
2. Define the following controls with examples.
   (i) Checkbox
   (ii) Choice
   (iii) Menu
   (iv) List
3. Define the component hierarchy of AWT.
4. Define gridBaglayout constraints.

*****

CHAPTER 10

GRAPHICS PROGRAMMING

A Graphics is the object of screen on which all primitive drawing takes place. Graphics brings life to applications. Java allows modification and creation of images using both awt and the newer java foundation classes (JFC 2D) architecture. The AWT supports a rich assortment of graphics methods that are drawn relative to a window. Graphics support a huge number of methods. We will almost always use the Graphics passed into a paint method when it is invoked by Java.

10.1 INTRODUCTION

Java contains a number of graphics primitives which are used to enable you to begin creating basic shapes and minimal on-screen graphics. Java needs to be made aware of the graphics object that is manipulating in order to draw an on-screen graphic. We start how to draw to the screen that is, how to produce lines, shapes and images with the built-in graphics primitive, how to print text using fonts, and how to use and modify color in our applets. The following points, we will discuss here.

(i) **Working of graphics system in Java:** Graphics system uses the Graphics class and the coordinate system to draw to the screen and how applets paint and repaint.

(ii) **Using graphics primitives:** including drawing and filling lines, ovals, rectangles, arcs and Strings.

(iii) **Setting fonts**: including how to draw characters and strings and how to find out the metrics of a given font for better layout.

(iv) **Setting colors:** including the Color class and how to set the foreground (drawing) and background color for your applet.

10.2 The Graphics Co-ordinate System

The graphical system uses a co-ordinate system that is used to specify how and where drawing operations take place. Java programs use an (x, y) coordinate system for all graphics operation. The x coordinate is the pixel distance from the left. The y coordinate is the pixel distance from the top. The coordinate system has the origin (0, 0) in the top-left corner. Positive values of x on X-axis are to the right and positive values of y on Y- axis are down. All pixel values are used as integers, no partial or fractional pixels.

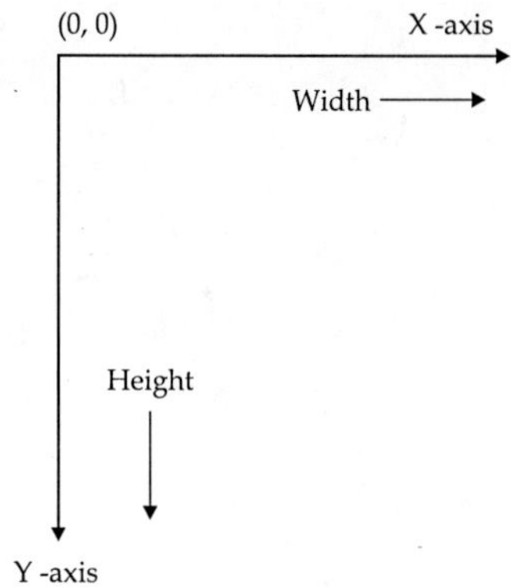

Figure 10.1: Graphics Co-ordinate System

When we have to draw an object on the screen, you call one of the drawing methods available in the `Graphics` class.

10.3 Java Color System

Java supports color in a portable, device-independent fashion. The Java color system is very similar to the physical system used by color monitors. The AWT color system allows you to specify any color you want. It forms unique colors by using varying intensities of the colors red, green, and blue. Therefore, Java colors are represented by the combinations of the numeric intensities of the primary colors (red, green, and blue). This color system is known as RGB (Red Green Blue) and is standard across most graphical computer systems. Color is encapsulated by the Color class. We can create our own colors, using one of the color constructors. The most commonly used are shown below:

Color(int red, int green, int blue)

This constructor takes three integers that specify the color as a mix of red, green and blue. These values must be between 0 and 255.

For example:

Color c=new Color(192,192,192); // light grey

Once we have created a color, we can use it to set the background and/or foreground color by using the setBackground( ) and/or setForeground( ) methods.

Table 10.1: RGB component values for some basic colors

Color	Red	Green	Blue
Red	255	0	0
Green	0	255	0
Blue	0	0	255
Yellow	255	255	0
Light Gray	192	192	192
Dark Gray	128	128	128
Purple	255	0	255
Black	0	0	0
White	255	255	255

We can obtain the red, green, and blue components of a color independently using the following methods.

int getRed( )
int getGreen( )
int getBlue( )

Each of these methods returns the RGB color component found in the invoking **Color** object in the lower 8 bits of an integer.

getRGB( )

To obtain a packed, RGB representation of a color, use **getRGB( )**, shown here:

int getRGB( )

Setting the Current Graphics Color

By default, graphics objects are drawn in the current foreground color. You can change this color by calling the **Graphics** method **setColor( )**:

void setColor(Color c)

Where, c specifies the new drawing color.

We can obtain the current color by calling **getColor( )**, shown below:

Color getColor( )

```
// color setting

import java.awt.*;
import java.applet.*;
public class setcolor extends Applet
{
public void paint(Graphics g)
{
Color x = new Color(255, 0, 0);
Color y = new Color(0, 255, 0);
Color z = new Color(0, 0, 255);
g.setColor(x);
g.drawLine(0, 30, 100, 30);
g.setColor(y);
g.drawLine(0, 50, 300, 50);
g.setColor(z);
g.drawLine(0, 80, 400, 80);
g.setColor(Color.red);
g.drawOval(10, 10, 100, 100);
}
}
/*
<applet code="setcolor" width=300 height=200>
</applet>
*/
```

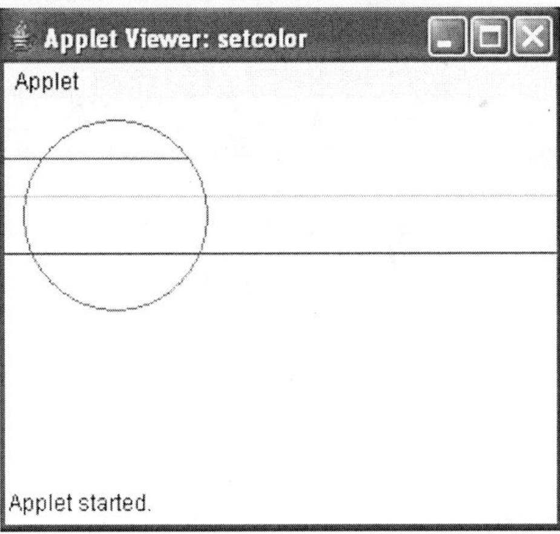

Working with Fonts

Fonts are encapsulated by the Font class. The AWT provides flexibility by abstracting font-manipulation operations and allowing for dynamic selection of fonts.

Constructors used:

Constructor	Description
Font(String fontname, int style, int size)	Creating a new Font

Here, fontname specifies the name of the desired font like Times new Roman, Sans Serif, Serif, Monospaced or other. The style of the font is specified by style. It may consist of one or more of these three constants: **Font.PLAIN**, **Font.BOLD**, and **Font.ITALIC**. To combine styles, OR them together. For example, **Font.BOLD | Font.ITALIC** specifies a bold, italics style. The size, in points, of the font is specified by size.

Methods used:

Method	Description
setFont(Font f)	Set the font
getFont( )	get the font
getFamily( )	Returns the name of the font family to which the invoking font belongs.
getFontName()	Returns the face name of the invoking font.

getName( )	Returns the logical name of the invoking font.
getSize( )	Returns the size, in points, of the invoking font.
getStyle( )	Returns the style values of the invoking font
isBold( )	Returns true if the font includes the BOLD style value. Otherwise, false is returned.
isItalic( )	Returns true if the font includes the ITALIC style value. Otherwise, false is returned.
isPlain( )	Returns true if the font includes the PLAIN style value. Otherwise, false is returned.
toString( ) Returns the string equivalent of the invoking font	Returns the string equivalent of the invoking font.
getAllFonts( )	Returns an array of Font objects for all of the available fonts

```
//program to set the fonts

import java.awt.*;
import java.applet.*;
public class setFonts extends Applet
{
Font f;
public void init()
{
f=new Font("Times New Roman", Font.BOLD, 20);
}

public void paint(Graphics g)
{
g.setFont(f);
g.setColor(Color.BLUE);
g.drawString("TANWEER ALAM",100,100);
}
}
/*
<applet code="setFonts" width=300 height=400>
</applet>
*/
```

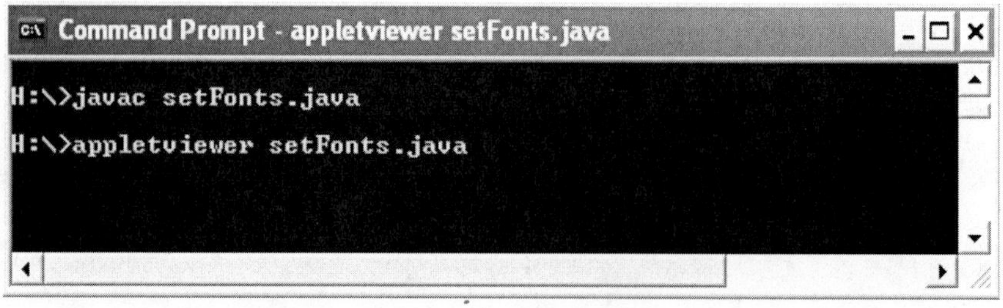

```
Command Prompt - appletviewer setFonts.java

H:\>javac setFonts.java

H:\>appletviewer setFonts.java
```

10.4 DRAWING AND FILLING

Filling a shape is just as easy as drawing it. You create the path using the standard path creation operators, but instead of calling stroke at the end, you invoke the fill operator. The fill operator will fill the path with the current ink settings.

Class Graphics

The Graphics class is the abstract base class for all graphics contexts that allow an application to draw onto components that are realized on various devices, as well as onto off-screen images.

A Graphics object encapsulates state information needed for the basic rendering operations that Java supports. This state information includes the following properties:

(i) The Component object on which to draw.

(ii) A translation origin for rendering and clipping coordinates.

(iii) The current clip.

(iv) The current color.

(v) The current font.

(vi) The current logical pixel operation function (XOR or Paint).

vii) The current XOR alternation color

Constructors used

Construct	Description
Graphics()	Constructs a new Graphics object.

Methods Used

Method	Description
translate(int x, int y)	Translates the origin of the graphics context to the point (x, y) in the current coordinate system.
toString()	Returns a String object representing this Graphics object's value.
setColor(Color c)	Sets this graphics context's current color to the specified color.
setFont(Font font)	Sets this graphics context's font to the specified font.
setPaintMode()	Sets the paint mode of this graphics context to overwrite the destination with this graphics context's current color.
setXORMode(Color c1)	Sets the paint mode of this graphics context to alternate between this graphics context's current color and the new specified color.
setClip(int x, int y, int width, int height)	Sets the current clip to the rectangle specified by the given coordinates.
setClip(Shape clip)	Sets the current clipping area to an arbitrary clip shape.
getColor()	Gets this graphics context's current color.
getFont()	Gets the current font.
getFontMetrics()	Gets the font metrics of the current font.
getFontMetrics(Font f)	Gets the font metrics for the specified font.
getClip()	Gets the current clipping area.
getClipBounds()	Returns the bounding rectangle of the current clipping area.
getClipBounds(Rectangle r)	Returns the bounding rectangle of the current clipping area.
finalize()	Disposes of this graphics context once it is no longer referenced.
fillRoundRect(int x, int y, int width, int height, int arcWidth, int arcHeight)	Fills the specified rounded corner rectangle with the current color.
fillRect(int x, int y, int width, int height)	Fills the specified rectangle.
fillRoundRect(int x, int y, int width, int height, int arcWidth, int arcHeight)	Fills the specified rounded corner rectangle with the current color.
fillPolygon(Polygon p)	Fills the polygon defined by the specified Polygon object with the graphics context's current color.
fillPolygon(int[] xPoints, int[] yPoints, int nPoints)	Fills a closed polygon defined by arrays of x and y coordinates.
fillOval(int x, int y, int width, int height)	Fills an oval bounded by the specified rectangle with the current color.
fillArc(int x, int y, int width, int height, int startAngle, int arcAngle)	Fills a circular or elliptical arc covering the specified rectangle.

fill3DRect(int x, int y, int width, int height, boolean raised)	Paints a 3-D highlighted rectangle filled with the current color.
drawString(String str, int x, int y)	Draws the text given by the specified string, using this graphics context's current font and color.
drawString(AttributedCharacterIterator iterator, int x, int y)	Draws the text given by the specified iterator, using this graphics context's current color.
drawRoundRect(int x, int y, int width, int height, int arcWidth, int arcHeight)	Draws an outlined round-cornered rectangle using this graphics context's current color.
drawRect(int x, int y, int width, int height)	Draws the outline of the specified rectangle.
drawPolyline(int[] xPoints, int[] yPoints, int nPoints)	Draws a sequence of connected lines defined by arrays of x and y coordinates.
drawPolygon(Polygon p)	Draws the outline of a polygon defined by the specified Polygon object.
drawPolygon(int[] xPoints, int[] yPoints, int nPoints)	Draws a closed polygon defined by arrays of x and y coordinates.
drawOval(int x, int y, int width, int height)	Draws the outline of an oval.
drawLine(int x1, int y1, int x2, int y2)	Draws a line, using the current color, between the points (x1, y1) and (x2, y2) in this graphics context's coordinate system.
drawImage(Image img, int x, int y, ImageObserver observer)	Draws as much of the specified image as is currently available.
drawChars(char[] data, int offset, int length, int x, int y)	Draws the text given by the specified character array, using this graphics context's current font and color.
drawArc(int x, int y, int width, int height, int startAngle, int arcAngle)	Draws the outline of a circular or elliptical arc covering the specified rectangle.
draw3DRect(int x, int y, int width, int height, boolean raised)	Draws a 3-D highlighted outline of the specified rectangle.
clearRect(int x, int y, int width, int height)	Clears the specified rectangle by filling it with the background color of the current drawing surface.
clipRect(int x, int y, int width, int height)	Intersects the current clip with the specified rectangle.
copyArea(int x, int y, int width, int height, int dx, int dy)	Copies an area of the component by a distance specified by dx and dy.
create()	Creates a new Graphics object that is a copy of this Graphics object.
create(int x, int y, int width, int height)	Creates a new Graphics object based on this Graphics object, but with a new translation and clip area.
dispose()	Disposes of this graphics context and releases any system resources that it is using.

The Graphics class provides a set of simple built-in graphics primitives for drawing, including lines, rectangles, polygons, ovals and arcs.

Syntax

The Graphics class is located in the **java.awt** package. To use the Graphics class, we have to pass a Graphics object in a components paint() method.

```
public void paint(Graphics g)
{
}
```

10.4.1 Drawing Lines

When we have to draw straight lines, use the drawLine() method. drawLine() method takes four arguments- the x and y coordinates of the starting point and the x and y coordinates of the ending point.

Syntax:

public abstract void drawLine(int x_1, int y_1, int x_2, int y_2)

Where (x_1, y_1) and (x_2, y_2) are the end points of a line.
x1 is the first point's x coordinate.
y1 is the first point's y coordinate.
x2 is the second point's x coordinate.
y2 is the second point's y coordinate.

Example:

The following applet draws twoseveral lines:

```
import java.awt.*;
import java.applet.*;
public class drawLines extends Applet
{
public void paint(Graphics g)
{
g.drawLine(0, 0, 100, 100);
g.drawLine(0, 100, 100, 0);
}
}
/*
<applet code="drawLines" width=200 height=200>
</applet>
*/
```

```
Command Prompt - appletviewer drawLines.java
H:\>javac drawLines.java
H:\>appletviewer drawLines.java
```

The output is as follows.

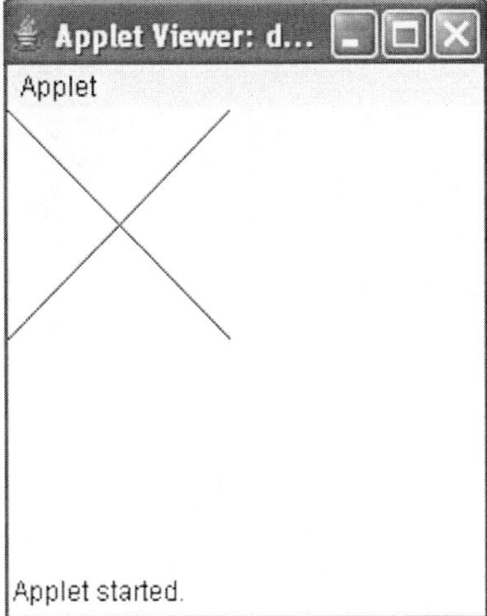

Another examples are as follows.

```
import java.awt.*;
import java.applet.*;

public class lines extends Applet
{
    void paint(Graphics g)
{
    g.setColor(Color.RED);
    g.drawLine(25,25,100,100);
  }
}
/*
<applet code="lines" width=200 height=200>
</applet>
*/
```

```
Command Prompt - appletviewer lines.java

H:\>javac lines.java

H:\>appletviewer lines.java
```

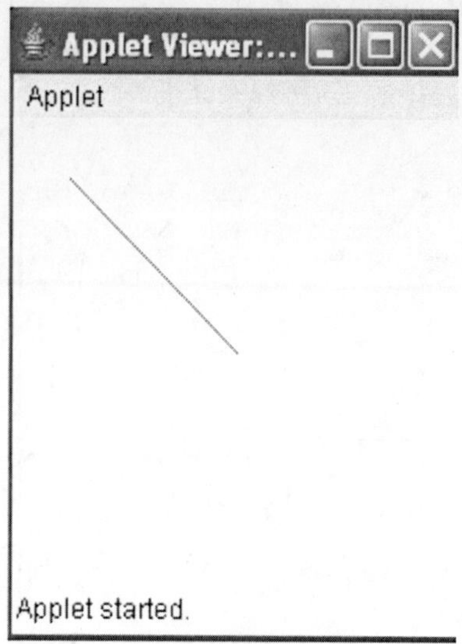

10.4.2 DRAWING RECTANGLES

When we have to draw rectangles, use the drawRect() method. drawRect() method takes four arguments.

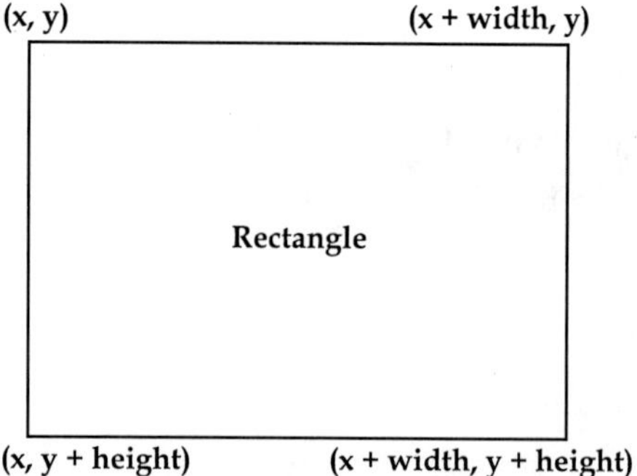

We have to draws the outline of the specified rectangle. The left and right edges of the rectangle are at x and x + width. The top and bottom edges are at y and y + height.

Syntax

The syntax is as follows.

public void drawRect(int x, int y, int width, int height)

where
x is the *x* coordinate of the rectangle to be drawn.
y is the *y* coordinate of the rectangle to be drawn.
width is the width of the rectangle to be drawn.
height is the height of the rectangle to be drawn.

//Example- Draw rectangle

```
import java.awt.*;
import java.applet.*;
public class rectangle extends Applet
{
public void paint(Graphics g)
{
g.drawRect(50, 50, 100, 100);
}
}
/*
<applet code="rectangle.class" width=200 height=200>
</applet>
*/
```

```
Command Prompt - appletviewer rectangle.java

H:\>javac rectangle.java

H:\>appletviewer rectangle.java
```

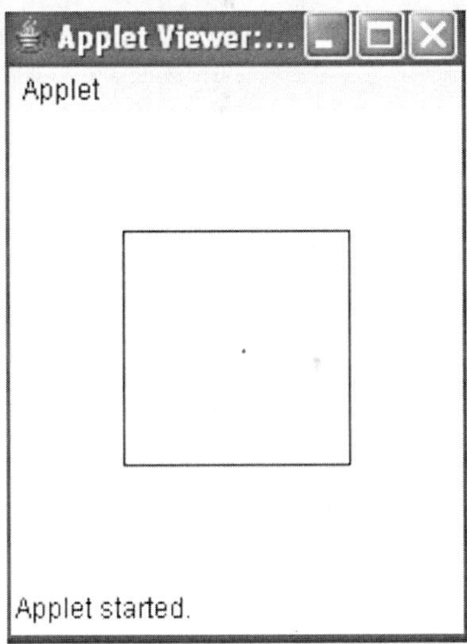

Other methods:

fillRect( ) method:

This method is used for fill the rectangle. The syntax is as follows.

void fillRect(int top, int left, int width, int height)

The upper-left corner of the rectangle is at top,left. The dimensions of the rectangle are specified by width and height.

//fill rectangle

```
import java.awt.*;
import java.applet.*;
public class fillRect extends Applet
{
public void paint(Graphics g)
{
g.fillRect(50, 50, 100, 100);
}
}

/*
<applet code="fillRect" width=300 height=200>
</applet>
*/
```

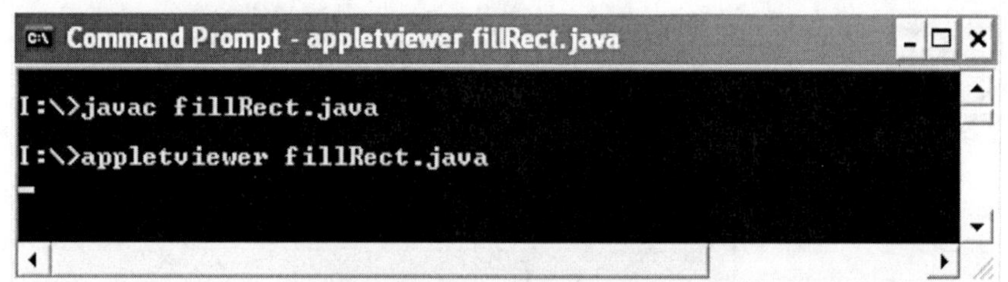

drawRoundRect( ) method:

This method is used to draw round rectangle. The syntax is as follows.

void drawRoundRect(int top, int left, int width, int height, int xDiam, int yDiam)

x - the x coordinate of the rectangle to be drawn.
y - the y coordinate of the rectangle to be drawn.
width - the width of the rectangle to be drawn.
height - the height of the rectangle to be drawn.
arcWidth - the horizontal diameter of the arc at the four corners.
arcHeight - the vertical diameter of the arc at the four corners.

A rounded rectangle has rounded corners. The upper-left corner of the rectangle is at top, left. The dimensions of the rectangle are specified by width and height. The diameter of the rounding arc along the X axis is specified by xDiam. The diameter of the rounding arc along the Y axis is specified by yDiam.

```
// Draw round rectangle

import java.awt.*;
import java.applet.*;

public class roundRect extends Applet
{
public void paint(Graphics g)
{
g.drawRoundRect(190, 10, 60, 50, 15, 15);
}
}
/*
<applet code="roundRect" width=300 height=200>
</applet>
*/
```

```
Command Prompt - appletviewer roundRect.java

I:\>javac roundRect.java

I:\>appletviewer roundRect.java
```

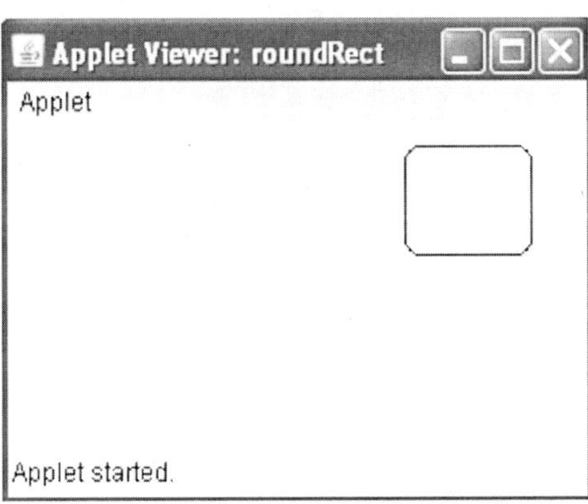

fillRoundRect( ) method:

This method is used for fill the round rectangle. The syntax is as follows.

void fillRoundRect(int top, int left, int width, int height, int xDiam, int yDiam)

// fill round rectangle

```
import java.awt.*;
import java.applet.*;
public class fillroundRect extends Applet
{
public void paint(Graphics g)
{
g.fillRoundRect(70, 90, 140, 100, 30, 40);
}
}
/*
<applet code="fillroundRect" width=300 height=200>
</applet>
*/
```

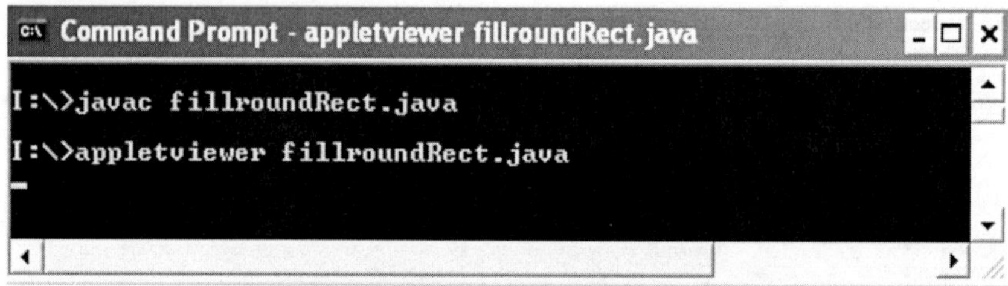

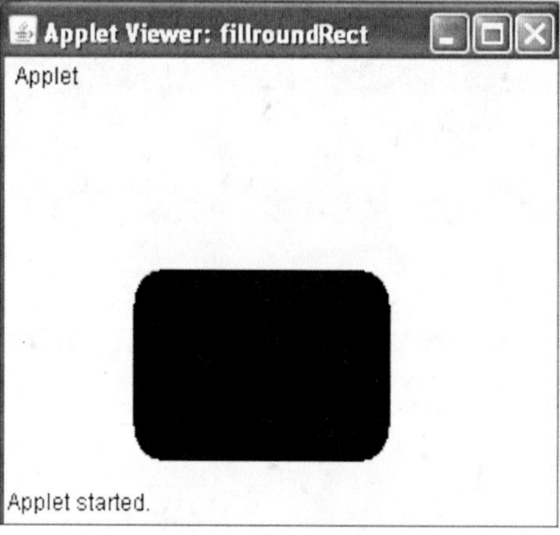

clearRect() method:

public abstract void clearRect(int x, int y, int width, int height)

Clears the specified rectangle by filling it with the background color of the current drawing surface. This operation does not use the current paint mode.

Beginning with Java 1.1, the background color of offscreen images may be system dependent. Applications should use setColor followed by fillRect to ensure that an offscreen image is cleared to a specific color.

Parameters:

`x` - the *x* coordinate of the rectangle to clear.
`y` - the *y* coordinate of the rectangle to clear.
`width` - the width of the rectangle to clear.
`height` - the height of the rectangle to clear.

```
//program

import java.awt.*;
import java.applet.*;
public class clearRect1 extends Applet
{
public void paint(Graphics g)
{
setBackground(Color.YELLOW);
g.setColor(Color.RED);
g.fillRect(50, 50, 150, 150);
g.clearRect(60,60,100,100);
}
}
/*
<applet code="clearRect1" width=300 height=200>
</applet>
*/
```

```
Command Prompt - appletviewer clearRect1.java

I:\>javac clearRect1.java

I:\>appletviewer clearRect1.java
_
```

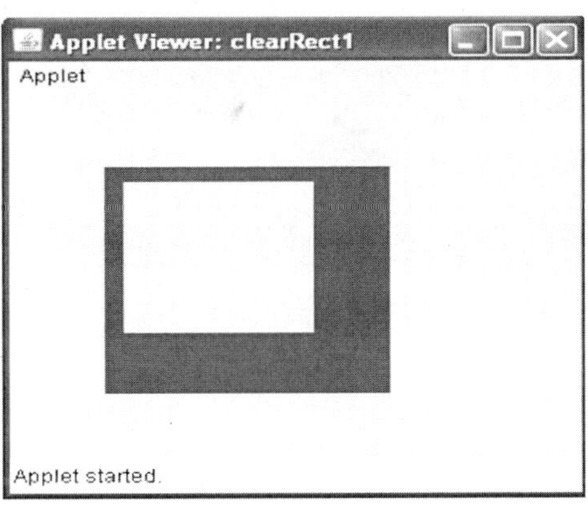

draw3DRect() method: (Three-dimensional rectangles, which are drawn with a shaded border)

Syntax:

public void draw3DRect(int x, int y, int width, int height, Boolean state)

where
x is the *x* coordinate of the rectangle to be drawn.
y is the *y* coordinate of the rectangle to be drawn.
width is the width of the rectangle to be drawn.
height is the height of the rectangle to be drawn.
Boolean state indicates whether the 3D effect is to raise the rectangle (**true**) or indent it (**false**).

These rectangles aren't really 3D; instead, they have a slight shadow effect that makes them appear either raised or indented from the surface of the applet.

```
//Program
import java.awt.*;
import java.applet.*;
public class tdRect extends Applet
{
  public void paint(Graphics g)
  {
setBackground(Color.YELLOW);
g.setColor(Color.RED);
g.draw3DRect(10,20,100,100,true);
  }
}
/*
<applet code="tdRect" width=300 height=200>
</applet>
*/
```

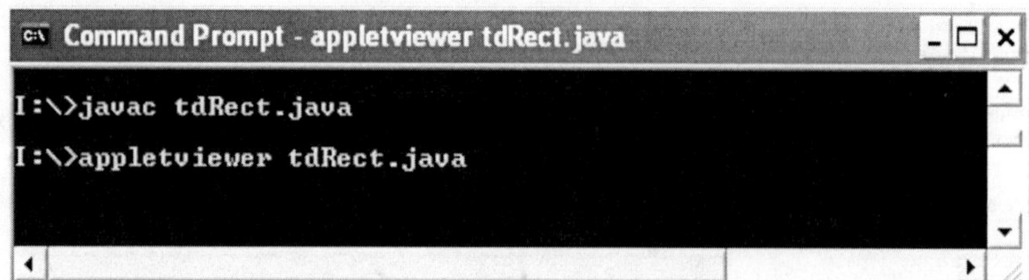

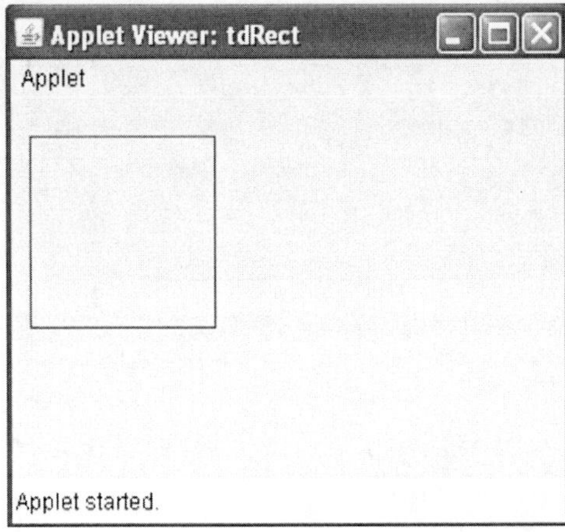

fill3DRect() Method:

Syntax:

public void fill3DRect(int x, int y, int width, int height, Boolean state)

where
x is the *x* coordinate of the rectangle to be drawn.
y is the *y* coordinate of the rectangle to be drawn.
width is the width of the rectangle to be drawn.
height is the height of the rectangle to be drawn.
Boolean state indicates whether the 3D effect is to raise the rectangle (**true**) or indent it (**false**).

These rectangles aren't really 3D; instead, they have a slight shadow effect that makes them appear either raised or indented from the surface of the applet.

```
//Program

import java.awt.*;
import java.applet.*;

public class filltdRect extends Applet
{
   public void paint(Graphics g)
   {
setBackground(Color.YELLOW);
g.setColor(Color.RED);
g.fill3DRect(10,20,100,100,true);
   }
}

/*
<applet code="filltdRect" width=300 height=200>
</applet>
*/
```

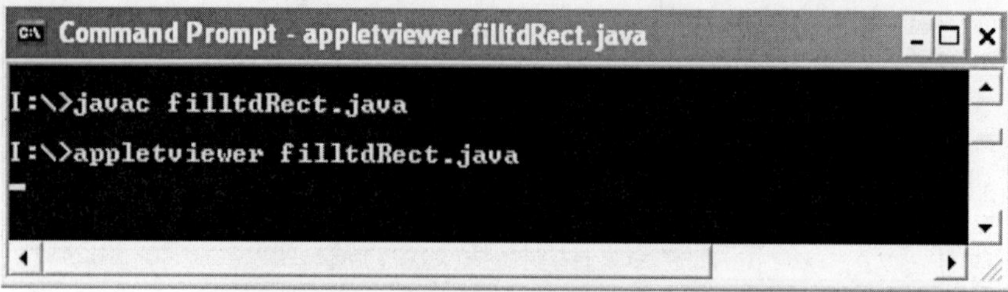

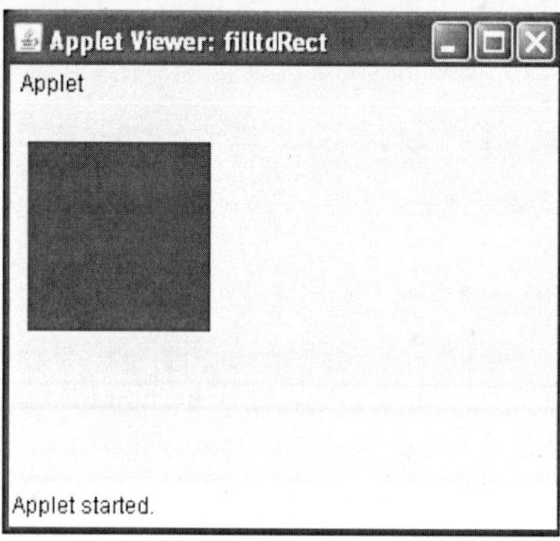

10.4.3 Drawing Ellipses and Circles

drawOval( ) method:

To draw an ellipse, use **drawOval( )**. The Syntax is as follows.

Syntax:

void drawOval(int top, int left, int width, int height)

The ellipse is drawn within a bounding rectangle whose upper-left corner is specified by top, left and whose width and height are specified by width and height.

```
//program

import java.awt.*;
import java.applet.*;

public class ellipse extends Applet
{
   public void paint(Graphics g)
   {
g.drawOval(100, 20, 100, 30);
   }
}

/*
```

```
<applet code="ellipse" width=300 height=200>
</applet>
*/
```

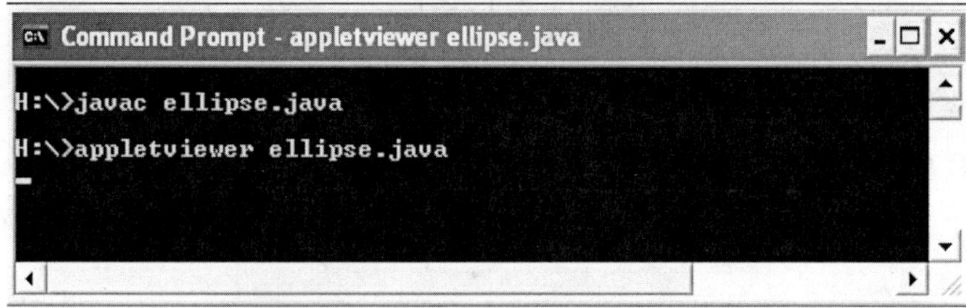

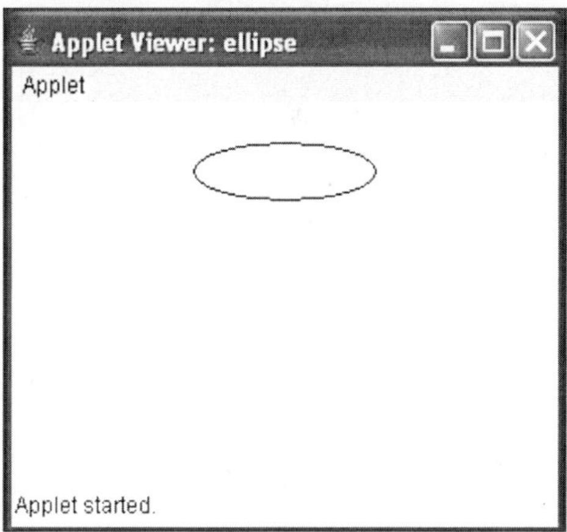

To draw a circle, specify a square as the bounding rectangle.

```
// Circle program

import java.awt.*;
import java.applet.*;

public class circle extends Applet
{
   public void paint(Graphics g)
   {
g.drawOval(50, 50, 100, 100);
   }
}
/*
<applet code="circle" width=300 height=200>
</applet>
*/
```

```
Command Prompt - appletviewer circle.java
H:\>javac circle.java
H:\>appletviewer circle.java
```

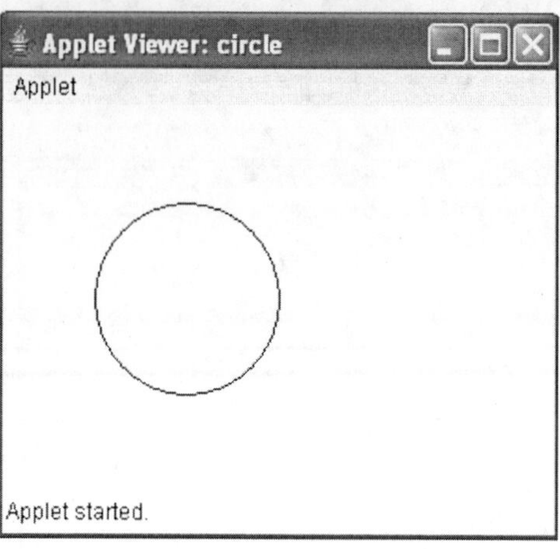

fillOval( ) method:

void fillOval(int top, int left, int width, int height)

// fill the oval

```
import java.awt.*;
import java.applet.*;
public class filloval extends Applet
{
   public void paint(Graphics g)
   {
g.setColor(Color.GREEN);
g.fillOval(50, 50, 100, 150);
   }
}
/*
<applet code="filloval" width=300 height=200>
</applet>
*/
```

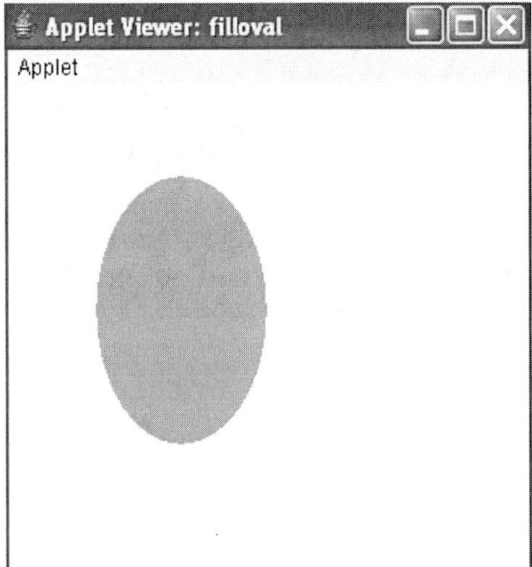

10.4.4 Drawing Arcs

drawArc() method:

Draws the outline of a circular or elliptical arc covering the specified rectangle.

Syntax:

public abstract void drawArc(int x, int y, int width, int height, int startAngle, int arcAngle)

where (x,y) is the center of the recrtangle and size is specified by the width and height arguments. The resulting arc begins at startAngle and extends for arcAngle degrees, using the current color.

The resulting arc covers an area width + 1 pixels wide by height + 1 pixels tall.

Parameters:

x - the x coordinate of the upper-left corner of the arc to be drawn.
y - the y coordinate of the upper-left corner of the arc to be drawn.
width - the width of the arc to be drawn.
height - the height of the arc to be drawn.
startAngle - the beginning angle.
arcAngle - the angular extent of the arc, relative to the start angle.

```
//program
import java.awt.*;
import java.applet.*;

public class drawarc extends Applet
{
   void paint(Graphics g)
   {
g.setColor(Color.GREEN);
g.drawArc(10, 40, 70, 70, 0, 75);
   }
}
/*
<applet code="drawarc" width=300 height=200>
</applet>
*/
```

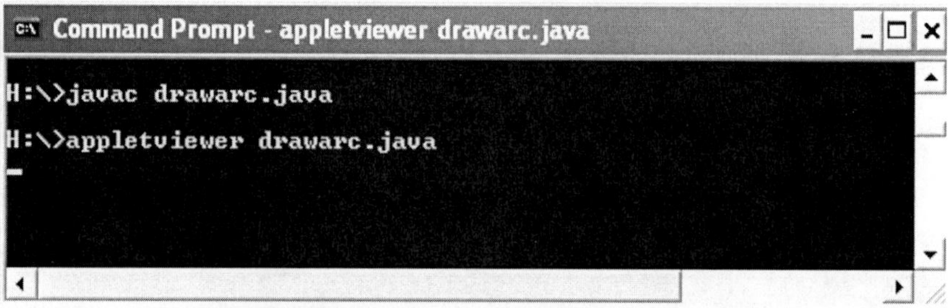

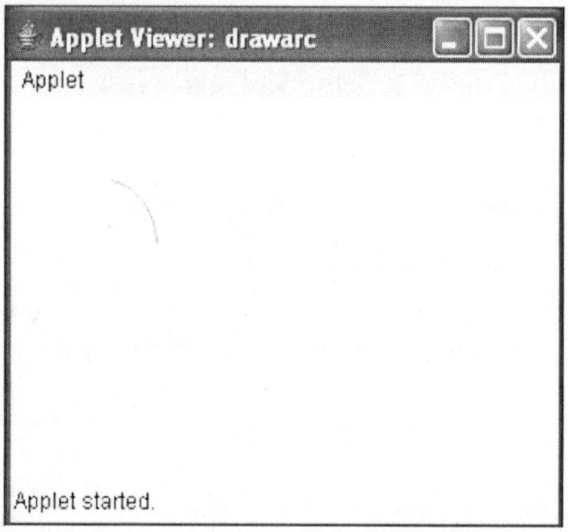

```
Command Prompt - appletviewer drawarc.java

H:\>javac drawarc.java

H:\>appletviewer drawarc.java
```

```
Applet Viewer: drawarc
Applet

Applet started.
```

fillArc() method:

Fills a circular or elliptical arc covering the specified rectangle. The arc is bounded by the rectangle whose upper-left corner is specified by top,left and whose width and height are specified by width and height. The arc is drawn from startAngle through the angular distance specified by sweepAngle. Angles are specified in degrees. Zero degrees is on the horizontal, at the three o'clock position. The arc is drawn counterclockwise if sweepAngle is positive, and clockwise if sweepAngle is negative. Therefore, to draw an arc from twelve o'clock to six o'clock, the start angle would be 90 and the sweep angle 180.

Syntax:

public abstract void fillArc(int x, int y, int width, int height, int startAngle, int arcAngle)

where

x - the *x* coordinate of the upper-left corner of the arc to be filled.

y - the *y* coordinate of the upper-left corner of the arc to be filled.

width - the width of the arc to be filled.

height - the height of the arc to be filled.

startAngle - the beginning angle.

arcAngle - the angular extent of the arc, relative to the start angle.

```
// fill Arcs

import java.awt.*;
import java.applet.*;
public class fillarc extends Applet
{
   public void paint(Graphics g)
   {
g.setColor(Color.GREEN);
g.fillArc(10, 40, 150, 150, 0, 75);
   }
}
/*
<applet code="fillarc" width=300 height=200>
</applet>
*/
```

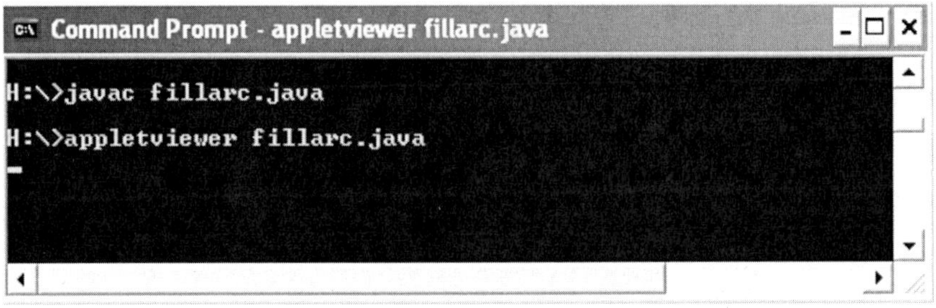

```
Command Prompt - appletviewer fillarc.java

H:\>javac fillarc.java

H:\>appletviewer fillarc.java
_
```

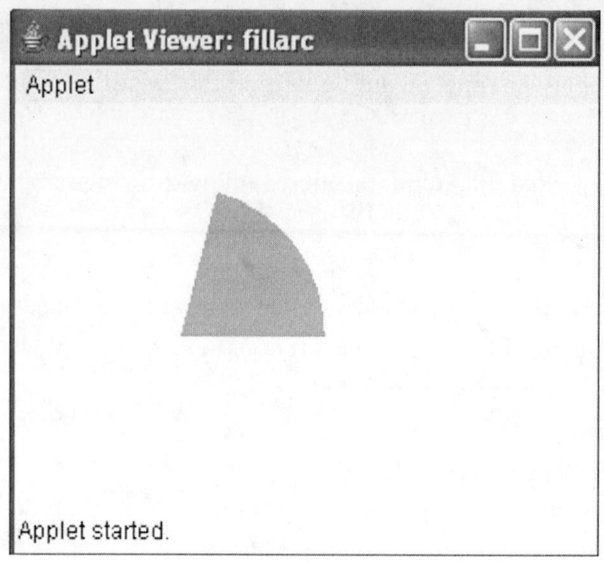

10.4.5 Drawing Polygons

drawPolygon( ) method:

void drawPolygon(int x[], int y[], int points)

where
x[] is an array of integers representing x coordinates
y[] is an array of integers representing y coordinates
point is an integer for the total number of points

To create a polygon object, you can either first create an empty polygon:

Polygon poly = new Polygon();

or create a polygon from a set of points using integer arrays, as in the previous example:

```
int x[] = { 30,90,98,150,50,60,25 };
int y[] = { 30,75,40,60,100,70,110 };
int p = x.length;
Polygon polygon = new Polygon(x[],y[],p);
```

we can add points to the polygon as follows:

```
polygon.addPoint(15,25);
```

// program to draw polygon

```
import java.awt.*;
import java.applet.*;

public class poly extends Applet
{
public void paint(Graphics g)
```

```
{
setBackground(Color.YELLOW);
g.setColor(Color.BLUE);
int x[] = {30, 200, 30, 200, 30};
int y[] = {30, 30, 200, 200, 30};
int n=5;
g.drawPolygon(x,y,n);
}
}
/*
<applet code="poly" width=300 height=300>
</applet>
*/
```

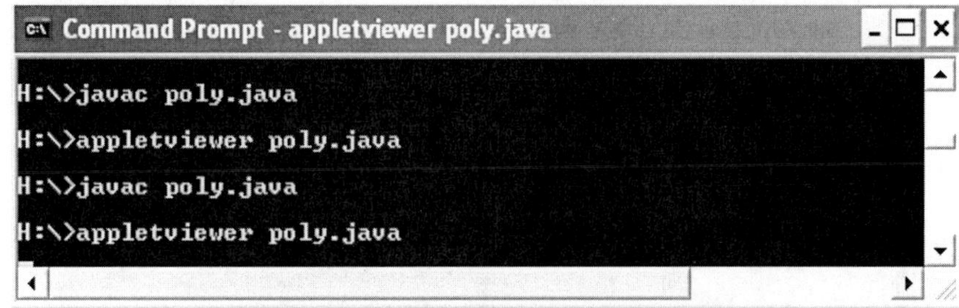

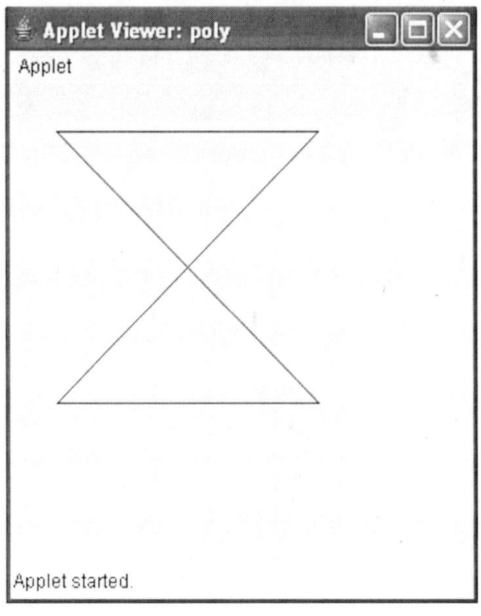

fillPolygon( ) method:

void fillPolygon(int x[ ], int y[ ], int points)

```
// fill Polygon
import java.awt.*;
import java.applet.*;
public class fillpoly extends Applet
{
public void paint(Graphics g)
{
setBackground(Color.YELLOW);
g.setColor(Color.BLUE);
int x[] = {30, 200, 30, 200, 30};
int y[] = {30, 30, 200, 200, 30};
int n=5;
g.fillPolygon(x,y,n);
}
}
/*
<applet code="fillpoly" width=300 height=300></applet>*/
```

```
Command Prompt - appletviewer fillpoly.java

        at java.awt.EventDispatchThread.pumpEvents(EventDispa
        at java.awt.EventDispatchThread.run(EventDispatchThre
H:\>javac fillpoly.java
H:\>appletviewer fillpoly.java
```

10.4.6 Resizing Graphics

We can fit the current size of the window in which it is drawn. The following steps are to be followed.

Firstly obtain the current dimensions of the window using **getSize( )** method. . It returns the dimensions of the window.

now scale the graphical output accordingly.

```
// Resizing output to fit the current size of a window.
import java.awt.*;
import java.awt.event.*;
import java.applet.*;
public class resizewindow extends Applet
{
final int increment = 25;
int max = 600;
int min = 100;
Dimension dim;
public resizewindow()
{
addMouseListener(new MouseAdapter()
{
public void mouseReleased(MouseEvent e)
{
int w = (dim.width + increment) > max?min :(dim.width + increment);
int h = (dim.height + increment) > max?min :(dim.height + increment);
setSize(new Dimension(w, h));
}
});
}
public void paint(Graphics g)
{
g.setColor(Color.BLUE);
dim = getSize();
g.drawLine(0, 0, dim.width-1, dim.height-1);
g.drawLine(0, dim.height-1, dim.width-1, 0);
g.drawRect(0, 0, dim.width-1, dim.height-1);
}
}
/*
<applet code="resizewindow" width=200 height=200>
</applet>
*/
```

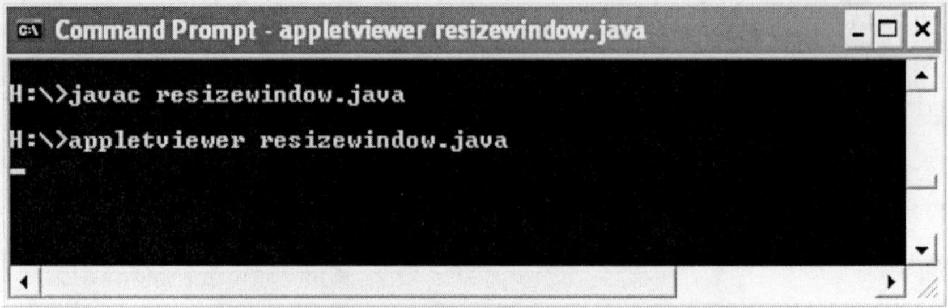
Command Prompt - appletviewer resizewindow.java
H:\>javac resizewindow.java
H:\>appletviewer resizewindow.java

Applet Viewer:...
Applet
Applet started.

Applet Viewer: resizewindow
Applet
Applet started.

SUMMARY

Java allows modification and creation of images using both awt and the newer java foundation classes (JFC 2D) architecture. The AWT supports a rich assortment of graphics methods that are drawn relative to a window. Graphics support a huge number of methods. Java supports color in a portable, device-independent fashion. The Java color system is very similar to the physical system used by color monitors. The AWT color system allows you to specify any color you want.

EXERCISE

1. What is Graphics Co-ordinate System?
2. What is AWT color System?
3. Write down the methods used in Font class.
4. Define 3D rectangle.

*****

CHAPTER 11

JAVA BEANS

JavaBeans technology is the component architecture for the Java 2 Platform, Standard Edition (J2SE). JavaBeans technology is based on the JavaBeans specification. The JavaBeans Specification includes the following definition of a bean: "a reusable software component that can be manipulated visually in a builder tool". A Java Bean is a reusable software component that can be visually manipulated in builder tools. The JavaBeans API provides a framework for defining reusable, embeddable, modular software components. JavaBeans are reusable software programs that we can develop and assemble easily to create sophisticated applications.

11.1 INTRODUCTION

JavaBeans brings component technology to the Java platform. JavaBeans are reusable software components for Java that can be manipulated visually in a builder tool. Beans can be used at three levels define as follows.

(i) If we are developing GUI editors, application builders or other "beanbox" tools, we need the JavaBeans API to manipulate beans within these tools. beanbox is the name of the sample bean manipulation program provided by Sun in its Beans Development Kit (BDK).

(ii) If we are writing actual beans, we need the JavaBeans API to write code that can be used in any conforming beanbox.

(iii) If we are writing applications that use beans developed by other programmers, or using a beanbox tool to combine those beans into an application, we do not actually need to be familiar with the JavaBeans API. We only need to be familiar with the documentation for individual beans that we are using.

11.2 BASIC BEAN CONCEPTS

Individual Java Beans will vary in functionality, but most share certain common defining features.

- Support for introspection allowing a builder tool to analyze how a bean works.
- Support for customization allowing a user to alter the appearance and behavior of a bean.

- Support for events allowing beans to fire events, and informing builder tools about both the events they can fire and the events they can handle.
- Support for properties allowing beans to be manipulated programmatically, as well as to support the customization mentioned above.
- Support for persistence allowing beans that have been customized in an application builder to have their state saved and restored. Typically persistence is used with an application builder's save and load menu commands to restore any work that has gone into constructing an application.

While Beans are intended to be used primarily with builder tools, they need not be. Beans can be manually manipulated by text tools through programmatic interfaces. All key APIs, including support for events, properties, and persistence, have been designed to be easily read and understood by human programmers as well as by builder tools.

11.3 APPLICATION BUILDER TOOLS

The primary purpose of beans is to enable the visual construction of applications. Java beans are look like Visual Basic, Visual Age or Delphi. These tools are referred to as visual application builder tools. These tools are used to make GUI applications. There is usually a palette of components available from which a program designer can drag items and place them on a form *or* client window.

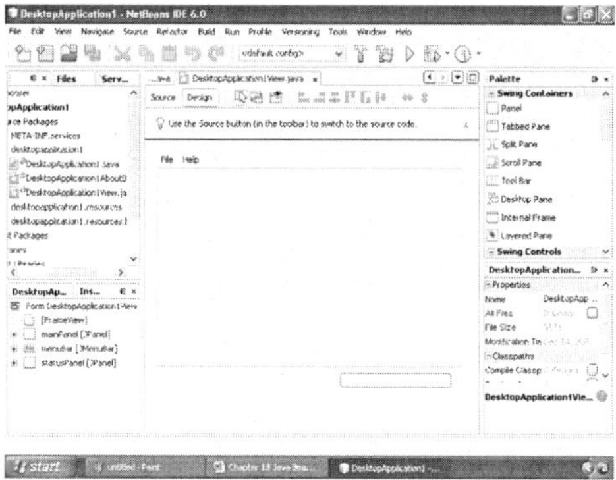

In windows environments the form is often called the client window area.

The form, or client window, represents the target application under construction and is presented, during design, as it will appear when it runs independently of the builder program. The window shared by many popular application builders is a property sheet, sometimes called a property editor or simply a properties window.

A property sheet is used to modify properties and events associated with components. In keeping with Java AWT terminology some property editors use the term action in place of event.

11.4 CREATE AN APPLICATION USING NETBEANS IDE 6.0

Select Start>>all programs>>NetBeans>>NetBeans IDE 6.0

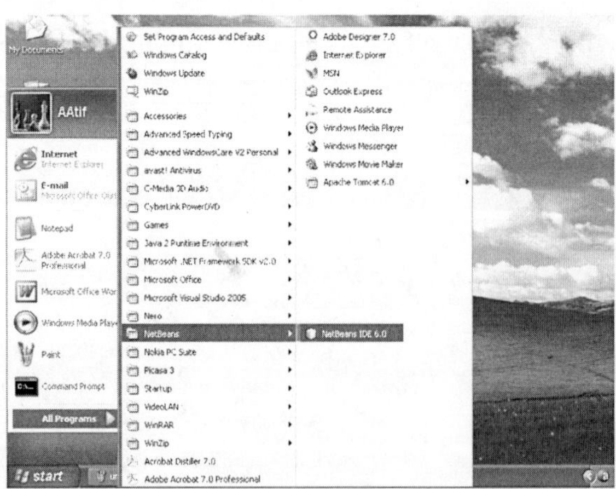

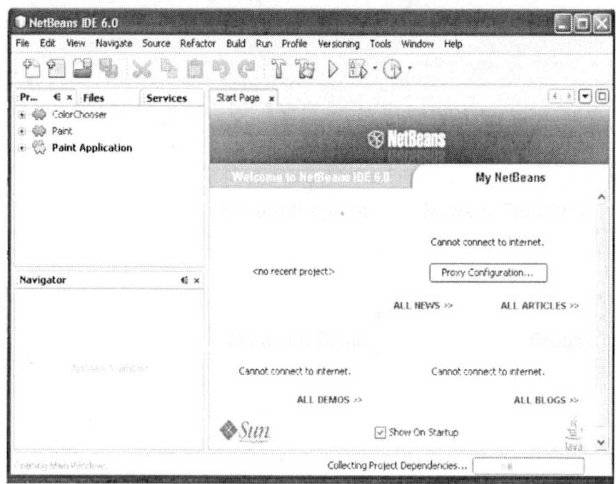

Click file and select New Project.

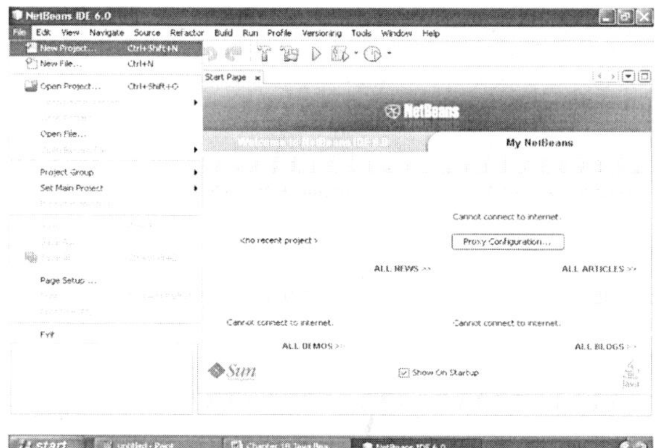

Now select Java Desktop Application.

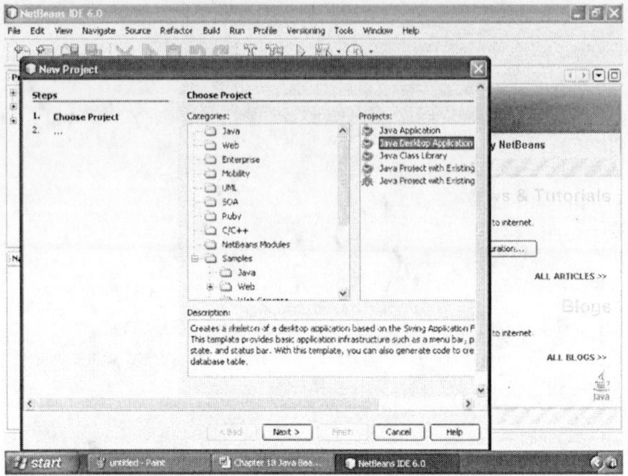

Click Next>.

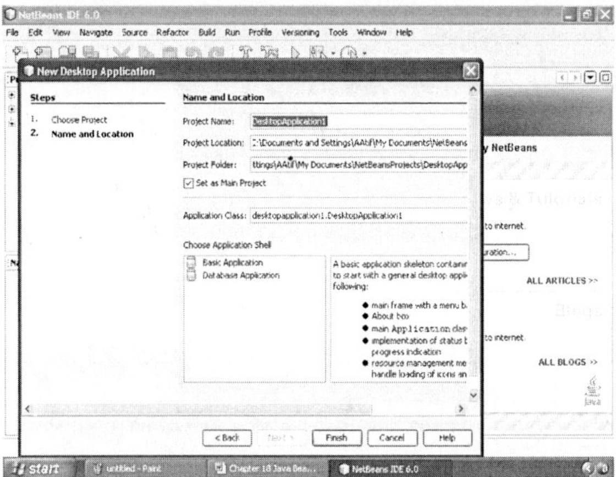

Enter project Name and Location. Now Click Finish.

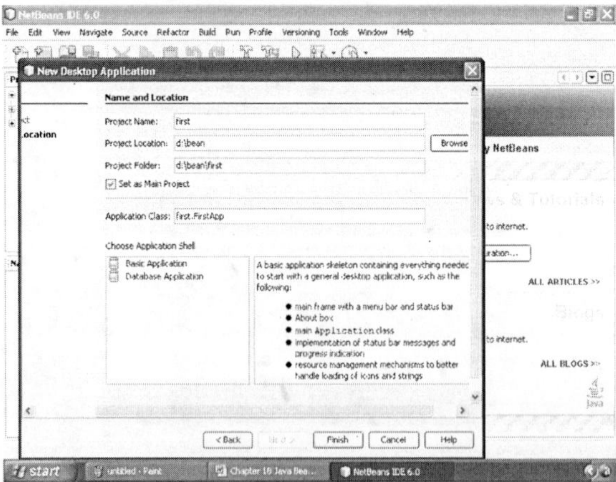

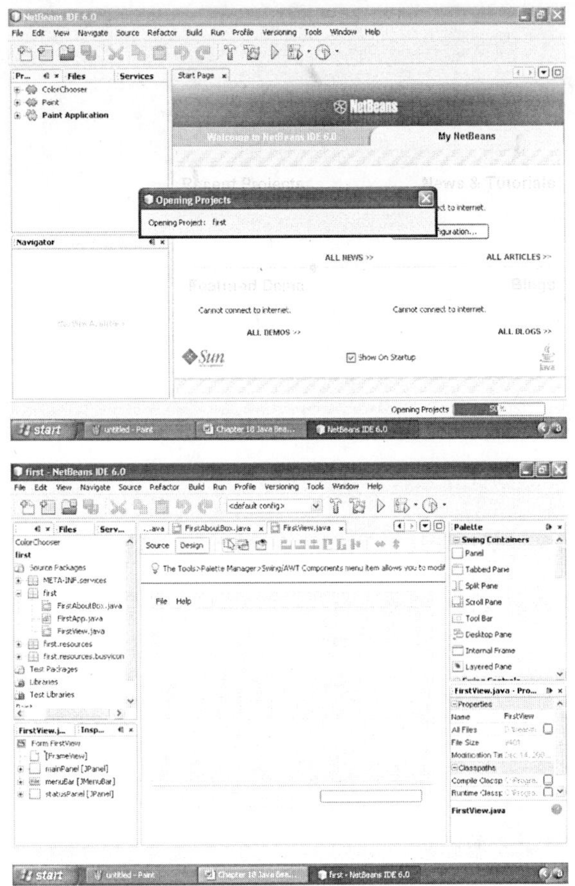

Now Design the application using palette and properties.

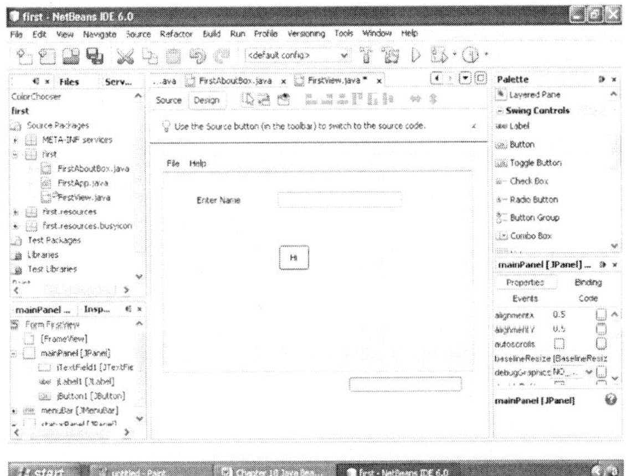

Now right click on button "Hi" and click Event>Action>actionPerformed.

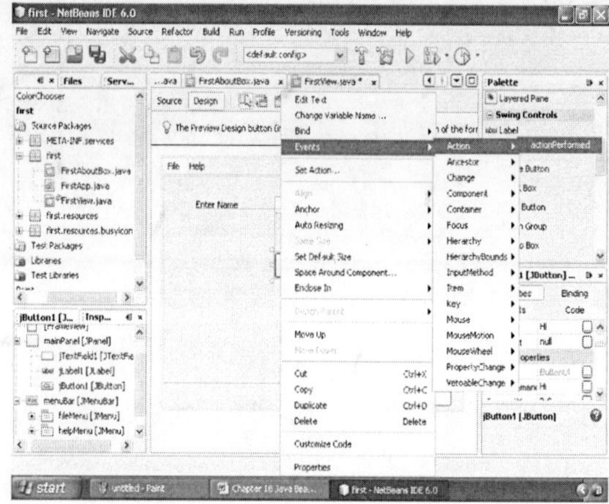

Now coding has been opened as follows.

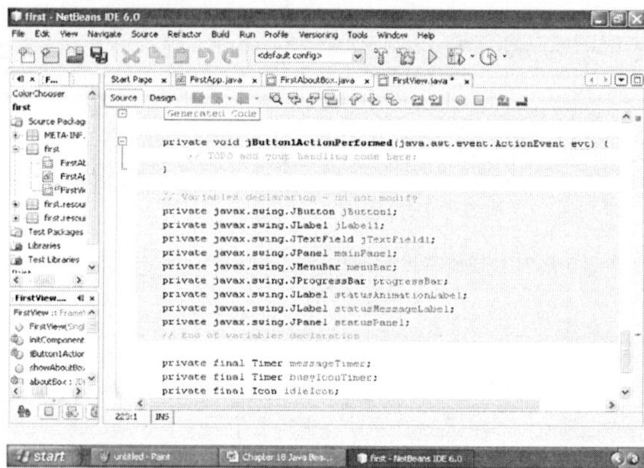

Now write the code as follows.

TextField1.setText("Hi Tanweer");

Now click Design.

Now Compile and run the Project as follows.

Select Build and click Build Main Project.

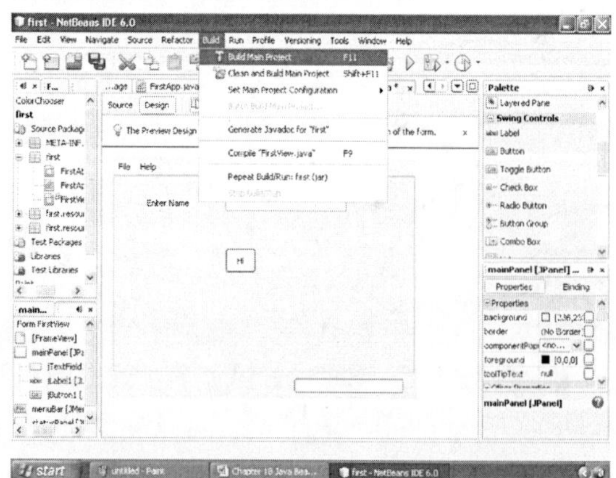

Now run the Project.

Click Run andRun Main Project.

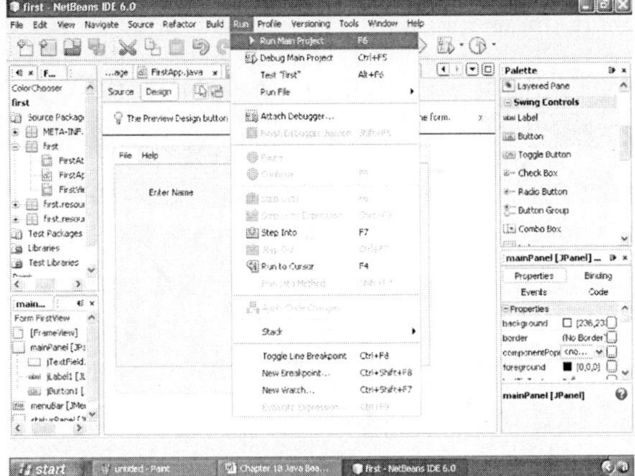

The output is as follows.

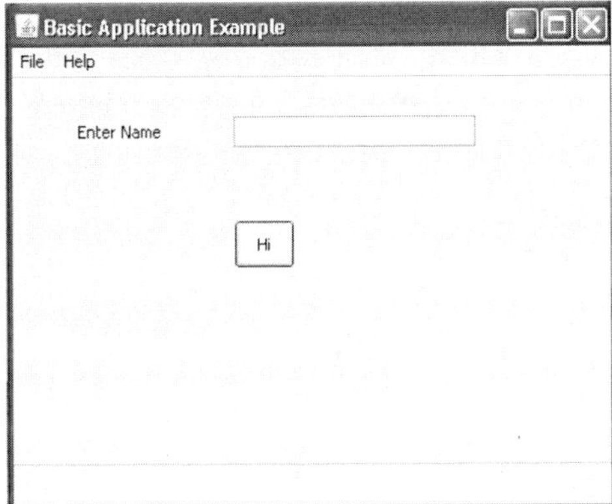

Click Hi Button.

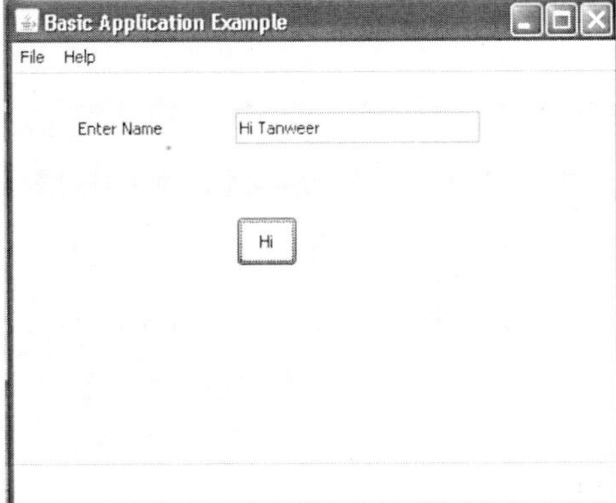

11.5 THE BEAN DEVELOPER KIT (BDK)

The BDK is delivered separately from the JDK. We can download the BDK freely from the sun web site. This site contains instructions for installing the BDK on your system. Here is a general description of the BDK files and directories:

(i) README.html contains an entry point to the BDK documentation

(ii) LICENSE.html contains the BDK license agreement

(iii) Beans/APIs contains

- (a) a java directory containing JavaBeans source files
- (b) a sun directory containing property editor source files

(iv) BeanBox contains

- (a) makefiles for building the BeanBox
- (b) scripts for running the BeanBox
- (c) a classes directory containing the BeanBox class files
- (d) a lib directory containing a BeanBox support jar file used by MakeApplet's produced code
- (e) sun and sunw directories containing BeanBox source (.java) files
- (f) a tmp directory containing automatically generated event adapter source and class files, .ser files, and applet files automatically generated by MakeApplet

(v) Beans/Demos contains

- (a) Make files for building the demo Beans.
- (b) an HTML directory containing an applet wrapper demo that must be run in appletviewer, HotJava, or JDK1.1-compliant browsers.
- (c) a sunw directory containing
  - (i) a wrapper directory containing a Bean applet wrapper
  - (ii) a demos directory containing demo source file

(vi) Beans/Doc contains

- (a) demos documentation
- (b) a javadoc directory containing JavaBeans and JavaBeans-related class and interface documentation
- (c) miscellaneous documentation

(vii) beans/jars contains jar files for demo Beans

Install the BDK on your system. This will create a directory called BDK1.1 and sub-directories BDK1.1/jars and BDK1.1\ beanbox together with some links to files in the Bean Development Kit installation directory.

Running the BeanBox

Change directory to BDK1.1/beanbox and type the command ./run.sh:

C:\ BDK1.1\beanbox>run.sh

The BeanBox starts and loads beans from the JAR files in the BDK1.1/jars directory. It then displays four windows on the screen:

(i) ToolBox

(ii) BeanBox

(iii) Properties sheet

(iv) MethodTracer

11.6 JAR FILES

JAR files are based on the ZIP file format. JAR files can be created and extracted using the "jar" command that comes with the JDK. JAR files are Java's version of ZIP files. There are two main uses for JAR files.

(i) To compress (make a smaller size) a number of files into one file (archiving).

(ii) To make a Java executable JAR file.

To compress (make a smaller size) a number of files into one file

The most common use for JAR files is to compress multiple files into a single JAR archive. JAR files can be opened with WinZip or WinRar. In terms of Java applications, the ability to archive any number of source or class files into one single archive represents the biggest advantage, distributing one file containing hundreds of files is so much easier than distributing hundreds of files separately.

The command to create a compressed JAR file:

cf archive.jar files

Where jar is the command to run the jar utility.

cf is to create a new archive with the file name specified.

The following list is represents the common options:

options	Description
- c	create new archive
- t	list table of contents for archive
- x	extract named (or all) files from archive
- u	update existing archive
- v	generate verbose output on standard output
- f	specify archive file name
- m	include manifest information from specified manifest file
- o	store only; use no ZIP compression
- M	do not create a manifest file for the entries
- i	generate index information for the specified jar files
- C	change to the specified directory

For example, A Java application consisting of three source files like:

a.java

```
public class A
{
public static void main()
{
System.out.println("Tanweer Alam");
}
}
```

b.java

```
public class B
{
public void displayB()
{
System.out.println("Method of class B");
}
}
```

c.java

```
public class C
{
public void displayC()
{
System.out.println("Method of class C");
}
}
```

Command Prompt

```
H:\java>javac A.java

H:\java>javac B.java

H:\java>javac C.java

H:\java>
```

Now make a jar file abc.jar. To make a JAR file with just One.java:

```
jar cf abc.jar a.java
```

To make a file with all three files listed separately:

```
jar cf abc.jar a.java b.java c.java
```

To make a file with all three files using a pattern match:

jar cf abc.jar *.java

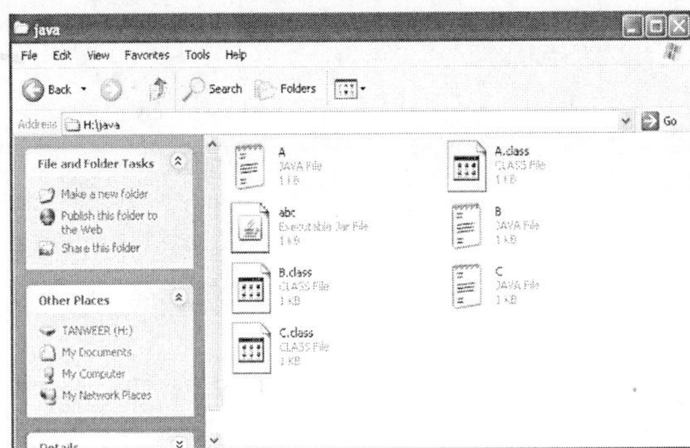

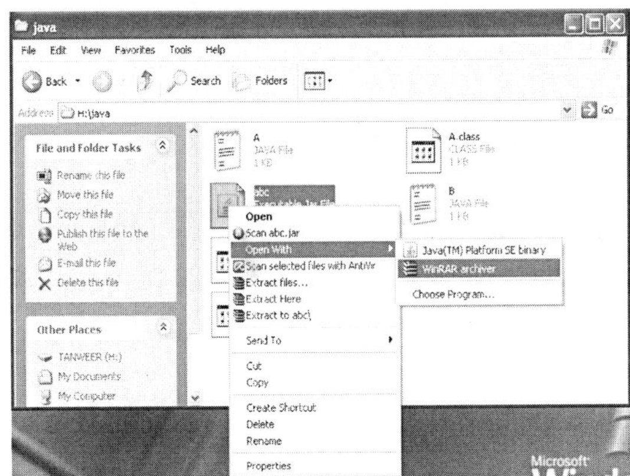

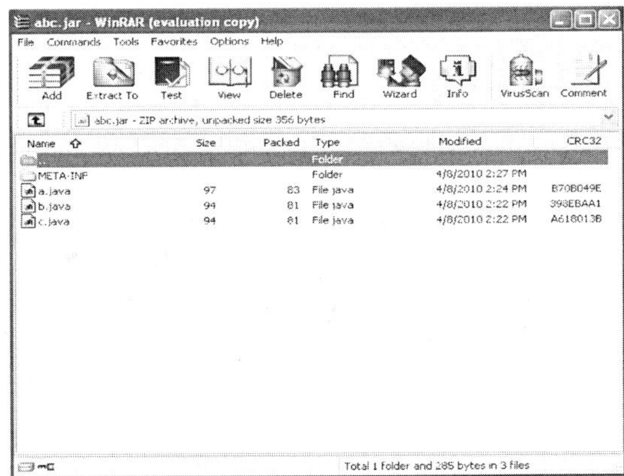

To make a Java executable JAR file

It is also possible to make an archive that can be executed by Java and even by a double click through your OS. To do this we must store compiled class files in the archive, as well as or instead of Java source files, since Java source files cannot be run. Now compile all Java source files as follows.

All JAR files contain something called a manifest file which holds information Java wants to know. One piece of information a manifest file may contain is the name of a class that will be run if the JAR file is executed. The steps are as follows.

(i) Create a text file that lists the class that has main method we want to execute. Write the following code in the text file.

Main-Class: a

Where a is the class name that have main method.

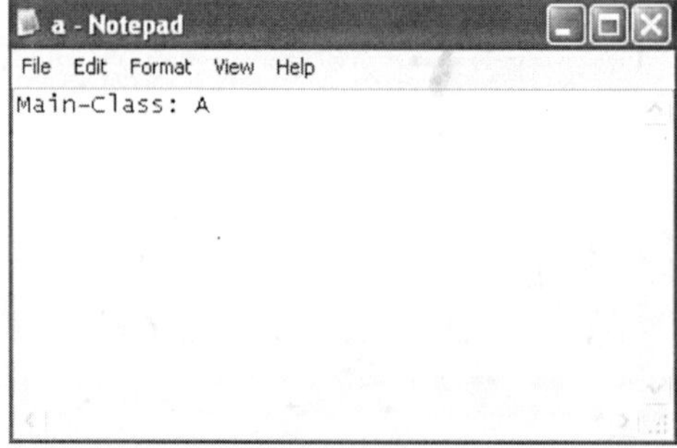

Now run the jar utility with this command line:

```
Command Prompt
H:\java>jar cmf A.txt xyz.jar *.class
H:\java>_
```

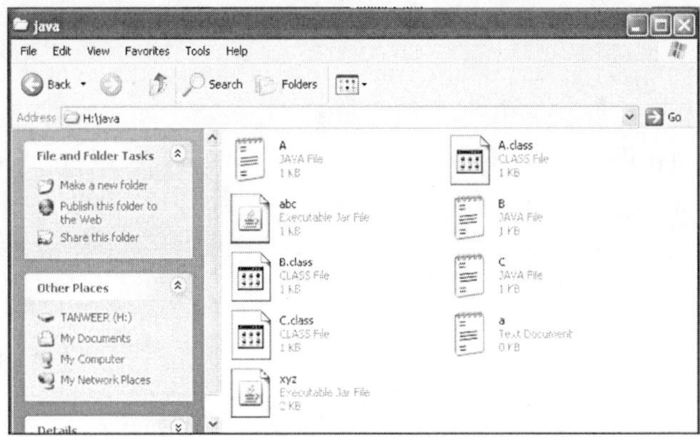

Now run the executable jar file as follows:

```
H:\java>java -jar xyz.jar
Tanweer Alam

H:\java>_
```

11.7 INTRODUCTION

Introspection is a core of Java Beans. It is a mechanism to get and use information at run-time. Introspection is the process of exposing the properties, methods, and events that a JavaBean component supports. This process is used at run-time, as well as by a visual development tool at design-time. This process controls the publishing and discovery of bean operations and properties. Introspection is the ability to ask a JavaBean component what properties and events it supports. By default, introspection is supported by reflection, where you name methods with certain naming patterns, like set/getProperty() and add/removeListener(). Introspector class is provided as part of the Beans class library.

The following are the advantages of Introspector.

Portability

Everything is done in the Java platform, so we can write components once, reuse them anywhere. We get all the advantages of the evolving Java APIs, while maintaining the portability of our components.

Reuse

We provide our component with reuse potential that possibly exceeds our expectations.

11.8 A SIMPLE BEAN

Java beans are usual java classes which adhere to certain coding convention. The following steps are used to develop a simple java bean.

(i) Creating a simple Bean
(ii) Compiling and saving the Bean into a Java Archive (JAR) file
(iii) Loading the Bean into the ToolBox
(iv) Dropping a Bean instance into the BeanBox
(v) Inspecting the Bean's properties, methods, and events
(vi) Generating an introspection report

Creating a simple Bean

The following steps are used to create a simple java bean.

(i) implements java.io.Srializable interface.
(ii) Provides no argument constructor.
(iii) Provides getter and setter methods for accessing its properties.

```
//Example FirstBean.java

import java.awt.*;
import java.io.Serializable;

public class FirstBean implements Serializable
{
   String name=null;
   int age=0;
   public FirstBean()
   {

   }
public String getName()
{
return name;
}
public void setName(String s)
{
name=s;
}
public int age()
{
return age;
}
public void setAge(int a)
{
```

```
age=a;
}
}
```

Compiling and saving the Bean into a Java Archive (JAR) file

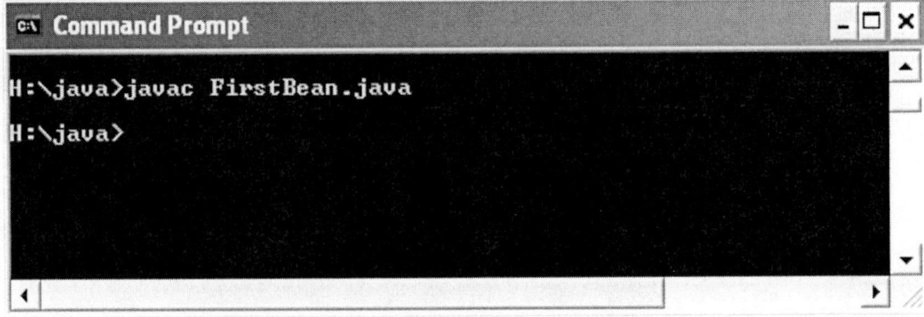

Create a manifest file

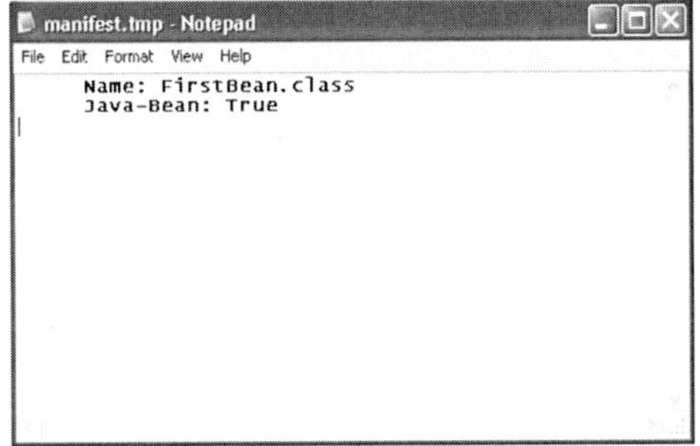

Create the JAR file.

Loading the Bean into the ToolBox

(i) Start NetBeans.

(ii) Select the newly created Form node in the Project Tree. A blank form opens in the GUI Builder view of an Editor tab.

(iii) Open the Palette Manager for Swing/AWT components by selecting Palette Manager in the Tools menu.

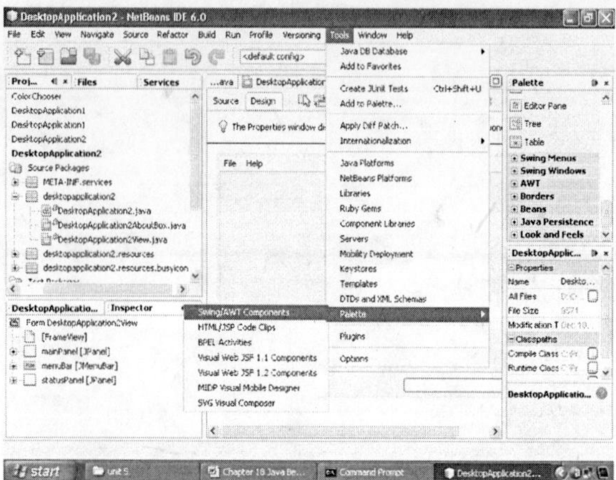

(iv) In the Palette Manager window select the beans components in the Palette tree and press the "Add from JAR" button.

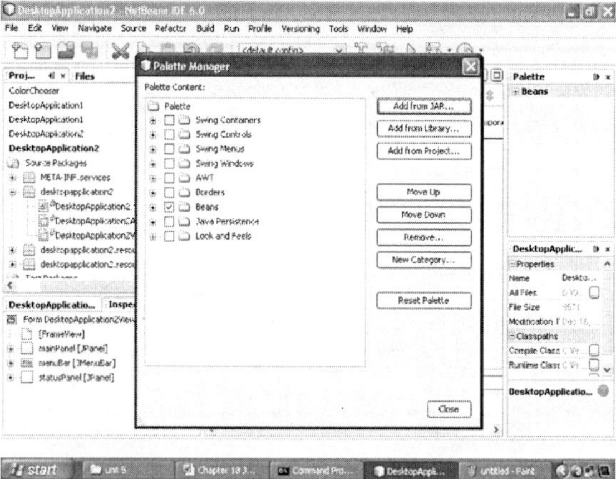

(v) Specify a location for your FirstBean JAR file and follow the Add from JAR Wizard instructions.

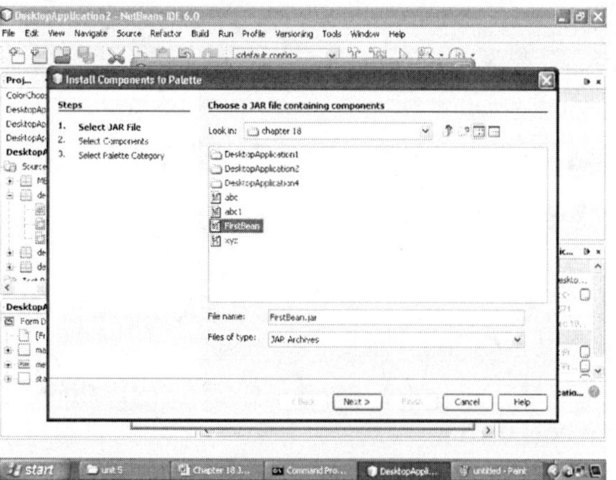

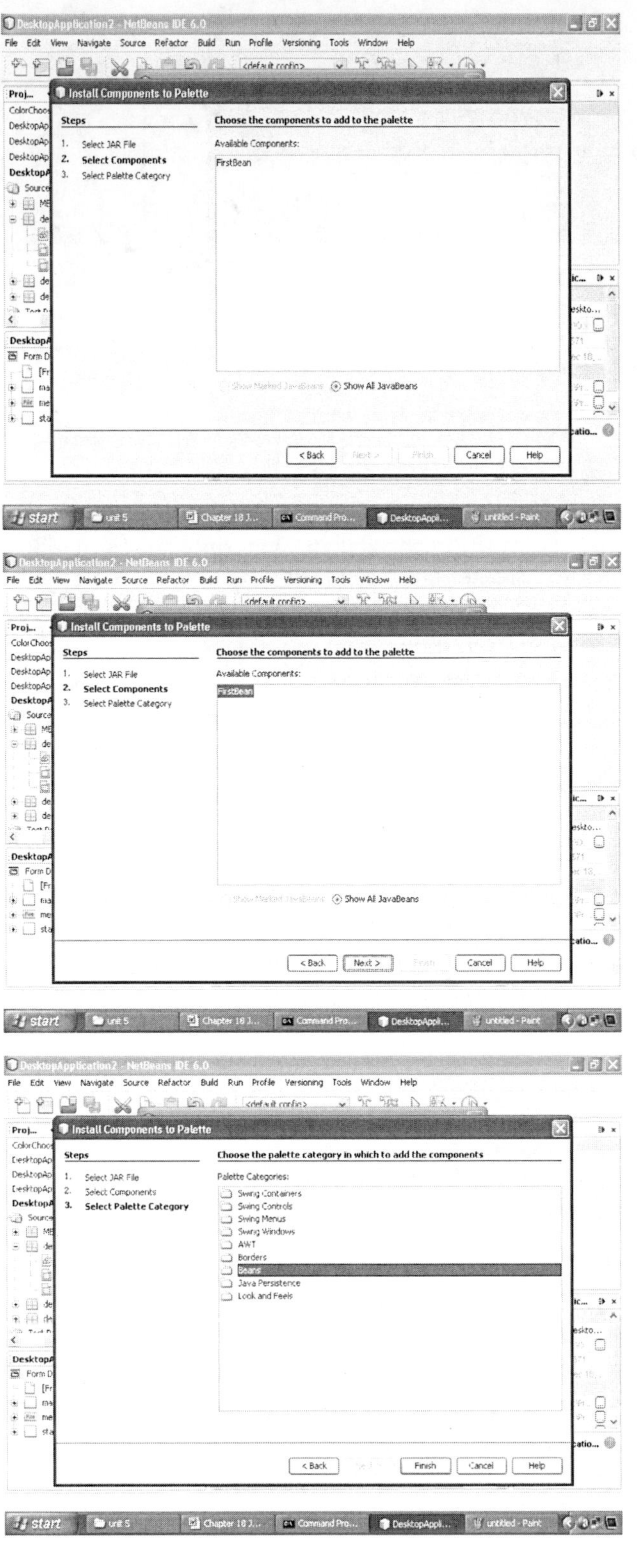

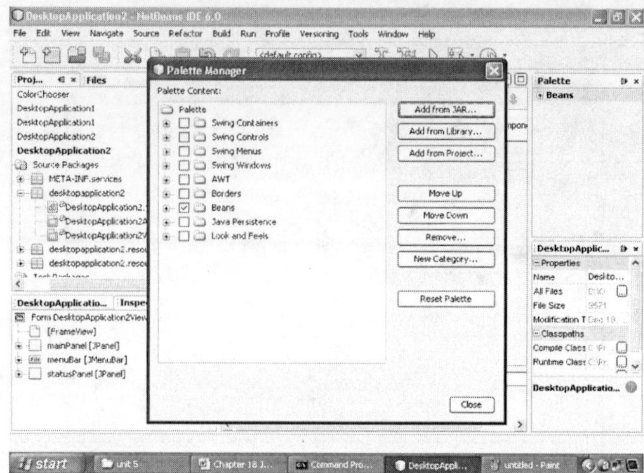

(vi) Select the Palette and Properties options from the Windows menu.

(vii) Expand the beans group in the Palette window. The SimpleBean object appears. Drag the FirstBean object to the GUI Builder panel.

Dropping a Bean instance into the BeanBox

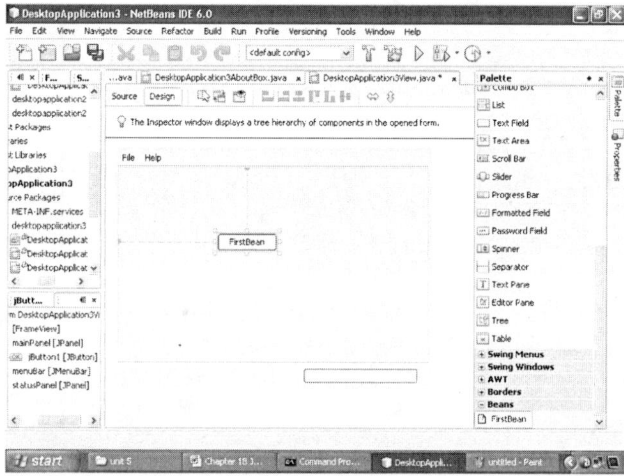

Inspecting the Bean's properties, methods, and events

The FirstBean properties will appear in the Properties window.

11.9 USING BOUND PROPERTIES

We can build Java Beans without any special API's. The bean building tool can then use introspection to determine the bean's methods, properties and events. Sometimes when a property of one bean is changed, another object might need to be notified of the change, and react to the change.

The BDK provides two classes and one interface for this purpose:

(i) **PropertyChangeSupport**. This supplies methods add/removePropertyChangeListener and firePropertyChange.

(ii) **PropertyChangeEvent**. This class provides 3 useful methods getNewValue, getOldValue and getPropertyName.

(iii) **PropertyChangeListener** This is an interface supplying one method, propertyChange.

Implementing Bound Property Support within a Bean

To implement a bound property in your application, follow these steps:

(i) import the java.beans package. Then we access the PropertyChangeSupport class.

(ii) Instantiate a PropertyChangeSupport object. This object maintains the property change listener list and fires property change events. We can also make our class a PropertyChangeSupport subclass.

(iii) implement methods to maintain the property change listener list. Since a PropertyChangeSupport subclass implements these methods, we merely wrap calls to the property-change support object's methods.

(iv) Modify a property's set method to fire a property change event when the property is changed.

11.10 THE JAVA BEANS API

Interface	Description
AppletInitializer	This interface is designed to work in collusion with java.beans.Beans. instantiate.
BeanInfo	A bean implementor who wishes to provide explicit information about their bean may provide a BeanInfo class that implements this BeanInfo interface and provides explicit information about the methods, properties, events, etc, of their bean.
Customizer	A customizer class provides a complete custom GUI for customizing a target Java Bean.
DesignMode	This interface is intended to be implemented by, or delegated from, instances of java.beans.beancontext.BeanContext, in order to propagate to its nested hierarchy of java.beans.beancontext. BeanContextChild instances, the current "designTime" property.
ExceptionListener	An ExceptionListener is notified of internal exceptions.
PropertyChangeListener	A "PropertyChange" event gets fired whenever a bean changes a "bound" property.
PropertyEditor	A PropertyEditor class provides support for GUIs that want to allow users to edit a property value of a given type.
VetoableChangeListener	A VetoableChange event gets fired whenever a bean changes a "constrained" property.
Visibility	Under some circumstances a bean may be run on servers where a GUI is not available.

Classes	Description
BeanDescriptor	A BeanDescriptor provides global information about a "bean", including its Java class, its displayName, etc.
Beans	This class provides some general purpose beans control methods.
DefaultPersistenceDelegate	The DefaultPersistenceDelegate is a concrete implementation of the abstract PersistenceDelegate class and is the delegate used by default for classes about which no information is available.
Encoder	An Encoder is a class which can be used to create files or streams that encode the state of a collection of JavaBeans in terms of their public APIs.
EventHandler	The EventHandler class provides support for dynamically generating event listeners whose methods execute a simple statement involving an incoming event object and a target object.
EventSetDescriptor	An EventSetDescriptor describes a group of events that a given Java bean fires.
Expression	An Expression object represents a primitive expression in which a single method is applied to a target and a set of arguments to return a result - as in "a.getFoo()".
FeatureDescriptor	The FeatureDescriptor class is the common baseclass for PropertyDescriptor, EventSetDescriptor, and MethodDescriptor, etc.
IndexedPropertyDescriptor	An IndexedPropertyDescriptor describes a property that acts like an array and has an indexed read and/or indexed write method to access specific elements of the array.
Introspector	The Introspector class provides a standard way for tools to learn about the properties, events, and methods supported by a target Java Bean.
MethodDescriptor	A MethodDescriptor describes a particular method that a Java Bean supports for external access from other components.
ParameterDescriptor	The ParameterDescriptor class allows bean implementors to provide additional information on each of their parameters, beyond the low level type information provided by the java.lang.reflect.Method class.
PersistenceDelegate	The PersistenceDelegate class takes the responsibility for expressing the state of an instance of a given class in terms of the methods in the class's public API.
PropertyChangeEvent	A "PropertyChange" event gets delivered whenever a bean changes a "bound" or "constrained" property.
PropertyChangeListenerProxy	A class which extends the EventListenerProxy specifically for adding a named PropertyChangeListener.
PropertyChangeSupport	This is a utility class that can be used by beans that support bound properties.
PropertyDescriptor	A PropertyDescriptor describes one property that a Java Bean exports via a pair of accessor methods.
PropertyEditorManager	The PropertyEditorManager can be used to locate a property editor for any given type name.

PropertyEditorSupport	This is a support class to help build property editors.
SimpleBeanInfo	This is a support class to make it easier for people to provide BeanInfo classes.
Statement	A Statement object represents a primitive statement in which a single method is applied to a target and a set of arguments - as in "a.setFoo(b)".
VetoableChangeListenerProxy	A class which extends the EventListenerProxy specifically for associating a VetoableChangeListener with a "constrained" property.
VetoableChangeSupport	This is a utility class that can be used by beans that support constrained properties.
XMLDecoder	The XMLDecoder class is used to read XML documents created using the XMLEncoder and is used just like the ObjectInputStream.
XMLEncoder	The XMLEncoder class is a complementary alternative to the ObjectOutputStream and can used to generate a textual representation of a JavaBean in the same way that the ObjectOutputStream can be used to create binary representation of Serializable objects.

Exception	Description
IntrospectionException	Thrown when an exception happens during Introspection.
PropertyVetoException	A PropertyVetoException is thrown when a proposed change to a property represents an unacceptable value.

11.11 INTRODUCTION TO ENTERPRISE JAVA BEANS (EJB)

An Enterprise JavaBean (EJB) is a reusable, portable J2EE component. Enterprise JavaBeans (EJB) provides the infrastructure for building enterprise-level server-side distributed Java components. One of the most important features of EJB is that enterprise beans have the ability to work with containers from different vendors. EJBs consist of methods that encapsulate business logic.

EJB Architecture

The EJB architecture is based on the concept of distributed computing or enterprise computing system. The EJB architecture is compose of

(i) An Enterprise Bean Server

(ii) An Enterprise Bean Container that runs on these server

(iii) An Enterprise Bean that run in these container

(iv) An Enterprise Bean Client

(v) EJB Home Interface

(vi) EJB Remote Interface

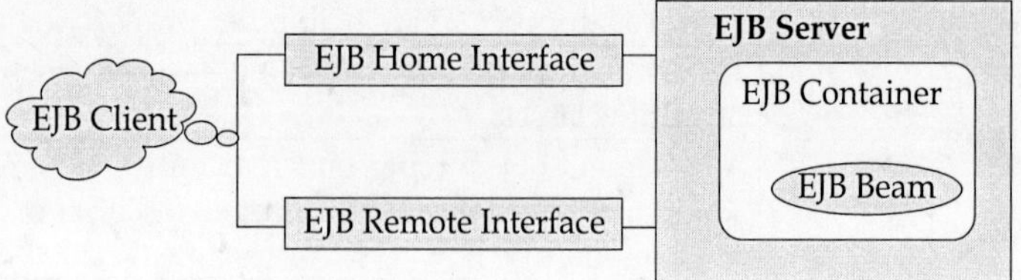

Figure 11.1: EJB Architecture

(i) **An Enterprise Bean Server**

It is a server that provides the service of EJB Beans to the EJB clients using EJB containers. An EJB server can have more than one container and each container in turn can accommodate more than one enterprise bean.

(ii) **An Enterprise Bean Container that runs on these server**

EJB Container provides the environment surrounds the beans on the EJB server is often referred to as the container. It acts as an intermediary between the bean class and the EJB server. The container manages bean resources and applies the primary services relevant to distributed systems to bean instances at run time.

(iii) **An Enterprise Bean that run in these container**

Bean Class has to implement the bean's business methods in the remote interface. An entity bean must implement javax.ejb.EntityBean and a session bean must implement javax.ejb.SessionBean. Both EntityBean and Session Bean extend javax.ejb.EnterpriseBean.

(iv) **An Enterprise Bean Client**

The EJB Client makes a request for a method on the bean. An EJB client sends the request to the EJB server. The EJB Server processes the request and sends it to the EJB Container and run the bean and sends back the result of client request.

(v) **EJB Home Interface**

The home interface extends javax.ejb.EJBHome, which in turn extends java.rmi.Remote. This interface defines the bean's life cycle methods such as creation of new beans, removal of beans and locating beans.

(vi) **EJB Remote Interface**

The remote interface extends javax.ejb.EJBObject, which in turn extends java.rmi.Remote. This interface for an enterprise bean defines the enterprise bean's business methods that clients for this bean can access.

Working Process

(i) Client makes a request for a method on the bean.

(ii) Container checks the client is in the approved list or not.

(iii) If the client is in approved list the container create the object of required bean.

(iv) Container informs the EJB Object that the bean is ready and passes the Client's method request to the bean.

Types of EJB

EJB has two types.

(i) Entity beans
(ii) Session beans

11.12 SESSION BEANS

Session beans are for managing processes or tasks. Session beans are typically used for business process or control logic that spans multiple entity beans.

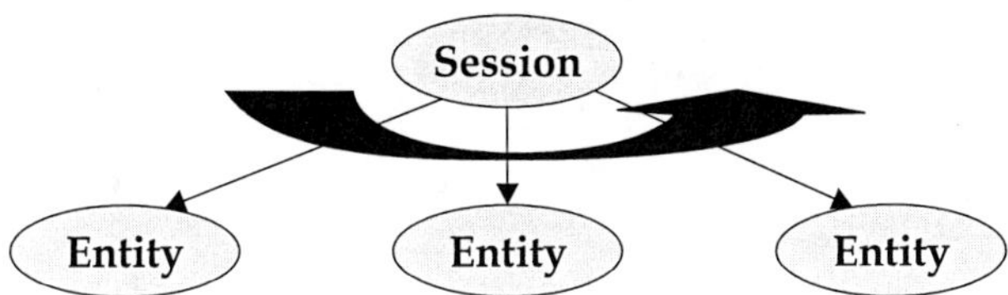

Figure 11.2: Session Beans

A session bean does not represent anything in a database, but it can access the database. A session bean is mainly for coordinating particular kinds of activities. That is, session beans are plain remote objects meant for abstracting business logic. The activity that a session bean represents is fundamentally transient. Session bean has two types.

(i) Stateful session beans
(ii) Stateless session beans

Life cycle of Stateless Session Bean

The following are two stages in the Lifecycle of Stateless Session Bean.

(a) **Does Not Exist Stage**

In this stage, bean does not have instance in the memory i.e. bean has not instantiated.

(b) **Method Ready Pool Stage**

In this stage bean has instance(s) in the memory of the EJB container and it is ready to serve clients. EJB container creates the new instance of the Bean and then sets the session context (setSessioncontext()) and it calls the ejbCreate() method to place the bean in the Method Ready Pool stage. Container calls the ejbRemove() method to move the bean into Does Not Exist state. The following Diagram shows the Life cycle of Stateless Session Bean.

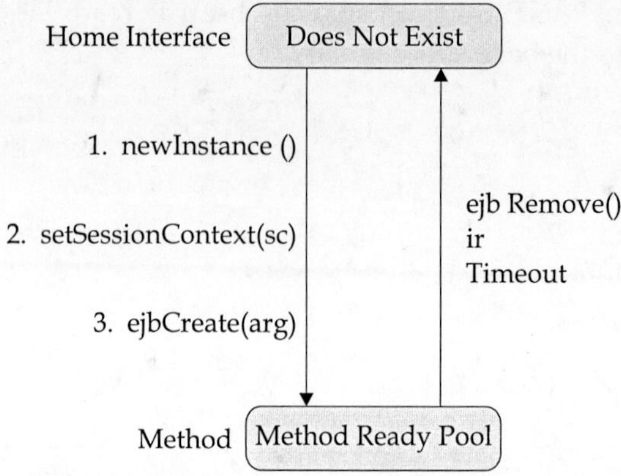

Figure 11.3: Life cycle of Stateless Session Bean

LIFE CYCLE OF STATEFUL SESSION BEAN

The following are three stages in the life cycle of Stateful Session bean.

(a) **Does Not Exist Stage:** In this stage, bean does not have instance in the memory i.e. bean has not instantiated.

(b) **Method Ready Pool Stage:** In this stage bean has instance in the memory of the EJB container and it is ready to serve client. Client Calls ejbCreate(arg) method on the Home Interface. Server creates new instance of the bean and sets the Session Context using setSessionContext. Container calls the ejbRemove() or Timeout method to move the bean into Does Not Exist state.

(c) **Passive state:** In this state the bean is passive to conserve the resource. The ejbpassivate() method is called before the instance enters in this state. After the ejbPassivate() method completes, the instance must be in a state that allows the container to use the Java Serialization protocol to externalize and store away the instance's state. Container calls the ejbRemove() or Timeout method to move the bean into Does Not Exist state. The following Diagram shows the Life cycle of Stateful Session Bean

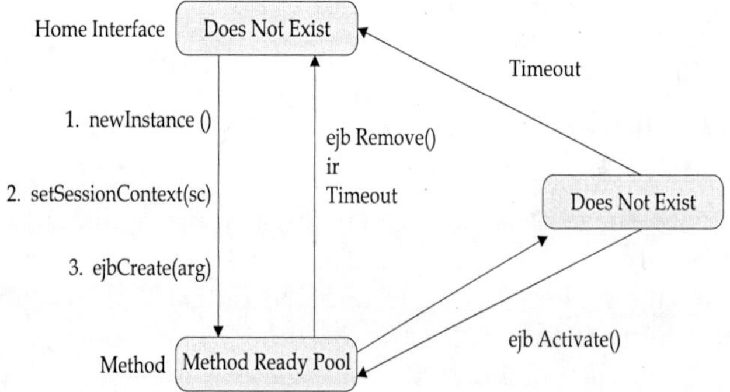

Figure 11.4: Life cycle of Statefull Session Bean

11.13 ENTITY BEANS

Entity beans provide an object-oriented interface that makes it easier for developers to create, modify, and delete data from the database. Entity beans should implement the javax.ejb. Since database operations involve create, update, load, delete and find operations, the EJB architecture requires entity beans to implement these operations. The EJB container tells the bean instance when it is safe to insert, update, and delete its data from the database, but it provides no other help. Container-managed beans have their persistence automatically managed by the EJB container. The container knows how a bean instance's fields map to the database and automatically takes care of inserting, updating, and deleting the data associated with entities in the database.

Ex. ATM

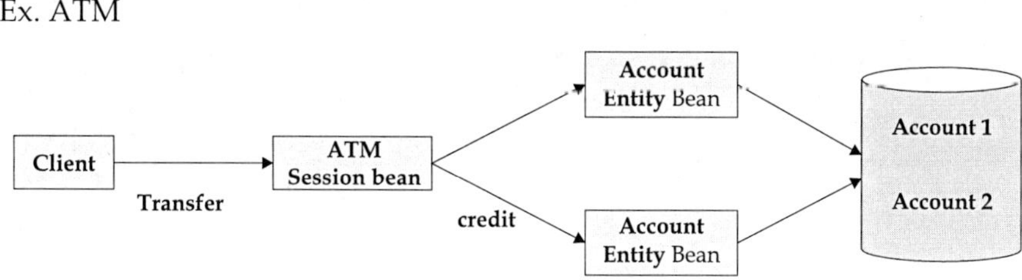

Figure 11.5: Entity Beans

11.14 DIFFERENCES BETWEEN ENTITY AND SESSION BEAN

Entity Bean	Session Bean
Entity bean has persistent state.	Session Bean does not have persistent state.
entity beans have a client-independent identity	Session beans does not have a client-independent identity
Entity beans are transaction-aware except for the fact that bean instances are not allowed to programmatically control transactions.	Session beans are transaction-aware.
Entity bean encapsulates persistent data.	Session bean does not encapsulate persistent data.
An Entity bean represents a row in a database.	A session bean does not represent anything in a database, but it can access the database.

SUMMARY

A Java Bean is a reusable software component that can be visually manipulated in builder tools. The JavaBeans API provides a framework for defining reusable, embeddable, modular software components. JavaBeans is architecture for both using and building components in Java. This architecture supports the features of software reuse, component models, and object orientation. JavaBeans are reusable software programs that we can develop and assemble easily to create sophisticated applications. The primary purpose of beans is to enable the visual construction of applications. Java beans are look like Visual Basic, Visual Age or Delphi. These tools are referred to as visual application builder tools. Introspection is the automatic process of analyzing a bean's design patterns to reveal the bean's properties, events, and methods. The JavaBeans API makes it possible to write component software in the Java programming language. Components are self-contained elements of software that can be controlled dynamically and assembled to form applications. JavaBeans is Java's component model. It allows users to construct applications by piecing components together either programmatically or visually (or both).

EXERCISE

1. Define java beans API.
2. What is bound properties in java beans?
3. Define EJB.
4. What is the difference between stateless session beans and statefull session beans?
5. What is Beans application builder tool?

*****

CHAPTER 12

SWING PROGRAMMING

Swing is part of Sun Microsystems' Java Foundation Classes (JFC), an API for providing a graphical user interface (GUI) for Java programs. The JFC was first announced at the 1997 JavaOne developer conference. Swing is a widget toolkit for Java. Swing refers to the new library of GUI controls (buttons, sliders, checkboxes, etc.) that replaces the somewhat weak and inflexible AWT controls. Swing provides a native look and feel that emulates the look and feel of several platforms and also supports a pluggable look and feel that allows applications to have a look and feel unrelated to the underlying platform.

12.1 INTRODUCTION

JFC is short form of Java Foundation classes that has a group of features to help people build graphical user interfaces (GUIs). All Swing components start with a capital J. JFC is defined as containing the following features.

(i) Lightweight: Swing components are light weighted.

(ii) Much bigger Library of built-in controls: Trees, ImageButton, TabbedPane, Slider, ToolBar, ColorChooser, Table, TextArea to display HTML or RTF, etc.

(iii) Much more customizable: Can change border, text alignment, or add image to almost any control. Can customize how minor features are drawn. Can separate internal representation from visual appearance.

(iv) Pluggable look and feel: Can change look and feel at runtime, or design own look and feel. Gives any program that uses Swing components a potentially wide choice of looks and feels, no matter what platform the program is running on.

(v) Many miscellaneous new features: Double-buffering built in, tool tips, dockable tool bars, keyboard accelerators, custom cursors, etc.

(vi) Java 2D graphics, text, and images in Java applications and applets.

12.2 Swing Definition

All Java Swing classes imports form the import javax.swing.*; package. The Swing package is part of the Java Foundation Classes (JFC) in the Java platform. The JFC encompasses a group of features to help people build GUIs. The Java Swing provides the multiple platform independent APIs interfaces for interacting between the users and GUIs components. The following steps are used to create a swing application.

(i) Setting up the top-level container
(ii) Setting up components
(iii) Adding components to containers
(iv) Handling events

The Swing controls can be divided as shown below.

GUI Category	Control	Swing Class Name
Basic Controls	Button CheckBox CheckBoxGroup Combo box List Menu MenuBar MenuItem Slider Toolbar TextField TextArea	JButton JCheckBox JRadioButton JComboBox JList JMenu JMenuBar JMenuItem JSlider JToolbar JTextField,JPasswordField JTextArea
Editable Display	Table Text Tree Color chooser File chooser	JTable JTextPane, JTextArea, JEditorPane JTree JColorChooser JFileChooser
Uneditable Display	Label Tooltip Progress bar	JLabel JToolTip JProgressBar
Space-Saving Containers	Scroll pane Split pane Tabbed pane	JScrollPane, JScrollBar JSplitPane JTabbedPane
Top-Level Containers	Frame Applet Dialog	JFrame JApplet JDialog, JOptionPane
Other Containers	Panel Internal Frame Layered pane Root pane	JPanel JInternalFrame JLayeredPane JRootPane

All swing components are the subclasses of JComponent. These classes are the controls or the building blocks from which you create your GUI.

(i) Add them to the content pane of a container (often JFrame or the JApplet) with a call like:

(a) Frame f=new Frame();

(b) Container c = f.getContentPane ();

(c) c.add (b);

(ii) Register your event-handler using the addXXXListener() method of the component.

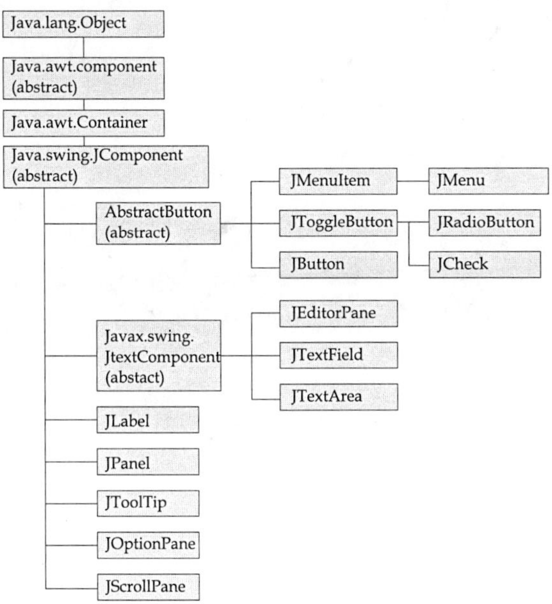

Figure 12.1: Swing Components

//Example

```
import java.awt.*;
import java.awt.event.*;
import javax.swing.*;
public class first
{
static JFrame f = new JFrame ("First Application");
public static void first()
{
   f.setSize (400,100);
   f.setVisible (true);
   f.getContentPane ().setLayout (new FlowLayout ());
   WindowListener wl = new WindowAdapter () {
      public void windowClosing (WindowEvent e) {
         System.exit (0);}
   };
   f.addWindowListener (wl);
}
```

```
public static void main(String[] args)
{
   first();
   JButton jb = new JButton("Click me");
   f.getContentPane().add(jb);
}
}
```

12.3 A SWING APPLET AND APPLICATION

A JApplet contains the ContentPane [in java: getContentPane()] in which to add components. Changing Properties also applies to the ContentPane. Most usage is the same as with Applet

(i) JApplet inherits from Applet
(ii) init, start, stop, etc. unchanged
(iii) Default layout manager is BorderLayout (like Frame and JFrame), not FlowLayout (like Applet). This is really the layout manager of the content pane.
(iv) Do drawing in paintComponent, not paint.

```
//JAppletApp.java
import java.awt.*;
import javax.swing.*;
public class JAppletApp extends JApplet
{
   public void init()
   {
      Container c = getContentPane();
      c.setBackground(Color.YELLOW);
      c.setLayout(new FlowLayout());
      c.add(new JLabel("My First JApplet"));
```

```
    }
}
/*<applet code="JAppletApp" width=300 height=300></applet>*/
```

Output

```
// change look and feel of an JApplet
import java.awt.*;
import javax.swing.*;
class WindowUtilities
{
public static void setNativeLookAndFeel()
{
try
{
UIManager.setLookAndFeel(UIManager.getSystemLookAndFeelClassName());
}
    catch(Exception e)
    {
    System.out.println(e);
```

```
      }
   }
}
public class JApp1 extends JApplet
{
   public void init()
   {
      WindowUtilities.setNativeLookAndFeel();
      Container c = getContentPane();
      c.setBackground(Color.YELLOW);
      c.setLayout(new FlowLayout());
      c.add(new JLabel("Hi, How r u?"));
      c.add(new JButton("Hi"));
   }
}
/*<Applet code=JApp1 width=300 height=300></Applet>*/
```

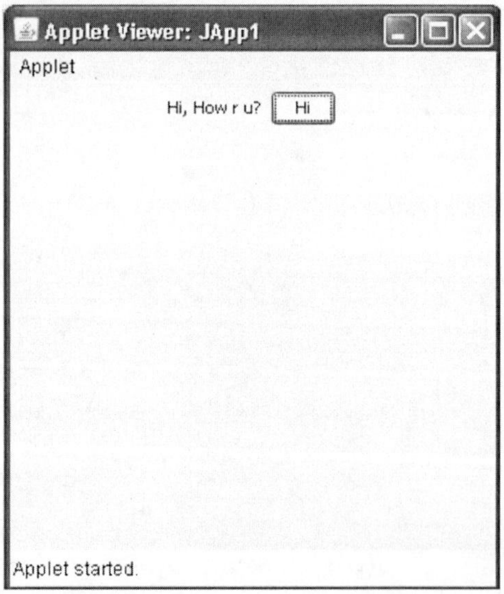

```
Command Prompt - appletviewer JApp1.java
P:\java>javac JApp1.java
P:\java>appletviewer JApp1.java
```

```
Applet Viewer: JApp1
Applet
Hi, How r u?  Hi
Applet started.
```

JFrame

JFrame extends the Frame and supports the swing components architecture. Components go in the contentpane, not directly in the frame.

Constructors used

Constructor	Description
JFrame()	Constructs a new Frame that is initially invisible.
JFrame(String title)	Constructs a new, initially invisible Frame with the specified title.

Methods used

Method	Description
addImpl(Component comp, Object constraints, int index)	By default, children may not be added directly to a this component, they must be added to its contentPane instead.
createRootPane()	Called by the constructor methods to create the default rootPane.
frameInit()	Called by the constructors to init the JFrame properly.
getAccessibleContext()	Get the AccessibleContext associated with this JFrame
getContentPane()	Returns the contentPane object for this frame.
getDefaultCloseOperation()	Returns the operation which occurs when the user initiates a "close" on this frame.
getGlassPane()	Returns the glassPane object for this frame.
getJMenuBar()	Returns the menubar set on this frame.
getLayeredPane()	Returns the layeredPane object for this frame.
getRootPane()	Returns the rootPane object for this frame.
isRootPaneCheckingEnabled()	Returns whether calls to add and setLayout cause an exception to be thrown.
paramString()	Returns a string representation of this JFrame.
processKeyEvent(KeyEvent e)	Processes key events occurring on this component and, if appropriate, passes them on to components in the frame which have registered interest in them.
processWindowEvent (WindowEvent e)	Processes window events occurring on this component.
remove (Component comp)	Removes the specified component from this container.
setContentPane (Container contentPane)	Sets the contentPane property.
setDefaultCloseOperation (int operation)	Sets the operation which will happen by default when the user initiates a "close" on this frame.
setGlassPane (Component glassPane)	Sets the glassPane property.
setJMenuBar (JMenuBar menubar)	Sets the menubar for this frame.
setLayeredPane (JLayeredPane layeredPane)	Sets the layeredPane property.
setLayout (LayoutManager manager)	By default the layout of this component may not be set, the layout of its contentPane should be set instead.

setRootPane (JRootPane root)	Sets the rootPane property.
setRootPaneCheckingEnabled (boolean enabled)	Determines whether calls to add and setLayout cause an exception to be thrown.
update(Graphics g)	Just calls paint(g).

Example:

```
import java.awt.*;
import javax.swing.*;
public class Jframe
{
   public static void main(String[] args)
   {
      JFrame f = new JFrame("JFrame");
      f.setSize(300, 300);
      Container c = f.getContentPane();
      c.setBackground(Color.YELLOW);
      c.setLayout(new FlowLayout());
      f.setVisible(true);
   }
}
```

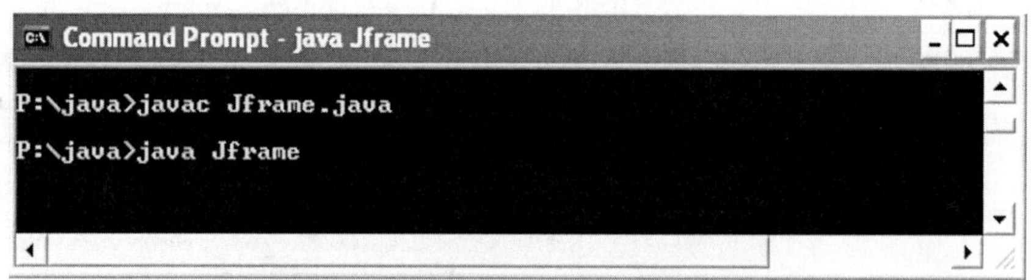

```
//Another Example
import javax.swing.*;
public class Jframe1
{
public static void main(String[] args)
{
JFrame frame = new JFrame("Hello, Swing!");
frame.setDefaultCloseOperation(JFrame.DISPOSE_ON_CLOSE);
JButton jb=new JButton("Hello");
frame.add(jb);
frame.pack();
frame.setVisible(true);
}
}
```

```
Command Prompt - java Jframe1
P:\java>javac Jframe1.java

P:\java>java Jframe1
```

H...
Hello

12.4 PROGRAMMING USING PANES

12.4.1 JRootPane

We can not create a JRootPane object directly. We get a JRootPane when we instantiate JInternalFrame or one of the top-level Swing containers, such as JApplet, JDialog or JFrame. The working process of root panes is to getting the content pane, setting its layout manager and adding Swing components to it.

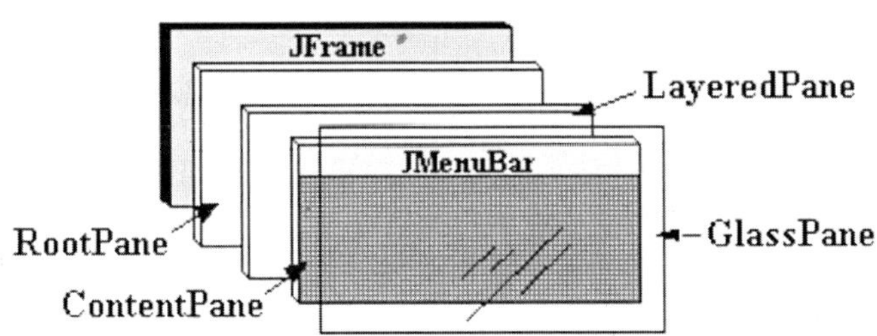

Figure 12.2: JRootPane

12.4.2 Parts of root pane

The following are the parts of root:

The glass pane

By default, glass pane is hidden. If we want to make the glass pane visible, then it's like a sheet of glass over all the other parts of the root pane. It is completely transparent sheet.

The layered pane

The position of layered pane is in between the rootpane and content pane. It serves to position its contents, which consist of the content pane and the optional menu bar.

The content pane

The content pane is a container that holds the visible components of the root pane excluding the menu bar.

The optional menu bar

If the container has a menu bar then use the setJMenuBar method of container to put the menu bar in the appropriate place.

12.4.3 The Root Pane API

The following table represent the list of API using root panes, glass panes and content panes.

Using a Root Pane

Method	Purpose
getRootPane()	Get the root pane of the applet, dialog, frame, internal frame, or window.
getRootPane(Component)	If the component contains a root pane, return that root pane. Otherwise, return the root pane (if any) that contains the component.
setDefaultButton(JButton)	Set button is the default button in the root pane.
JButton getDefaultButton()	Get the default button in the root pane.

Setting or Getting the Root Pane's Contents

Method	Purpose
setGlassPane(Component)	Set the glass pane.
getGlassPane()	Get the glass pane.
setLayeredPane(JLayeredPane)	Set the layered pane.
Container getLayeredPane()	Get the layered pane.
setContentPane(Container)	Set the content pane.

getContentPane()	Get the content pane.
setJMenuBar(JMenuBar)	Set the menu bar.
getJMenuBar()	Get the menu bar.

12.5 Pluggable Look and feel

LookAndFeel provides the dramatically changes in the component like frame related to the graphics for the application. Through this the application can be done very efficient and easier.

WindowUtilities.java

```
import javax.swing.*;
import java.awt.*;
import java.awt.event.*;

class ExitListener extends WindowAdapter
{
   public void windowClosing(WindowEvent event)
   {
      System.exit(0);
   }
}

public class WindowUtilities
{
   public static void setNativeLookAndFeel()
{
   try
   {
   UIManager.setLookAndFeel(UIManager.getSystemLookAndFeelClassName());
   }
      catch(Exception e) {
      System.out.println(e);
   }
   }

   ublic static void setJavaLookAndFeel()
{
try
{
   UIManager.setLookAndFeel(UIManager.
               getCrossPlatformLookAndFeelClassName());
   }
   catch(Exception e)
   {
```

```
    System.out.println(e);
    }
    }
    public static void setMotifLookAndFeel()
  {
      try
      {
        UIManager.setLookAndFeel("com.sun.java.swing.plaf.motif.
                MotifLookAndFeel");
      }
      catch(Exception e)
      {
      System.out.println(e);
    }
  }
    public static JFrame openInJFrame(Container content, int width, int height, String
          title,Color bgC)
    {
      JFrame f = new JFrame(title);
      f.setBackground(bgC);
      content.setBackground(bgC);
      f.setSize(width, height);
      f.setContentPane(content);
      f.addWindowListener(new ExitListener());
      f.setVisible(true);
      return(f);
    }
    static JFrame openInJFrame(Container content, int width, int height, String title)
  {
    return(openInJFrame(content, width, height, title, Color.white));
  }
    public static JFrame openInJFrame(Container content, int width, int height)
  {
    return(openInJFrame(content, width, height, content.getClass().getName(),
          Color.white));
    }
  }
```

```
//implement look and feel
//JApplet2.java
import java.awt.*;
import javax.swing.*;

public class JApplet2 extends JApplet
{
   public void init()
   {
      WindowUtilities.setNativeLookAndFeel();
      Container c = getContentPane();
      c.setBackground(Color.white);
      c.setLayout(new FlowLayout());
      c.add(new JButton(“Hi”));
      c.add(new JButton(“Look & Feel”));
      c.add(new JButton(“OK”));
   }
}
/*<applet code=JApplet2 width=300 height=300></applet>*/
```

```
Command Prompt - appletviewer JApplet2.java

P:\java>javac JApplet2.java

P:\java>appletviewer JApplet2.java
```

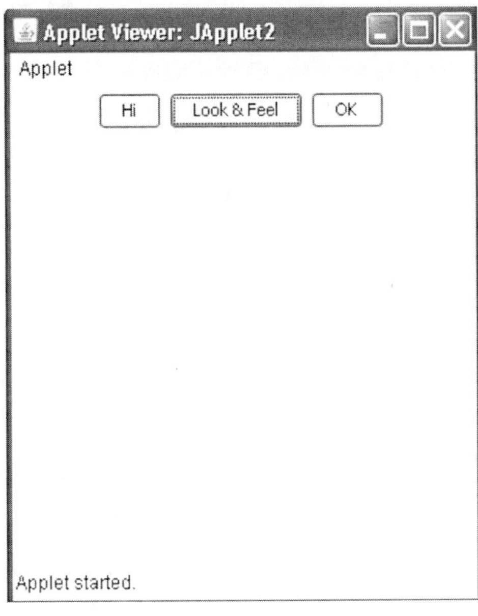

```
//JFrame2.java
import java.awt.*;
import javax.swing.*;
import java.awt.event.*;
public class JFrame2
{
  public static void main(String[] args)
{
      WindowUtilities.setNativeLookAndFeel();
      JFrame f = new JFrame("Hi Look and Feel");
      f.setSize(300, 300);
      Container c = f.getContentPane();
      c.setBackground(Color.white);
      c.setLayout(new FlowLayout());
      c.add(new JButton("Hi"));
      c.add(new JButton("Look and Feel"));
      c.add(new JButton("OK"));
      f.addWindowListener(new ExitListener());
      f.setVisible(true);
  }
}
```

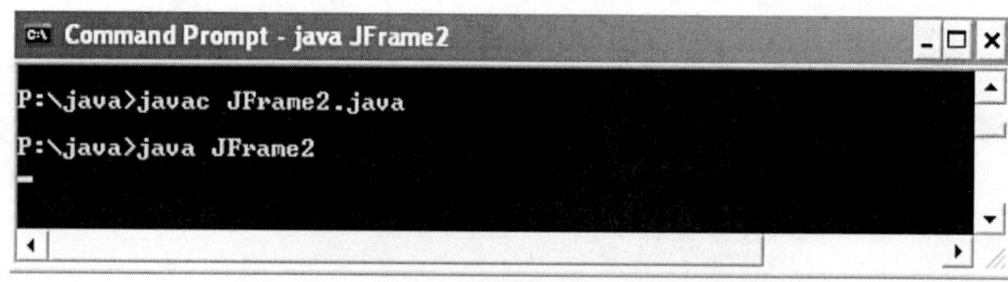

12.6 JLabel

The JLabel is the Swing equivalent of the AWT Label. JLabel is the simplest JComponent. It is just a string, image or both that appears on screen. The contents can be left, right, or center aligned according to an argument to the constructor. The default is left aligned. JLabel is cheap, fast way to get a picture or text on the screen.

Constructors used

Constructor	Description
JLabel()	Creates a JLabel instance with no image and with an empty string for the title.
JLabel(Icon i)	Creates a JLabel instance with the specified image.
JLabel(Icon i, int align)	Creates a JLabel instance with the specified image and horizontal alignment.
JLabel(String s)	Creates a JLabel instance with the specified text.
JLabel(String s, int align)	Creates a JLabel instance with the specified text and horizontal alignment.
JLabel(String s, Icon i, int align)	Creates a JLabel instance with the specified text, image, and horizontal alignment.

Methods used

Method	Description
setText(String)	Defines the single line of text this component will display.
getText()	Returns the text string that the label displays.
setIcon(Icon)	Sets the icon this component will display.
getIcon()	Returns the icon that the label displays.
setDisplayedMnemonic(char)	Specifies the displayedMnemonic as a char value.
getDisplayedMnemonic()	Return the keycode that indicates a mnemonic key.
setDisabledIcon(Icon)	Set the icon to be displayed if this JLabel is disabled.
getDisabledIcon()	Returns the value of the disabledIcon.
setHorizontalAlignment(int)	Set the horizontal alignment of the label.
setVerticalAlignment(int)	Set the vertical alignment of the label.
getHorizontalAlignment()	Get the horizontal alignment of the label.
getVerticalAlignment()	Get the vertical alignment of the label.
setHorizontalTextPosition(int)	Sets the horizontal position of the label's text.
setVerticalTextPosition(int)	Sets the vertical position of the label's text.
getHorizontalTextPosition()	Returns the horizontal position of the label's text.
getVerticalTextPosition()	Returns the vertical position of the label's text.
setIconTextGap(int)	Sets the number of pixels between the label's text and its image.
getIconTextGap()	Gets the number of pixels between the label's text and its image.
setLabelFor(Component)	Sets which component the label describes.
getLabelFor()	Gets which component the label describes.

Example:

```
import java.awt.*;
import javax.swing.*;
public class Jlabel
{
   static void main(String[] args)
{
      JFrame f = new JFrame("JLabel");
      f.setSize(300, 300);
      Container c = f.getContentPane();
      c.setBackground(Color.YELLOW);
      c.setLayout(new FlowLayout());
      c.add(new JLabel("Hello,How are you?"));
      f.setVisible(true);
   }
}
```

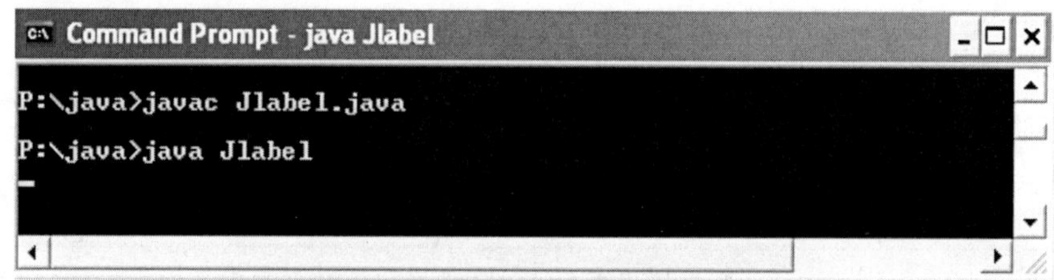

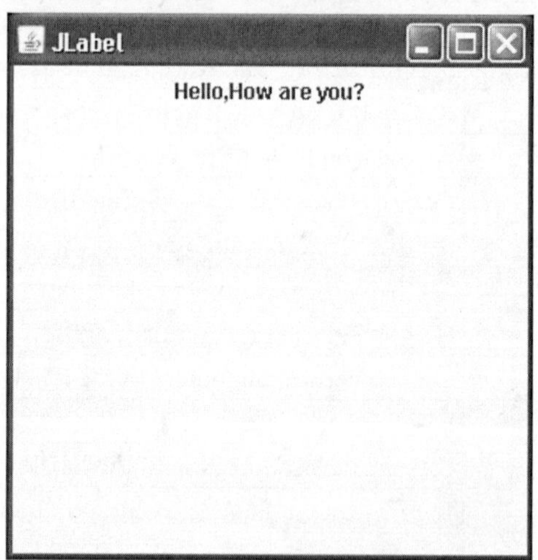

12.7 JTextField

The JTextField acts like any other ordinary text field of the AWT, except the fact that it can't be used as a PasswordTextField. SWING provides us with an additional class

JPasswordField.

Constructors used

Constructor	Description
JTextField()	Constructor of a JTextField
JTextField(int columns)	Constructor of a JTextField.
JTextField(java.lang.String text)	Constructor of a JTextField.
JTextField(java.lang.String text, int columns)	Constructor of a JTextField.

Methods used

Method	Description
getByte()	Returns a byte from the JTextField
getDouble()	Returns a double from the JTextField.
getFloat()	Returns a float from the JTextField.
getInt()	Returns an int from the JTextField.
getLong()	Returns a long from the JTextField.
getShort()	Returns a short from the JTextField.
isByte()	Checks if the JTextField contains a byte.
isDouble()	Checks if the JTextField contains a double.
isEmpty()	Tests if the JTextField is empty or not.
isFloat()	Checks if the JTextField contains a float.
isInt()	Checks if the JTextField contains an int.
isLong()	Checks if the JTextField contains a long.
isShort()	Checks if the JTextField contains a short.
setAutoSelection(boolean aBoolean)	Sets or unsets the autoselection for this JTextField.
setText(byte b)	Sets the text of the JTextField.
setText(double d)	Sets the text of the JTextField.
setText(float f)	Sets the text of the JTextField.
setText(int i)	Sets the text of the JTextField.
setText(long l)	Sets the text of the JTextField.
setText(short s)	Sets the text of the JTextField.

Example:

```
import java.awt.*;
import javax.swing.*;
public class Jtextfield
{
   public static void main(String[] args)
{
       JFrame f = new JFrame("JTextField");
       f.setSize(300, 300);
       Container c = f.getContentPane();
```

```
        c.setBackground(Color.YELLOW);
        c.setLayout(new FlowLayout());
        c.add(new JTextField("Hello"));
        f.setVisible(true);
    }
}
```

]12.8 JButton

The JButton is the Swing equivalent of the AWT Button. Simple uses of JButton are very similar to Button. We can add Icons to our Buttons. In order to add an Icon we need to pass the ImageIcon to the constructor. We create a JButton with a String as a label, and then drop it in a window. Events are normally handled just as with a Button: you attach an ActionListener via the addActionListener method. JToolTip is a text string that acts as a hint or further explanation.

The code to create it:

```
B1.setToolTipText ("click here");
```

Constructors used

Constructor	Description
JButton()	Creates a button with no set text or icon.
JButton(Action a)	Creates a button where properties are taken from the Action supplied.
JButton(Icon icon)	Creates a button with an icon.
JButton(String text)	Creates a button with text.
JButton(String text, Icon icon)	Creates a button with initial text and an icon.

Methods used

Method	Description
configurePropertiesFromAction (Action a)	Sets the AbstractButton's properties according to values from the Action instance.
getAccessibleContext()	Gets the AccessibleContext associated with this JButton.
getUIClassID()	Returns a string that specifies the name of the L&F class that renders this component.
isDefaultButton()	Gets the value of the defaultButton property.
isDefaultCapable()	Gets the value of the defaultCapable property.
paramString()	Returns a string representation of this JButton.
removeNotify()	Overrides JComponent.removeNotify to check if this button is currently set as the default button on the RootPane.
setDefaultCapable(boolean d)	Sets the defaultCapable property, which determines whether this button can be made the default button for its root pane.
updateUI()	Resets the UI property to a value from the current look and feel.

Example:

```
import java.awt.*;
import javax.swing.*;
public class Jbutton
{
   public static void main(String[] args)
{
      JFrame f = new JFrame("JButton ");
      f.setSize(300, 300);
      Container c = f.getContentPane();
      c.setBackground(Color.YELLOW);
      c.setLayout(new FlowLayout());
      c.add(new JButton("Hello"));
      f.setVisible(true);
   }
}
```

12.9 JToggleBtton

JToggleButton has two states, Selected or Deselected. When we press a ToggleButton it stays on until we switch it off again. Because of this, it uses a different listener to the one we use for a JButton as it maintains a state of 'Selected' or 'Deselected'. The Event Listener used in this case is an Item Listener. We instantiate the JToggleButton just like a normal button, with the String argument being passed as the string in the middle of the button.

Constructors used

Constructor	Description
JToggleButton()	Creates an initially unselected toggle button without setting the text or image.
JToggleButton(Action)	Creates a toggle button where properties are taken from the Action supplied.
JToggleButton(Icon)	Creates an initially deselected toggle button with the specified image but no text
JToggleButton(Icon, boolean)	Creates a toggle button with the specified image and selection state, but no text.
JToggleButton(String)	Creates an unselected toggle button with the specified text.
JToggleButton(String,boolean)	Creates a toggle button with the specified text and selection state.
JToggleButton(String, Icon)	Creates a toggle button that has the specified text and image and that is initially deselected.
JToggleButton(String,Icon, boolean)	Creates a toggle button with the specified text, image, and selection state.

Methods used

Method	Description
getAccessibleContext()	Gets the AccessibleContext associated with this JToggleButton.
getUIClassID()	Returns a string that specifies the name of the look and feel class that renders this component.
paramString()	Returns a string representation of this JToggleButton.
updateUI()	Resets the UI property to a value from the current look and feel.

Example:

```
import java.awt.*;
import javax.swing.*;
public class Jtogglebutton
{
   public static void main(String[] args)
{
      JFrame f = new JFrame("JToggleButton");
      f.setSize(300, 300);
      Container c = f.getContentPane();
      c.setBackground(Color.YELLOW);
      c.setLayout(new FlowLayout());
      c.add(new JToggleButton("On/Off"));
      f.setVisible(true);
   }
}
```

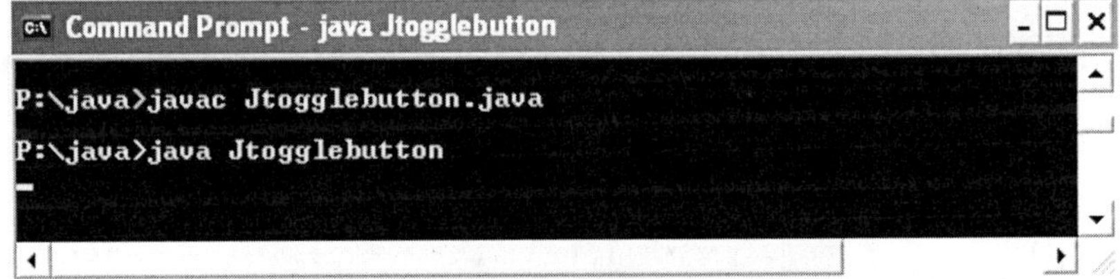

12.10 JCheckbox

A CheckBox screen object that represents a Boolean choice: pressed, not pressed, on, or off. Usually some text explains the choice. For example, JLabel would have a JCheckBox "Button" allowing yes or no.

The code to create it

```
JCheckBox b1 = new JCheckBox ("Yes");
JCheckBox b2 = new JCheckBox ("No");
Container c = frame.getContentPane ();
c.add (b1);
c.add(b2);
....
```

The code to retrieve user input from it

CheckBox generates bot ActionEvent and ItemEvent every time you change it.

Constructors used

Constructor	Description
JCheckBox()	Creates an initially unselected check box button with no text, no icon.
JCheckBox(Action)	Creates a check box where properties are taken from the Action supplied.
JCheckBox(Icon)	Creates an initially unselected check box with an icon.
JCheckBox(Icon, boolean)	Creates a check box with an icon and specifies whether or not it is initially selected.
JCheckBox(String)	Creates an initially unselected check box with text.
JCheckBox(String, boolean)	Creates a check box with text and specifies whether or not it is initially selected.
JCheckBox(String, Icon)	Creates an initially unselected check box with the specified text and icon.
JCheckBox(String, Icon, boolean)	Creates a check box with text and icon, and specifies whether or not it is initially selected.

Methods used

Method	Description
configurePropertiesFromActio n(Action a)	Factory method which sets the ActionEvent source's properties according to values from the Action instance.
createActionPropertyChangeLi stener(Action)	Factory method which creates the PropertyChangeListener used to update the ActionEvent source as properties change on its Action instance.
getAccessibleContext()	Gets the AccessibleContext associated with this JCheckBox.
getUIClassID()	Returns a string that specifies the name of the L&F class that renders this component.
isBorderPaintedFlat()	Returns whether the border should be painted flat.
paramString()	Returns a string representation of this JCheckBox.
setBorderPaintedFlat(boolean)	Sets whether the border should be painted flat.
updateUI()	Notification from the UIFactory that the L&F has changed.

Example:

```
import java.awt.*;
import javax.swing.*;
public class Jcheckbox
{
   public static void main(String[] args)
{
      JFrame f = new JFrame("JCheckBox");
      f.setSize(300, 300);
      c = f.getContentPane();
      c.setBackground(Color.YELLOW);
      c.setLayout(new FlowLayout());
      c.add(new JCheckBox("Yes"));
      c.add(new JCheckBox("No"));
      f.setVisible(true);
   }
}
```

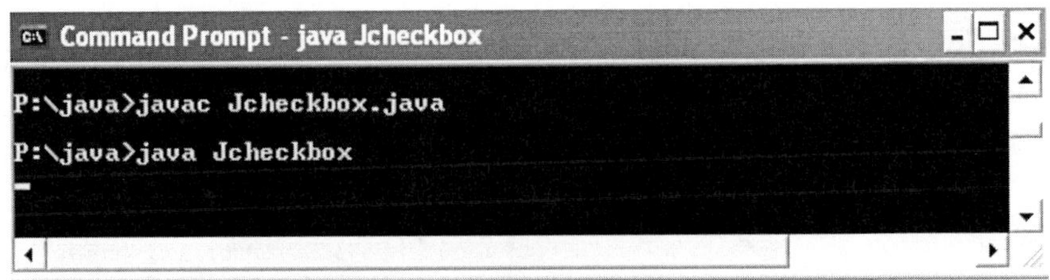

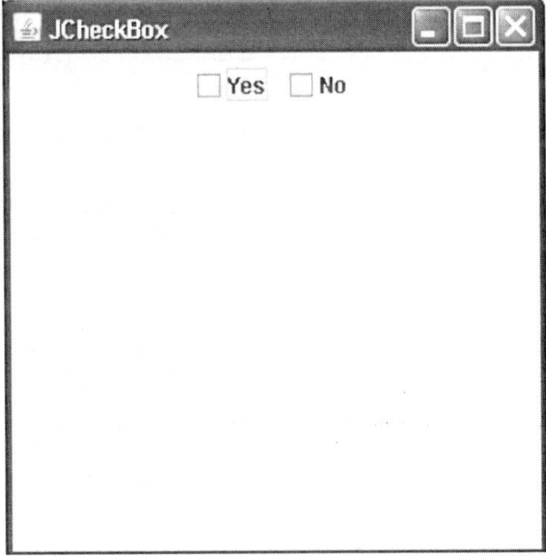

12.11 JRADIOBUTTON

JRadioButton is used to create radio buttons as well as check box. if we add more than one radio button to a JRadioButtonGroup then from all those buttons we can select one of them.

Constructors used

Constructor	Description
JRadioButton()	Creates an initially unselected radio button with no set text.
JRadioButton(Action)	Creates a radiobutton where properties are taken from the Action supplied.
JRadioButton(Icon)	Creates an initially unselected radio button with the specified image but no text.
JRadioButton(Icon, boolean)	Creates a radio button with the specified image and selection state, but no text.
JRadioButton(String)	Creates an unselected radio button with the specified text.
JRadioButton(String, boolean)	Creates a radio button with the specified text and selection state.
JRadioButton(String, Icon)	Creates a radio button that has the specified text and image, and that is initially unselected.
JRadioButton(String, Icon, boolean)	Creates a radio button that has the specified text, image, and selection state.

Methods used

Method	Description
configurePropertiesFromAction(Action a)	Sets the ActionEvent source's properties according to values from the Action instance.
createActionPropertyChangeListener(Action a)	Creates the PropertyChangeListener used to update the ActionEvent source as properties change on its Action instance.
getAccessibleContext()	Gets the AccessibleContext associated with this JRadioButton.
getUIClassID()	Returns the name of the L&F class that renders this component.
paramString()	Returns a string representation of this JRadioButton.
updateUI()	Notification from the UIFactory that the liik and feel has changed.

Example:

```
import java.awt.*;
import javax.swing.*;
public class Jradiobutton
{
   public static void main(String[] args)
{
      JFrame f = new JFrame("JRadioButton");
      f.setSize(300, 300);
      Container c = f.getContentPane();
      c.setBackground(Color.YELLOW);
      c.setLayout(new FlowLayout());
```

```
        c.add(new JRadioButton("Yes"));
        c.add(new JRadioButton("No"));
        f.setVisible(true);
    }
}
```

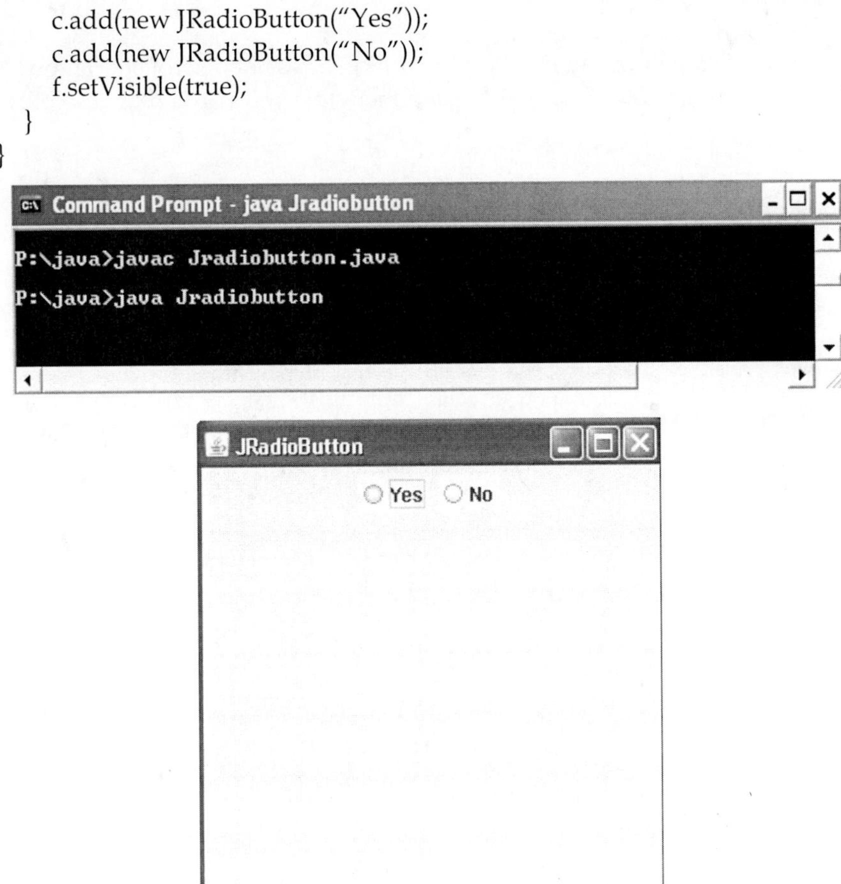

12.12 JVIEWPORT

View port is an area to represents the viewing of swing components. The View Port is the primary place view information. It shows all the information stored on reference in a concise and to the point manner. The JViewport class is the container that is really responsible for displaying a specific visible region of the component in JScrollPane.

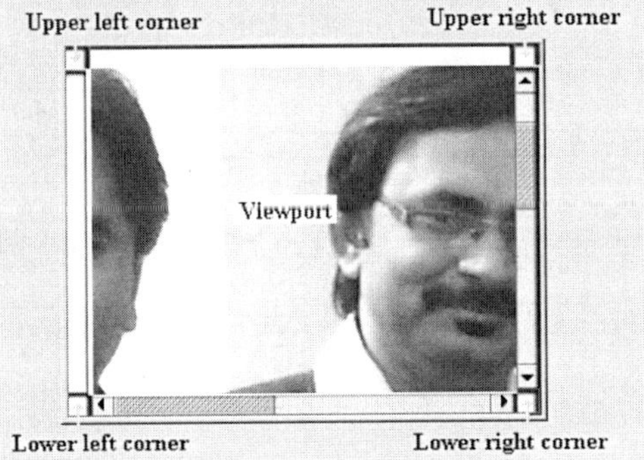

Figure 12.3: JViewport

12.13 JSCROLLPANE

Any component or container can be placed in a JScrollPane and scrolled. Simply create a JScrollPane by passing its constructor the component that we would like to scroll:

JScrollPane jsp = new JScrollPane(list);

Constructors used

Constructor	Description
JScrollPane()	Creates an empty JScrollPane where both horizontal and vertical scrollbars appear when needed.
JScrollPane(Component c)	Creates a JScrollPane that displays the contents of the specified component, where both horizontal and vertical scrollbars appear whenever the component's contents are larger than the view.
JScrollPane (Component c,int vsb, int hsb)	Creates a JScrollPane that displays the view component in a viewport whose view position can be controlled with a pair of scrollbars.
JScrollPane(int vsb, int hsb)	Creates an empty JScrollPane with specified scrollbar policies.

Methods used

Method	**Description**
createHorizontalScrollBar()	Returns a JScrollPane.ScrollBar by default.
createVerticalScrollBar()	Returns a JScrollPane.ScrollBar by default.
createViewport()	Returns a new JViewport by default.
getColumnHeader()	Returns the column header.
getCorner(String key)	Returns the component at the specified corner.
getHorizontalScrollBar()	Returns the horizontal scroll bar that controls the viewport's horizontal view position.
getHorizontalScrollBarPolicy()	Returns the horizontal scroll bar policy value.
getRowHeader()	Returns the row header.
getVerticalScrollBar()	Returns the vertical scroll bar that controls the viewports vertical view position.
getVerticalScrollBarPolicy()	Returns the vertical scroll bar policy value.
getViewport()	Returns the current JViewport.
getViewportBorder()	Returns the Border object that surrounds the viewport.
getViewportBorderBounds()	Returns the bounds of the viewport's border.
isValidateRoot()	Calls revalidate on any descendant of this JScrollPane.
isWheelScrollingEnabled()	Indicates whether or not scrolling will take place in response to the mouse wheel.
paramString()	Returns a string representation of this JScrollPane.
setHorizontalScrollBar(JScrollBar sb)	Adds the scrollbar that controls the viewport's horizontal view position to the scrollpane.

setComponentOrientation(ComponentOrientation co)	Sets the orientation for the vertical and horizontal scrollbars as determined by the ComponentOrientation argument.
setCorner(String key, Component c)	Adds a child that will appear in one of the scroll panes corners, if there's room.
setHorizontalScrollBarPolicy(int policy)	Determines when the horizontal scrollbar appears in the scrollpane.
setLayout(LayoutManager layout)	Sets the layout manager for this JScrollPane
setRowHeader(JViewport rowHeader)	Removes the old rowHeader, if it exists.
setRowHeaderView(Component view)	Sets row-header viewport to the scrollpane.
setVerticalScrollBar(JScrollBar verticalScrollBar)	Adds the scrollbar that controls the viewports vertical view position to the scrollpane.
setVerticalScrollBarPolicy(int policy)	Determines when the vertical scrollbar appears in the scrollpane.
setViewport(JViewport v)	Sets the scrollbars and headers with the new viewport.
setViewportBorder(Border b)	Adds a border around the viewport.
setWheelScrollingEnabled (boolean handleWheel)	Enables/disables scrolling in response to movement of the mouse wheel.

Example:

```
import java.awt.*;
import javax.swing.*;
public class Jscrollpane
{
   public static void main(String[] args)
   {
      JFrame f = new JFrame("JScrollPane ");
      f.setSize(300, 300);
      Container c = f.getContentPane();
      c.setBackground(Color.YELLOW);
      c.setLayout(new FlowLayout());
      JPanel jp= new JPanel();
      jp.add(new JButton("Hi"));
      jp.add(new JButton("Hello"));
      c.add(new JScrollPane(jp));
      f.setVisible(true);
   }
}
```

```
Command Prompt - java Jscrollpane

P:\java>javac Jscrollpane.java

P:\java>java Jscrollpane
```

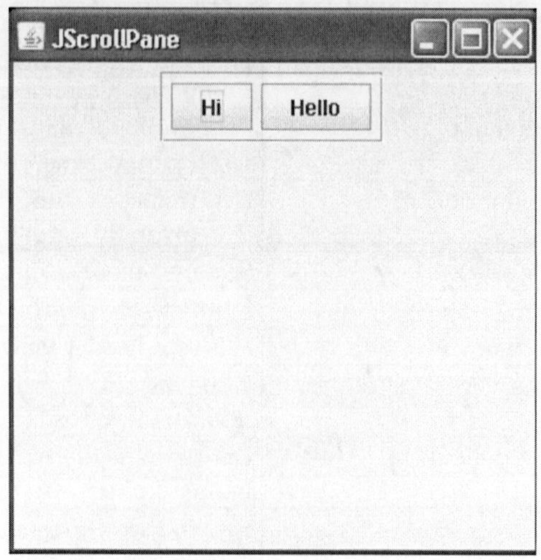

12.14 JSCROLLBAR

JScrollBar class used to create a scroll bar. It provides the view content area where we want to show the content to scroll this.

Constructors used

Constructor	Description
JScrollBar()	Creates a vertical scrollbar with the following initial values:
JScrollBar(int alignment)	Creates a scrollbar with the specified orientation and the following initial values:
JScrollBar(int alignment, int value, int extent, int min, int max)	Creates a scrollbar with the specified orientation, value, extent, minimum, and maximum.

Methods used

Method	Description
addAdjustmentListener(AdjustmentListener)	Adds an AdjustmentListener.
getAccessibleContext()	Gets the AccessibleContext associated with this JScrollBar.
getAdjustmentListeners()	Returns an array of all the AdjustmentListeners added to this JScrollBar with addAdjustmentListener().
getBlockIncrement()	For backwards compatibility with java.awt.Scrollbar.
getBlockIncrement(int)	Returns the amount to change the scrollbar's value by, given a block (usually "page") up/down request.
getMaximum()	The maximum value of the scrollbar is maximum - extent.
getMaximumSize()	The scrollbar is flexible along it's scrolling axis and rigid along the other axis.
getMinimum()	Returns the minimum value supported by the scrollbar (usually zero).

getMinimumSize()	The scrollbar is flexible along it's scrolling axis and rigid along the other axis.
getModel()	Returns data model that handles the scrollbar's four fundamental properties: minimum, maximum, value, extent.
getOrientation()	Returns the component's orientation (horizontal or vertical).
getValue()	Returns the scrollbar's value.
getValueIsAdjusting()	True if the scrollbar knob is being dragged.
paramString()	Returns a string representation of this JScrollBar.
removeAdjustmentListener(AdjustmentListener)	Removes an AdjustmentEvent listener.
setBlockIncrement(int)	Sets the blockIncrement property.
setEnabled(boolean)	Enables the component so that the knob position can be changed.
setMaximum(int maximum)	Sets the model's maximum property.
setMinimum(int minimum)	Sets the model's minimum property.
setOrientation(int orientation)	Set the scrollbar's orientation to either VERTICAL or HORIZONTAL.
setUnitIncrement (int unitIncrement)	Sets the unitIncrement property.
setValue(int value)	Sets the scrollbar's value.

Example:

```
import java.awt.*;
import javax.swing.*;
public class Jscrllbar
{
   public static void main(String[] args)
{
      JFrame f = new JFrame("JScrollBar");
      f.setSize(300, 300);
      Container c = f.getContentPane();
      c.setBackground(Color.YELLOW);
      c.setLayout(new FlowLayout());
      c.add(new JScrollBar());
      f.setVisible(true);
   }
}
```

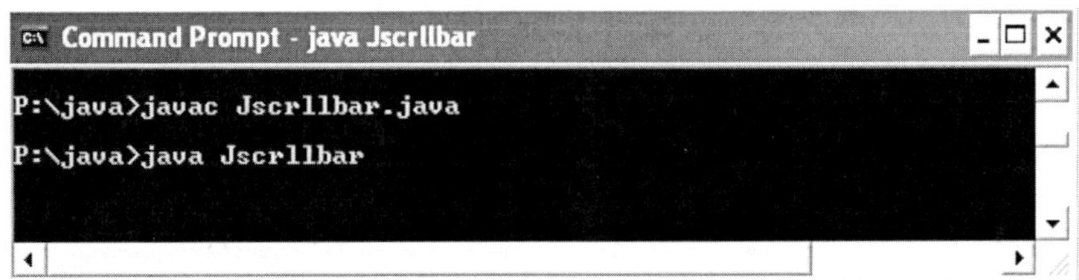

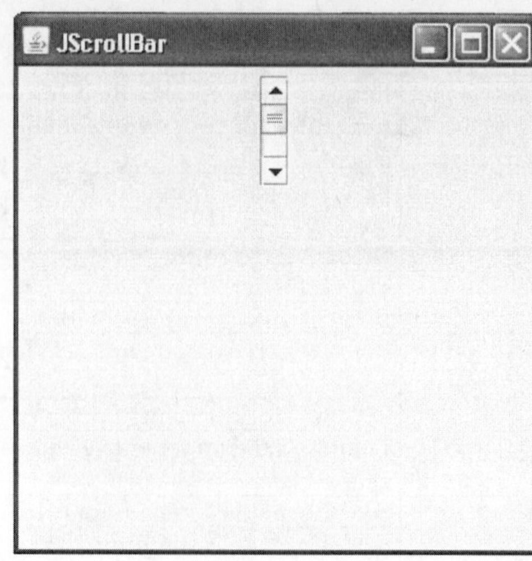

12.15 JLIST

The JList is another complex component which provides a list of data elements. We can select any number of items at the same time. We can display the list of data vertically or horizontally.

Constructors used

Constructor	Description
JList()	Constructs a JList with an empty model.
JList (ListModel dataModel)	Constructs a JList that displays the elements in the specified, non-null model.
JList(Object[] listData)	Constructs a JList that displays the elements in the specified array.
JList(Vector listData)	Constructs a JList that displays the elements in the specified Vector.

Methods used

Method	Description
addSelectionInterval(int anchor, int lead)	Sets the selection to be the union of the specified interval with current selection.
clearSelection()	Clears the selection.
getCellBounds(int index0, int index1)	Returns the bounds of the specified range of items in JList coordinates.
getCellRenderer()	Returns the object that renders the list items.
getDragEnabled()	Gets the dragEnabled property.
getFirstVisibleIndex()	Returns the index of the first visible cell.
getListSelectionListeners()	Returns an array of all the ListSelectionListeners added to this JList with addListSelectionListener().
getMaxSelectionIndex()	Returns the largest selected cell index.

getMinSelectionIndex()	Returns the smallest selected cell index.
getPrototypeCellValue()	Returns the cell width.
getSelectedIndices()	Returns an array of all of the selected indices in increasing order.
getSelectedValue()	Returns the first selected value or null if the selection is empty.
getSelectedValues()	Returns an array of the values for the selected cells.
getSelectionBackground()	Returns the background color for selected cells.
getSelectionForeground()	Returns the selection foreground color.
getSelectionMode()	Returns whether single-item or multiple-item selections are allowed.
getSelectionModel()	Returns the value of the current selection model.
getToolTipText(MouseEvent event)	Allow the renderer's tips to be used if it has text set.
getValueIsAdjusting()	Returns the value of the data model's isAdjusting property.
getVisibleRowCount()	Returns the preferred number of visible rows.
isSelectedIndex(int index)	Returns true if the specified index is selected.
isSelectionEmpty()	Returns true if nothing is selected.
paramString()	Returns a string representation of this JList.
setListData(Object[] listData)	Constructs a ListModel from an array of objects and then applies setModel to it.
setListData(Vector listData)	Constructs a ListModel from a Vector and then applies setModel to it.
setModel(ListModel model)	Sets the model that represents the contents.
setSelectedIndex(int index)	Selects a single cell.
setSelectedIndices(int[])	Selects a set of cells.
setSelectedValue(Object, boolean)	Selects the specified object from the list.
setSelectionBackground (Color selectionBackground)	Sets the background color for selected cells.
setSelectionForeground (Color selectionForeground)	Sets the foreground color for selected cells.
setVisibleRowCount (int visibleRowCount)	Sets the preferred number of rows.

Example:

```
import java.awt.*;
import javax.swing.*;
public class Jlist
{
   public static void main(String[] args)
{
      JFrame f = new JFrame("JScrollBar");
```

```
        f.setSize(300, 300);
        Container c = f.getContentPane();
        c.setBackground(Color.YELLOW);
        c.setLayout(new FlowLayout());
        String a[];
        a=new String[3];
        a[0]="Tanweer";
        a[1]="Anjum";
        a[2]="AAtif";
        JList jl=new JList(a);
        jl.setBackground(Color.RED);
        .add(jl);
        f.setVisible(true);
    }
}
```

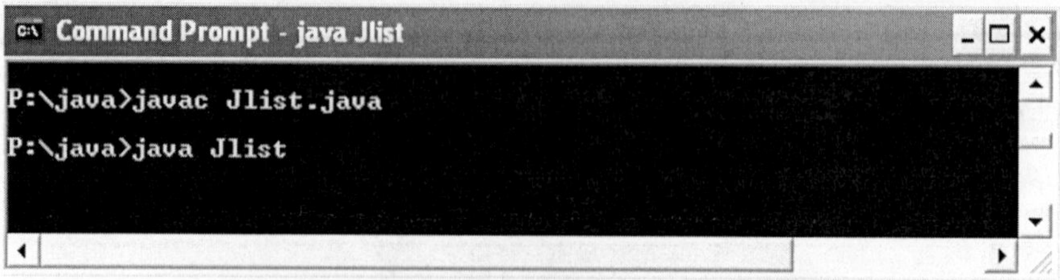

```
Command Prompt - java Jlist
P:\java>javac Jlist.java
P:\java>java Jlist
```

JList

Tanweer
Anjum
AAtif

12.16 JCOMBOBOX

JComboBox provides the drop-down list where user selects only one item or value at a time. But combo box is a combination of multiple text or buttons etc.

Constructors used

Constructor	Description
JComboBox()	Creates a JComboBox with a default data model.
JComboBox(ComboBoxModel aModel)	Creates a JComboBox that takes its items from an existing ComboBoxModel.
JComboBox(Object[] items)	Creates a JComboBox that contains the elements in the specified array.
JComboBox(Vector items)	Creates a JComboBox that contains the elements in the specified Vector.

Methods used

Method	Description
actionPerformed(ActionEvent)	This method is public as an implementation side effect.
addActionListener(ActionListener)	Adds an ActionListener.
addItem(Object anObject)	Adds an item to the item list.
addItemListener(ItemListener)	Adds an ItemListener.
addPopupMenuListener(PopupMenuListener)	Adds a PopupMenu listener.
getAction()	Returns the currently set Action for this ActionEvent source, or null if no Action is set.
getActionCommand()	Returns the action command
getActionListeners()	Returns an array of all the ActionListeners.
getEditor()	Returns the editor used to paint and edit the selected item in the JComboBox field.
getItemAt(int index)	Returns the list item at the specified index.
getItemCount()	Returns the number of items in the list.
getItemListeners()	Returns an array of all the ItemListeners.
getKeySelectionManager()	Returns the list's key-selection manager.
getMaximumRowCount()	Returns the maximum number of items the combo box can display without a scrollbar
getModel()	Returns the data model currently used by the JComboBox.
getPopupMenuListeners()	Returns an array of all the PopupMenuListeners
getSelectedIndex()	Returns the first item in the list that matches the given item.
getSelectedItem()	Returns the current selected item.
getSelectedObjects()	Returns an array containing the selected item.
insertItemAt(Object anObject, int index)	Inserts an item into the item list at a given index.
intervalAdded(ListDataEvent e)	This method is public as an implementation side effect.
intervalRemoved ListDataEvent e)	This method is public as an implementation side effect.
isEditable()	Returns true if the JComboBox is editable.
isPopupVisible()	Determines the visibility of the popup.

paramString()	Returns a string representation of this JComboBox.
removeActionListener (ActionListener l)	Removes an ActionListener.
removeAllItems()	Removes all items from the item list.
removeItem(Object anObject)	Removes an item from the item list.
removeItemAt(int anIndex)	Removes the item at anIndex This method works only if the JComboBox uses a mutable data model.
removeItemListener (ItemListener aListener)	Removes an ItemListener.
removePopupMenuListener (PopupMenuListener l)	Removes a PopupMenuListener.
selectedItemChanged()	This protected method is implementation specific.
setAction(Action a)	Sets the Action for the ActionEvent source.
setActionCommand (String aCommand)	Sets the action command that should be included in the event sent to action listeners.
setEditable(boolean aFlag)	Determines whether the JComboBox field is editable.
setEditor(ComboBoxEditor anEditor)	Sets the editor used to paint and edit the selected item in the JComboBox field.
setEnabled(boolean b)	Enables the combo box so that items can be selected.
setMaximumRowCount(int count)	Sets the maximum number of rows the JComboBox displays.
setPopupVisible(boolean v)	Sets the visibility of the popup.
setSelectedIndex(int anIndex)	Selects the item at index anIndex.
setSelectedItem(Object anObject)	Sets the selected item in the combo box display area to the object in the argument.

Example:

```
import java.awt.*;
import javax.swing.*;
public class Jcombobox
{
   public static void main(String[] args)
{
      JFrame f = new JFrame("JComboBox");
      f.setSize(300, 300);
      Container c = f.getContentPane();
      c.setBackground(Color.YELLOW);
      c.setLayout(new FlowLayout());
      JComboBox jb=new JComboBox();
      jb.addItem("item1");
      jb.addItem("item2");
```

```
        c.add(jb);
        f.setVisible(true);
    }
}
```

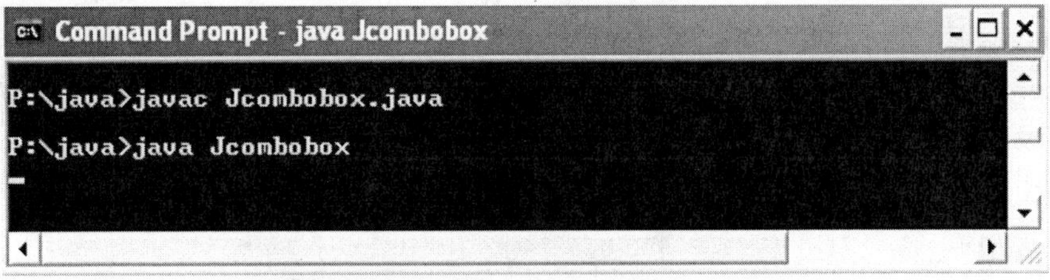

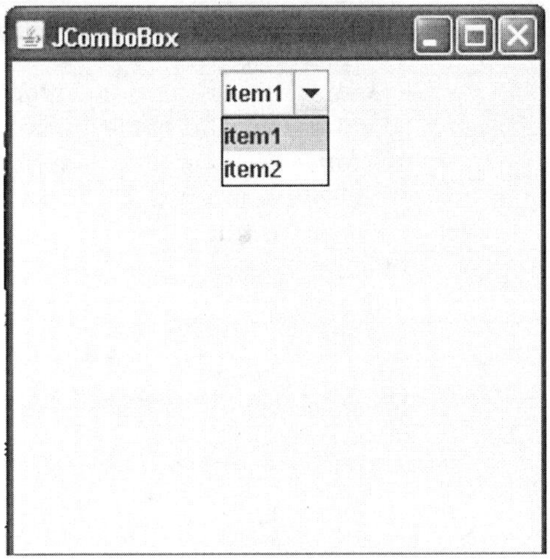

12.17 JPROGRESSBAR

JProgressBar shows the integer types values in percent within a bounded range to determine the working process.

Constructors used

Constructor	Description
JProgressBar()	Creates a horizontal progress bar that displays a border but no progress string.
JProgressBar(Bounded RangeModel newModel)	Creates a horizontal progress bar that uses the specified model to hold the progress bar's data.
JProgressBar(int orient)	Creates a progress bar with the specified orientation, which can be either JProgressBar. VERTICAL or JProgressBar.HORIZONTAL.
JProgressBar(int min, int max)	Creates a horizontal progress bar with the specified minimum and maximum.
JProgressBar(int orient, int min, int max)	Creates a progress bar using the specified orientation, minimum, and maximum.

Methods used

Method	Description
addChangeListener(ChangeListener)	Adds the specified ChangeListener to the progress bar.
getChangeListeners()	Returns an array of all the ChangeListeners added to this progress bar with addChangeListener.
getMaximum()	Returns the progress bar's maximum value.
getMinimum()	Returns the progress bar's minimum value.
getModel()	Returns the data model used by this progress bar.
getOrientation()	Returns JProgressBar.VERTICAL or JProgressBar. HORIZONTAL, depending on the orientation of the progress bar.
getPercentComplete()	Returns the percent complete for the progress bar.
getString()	Returns the current value of the progress string.
getValue()	Returns the progress bar's current value.
isBorderPainted()	Returns the borderPainted property.
isIndeterminate()	Returns the value of the indeterminate property.
isStringPainted()	Returns the value of the stringPainted property.
paintBorder(Graphics g)	Paints the progress bar's border if the borderPainted property is true.
paramString()	Returns a string representation of this JProgressBar.
removeChangeListener (ChangeListener l)	Removes a ChangeListener from the progress bar.
setBorderPainted(boolean b)	Sets the borderPainted property, which is true if the progress bar should paint its border.
setIndeterminate (boolean newValue)	Sets the indeterminate property of the progress bar.
setMaximum(int n)	Sets the progress bar's maximum value
setMinimum(int n)	Sets the progress bar's minimum value (stored in the progress bar's data model) to n.
setModel (BoundedRangeModel newModel)	Sets the data model used by the JProgressBar.
setOrientation(int Orientation)	Sets the progress bar's orientation to newOrientation.
setString(String s)	Sets the value of the progress string.
setStringPainted(boolean b)	Sets the value of the stringPainted property.
setValue(int n)	Sets the progress bar's current value.

Example:

```
import java.awt.*;
import javax.swing.*;
public class Jprogressbar
{
    public static void main(String[] args)
{
        JFrame f = new JFrame("JProgressBar");
        f.setSize(300, 300);
        Container c = f.getContentPane();
        c.setBackground(Color.YELLOW);
        c.setLayout(new FlowLayout());
```

```
        c.add(new JProgressBar(0,100));
        f.setVisible(true);
    }
}
```

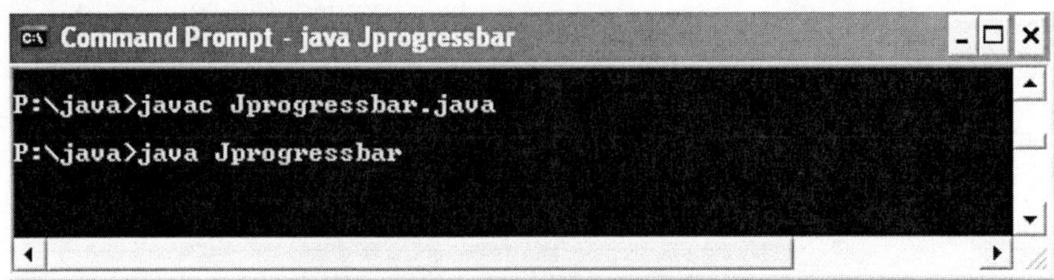

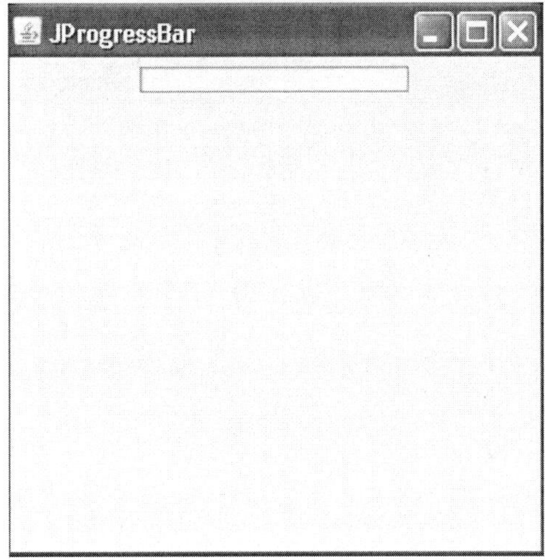

12.18 JMENU

JMenu class used to create a new menu where we add the JMenuItems. When we select the item then shows the popup menu items in the JMenuBar.

Constructors used

Constructor	Description
JMenuBar()	Creates a new menu bar.

Methods used

Method	Description
add(JMenu c)	Appends the specified menu to the end of the menu bar.
addNotify()	Overrides JComponent.addNotify to register the menu bar.

getAccessibleContext()	Gets the AccessibleContext associated with this JMenuBar.
getComponent()	Implemented to be a MenuElement.
getComponentIndex(Component c)	Returns the index of the specified component.
getHelpMenu()	Gets the help menu for the menu bar.
getMargin()	Returns the margin between the menubar's border and its menus.
getMenu(int index)	Returns the menu at the specified position in the menu bar.
getMenuCount()	Returns the number of items in the menu bar.
isBorderPainted()	Returns true if the menu bars border should be painted.
isSelected()	Returns true if the menu bar currently has a component selected.
menuSelectionChanged(boolean isIncluded)	Implemented to be a MenuElement -- does nothing.
paintBorder(Graphics g)	Paints the menubar's border if BorderPainted property is true.
paramString()	Returns a string representation of this JMenuBar.
setBorderPainted(boolean b)	Sets whether the border should be painted.
setHelpMenu(JMenu menu)	Sets the help menu that appears when the user selects the "help" option in the menu bar.
setMargin(Insets m)	Sets the margin between the menubar's border and its menus.
setSelected(Component sel)	Sets the currently selected component, producing a a change to the selection model.

Example:

```
import java.awt.*;
import javax.swing.*;
public class Jmenu
{
   public static void main(String[] args)
{
      JFrame f = new JFrame("JMenu");
      f.setSize(300, 300);
      JMenuBar mb=new JMenuBar();
      JMenu menu=new JMenu("File");
      JMenuItem m1=new JMenuItem("New");
      JMenuItem m2=new JMenuItem("Open");
      menu.add(m1);
      menu.add(m2);
      mb.add(menu);
      f.setJMenuBar(mb);
```

```
        f.setVisible(true);
    }
}
```

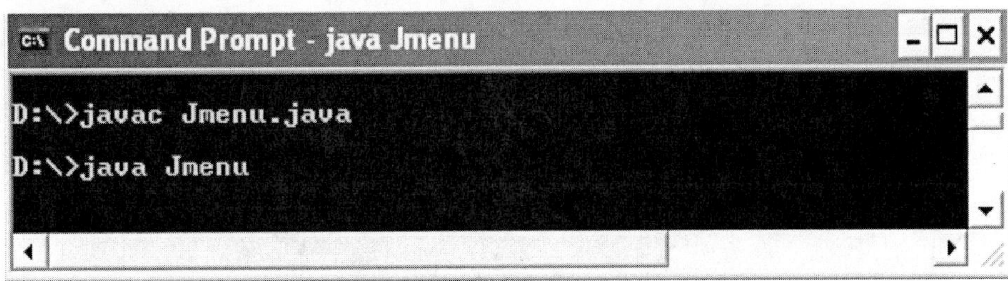

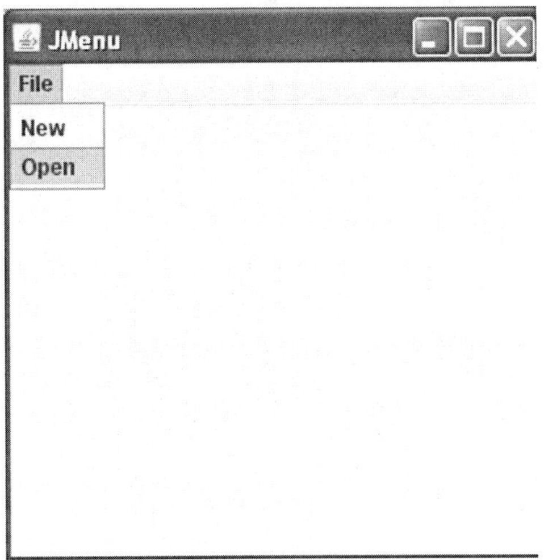

Example:

```
import java.awt.*;
import javax.swing.*;
public class Jmenu
{
    public static void main(String[] args)
    {
        JFrame f = new JFrame("JMenu");
        f.setSize(300, 300);
        Container c = f.getContentPane();
        c.setBackground(Color.YELLOW);
        c.setLayout(new FlowLayout());
        JMenuBar mb=new JMenuBar();
        JMenu menu=new JMenu();
        JMenuItem m1=new JMenuItem("File");
        JMenuItem m2=new JMenuItem("New");
        menu.add(m1);
```

```
        menu.add(m2);
        mb.add(menu);
        c.add(mb);
        f.setVisible(true);
    }
}
```

```
P:\java>javac Jmenu.java

P:\java>java Jmenu
```

12.19 JTOOLBAR

JToolbar class provides set of command buttons icons that performs the different actions or controls.

Constructors used

Constructor	Description
JToolBar()	Creates a new tool bar; orientation defaults to HORIZONTAL
JToolBar(int orientation)	Creates a new tool bar with the specified orientation.
JToolBar(String name)	Creates a new tool bar with the specified name.
JToolBar(String name, int orientation)	Creates a new tool bar with a specified name and orientation.

Methods used

Method	Description
add(Action a)	Adds a new JButton which dispatches the action.
addImpl(Component comp, Object constraints, int index)	If a JButton is being added, it is initially set to be disabled.
addSeparator()	Appends a separator of default size to the end of the tool bar.
addSeparator(Dimension size)	Appends a separator of a specified size to the end of the tool bar.
getMargin()	Returns the margin between the tool bar's border and its buttons.
getOrientation()	Returns the current orientation of the tool bar.
isBorderPainted()	Gets the borderPainted property.
isFloatable()	Gets the floatable property.
isRollover()	Returns the rollover state.
paintBorder(Graphics g)	Paints the tool bar's border if the borderPainted property is true.
paramString()	Returns a string representation of this JToolBar.
setBorderPainted(boolean b)	Sets the borderPainted property, which is true if the border should be painted.
setFloatable(boolean b)	Sets the floatable property, which must be true for the user to move the tool bar.
setLayout(LayoutManager mgr)	Sets the layout manager for this container.
setMargin(Insets m)	Sets the margin between the tool bar's border and its buttons.
setOrientation(int o)	Sets the orientation of the tool bar.
setRollover(boolean rollover)	Sets the rollover state of this toolbar.

Example:

```
import java.awt.*;
import javax.swing.*;
public class Jtoolbar
{
   public static void main(String[] args)
   {
      JFrame f = new JFrame("JToolBar");
      f.setSize(300, 300);
      Container c = f.getContentPane();
      c.setBackground(Color.YELLOW);
      c.setLayout(new FlowLayout());
      JToolBar jtb=new JToolBar("File");
      c.add(jtb);
      f.setVisible(true);
   }
}
```

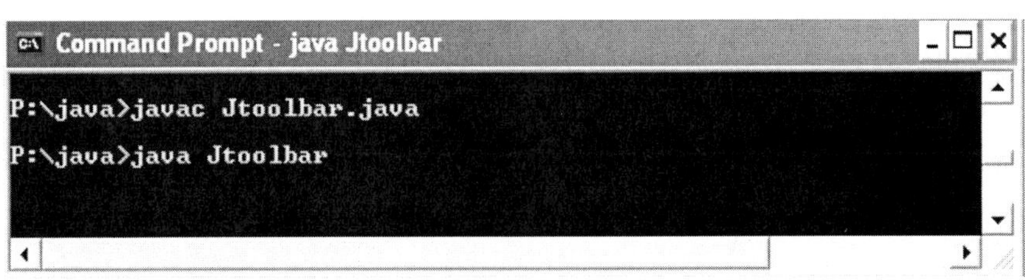

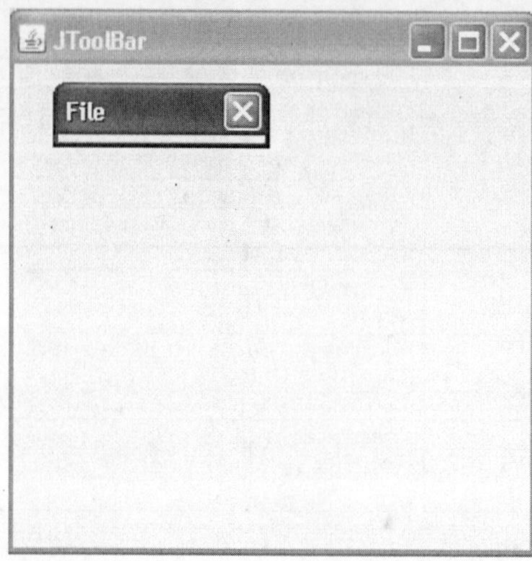

12.20 JLayeredPane

JLayeredPane has JFC/Swing container that can be used to overlap the components to each other.

Constructors used

Constructor	Description
JLayeredPane()	Create a new JLayeredPane

Methods used

Method	Description
addImpl(Component c,Object o, int index)	Adds the specified component to this container at the specified index.
getComponentCountInLayer(int layer)	Returns the number of children currently in the specified layer.
getComponentsInLayer(int layer)	Returns an array of the components in the specified layer.
getComponentToLayer()	Returns the hashtable that maps components to layers.
getIndexOf(Component c)	Returns the index of the specified Component.
getLayer(Component c)	Returns the layer attribute for the specified Component.
getLayer(JComponent c)	Gets the layer property for a JComponent.
getObjectForLayer(int layer)	Returns the Integer object associated with a specified layer.
getPosition(Component c)	Get the relative position of the component within its layer.
highestLayer()	Returns the highest layer value from all current children.
lowestLayer()	Returns the lowest layer value from all current children.

moveToBack(Component c)	Moves the component to the bottom of the components.
moveToFront(Component c)	Moves the component to the top of the components in its current layer (position 0).
paint(Graphics g)	Paints this JLayeredPane within the specified graphics context.
paramString()	Returns a string representation of this JLayeredPane.
putLayer(JComponent c, int layer)	Sets the layer property on a JComponent.
remove(int index)	Remove the indexed component from this pane.
setLayer(Component c, int layer)	Sets the layer attribute on the specified component.
setLayer(Component c, int layer, int position)	Sets the layer attribute for the specified component.
setPosition(Component c, int position)	Moves the component to position within its current layer, where 0 is the topmost position within the layer and -1 is the bottommost position.

12.21 JTABBEDPANE

JTabbedPane class provides the tab component through which we can switch from one component to another component regarding to the specific tab button by clicking on that.

Constructors used

Constructor	Description
JTabbedPane.AccessibleJTabbedPane()	Constructs an AccessibleJTabbedPane

Methods used

Method	Description
addAccessibleSelection(int i)	Adds the specified Accessible child of the object to the object's selection.
clearAccessibleSelection()	Clears the selection in the object, so that no children in the object are selected.
getAccessibleAt(Point p)	Returns the Accessible child contained at the local coordinate Point, if one exists.
getAccessibleChild(int i)	Return the specified Accessible child of the object.
getAccessibleChildrenCount()	Returns the number of accessible children in the object.
getAccessibleRole()	Get the role of this object.
getAccessibleSelection()	Gets the AccessibleSelection associated with this object.
getAccessibleSelection(int i)	Returns an Accessible representing the specified selected child of the object.
getAccessibleSelectionCount()	Returns the number of Accessible children currently selected.
isAccessibleChildSelected(int i)	Determines if the current child of this object is selected.
removeAccessibleSelection(int i)	Removes the specified child of the object from the object's selection.

selectAllAccessibleSelection()	Causes every child of the object to be selected if the object supports multiple selections.
stateChanged(ChangeEvent e)	Invoked when the target of the listener has changed its state.

12.22 JSPLITPANE

JSplitPane class used to divides the two components graphically like: top and button, left and right.

Constructors used

Constructor	Description
JSplitPane()	Creates a new JSplitPane.
JSplitPane(int Orientation)	Creates a new JSplitPane with the specified orientation and no continuous layout.
JSplitPane(int Orientation, boolean newContinuousLayout)	Creates a new JSplitPane with the specified orientation and redrawing style.
JSplitPane(int Orientation, boolean layout,Component c1, Component c2)	Creates a new JSplitPane with the specified orientation and redrawing style, and with the specified components.
JSplitPane(int newOrientation, Component newLeftComponent, Component newRightComponent)	Creates a new JSplitPane with the specified orientation and with the specified components that do not do continuous redrawing.

Methods used

Method	Description
addImpl(Component c, Object constraints, int index)	Adds the specified component to this split pane.
getAccessibleContext()	Gets the AccessibleContext associated with this JSplitPane.
getBottomComponent()	Returns the component below, or to the right of the divider.
getDividerLocation()	Returns the last value passed to setDividerLocation.
getDividerSize()	Returns the size of the divider.
getLastDividerLocation()	Returns the last location the divider was at.
getLeftComponent()	Returns the component to the left (or above) the divider.
getMaximumDividerLocation()	Returns the maximum location of the divider.
getMinimumDividerLocation()	Returns the minimum location of the divider.
getOrientation()	Returns the orientation.
getResizeWeight()	Returns the number that determines how extra space is distributed.
getRightComponent()	Returns the component to the right (or below) the divider.
getTopComponent()	Returns the component above, or to the left of the divider.
isContinuousLayout()	Gets the continuousLayout property.

isOneTouchExpandable()	Gets the oneTouchExpandable property.
paramString()	Returns a string representation of this JSplitPane.
remove(Component component)	Removes the child component, component from the pane.
remove(int index)	Removes the Component at the specified index.
removeAll()	Removes all the child components from the split pane.
setBottomComponent(Component comp)	Sets the component below, or to the right of the divider.
setContinuousLayout (boolean newContinuousLayout)	Sets the value of the continuousLayout property.
setDividerLocation(double proportionalLocation)	Sets the divider location as a percentage of the JSplitPane's size.
setDividerLocation(int location)	Sets the location of the divider.
setDividerSize(int newSize)	Sets the size of the divider.
setLastDividerLocation(int newLastLocation)	Sets the last location the divider was at to newLastLocation.
setLeftComponent(Component comp)	Sets the component to the left (or above) the divider.
setOrientation(int orientation)	Sets the orientation, or how the splitter is divided.
setResizeWeight(double value)	Specifies how to distribute extra space when the size of the split pane changes.
setRightComponent(Component comp)	Sets the component to the right (or below) the divider.
setTopComponent(Component comp)	Sets the component above, or to the left of the divider.

Example:

```
import java.awt.*;
import javax.swing.*;
public class Jsplit
{
   public static void main(String[] args)
   {
      JFrame f = new JFrame("JSplitPane");
      f.setSize(300, 300);
      Container c = f.getContentPane();
      c.setBackground(Color.YELLOW);
      c.setLayout(new FlowLayout());
      JSplitPane jtp=new JSplitPane();
      c.add(jtp);
      .setVisible(true);
   }
}
```

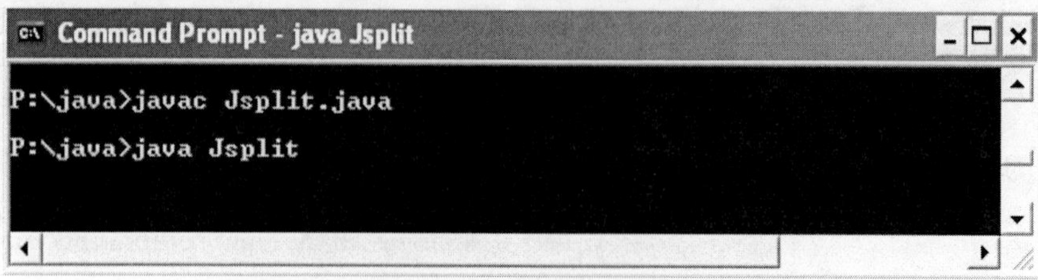

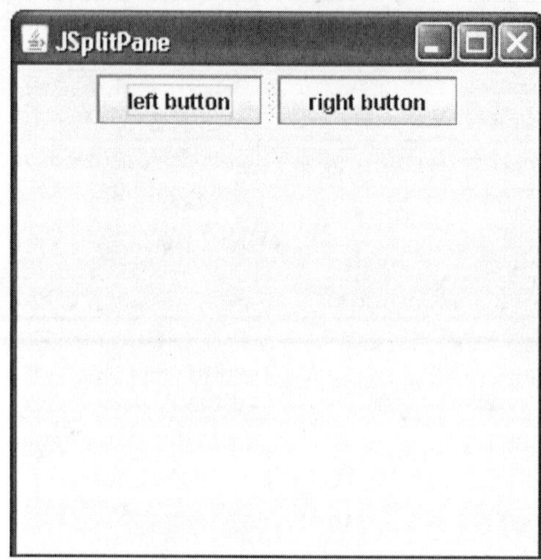

12.23 JDIALOGBOX

JDialogBox class used to create the dialog window and when you want to create the custom dialog window with the help of JOptionPane method.It extends the Dialog.

Constructors used

Constructor	Description
JDialog()	Creates a non-modal dialog without a title and without a specified Frame.
JDialog(Dialog d)	Creates a non-modal dialog without a title with the specified Dialog.
JDialog(Dialog d, boolean modal)	Creates a modal or non-modal dialog without a title and with the specified dialog.
JDialog(Dialog d, String title)	Creates a non-modal dialog with the specified title and with the specified dialog.
JDialog(Dialog d,String title,boolean modal)	Creates a modal or non-modal dialog with the specified title and the specified frame.
JDialog(Dialog d,String title,boolean modal, GraphicsConfiguration gc)	Creates a modal or non-modal dialog with the specified title, Dialog, and GraphicsConfiguration.
JDialog(Frame f)	Creates a non-modal dialog without a title with the specified Frame.

JDialog(Frame f, boolean modal)	Creates a modal or non-modal dialog without a title and with the specified owner Frame.
JDialog(Frame f, String title)	Creates a non-modal dialog with the specified title and with the specified frame.
JDialog(Frame f,String title, boolean modal)	Creates a modal or non-modal dialog with the specified title and the specified Frame.
JDialog(Frame f,String title, boolean modal, GraphicsConfiguration gc)	Creates a modal or non-modal dialog with the specified title, Frame, and GraphicsConfiguration.

Methods used

Method	Description
addImpl(Component comp, Object constraints, int index)	Adds the specified child Component.
createRootPane()	Called by the constructor methods to create the default rootPane.
dialogInit()	Called by the constructors to init the JDialog properly.
getAccessibleContext()	Gets the AccessibleContext associated with this JDialog.
getContentPane()	Returns the contentPane object for this dialog
getDefaultCloseOperation()	Returns the operation which occurs when the user initiates a close on this dialog.
getGlassPane()	Returns the glassPane object for this dialog.
getJMenuBar()	Returns the menubar set on this dialog.
getLayeredPane()	Returns the layeredPane object for this dialog.
getRootPane()	Returns the rootPane object for this dialog.
isRootPaneCheckingEnabled()	Returns whether calls to add and setLayout are forwarded to the contentPane.
paramString()	Returns a string representation of this JDialog.
remove(Component comp)	Removes the specified component from the container.
setContentPane(Container contentPane)	Sets the contentPane property.
setDefaultCloseOperation(int operation)	Sets the operation which will happen by default when the user initiates a "close" on this dialog.
setGlassPane(Component glassPane)	Sets the glassPane property.
setJMenuBar(JMenuBar menu)	Sets the menubar for this dialog.
setLayeredPane(JLayeredPane layeredPane)	Sets the layeredPane property.
setLayout(LayoutManager manager)	Sets the LayoutManager.
setRootPane(JRootPane root)	Sets the rootPane property.

12.24 JINTERNALFRAME

This class extends from the JComponent and provides the facility to dragging, closing, resizing and menubar of the internal frame. The JInternalFrame added into the JDesktopPane.

12.25 JSLIDER

JSlider is a component that lets the user graphically select a value by sliding a knob within a bounded interval. We can create a JSlidter in a similar manner to Scrollbar: the zero-argument constructor creates a horizontal slider with a range from 0 to 100 and an initial value of 50. We can also supply the orientation (via JSlider.HORIZONTAL or JSlider.VERTICAL) and the range and initial value to the constructor. We handle events by attaching a ChangeListener. Its stateChanged method normally calls getValue to look up the current JSlider value.

Constructors used

Constructor	Description
JSlider()	Creates a horizontal slider with the range 0 to 100 and an initial value of 50.
JSlider(BoundedRangeModel brm)	Creates a horizontal slider using the specified BoundedRangeModel.
JSlider(int orientation)	Creates a slider using the specified orientation with the range 0 to 100 and an initial value of 50.
JSlider(int min, int max)	Creates a horizontal slider using the specified min and max with an initial value equal to the average of the min plus max.
JSlider(int min, int max, int value)	Creates a horizontal slider using the specified min, max and value.
JSlider(int orientation, int min, int max, int value)	Creates a slider with the specified orientation and the specified minimum, maximum, and initial values.

Methods used

Method	Description
addChangeListener(ChangeListener l)	Adds a ChangeListener to the slider.
createStandardLabels(int increment)	Creates a hashtable that will draw text labels starting at the slider minimum using the increment specified.
createStandardLabels (int increment,int start)	Creates a hashtable that will draw text labels starting at the start point specified using the increment specified.
getChangeListeners()	Returns an array of all the ChangeListeners added to this JSlider with addChangeListener().
getMajorTickSpacing()	This method returns the major tick spacing.
getMaximum()	Returns the maximum value supported by the slider.
getMinimum()	Returns the minimum value supported by the slider.
getMinorTickSpacing()	This method returns the minor tick spacing.
getModel()	Returns data model that handles the sliders three fundamental properties: minimum, maximum, value.
getOrientation()	Return this slider's vertical or horizontal orientation.
getPaintLabels()	Tells if labels are to be painted.
getPaintTicks()	Tells if tick marks are to be painted.
getPaintTrack()	Tells if the track (area the slider slides in) is to be painted.
getSnapToTicks()	Returns true if the knob (and the data value it represents) resolve to the closest tick mark next to where the user positioned the knob.
getValue()	Returns the sliders value.
getValueIsAdjusting()	True if the slider knob is being dragged.
paramString()	Returns a string representation of this JSlider.
removeChangeListener(ChangeListener l)	Removes a ChangeListener from the slider.
setExtent(int extent)	Sets the size of the range "covered" by the knob.
setInverted(boolean b)	Specify true to reverse the value-range shown for the slider and false to put the value range in the normal order.
setLabelTable(Dictionary labels)	Used to specify what label will be drawn at any given value.
setMajorTickSpacing(int n)	This method sets the major tick spacing.
setMaximum(int maximum)	Sets the models maximum property.
setMinimum(int minimum)	Sets the models minimum property.

setMinorTickSpacing(int n)	This method sets the minor tick spacing.
setModel(BoundedRangeModel newModel)	Sets the model that handles the sliders three fundamental properties: minimum, maximum, value.
setOrientation(int orientation)	Set the scrollbars orientation to either VERTICAL or HORIZONTAL.
setPaintLabels(boolean b)	Determines whether labels are painted on the slider.
setPaintTicks(boolean b)	Determines whether tick marks are painted on the slider.
setPaintTrack(boolean b)	Determines whether the track is painted on the slider.
setSnapToTicks(boolean b)	Specifying true makes the knob (and the data value it represents) resolve to the closest tick mark next to where the user positioned the knob.
setValue(int n)	Sets the sliders current value.
setValueIsAdjusting(boolean b)	Sets the models valueIsAdjusting property.

Example:

```
import java.awt.*;
import javax.swing.*;
public class Jslider
{
   public static void main(String[] args)
   {
      JFrame f = new JFrame("JSlider");
      f.setSize(300, 300);
      Container c = f.getContentPane();
      c.setBackground(Color.YELLOW);
      c.setLayout(new FlowLayout());
      JSlider js=new JSlider(0,100,10);
      c.add(js);
      f.setVisible(true);
   }
}
```

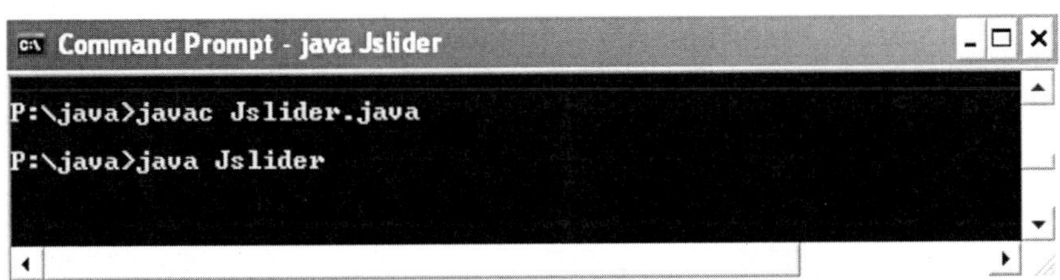

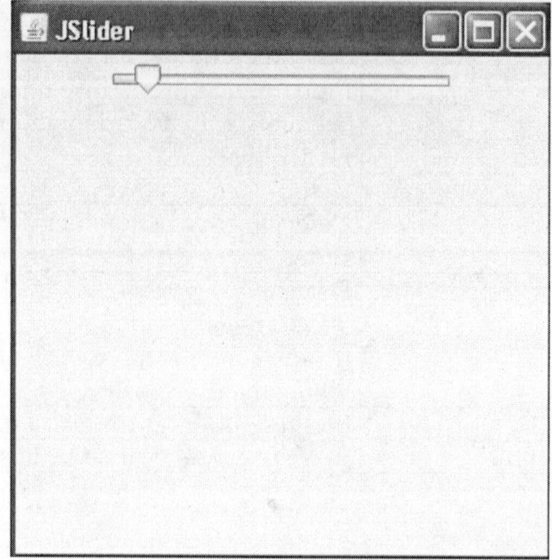

SUMMARY

Java provides interactive features for design the GUIs toolkit or components like: labels, buttons, text boxes, checkboxes, combo boxes, panels and sliders etc. Swing is part of Sun Microsystems' Java Foundation Classes (JFC), an API for providing a graphical user interface (GUI) for Java programs. The Swing package is part of the Java Foundation Classes (JFC) in the Java platform. The JFC encompasses a group of features to help people build GUIs. The Java Swing provides the multiple platform independent APIs interfaces for interacting between the users and GUIs components. Containers are the objects that are displayed directly on the screen. Controls must be added to a container if you want to see them. The container in this example driver program is called JFrame.

EXERCISE

1. Write short notes on the following. Explain with examples.

   (i) JButton (ii) JProgressBar

   (iii) JTree (iv) JApple

2. What are the differences between AWT and Swing? Explain.
3. How can you create a Button with an image, loaded on it and how do you set a tool tip to a button control?

*****

CHAPTER 13

JAVA SERVLETS

Servlets are server side programs that run in an enterprise environment of J2EE application server. Servlets provide a powerful mechanism for developing server side programs. Servlets provide component-based, platform-independent methods for building the Web-based applications. Servlets run entirely inside the Java Virtual Machine so these are safe and portable. Since the Servlet runs at server side so it does not checks the browser for compatibility. Servlets can access the entire family of Java APIs, including the JDBC API to access enterprise databases.

13.0 INTRODUCTION

A servlet is a Java program. Servlets are used with web servers like Tomcat 6.0 and run inside a Java Virtual Machine (JVM) on the server so these are safe. A Servlet is an object that is used to receive a request and generates a response based on that request. Servlets can be generated automatically by JavaServer Pages (JSP) compiler, or alternately by template engines such as ServletRunner. Client sends the request to the Servlet. The servlet processes the client request and sends the response back to the server/Servlet container, which is routed to the client.

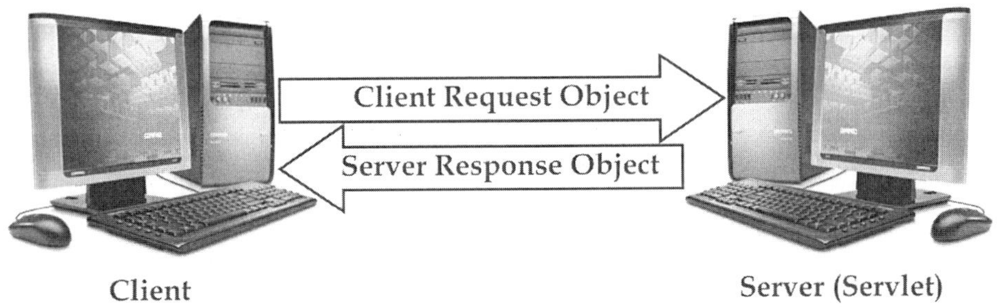

Figure 13.1: HTTP request response model.

The HTTP protocol is a stateless protocol based on a request and response model with a small, finite number of request methods like GET, POST, HEAD, OPTIONS, PUT, TRACE, DELETE and CONNECT etc. Most of the servlet-based web applications are built around the framework of the HTTP request/response model.

13.1 ADVANTAGES OF SERVLETS

The following are the advantages of Servlet.

(i) The servlet request and response objects provide a convenient way to handle HTTP requests and send data back to the client.

(ii) Servlet is a popular standard, effectively replacing early techniques, such as CGI scripts, for generating dynamic HTML.

(iii) Servlets are fully integrated into the J2EE framework.

(iv) Servlets are fully integrated with the Java. The J2EE framework provides an extensive set of services that your Web application can use, such as RMI, security etc.

(v) A servlet handles concurrent requests. There is only a single instance of each servlet, and servlet have a well-defined lifecycle.

13.2 SERVLET AND SERVLETCONTAINER

Servlets augment the functionality of a web application. They are dynamically loaded by the server's Java runtime environment when needed. On receiving an incoming request from the client, the ServletContainer initiates the required servlet. The Older 2-tier systems, such as in the following figure, were made of a servlet container and the web browser.

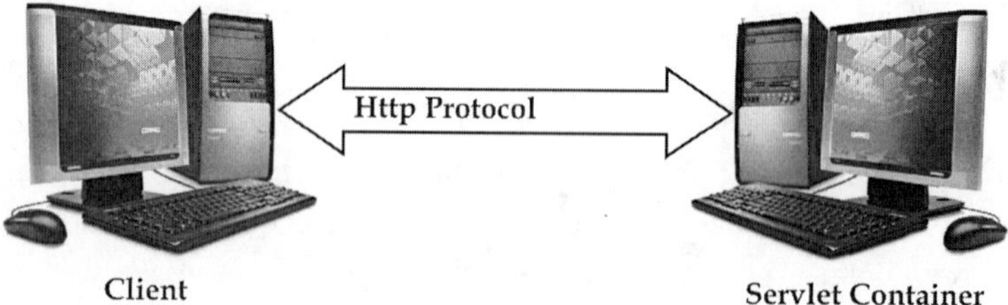

Figure 13.2: 2-Tier Architecture

The application server is an extension of the 2-tier client/server model into an N-tier approach. The application server has a built-in web server/servlet container and Application container. An example of this model is the J2EE application model (Java 2 Enterprise Edition). This model is implemented in application servers like IBM Web Sphere, BEA Web Logic, etc. the following figure demonstrates the N-tier approach.

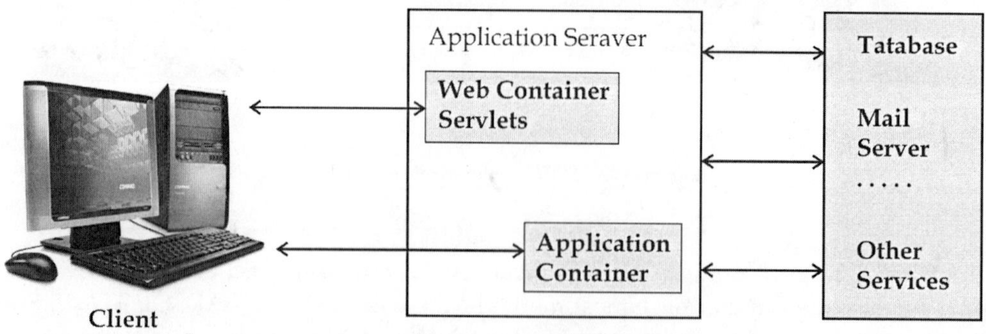

Figure 13.3: N-tier Architecture

A servlet must execute under the control of a servlet container, because it is the container that calls servlet methods and provides services that the servlet needs when executing.

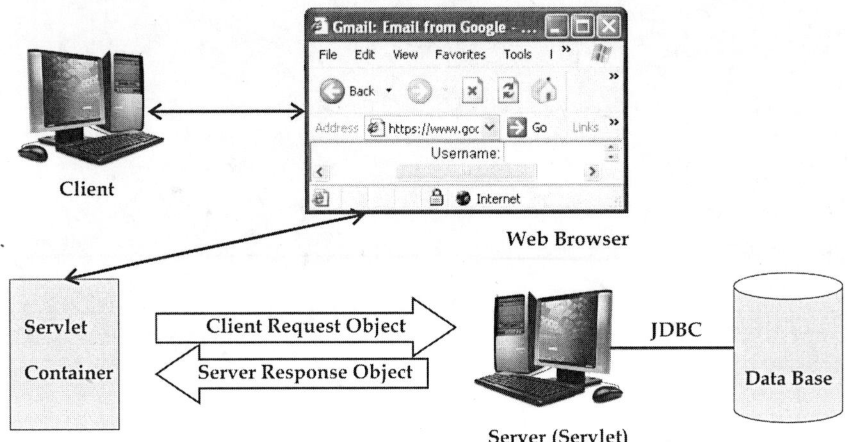

Figure 13.4: Servlets and the Servlet Container

A servlet container is nothing but a compiled, executable program. It is a specialized web server that supports Servlet execution. The main function of the Servlet container is to load, initialize and execute servlet programs. The servlet container loads the servlet class and calls the init method of the servlet as soon as the servlet is called for the first time.

Individual Servlets are registered with a Servlet container. The Servlet container is then able to initialize the Servlet as necessary and deliver requests to the Servlet as they arrive. Servlet containers are also called web containers or web engines.

Working Process

The servlet container loads the servlet class and calls the init method of the servlet as soon as the servlet is called for the first time.

(i) Then this container makes an instance of javax.servlet.ServletRequest and javax.servlet.ServletResponse for each request.

(ii) Then it passes the ServletRequest and ServletResponse objects by invoking the servlet's service method.

(iii) Finally, it calls the destroy method and unload the servlet class when the servlet class is to be shut down.

13.3 SERVLETRUNNER

The servletrunner is a small program that is used to test servlets program before deploying them to a web server. ServletRunner is multithreaded, so it can run more than one servlet program at same time. So it runs multiple servlets simultaneously, or to test one servlet that calls other servlets in order to satisfy client requests. The servletrunner is located in the bin directory of the JSDK2.0. So path of servletrunner is as C:\JSDK2.0\BIN. We get help on using the servletrunner.

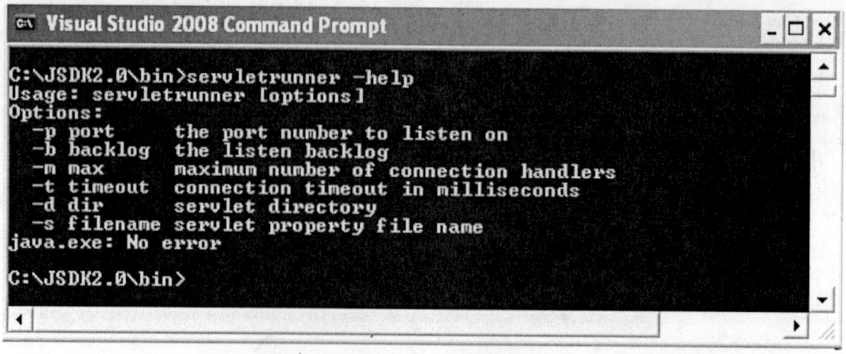

```
Visual Studio 2008 Command Prompt

C:\JSDK2.0\bin>servletrunner -help
Usage: servletrunner [options]
Options:
  -p port      the port number to listen on
  -b backlog   the listen backlog
  -m max       maximum number of connection handlers
  -t timeout   connection timeout in milliseconds
  -d dir       servlet directory
  -s filename  servlet property file name
java.exe: No error

C:\JSDK2.0\bin>
```

To see the default values of these options, start the servletrunner with the **-v** switch.

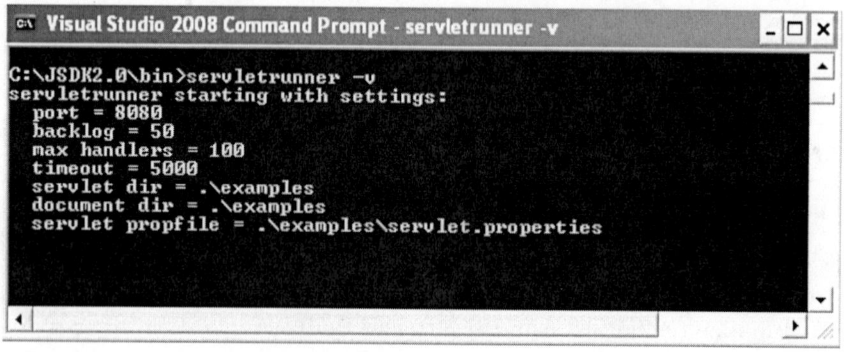

```
Visual Studio 2008 Command Prompt - servletrunner -v

C:\JSDK2.0\bin>servletrunner -v
servletrunner starting with settings:
  port = 8080
  backlog = 50
  max handlers = 100
  timeout = 5000
  servlet dir = .\examples
  document dir = .\examples
  servlet propfile = .\examples\servlet.properties
```

13.4 Steps to run Servlet Program

The following steps are used to run the servlet program.

(i) install the software JSDK2.0

(ii) Sets the class path.

(iii) Write the servlet code and save with extension .java.

(iv) Compile the servlet program.

(v) Run the ServletRunner.exe at the specific port.

(vi) Now open Internet Explorer and write the url as http://localhost:portno/directory_name/programName

(i) install the software JSDK2.0

When JSDK2.0 is installed on our machine, then a directory is created on c:\ as follows.

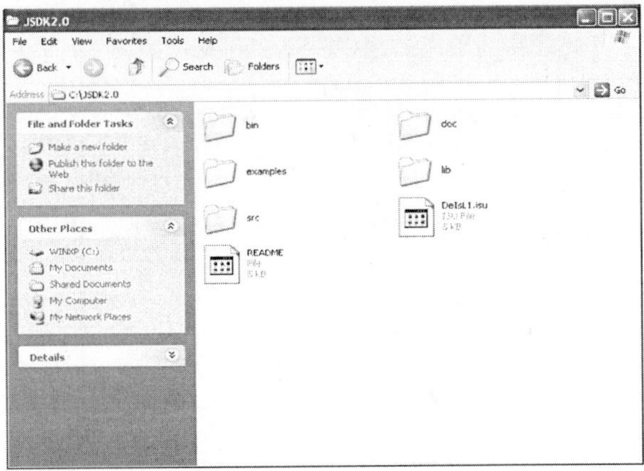

(ii) Sets the class path:

Now sets the class path, the steps are as follows.

Right click on My Computer.

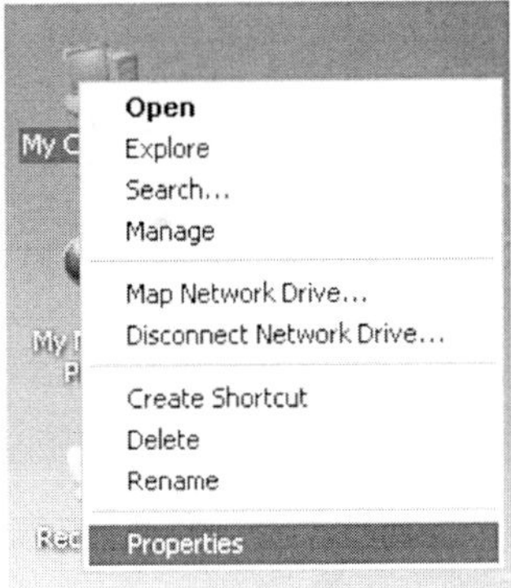

Now click on advance.

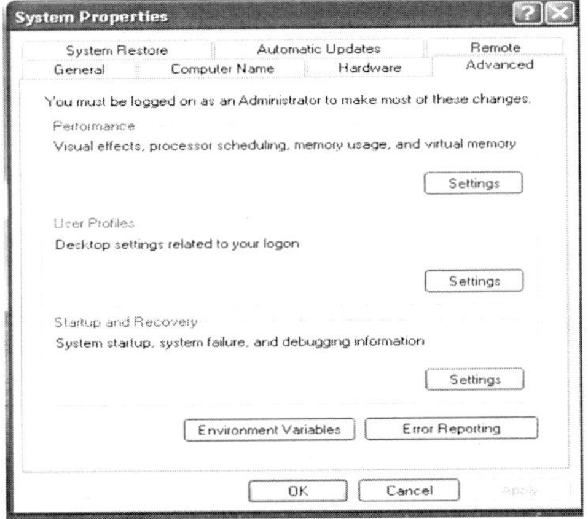

Now click on Environmental variable.

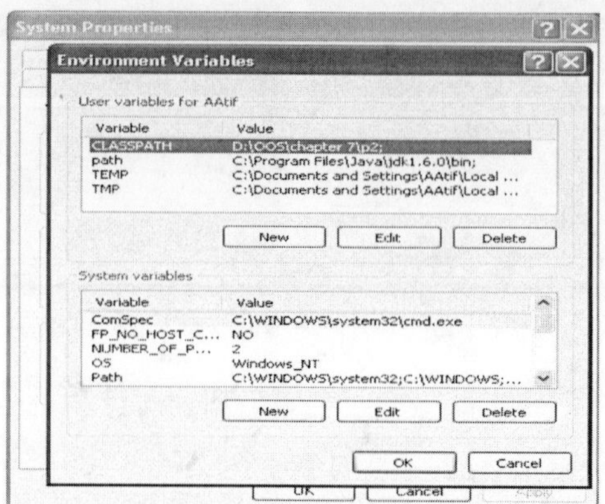

Click new and write the variable name is CLASSPATH and variable value is C:\ JSDK2.0\src; and click OK.

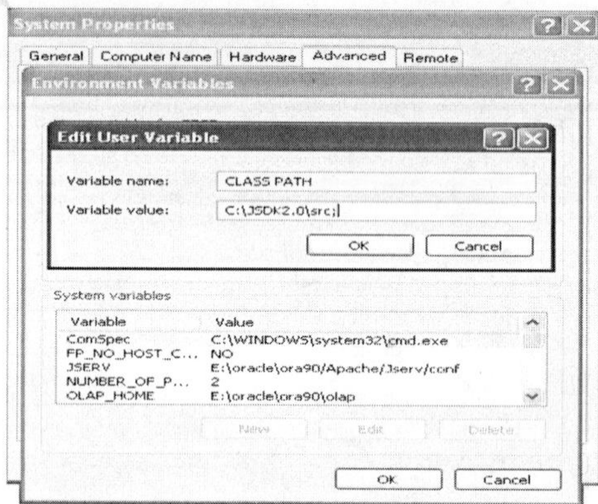

(iii) Write the servlet code and save with extension .java.

```
import javax.servlet.*;
import javax.servlet.http.*;
import java.io.*;
public class program extends HttpServlet
{
public void doGet(HttpServletRequest req, HttpServletResponse res)throws
        IOException
{
res.setContentType(“text/HTML”);
PrintWriter out=res.getWriter();
out.println(“<HTML><HEAD><TITLE>My First servlet</TITLE></
        HEAD><BODY>”);
out.println(“<b>servlet output</b></BODY></HTML>”);
}
}
```

Save the above program as program.java.

(iv) Compile the servlet program.

Compile the servlet program using javac compiler as follows.

(v) Run the ServletRunner.exe at the specific port.

Create a directory servlet at d:\ and save the program.java file to this directory. Now run the servletrunner as follows.

Command Prompt - servletrunner -p 100 -d D:\servlet

```
C:\JSDK2.0\bin>servletrunner -p 100 -d D:\servlet
servletrunner starting with settings:
  port = 100
  backlog = 50
  max handlers = 100
  timeout = 5000
  servlet dir = D:\servlet
  document dir = .\examples
  servlet propfile = D:\servlet\servlet.properties
```

(vi) Now open Internet Explorer and write the url as http://localhost:portno/directory_name/programName

Now open the internet explorer and write the following url to the url address locator.

http://localhost:100/servlet/program

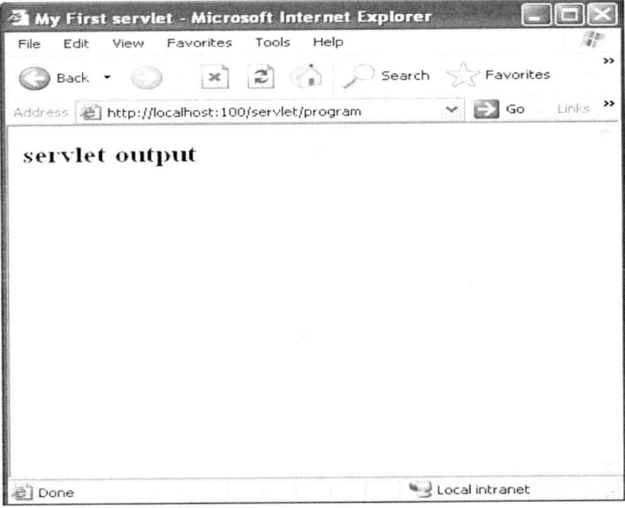

13.5 LIFECYCLE OF A SERVLET

The lifecycle of Servlet consists of the following steps:

(i) The container load Servlet class during start-up.

(ii) The container calls the init() method to initializes the servlet and must be called before service any requests. In the entire life of a servlet, the init() method is called only once.

(iii) After initialization, the servlet can service client-requests. The container calls the service() method of the servlet for every request. The service() method determines the kind of request being made and dispatches it to an appropriate method to handle the request.

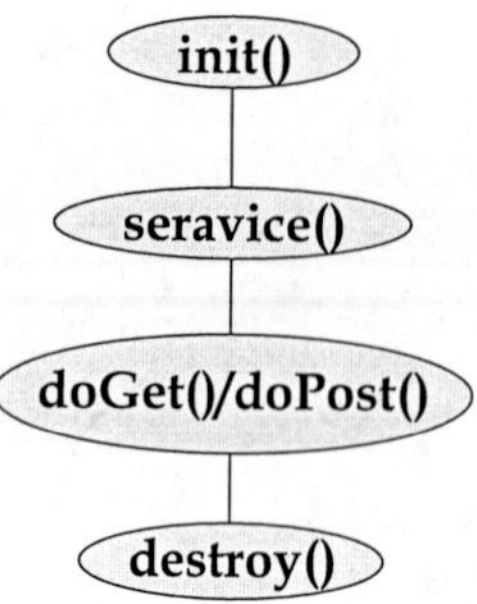

Figure 13.6: Lifecycle of Servlet

Finally, the container calls the destroy() method which takes the servlet out of service. The destroy() method like init() is called only once in the lifecycle of a Servlet.

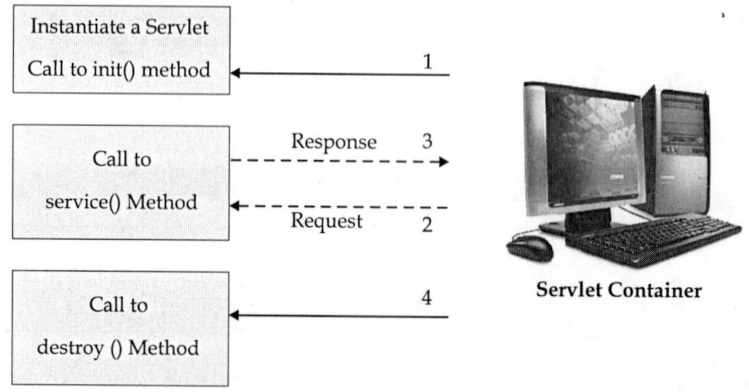

Figure 13.7: Servlet Lifecycle

13.6 SERVLET API

The servlet overrides the appropriate methods from the servlet base class--javax.servlet. HttpServlet class for HTTP servlets, or possibly javax.servlet.GenericServlet for protocol-independent servlets--in order to process the request and return the response. For example, most servlets override the HttpServlet doGet() method or doPost() method or both to process HTTP GET and POST requests.

Servlet API	Description
javax.servlet	The javax.servlet package contains a number of classes and interfaces that describe and define the contracts between a servlet class and the runtime environment provided for an instance of such a class by a conforming servlet container.
javax.servlet.http	The javax.servlet.http package contains a number of classes and interfaces that describe and define the contracts between a servlet class running under the HTTP protocol and the runtime environment provided for an instance of such a class by a conforming servlet container.

The package javax.servlet.http defines HTTP-specific subclasses of the generic servlet elements, including session management objects that track multiple requests and responses between the Web server and a client. A Generic servlet contains the following five methods:

Method	Description
init()	The init() method is called only once by the servlet container throughout the life of a servlet.
service()	Once the servlet starts getting the requests, the service() method is called by the servlet container to respond.
getServletConfig()	This method contains parameters for initialization and startup of the servlet and returns a ServletConfig object.
getServletInfo()	The information about the servlet is returned by this method like version, author etc.
destroy()	This method is called when we need to close the servlet.

Syntax

(i) **public void init(ServletConfig config) throws ServletException**

The init() method takes a ServletConfig object that contains the initialization parameters and servlet's configuration and throws a ServletException if an exception has occurred.

(ii) **public void service(ServletRequest req, ServletResponse res) throws ServletException, IOException**

The servlet services the client's request with the help of two objects. These two objects javax.servlet.ServletRequest and javax.servlet.ServletResponse are passed by the servlet container.

(iii) **public ServletConfig getServletConfig()**

This object is passed to the init method. When this interface is implemented then it stores the ServletConfig object in order to return it. It is done by the generic class which implements this inetrface.

(iv) **public String getServletInfo()**

This method returns a string which should be in the form of plain text and not any kind of markup.

(v) **public void destroy()**

That is before removing a servlet instance from service, the servlet container calls the destroy() method. Once the servlet container calls the destroy() method, no service methods will be then called .

Some Servlet Programs

//Program 1

We have design the html form as follows.

SerLogin.html

```
<HTML>
<HEAD><TITLE>Login Form</TITLE></HEAD>
<BODY>
<FORM METHOD=GET ACTION="http://localhost:100/servlet/SerLogin">
What is your name?
<INPUT TYPE=TEXT NAME=t1 SIZE=20>
<INPUT TYPE=TEXT NAME=t2 SIZE=20>
<INPUT TYPE=SUBMIT VALUE="Login">
</FORM>
</BODY>
</HTML>
```

Write the servlet program as follows.

SerLogin.java

```
import javax.servlet.*;
import java.io.*;
import java.util.*;
public class SerLogin extends GenericServlet
{
   public void service(ServletRequest req,ServletResponse res)
   {
      try{
         res.setContentType("text/html");
         PrintWriter out=res.getWriter();
         out.write("<html><head><title>Servlet Example</title></
             head><body>");
         out.write("<h1>Servlet output</h1><hr>");
         String s1=req.getParameter("t1");
         String s2=req.getParameter("t2");
         if(s1.equals("ADMIN") && s2.equals("admin"))
         {
            out.write("Welcome Administrator!");
         }
         else if(s1.equals("tanweer03") && s2.equals("tanweer"))
         {
            out.write("Welcome Tanweer!");
```

```
            }
            out.write("</body></html>");
        }catch(Exception e){}
    }
}
```

Now compile the servlet program as follows.

Now start the servletrunner as follows.

```
Command Prompt - servletrunner -p 100 -d D:\servlet
C:\JSDK2.0\bin>servletrunner -p 100 -d D:\servlet
servletrunner starting with settings:
  port = 100
  backlog = 50
  max handlers = 100
  timeout = 5000
  servlet dir = D:\servlet
  document dir = .\examples
  servlet propfile = D:\servlet\servlet.properties
program: init
Ser4: init
SerLogin: init
```

Now run the program.

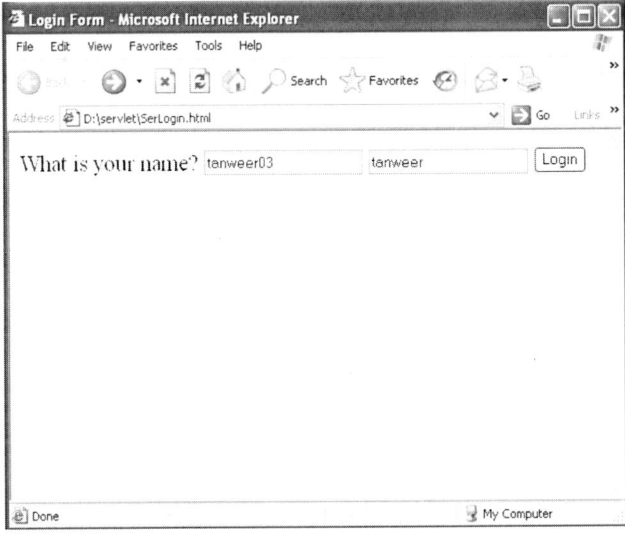

Now click on login button. The output is as follows.

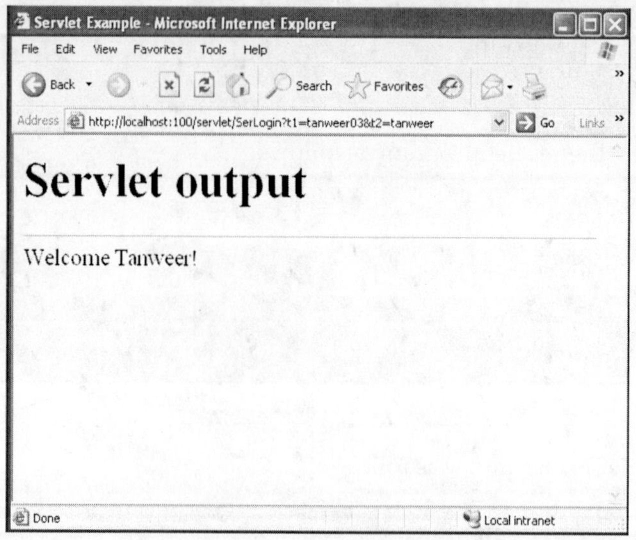

//Program 2

We have design the html form as follows.

HelloSer.html

```
<HTML>
<HEAD><TITLE>Greetings Form</TITLE></HEAD>
<BODY>
<FORM METHOD=GET ACTION="http://localhost:100/servlet/
HelloServlet1">
What is your name?
<INPUT TYPE=TEXT NAME=username SIZE=20>
<INPUT TYPE=SUBMIT VALUE="Click Here">
</FORM>
</BODY>
</HTML>
```

Write the servlet program as follows.

HelloServlet1.java

```
import javax.servlet.*;
import javax.servlet.http.*;
import java.io.*;
public class HelloServlet1 extends HttpServlet {
public void doGet(HttpServletRequest req, HttpServletResponse resp) throws
        ServletException, IOException
{
resp.setContentType("text/html");
PrintWriter out = resp.getWriter();
```

```
out.println("<HTML>");
out.println("<HEAD><TITLE>Finally,interaction!</TITLE></HEAD>");
out.println("<BODY><H1>Hello, " + req.getParameter("username") + "!<br>
Greetings,You are visiting our website first time.<br> Have a Nice Day.</H1>");
out.println("</BODY></HTML>");
}
}
```

Now compile the servlet program as follows.

Now start the servletrunner as follows.

```
Command Prompt - servletrunner -p 100 -d D:\servlet
C:\JSDK2.0\bin>servletrunner -p 100 -d D:\servlet
servletrunner starting with settings:
  port = 100
  backlog = 50
  max handlers = 100
  timeout = 5000
  servlet dir = D:\servlet
  document dir = .\examples
  servlet propfile = D:\servlet\servlet.properties
HelloServlet1: init
```

Now run the program.

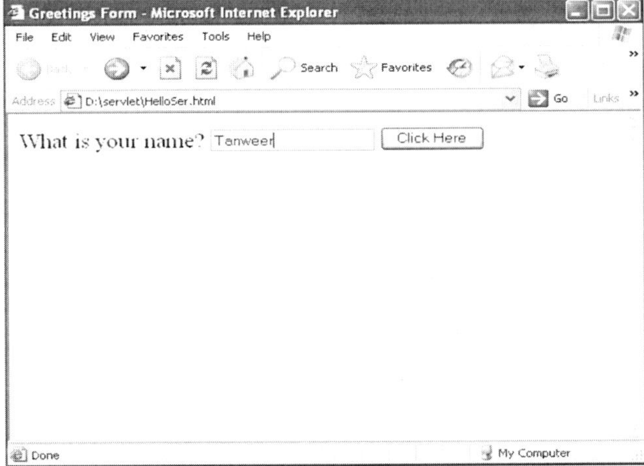

Now click on login button. The output is as follows.

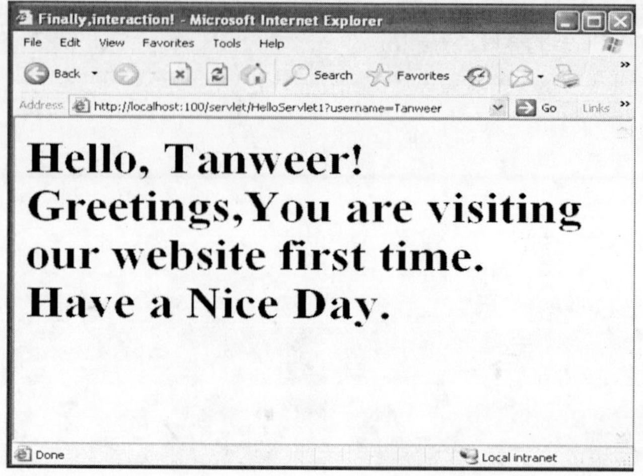

13.7 THREAD-SAFE SERVLETS

A thread is a single execution process i.e. an individual, sequential flow of control within a program. When we say that a program is multithreaded, we are not implying that the program runs two separate instances simultaneously (as if you concurrently executed the program twice from the command line). Rather, we are saying that the same instance (executed only once) spawns multiple threads that process this single instance of code. This means that more than one sequential flow of control runs through the same memory block. So what do we mean by thread-safe, you ask? When multiple threads execute a single instance of a program and therefore share memory, multiple threads could possibly be attempting to read and write to the same place in memory. If requests to your webpage may and probably will occur concurrently which means multiple threads will be running your code simultaneously. This means you have to take care that one thread do not interfere with processing of other threads, therefore thread-safety is an important issue in web application. Developers should be aware of this issue and should make sure their code works in a thread-safe way.

```
import javax.servlet.*;
import javax.servlet.http.*;
import java.io.*;

public class threadSafeServlet extends HttpServlet implements
        SingleThreadModel
{
    private ServletConfig config;
    public void init (ServletConfig config) throws ServletException
{
        this.config = config;
        }
```

```
public void doGet (HttpServletRequest req,HttpServletResponse res) throws
        ServletException,IOException
{
    res.setContentType(“text/html”);
    PrintWriter out = res.getWriter();
    out.println( “<html>” );
    out.println( “<head>” );
    out.println( “<title>This is A Thread safe Servlet</title>” );
    out.println( “</head>” );
    out.println( “<body>” );
    out.println( “<h1>A Thread Safe Servlet</h1>” );
    out.println( “</body>” );
    out.println( “</html>” );
    out.close();
}
}
```

Command Prompt

```
D:\servlet>javac threadSafeServlet.java

D:\servlet>_
```

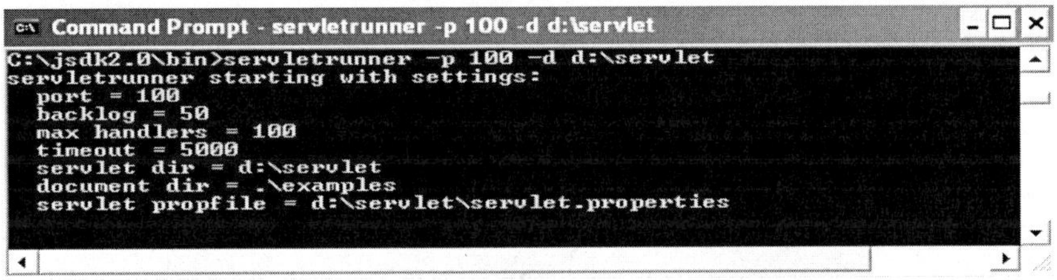

Command Prompt - servletrunner -p 100 -d d:\servlet

```
C:\jsdk2.0\bin>servletrunner -p 100 -d d:\servlet
servletrunner starting with settings:
  port = 100
  backlog = 50
  max handlers = 100
  timeout = 5000
  servlet dir = d:\servlet
  document dir = .\examples
  servlet propfile = d:\servlet\servlet.properties
```

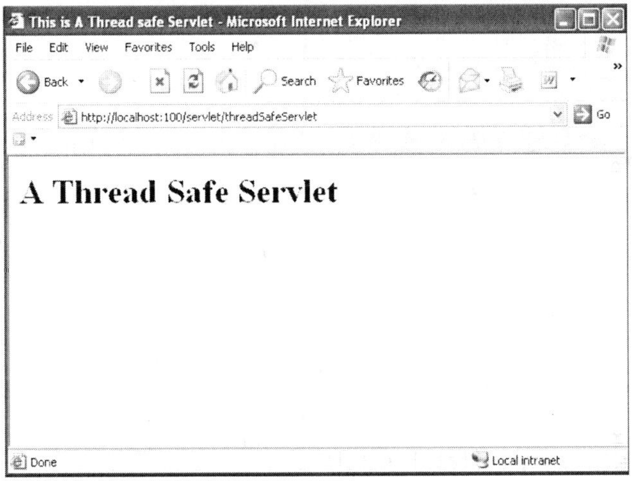

This is A Thread safe Servlet - Microsoft Internet Explorer

File Edit View Favorites Tools Help

Back Search Favorites

Address http://localhost:100/servlet/threadSafeServlet Go

A Thread Safe Servlet

Done Local intranet

13.8 HTTP Redirects

HTTP Redirects is done by sending instructions for the client to use another URL in the responses. Redirection is generally used when a document moves for load balancing or for simple randomization.

//Program

```
import java.io.*;
import javax.servlet.*;
import javax.servlet.http.*;

public class redirect1 extends HttpServlet
{
  public void doGet(HttpServletRequest req, HttpServletResponse res) throws
        ServletException, IOException
  {
  PrintWriter out = res.getWriter();
  res.setContentType("text/html");
  out.println("<html><body>");
  out.println("<H1>HTTP Redirect</H1><BR>");
  out.println("<H4>Click Here to open our website</H4><BR>");
  out.println("<a href=\"http://www.miet.ac.in\">Click here</a>");
  out.println("</body></html>");
  return;
  }
}
```

Command Prompt

```
D:\servlet>javac redirect1.java

D:\servlet>_
```

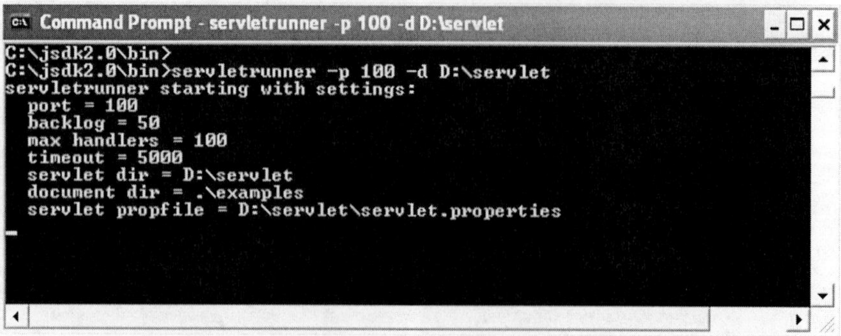

Command Prompt - servletrunner -p 100 -d D:\servlet

```
C:\jsdk2.0\bin>
C:\jsdk2.0\bin>servletrunner -p 100 -d D:\servlet
servletrunner starting with settings:
  port = 100
  backlog = 50
  max handlers = 100
  timeout = 5000
  servlet dir = D:\servlet
  document dir = .\examples
  servlet propfile = D:\servlet\servlet.properties
_
```

Redirect to New Location

```
import java.io.*;
import javax.servlet.*;
import javax.servlet.http.*;

public class redirect2 extends HttpServlet
{
   public void doGet(HttpServletRequest request, HttpServletResponse response)
          throws ServletException, IOException
   {
   PrintWriter out = response.getWriter();
   response.setStatus(HttpServletResponse.SC_MOVED_TEMPORARILY);
   response.setHeader("Location", "http://www.miet.ac.in");
   response.setContentType("text/html");
   return;
```

```
    }
}
```

```
Command Prompt

D:\servlet>javac redirect2.java

D:\servlet>_
```

```
Command Prompt - servletrunner -p 100 -d D:\servlet
C:\jsdk2.0\bin>
C:\jsdk2.0\bin>servletrunner -p 100 -d D:\servlet
servletrunner starting with settings:
  port = 100
  backlog = 50
  max handlers = 100
  timeout = 5000
  servlet dir = D:\servlet
  document dir = .\examples
  servlet propfile = D:\servlet\servlet.properties
redirect1: init
Servlet not found: redirect2
Servlet not found: redirect2
redirect2: init
_
```

Write the following url at the url locator of internet explorer.

http://localhost:100/servlet/redirect2

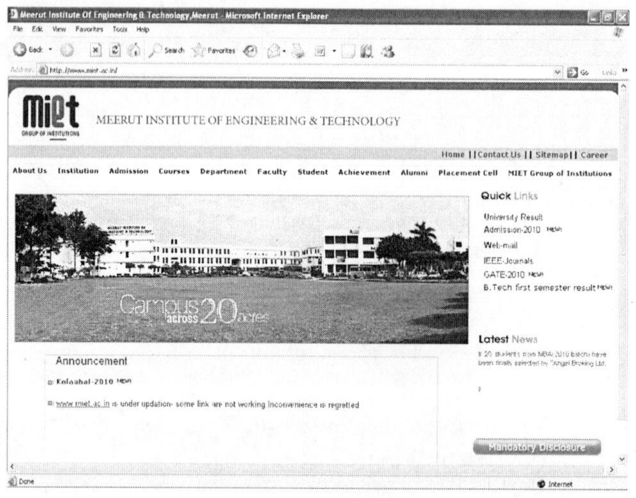

//Another program

```
<HTML>
<HEAD><TITLE>Login Form</TITLE></HEAD>
<BODY>
```

```
<FORM METHOD=GET ACTION="http://localhost:100/servlet/redirect4">
Enter UserId:
<INPUT TYPE=TEXT NAME="user" SIZE=20>
<br>Enter password:
<INPUT TYPE=TEXT NAME="pass" SIZE=20><br>
<INPUT TYPE=SUBMIT VALUE="Login">
</FORM>
</BODY>
</HTML>
```

```
import java.io.*;
import javax.servlet.*;
import javax.servlet.http.*;

public class redirect4 extends HttpServlet
{
  public void doGet(HttpServletRequest req, HttpServletResponse res) throws
        ServletException,IOException
  {
  PrintWriter out = res.getWriter();
  res.setContentType("text/html");
  out.println("<html><body>");
  String name = req.getParameter("user");
  String password = req.getParameter("pass");
if(name.equals("tanweer")&& password.equals("alam"))
{
  out.println("Successfully logon!");
}
else
{
out.println("uInvalid username or Password!<br> Try again!");
}
  out.println("</body></html>");
  }
}
```

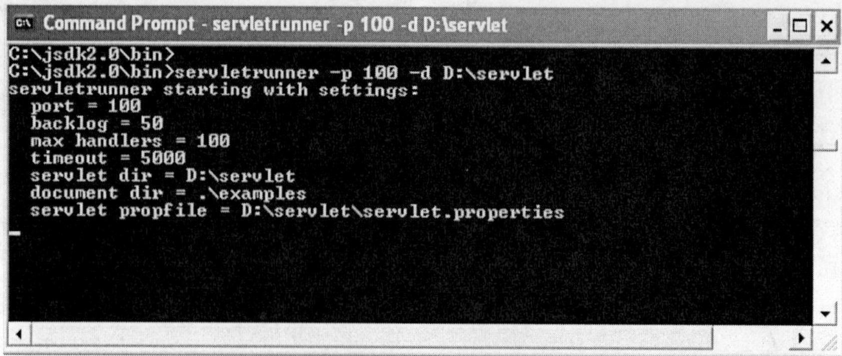
Command Prompt - servletrunner -p 100 -d D:\servlet
C:\jsdk2.0\bin>
C:\jsdk2.0\bin>servletrunner -p 100 -d D:\servlet
servletrunner starting with settings:
port = 100
backlog = 50
max handlers = 100
timeout = 5000
servlet dir = D:\servlet
document dir = .\examples
servlet propfile = D:\servlet\servlet.properties

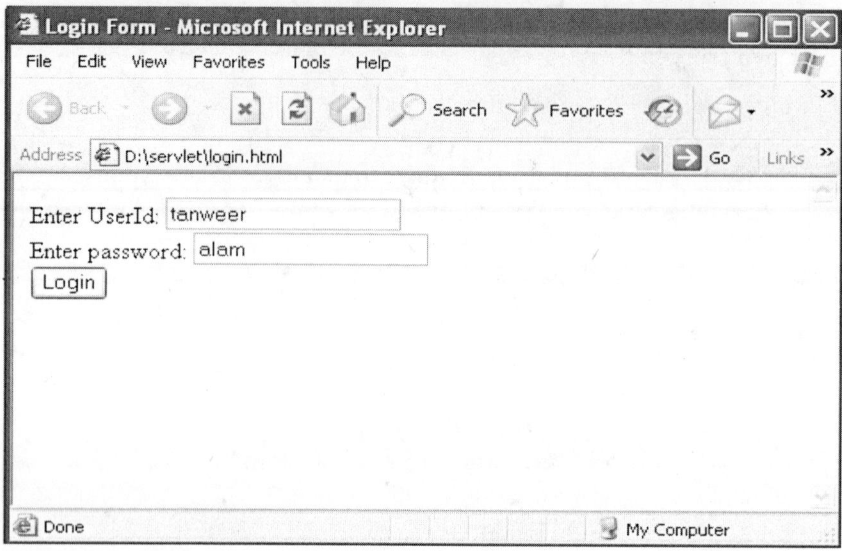
Login Form - Microsoft Internet Explorer
File Edit View Favorites Tools Help
Back Search Favorites
Address D:\servlet\login.html Go Links
Enter UserId: tanweer
Enter password: alam
Login
Done
My Computer

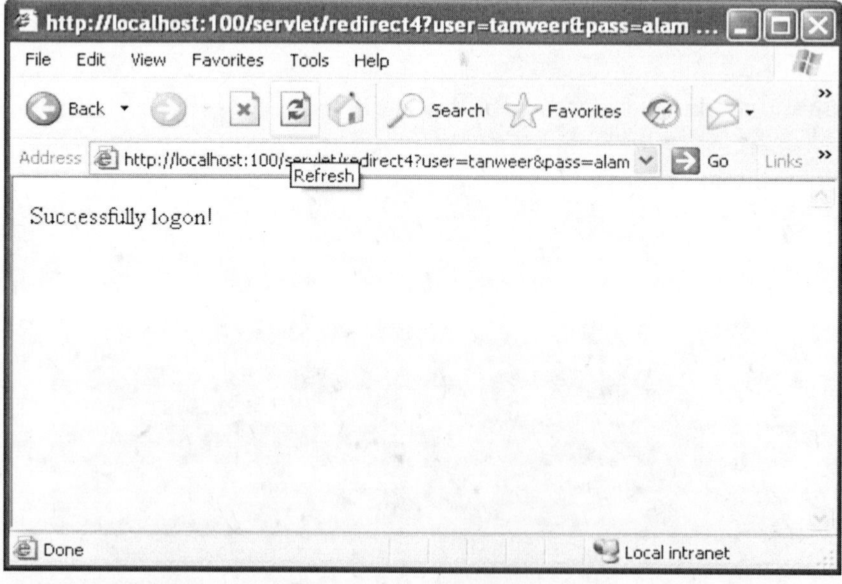
http://localhost:100/servlet/redirect4?user=tanweer&pass=alam ...
File Edit View Favorites Tools Help
Back Search Favorites
Address http://localhost:100/servlet/redirect4?user=tanweer&pass=alam Go Links
Refresh
Successfully logon!
Done
Local intranet

13.9 COOKIES

Cookie is a small amount of information sent by a Servlets to a Web browser, saved by the web browser and later sent back to the server. A cookie has a name, a single value and optional attributes such as a comment, path and domain qualifiers, a maximum age and a version number. The value of cookie can uniquely identify a client, so cookies are commonly used for session management. The browser returns cookies to the servlet by adding fields to HTTP request headers. The servlet sends cookies to the browser by using the HttpServletResponse.addCookie(javax.servlet.http.Cookie) method, which adds fields to HTTP response headers to send cookies to the browser, one at a time. The browser is expected to support 20 cookies for each Web server, 300 cookies total, and may limit cookie size to 4 KB each. Cookies can be retrieved from a request by using the HttpServletRequest. getCookies() method. Several cookies might have the same name but different path attributes.

Constructor	Description
cookie(String name, string value)	Constructs a cookie with a specified name and value.

Methods used

Method	Description
getName()	Returns the name of the cookie.
getMaxAge()	Returns the maximum age of the cookie, specified in seconds, By default, -1 indicating the cookie will persist until browser shutdown.
getDomain()	Returns the domain name set for this cookie.
getComment()	Returns the comment describing the purpose of this cookie, or null if the cookie has no comment.
getPath()	Returns the path on the server to which the browser returns this cookie.
getValue()	Returns the value of the cookie.
getVersion()	Returns the version of the protocol this cookie complies with.
setComment(java.lang.String purpose)	Specifies a comment that describes a cookie's purpose.
setMaxAge(int expiry)	Sets the maximum age of the cookie in seconds.
setPath(java.lang.String uri)	Specifies a path for the cookie to which the client should return the cookie.
setValue(java.lang.String newValue)	Assigns a new value to a cookie after the cookie is created.
setVersion(int v)	Sets the version of the cookie protocol this cookie complies with.
clone()	return a copy of this cookie.

A servlet uses the getCookies() method of HTTPServletRequest to retrieve cookies as request. The addCookie() method of HTTPServletResponse sends a new cookie to the browser. We can set the age of cookie by setMaxAge() method.

Example:

```
import java.io.*;
import javax.servlet.*;
import javax.servlet.http.*;
public class addcookie extends HttpServlet
{
public void doGet(HttpServletRequest request,HttpServletResponse response)
throws ServletException, IOException
{
PrintWriter out;
   response.setContentType("text/html");
   out = response.getWriter();
   Cookie c1 = new Cookie("Tanweer","30");
   Cookie c2 = new Cookie("AAtif","02");
   response.addCookie(c1);
   response.addCookie(c2);
   out.println("<HTML><HEAD><TITLE>");
   out.println(" This output is generated from a Servlet");
   out.println("</TITLE></HEAD><BODY>");
   out.println("<h2> This Program add two Cookies<h2>");
   out.println("</BODY></HTML>");
   out.close();
   }
}
```

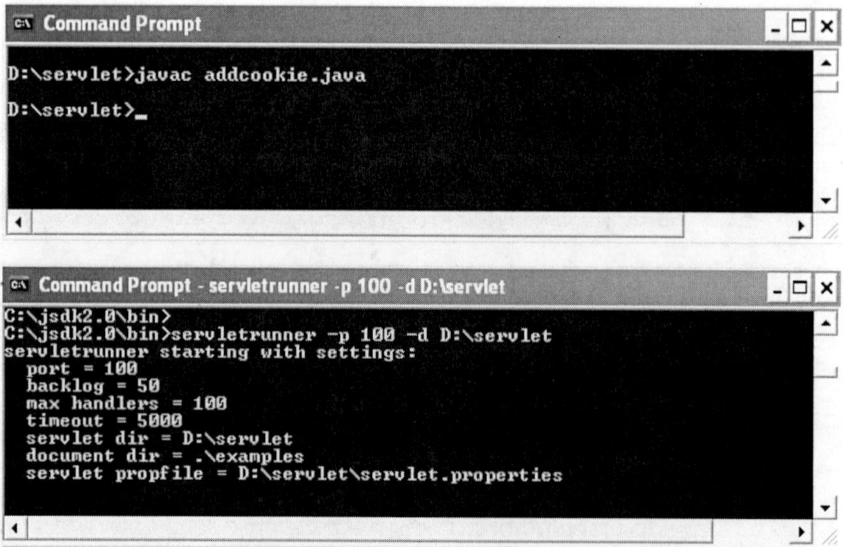

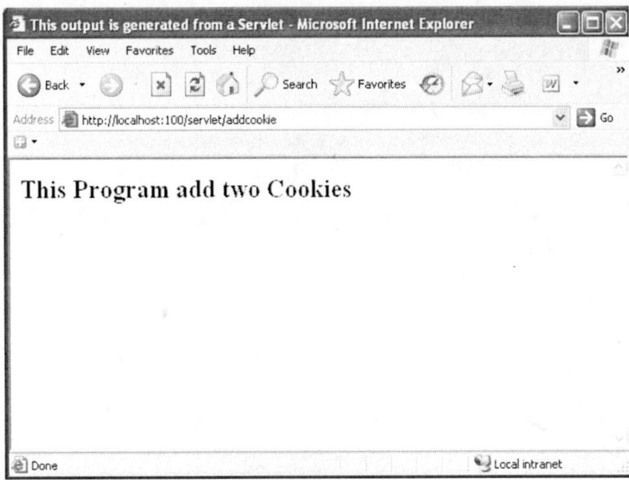

Read Cookies from Servlet

The Cookie Class provides an easy way to read Cookies. You can use **getCookies()** method to retrieve all the cookies in your servlet program.

This getCookies() method returns an array of cookie objects. In this example we will show you how you can retrieve all the cookies and display using servlets.

Here is the code of ReadCookies.java

```
import javax.servlet.*;
import javax.servlet.http.*;
import java.io.*;
public class ReadCookies extends HttpServlet
{
public void doGet(HttpServletRequest request, HttpServletResponse response)
        throws ServletException, java.io.IOException
{
   String cname[]=new String[20];
   String cvalue[]=new String[20];
   Cookie[] c = request.getCookies();
   for(int i=0;i<c.length;i++)
{
cname[i]=c[i].getName();
cvalue[i]=c[i].getValue();
}
   response.setContentType("text/html");
   PrintWriter out = response.getWriter();
   out.println("<html>");
   out.println("<head>");
   out.println("<title>Read Cookie</title>");
```

```
   out.println("</head>");
   out.println("<body>");
for(int i=0;i<c.length;i++)
{
out.println("<B>"+cname[i]+" "+cvalue[i]+"</B>");
}
      out.println("</body>");
      out.println("</html>");
   }
}
```

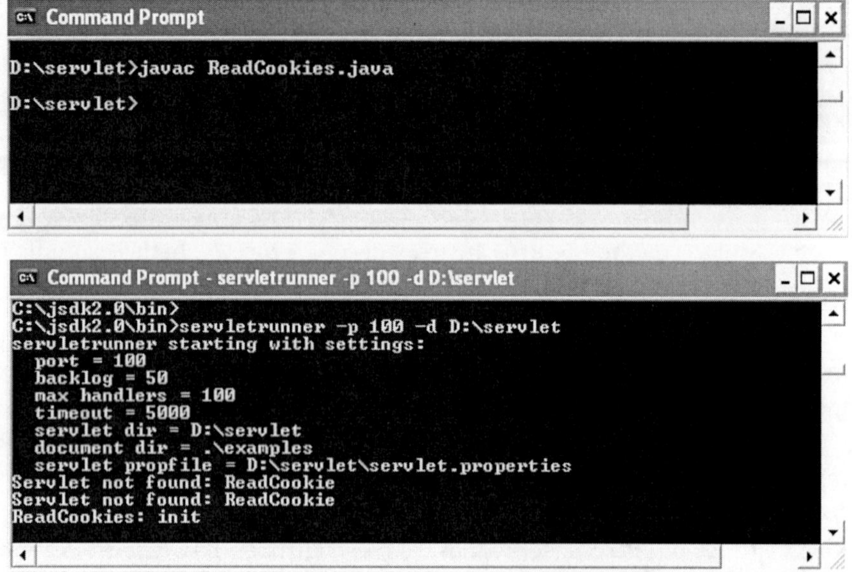

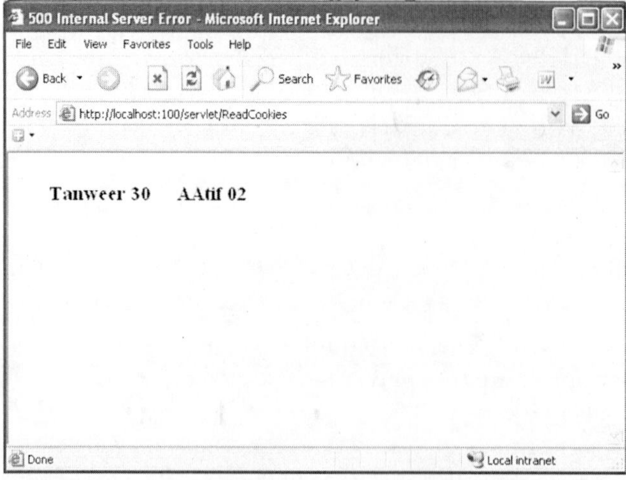

SUMMARY

Servlets provide component-based, platform-independent methods for building the Web-based applications. Servlets run entirely inside the Java Virtual Machine so these are safe and portable. Since the Servlet runs at server side so it does not checks the browser for compatibility. Servlets augment the functionality of a web application. They are dynamically loaded by the server's Java runtime environment when needed. On receiving an incoming request from the client, the ServletContainer initiates the required servlet. The servletrunner is a small program that is used to test servlets program before deploying them to a web server. ServletRunner is multithreaded, so it can run more than one servlet program at same time. So it runs multiple servlets simultaneously, or to test one servlet that calls other servlets in order to satisfy client requests.

EXERCISE

1. What is servletrunner?
2. Define servlet life cycle.
3. What is HTTP redirects?
4. Write the steps to run the Servlet program.

*****

CHAPTER 14

JAVA SERVER PAGES

JSP is stand for Java Server Pages, is Sun's solution for developing dynamic web sites. In today's environment most web sites servers dynamic pages based on user request. JSP is made operable by having their contents (JSP tags, HTML tags and scripts) translated into a servlet by the application server. This process is responsible for translating JSP file (both the dynamic and static elements) into Java servlet code that delivers the translated contents through the Web server output stream to the browser. JSP makes the development process very simple and its maintenance also becomes very easy. JSP provide excellent server side scripting support for creating database driven web applications. JDBC provide excellent database connectivity in heterogeneous database environment. Using JSP and JDBC it's very easy to develop database driven web application.

14.1 INTRODUCTION

JSP is an extremely powerful choice for web development. JSP pages usually contain a mixture of both static data and dynamic elements. It is important to understand the distinction between the two forms. Static data is never changed in the server page and dynamic elements will always be interpreted and replaced before reaching the client. JSP is a technology using server side scripting that is actually translated into Servlets and compiled before they are run. JSP is used to develop the web application in more efficient way than Servlets. JSP pages provide tags that allow developers to perform most dynamic content operations without writing complex java code. Advanced developers can add the full power of the java programming language to perform advanced operations in JSP pages. JSP pages are efficient, it loads into the web server's memory on receiving the request very first time and the subsequent calls are served within a very short period of time.

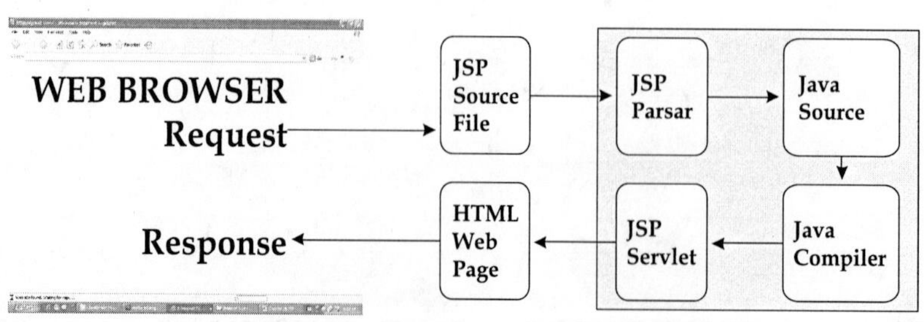

14.2 JSP PAGE'S COMPONENTS

JSP page is built using the following components:

(i) Directives
(ii) Declarations
(iii) Scriplets
(iv) Expressions
(v) Standard Actions
(vi) Custom Tags

Directives

Listing some of them as follows:

1. Page

Syntax:

< %@ page Language="Java" extends="<Class name>" import="<class> or <package>" %>

Attributes:

a. Language = "Java"

b. Import = "Class"

c. Buffersize = ""

d. Scope = "REQUEST/PAGE/SESSION/APPLICATION"

e. And etc....

Page directive is aimed to define certain attribute of a JSP page for e.g. Language of the page in which the page content should be written , which class to be imported so that it can be used within the JSP page.

2. Include

Syntax:

<%@ include file="<filename>" %>

Attributes:

a. file = "<filename>"

This directive is to include the a HTML, JSP or Sevlet file into a JSP file. This is a static inclusion of file i.e. it will be included into the JSP file at the time of compilation and once the JSP file is compiled any changes in the included the file will not the reflected.

Declarations

Syntax: <%! Declare all the variables here %>

Scriplets:

Syntax: <% All your scripts will come here %>

Expressions

Syntax: <%= expression evaluation and display the variable %>

Standard Action

Syntax:

Include <jsp:include page ="<filename>" />

This inclusion of file is dynamic and the specified file is included in the JSP file at run-time i.e. out put of the included file is inserted into the JSP file.

Forward <jsp:forward page="<filename>" />

This will redirect to the different page without notifying browser. And many more.

Custom Tags:

taglib

Syntax: <%@ taglib uri="<tag library uri>" prefix="<tagprefix>" %>

Attributes:

a. uri = "<relative path of the tag library uri>"

b. prefix = "<tagprefix>"

prefix is alias name for the tag library name.

14.3 COMMENTS AND CHARACTER QUOTING CONVENTIONS

The following table represents the comments and character conventions.

Syntax	Purpose
<%-- comment --%>	A JSP comment. Ignored by JSP-to-scriptlet translator. Any embedded JSP scripting elements, directives, or actions are ignored.
<!-- comment -->	An HTML comment. Passed through to resultant HTML. Any embedded JSP scripting elements, directives, or actions are executed normally.
<\%	Used in template text (static HTML) where you really want "<%".
%\>	Used in scripting elements where you really want "%>".
\'	A single quote in an attribute that uses single quotes. Remember, however, that you can use either single or double quotes, and the other type of quote will then be a regular character.
\"	A double quote in an attribute that uses double quotes. Remember, however, that you can use either single or double quotes, and the other type of quote will then be a regular character.
%\>	%> in an attribute.
<\%	<% in an attribute

14.4 JSP OBJECTS

JSP provides certain Implicit Objects listed below.

Objects	Of kind
Out	JSP writer
Request	Http Servlet Request
Response	HTTP Servlet Response
Session	HTTP Session
Application	Servlet Context
Config	Servlet config
Page	Object
Page Context	Responsible for generating all other implicit objects.

JSP Provides certain implicit objects listed below:

Out: Out object is instantiated implicitly from JSP writer class and can be used for displaying anything on the browser.

For Example- out.println("Hi, AAtif");

Request: It is also an implicit object of class HttpServletRequest class and using this object request parameters can be accessed.

For Example- in case of retrieval of parameters from another form is as follows.

Request.getParameters("Name");

Response: It is also an implicit object of class HttpServletResponse class and using this object response parameters can be modified or set.

For example: - set the buffer size.

Response.setBufferSize ("100");

Session: Session object is of class HttpSession and used to maintain the session information. It stores the information in Name-value pair.

For example:

Session.setValue ("name","Aatif");

Session.setValue ("age","2");

Application: Application object belongs to the class ServletContext and used to maintain certain information throughout the scope of the Application.

For example: set the value of server using this object as follows.

Application.setValue ("ServerName","www.myserver.com");

Page: Objects with page scope are accessible only as part of the page that they created in references to objects with a scope of pages is released after the response is sent back to the client from the JSP page.

14.5 STEPS TO DEVELOP FIRST JSP APPLICATION

Step1: Install the Apache Tomcat Server

Now click start>>All Programs>>Apache Tomcat 6.0>> Monitor Tomcat

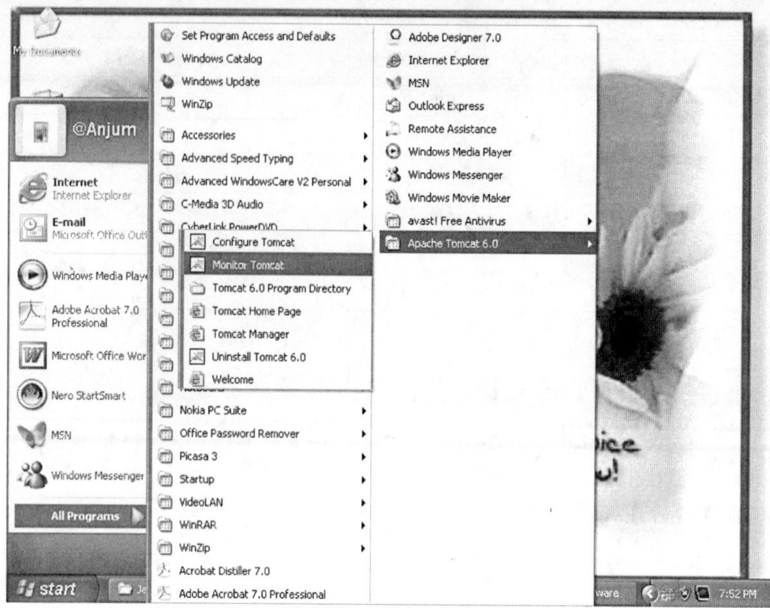

The green icon is automatically generated in right bottom corner as follows.

Tomcat Icon(Green Icon)

Step 2: Go To the following path.

C:\Program Files\Apache Software Foundation\Tomcat 6.0\webapps

In webapps directory, make a new directory where you want to save all JSP programs. Like MyJSP. Now creates a blank directory in MyJSP directory named WEB-INF. Again create a new blank directory in WEB-INF named classes.

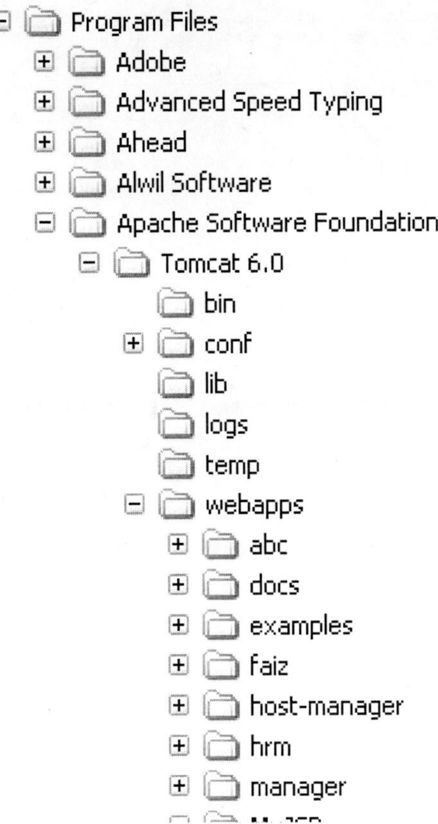

Step 3: Write a JSP program as follows.

```
<html>
<body>
<H1>MY First JSP Program</H1>
<font color=red size=7>MY First JSP Program</font><BR>
<%
for(int i=1;i<=4;i++)
{
   out.write("Hello Tanweer <br>");
}
%>
</body>
</html>
```

Save above program with named First.jsp at the location C:\Program Files\Apache Software Foundation\Tomcat 6.0\webapps\MyJSP.

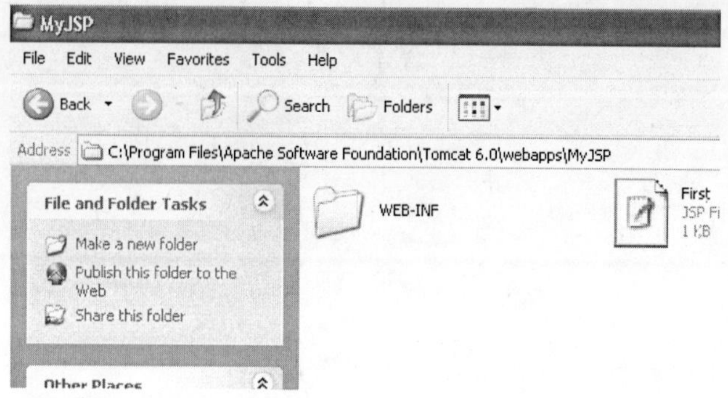

Step 4: Now open Internet Explorer and write the following URL.

http://localhost:8080/MyJSP/First.jsp

Now Press Enter.

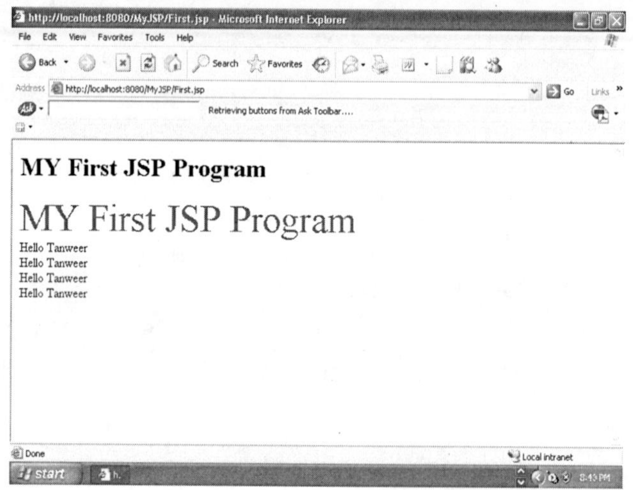

14.6 LIFECYCLE OF JSP

The JSP architecture is based on the Servlet architecture. Actually JSP page is a text file stored on the web server (Tomcat Server) and accessed via their path. The following URL is used to open the file First.jsp.

http://localhost:8080/MyFolder/First.jsp

The web server (Tomcat Server) is bound to port 8080 on local host, when the JSP page is requested. The following steps are used in life cycle of JSP.

Step1): The JSP engine uses the content of the JSP file to generate the required source code of Servlet.

Step2): This source code is then compiled and run by the Servlet engine of web server. **Step3):** Servlet code execution services a request of clients.

Once JSP code has been converted to a Servlet and Servlet Code has been compiled, the compiled version is saved and used to service additional client requests according to the standard Servlet life cycle.

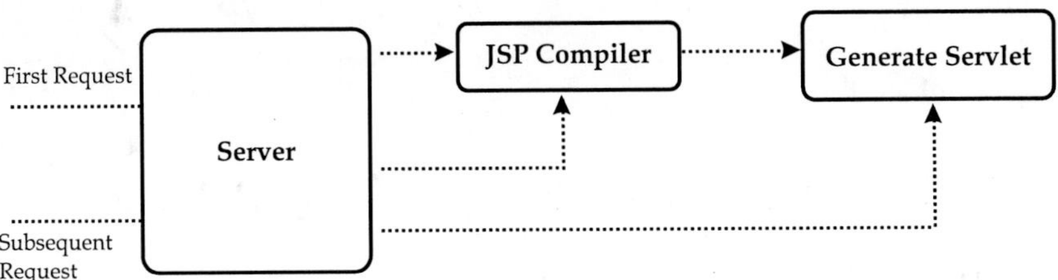

Figure: Life Cycle of JSP

The following are the states of JSP lifecycle.

jspInit: works like servlet init method.

```
public void jspInit()
{
}
```

jspTransleted: used to translate the JSP into Servlet and in case of Tomcat server, that's translated servlets goes in work directory.

```
public void jspTransleted ()
{
}
```

_jspService: Its works like servlet's service method.

```
public void _jspService ()
{
}
```

jspDestory: same as servlets destory method.

```
public void jspDestory ()
{
}
```

Life of the the jsp page is just same as the Servlet life cycle. After get translated the jsp file is just like a Servlet.

The code of the program is given below:

```
<html>
<head>
<title>The lifecycle of JSP page</title>
</head>
<body>
<h1>Showing the life cycle of JSP</h1>
```

```
<%!
String s;
public void jspInit()
{
s="init";
}
public void jspTransleted()
{
s=s+" "+"Translated";
}
public void _jspService()
{
s=s+" "+"Service";
}

public void jspDestroy()
{
s=s+" "+"Destroy";
}
%>
<%
out.println("You are in <B>"+s+"</B> JSP State "+"<br>");
%>
</body>
</html>
```

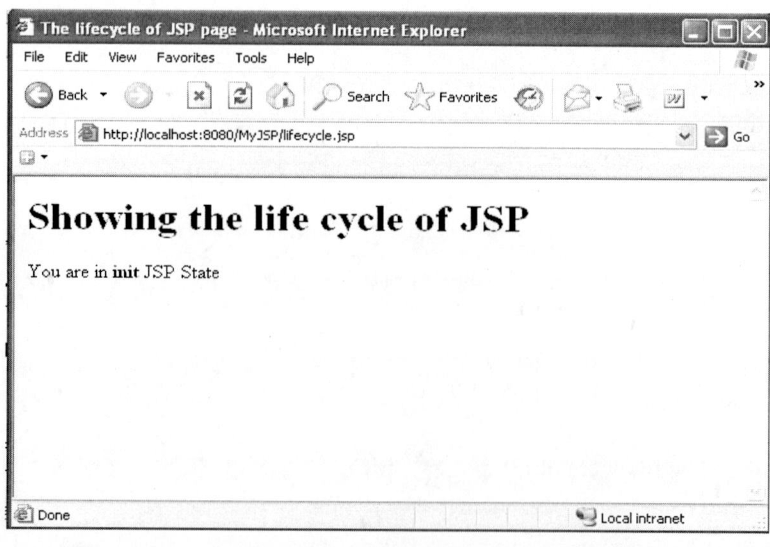

14.7 HOW DOES JSP EXECUTE?

Consider the following programs.

1. entry.html

```
<html>
<body>
<b> How Many Times?</b>
<FORM METHOD="GET" ACTION="http://localhost:8080/MyJSP/print.jsp">
<INPUT TYPE=TEXT SIZE=20 Name="xx">
<INPUT TYPE="SUBMIT" VALUE="PRINT">
</FORM>
</body>
</html>
```

print.jsp

```
<html>
<body>
<%
int num=Integer.parseInt(request.getParameter("xx"));
for(int i=0;i<num;i++)
{
out.write("Hello Aatif<br>");
}
%>
</body>
</html>
```

Output: the output of above programs is as follows.

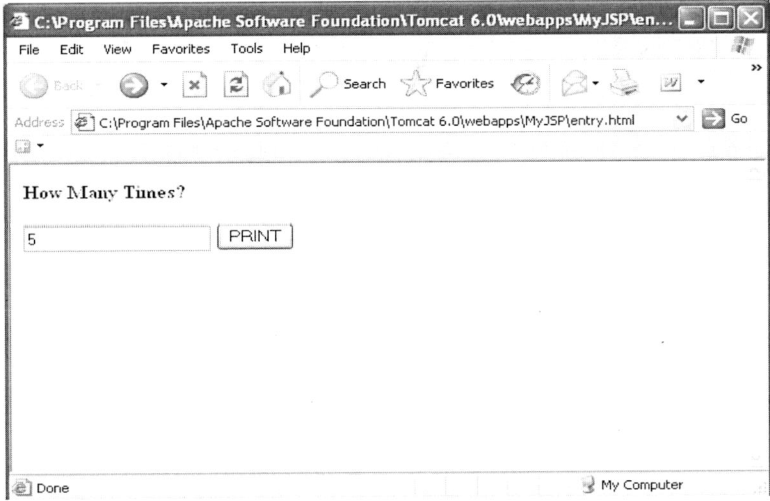

Click on PRINT button.

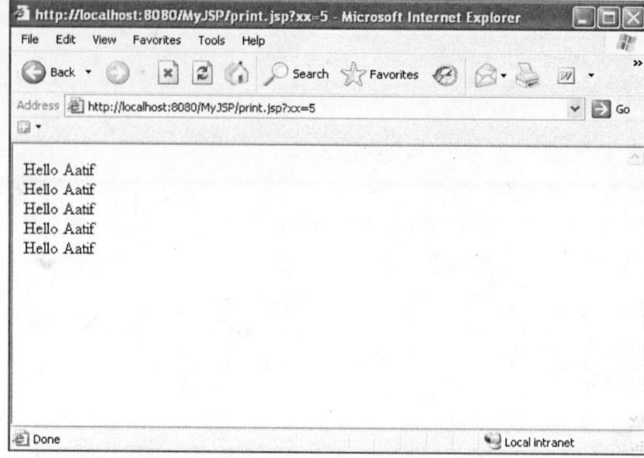

The following happens when a user requests print.jsp, the browser sends its request to the web server as http://localhost:8080/MyJSP/print.jsp?xx=5 this specifies the value of xx as a GET parameter. This web server recognizes the print.jsp file in the URL sent by the browser. The web server recognizes print.jsp and information delivered by the browser encoded in the URL must be passed on to print.jsp. print.jsp is then translated into a java class by the JSP engine i.e. compilation occur. This translation and compilation phase occurs only when the JSP file is first called (or it is subsequently changed). Hence there will be a slight delay the first time that print.jsp is run. For every subsequent request for that JSP page therefore, there is no delay because the request is forwarded directly to the Servlet byte code already in memory. Whenever the JSP file changes, the web server automatically detects the change and rebuilds the corresponding Servlet. The JSP to Servlet compilation phase imposes a slight delay the first time a page is retrieved.

14.8 CALLING A SERVLET FROM A JSP

We can invoke a Servlet from a JSP page using an action on a form. The following steps are used to call Servlet program from JSP page.

Step 1. create a Servlet program and save as program.java.

```
import javax.servlet.*;
import javax.servlet.http.*;
import java.io.*;
public class program extends HttpServlet
{
public void doGet(HttpServletRequest req, HttpServletResponse res)throws
        IOException
{
res.setContentType("text/HTML");
PrintWriter out=res.getWriter();
out.println("<HTML><HEAD><TITLE>My       First       servlet</TITLE></
    HEAD><BODY>");
```

```
out.println("<b>servlet output</b></BODY></HTML>");
}
}
```

Step2. Now compile this program using javac compiler.

```
Command Prompt

D:\servlet>javac program.java

D:\servlet>_
```

Step 3. Now set the path for Servlet as follows.

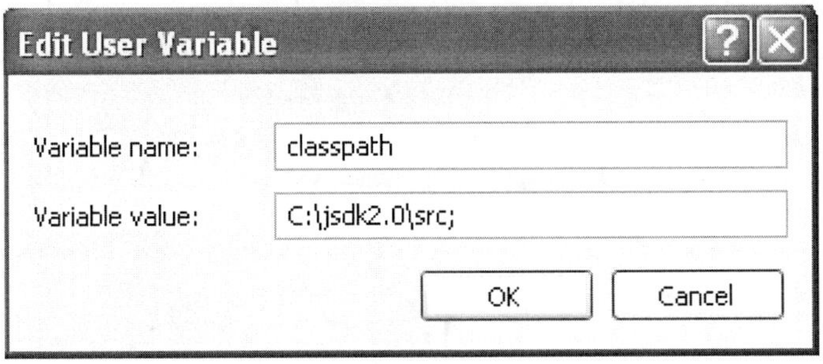

Edit User Variable

Variable name: classpath

Variable value: C:\jsdk2.0\src;

OK Cancel

Step 4: start Servletrunner as follows.

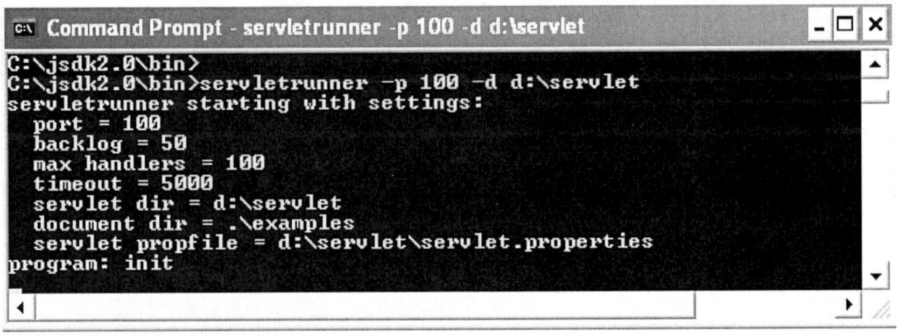

```
Command Prompt - servletrunner -p 100 -d d:\servlet
C:\jsdk2.0\bin>
C:\jsdk2.0\bin>servletrunner -p 100 -d d:\servlet
servletrunner starting with settings:
  port = 100
  backlog = 50
  max handlers = 100
  timeout = 5000
  servlet dir = d:\servlet
  document dir = .\examples
  servlet propfile = d:\servlet\servlet.properties
program: init
```

Step 5: write the code of JSP Program as Follows.

Save the following program as callservlet.jsp.

```
<HTML>
<HEAD> <TITLE> Call Servlet from JSP </TITLE> </HEAD>
<CENTER>
<H1> Call Servlet from JSP </H1>
<FORM method="GET"
action="http://localhost:100/servlet/program">
<%out.write("<H2> Servlet Launcher </H2>");%>
```

```
Click the button below to display the Servlet Output
<P> <INPUT type="submit" name="Submit" value="Call the Servlet">
</FORM>
</CENTER>
</BODY>
</HTML>
```

Step 6. Run the callservlet.jsp program as follows.

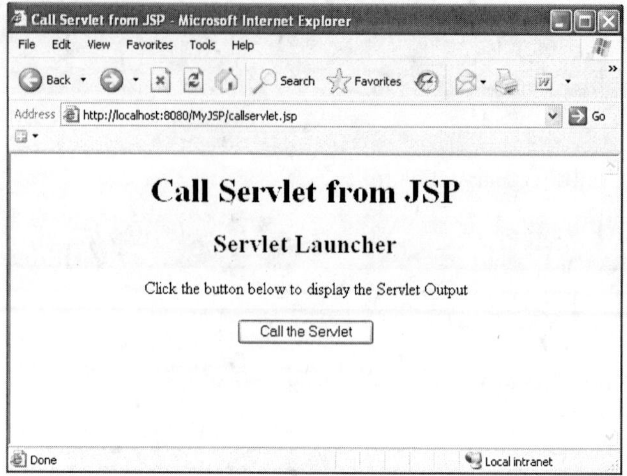

Now click on call the Servlet button.

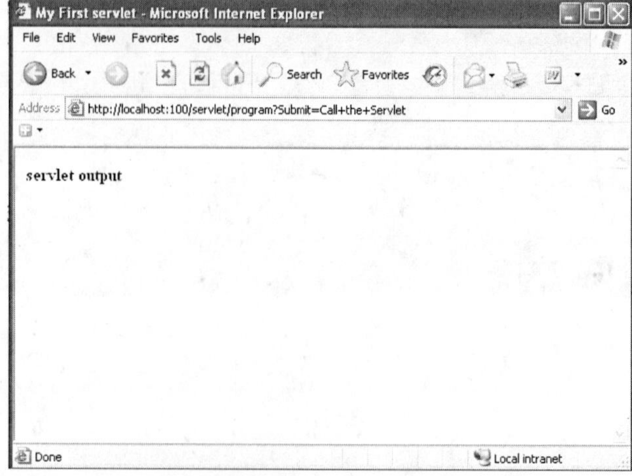

14.9 ACCESSING A DATABASE FROM A JSP PAGE

The following steps are used to connect the JSP page with database.

Step 1. Declaring Variables

Import java.sql.* package as follows.

```
<%@ page language="java" import="java.sql.*" %>
```

Step 2. Load the Driver.

Load database driver. This is achieved using the single line of code as follows. For Example.

String database="c:\\student1.mdb";

String url="jdbc:odbc:Driver={Microsoft Access Driver (*.mdb)};DBQ=" + database + ";DriverID=22;READONLY=true";

Class.forName("sun.jdbc.odbc.JdbcOdbcDriver");

Step 3. Connection to database

Make a connection as follows.

Connection con=DriverManager.getConnection(url,"","");

When url is passed into getConnection() method of DriverManager class it returns connection object.

Step 4. Executing Query or Accessing data from database

This is done using following code.
Statement stmt=con.createStatement();

ResultSet rs=stmt.executeQuery("select *from student");

A query is always executed on a Statement object. The two most important methods of this Statement interface are executeQuery() and executeUpdate(). The executeQuery() method executes an SQL statement that returns a single ResultSet object. The executeUpdate() method executes an insert, update, and delete SQL statement.

Step 5. Reading values from a ResultSet

```
while(rs.next())
      {
         String s1=rs.getString(1);
         String s2=rs.getString(2);
         String s3=rs.getString(3);
         out.write("<tr>");
   out.write("<td>"+s1+"</td>");
   out.write("<td>"+s2+"</td>");
   out.write("<td>"+s3+"</td>");
   out.write("</tr>");
      }
```

For Example:

Database

we create a database named student1 and it contains information about Name, Address & MobileNo.

Table: Student

Student : Table

Name	Address	MobileNo
Tanweer	MIET	09319398037
Aatif	MIET	09319398037

Coding

```
conn11.jsp
<%@ page language=”java” import=”java.sql.*” %>
<html><head></head><body>
<%
 try
   {
     String database=”c:\\student1.mdb”;
     String url=”jdbc:odbc:Driver={Microsoft Access Driver (*.mdb)};DBQ=” +
            database + “;DriverID=22;READONLY=true”;
     Class.forName(“sun.jdbc.odbc.JdbcOdbcDriver”);
     Connection con=DriverManager.getConnection(url,””,””);
     Statement stmt=con.createStatement();
     ResultSet rs=stmt.executeQuery(“select *from student”);
     out.write(“<table border=1 align=center><tr><th>Name</
            th><th>Address</th><th>MobileNo</th></tr>”);
 while(rs.next())
          {
            String s1=rs.getString(1);
            String s2=rs.getString(2);
            String s3=rs.getString(3);
            out.write(“<tr>”);
   out.write(“<td>”+s1+”</td>”);
   out.write(“<td>”+s2+”</td>”);
   out.write(“<td>”+s3+”</td>”);
   out.write(“</tr>”);
          }
     }
     catch(Exception e)
     {
            out.write(e.getMessage());
     }
%>
</table>
</body></html>
```

Output:

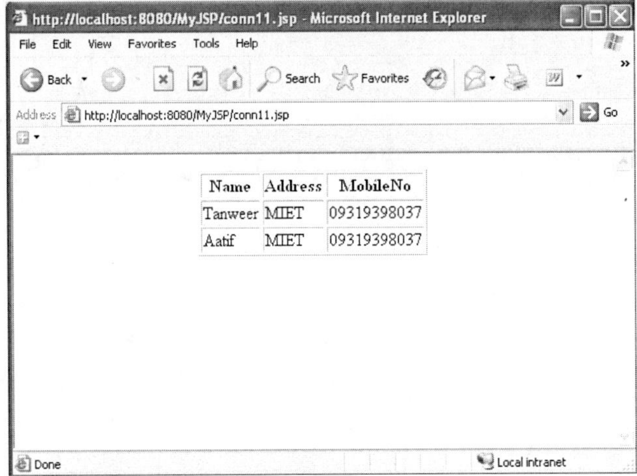

Name	Address	MobileNo
Tanweer	MIET	09319398037
Aatif	MIET	09319398037

Another Example:

Here I am going to discuss the connectivity from MSAccess database with JSP. We take an example of BookDetails database. This database contains a table named bookinfo. This table contains three fields- BookId, Title and AuthorName. We write an html page for inserting the values in student table in database. After submitting values a table will be showed that contains the student name and author name.

Database

we create a database named books and it contains information about Title & AuthorName.

Table: bookinfo

bookinfo : Table

	ID	Title	AuthorName
	1	Computer Graphics	Tanweer Alam
	2	Computer Graphics and Animation	Tanweer Alam
	3	Computer Based Optimization Techniques	Tanweer Alam
▶	(AutoNumber)		

Coding

Save the following code as BookEntryForm.jsp.

```
<%@ page language="java" import="java.sql.*" %>
<%
     String database="c:\\BookDetails.mdb";
   String url="jdbc:odbc:Driver={Microsoft Access Driver (*.mdb)};DBQ=" +
      database + ";DriverID=22;READONLY=true";
     Class.forName("sun.jdbc.odbc.JdbcOdbcDriver");
```

```
Connection con=null;
   ResultSet rs=null;
   Statement stmt=null;
try{

      con=DriverManager.getConnection(url);
      stmt=con.createStatement();
   }
   catch(Exception e){
      System.out.println(e.getMessage());
   }
if(request.getParameter("action") != null){
      String bookname=request.getParameter("Title");
      String author=request.getParameter("AuthorName");
      stmt.executeUpdate("insert into bookinfo values('"+bookname+"','"+author+
"')");
      rs=stmt.executeQuery("select * from bookinfo");
      %>
<html>
      <body>
      <center>
         <h2>Books List</h2>
         <table border="1" cellspacing="0" cellpadding
="0">
         <tr>
            <td><b>S.No</b></td>
            <td><b>Book Name</b></td>
            <td><b>Author</.b></td>
         </tr>
            <%
            int no=1;
            while(rs.next()){
            %>
            <tr>
             <td><%=no%></td>
             <td><%=rs.getString("Title")%></td>
             <td> <%=rs.getString("AuthorName")
%> </td>
            </tr>
            <%
            no++;
   }
   rs.close();
```

```
  stmt.close();
  con.close();
%>
        </table>
        </center>
      </body>
  </html>
<%}else{%>
  <html>
  <head>
     <title>Book Entry Form</title>
     <script language="javascript">
      function validate(objForm){
        if(objForm.bookname.value.length==0){
        alert("Please enter Book Name!");
        objForm.bookname.focus();
        return false;
        }
        if(objForm.author.value.length==0){
        alert("Please enter Author name!");
        objForm.author.focus();
        return false;
        }
        return true;
           }
        </script>
     </head>

     <body>
        <center>
<form     action="BookEntryForm.jsp"     method="post"     name="entry"
onSubmit="return
 validate(this)">
   <input type="hidden" value="list" name="action">
   <table border="1" cellpadding="0" cellspacing="0">
   <tr>
      <td>
         <table>
            <tr>
            <td colspan="2" align="center">
<h2>Book Entry Form</h2></td>
            </tr>
            <tr>
```

```
            <td colspan="2"> </td>
            </tr>
            <tr>
            <td>Book Name:</td>
            <td><input name="Title" type=
"text" size="50"></td>
            </tr>
            <tr>
            <td>Author:</td><td><input name=
"AuthorName" type="text" size="50"></td>
            </tr>
            <tr>
              <td colspan="2" align="center">
<input type="submit" value="Insert"></td>
              </tr>
            </table>
          </td>
        </tr>
      </table>
</form>
          </center>
        </body>
      </html>
<%}%>
```

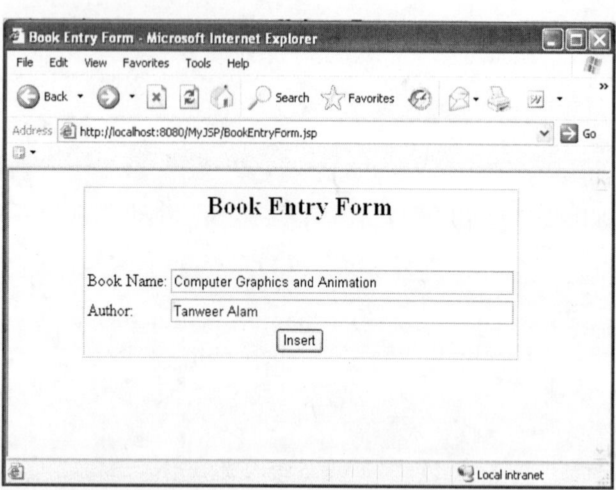

Fill the Book Name and Author fields and press Submit button. A page will open and show a table of book name and authors as follows.

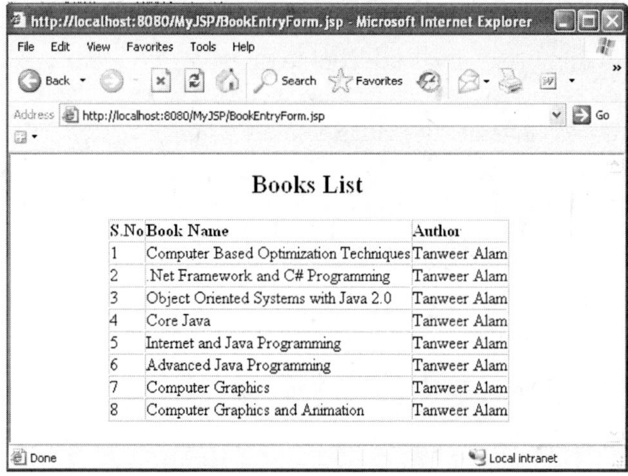

14.8 WORKING WITH COOKIE IN JSP

Cookie is a small program which is stored in client's computer. Web server uses cookie to identify the user in the next time visit. Each time user visits a website which cookie is enabling; the web server adds extra data into the HTTP header and responds to the web browser. In the next time when user visits the same site again, the web browser also sends cookie in the HTTP request header to the web server. Cookie is stored in the user's computer as a string of name/value. JSP provides API to allow you to work with cookie effectively through object of the class javax.servlet.http.Cookie.

Cookies can be constructed using the following code:

Cookie(String name, String value)

Cookie objects have the following methods.

Method	Description
getName()	Returns the name of the cookie.
getMaxAge()	Returns the maximum specified age of the cookie.
getValue()	Returns the value of the cookie.
getPath()	Returns the prefix of all URLs for which this cookie is targeted.
getComment()	Returns the comment describing the purpose of this cookie, or null if no such comment has been defined.
setMaxAge(int)	Sets the maximum age of the cookie. The cookie will expire after that many seconds have passed. Negative values indicate the default behavior: the cookie is not stored persistently, and will be deleted when the user web browser exits. A zero value causes the cookie to be deleted
setValue(String)	Sets the value of the cookie
setPath(String)	This cookie should be presented only with requests beginning with this URL.
setComment(String)	If a web browser presents this cookie to a user, the cookie's purpose will be described using this comment.

Sending cookie from the web server to the client's computer.

Save the following program as addcookie.jsp.

```
<%@page import="javax.servlet.http.Cookie" %>
<html>
 <head>
 <title>Add Cookie</title>
 </head>
 <body>
 <%
 Cookie c = new Cookie("userId","Tanweer");
 c.setMaxAge(2100);
 response.addCookie(c);
 %>
 A Cookie is Added, Thanks.
 </body>
```

Now run the program.

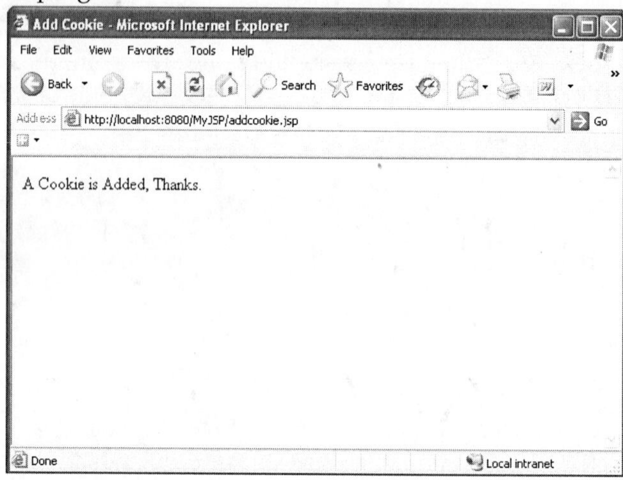

Reading cookie

To read cookie from a HTTP request, we first call the method *getCookies()* of the *request* object. This method returns you a list of available cookies in the request header and then you can walk through all of them.

Save the following program as readcookie.jsp.

```
<%@page import="javax.servlet.http.Cookie" %>
<html>
 <head>
 <title>Read Cookie</title>
 </head>
```

```
<body>
<%
Cookie[] list = request.getCookies();
if(list != null){
for(int i = 0; i < list.length;i++){
out.println(list[i].getName() + ":" + list[i].getValue()+"<br>");
}
}
%>
</body>
</html>
```

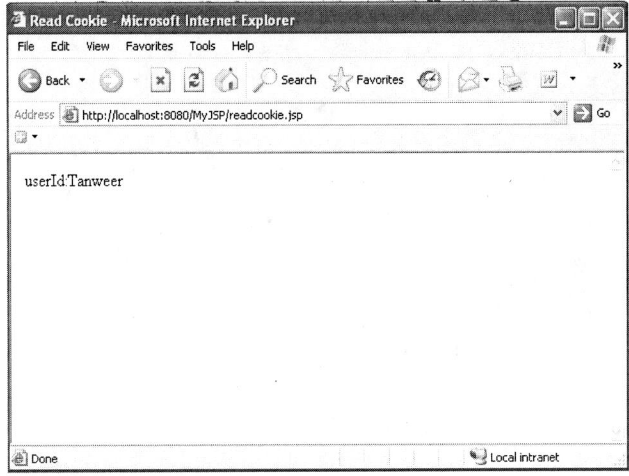

Removing existing cookie

If we want to remove an existing cookie then we can use the method *setMaxAge()* of that cookie object to set its timeout to zero.

Save the following program as removecookie.jsp.

```
<%@page import="javax.servlet.http.Cookie"%>
<html>
 <head>
 <title>Removing existing cookie</title>
 </head>
 <body>
 <%
 Cookie[] list = request.getCookies();
 if (list != null) {
 for (int i = 0; i < list.length; i++) {
 list[i].setMaxAge(0);
 out.write(list[i].getName() + " cookie is removed <br>");
```

```
}
}
%>
</body>
</html>
```

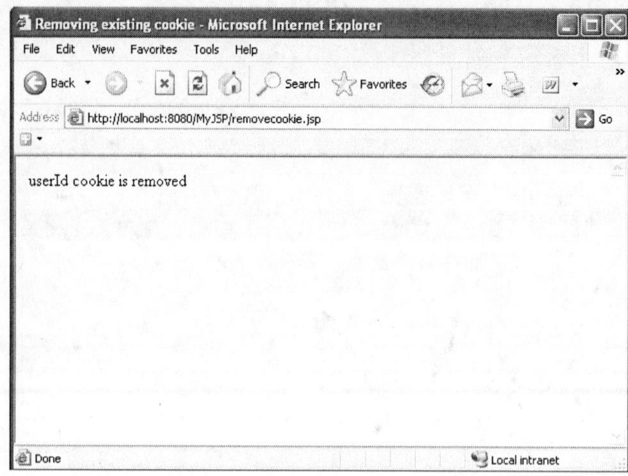

Example Using Cookies

No we will write code in JSP file to set and then display the cookie.

Create Form

The following form entrycookie.html prompts the user to enter name.

```
<%@ page language="java" %>
<html>
<head>
<title>Cookie Input Form</title>
</head>
<body>
<form method="post" action="http://localhost:8080/MyJSP/setcookie.jsp">
<p><b>Enter Your Name: </b><input type="text" name="username"><br>
<input type="submit" value="Submit">
</form>
</body>
</html>
```

Above form prompts the user to enter the user name. User input are posted to the setcookie.jsp file, which sets the cookie.

```
<%@ page language="java" import="java.util.*"%>
<%
String username=request.getParameter("username");
```

```
if(username==null) username="";
Date now = new Date();
String timestamp = now.toString();
Cookie cookie = new Cookie ("username",username);
cookie.setMaxAge(365 * 24 * 60 * 60);
response.addCookie(cookie);
%>
<html>
<head>
<title>Cookie Saved</title>
</head>
<body>
<p><a href="http://localhost:8080/MyJSP/showcookie.jsp">Click Here to show
the cookie value</a><p>
</body>
</html>
```

Now displays a link to view cookie page. Here is the code of display cookie page (showcookie.jsp):

```
<%@ page language="java" %>
<%
String cookieName = "username";
Cookie cookies [] = request.getCookies ();
Cookie myCookie = null;
if (cookies != null)
{
for (int i = 0; i < cookies.length; i++)
{
if (cookies [i].getName().equals (cookieName))
{
myCookie = cookies[i];
break;
}
}
}
%>
<html>
<head>
<title>Show Saved Cookie</title>
</head>
<body>
<%
if (myCookie == null) {
```

```
%>
No Cookie found with the name <%=cookieName%>
<%
} else {
%>
<p>Welcome: <%=myCookie.getValue()%><br> You are visiting our web site first
time<br>Have a Nice Day..
<%
}
%>
</body>
</html>
```

When user navigates to the above the page, cookie value is displayed.

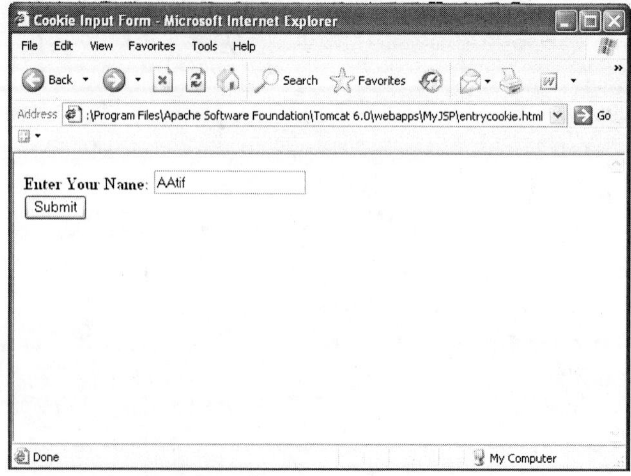

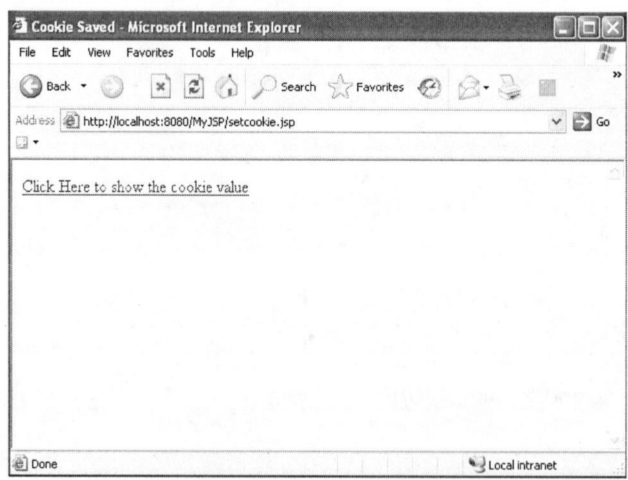

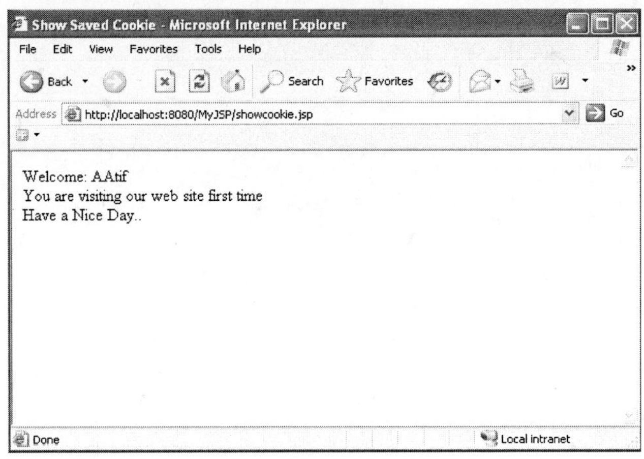

14.9 SOME JSP PROGRAMS

Program 1: Add two numbers in JSP

```
<%@ page language="java"%>
<html>
<head>
<title>Add Two numbers in JSP</title>
</head>
<body>
<%
int a=10;
int b=20;
int result=a+b;
out.print("Additon of a and b :"+result);
%>
</body>
</html>
```

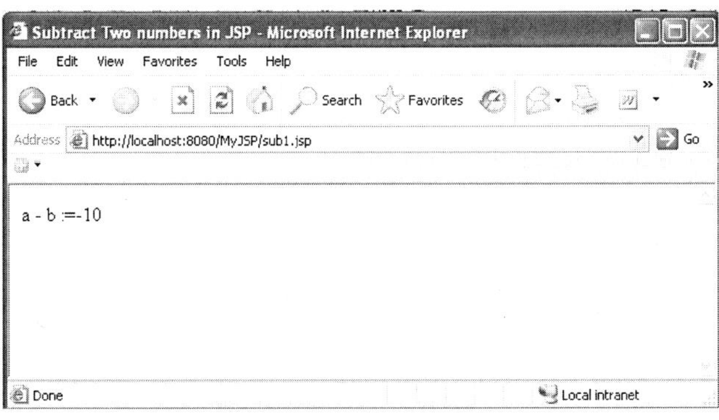

Program 2: Subtract two numbers in JSP

```
<%@ page language="java"%>
<html>
<head>
<title>Subtract Two numbers in JSP</title>
</head>
<body>
<%
int a=10;
int b=20;
int result=a-b;
out.print("a - b :="+result);
%>
</body>
</html>
```

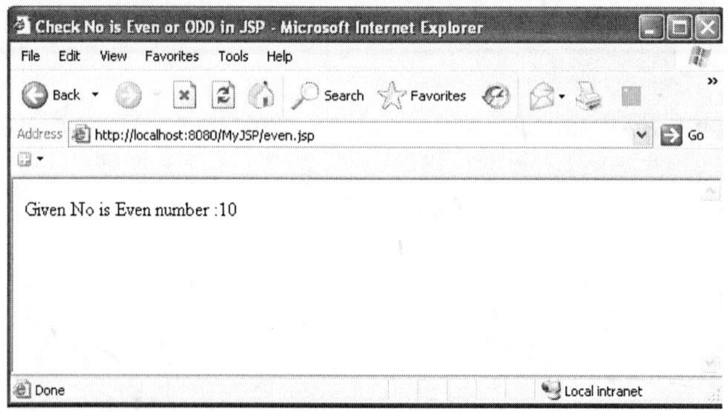

Program 3: Check given No is EVEN or ODD in JSP

```
<%@ page language="java"%>
<html>
<head>
<title>Check No is Even or ODD in JSP</title>
</head>
<body>
<%
   int i=10;
   if((i%2)==0)
   {
   out.print("Given No is Even number :"+i);
   out.print("<br>");
   }
   else
out.print("Given No is ODD number :"+i);
%>
</body>
</html>
```

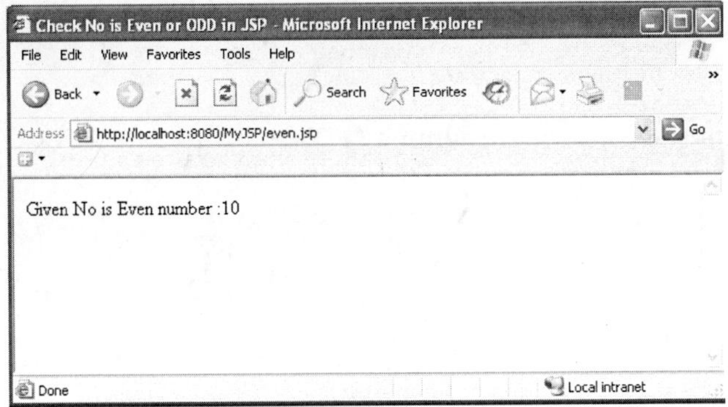

Program 4: Print all odd numbers between 0 to 10 in JSP

```
<%@ page language="java"%>
<html>
<head>
<title>Odd number program in JSP</title>
</head>
<body>
<%
for(int i=0;i<=10;i++)
{
if((i%2)!=0)
   {
   out.print("Odd number :"+i);
   out.print("<br>");
   }
}
%>
</body>
</html>
```

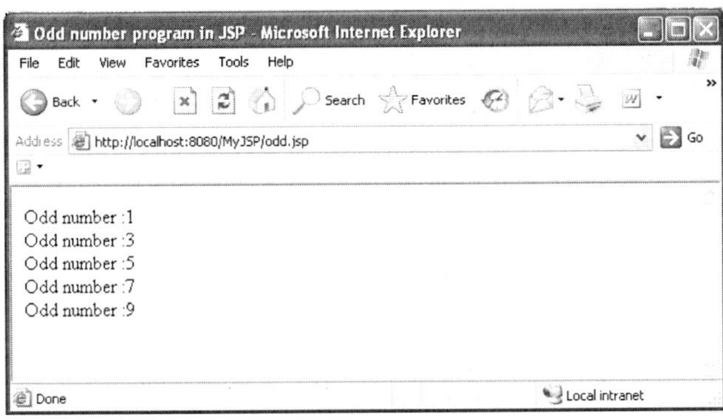

Program 5: Display Date and Time

```
<HTML>
<HEAD>
<TITLE>Date and Time JSP Program</TITLE>
</HEAD>
<BODY BGCOLOR="ffddcc">
<CENTER>
<H2>Date and Time</H2>
<%
java.util.Date today = new java.util.Date();
out.println("Today's date is: "+today);
%>
</CENTER>
</BODY>
</HTML>
```

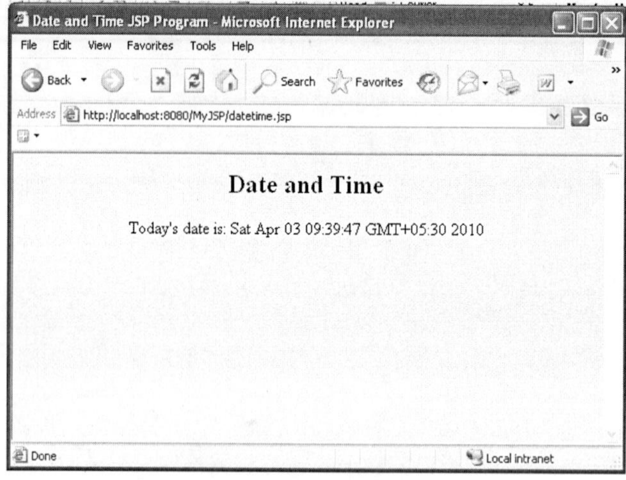

Program 6: Print Name with different colors.

```
<html>
<body>
<h1>Hello Tanweer</h1>
<font color=red size=7>Hello Anjum</font><br>
<font color=blue size=7>Hello AAtif </font>
<%
for(int i=1;i<=10;i++)
{
   out.write("Bye<br>");
}
%>
</body>
</html>
```

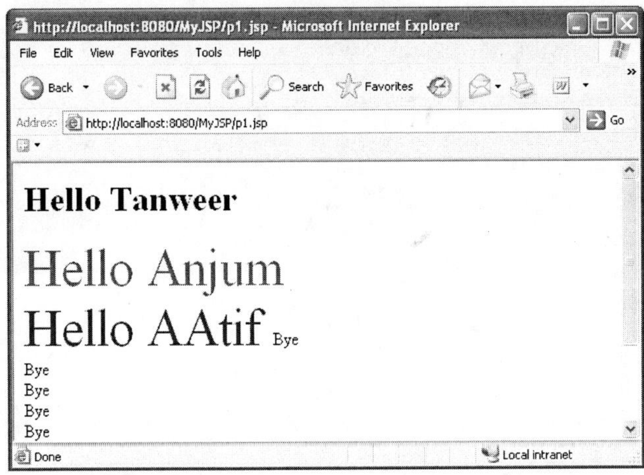

Program 7: Send data from one form to another

```
//p7.jsp
<html>
<body>
<form method=post action=http://localhost:8080/MyJSP/p8.jsp>
Name:<input type=text name="name"><br>
Course:<input type=text name="course"><br>
Age:<input type=text name="age"><br>
<input type=Submit name="Submit"><br>
</form>
</body>
</html>
```

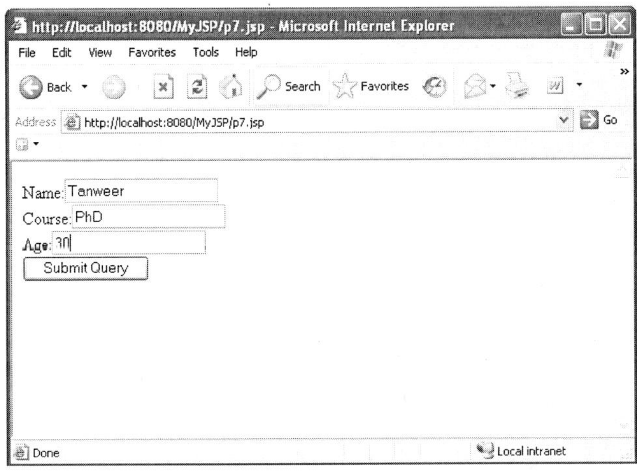

```
//p8.jsp
<%@ page language="java" %>
<html><body>
<%
   String s1=request.getParameter("name");
   String s2=request.getParameter("course");
   String s3=request.getParameter("age");
   out.write("Name is ::"+s1+"<BR>");
 out.write("Course is ::"+s2+"<BR>");
 out.write("Age is ::"+s3+"<BR>");
%>
</body></html>
```

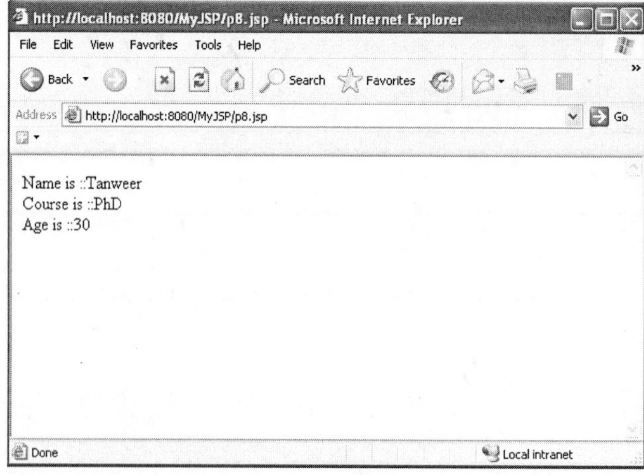

Program 8: add another file to your JSP file.

Headerfooter.jsp

```
<%@ page language="java" %>
<html>
<body>
<jsp:include page="head.jsp" />
You are visiting our website fist time,<br><h3> Have a nice day.</h3>
<jsp:include page="footer.jsp" />
</body>
</html>
```

Header.jsp

```
<h1 align='Center'>College Management System</h1>
<p align=right>
<%
   out.write("<a href=logout.jsp>Logout</a>");
%>
</p>
```

```
<hr>
```

Footer.jsp

```
<hr>
<h6 align=center>All rights reserved</h6>
```

Logout.jsp

```
<html>
<body>
<%
   out.write("Successfully logout your accont");
%>
</body>
</html>
```

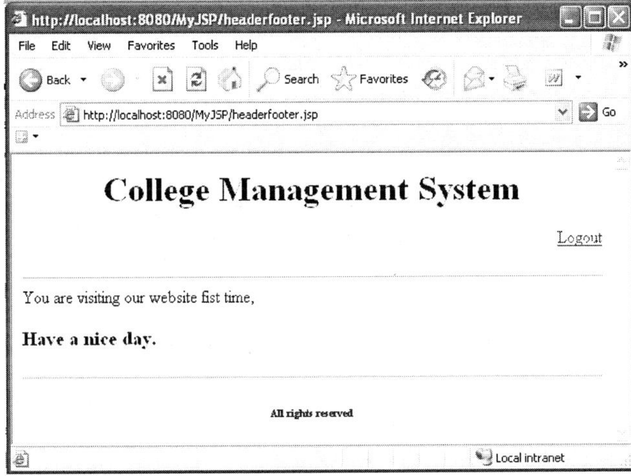

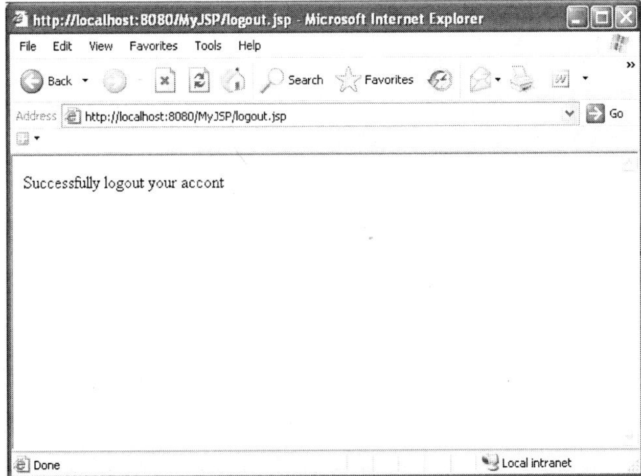

Program 9: How to Open Internet using JSP file.

Web.html

```
<html>
<body>
<H1>Open any Website from Internet using JSP </H1>
<b> Enter WeB site Name</b>
<FORM   METHOD="GET"    ACTION="http://localhost:8080/MyJSP/website.
jsp">
<INPUT TYPE=TEXT SIZE=50 Name="web">
<INPUT TYPE="SUBMIT" VALUE="Open">
</FORM>
</body>
</html>
```

Website.jsp

```
<html>
<body>
<%
String s="http://www."+request.getParameter("web");
out.println("<H4>Click Here to open our website</H4><BR>");
out.println("<a href="+s+">Click here</a>");
%>
</body>
</html>
```

Output

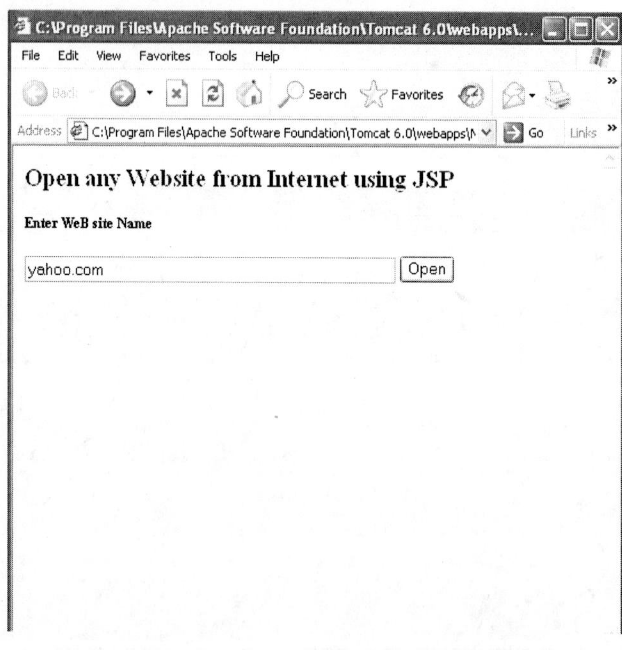

Enter the website name and click Open button.

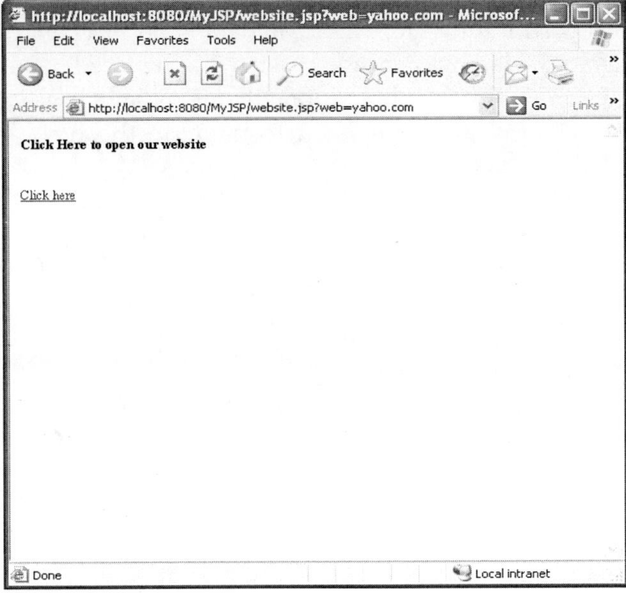

Now single click on click here hyperlink.

SUMMARY

JSP provide excellent server side scripting support for creating database driven web applications. JDBC provide excellent database connectivity in heterogeneous database environment. Using JSP and JDBC it's very easy to develop database driven web application. JSP is an extremely powerful choice for web development. JSP pages usually contain a mixture of both static data and dynamic elements. It is important to understand the distinction between the two forms. Static data is never changed in the server page and dynamic elements will always be interpreted and replaced before reaching the client. JSP is a technology using server side scripting that is actually translated into Servlets and compiled before they are run. JSP is used to develop the web application in more efficient way than Servlets.

EXERCISE

1. What are the implicit objects of JSP?
2. What are differences between Servlet and JSP?
3. Explain JSP.
4. How to Develop a JSP Application?
5. What are Cookies in JSP? Explain with suitable example.

*****

CHAPTER 15

WORKING WITH DATABASE

Java Database Connectivity in short called as JDBC. JDBC is commonly used to connect a user program to a database. JDBC is Java application programming interface that allows the Java programmers to access database management system from Java programs. It is a java API which enables the java programs to execute SQL statements. It is an application programming interface that defines how a java programmer can access the database in matrix form from Java code using a set of standard interfaces and classes written in Java.

15.0 INTRODUCTION

JDBC was developed by JavaSoft, a subsidiary of Sun Microsystems. JavaSoft responded with the first release of the JDBC specification in May, 1996. JDBC provides a vendor-neutral, universal framework for vendors to use in building tools that allow clients to access databases. JDBC sends a request to a database server using the appropriate SQL command and processes the results. A database that another program links to is called a data source. Many data sources, including products produced by Microsoft and Oracle, already use a standard called Open Database Connectivity (ODBC). JDBC is a low-level API and a base for higher-level APIs. Two higher-level APIs under development are:

(i) An embedded SQL for Java

An embedded SQL preprocessor allows a programmer to instead mix SQL statements directly with Java. JDBC requires that the SQL statements be passed as Strings to Java methods: for example, a Java variable can be used in a SQL statement to receive or provide SQL values. The embedded SQL preprocessor then translates this Java/SQL mix into Java with JDBC calls.

(ii) A direct mapping of relational database tables to Java classes

This is a relational mapping, in which each row of the table becomes an instance of that class and each column value corresponds to an attribute of that instance. Programmers can then operate directly on Java objects; the required SQL calls to fetch and store data automatically.

15.1 JAVA DATABASE CONNECTIVITY

JDBC is a programming framework for writing programs that access information stored in databases, spreadsheets, and flat files. Database access, for many developers, is an essential part of the tools of software development. Accessing a database in Java doesn't have to be a difficult task. Using Java Database Connectivity (JDBC) you can easily access databases in your applications and applets via special drivers. A database that another program links to is called a data source. The JDBC API standard defines a set of Java classes required to perform standard relational database operations such as managing database connections, SQL statements, result sets, and metadata. JDBC sends a request to a database server using the appropriate SQL command and then processes the results. JDBC makes it possible by using the following steps:

(i) establish a connection with a database

(ii) send SQL statements

(iii) process the results

15.2 JDBC ARCHITECTURE

JDBC is an API (application Programming Interface) for Java Programming language that defines how a client may access a database. An API helps us access database from our java program or simply embed queries in code. The JDBC API was presented as primary technique for connecting Java applications to the data base System.

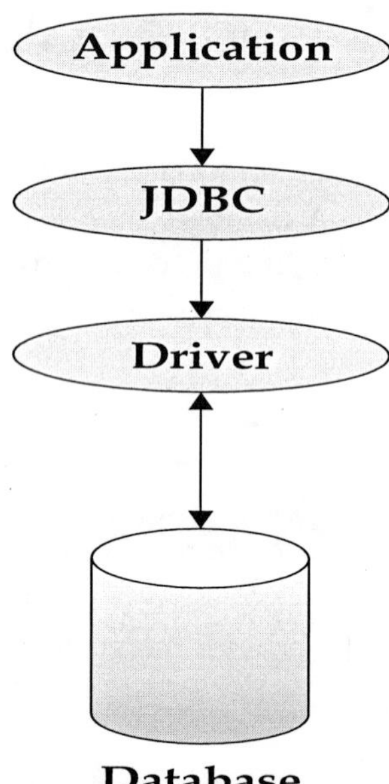

Figure 15.1: JDBC Architecture

Different languages have different APIs for the purpose. The JDBC Architecture consists of two layers:

(i) The JDBC API, which provides the application-to-JDBC Manager connection

(ii) The JDBC Driver API, which supports the JDBC Manager-to-Driver Connection.

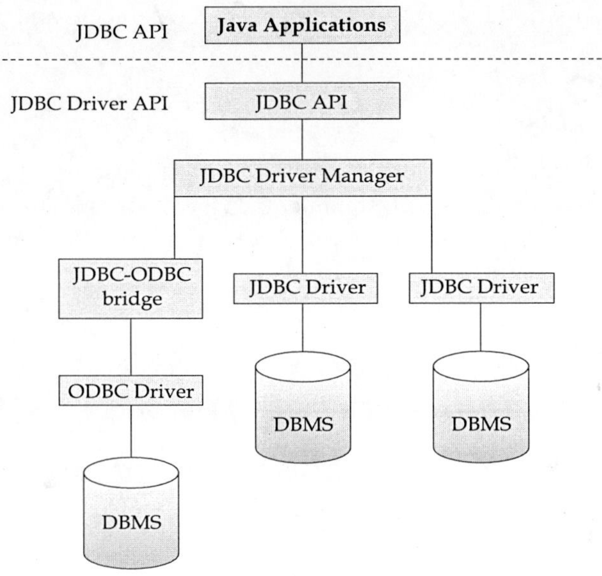

Figure 15.2: JDBC API

The JDBC API supports both two-tier and three-tier models for database access. In other words, JDBC can either be used directly from your application or as part of a middle-tier server application.

15.2.1 The Two-Tier Model

In the two-tier model, a Java application interacts directly with the database. This requires a JDBC driver that can communicate with the particular database management system being accessed. The Functionality of two tier model is divided into these two layers:

(i) Application layer, including the JDBC driver, business logic, and user interface.

(ii) Database layer, including the RDBMS

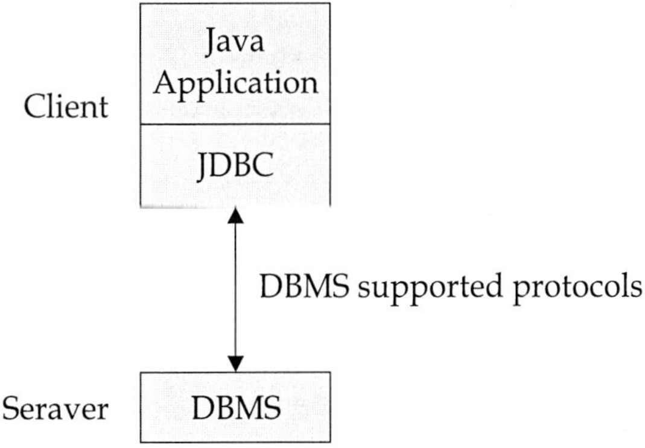

Figure 15.3: Two-Tier Model

Client sends a request using SQL statements to the database and the results are sent back to the client.

15.2.2 The Three-Tier Model

In the three-tier model, commands are sent to an application server (middle tier service). The application server then sends SQL statements to the database. The database processes the SQL statements and sends the results back to the middle tier (Application Server), which then sends them to the user.

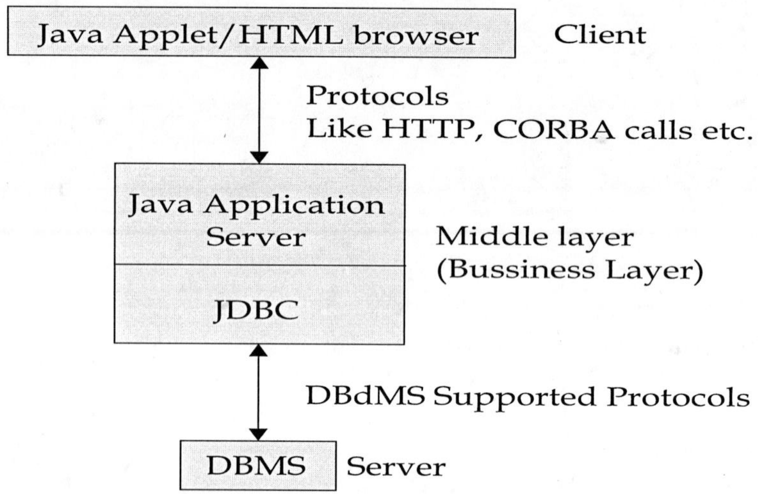

Figure 15.4: Three-Tier Model

The following are some advantages of three-tier architecture:

(i) User can employ an easy-to-use higher-level API which is translated by the middle tier into the appropriate low-level calls.

(ii) Provide improved performance.

(iii) Business logic is clearly separated from the database.

(iv) Client applications can use a simple protocol such as CGI to access services.

The three-tier model is common in Web applications, where the client tier is frequently implemented in a web browser on a client machine, the middle tier is implemented in a Web server with a servlet engine, and the database management system runs on a dedicated database server.

15.3 JDBC API

JDBC is a core part of the Java platform and is included in the standard JDK distribution. API- stands for application Programming Interface. An API helps us access database from our java program or simply embed queries in code. JDBC is an API for Java Programming language that defines how a client may access a database. There are two layers in JDBC API.

(i) Driver Layer
ii) Application Layer

(i) Driver Layer

Driver Layer has two components, the Driver manage and Driver. The Driver Manager is responsible for loading and unloading drivers and making connections through the drivers. It also provides logging and database login time on second is Driver, it is where the connection to the database is made.

(ii) Application Layer

Application is used by the database application developers. The Connection, PreparedStatement, Statement, CallableStatement and ResultSet are used in application layer.

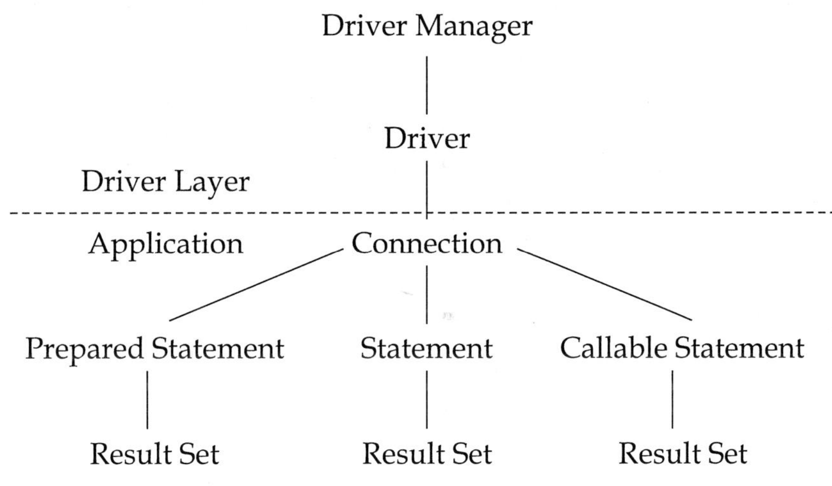

Figure 15.5: Driver Manager

The following are the JDBC API interface:

(i) java.sqlDriverManager
(ii) java. Sql.Connection
(iii) java. sql.Statement
(iv) java.sql.Resultset

The following support interfaces are also available:

(i) java.sql.Driver
(ii) java. sql.PreparedStatement
(iii) java.sql.Callablestatement
(iv) java. sql.ResultSetMetaData
(v) java. Sql.DriverPropertymfo

(vi) java. sql.DatabaseMetaData

(vii) java.sql.Date

(viii) java.sql.Time

(ix) java. sql.Timestamp

(x) java.sql.Types

(xi) java. sql.Numeric

DriverManager

The DriverManager class works between the user and the drivers. DriverManager is a very important class. Its main purpose is to provide a means of managing the different types of JDBC database driver on running an application. When opening a connection to a database it is the DriverManager's role to choose the most appropriate driver from the previously loaded drivers. java.sql.DriverManager handles the loading and unloading of the appropriate database drivers required to make the connection. The driver is loaded by calling the Class.forName() method.

Table 15.1: DriverManager

Method	Description
getDriver(String url)	It attempts to locate the driver by the given string.
getDrivers()	It retrieves the enumeration of the drivers which has been registered with the DriverManager class.
getConnection(String url)	It tries to establish the connection to a given database URL.
getConnection(String url, Sting user, String password)	It tries to establish the connection to a given database URL.
getConnection(String url, Properties info)	It tries to establish the connection to a given database URL.
registerDriver(Driver driver)	It registers the driver with the DriverManager class.
deregisterDriver(Driver driver)	It drops the driver from the list of drivers registered in the DriverManager class.

Connection

When a connection is opened, this represents a single instance of a particular database session. As long as the connection remains open, SQL queries may be executed and results obtained. This interface can be used to retrieve information regarding the table descriptions, and any other information about the database to which you are connected. java.sql.Connection exposes the database to the developer, representing the connection as an accessible Java component.

Statement

The objective of the Statement interface is to pass to the database the SQL string for execution and to retrieve any results from the database in the form of a ResultSet. Only one ResultSet can be open per statement at any one time. java.sql.Statement: provides a container for executing SQL statements using a connection.

Three kinds of Statements

(i) Statement:

Execute simple sql queries without parameters.
Statement createStatement()
Creates an SQL Statement object.

(ii) Prepared Statement:

Execute precompiled sql queries with or without parameters.
PreparedStatement prepareStatement(String sql)
returns a new PreparedStatement object. PreparedStatement objects are precompiled SQL statements.

(iii) Callable Statement:

Execute a call to a database stored procedure.
CallableStatement prepareCall(String sql)
returns a new CallableStatement object.
CallableStatement objects are SQL stored procedure call statements.

ResultSet

A ResultSet is the retrieved data from a currently executed SQL statement. The data from the query is delivered in the form of a table. The rows of the table are returned to the program in sequence. Within any one row, the multiple columns may be accessed in any order. java.sql.ResultSet: exposes the data that returns from the database server to the Java application.

ResultSet navigation methods

Table 15.2: ResultSet navigation methods

Method	Description
next()	Moves cursor to next row.
first()	Moves cursor to first row.
last()	Moves cursor to last row.
previous()	Moves cursor to previous row.
beforeFirst()	Moves cursor to just before the first row.
afterLast()	Moves cursor to just before the last row.
absolute(int)	Moves cursor to a row index, positive value from the front, negative value from the back.
relative(int)	Moves cursor relative number of row, positive and negative value from the current position.

15.4 HOW JDBC WORKS

Steps for Creating the Database in MSAccess

Click on start>All Programs>Microsoft Office> Microsoft Office Access 2003

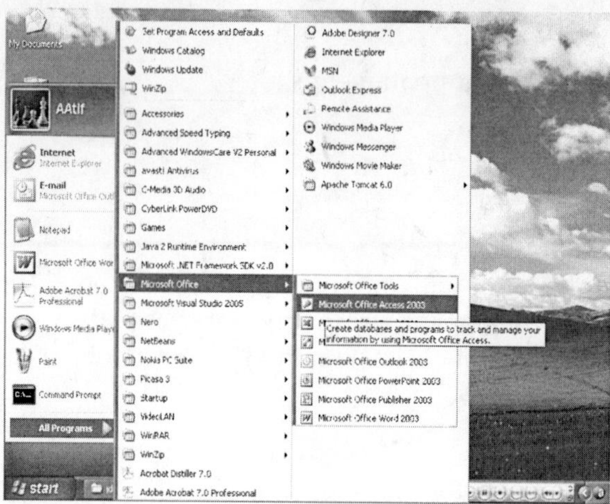

Click File and select New.

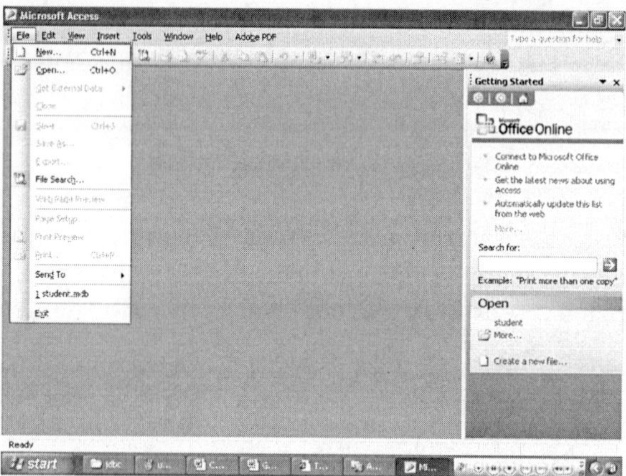

Click on Blank Database

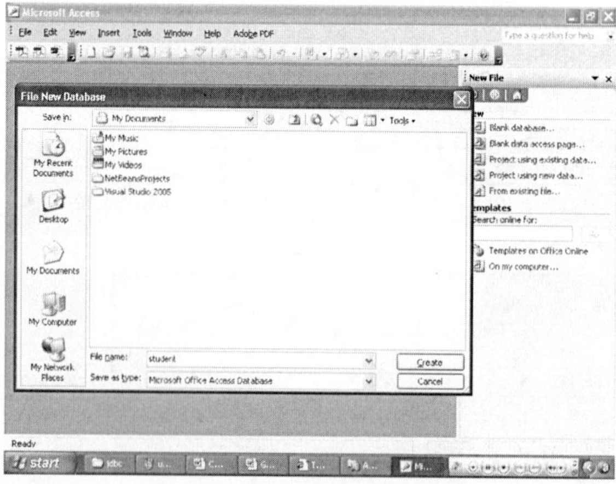

Enter the name of database and click Create button.

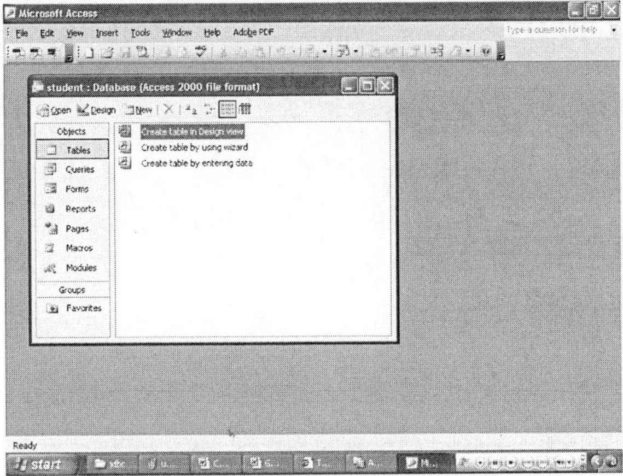

Double click on "Create table in Design view".

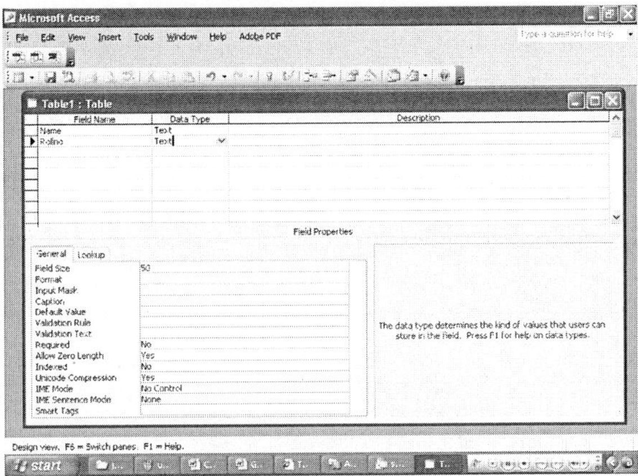

Close this window.

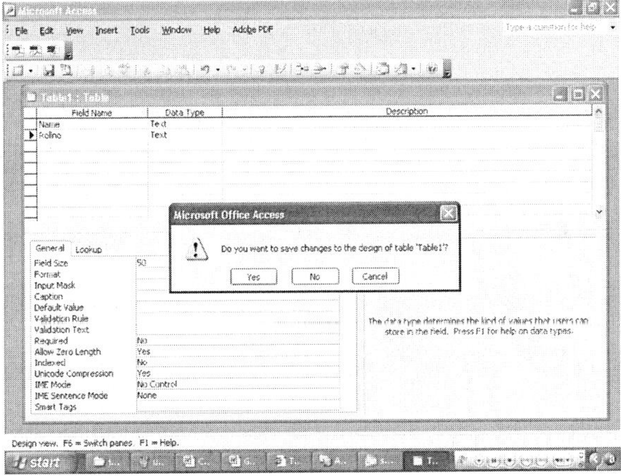

Click yes.

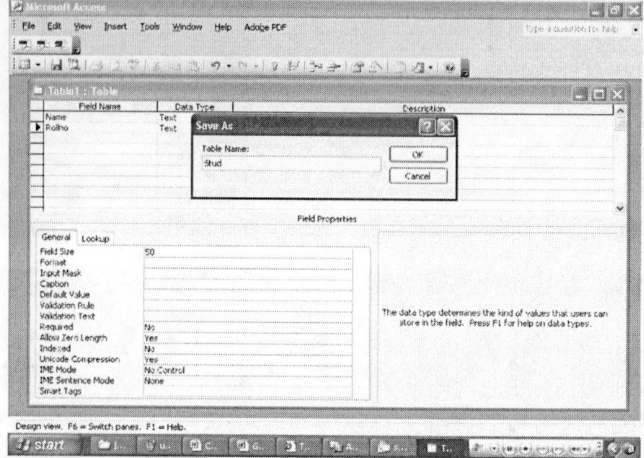

Enter the table name and click OK.

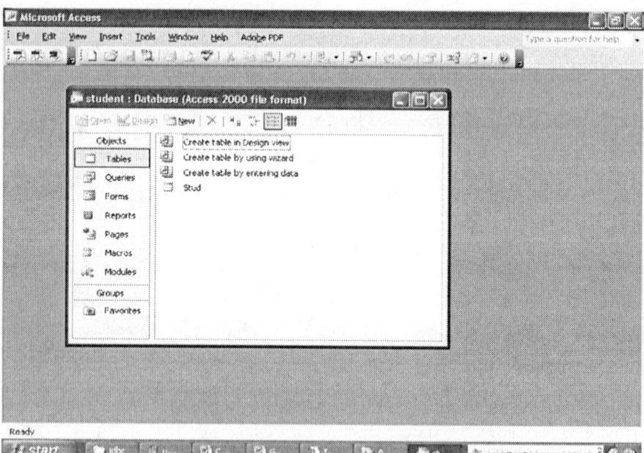

Double click on Stud.

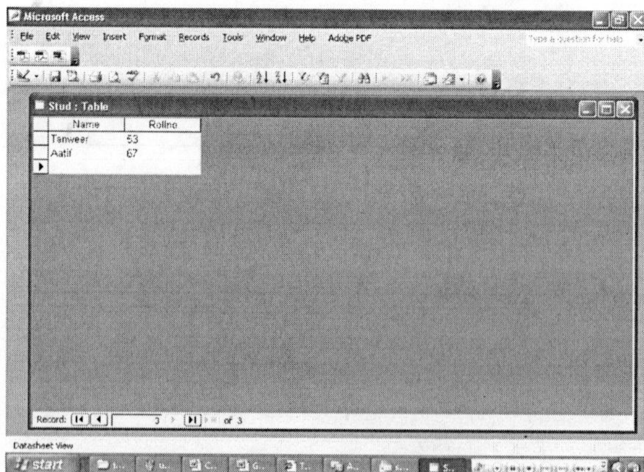

15.5 Steps for Creating the ODBC DSN

Double click on Data Source (ODBC).

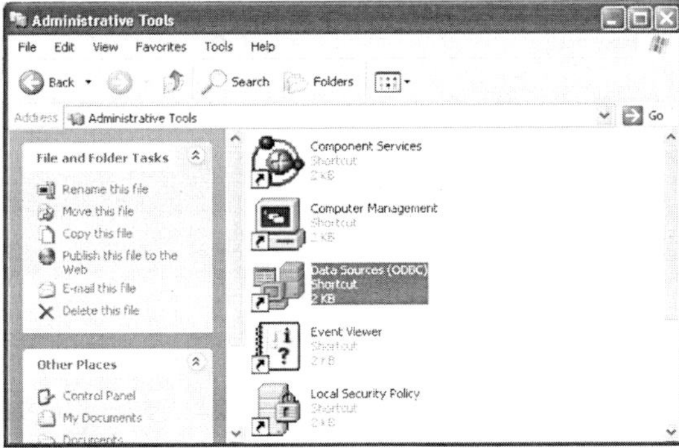

Now click Add.

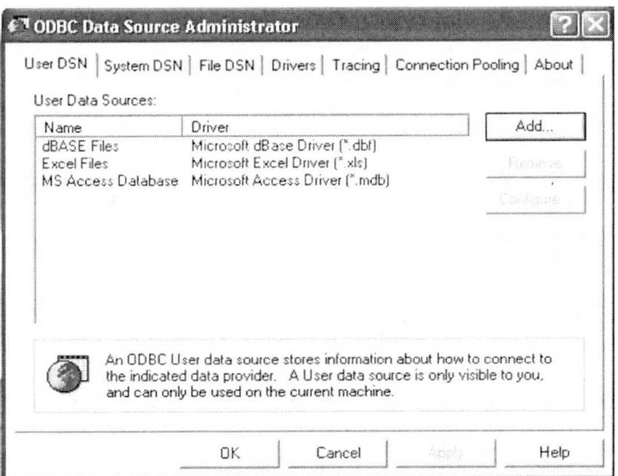

Select Microsoft do access (*.mdb).

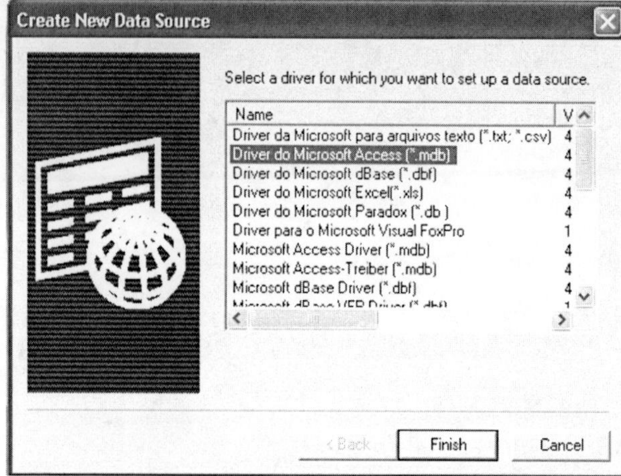

Enter the Data Source Name with description and click select.

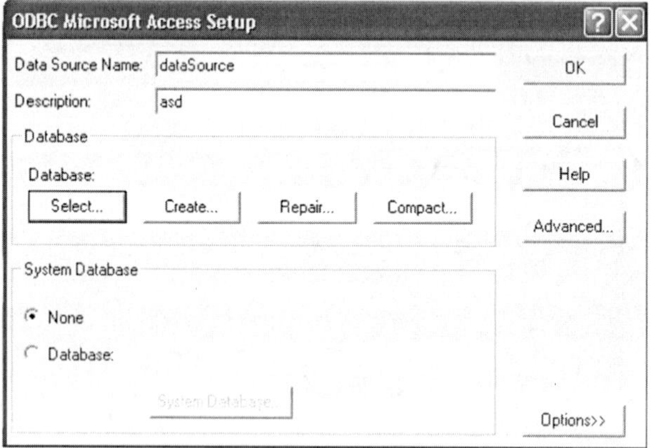

Now select the database and click OK.

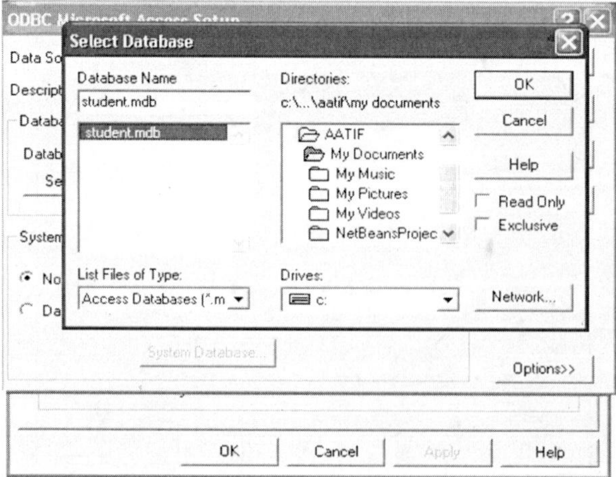

Again click OK.

Click OK.

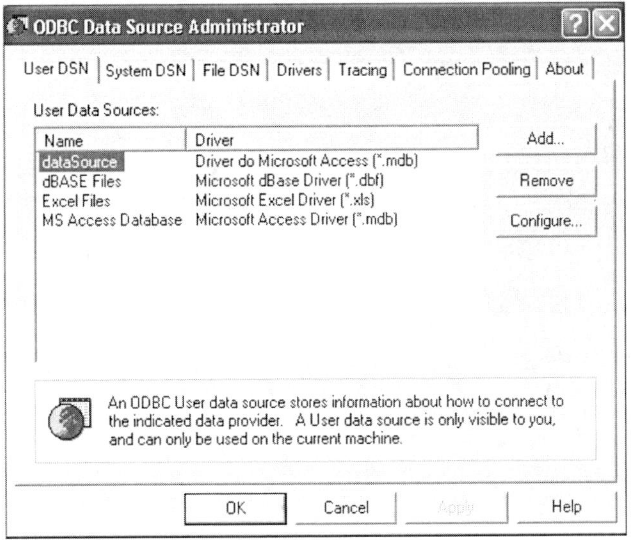

15.6 JDBC CONNECTIVITY

To use the JDBC in a Java Language application, the following steps are to be followed. They are:

Step 1. Import the java.sql package

The first step is importing the java.sql package.

import java.sql.*;

Step 2. Load the Driver

Loading of the driver is done using the following method.

Class.forName("sun.jdbc.odbc.JdbcOdbcDriver");

Step 3. Establish Connection

Connection is established with the database using the following method defines in the Driver Manager Class.

Connection c=DriverManager.getConnection("jdbc:odbc:dataSource");

When "jdbc:odbc:dataSource" is the database URL object specifying the protocol, sub protocol and data Source Name.

Step 4. Prepare statement

In this step, statement object that is required to send a query to the database is prepared. This statement is prepared using the following method defined in connection interface

Statement st=c.createStatement();

Step 5. Extend Query

The sql query that is to be sent to the database is executed by calling the following method on statement object, which refers a ResultSet object:

ResultSet rs=st.executeQuery("select * from Stud");

Step 6. Retrive the result

The result retered by the database to the query executed are extracted from resulset using the get method defined in resultset interface.

```
while(rs.next())
        {
           System.out.println(rs.getString("Name"));
        }
```

Step 7. Close the statement and Connection

Using the close method the statement and connection are closed

```
st.close ();
c.close ();
```

```
//Program
import java.sql.*;
class Connectivity1
{
```

```
            System.out.println(rs.getString("Name"));
         }
      }
      catch(Exception e)
      {
System.out.println(e);
      }
   }
}
```

```
P:\java>javac Connectivity3.java

P:\java>java Connectivity3
updated
Anjum
alam

P:\java>_
```

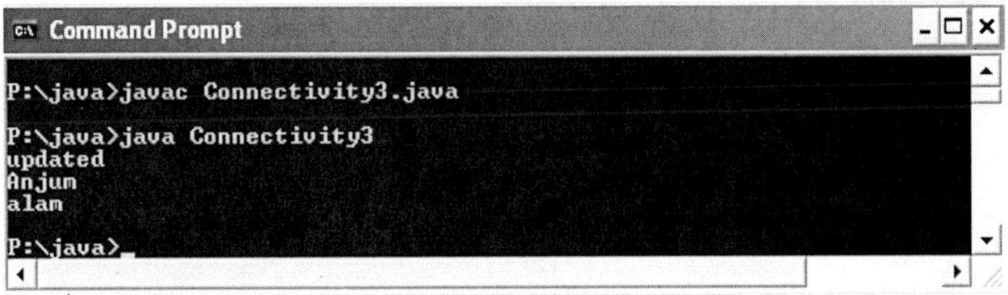

//insert a record

```
import java.sql.*;
class Connectivity4
{
   public static void main(String[] args)
   {
      ResultSet rs;
   try
 {
       Class.forName("sun.jdbc.odbc.JdbcOdbcDriver");
         Connection c=DriverManager.getConnection("jdbc:odbc:dataSource");
         Statement st=c.createStatement();
st.executeUpdate("insert into Stud values('alam','52')");
System.out.println("inserted");
         rs=st.executeQuery("select * from Stud");
         while(rs.next())
         {
            System.out.println(rs.getString("Name"));
         }
      }
      catch(Exception e)
      {
 System.out.println(e);
      }
   }
}
```

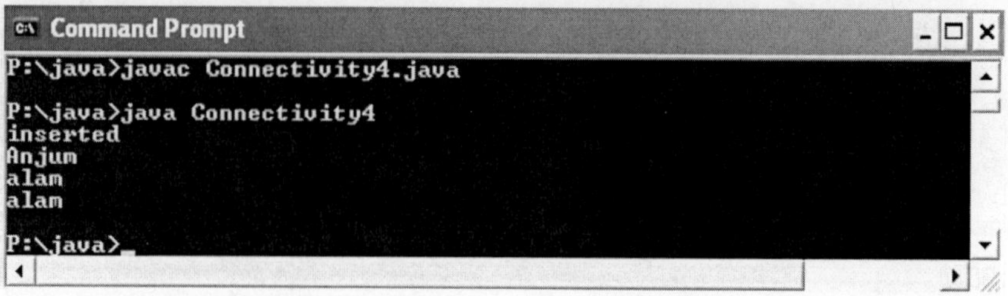

```
Command Prompt
P:\java>javac Connectivity4.java

P:\java>java Connectivity4
inserted
Anjum
alam
alam

P:\java>_
```

15.7 DSN less Connections with the JDBC-ODBC "Bridge" Driver

MS Access Example

```
String driver = "DRIVER= {Microsoft Access Driver (*.mdb)};"
                + "DBQ=C:\\mydbs\\db1.mdb";
    Connection c = DriverManager.getConnection(driver);
    // Code
```

The database is as follows.

bookinfo : Table

Title	AuthorName
Computer Based Optimization Techniques	Tanweer Alam
.Net Framework and C# Programming	Tanweer Alam
Object Oriented Systems with Java 2.0	Tanweer Alam
Core Java	Tanweer Alam
Internet and Java Programming	Tanweer Alam
Advanced Java Programming	Tanweer Alam
Computer Graphics	Tanweer Alam
Computer Graphics and Animation	Tanweer Alam

The coding is as follows

```
import java.sql.*;
public class Connectivity5
{
   public static void main(String[] args)
   {
 try{
 String database="c:\\BookDetails.mdb";
String url="jdbc:odbc:Driver={Microsoft Access Driver (*.mdb)};DBQ=" + database
+ ";DriverID=22;READONLY=true";
      Class.forName("sun.jdbc.odbc.JdbcOdbcDriver");
 Connection con=null;
    ResultSet rs=null;
    Statement stmt=null;
      con=DriverManager.getConnection(url);
```

```
        stmt=con.createStatement();
    rs=stmt.executeQuery("select * from bookinfo");
            while(rs.next())
            {
                System.out.println(rs.getString("Title")+" By "+rs.
getString("AuthorName"));
            }
    }
    catch(Exception e)
    {
        System.out.println(e.getMessage());
    }
}
}
```

The output is as follows

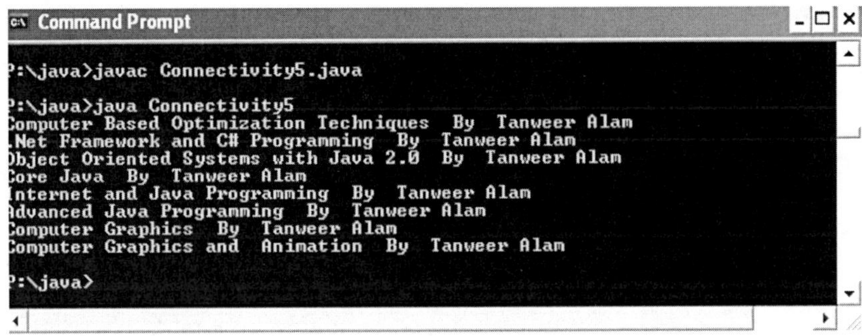

ODBC Driver for Oracle (from Oracle)

String driver = "Driver= {Oracle ODBC Driver};" & "Dbq=myDBName;" & "Uid=scottt;" & "Pwd=tiger";

Connection c = DriverManager.getConnection(driver);

Where: The DBQ name must be defined in the tnsnames.ora file

ODBC Driver for Oracle (from Microsoft)

For the current Oracle ODBC Driver from Microsoft

String driver="Driver={Microsoft ODBC for Oracle};"&"Server=OracleServer.world;" & "Uid=scott" & "Pwd=tiger";

For the older Oracle ODBC Driver from Microsoft

String driverInfo = "Driver={Microsoft ODBC Driver for Oracle};" & _
"ConnectString=OracleServer.world;" & "Uid=scott;" &
"Pwd=tiger"

ODBC Driver for Excel

String driverInfo = "Driver={Microsoft Excel Driver (*.xls)};" & "DriverId=790;" & "Dbq=c:\somepath\mySpreadsheet.xls;" & "DefaultDir=c:\ path"

15.8 JDBC DRIVERS

A JDBC driver is a piece of software that exactly knows how to talk to database. A JDBC client does not make a direct link to a DBMS Server. A JDBC makes use of ODBC to Connect to DBMS Server. The bridge between a Java Program and a database is called JDBC-ODBC Bridge. There may be different drivers available for same database. A client send SQL request to a database server and get SQL result. A Conceptual Structure of using a Java API in a client to handle a database in a server is shown below.

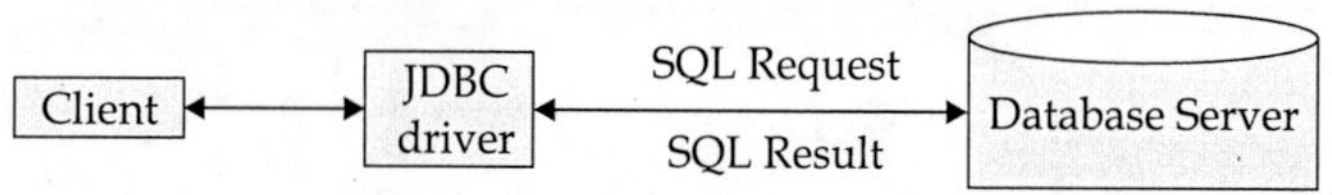

Figure 15.6: JDBC Drivers

Types of Driver

Java has different types of drivers to access a DBMS. The JDBC Drivers are classified into four types. They are classified based on the technique used to access a DBMS.

Type1: JDBC-ODBC Bridge Driver

The JDBC type I driver is also known as the JDBC-ODBC Bridge Driver. A JDBC-ODBC bridge acts as an interface between a client and a database server. The driver converts JDBC method calls into ODBC method calls and sends it to the database server. The bridge is usually used when there is no pure-Java driver available for a particular database. An application in a client makes use of the Java API to send the requests to a database to the JDBC-ODBC Bridge. The reply obtained from the database server is sent to the client via JDBC-ODBC driver.

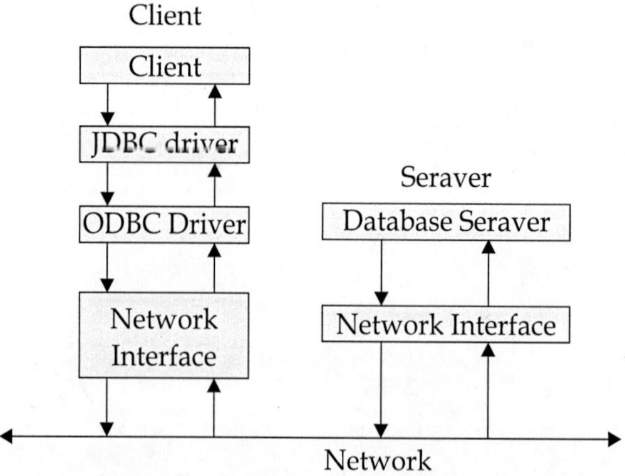

Figure 15.7: JDBC-ODBC Bridge Driver

Advantages

(i) Almost any database, for which ODBC driver is installed, can be accessed.

(ii) It will be faster because it is running on kernel layer not on application layer

Disadvantages

(i) Performance overhead since the calls have to go through the JDBC overhead bridge to the ODBC driver.

(ii) ODBC driver allows us limited to do.

Type II: Native-API-Partly-Java Driver

The JDBC type II driver is also known as the **Native-API-Partly-Java driver.** It is a database driver implementation that uses the client-side libraries of the database. In this type of driver, the JDBC requests are translated to the cal Level Interface (CLI) of the database installed in the client machine to Communicate with a database. When the database receives the requests, they are processed and sent back. The driver converts JDBC method calls into native calls of the database API. This result in the native format of the database is converted to JDBC format and sent to the application in running in a client. This type of Driver offers a faster response them type I drivers

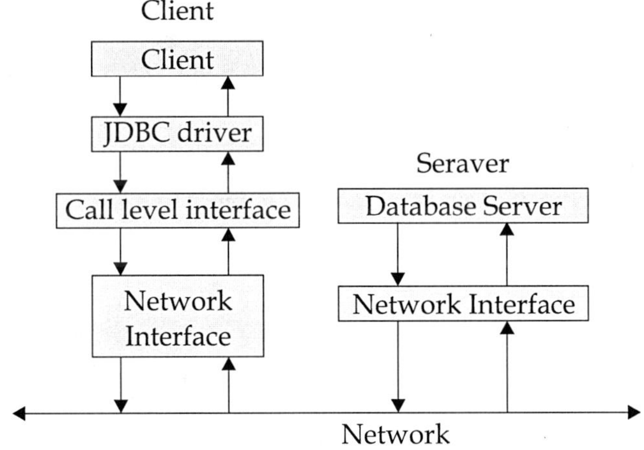

Figure 15.8: Native-API-Partly-Java Driver

Advantage

(i) Better performance than Type 1 since no JDBC to ODBC translation is needed

(ii) Vendor can make better interface to use full potential of their database

Disadvantages

(i) Limited to a particular database

Type III:JDBC-NET-ALL-Java Driver

The JDBC type III driver is also known as the JDBC-NET-ALL-Java Driver. It is similar to type II driver. The only difference is that JDBC for server and Native Database Library (CLI) is stored in a remote server. Communication between the client and the server takes place using JDBC driver network protocol are shown below.

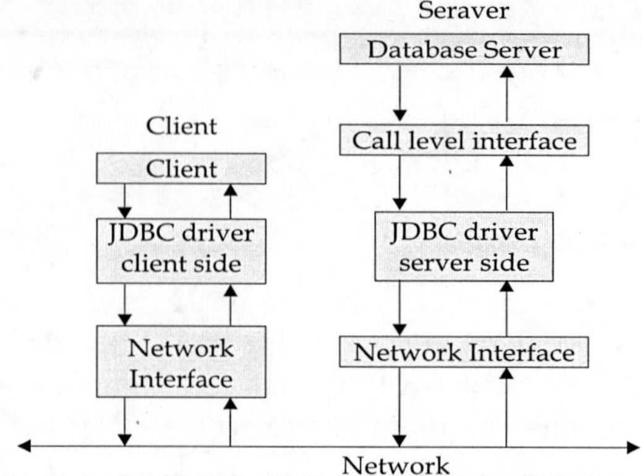

Figure 15.9: JDBC-NET-ALL-Java Driver

Advantage

The advantage of this driver is that the client need not access any Local disk to get the CLI. Hence an application can be used to access a database over a network.

Disadvantages

An extra layer added may result in a time-bottleneck.

Type IV: Native-Protocol-All-Java Driver

This type of a driver is 100% Java and does not make use of any CLI native Libraries. In this type, no translation takes place. A JDBC makes a call directs to the database. It makes use of its own DB protocol written in Java for network Communication.

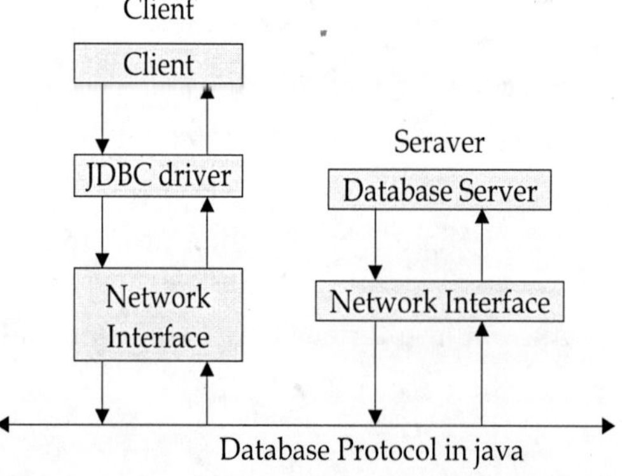

Figure 15.10: Native-Protocol-All-Java Driver

Advantages

(i) These drivers don't translate the requests into database request to ODBC or pass it to client API. Thus the performance is considerably improved.

(ii) They come as .jar file so they are easy to deploy.

Disadvantage

(i) If data is sensitive and encryption is required, it comes back to database support for encryption

15.9 JAVA.SQL PACKAGE

The Java.sql package provides the API for accessing and processing data stored in a data source. It contains several classes and interface that help in connecting to a database, sending SQL statement to a database and processing query result. JDBC API provides for reading and writing data from any data source with a tabular format. The reader/writer facility, available through the javax.sql.RowSet group of interfaces, can be customized to use and update data from a spread sheet, flat file, or any other tabular data source.

Interfaces used:

Table 15.3 : Java.sql package Interfaces

Interface	Description
Array	Mapping for SQL ARRAY.
Blob	Mapping for SQL BLOB.
CallableStatement	The interface used to execute SQL stored procedures.
Clob	Mapping for SQL CLOB.
Connection	A connection (session) with a specific database.
DatabaseMetaData	Comprehensive information about the database as a whole.
Driver	The interface that every driver class must implement. It provides the API for registering and connecting drivers based on JDBC technology ("JDBC drivers"); generally used only by the DriverManager class.
ParameterMetaData	An object that can be used to get information about the types and properties of the parameters in a PreparedStatement object.
PreparedStatement	An object that represents a precompiled SQL statement. It used to send prepared statements or basic SQL statements (derived from Statement)
Ref	Mapping for SQL REF.
ResultSet	A table of data representing a database result set, which is usually generated by executing a statement that queries the database.
ResultSetMetaData	An object that can be used to get information about the types and properties of the columns in a ResultSet object.
Savepoint	The representation of a savepoint, which is a point within the current transaction that can be referenced from the Connection.rollback method.
SQLData	The interface used for the custom mapping of an SQL user-defined type (UDT) to a class in the Java programming language.
SQLInput	An input stream that contains a stream of values representing an instance of an SQL structured type or an SQL distinct type.
SQLOutput	The output stream for writing the attributes of a user-defined type back to the database.
Statement	Used to send basic SQL statements.
Struct	Mapping for SQL STRUCT.

Classes used:

Table 15.4 : Java.sql package Classes

Class	**Description**
Date	Mapping for SQL DATE.
DriverManager	makes a connection with a driver
DriverPropertyInfo	Driver properties for making a connection. It provides properties for a JDBC driver; not used by the general user.
SQLPermission	Provides permission when code running within a Security Manager, such as an applet, attempts to set up a logging stream through the DriverManager.
Time	Mapping for SQL TIME.
Timestamp	A thin wrapper around java.util.Date that allows the JDBC API to identify this as an SQL TIMESTAMP value.
Types	The class that defines the constants that are used to identify generic SQL types, called JDBC types.

Exception Summary

Table 15.5 : Java.sql package Exceptions

Exception	Description
BatchUpdateException	An exception thrown when an error occurs during a batch update operation.
DataTruncation	An exception that reports a DataTruncation warning (on reads) or throws a DataTruncation exception (on writes) when JDBC unexpectedly truncates a data value.
SQLException	An exception that provides information on a database access error or other errors.
SQLWarning	An exception that provides information on database access warnings.

15.10 JDBC CONNECTIVITY WITH JAVA SCRIPT

To use the JDBC in a Java Language application, the following steps are to be followed. They are:

The following steps are used.

Step 1: Create a Connection

var cn = new ActiveXObject("ADODB.Connection");

var strConn = "Provider=Microsoft.Jet.OLEDB.4.0;Data Source = C:\\mydatabase.mdb";

Step 2: Create a resultset and Command

var rs = new ActiveXObject("ADODB.Recordset");

var SQL = "select * from stud";

Step 3: Open the Connection

```
cn.Open(strConn);
rs.Open(SQL,cn);
```

Step 4: Display the Records.

```
while(!rs.EOF)
{
document.write(rs(0) + " " +rs(1)+"<br>");
rs.MoveNext();
}
```

Step 5: Close the resultset and Connection.

```
rs.Close();
cn.Close();
```

Select:

We can display all records of database using select command.

Database:

stud : Table

Name	RollNo
Tanweer	53
Aatif	01
Sameer	02

Coding

```
<html>
<head>
<title>Entitled Document</title>
<script language="JavaScript">
function getSubmit()
{ var i=0;
var cn = new ActiveXObject("ADODB.Connection");
var strConn = "Provider=Microsoft.Jet.OLEDB.4.0;Data Source = C:\\mydatabase.
mdb";
var rs = new ActiveXObject("ADODB.Recordset");
var SQL = "select * from stud";
```

```
cn.Open(strConn);
rs.Open(SQL,cn);
alert("Display Record");
while(!rs.EOF)
{
document.write(rs(0) + " " +rs(1)+"<br>");
rs.MoveNext();
}
rs.Close();
cn.Close();
}
</script>
</head>
<body onLoad="getSubmit()"></body>
</html>
```

Output

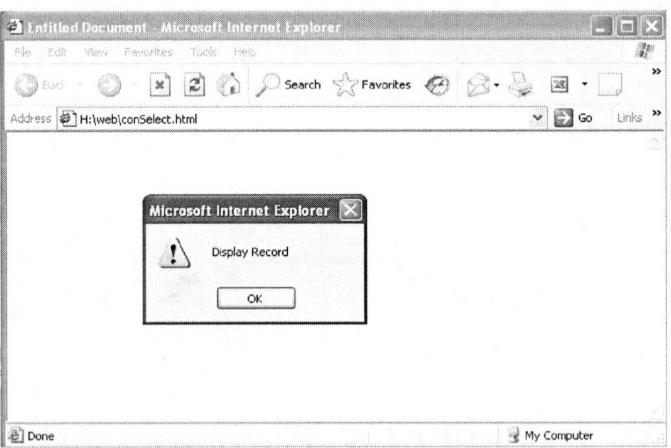

Click OK.

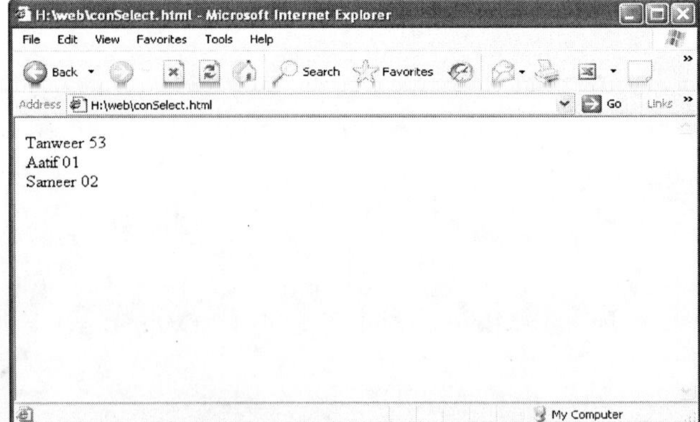

Update:

We can update any record of database using update command.

The database is as follows.

stud : Table

Name	RollNo
Tanweer	53
Aatif	01
Sameer	02

Coding:

```
<html>
<head>
<title>Entitled Document</title>
<script language="JavaScript">
function getSubmit()
{
var cn = new ActiveXObject("ADODB.Connection");
var strConn = "Provider=Microsoft.Jet.OLEDB.4.0;Data Source = C:\\mydatabase.
mdb";
var rs = new ActiveXObject("ADODB.Recordset");
var SQL = "UPDATE stud SET Name='Anjum' WHERE Name='Tanweer'";
cn.Open(strConn);
rs.Open(SQL, cn);
alert("Database Updated");
rs.Close();
cn.Close();
}
</script>
</head>
<body onLoad="getSubmit()"></body>
</html>
```

Output:

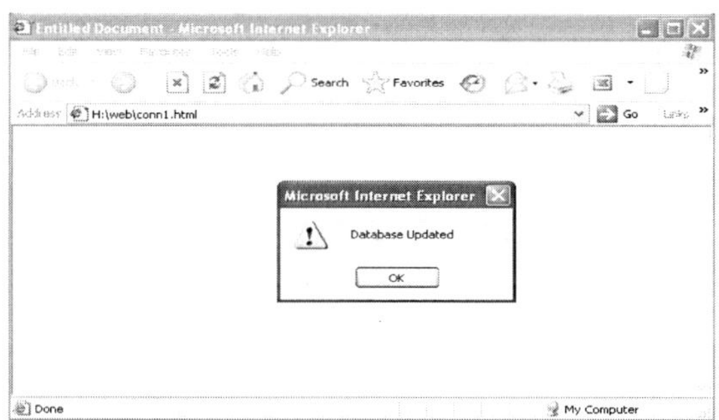

Now updated database is

stud : Table

Name	RollNo
Anjum	53
Aatif	01
Sameer	02

Insert:

We can insert any record into database using insert command.

Coding:

```
<html>
<head>
<title>Entitled Document</title>
<script language="JavaScript">
function getSubmit()
{
var cn = new ActiveXObject("ADODB.Connection");
var strConn = "Provider=Microsoft.Jet.OLEDB.4.0;Data Source = C:\\mydatabase.
mdb";
var rs = new ActiveXObject("ADODB.Recordset");
var SQL = "insert into stud values('Alam','43')";
cn.Open(strConn);
rs.Open(SQL, cn);
alert("Record Inserted");
rs.Close();
cn.Close();
}
</script>
</head>
<body onLoad="getSubmit()"></body>
</html>
```

Output:

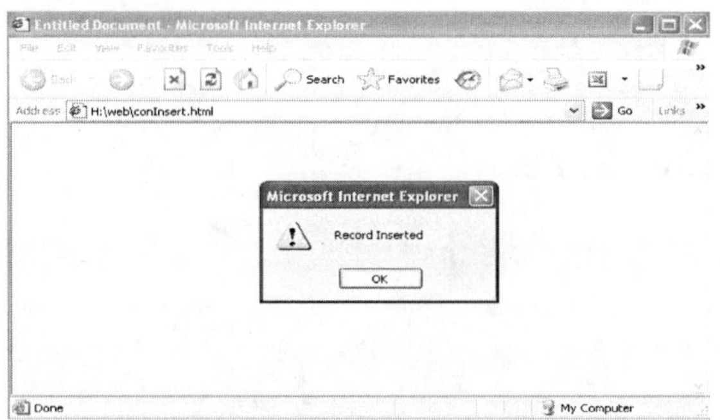

Now database is as follows.

stud : Table

Name	RollNo
Anjum	53
Aatif	01
Sameer	02
Alam	43

Delete:

Coding:

```
<html>
<head>
<title>Entitled Document</title>
<script language="JavaScript">
function getSubmit()
{
var cn = new ActiveXObject("ADODB.Connection");
var strConn = "Provider=Microsoft.Jet.OLEDB.4.0;Data Source = C:\\mydatabase.
mdb";
var rs = new ActiveXObject("ADODB.Recordset");
var SQL = "delete from stud where RollNo='43'";
cn.Open(strConn);
rs.Open(SQL, cn);
alert("Record Deleted");
rs.Close();
cn.Close();
}
</script>
</head>
<body onLoad="getSubmit()"></body>
</html>
```

Output:

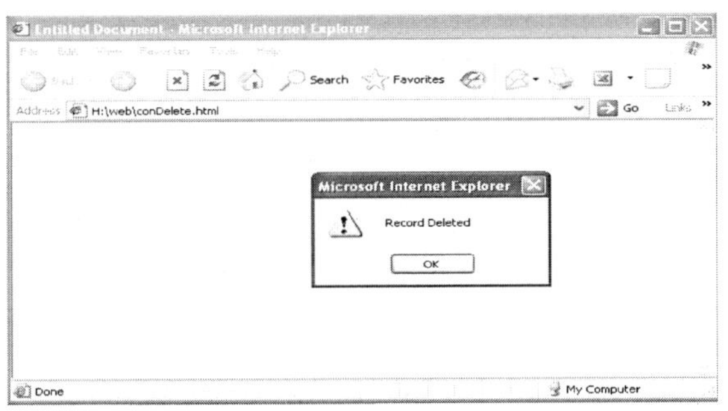

Now database is as follows.

stud : Table

	Name	RollNo
	Anjum	53
	Aatif	01
	Sameer	02
▶		

15.11 JDBC CONNECTIVITY WITH JSP

The following steps are used to connect the JSP page with database.

Step 1. Declaring Variables

Import java.sql.* package as follows.

```
<%@ page language="java" import="java.sql.*" %>
```

Step 2. Load the Driver.

Load database driver. This is achieved using the single line of code as follows. For Example.

```
String database="c:\\student1.mdb";
String url="jdbc:odbc:Driver={Microsoft Access Driver (*.mdb)};DBQ=" + database
+ ";DriverID=22;READONLY=true";
Class.forName("sun.jdbc.odbc.JdbcOdbcDriver");
```

Step 3. Connection to database

Make a connection as follows.

```
Connection con=DriverManager.getConnection(url,"","");
```

When url is passed into getConnection() method of DriverManager class it returns connection object.

Step 4. Executing Query or Accessing data from database

This is done using following code.

```
Statement stmt=con.createStatement();
ResultSet rs=stmt.executeQuery("select *from student");
```

A query is always executed on a Statement object. The two most important methods of this Statement interface are executeQuery() and executeUpdate(). The executeQuery() method executes an SQL statement that returns a single ResultSet object. The executeUpdate() method executes an insert, update, and delete SQL statement.

Step 5. Reading values from a ResultSet

```
while(rs.next())
        {
```

```
            String s1=rs.getString(1);
            String s2=rs.getString(2);
            String s3=rs.getString(3);
            out.write("<tr>");
   out.write("<td>"+s1+"</td>");
   out.write("<td>"+s2+"</td>");
   out.write("<td>"+s3+"</td>");
   out.write("</tr>");
        }
```

For Example:

Database

we create a database named student1 and it contains information about Name, Address & MobileNo.

Table: Student

Student : Table

Name	Address	MobileNo
Tanweer	MIET	09319398037
Aatif	MIET	09319398037

Coding

```
conn11.jsp
<%@ page language="java" import="java.sql.*" %>
<html><head></head><body>
<%
 try
   {
      String database="c:\\student1.mdb";
String url="jdbc:odbc:Driver={Microsoft Access Driver (*.mdb)};DBQ=" + database
+ ";DriverID=22;READONLY=true";
      Class.forName("sun.jdbc.odbc.JdbcOdbcDriver");
      Connection con=DriverManager.getConnection(url,"","");
      Statement stmt=con.createStatement();
      ResultSet rs=stmt.executeQuery("select *from student");
      out.write("<table          border=1          align=center><tr><th>Name</
         th><th>Address</th><th>MobileNo</th></tr>");
 while(rs.next())
        {
           String s1=rs.getString(1);
           String s2=rs.getString(2);
```

```
            String s3=rs.getString(3);
            out.write("<tr>");
      out.write("<td>"+s1+"</td>");
      out.write("<td>"+s2+"</td>");
      out.write("<td>"+s3+"</td>");
      out.write("</tr>");
          }

        }
        catch(Exception e)
        {
            out.write(e.getMessage());
        }

%>
</table>
</body></html>
```

Output:

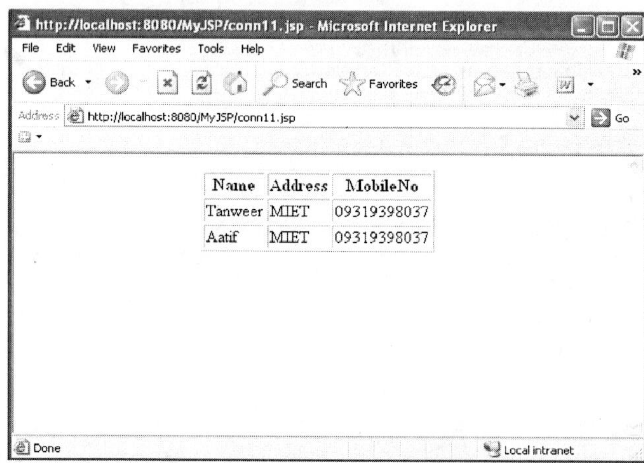

Another Example:

Here I am going to discuss the connectivity from MSAccess database with JSP. We take an example of BookDetails database. This database contains a table named bookinfo. This table contains three fields- BookId, Title and AuthorName. We write an html page for inserting the values in student table in database. After submitting values a table will be showed that contains the student name and author name.

Database

we create a database named books and it contains information about Title & AuthorName.

Table: bookinfo

bookinfo : Table

ID	Title	AuthorName
1	Computer Graphics	Tanweer Alam
2	Computer Graphics and Animation	Tanweer Alam
3	Computer Based Optimization Techniques	Tanweer Alam
(AutoNumber)		

Coding

Save the following code as BookEntryForm.jsp.

```
<%@ page language="java" import="java.sql.*" %>
<%
 String database="c:\\BookDetails.mdb";
 String url="jdbc:odbc:Driver={Microsoft Access Driver (*.mdb)};DBQ=" + database
        + ";DriverID=22;READONLY=true";
      Class.forName("sun.jdbc.odbc.JdbcOdbcDriver");
 Connection con=null;
    ResultSet rs=null;
    Statement stmt=null;
 try{
      con=DriverManager.getConnection(url);
      stmt=con.createStatement();
   }
   catch(Exception e){
      System.out.println(e.getMessage());
   }
if(request.getParameter("action") != null){
      String bookname=request.getParameter("Title");
      String author=request.getParameter("AuthorName");
      stmt.executeUpdate("insert into bookinfo values('"+bookname+"','"+author+
          "')");
      rs=stmt.executeQuery("select * from bookinfo");
      %>
<html>
      <body>
      <center>
         <h2>Books List</h2>
         <table border="1" cellspacing="0" cellpadding
="0">
         <tr>
            <td><b>S.No</b></td>
            <td><b>Book Name</b></td>
            <td><b>Author</.b></td>
         </tr>
            <%
            int no=1;
```

```
            while(rs.next()){
            %>
            <tr>
             <td><%=no%></td>
             <td><%=rs.getString("Title")%></td>
             <td> <%=rs.getString("AuthorName")
%> </td>
            </tr>
            <%
            no++;
   }
   rs.close();
   stmt.close();
   con.close();
%>
         </table>
         </center>
      </body>
   </html>
<%}else{%>
   <html>
   <head>
      <title>Book Entry Form</title>
      <script language="javascript">
       function validate(objForm){
         if(objForm.bookname.value.length==0){
         alert("Please enter Book Name!");
         objForm.bookname.focus();
         return false;
         }
         if(objForm.author.value.length==0){
         alert("Please enter Author name!");
         objForm.author.focus();
         return false;
         }
         return true;
            }
         </script>
      </head>

      <body>
         <center>
<form action="BookEntryForm.jsp" method="post" name="entry"
        onSubmit="return
 validate(this)">
   <input type="hidden" value="list" name="action">
```

```
    <table border="1" cellpadding="0" cellspacing="0">
    <tr>
      <td>
        <table>
          <tr>
          <td colspan="2" align="center">
<h2>Book Entry Form</h2></td>
          </tr>
          <tr>
          <td colspan="2"> </td>
          </tr>
          <tr>
          <td>Book Name:</td>
          <td><input name="Title" type=
"text" size="50"></td>
          </tr>
          <tr>
          <td>Author:</td><td><input name=
"AuthorName" type="text" size="50"></td>
          </tr>
          <tr>
            <td colspan="2" align="center">
<input type="submit" value="Insert"></td>
            </tr>
          </table>
        </td>
      </tr>
    </table>
</form>
        </center>
      </body>
    </html>
<%}%>
```

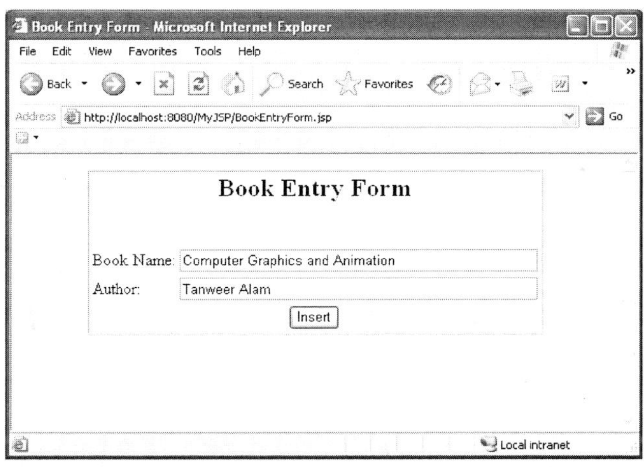

Fill the Book Name and Author fields and press Submit button. A page will open and show a table of book name and authors as follows.

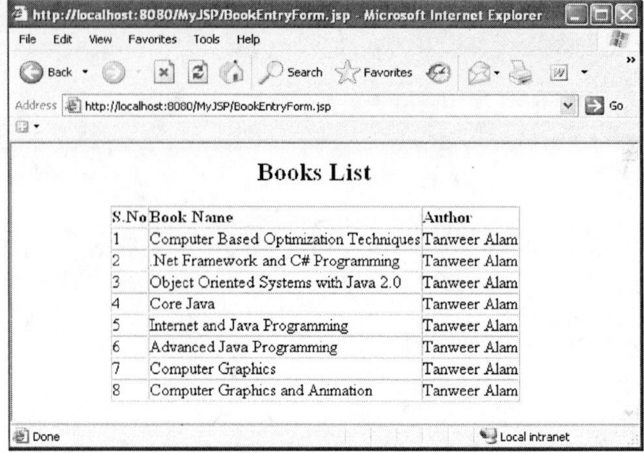

Books List

S.No	Book Name	Author
1	Computer Based Optimization Techniques	Tanweer Alam
2	.Net Framework and C# Programming	Tanweer Alam
3	Object Oriented Systems with Java 2.0	Tanweer Alam
4	Core Java	Tanweer Alam
5	Internet and Java Programming	Tanweer Alam
6	Advanced Java Programming	Tanweer Alam
7	Computer Graphics	Tanweer Alam
8	Computer Graphics and Animation	Tanweer Alam

SUMMARY

JDBC is Java application programming interface that allows the Java programmers to access database management system from Java programs. It is a java API which enables the java programs to execute SQL statements. It is an application programming interface that defines how a java programmer can access the database in matrix form from Java code using a set of standard interfaces and classes written in Java. JDBC sends a request to a database server using the appropriate SQL command and processes the results. A database that another program links to is called a data source. Many data sources, including products produced by Microsoft and Oracle, already use a standard called Open Database Connectivity (ODBC). JDBC is a low-level API and a base for higher-level APIs. JDBC is a programming framework for writing programs that access information stored in databases, spreadsheets, and flat files. Database access, for many developers, is an essential part of the tools of software development.

EXERCISE

1. Assume that there is a table named as student in MS-Access with the fields: name,rollno. Write a java program to insert and then display the records of this table using JDBC.
2. Explain JDBC drivers also write the procedure for establishing a connection with JDBC.
3. What are statements? Explain.
4. Define java.sql package.
5. What is JDBC Architecture?

*****

CHAPTER 16

DEVELOPING JAVA BEANS IN JSP PAGE

Java is one of the leading platforms for developing web applications. Servlet and JSP allow us to develop web applications that will run across multiple web servers and operating systems. Java Beans are reusable components. They are used to separate Business logic from the Presentation logic. Java Beans is architecture for both using and building components in Java. This architecture supports the features of software reuse, component models and object orientation.

16.0 INTRODUCTION

Java Beans are reusable components. JavaBeans components can be used to give World Wide Web pages interactive capabilities such as computing interest rates or browser characteristics. They are used to separate Business logic from the Presentation logic. Internally, a bean is just an instance of a class.

16.1 JAVA BEANS IN JSP PAGES

The Java bean is not much different from a java program. The main differences are the signature methods being used in a bean. Bean has to be a corresponding get/set method for every parameter. These methods are known as accessors. JSP has three basic tags for working with Java Beans.

Following are the three tags:

```
<jsp:useBean>
<jsp:setProperty>
<jsp:getProperty>
```

(i) <jsp:useBean>

This tag is used to declare and instantiate the JavaBean class. It's syntax is as follows :

```
<jsp:useBean
   id="object-name"
   scope="page | request | session | application"
   type="type-of-object"
```

```
    class="fully-qualified-classname"
    beanName="fully-qualified-beanName"
/>
```

- id - name of the object e.g.

  String name = null;

  In the above code, name is the 'id' we are talking about.
- scope - an optional attribute by which you can control when your JavaBean object will be destroyed. Default is page, which means every page view will create a new JavaBean.
- type - type of the object which can be the same class, a super class or an interface which the class implements. This parameter is optional. e.g.

  String name = "Faisal Khan";

  In the above code, String is the 'type' we are talking about.
- class - a fully qualified class name e.g.

  Date d = new java.util.Date();

  In the above code, java.util.Date is the 'class' we are talking about.
- beanName - it is also fully qualified class name just like 'class' attribute above. Only difference is that the class name in the case of 'beanName' can be provided at request time.

(ii) <jsp:setProperty>

This tag is used to set the value of one or all the properties of given JavaBean. It's syntax is as follows :

```
<jsp:setProperty
    name="id-of-the-JavaBean"
    property="name-of-property"
    param="name-of-request-parameter-to-use"
    value="new-value-of-this-property"
/>
```

Let us now see what the different attributes mean :

- name - 'id' of the <jsp:useBean> tag you set above.
- property - name of the property whose value you want to set.
- param - name of the request paramter you want to use to set the value of this property.
- value - the new value you want to set for this property.

(iii) <jsp:getProperty>

This tag is used to retrieve the value of a given property from the given JavaBean. It's syntax is as follows:

```
<jsp:getProperty
   name="name-of-the-object"
   property="name-of-property"
/>
```

Let us see what are the different attributes for this tag :

- name - 'id' of the <jsp:useBean> tag we set above.
- property - name of the property whose value you want to retrieve.

Example

```
<%@ page language="java" contentType="text/html" %>
<HTML>
<HEAD>
<TITLE>JSP: Beans Example 1</TITLE>
</HEAD>
<BODY BGCOLOR="YELLOW">
<H1>Developing Java Beans in a JSP page</H1>
 <jsp:useBean id="d" class="java.util.Date" />
 The current day and time is:
 <UL>
  <LI> Date: <jsp:getProperty name="d" property="date"/>
  <LI> Month: <jsp:getProperty name="d" property="month"/>
  <LI> Year: <jsp:getProperty name="d" property="year"/>
  <LI> Hours: <jsp:getProperty name="d" property="hours"/>
  <LI> Minutes: <jsp:getProperty name="d" property="minutes"/>
 </UL>
 </BODY>
</HTML>
```

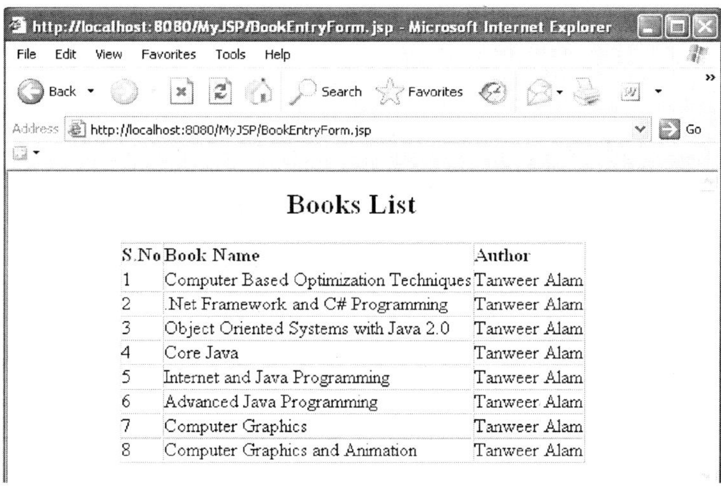

Books List

S.No	Book Name	Author
1	Computer Based Optimization Techniques	Tanweer Alam
2	.Net Framework and C# Programming	Tanweer Alam
3	Object Oriented Systems with Java 2.0	Tanweer Alam
4	Core Java	Tanweer Alam
5	Internet and Java Programming	Tanweer Alam
6	Advanced Java Programming	Tanweer Alam
7	Computer Graphics	Tanweer Alam
8	Computer Graphics and Animation	Tanweer Alam

16.2 BEANS SCOPE

The following options are defined the scope of bean.

(i) Page scope

By default all beans have page scope. When current page finishes generating then the object whose scope is the page will disappear. The object with a page scope may be modified but the changes are lost as soon as the page exists.

(ii) Request scope

If the scope defined is of Request scope then JSP page uses an jsp:forward tag, then the bean should be applicable in the forwarded JSP.

(iii) The Session scope

In JSP, user has session scope. A session does not correspond directly to the user but it corresponds with a particular period of time the user spends at a site.

16.3 BEAN STRUCTURE

JSP using the client server approach. Client-Server approach is also called page-centric approach. In Client-Server approach, the application lies on the client side and services the requests connecting to the server application.

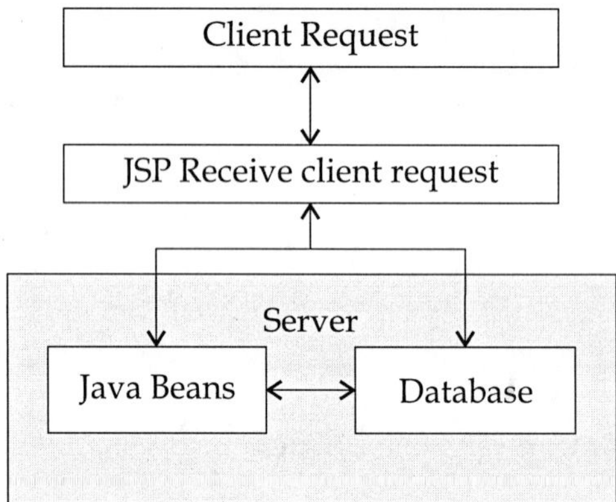

Figure 16.1: BEAN Structure

The procedure is as follows.

(i) Client makes a request.

(ii) The JSP page takes the request from client and processes it.

(iii) JSP accesses the database using Java Beans.

(iv) The requests are processed and the serviced results are sent back to client by JSP.

SUMMARY

A key advantage of JavaServer Pages technology is the ability to separate the Java code containing the business logic and determining the dynamic content from the HTML code containing the request processing, presentation logic, and static content. This separation allows HTML experts to focus on presentation, while Java experts focus on business logic in JavaBeans that are called from the JSP page.

A typical JSP page will have only brief snippets of Java code, usually for Java functionality for request processing or presentation. Data access, such as in the runQuery() method in the sample, is usually more appropriate in a JavaBean. However, the formatResult() method in the sample, which formats the output, is more appropriate for the JSP page itself.

EXERCISE

1. Explain the Java Beans in JSP Pages.
2. How to develop java beans in a jsp page?
3. Explain bean scope.
4. What is bean structure?

*****

CHAPTER 17

INTRODUCTION TO STRUTS FRAMEWORKS

Apache Struts is a free open-source framework for creating well-architected web applications. Web applications differ from conventional websites because web applications can create a dynamic response while many websites deliver only static pages. A web application can interact with databases and business logic layer to customize a response.

17.0 INTRODUCTION

Apache Struts is based on the Model-View-Controller (MVC) design pattern. MVC is divided into three levels. These are Model, View and Control.

(i) Model

Model is used to provide the data from the database and saving the data into the data store. In the Model, All the business logics are implemented. Data are entered by the user through View. Data are checked in the model before saving into the database. Model is divided into three parts. These are Data access, Data saving and the Data validation logic.

(ii) View

Data are entered by the user through View. HTML, JSPs, Custom Tag Libraries and Resources files are the parts of view component. It is responsible for the following.

(i) Taking the input from the user

(ii) Sending the request to the controller

(iii) Receiving the response from the controller

(iv) Displaying the result to the user.

(iii) Controller

Controller is an interface between Model and View. Action, ActionServlet, ActionForm and struts-config.xml are the part of Controller. Controller is responsible for the following.

(i) Receiving the request from client.

(ii) Once request is received from client it executes the appropriate business logic from the Model

(iii) Produce the output to the user using the View component.

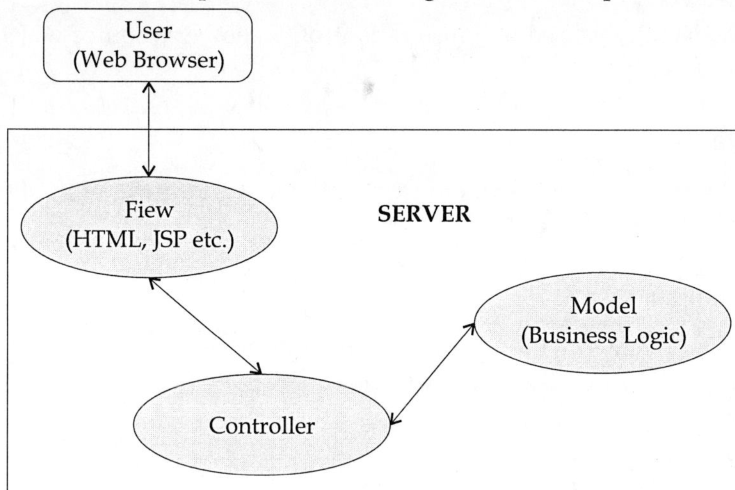

17.1 STRUTS DEFINITION

Apache Struts is a framework that promotes the use of the Model-View-Controller (MVC) architecture for designing large scale web applications. MVC is divided into three levels. These are Model, View and Control. The Model represents the business or database layer, the View represents the page design layer and the Controller represents the navigational layer.

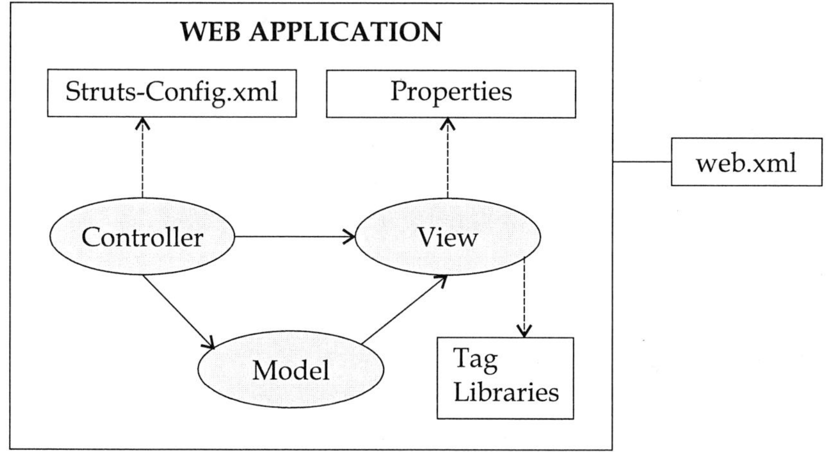

Figure: Struts framework

The framework provides the following three components.

(i) Request

Request handler provided by the application developer.

(ii) Response

Response handler is used to transfers control to another resource which completes the response.

(iii) Tag Library

A tag library helps developers to create interactive form-based applications with server pages.

17.2 Struts configuration

Struts will be configured with the following configuration files.

(i) web.xml

We can configure the web server with the web.xml file for the struts application. In this file we can set where the web server find the struts-config.xml and other global properties.

(ii) struts-config.xml

The controller calls the Model or a view. The names are allocated to the action classes or JSP Files (Views) that are set in the struts-config.xml. If we change a class name, we only have to change the name in the struts-config.xml.

(iii) Struts-Tag-Libraries

The Struts-Tag-Libraries are the summary of functions that extends the functionality of JSP's.

(iv) Properties files

These files will be used to keep the multi languages text of our web application. We can create a separate properties file for each language that contains all texts of the application.

17.3 Install the Software

The following steps are used.

1. **Download the Struts zip file**

   Download the struts software from the struts website. http://jakarta.apache.org/struts/.

2. **Unzip into a directory of your choice**

   For example, unzip into C:\ struts.

17.4 How to set Path

Right click on my computer and select properties.

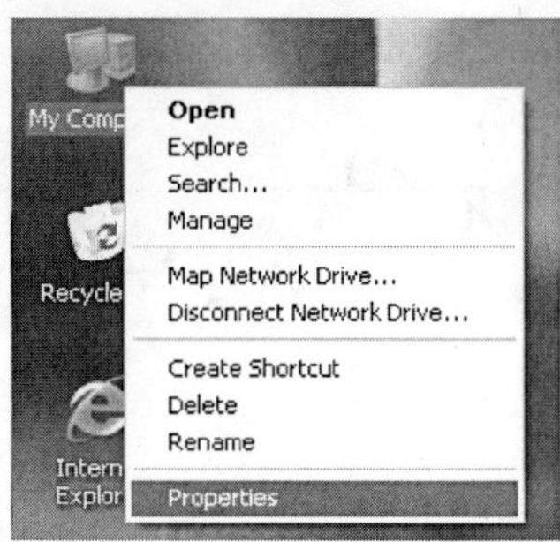

Select advanced and click on Environmental Variable.

System Properties
System Restore | Automatic Updates | Remote
General | Computer Name | Hardware | Advanced
You must be logged on as an Administrator to make most of these changes.
Performance
Visual effects, processor scheduling, memory usage, and virtual memory
Settings
User Profiles
Desktop settings related to your logon
Settings
Startup and Recovery
System startup, system failure, and debugging information
Settings
Environment Variables | Error Reporting
OK | Cancel | Apply

Click OK then click New.

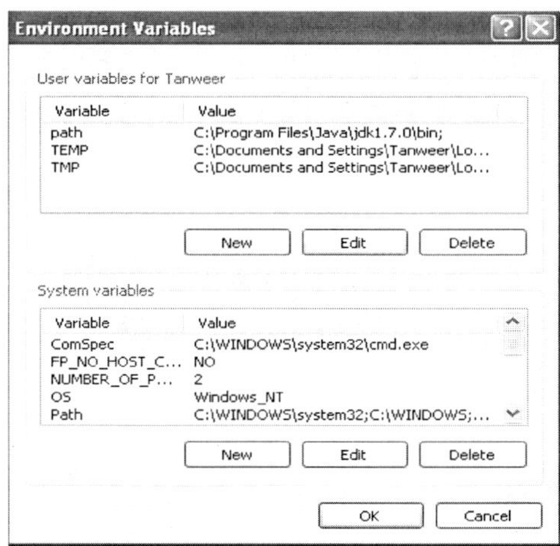

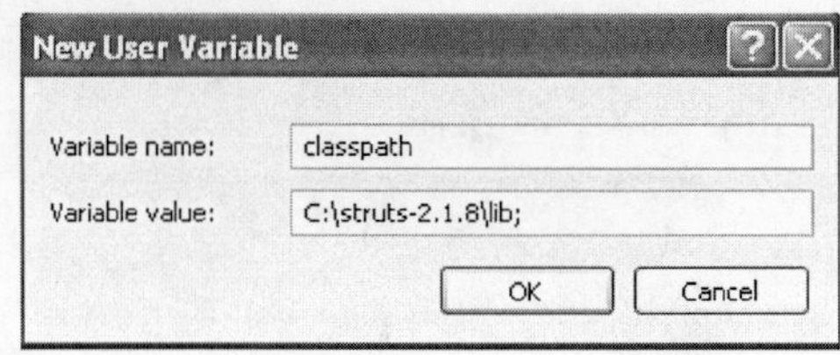

Now click OK.

17.5 Struts Tags

Struts framework has the following attributes:

Attribute	Description
id	Bean name for temporary use
name	name of a pre-existing bean
property	property of the bean named in the name attribute
scope	scope to search for the bean named in the name attribute

17.6 CREATING BEANS

The struts-bean tag library contains JSP custom tags useful in defining new beans. Struts-beans can be created with the <jsp:useBean></jsp:useBean> tag.

Bean Properties

JSP tags use the bean properties <jsp:getProperty> and <jsp:setProperty>). For example a property named address.state returns the value retrieved by the Java expression getAddress().getState().

Bean Creation

Now new JSP beans can be created from a variety of APIs and objects associated with the current request.

Bean Output

Bean output is supports the rendering of textual output that will be included in the response being created by JSP page. The <bean:message> and <bean:write> tags will write bean and application resources properties into the current HttpResponse object.

Other Bean Tags

The Struts framework provides other tags like cookies, request headers, request parameters, Struts configuration objects and web application resources. These tags are as follows.

Other Bean Tags
<bean:cookie ... >
<bean:page ... >
<bean:parameter ... >
<bean:header ... >
<bean:resource ... >
<bean:struts ... >

17.7 CREATING HTML FORMS

Working with html in struts framework described in the following steps.

HTML form is used to get the user input data.

Data corresponding to the user input is stored in an ActionForm class.

struts-config.xml file is used to define exactly how the user input are processed.

Data is stored in Action class.

Display the result at JSP Page.

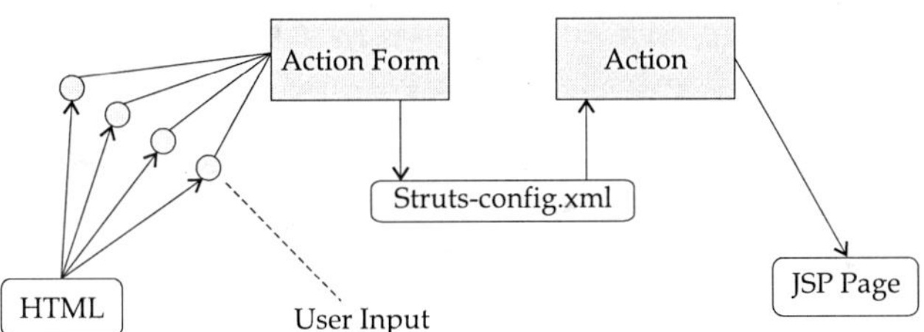

The html tags of Struts are used to gather the users input data. Some tags are used to create a form element, body elements, images, links and other as well as displaying errors. HTML tags used in struts framework are as follows.

(i) <html:base>

This tag is used to generate <base> tag. It is used inside <head> tag.

(ii) <html:form>

It generates html <form>.

(iii) <html:text>

Name	Tanweer
Roll No	53

It generates <input type="text">.

(iv) <html:password>

It generates <input type="password">.

(v) <html:textarea>

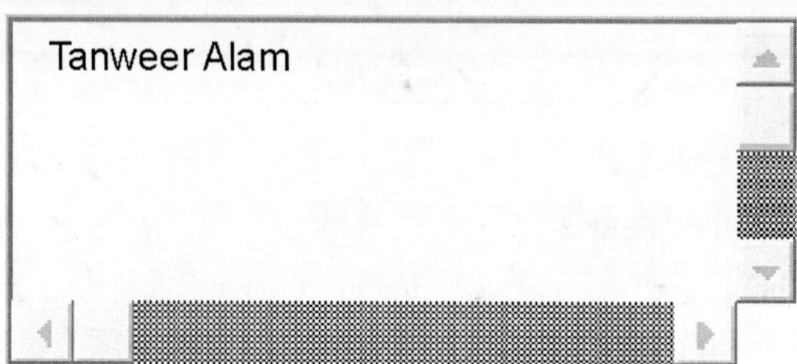

It generates <textarea>.

(vi) <html:button>

This tag is used to generate an <input type="button"> tag. It should be used inside a <form> element.

(vii) <html:cancel>

Cancel

This tag is used to generate an <input type="submit"> tag. It is used inside a <form> element.

(viii) <html:submit>

Submit

It generates <input type="submit"> to submit form data entered by the user.

(ix) <html:checkbox>

It is used to generates an <input type="checkbox">.

<html:multibox> also generates an <input type="checkbox">.

(x) <html:errors>

It generates html to display any errors that may have occurred during invocation of the validate() method.

(xi) <html:hidden>

It generates <input type="hidden">.There is a hidden element that is invisible.

(xii) <html:html>

It generates <html>.

(xiii) <html:image>

(xiv) <html:link>

It generates an html link.

(xv) <html:radio>

Yes No

It generates a radio button (<input type="radio">).

(xvi) <html:reset>

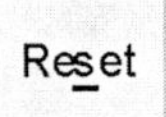

It generates <input type="reset">.

(xvii) (<html:select>

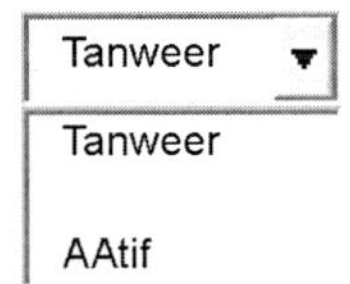

<html:select> It generates <select>.

<html:options> It generates html for an entire list of <option> tags.

<html:option> It generates a single <option>.

17.8 WORKING WITH STRUTS

The following steps are used to work with struts.

Step 1: Download Struts software from the struts site http://struts.apache.org/download.cgi

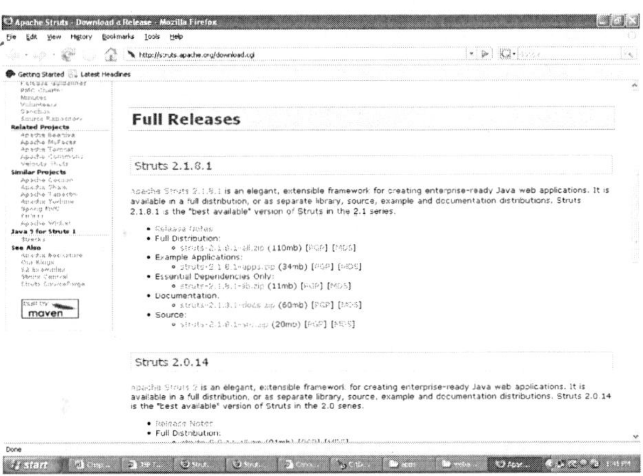

We will download the Struts 2.1.8.1 (struts-2.1.8.1 -all.zip).

Step 2: Now we will download the latest version of tomcat from http://tomcat.apache.org/download-55.cgi. We will download apache-tomcat-5.5.29.zip.

Step 3: Install latest version of Java.

Step 4: Run the C:\apache-tomcat-5.5.29\bin\startup.bat to start the tomcat.

Now double click on tomcat6.exe

Click OK.

```
C:\DOCUME~1\Test\LOCALS~1\Temp\Rar$EX02.328\apache-tomcat-5.5.29\bin\tomcat5.exe
INFO: XML validation disabled
May 10, 2010 2:09:42 PM org.apache.catalina.startup.HostConfig deployWAR
INFO: Deploying web application archive struts2-blank-2.1.8.1.war
May 10, 2010 2:09:42 PM com.opensymphony.xwork2.util.logging.commons.CommonsLogg
er info
INFO: Parsing configuration file [struts-default.xml]
May 10, 2010 2:09:42 PM com.opensymphony.xwork2.util.logging.commons.CommonsLogg
er info
INFO: Unable to locate configuration files of the name struts-plugin.xml, skippi
ng
May 10, 2010 2:09:42 PM com.opensymphony.xwork2.util.logging.commons.CommonsLogg
er info
INFO: Parsing configuration file [struts-plugin.xml]
May 10, 2010 2:09:42 PM com.opensymphony.xwork2.util.logging.commons.CommonsLogg
er info
INFO: Parsing configuration file [struts.xml]
May 10, 2010 2:09:42 PM org.apache.coyote.http11.Http11AprProtocol start
INFO: Starting Coyote HTTP/1.1 on http-8080
May 10, 2010 2:09:42 PM org.apache.coyote.ajp.AjpAprProtocol start
INFO: Starting Coyote AJP/1.3 on ajp-8009
May 10, 2010 2:09:42 PM org.apache.catalina.storeconfig.StoreLoader load
INFO: Find registry server-registry.xml at classpath resource
May 10, 2010 2:09:42 PM org.apache.catalina.startup.Catalina start
INFO: Server startup in 1266 ms
```

Step 5: Test Tomcat.

Type http://localhost:8080/ url in your browser, it shows the welcome page in the browser window as follows.

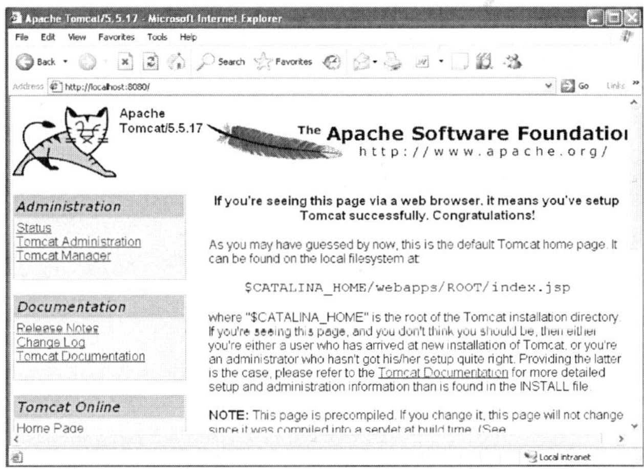

Step 6: Extract the downloaded struts into your directory.

For example

Extract at c:\struts-2.1.8.1

Now goto c:\struts-2.1.8.1\struts-2.0.6-all\struts-2.0.6\apps

Copy the struts2-blank-2.1.8.1.war file and paste it at the following location.

C:\Program Files\Apache Software Foundation\Tomcat 5.5\webapps as follows.

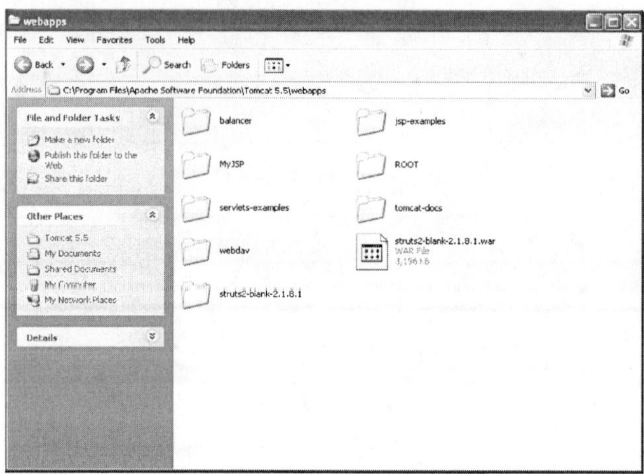

Tomcat will automatically deploy the application.

```
C:\DOCUME~1\Test\LOCALS~1\Temp\Rar$EX02.328\apache-tomcat-5.5.29\bin\tomcat5.exe
INFO: Unable to locate configuration files of the name struts-plugin.xml, skippi
ng
May 10, 2010 2:09:42 PM com.opensymphony.xwork2.util.logging.commons.CommonsLogg
er info
INFO: Parsing configuration file [struts-plugin.xml]
May 10, 2010 2:09:42 PM com.opensymphony.xwork2.util.logging.commons.CommonsLogg
er info
INFO: Parsing configuration file [struts.xml]
May 10, 2010 2:09:42 PM org.apache.coyote.http11.Http11AprProtocol start
INFO: Starting Coyote HTTP/1.1 on http-8080
May 10, 2010 2:09:42 PM org.apache.coyote.ajp.AjpAprProtocol start
INFO: Starting Coyote AJP/1.3 on ajp-8009
May 10, 2010 2:09:42 PM org.apache.catalina.storeconfig.StoreLoader load
INFO: Find registry server-registry.xml at classpath resource
May 10, 2010 2:09:42 PM org.apache.catalina.startup.Catalina start
INFO: Server startup in 1266 ms
May 10, 2010 2:15:02 PM org.apache.catalina.startup.HostConfig checkResources
INFO: Undeploying context [/struts2-blank-2.1.8.1]
```

Step 7: To test the struts-blank application. We have type the url http://localhost:8080/struts2-blank-2.1.8.1 in the browser and the struts-blank application get displayed in our browser window.

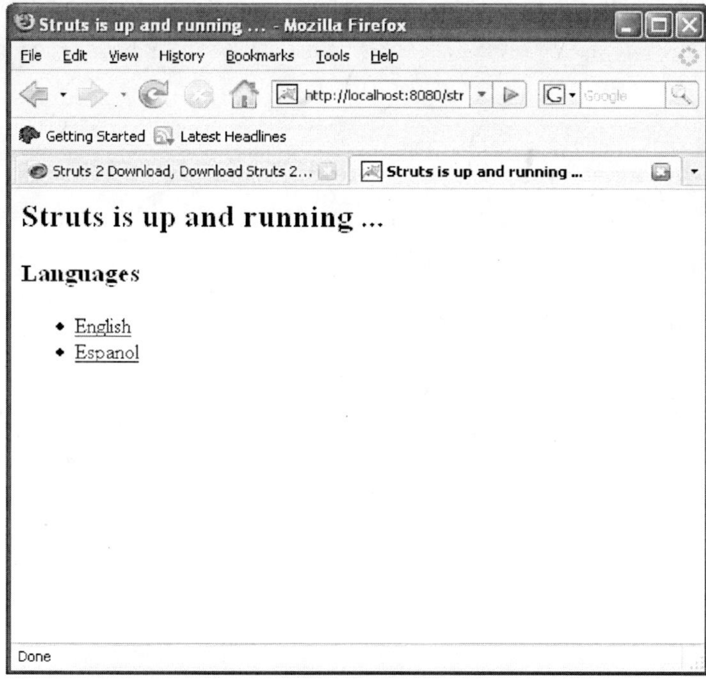

Click the English link and start Struts Blank sample application.

We can simply copy these files to the webapps directory of our tomcat server. Tomcat will automatically deploy these applications and then we can test these applications.

Copy struts2-mailreader-2.0.6.war and paste it to webapps.

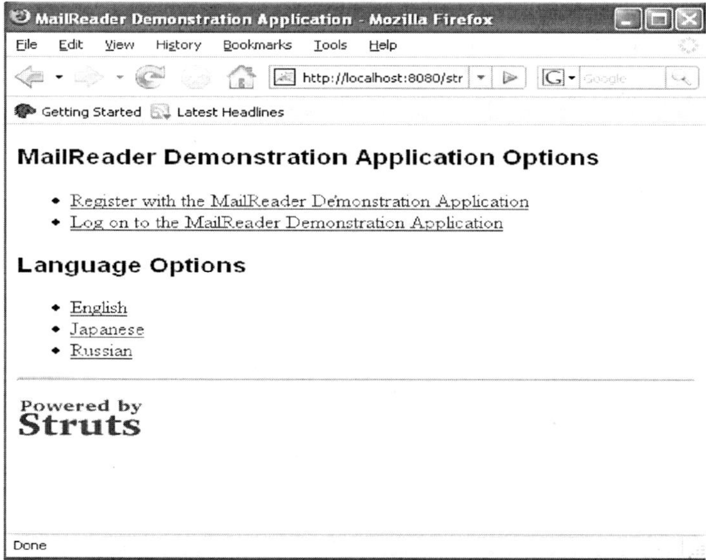

Click on register with the Mail reader.

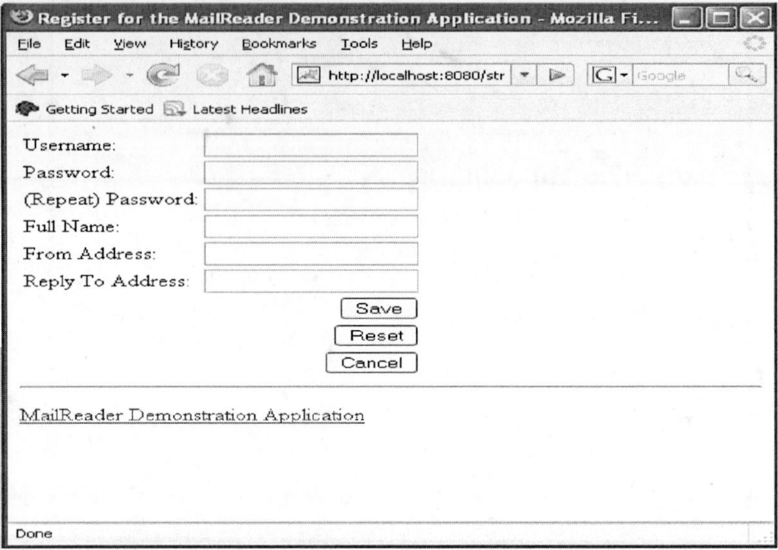

Click on login.

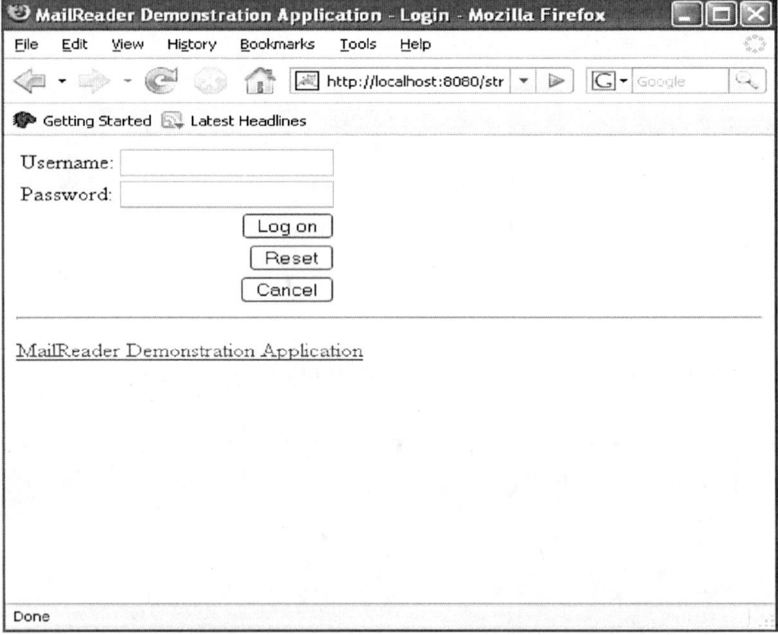

Similarly copy struts2-showcase-2.0.6.war and paste it to the webapps.

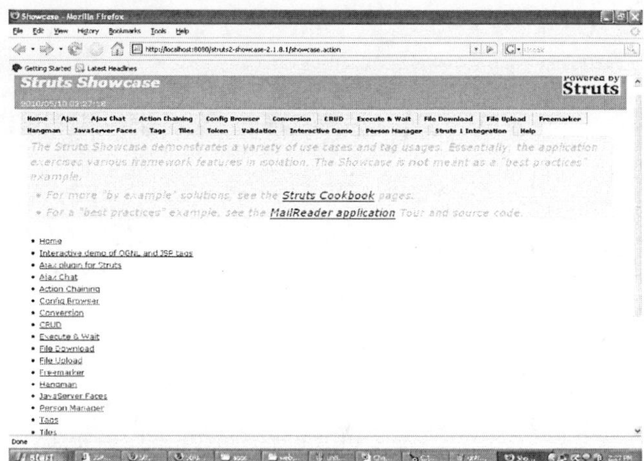

17.9 CREATING DIRECTORY STRUCTURE FOR THE PROJECT

The following steps are used to create directory structure of struts application.

Step 1: Firstly extract struts 2.1.8.1 download and copy struts2-blank-2.1.8.1.war to webapps directory. Rename struts2-blank-2.1.8.1.war to struts2 and unzip it in the webapps directory. Now start the tomcat and type http://localhost:8080/struts2/ into your browser.

Step 2: Now we delete the content of struts2\WEB-INF\src and struts2\WEB-INF\classes directories, we don't need these files for struts 2 blank application.

Step 3: Create build.xml file in the struts2\WEB-INF\src and paste the following content in the build.xml file.

```
<project name="struts2" basedir="../" default="all">
  <!-- Project settings -->
  <property name="project.title" value="Developed by Tanweer Alam"/>
  <property name="project.jar.file" value="struts2.jar"/>
```

```
 <path id="class.path">
<fileset dir="lib">
   <include name="**/*.jar"/>
</fileset>
  <fileset dir="libext">
   <include name="**/*.jar"/>
  </fileset>
 </path>
  <!-- Classpath for Project -->
<path id="compile.classpath">
     <pathelement path ="lib/commons-beanutils.jar"/>

     <pathelement path ="lib/commons-digester.jar"/>
     <pathelement path ="lib/struts.jar"/>
     <pathelement path ="libext/servlet-api.jar"/>
     <pathelement path ="libext/catalina-ant.jar"/>
     <pathelement path ="classes"/>
     <pathelement path ="${classpath}"/>
  </path>
  <!-- Check timestamp on files -->
  <target name="prepare">
     <tstamp/>
     <copy
        file="src/struts.xml"
        todir="src/classes"/>

  </target>
  <!-- Copy any resource or configuration files -->
  <target name="resources">
  <copy todir="src/classes" includeEmptyDirs="no">
        <fileset dir="src/java">
        <patternset>
           <include name="**/*.conf"/>
           <include name="**/*.properties"/>
           <include name="**/*.xml"/>
        </patternset>
        </fileset>
     </copy>
  </target>
  <!-- Normal build of application -->
  <target name="compile" depends="prepare,resources">
     <javac srcdir="src" destdir="src/classes"
              debug="true" debuglevel="lines,vars,source">
        <classpath refid="class.path"/>
```

```
</javac>
   <jar
   jarfile="lib/${project.jar.file}"
basedir="src/classes"/>
</target>
<!-- Remove classes directory for clean build -->
<target name="clean"
 description="Prepare for clean build">
 <delete dir="classes"/>
 <mkdir  dir="classes"/>
</target>
<!-- Build Javadoc documentation -->
<target name="javadoc"
 description="Generate JavaDoc API docs">
<delete dir="./doc/api"/>
   <mkdir dir="./doc/api"/>
   <javadoc sourcepath="./src/java"
      destdir="./doc/api"
      classpath="${servlet.jar}:${jdbc20ext.jar}"
      packagenames="*"
      author="true"
      private="true"
      version="true"
      windowtitle="${project.title} API Documentation"
      doctitle="&lt;h1&gt;${project.title}
            Documentation (Version ${project.version})&lt;/h1&gt;"
      bottom="Copyright &#169; 2002">
   <classpath refid="compile.classpath"/>
   </javadoc>
</target>
<!-- Build entire project -->
<target name="project" depends="clean,prepare,compile"/>
<!-- Create binary distribution -->
<target name="dist"
   description="Create binary distribution">
 <mkdir
   dir="${distpath.project}"/>
 <jar
   jarfile="${distpath.project}/${project.distname}.jar"
   basedir="./classes"/>
 <copy
   file="${distpath.project}/${project.distname}.jar"
```

```
        todir="${distpath.project}"/>
          <war
        basedir="../"
        warfile="${distpath.project}/${project.distname}.war"
        webxml="web.xml">
        <exclude name="${distpath.project}/${project.distname}.war"/>
       </war>
  </target>
  <!-- Build project and create distribution-->
  <target name="all" depends="project"/>
    </project>
```

Step 4: Create directory **libext** under the **struts2\WEB-INF** then you copy latest Servlets-api.jar file over there. This library file will be used to compile Servlets in our application.

Step 5: Now we create directories named java and classes under struts2\WEB-INF\src. The directory struts2\WEB-INF\src\java will be used to put the entire java sources file and directory struts2\WEB-INF\src\classes will be used by ant build utility to store compiled java files.

Now directory structure has been completed.

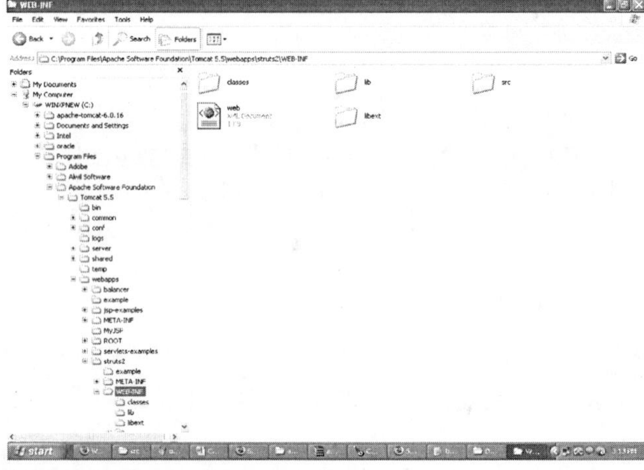

17.10 WRITING THE FIRST STRUTS APPLICATION

The following steps are used to develop struts application.

Step 1: Develop the view (JSP File)

Write the following code to the file first.jsp at the location C:\Program Files\Apache Software Foundation\Tomcat 5.5\webapps\struts2.

```
<%@ taglib prefix="s" uri="/struts-tags" %>
<html>
<head>
```

```
<title>Congratulation, Your First Struts Application!</title>
</head>
   <body>
   <h2><s:property value="message" /></h2>
<p>Current date and time is: <b><s:property value="currentTime" /></b>
</body>
</html>
```

Step 2: Develop Action class

Now create Fiststruts.java and saves it to the "struts2\WEB-INF\src\java\net\tanweer" directory. This action class creates the message to be displayed on the screen. Here is the code of Fiststruts.java:

```
package net.tanweer;
import com.opensymphony.xwork2,ActionSupport;
import java.util.Date;
public class Fiststruts extends ActionSupport {
  public static final String MESSAGE = "Struts 2 Hello World Tutorial!";
  public String execute() throws Exception {
    setMessage(MESSAGE);
    return SUCCESS;
  }
  private String message;
  public void setMessage(String message){
    this.message = message;
  }
  public String getMessage() {
    return message;
  }
 public String getCurrentTime(){
   return new Date().toString();
 }
}
```

Step 3: Develop Controller Configuration File

Struts 2 uses the **struts.xml** file for configuring the application. Create **struts.xml** file and save it in the "**struts2\WEB-INF\src**" directory with the following content.

```
<?xml version="1.0" encoding="UTF-8" ?>
<!DOCTYPE struts PUBLIC
"-//Apache Software Foundation//DTD Struts Configuration 2.0//EN"
"http://struts.apache.org/dtds/struts-2.0.dtd">
<struts>
<constant name="struts.enable.DynamicMethodInvocation" value="false" />
<constant name="struts.devMode" value="true" />
```

```
<package name="tanweer" namespace="/tanweer" extends="struts-default">
<action name="HelloWorld" class="net.tanweer.Firststruts">
<result>/pages/First.jsp</result>
</action>
<!-- Add actions here -->
</package>
<!-- Add packages here -->
</struts>
```

The struts.xml file should be present in the class path of the application, you can either include it in the jar and place in the lib directory of the application or place it in the classes directory of the web application. In our application we are using ant build tool which is including it in the jar file.

Step 4: Install Ant Build Tool

Unzip ant build tool to c:\ as follows.

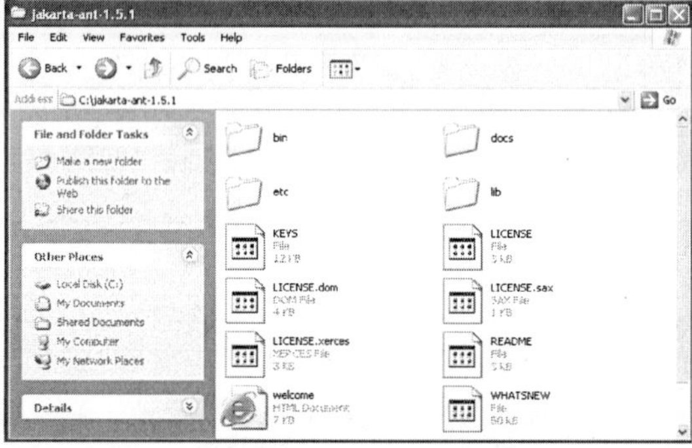

Copy the bin and lib directory to the new directory named ANT_HOME at c:\.

Now set the path as follows.

Environment name: path

Environment value: C:\ANT_HOME\bin;C:\Program Files\Java\jdk1.7.0\bin;C:\Program Files\Java\jdk1.7.0\lib;

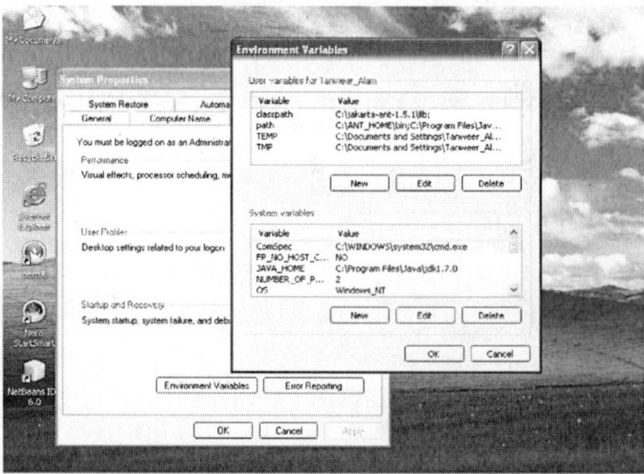

Set the JAVA_HOME variable.

In system variable click new enter JAVA_HOME to the variable name and value is C:\Program Files\Java\jdk1.7.0\bin;C:\Program Files\Java\jdk1.7.0

Remember: not use the semicolon (;) after the end of variable value.

Now test the ant build tool as follows.

Just write ant to the command prompt.

```
Command Prompt
Microsoft Windows XP [Version 5.1.2600]
(C) Copyright 1985-2001 Microsoft Corp.

C:\Documents and Settings\Tanweer_Alam>ant
Buildfile: build.xml does not exist!
Build failed
C:\Documents and Settings\Tanweer_Alam>_
```

Step 5: Building the application

To build the application open command prompt and go to C:\Program Files\Apache Software Foundation\Tomcat 6.0\webapps\struts2\WEB-INF\src directory of the web application and issue the "ant" command. The ant build tool will compile the java file and create jar file "**struts2.jar**" into the lib directory of our web application. The following is the output of ant build tool:

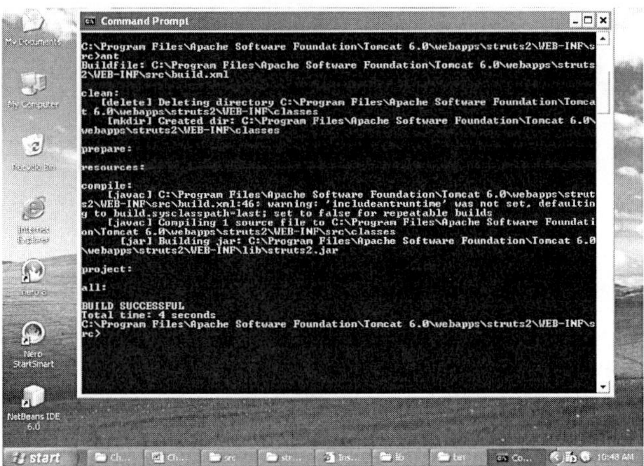

Step 6: Test Struts2 Application

Now we will test our application. To test the application starts the tomcat server.

Now type http://localhost:8080/struts2/ and press enter.

Now select "Struts2 Hello World Application" from the list. The application will display message "Struts2 Hello World!" along with current date and time of the server.

SUMMARY

Web applications differ from conventional websites because web applications can create a dynamic response while many websites deliver only static pages. A web application can interact with databases and business logic layer to customize a response. Apache Struts is a free open-source framework for creating well-architected web applications. It is based on the Model-View-Controller (MVC) design pattern. MVC is divided into three levels. These are Model, View and Control. The Model represents the business or database layer, the View represents the page design layer and the Controller represents the navigational layer.

EXERCISE

1. Explain Struts.
2. Define struts framework.
3. How to make the struts application?
4. How to create directory structure for the project?

*****

APPENDIX
Test Your Knowledge

1. What do you mean by protocol ? Explain the role of HTTP and TCP/IP protocols in web.
2. What do mean by port? List the common Well-Known port assignments.
3. What are the internet Addresses? List the Common Top-Level Domains.
4. Discuss, in detail, about Cyber laws of India.
5. Write short notes on:
   (i) Common Gateway Interface
   (ii) Name Resolution
   (iii) Firewalls
   (iv) Proxy Servers
6. What are the Web Project Characteristics? Explain in detail.
7. What are the skills Web Team must have? What are the roles of the team and how do the team members interact?
8. What is four stage Web Project Developing process? Explain with suitable figure.
9. Write short notes on
   - Feasibility and Software Testing.
   - Technical Specifications.
10. What do you mean by Platform Independence in JAVA?
11. What do you mean by Class and Object? Explain using a suitable example.
12. Write a program in JAVA to read the contents of one file and write it into another file.
13. What do you mean by heavy weight and light weight process? Explain
14. Write a Java Program using: Default Constructor, Argument Constructor & Copy Constructor.

15. Write a program in java to get the input from the keyboard and display it on the screen without using java.io package.

16. Write down the applet life cycle.

17. What is Thread? Draw the figure to display the all the Thread States and explain each in short.

18. Trace the following code, and find out the errors if any:

```
public class Hello
{
  public static int main(String[] uptu)
  {
    System.out.err("this is an error");
    System.out.write("this method is right");
  }
}
```

19. What do mean by Applet? Draw the Applet Life cycle and Explain. Write an Applet that get the input from the User for principle amount, rate and year to calculate simple interest and display it on the screen. Write a HTML page and test the applet.

20. What do you mean by Streams? Write the default constructors of all Input and Output Streams.

21. What is the use of super keyword? Write a program in JAVA to call Default Constructor, Overloaded constructor of super class from child class Constructors.

22. What is AWT? Draw the Hierarchy of AWT Components and explain each in short.

23. How HTML is used with JAVA programs? Explain using a suitable example.

24. What is the difference between Socket and Server Socket? Write the default constructors for both.

25. What is Event Handling? Explain any Event by using a suitable example.

26. Write the steps to create a new user defined bean.

27. Explain any two methods available in HTTPServlet package.

28. What is the relationship between AWT and Swing?

29. Write down the similarities in C++ features and JAVA features.

30. Write a program to display the name of the Java files in C-drive.

31. Write a short note on Lavatron applet.

32. Write a short note on image based menu.

33. How many types of statements are available in java.sql package?

34. Explain brief functioning of upper layer E-mail and their applications.

35. What is the definition of java beans. Give its advantages? Explain it.

36. What are JAR flies? Write down about the following command options:

    (a). jar cf file / .jar

    (b). jar it file / .jar

    (c). 'c' option is used for ....

    (d). 'C' option is used for ....

    (e). 'M' option is used for ....

    (f). '0' option is used for ....

    (g). 'U' option is used for ....

37. What is Introspection? How can we create a new Bean? Explain it with an example.

38. What are Java Beans API? Explain it with its various Interfaces.

39. Write short notes on :

    (a) Java Swing

    (b) Java Servlets

    (c) JDBC

    (d) Enterprise java beans

    (e) Web Browser.

40. What is the difference between CGI and Servlets ? (V. Imp)

41. Explain the life cycle of a Servlet.

42. Write down brief notes on:

    Session Tracking and cookies.

43. Write down most Important Omitted features done by java ? (Imp)

44. Explain the following with the help of suitable examples:

    (a) Dynamic Billboard Applet

    (b) Lavatron Applet.

45. What is Scrabblet ? Which type of security it provides? Give the Basic approach of this game.

46. What are the types of JDBC drivers? Explain in brief.

47. What is java Bean? What are the various steps which are needed to create a new bean?
48. Explain SMTP (e-mail application protocol). Show its functionality.
49. Explain SNMP (Network Management Protocol) and show its functionality.

*****

INDEX

D

E

F

G

H